Texts in Theoretical Computer Science
An EATCS Series

Editors: W. Brauer J. Hromkovič G. Rozenberg A. Salomaa
On behalf of the European Association
for Theoretical Computer Science (EATCS)

Advisory Board:
G. Ausiello M. Broy C.S. Calude A. Condon
D. Harel J. Hartmanis T. Henzinger T. Leighton
M. Nivat C. Papadimitriou D. Scott

T0223952

Fred Kröger · Stephan Merz

Temporal Logic and State Systems

Springer

Prof. Dr. Fred Kröger
Institut für Informatik
Ludwig-Maximilians-Universität München
Oettingenstr. 67
80538 München, Germany
kroeger@informatik.uni-muenchen.de

Dr. Stephan Merz
INRIA Lorraine & LORIA
615, rue du Jardin Botanique
54602 Villers-lés-Nancy, France
stephan.merz@loria.fr

ISBN 978-3-642-08680-9

e-ISBN 978-3-540-68635-4

Texts in Theoretical Computer Science. An EATCS Series. ISSN 1862-4499

ACM Computing Classification: D.2.4, F.3.1, F.4.1

Softcover reprint of the hardcover 1st edition 2008

Cover Design: KünkelLopka GmbH, Heidelberg

Printed on acid-free paper

9 8 7 6 5 4 3 2 1

springer.com

Preface

Following the *Stanford Encyclopedia of Philosophy*,

> "the term *temporal logic* has been broadly used to cover all approaches to the representation of temporal information within a logical framework".

Applications of temporal logic include philosophical issues about time, the semantics of tenses in natural languages, and its use as a formal framework for the treatment of behavioural aspects of computerized systems.

In a more narrow sense, temporal logic is understood as a *modal-logic* type of approach: temporal relationships between different assertions are expressed by applying particular temporal logic operators to them. This book focuses on this type of temporal logic and we will study computer science applications to what we call *state systems*: systems which involve "states" and exhibit "behaviours" by "running" through sequences of such states.

One of the most challenging problems facing today's software engineers and computer scientists is to find ways and establish techniques to reduce the number of errors in the systems they build. It is widely acknowledged that formal methods may contribute to solving this challenge with significant success. In particular, temporal logic is a well-established and successfully used formal tool for the *specification* and *verification* of state systems. Its formulas are interpreted over "runs" of such systems and can thus express their behavioural properties. The means induced by the (semantical and deductive) logical apparatus provide methods to formally prove such properties.

This monograph is written in the tradition of the first author's textbook [83]

> *Temporal Logic of Programs*

and the two volumes

> *The Temporal Logic of Reactive and Concurrent Systems – Specification* and
> *The Temporal Logic of Reactive and Concurrent Systems – Safety*

of Manna and Pnueli [102, 104]. This means that we will present the "mathematics" of temporal logic in considerable detail and we will then systematically study specification and verification methods, which will be illustrated by fully elaborated examples.

Compared with those books, however, the topics and their presentation are rearranged and we have included significant new material and approaches. In particular, branching time logics, expressiveness issues of temporal logic, aspects related to Lamport's *Temporal Logic of Actions* (TLA), and model checking methods are additionally presented.

There is a wealth of relevant and interesting material in the field. The "main text" of this book presents topics that – in our opinion – constitute a "canonical" exposition of the field. In additional *Second Reading* paragraphs we have occasionally inserted short "excursions" that expand on related or advanced themes or that present interesting complements. These paragraphs can be skipped without loss of continuity in the main presentation.

The first chapter of this book gives a short overview of basic concepts and notions of (mathematical) logic. This is not only to introduce the reader not familiar with logic into that world, it also defines basic terminology and notation that we use throughout the remaining text.

Chapters 2–5 and 10 form the purely logical part of the book. Even when restricted to the modal-logic type as mentioned above, there are many different versions and variants of temporal logic. We start in Chap. 2 with the basic propositional linear temporal logic and study in Chap. 3 some important propositional extensions. It should be mentioned that even the borderline between temporal logic(s) and modal logics is not really well defined. Some relationships concerning this are briefly discussed in Second Reading paragraphs.

Chapter 4 is devoted to the expressiveness of propositional linear temporal logics. In particular, the logics are compared with other description formalisms: classical predicate logic and ω-automata.

Chapter 5 introduces first-order linear temporal logic together with some additional useful extensions. Chapter 10 discusses some other temporal logics and, particularly, introduces branching time logics.

The remaining Chaps. 6–9 and 11 deal with applications of temporal logics to state systems. Various versions of *transition systems* – as formal representations of such systems – are introduced in Chap. 6, and Chap. 7 gives a general systematic presentation of (deductive) temporal logic verification methods for them. Chapter 8 applies the methods to the special ("classical") case of the verification of concurrent programs.

Chapter 9 addresses aspects that arise when system specifications are "structured". Particularly, the refinement of specifications is considered and we study how this can be described in the logic TLA.

The "semantical" model checking approach to system verification offers an alternative to deductive methods. It has attracted much interest, largely because it can be fully automated in a way that scales to systems of interesting complexity. Chapter 11 presents the essential concepts and techniques underlying this approach.

Every chapter ends with some bibliographical notes referring to the relevant literature. After the last chapter we include an extensive list of formal laws of the various temporal logics studied in this book.

We have used drafts of this book as supports for courses at the advanced undergraduate and the graduate level. Different selections of the material are possible, depending on the audience and the orientation of the course. The book is also intended as an introduction and reference for scientists and practicing software engineers who want to familiarize themselves with the field. We have aimed to make the presentation as self-contained as possible.

We are indebted to P. Fontaine, M. Hammer, A. Knapp, and H. Störrle for helpful remarks during the preparation of this text.

Finally, we thank Springer-Verlag for the interest in publishing this book and the overall support during its completion.

Munich and Nancy,
January 2008

Fred Kröger
Stephan Merz

Contents

1

Basic Concepts and Notions of Logics

In this book various temporal logics will be studied. In preparation, we first introduce some basic concepts, notions, and terminology of logics in general by means of a short overview of *classical logic*. Particularly, items are addressed which will be of relevance in subsequent considerations. This includes some well-known results from classical logic which we list here without any proofs.

1.1 Logical Languages, Semantics, and Formal Systems

A logic formalizes the reasoning about "statements" within some area of application. For this purpose, it provides formal languages containing *formulas* for the representation of the statements in question and formal concepts of reasoning like *consequence* and *derivability* relations between formulas.

Classical (mathematical) logic applies to mathematical systems: number systems such as the natural or real numbers, algebraic systems such as groups or vector spaces, etc. In a separable "nucleus" of this logic, called *propositional logic* PL, the effect of building formulas with boolean operators like *and*, *or*, *implies*, etc. is studied, while the atomic building blocks of such formulas are viewed as "black boxes" without any further internal structure.

Generally, a logical language is given by an alphabet of different symbols and the definition of the set of formulas which are strings over the alphabet. Given a set $\mathbf{V}$ whose elements are called *propositional constants*, a *language* $\mathcal{L}_{\mathrm{PL}}(\mathbf{V})$ (also shortly: $\mathcal{L}_{\mathrm{PL}}$) *of propositional logic* can be defined as follows.

Alphabet

- All propositional constants of $\mathbf{V}$,
- the symbols **false** | $\rightarrow$ | (|).

(The stroke | is not a symbol but only used for separating the symbols in the list.)

Formulas

1. Every propositional constant of **V** is a formula.
2. **false** is a formula.
3. If A and B are formulas then $(A \to B)$ is a formula.

The clauses 1–3 (also called *formation rules*) constitute an *inductive* definition which may be understood to work like a set of production rules of a formal grammar: a string over the alphabet is a formula if and only if it can be "produced" by finitely many applications of the rules 1–3.

The set **V** is a parameter in this definition. For concrete applications, **V** has to be fixed yielding some particular language tailored for the "universe of discourse" in question. There are no assumptions on how many elements **V** may have. This most general setting may sometimes cause some technical complications. In applications studied in this book we do not need the full generality, so we actually may restrict **V** to be finite or "at most" denumerable.

In general, a logical language is called *countable* if its alphabet is finite or denumerable. We will tacitly assume that all the languages still to be defined subsequently will be countable in this sense.

The symbol $\to$ is a (binary) *logical operator*, called *implication*; **false** is a special formula. Further logical operators and another distinguished formula **true** can be introduced to abbreviate particular formulas.

Abbreviations

$$\begin{aligned}
\neg A &\equiv A \to \mathbf{false},\\
A \vee B &\equiv \neg A \to B,\\
A \wedge B &\equiv \neg(A \to \neg B),\\
A \leftrightarrow B &\equiv (A \to B) \wedge (B \to A),\\
\mathbf{true} &\equiv \neg\, \mathbf{false}.
\end{aligned}$$

(We have omitted surrounding parentheses and will do so also in the following. By $\equiv$ we denote equality of strings.) The operators $\neg$, $\vee$, $\wedge$, and $\leftrightarrow$ are called *negation*, *disjunction*, *conjunction*, and *equivalence*, respectively.

The symbols A and B in such definitions are not formulas (of some $\mathcal{L}_{\mathrm{PL}}$) themselves but *syntactic variables* ranging over the set of formulas. Accordingly, a string like $\neg A \to B$ is not a formula either. It yields a formula by substituting proper formulas for A and B. Nevertheless, we freely use wordings like "formula A" or "formula $\neg A \to B$" to avoid more precise but complicated formulations like "formula of the form $\neg A \to B$ where A and B stand for formulas". Moreover, we speak of formulas "of PL" since the concrete language $\mathcal{L}_{\mathrm{PL}}$ is not relevant in this notation. In all the other logics developed subsequently, we will adopt these conventions accordingly.

The language definition of a logic constitutes its *syntax*. Its *semantics* is based on formal *interpretations* J of the syntactical elements together with a notion of *validity in* (or *satisfaction by*) J.

In the case of PL, interpretations are provided by (*boolean*) *valuations*. Given two distinct *truth values*, denoted by ff ("false") and tt ("true"), a valuation B for a set $\mathbf{V}$ of propositional constants is a mapping

$$\mathsf{B} : \mathbf{V} \rightarrow \{\mathsf{ff}, \mathsf{tt}\}.$$

Every such B can be inductively extended to the set of all formulas of $\mathcal{L}_{\mathrm{PL}}(\mathbf{V})$:

1. $\mathsf{B}(v)$ for $v \in \mathbf{V}$ is given.
2. $\mathsf{B}(\mathbf{false}) = \mathsf{ff}$.
3. $\mathsf{B}(A \rightarrow B) = \mathsf{tt} \;\Leftrightarrow\; \mathsf{B}(A) = \mathsf{ff}$ or $\mathsf{B}(B) = \mathsf{tt}$.

(We use $\Leftrightarrow$ as an abbreviation for "if and only if"; later we will also use $\Rightarrow$ for "if... then...".) This also defines B for the formula abbreviations above:

4. $\mathsf{B}(\neg A) = \mathsf{tt} \;\Leftrightarrow\; \mathsf{B}(A) = \mathsf{ff}$.
5. $\mathsf{B}(A \vee B) = \mathsf{tt} \;\Leftrightarrow\; \mathsf{B}(A) = \mathsf{tt}$ or $\mathsf{B}(B) = \mathsf{tt}$.
6. $\mathsf{B}(A \wedge B) = \mathsf{tt} \;\Leftrightarrow\; \mathsf{B}(A) = \mathsf{tt}$ and $\mathsf{B}(B) = \mathsf{tt}$.
7. $\mathsf{B}(A \leftrightarrow B) = \mathsf{tt} \;\Leftrightarrow\; \mathsf{B}(A) = \mathsf{B}(B)$.
8. $\mathsf{B}(\mathbf{true}) = \mathsf{tt}$.

A formula A of $\mathcal{L}_{\mathrm{PL}}$ is called *valid in* B (or B *satisfies* A), denoted by $\models_{\mathsf{B}} A$, if $\mathsf{B}(A) = \mathsf{tt}$.

Based on this notion, the *consequence relation* and *(universal) validity* in PL are defined. Let A be a formula, $\mathcal{F}$ a set of formulas of $\mathcal{L}_{\mathrm{PL}}$.

- A is called a *consequence of* $\mathcal{F}$ if $\models_{\mathsf{B}} A$ holds for every valuation B with $\models_{\mathsf{B}} B$ for all $B \in \mathcal{F}$.
- A is called *(universally) valid* or a *tautology* if it is a consequence of the empty set of formulas, i.e., if $\models_{\mathsf{B}} A$ holds for every B.

The pattern of this definition will occur analogously for all other subsequent logics with other interpretations. For any logic,

$$\mathcal{F} \models A, \text{ also written } B_1, \ldots, B_n \models A \text{ if } \mathcal{F} = \{B_1, \ldots, B_n\}, n \geq 1$$

will denote that A is a consequence of $\mathcal{F}$, and

$$\models A$$

will denote that A is valid.

With these definitions there are two possible formal statements (in PL) of what informally is expressed by a phrase like "B follows from A". The first one is asserted by implication within the language:

$$A \rightarrow B.$$

The second one is given by the consequence relation:

$$A \models B.$$

A fundamental fact of classical (propositional) logic is that these notions are equivalent:

$$A \models B \;\Leftrightarrow\; \models A \to B$$

or more generally ($\mathcal{F}$ being an arbitrary set of formulas):

$$\mathcal{F} \cup \{A\} \models B \;\Leftrightarrow\; \mathcal{F} \models A \to B$$

which can be "unfolded" for finite $\mathcal{F}$ to

$$A_1, \ldots, A_n \models B \;\Leftrightarrow\; \models A_1 \to (A_2 \to \ldots \to (A_n \to B) \ldots)$$

or, equivalently, to the more readable

$$A_1, \ldots, A_n \models B \;\Leftrightarrow\; \models (A_1 \wedge \ldots \wedge A_n) \to B.$$

Note that we write $(A_1 \wedge \ldots \wedge A_n)$ without inner parentheses, which is syntactically not correct but justified as a shortcut by the fact that the real bracketing is of no relevance (more formally: the operator $\wedge$ is associative). The analogous notation will be used for disjunctions.

Validity and consequence are key notions of any logic. Besides their semantical definitions they can (usually) be described in a *proof-theoretical* way by *formal systems*. A formal system Σ for a logical language consists of

- a set of formulas of the language, called *axioms*,
- a set of (*derivation*) *rules* of the form $A_1, \ldots, A_n \vdash B \;\; (n \geq 1)$.

The formulas $A_1, \ldots, A_n$ are called the *premises*, the formula B is the *conclusion* of the rule. To distinguish it from other existing forms, a formal system of this kind is called *Hilbert-like*. Throughout this book we will use only this form.

The *derivability* (in formal system Σ) of a formula A *from* a set $\mathcal{F}$ of formulas (*assumptions*), denoted by $\mathcal{F} \vdash_{\Sigma} A$ or $\mathcal{F} \vdash A$ when Σ is understood from the context, is defined inductively:

1. $\mathcal{F} \vdash A$ for every axiom.
2. $\mathcal{F} \vdash A$ for every $A \in \mathcal{F}$.
3. If $\mathcal{F} \vdash A$ for all premises A of a rule then $\mathcal{F} \vdash B$ for the conclusion of this rule.

A formula A is called *derivable*, denoted by $\vdash_{\Sigma} A$ or $\vdash A$, if $\emptyset \vdash A$. If A is derivable from some $A_1, \ldots, A_n$ then the "relation" $A_1, \ldots, A_n \vdash A$ can itself be used as a *derived rule* in other derivations.

For languages of PL there are many possible formal systems. One of them, denoted by Σ_{PL}, is the following.

Axioms

- $A \to (B \to A)$,
- $(A \to (B \to C)) \to ((A \to B) \to (A \to C))$,
- $((A \to \mathbf{false}) \to \mathbf{false}) \to A$.

Rule

- $A, A \to B \vdash B$ *(modus ponens)*.

We remark once more that the strings written down are not formulas. So, for example, $A \to (B \to A)$ is not one axiom but an *axiom scheme* which yields infinitely many axioms when formulas are substituted for A and B. Actually, Σ_{PL} is written in a form which is independent of the concrete language of PL. So we may call Σ_{PL} a formal system "for PL". In the same sense we will subsequently give formal systems for other logics. A formal system for a logic is also called its *axiomatization*.

Like the semantical consequence relation $\models$, derivability is related to implication in the following sense:

$$\mathcal{F} \cup \{A\} \vdash B \;\Leftrightarrow\; \mathcal{F} \vdash A \to B.$$

The only if part of this fact is called the *Deduction Theorem* (of PL).

An indispensable requirement of any reasonable formal system is its *soundness* with respect to the semantical notions of the logic. Σ_{PL} is in fact sound, which means that

$$\mathcal{F} \vdash_{\Sigma_{\mathrm{PL}}} A \;\Rightarrow\; \mathcal{F} \models A$$

holds for every $\mathcal{F}$ and A. Moreover, it can also be shown that

$$\mathcal{F} \models A \;\Rightarrow\; \mathcal{F} \vdash_{\Sigma_{\mathrm{PL}}} A$$

which states the *completeness* of Σ_{PL}. As a special case both facts imply

$$\vdash_{\Sigma_{\mathrm{PL}}} A \;\Leftrightarrow\; \models A$$

for every formula A.

A formal system allows for "producing" formulas by applying rules in a "mechanical" way. So, a particular effect of the latter relationship is that the set of valid formulas of (any language of) PL can be "mechanically generated" (in technical terms: it is *recursively enumerable*). Moreover, this set is *decidable* (shortly: PL is decidable), i.e., there is an algorithmic procedure to decide for any formula whether it is valid.

We illustrate the main concepts and notions of this section by an example. A simple logical principle of reasoning is informally expressed by

"If B follows from A and C follows from B then C follows from A".

This *chaining rule* can formally be stated and verified in several ways: we can establish the formula

$$F \equiv ((A \to B) \land (B \to C)) \to (A \to C)$$

as valid, i.e., $\models F$ (speaking semantically), or as derivable, i.e., $\vdash F$ (speaking proof-theoretically), or we can express it by

$$A \to B, B \to C \models A \to C \quad (\text{or } A \to B, B \to C \vdash A \to C).$$

The proofs for the semantical formulations are straightforward from the definitions. As an example of a formal derivation within the formal system Σ_{PL} and in order to introduce our standard format of such proofs we derive $A \to C$ from $A \to B$ and $B \to C$, i.e., we show that $A \to B, B \to C \vdash A \to C$:

(1)	$A \to B$	assumption
(2)	$B \to C$	assumption
(3)	$(B \to C) \to (A \to (B \to C))$	axiom
(4)	$A \to (B \to C)$	modus ponens,(2),(3)
(5)	$(A \to (B \to C)) \to ((A \to B) \to (A \to C))$	axiom
(6)	$(A \to B) \to (A \to C)$	modus ponens,(4),(5)
(7)	$A \to C$	modus ponens,(1),(6)

In each of the numbered steps (lines) we list some derivable formula and indicate on the right-hand side if it is an axiom or an assumption or by what rule applied to previous lines it is found.

We add a selection of some more valid formulas. These and other tautologies will (very often implicitly) be used in the subsequent chapters.

- $A \vee \neg A$,
- $\neg\neg A \leftrightarrow A$,
- $(A \wedge (B \vee C)) \leftrightarrow ((A \wedge B) \vee (A \wedge C))$,
- $\neg(A \wedge B) \leftrightarrow (\neg A \vee \neg B)$,
- $((A \wedge B) \to C) \leftrightarrow (A \to (B \to C))$,
- $(A \to B) \leftrightarrow (\neg B \to \neg A)$,
- $(A \wedge \textbf{true}) \leftrightarrow A$,
- $(A \vee \textbf{false}) \leftrightarrow A$,
- $(A \to C) \to ((A \wedge B) \to C)$,
- $((A \vee B) \to C) \to (A \to C)$.

As mentioned at the beginning, PL formalizes (a part of) reasoning about statements in mathematical systems. Its semantics formalizes the natural basic point of view of "usual" mathematics that a statement is something which is either "false" or "true". We still remark that, for specific applications or propagated by philosophical considerations, there are other "non-standard" semantical concepts as well. Examples are *three-valued logic* (a statement can have three different truth values which may be understood as "false", "possible", or "true"), *probabilistic logic* (truth is given with a certain probability), or *intuitionistic logic* (statements are interpreted *constructively* which, e.g., means that the *tertium non datur* formula $A \vee \neg A$ is no longer valid since it might be that neither the truth nor the falsity of A can be found in a constructive way).

1.2 Classical First-Order Logic

Mathematical statements and argumentations usually need more means than can be represented in propositional logic. These are provided by extending PL to *predicate logic* which investigates a more detailed structure of formulas dealing with *objects, functions*, and *predicates*, and includes the concept of *quantification* with operators like *for some* and *for all*.

The standard form of predicate logic is *first-order logic* FOL which we describe in its *many-sorted* version as follows.

A *signature* $SIG = (\mathbf{S}, \mathbf{F}, \mathbf{P})$ is given by

- a set $\mathbf{S}$ of *sorts*,
- $\mathbf{F} = \bigcup_{\vec{s} \in \mathbf{S}^*, s \in \mathbf{S}} \mathbf{F}^{(\vec{s},s)}$ where $\mathbf{F}^{(\vec{s},s)}$, for every $\vec{s} \in \mathbf{S}^*$ and $s \in \mathbf{S}$, is a set of *function symbols* (also called *individual constants* in the case of $\vec{s} = \varepsilon$),
- $\mathbf{P} = \bigcup_{\vec{s} \in \mathbf{S}^*} \mathbf{P}^{(\vec{s})}$ where $\mathbf{P}^{(\vec{s})}$, for every $\vec{s} \in \mathbf{S}^*$, is a set of *predicate symbols* (also called *propositional constants* in the case of $\vec{s} = \varepsilon$).

($\mathbf{S}^*$ denotes the set of finite strings over $\mathbf{S}$; ε is the empty string.) For $f \in \mathbf{F}$ we will often write $f^{(\vec{s},s)}$ to indicate that f belongs to $\mathbf{F}^{(\vec{s},s)}$, and analogously for $p \in \mathbf{P}$.

Given a signature $SIG = (\mathbf{S}, \mathbf{F}, \mathbf{P})$, a *first-order language* $\mathcal{L}_{\mathrm{FOL}}(SIG)$ (also shortly: $\mathcal{L}_{\mathrm{FOL}}$) is given by the following syntax.

Alphabet

- All symbols of $\mathbf{F}$ and $\mathbf{P}$,
- for every $s \in \mathbf{S}$ denumerably many (*individual*) *variables*,
- the *equality symbol* $=$,
- the symbols $\mathbf{false} \mid \rightarrow \mid \exists \mid , \mid (\mid)$.

We will denote the set of variables for $s \in \mathbf{S}$ by $\mathcal{X}_s$ and define $\mathcal{X} = \bigcup_{s \in \mathbf{S}} \mathcal{X}_s$. Strictly speaking, $\mathcal{L}_{\mathrm{FOL}}(SIG)$ does not only depend on the given signature SIG but also on the choice of (the notations for) all these variables. We do not display this dependence since $\mathcal{X}$ could also be fixed for all languages. Note that requesting each $\mathcal{X}_s$ to be denumerable is only for having "enough" variables available.

Terms and *their sorts* (inductively defined):

1. Every variable of $\mathcal{X}_s$ is a term of sort s.
2. If $f \in \mathbf{F}^{(s_1 \ldots s_n, s)}$ is a function symbol and t_i are terms of sorts s_i for $1 \le i \le n$ then $f(t_1, \ldots, t_n)$ is a term of sort s.

An *atomic formula* is a string of the form

- $p(t_1, \ldots, t_n)$, where $p \in \mathbf{P}^{(s_1 \ldots s_n)}$ is a predicate symbol and t_i are terms of sorts s_i for $1 \le i \le n$, or
- $t_1 = t_2$, where t_1 and t_2 are terms of the same sort.

Formulas (inductively defined):

1. Every atomic formula is a formula.

2. **false** is a formula, and if A and B are formulas then $(A \to B)$ is a formula.
3. If A is a formula and x is a variable then $\exists x A$ is a formula.

We reuse the abbreviations from $\mathcal{L}_{\mathrm{PL}}$ and introduce two more:

$$\begin{aligned} \forall x A &\equiv \neg \exists x \neg A, \\ t_1 \neq t_2 &\equiv \neg\, t_1 = t_2. \end{aligned}$$

Furthermore, we will write f instead of $f()$ for individual constants $f \in \mathbf{F}^{(\varepsilon,s)}$ and p instead of $p()$ for propositional constants $p \in \mathbf{P}^{(\varepsilon)}$; x, y and the like will be used to denote variables.

A variable x (more precisely: an occurrence of x) in a formula A is called *bound* if it appears in some part $\exists x B$ of A; otherwise it is called *free*. If t is a term of the same sort as x then $A_x(t)$ denotes the result of substituting t for every free occurrence of x in A. When writing $A_x(t)$ we always assume implicitly that t does not contain variables which occur bound in A. (This can always be achieved by replacing the bound variables of A by others.) A formula without any free variables is called *closed*. If A is a formula that contains no free occurrences of variables other than $x_1, \ldots, x_n$ then the (closed) formula $\forall x_1 \ldots \forall x_n A$ is called the *universal closure* of A.

As an example of a first-order language consider the signature

$$SIG_{gr} = (\{GR\}, \{NEL^{(\varepsilon,GR)}, \circ^{(GR\,GR,GR)}, INV^{(GR,GR)}\}, \emptyset).$$

The terms of $\mathcal{L}_{\mathrm{FOL}}(SIG_{gr})$ are the variables $x \in \mathcal{X}_{GR} = \mathcal{X}$ of the language, the individual constant NEL, and expressions of the form $\circ(t_1, t_2)$ or $INV(t)$ with terms t, t_1, t_2. All terms are of the sole sort GR. Since SIG_{gr} contains no predicate symbols the only atomic formulas are "equalities" $t_1 = t_2$ with terms t_1, t_2. The string

$$\forall x \circ(NEL, x) = x$$

is an example of a formula.

For the semantics of FOL, interpretations are given by *structures* which generalize the valuations of PL to the new situation. A structure S for a signature $SIG = (\mathbf{S}, \mathbf{F}, \mathbf{P})$ consists of

- $|\mathsf{S}| = \bigcup_{s \in \mathbf{S}} |\mathsf{S}|_s$ where $|\mathsf{S}|_s$ is a non-empty set (called *domain*) for every $s \in \mathbf{S}$,
- mappings $f^{\mathsf{S}} : |\mathsf{S}|_{s_1} \times \ldots \times |\mathsf{S}|_{s_n} \to |\mathsf{S}|_s$ for all function symbols $f \in \mathbf{F}^{(s_1 \ldots s_n, s)}$,
- mappings $p^{\mathsf{S}} : |\mathsf{S}|_{s_1} \times \ldots \times |\mathsf{S}|_{s_n} \to \{\mathsf{ff}, \mathsf{tt}\}$ for all predicate symbols $p \in \mathbf{P}^{(s_1 \ldots s_n)}$.

Note that for individual constants $f \in \mathbf{F}^{(\varepsilon,s)}$ we obtain $f^{\mathsf{S}} \in |\mathsf{S}|_s$. For $p \in \mathbf{P}^{(\varepsilon)}$ we have $p^{\mathsf{S}} \in \{\mathsf{ff}, \mathsf{tt}\}$ which justifies these p again being called propositional constants.

A *variable valuation* ξ (with respect to S) assigns some $\xi(x) \in |\mathsf{S}|_s$ to every variable $x \in \mathcal{X}_s$ (for all $s \in \mathbf{S}$). A structure together with a variable valuation ξ defines inductively a value $\mathsf{S}^{(\xi)}(t) \in |\mathsf{S}|$ for every term t:

1. $\mathsf{S}^{(\xi)}(x) = \xi(x)$ for $x \in \mathcal{X}$.
2. $\mathsf{S}^{(\xi)}(f(t_1, \ldots, t_n)) = f^{\mathsf{S}}(\mathsf{S}^{(\xi)}(t_1), \ldots, \mathsf{S}^{(\xi)}(t_n))$.

Furthermore, we can define $\mathsf{S}^{(\xi)}(A) \in \{\mathsf{ff}, \mathsf{tt}\}$ for every atomic formula:

1. $\mathsf{S}^{(\xi)}(p(t_1, \ldots, t_n)) = p^{\mathsf{S}}(\mathsf{S}^{(\xi)}(t_1), \ldots, \mathsf{S}^{(\xi)}(t_n))$.
2. $\mathsf{S}^{(\xi)}(t_1 = t_2) = \mathsf{tt} \Leftrightarrow \mathsf{S}^{(\xi)}(t_1)$ and $\mathsf{S}^{(\xi)}(t_2)$ are equal values in $|\mathsf{S}|_s$ (where s is the sort of t_1 and t_2).

Analogously to the valuations B in PL, $\mathsf{S}^{(\xi)}$ can be inductively extended to all formulas of $\mathcal{L}_{\mathrm{FOL}}$. Defining the relation $\sim_x$ for $x \in \mathcal{X}$ between variable valuations by

$$\xi \sim_x \xi' \Leftrightarrow \xi(y) = \xi'(y) \text{ for all } y \in \mathcal{X} \text{ other than } x,$$

the inductive clauses are:

1. $\mathsf{S}^{(\xi)}(A)$ for atomic formulas is already defined.
2. $\mathsf{S}^{(\xi)}(\mathbf{false}) = \mathsf{ff}$.
3. $\mathsf{S}^{(\xi)}(A \to B) = \mathsf{tt} \Leftrightarrow \mathsf{S}^{(\xi)}(A) = \mathsf{ff}$ or $\mathsf{S}^{(\xi)}(B) = \mathsf{tt}$.
4. $\mathsf{S}^{(\xi)}(\exists x A) = \mathsf{tt} \Leftrightarrow$ there is a ξ' such that $\xi \sim_x \xi'$ and $\mathsf{S}^{(\xi')}(A) = \mathsf{tt}$.

The truth values for formulas like $\neg A$, $A \vee B$, etc. result from these definitions as in PL, and for $\forall x A$ we obtain:

5. $\mathsf{S}^{(\xi)}(\forall x A) = \mathsf{tt} \Leftrightarrow \mathsf{S}^{(\xi')}(A) = \mathsf{tt}$ for all ξ' with $\xi \sim_x \xi'$.

The value $\mathsf{S}^{(\xi)}(A)$ depends only on the valuation of variables that have free occurrences in A. In particular, $\mathsf{S}^{(\xi)}(A)$ does not depend on the variable valuation ξ when A is a closed formula. This observation justifies our convention that bound variables are suitably renamed before a substitution $A_x(t)$ is performed.

A formula A of $\mathcal{L}_{\mathrm{FOL}}$ is called *valid in* S (or S *satisfies* A), denoted by $\models_{\mathsf{S}} A$, if $\mathsf{S}^{(\xi)}(A) = \mathsf{tt}$ for every variable valuation ξ. Following the general pattern from Sect. 1.1, A is called a *consequence of* a set $\mathcal{F}$ of formulas ($\mathcal{F} \models A$) if $\models_{\mathsf{S}} A$ holds for every S with $\models_{\mathsf{S}} B$ for all $B \in \mathcal{F}$. A is called (*universally*) *valid* ($\models A$) if $\emptyset \models A$.

Continuing the example considered above, a structure Z for the signature SIG_{gr} could be given by

$$|\mathsf{Z}| = |\mathsf{Z}|_{GR} = \mathbb{Z} \text{ (the set of integers)},$$
$$NEL^{\mathsf{Z}} = 0 \in \mathbb{Z},\ \circ^{\mathsf{Z}}(k,l) = k + l,\ INV^{\mathsf{Z}}(k) = -k \text{ (for } k, l \in \mathbb{Z}).$$

The formula $\forall x \circ(NEL, x) = x$ is valid in Z but not universally valid: consider the structure S that differs from Z by defining $NEL^{\mathsf{S}} = 1$. An example of a valid formula is

$$\circ(x, y) = INV(y) \to INV(y) = \circ(x, y).$$

More generally,

$$t_1 = t_2 \to t_2 = t_1$$

is a valid formula ("scheme") for arbitrary terms t_1, t_2 (of the same sort), and this formulation is in fact independent of the concrete signature SIG in the sense that it is valid in every $\mathcal{L}_{\mathrm{FOL}}(SIG)$ for terms t_1, t_2 that can be built within SIG.

The fundamental relationship

$$\mathcal{F} \cup \{A\} \models B \;\Leftrightarrow\; \mathcal{F} \models A \rightarrow B$$

between implication and consequence stated in Sect. 1.1 for PL has to be modified slightly in FOL. It holds if A does not contain free variables.

In contrast to PL, FOL is not decidable (for arbitrary first-order languages), but there exist again sound and complete axiomatizations of FOL. An example is given by the following formal system Σ_{FOL} (which uses x and y to denote variables).

Axioms

- All axioms of Σ_{PL},
- $A_x(t) \rightarrow \exists x A$,
- $x = x$,
- $x = y \rightarrow (A \rightarrow A_x(y))$.

Rules

- $A, A \rightarrow B \vdash B$,
- $A \rightarrow B \vdash \exists x A \rightarrow B$ if there is no free occurrence of x in B (*particularization*).

According to the remark above, the Deduction Theorem for FOL must be formulated with somewhat more care than in PL. A possible formulation is:

$\mathcal{F} \cup \{A\} \vdash B \;\Rightarrow\; \mathcal{F} \vdash A \rightarrow B$ if the derivation of B from $\mathcal{F} \cup \{A\}$ contains no application of the particularization rule involving a variable that occurs free in A.

Note in particular that the condition for the applicability of this rule is trivially fulfilled if A is a closed formula.

The converse connection holds without any restrictions (as in PL).

Again we list some valid formulas (now of FOL) in order to give an impression what kinds of such predicate logical facts may be used subsequently.

- $t_1 = t_2 \leftrightarrow t_2 = t_1$,
- $t_1 = t_2 \wedge t_2 = t_3 \rightarrow t_1 = t_3$,
- $\forall x A \rightarrow A_x(t)$,
- $\forall x(A \rightarrow B) \rightarrow (\forall x A \rightarrow \forall x B)$,
- $\exists x(A \vee B) \leftrightarrow (\exists x A \vee \exists x B)$,
- $\exists x(A \rightarrow B) \leftrightarrow (\forall x A \rightarrow B)$, x not free in B,
- $\exists x \forall y A \rightarrow \forall y \exists x A$.

Finally we note a derivable rule, called *generalization*, which is "dual" to the above particularization rule:

- $A \rightarrow B \vdash A \rightarrow \forall x B$ if there is no free occurrence of x in A.

1.3 Theories and Models

Languages of predicate logic provide a general linguistic framework for the description of mathematical systems. This framework is instantiated to specific systems by fixing an according signature. For example, the language $\mathcal{L}_{\mathrm{FOL}}(SIG_{gr})$ with

$$SIG_{gr} = (\{GR\}, \{NEL^{(\varepsilon,GR)}, \circ^{(GR\,GR,GR)}, INV^{(GR,GR)}\}, \emptyset),$$

mentioned in the previous section, is an appropriate language for formalizing groups: GR represents the underlying set of the group, NEL should be interpreted as the neutral element, $\circ$ as the group product, and INV as the inverse operation. This interpretation is formally performed by a structure, and in fact, the sample structure Z for SIG_{gr} of Sect. 1.2 is a group.

Valid formulas hold in all structures. Structures that "fit" the mathematical system in question can be distinguished by a set of formulas that are valid in those structures, though not necessarily universally valid. Formalizing this concept, a *(first-order) theory* $Th = (\mathcal{L}_{\mathrm{FOL}}(SIG), \mathcal{A})$ is given by a language $\mathcal{L}_{\mathrm{FOL}}(SIG)$ and a set $\mathcal{A}$ of formulas of $\mathcal{L}_{\mathrm{FOL}}(SIG)$, called the *non-logical axioms* of Th. A structure S for SIG satisfying all formulas of $\mathcal{A}$ is called a *model* of the theory Th. Given a class $\mathcal{C}$ of structures for a signature SIG, a $\mathcal{C}$*-theory* is a theory $Th = (\mathcal{L}_{\mathrm{FOL}}(SIG), \mathcal{A}_{\mathcal{C}})$ such that all structures of $\mathcal{C}$ are models of Th. A formula F of $\mathcal{L}_{\mathrm{FOL}}(SIG)$ is valid in all structures of $\mathcal{C}$ if

$$\mathcal{A}_{\mathcal{C}} \vdash_{\Sigma_{\mathrm{FOL}}} F$$

since Σ_{FOL} is sound and therefore $\mathcal{A}_{\mathcal{C}} \vdash_{\Sigma_{\mathrm{FOL}}} F$ implies $\mathcal{A}_{\mathcal{C}} \models F$.

With these definitions, the theory $Group = (\mathcal{L}_{\mathrm{FOL}}(SIG_{gr}), \mathcal{G})$ with $\mathcal{G}$ consisting of the formulas

$$\begin{aligned}
&(x_1 \circ x_2) \circ x_3 = x_1 \circ (x_2 \circ x_3),\\
&NEL \circ x = x,\\
&INV(x) \circ x = NEL
\end{aligned}$$

– where we write $x_1 \circ x_2$ instead of $\circ(x_1, x_2)$ – is a (first-order) group theory. More precisely, $Group$ is a $\mathcal{C}_{gr}$-theory where $\mathcal{C}_{gr}$ is the class of all structures G for SIG_{gr} such that the set $|\mathsf{G}| = |\mathsf{G}|_{GR}$ together with the interpretations NEL^{G}, $\circ^{\mathsf{G}}$, and INV^{G} form a group. The non-logical axioms of $\mathcal{G}$ are just well-known group axioms. Formulas F valid in groups can be obtained within the logical framework by derivations

$$\mathcal{G} \vdash_{\Sigma_{\mathrm{FOL}}} F.$$

The axioms of $\mathcal{G}$ contain free variables. Sometimes it might be convenient to write such axioms in "closed form" by taking their universal closures, e.g.,

$$\forall x_1 \forall x_2 \forall x_3((x_1 \circ x_2) \circ x_3 = x_1 \circ (x_2 \circ x_3))$$

instead of the first axiom above. The definition of validity in a structure implies that any structure satisfies a formula A if and only if it satisfies the universal closure of A; therefore the two versions of how to write the axioms are in fact equivalent.

We give some more examples of theories: let

$$SIG_{lo} = (\{ORD\}, \emptyset, \{\prec^{(ORD\ ORD)}\}),$$
$$LinOrd = (\mathcal{L}_{\mathrm{FOL}}(SIG_{lo}), \mathcal{O})$$

with $\mathcal{O}$ consisting of the axioms (in non-closed form)

$$\neg\, x \prec x,$$
$$(x_1 \prec x_2 \wedge x_2 \prec x_3) \rightarrow x_1 \prec x_3,$$
$$x_1 \neq x_2 \rightarrow (x_1 \prec x_2 \vee x_2 \prec x_1).$$

(As for $\circ$ in $\mathcal{L}_{\mathrm{FOL}}(SIG_{gr})$, we mostly use infix notation – here and in the following – for "binary" function and predicate symbols.) Every structure O where $|\mathsf{O}| = |\mathsf{O}|_{ORD}$ is a non-empty set and $\prec^{\mathsf{O}}$ is a (strict) linear order on $|\mathsf{O}|$ is a model of $LinOrd$ which, hence, may be called a linear order theory.

A natural number theory Nat is based on a signature

$$SIG_{Nat} = (\{NAT\}, \mathbf{F}, \emptyset)$$

with

$$\mathbf{F} = \{0^{(\varepsilon, NAT)}, SUCC^{(NAT, NAT)}, +^{(NAT\ NAT, NAT)}, *^{(NAT\ NAT, NAT)}\}.$$

In the intended structure N for SIG_{Nat}, $|\mathsf{N}| = |\mathsf{N}|_{NAT}$ is the set $\mathbb{N}$ of natural numbers (including zero), 0^{N} is the number zero, $SUCC^{\mathsf{N}}$ is the successor function on natural numbers, and $+^{\mathsf{N}}$ and $*^{\mathsf{N}}$ are addition and multiplication, respectively. $Nat = (\mathcal{L}_{\mathrm{FOL}}(SIG_{Nat}), \mathcal{N})$ is an $\{\mathsf{N}\}$-theory if we let $\mathcal{N}$ contain the following axioms:

$$SUCC(x) \neq 0,$$
$$SUCC(x) = SUCC(y) \rightarrow x = y,$$
$$x + 0 = x,$$
$$x + SUCC(y) = SUCC(x + y),$$
$$x * 0 = 0,$$
$$x * SUCC(y) = (x * y) + x,$$
$$(A_x(0) \wedge \forall x(A \rightarrow A_x(SUCC(x)))) \rightarrow \forall x A.$$

The notion of $\mathcal{C}$-theories is not very sharp. If $Th = (\mathcal{L}_{\mathrm{FOL}}, \mathcal{A})$ is a $\mathcal{C}$-theory then, by definition, so is every $(\mathcal{L}_{\mathrm{FOL}}, \mathcal{A}')$ where $\mathcal{A}' \subseteq \mathcal{A}$. Hence, in general, a $\mathcal{C}$-theory does not really "characterize" the class $\mathcal{C}$ of structures. The reason is that in the definition we only required that all structures of $\mathcal{C}$ satisfy the non-logical axioms, but not that these structures be the only models of the theory.

The theories *Group* and $LinOrd$ actually satisfy this stronger requirement: somewhat roughly speaking, a structure is a model of *Group* or $LinOrd$ if and only if it is a group or a linearly ordered set, respectively. The theories characterize these mathematical systems and we may call them *theory of groups* and *theory of linear orders* (instead of "$\mathcal{C}$-theories").

In the case of Nat, however, the situation is fundamentally different. The structure N cannot be characterized in this way: every first-order theory which has N as a model has also other (even "essentially" different) models. This is a consequence of the famous *(First) Gödel Incompleteness Theorem* which (particularly) says that N cannot be completely axiomatized in first-order logic. More precisely: for any first-order $\{\mathsf{N}\}$-theory whose non-logical axiom set $\mathcal{A}$ is decidable there are formulas F of SIG_{Nat} such that $\models_{\mathsf{N}} F$ but F is not derivable from $\mathcal{A}$ in Σ_{FOL}.

In the presence of different models for natural number theories, N is usually called the *standard model.* This model, together with its underlying signature SIG_{Nat}, will frequently occur in subsequent sections. If necessary, we will feel free to assume (without explicitly mentioning) that the signature may also be enriched by more symbols than shown above (e.g., symbols for other individual constants like $1, 2, \ldots$, for subtraction, division, order relations, etc.) together with their standard interpretations in N. Furthermore, we will overload notation by denoting the interpretations of syntactic symbols by these same symbols (e.g., $+^{\mathsf{N}}, *^{\mathsf{N}}, 1^{\mathsf{N}}, 2^{\mathsf{N}}, \ldots$ will be denoted by $+, *, 1, 2, \ldots$).

Besides formalizing mathematical systems such as groups and linear orders, the concept of logical theories also finds applications in computer science. For example, the theory Nat (perhaps presented with some extra "syntactic sugar") would typically be called an *algebraic specification* of the natural numbers. In general, an algebraic specification of an *abstract data type* (in a *functional* setting) is just the same as a theory.

A further example is given by the signature

$$SIG_{st} = (\{OBJ, STACK\}, \mathbf{F}, \emptyset)$$

with

$$\mathbf{F} = \{EMPTY^{(\varepsilon,STACK)}, PUSH^{(STACK\ OBJ,STACK)}, \\ POP^{(STACK,STACK)}, TOP^{(STACK,OBJ)}\}$$

and the theory (or algebraic specification)

$$Stack = (\mathcal{L}_{\mathrm{FOL}}(SIG_{st}), \mathcal{S})$$

with $\mathcal{S}$ consisting of the axioms

$$PUSH(x, y) \neq EMPTY, \\ POP(PUSH(x, y)) = x, \\ TOP(PUSH(x, y)) = y$$

(where $x \in \mathcal{X}_{STACK}, y \in \mathcal{X}_{OBJ}$). Clearly, $Stack$ is a theory of stacks: the domain $|\mathsf{S}|_{STACK}$ of its (standard) models consists of stacks of objects from $|\mathsf{S}|_{OBJ}$ and $EMPTY^{\mathsf{S}}$, $PUSH^{\mathsf{S}}$, POP^{S}, and TOP^{S} are functions implementing the usual stack operations.

Note that the semantical definitions in the previous section obviously assume that the mappings which interpret function and predicate symbols are total since otherwise the evaluation $\mathsf{S}^{(\xi)}$ would not always be defined. In this example, on the other hand, *pop* and *top* are usually understood to be partial (not defined on the empty stack). To solve this technical problem in a trivial way, we assume that *pop* and *top* deliver some arbitrary values when applied to the empty stack and, hence, are total. In subsequent similar situations we will always tacitly make corresponding assumptions.

In some computer science texts, specifications like *Nat* or *Stack* additionally contain (or "use") an explicit specification of a data type *Boolean* containing the boolean values and the usual boolean operators. Because *Boolean* is implicitly contained in the propositional fragment of first-order logic, it does not have to be an explicit part of a first-order theory.

We have introduced the concept of theories in the framework of classical first-order logic. Of course, it can be defined in the same way for any other logic as well. For example, a theory could also be based on propositional logic. Such *propositional theories* are of minor interest in mathematics. In computer science, however, this changes, particularly because of the decidability of PL. A typical situation arises by first-order theories of structures with finite domains. These can be encoded as propositional theories (essentially by expressing a quantification $\exists x A$ by a disjunction of all instantiations of A with the finitely many possible values $\xi(x)$ of x) and can then be accessible to appropriate algorithmic treatments. We will investigate this aspect in the context of temporal logic in Chap. 11 and content ourselves here with a toy example of the kind which typically serves as a measure for automatic proof systems. Consider the following criminal story:

> Lady Agatha was found dead in her home where she lived together with her butler and with uncle Charles. After some investigations of the detective, the following facts are assured:
>
> 1. Agatha was killed by one of the inhabitants.
> 2. Nobody kills somebody without hating him or her.
> 3. The perpetrator is never richer than the victim.
> 4. Charles hates nobody whom Agatha was hating.
> 5. Agatha hated all inhabitants except perhaps the butler.
> 6. The butler hates everybody not richer than Agatha or hated by Agatha.
> 7. No inhabitant hates (or hated) all inhabitants.
>
> Who killed Agatha?

In order to fix a language of propositional logic we have to determine the set $\mathbf{V}$ of propositional constants. For our story we represent the persons Agatha, the butler, and Charles by a, b, and c, respectively, and let $\mathbb{P} = \{a, b, c\}$ and

$$\mathbf{V}_{murder} = \{kill_{ij}, hate_{ij}, richer_{ij} \mid i, j \in \mathbb{P}\}.$$

The elements of $\mathbf{V}_{murder}$ represent the propositions "i killed j", "i hates (or hated) j", and "i is (was) richer than j" for $i, j \in \mathbb{P}$, respectively. With this in mind we get a propositional theory $(\mathcal{L}_{\mathrm{PL}}(\mathbf{V}_{murder}), \mathcal{M})$ by collecting in $\mathcal{M}$ the following formulas which formally express the above facts:

1. $kill_{aa} \vee kill_{ba} \vee kill_{ca}$,
2. $kill_{ij} \to hate_{ij}$ for all $i, j \in \mathbb{P}$,
3. $kill_{ij} \to \neg richer_{ij}$ for all $i, j \in \mathbb{P}$,
4. $hate_{aj} \to \neg hate_{cj}$ for all $j \in \mathbb{P}$,
5. $hate_{aa} \wedge hate_{ac}$,
6. $(\neg richer_{ja} \vee hate_{aj}) \to hate_{bj}$ for all $j \in \mathbb{P}$,
7. $\neg hate_{ia} \vee \neg hate_{ib} \vee \neg hate_{ic}$ for all $i \in \mathbb{P}$.

The case can be solved semantically by showing that for any model M of the theory, which in this propositional situation is just a valuation $\mathsf{M} : \mathbf{V}_{murder} \to \{\mathsf{ff}, \mathsf{tt}\}$, $\mathsf{M}(kill_{aa}) = \mathsf{tt}$ must hold whereas $\mathsf{M}(kill_{ba}) = \mathsf{M}(kill_{ca}) = \mathsf{ff}$, or proof-theoretically by showing that

$$\mathcal{M} \vdash_{\Sigma_{\mathrm{PL}}} kill_{aa} \wedge \neg kill_{ba} \wedge \neg kill_{ca} .$$

Anyway, the conclusion is that Agatha committed suicide. One should also convince oneself by exhibiting a model M for $\mathcal{M}$ that the assumed facts are not contradictory: otherwise, the conclusion would hold trivially.

1.4 Extensions of Logics

The logic FOL extends PL in the sense that every formula of (any language $\mathcal{L}_{\mathrm{PL}}(\mathbf{V})$ of) PL is also a formula of (some language containing the elements of $\mathbf{V}$ as propositional constants of) FOL. Furthermore, PL is a *sublogic* of FOL: all consequence relationships and, hence, universal validities in PL hold in FOL as well. The logics to be defined in the next chapters will be extensions of PL or even FOL in the same way.

Staying within the classical logic framework, we still want to mention another extension of FOL which allows for addressing the non-characterizability of the standard model of natural numbers in FOL as pointed out in the previous section. The reason for this deficiency is that FOL is too weak to formalize the fundamental *Peano Postulate* of natural induction which states that for every set $\mathbb{M}$ of natural numbers,

> if $0 \in \mathbb{M}$ and if for every $n \in \mathbb{N}$, $n+1 \in \mathbb{M}$ can be concluded from the assumption that $n \in \mathbb{M}$, then $\mathbb{M} = \mathbb{N}$.

This is only incompletely covered by the *induction axiom*

$$(A_x(0) \wedge \forall x(A \to A_x(SUCC(x)))) \to \forall x A$$

of the theory Nat. In our assumed framework of countable languages (cf. Sect. 1.1) this fact is evident since A (which "represents" a set $\mathbb{M}$) then ranges only over denumerably many formulas whereas the number of sets of natural numbers is uncountable. But even in general, the Peano Postulate cannot be completely described in FOL.

An extension of FOL in which the Peano Postulate can be described adequately is *(classical) second-order logic* SOL. Given a signature $SIG = (\mathbf{S}, \mathbf{F}, \mathbf{P})$, a *second-order language* $\mathcal{L}_{\mathrm{SOL}}(SIG)$ (again shortly: $\mathcal{L}_{\mathrm{SOL}}$) is defined like a first-order language with the following additions: the alphabet is enriched by

- denumerably many *predicate variables* for every $\vec{s} \in \mathbf{S}^*$.

Let the set of predicate variables for $\vec{s} \in \mathbf{S}^*$ be denoted by $\mathcal{R}_{\vec{s}}$ and $\mathcal{R} = \bigcup_{\vec{s} \in \mathbf{S}^*} \mathcal{R}_{\vec{s}}$. These new symbols allow for building additional atomic formulas of the form

- $r(t_1, \ldots, t_n)$, where $r \in \mathcal{R}_{s_1 \ldots s_n}$ is a predicate variable and t_i are terms of sorts s_i for $1 \leq i \leq n$,

and the inductive definition of formulas in FOL is extended by the clause

- If A is a formula and r is a predicate variable then $\exists r A$ is a formula.

$\forall r A$ abbreviates $\neg \exists r \neg A$.

The semantics of a language $\mathcal{L}_{\mathrm{SOL}}(SIG)$ is again based on the concept of a structure S for SIG. Variable valuations are redefined to assign for all $s \in \mathbf{S}$ and $s_1 \ldots s_n \in \mathbf{S}^*$

- some $\xi(x) \in |\mathsf{S}|_s$ to every individual variable $x \in \mathcal{X}_s$ (as in FOL),
- some mapping $\xi(r) : |\mathsf{S}|_{s_1} \times \ldots \times |\mathsf{S}|_{s_n} \to \{\mathsf{ff}, \mathsf{tt}\}$ to every predicate variable $r \in \mathcal{R}_{s_1 \ldots s_n}$.

The definition of $\mathsf{S}^{(\xi)}(A)$ is extended to the new kind of formulas by

- $\mathsf{S}^{(\xi)}(r(t_1, \ldots, t_n)) = \xi(r)(\mathsf{S}^{(\xi)}(t_1), \ldots, \mathsf{S}^{(\xi)}(t_n))$,
- $\mathsf{S}^{(\xi)}(\exists r A) = \mathsf{tt} \;\Leftrightarrow\;$ there is a ξ' such that $\xi \sim_r \xi'$ and $\mathsf{S}^{(\xi')}(A) = \mathsf{tt}$

where $r \in \mathcal{R}$ and $\xi \sim_r \xi' \;\Leftrightarrow\; \xi(\bar{r}) = \xi'(\bar{r})$ for all $\bar{r} \in \mathcal{R}$ other than r. Finally the notions of validity and consequence from FOL are transferred verbatim to SOL.

A *second-order theory* $(\mathcal{L}_{\mathrm{SOL}}, \mathcal{A})$ consists of a second-order language $\mathcal{L}_{\mathrm{SOL}}$ and a set $\mathcal{A}$ of non-logical axioms (formulas of $\mathcal{L}_{\mathrm{SOL}}$). Models of such theories are defined as in FOL. Any first-order theory can be viewed as a second-order theory as well. E.g., the theory *LinOrd* of the previous section can be made into a *second-order theory of linear orders* just by replacing $\mathcal{L}_{\mathrm{FOL}}(SIG_{lo})$ by $\mathcal{L}_{\mathrm{SOL}}(SIG_{lo})$.

A proper second-order theory for the natural numbers takes the signature SIG_{Nat} and the first six axioms of the first-order theory *Nat* together with the new induction axiom

$$\forall r(r(0) \land \forall x(r(x) \to r(SUCC(x))) \to \forall x\, r(x))$$

where $r \in \mathcal{R}_{NAT}$ is a predicate variable. The standard model N is a model of this theory and in fact it is the only one (up to "isomorphism"; this relation will be made more precise in Sect. 5.3). So this theory really characterizes the natural numbers.

But the background of Gödel's Incompleteness Theorem is some inherent incompleteness of *Peano arithmetic* and this now becomes manifest at another place: in contrast to FOL, SOL cannot be completely axiomatized, i.e., there is no sound and complete formal system for SOL, not even in the simple sense that every valid formula should be derivable.

This statement has to be taken with some care, however. If we took all valid formulas of SOL as axioms of a formal system then this would be trivially sound and complete in that sense. But this is, of course, not what is intended by a formal system: to allow for "mechanical" generation of formulas. This intention implicitly supposes that in a formal system the set of axioms is decidable and for any finite sequence $A_1, \ldots, A_n, B$ of formulas it is decidable whether $A_1, \ldots, A_n \vdash B$ is a rule. Since SOL (like FOL) is undecidable, the above trivial approach does not meet this requirement.

To sum up, a logic LOG with a consequence relation $\models$ is called *incomplete* if there is no formal system Σ for LOG in this sense such that

$$\models A \;\Leftrightarrow\; \vdash_{\Sigma} A$$

for every formula A of (any language of) LOG. According to this definition, SOL is incomplete.

We finally note that the above considerations are not restricted to SOL. In fact, the incompleteness result of Gödel may be extended to the following general principle:

Gödel Incompleteness Principle. *Let LOG be a logic with a consequence relation* $\models$ *and* $\mathcal{L}_{\mathrm{LOG}}$ *a language of LOG such that every formula of* $\mathcal{L}_{\mathrm{FOL}}(SIG_{Nat})$ *is a formula of* $\mathcal{L}_{\mathrm{LOG}}$*. If there is a decidable set* $\mathcal{F}$ *of formulas of* $\mathcal{L}_{\mathrm{LOG}}$ *such that*

$$\mathcal{F} \models A \;\Leftrightarrow\; \models_{\mathsf{N}} A$$

holds for every closed formula A *of* $\mathcal{L}_{\mathrm{FOL}}(SIG_{Nat})$ *then* LOG *is incomplete.*

(As before, $SIG_{Nat} = (\{NAT\}, \{0, SUCC, +, *\}, \emptyset)$ and N is the standard model of natural numbers.) This shows the fundamental "trade-off" between logical completeness and characterizability of the natural numbers.

Bibliographical Notes

Logic is a discipline with a long history of more than 2,000 years. *Mathematical* logic as we understand it nowadays – investigating mathematical reasoning and itself grounded in rigorous mathematical methods – began at the end of the nineteenth century with Frege's *Begriffsschrift* [50], the *Principia Mathematica* [158] by Whitehead and Russell, and other pioneering work. For some time, logicians then had the "vision" that it should be possible to "mechanize" mathematics by completely formalizing it within logic. Gödel's work, particularly his famous incompleteness result [57], showed that there are fundamental bounds to this idea.

In the present-day literature, there is a huge number of textbooks on mathematical logic. The selection of contents and the usage of notions and terminology is not uniform in all these texts. In our presentation we mainly refer to the books [43, 60, 105, 137].

2

Basic Propositional Linear Temporal Logic

We now begin to present temporal logics. Being the focus of our attention, the original and perhaps best elaborated *linear (time) temporal logic* will be studied at great length in the subsequent chapters. Other frameworks for modeling time will be considered in Chap. 10.

There are many versions of linear temporal logic. In order to provide a systematic presentation we choose a "modular" way: we start in this chapter with the basic "building block". Various extensions will be studied in later chapters.

Temporal logic is a branch of *modal logic*. In a Second Reading paragraph in Sect. 2.3 we will give some short explanations of this relationship.

2.1 The Basic Language and Its Normal Semantics

Classical logic formalizes mathematical systems – (functional) data types in the wording of computer science – that consist of domains of objects and functions and predicates over these objects. The canonical application area of temporal logic is the formalization of *state systems*. Roughly speaking (precise formalizations will be given in Chap. 6), a state system generates (temporal) "runs" or "sequences" of "states". Consider the following well-known toy example of the *Towers of Hanoi* puzzle:

> A number of stones of pairwise different size are piled one on another with decreasing size from the bottom to the top. This tower, which is initially standing on some place, is to be transferred to another place by a sequence of moves, possibly using one more auxiliary place. In each move only the top stone of a tower on one of the three places may be taken and put on a free place or on another tower whose topmost stone is bigger than the added stone.

This puzzle may be viewed as a state system: the states are given by the different configurations of which stones are on which places, and moves produce sequences of states.

In order to formalize and argue about the "behaviour" of this system we would like to express and reason about statements of the kind

> "if the topmost stone ts on some place is bigger than the topmost stone on another place then in the next state ts cannot be the topmost stone on this latter place"

or

> "in all states, on each of the three places the stones will be piled up with decreasing size",

and the like. The structure of these statements is of the form

> if A then *in the next state* B,
> *in all states* C,

respectively, where the parts A, B, and C can easily be formulated in classical (first-order) logic. The phrases *in the next state*, *in all states* (and the like) are the focus of the temporal logic approach. They allow for building new statements from other ones. More formally, they are (propositional) logical operators for formulating new statements about the truth or falsity of other statements in states (or "points in time") which are related to the *present* state ("point in time") in particular ways.

In a first-order language, state sequences (the "flow of time") could be formalized using a distinguished sort and appropriate predicate symbols; cf. also Sect. 4.2. Instead, temporal logic adds such operators at the propositional level. Among several different approaches to this, *linear temporal logic* follows the idea of state runs as above. More formally, it adopts the paradigm of *linearly ordered, discrete time.*

Let $\mathbf{V}$ be a set of *propositional constants.* The alphabet of a *basic language* $\mathcal{L}_{\mathrm{LTL}}(\mathbf{V})$ (also shortly: $\mathcal{L}_{\mathrm{LTL}}$) *of propositional linear temporal logic* LTL is given by

- all propositional constants of $\mathbf{V}$,
- the symbols **false** $\mid \rightarrow \mid \bigcirc \mid \Box \mid (\mid)$.

Inductive Definition of *formulas* (of $\mathcal{L}_{\mathrm{LTL}}(\mathbf{V})$).

1. Every propositional constant of $\mathbf{V}$ is a formula.
2. **false** is a formula.
3. If A and B are formulas then $(A \rightarrow B)$ is a formula.
4. If A is a formula then $\bigcirc A$ and $\Box A$ are formulas.

Further operators can be introduced as abbreviations:

$$\neg, \vee, \wedge, \leftrightarrow, \textbf{true} \text{ as in classical logic,}$$
$$\Diamond A \equiv \neg\Box\neg A.$$

The temporal operators $\bigcirc$, $\Box$, and $\Diamond$ are called *nexttime*, *always* (or *henceforth*), and *sometime* (or *eventuality*) operators, respectively. Formulas $\bigcirc A$, $\Box A$, and $\Diamond A$ are typically read "next A", "always A", and "sometime A".

For notational simplicity we establish a priority order of the operators:

$$\begin{array}{lll} \vee, \wedge & \text{have} & \text{higher priority than} \rightarrow \text{and} \leftrightarrow, \\ \rightarrow & \text{has} & \text{higher priority than} \leftrightarrow. \end{array}$$

(Note that $\neg$, $\bigcirc$, $\Box$, and $\Diamond$ are binding stronger than $\vee$, $\wedge$, $\rightarrow$, and $\leftrightarrow$ by definition.) Accordingly, we will omit superfluous parentheses, including the outermost.

Example. Instead of the fully parenthesized formula

$$(((\Box A_1 \wedge A_2) \rightarrow A_3) \leftrightarrow (\Diamond(\bigcirc A_4 \vee \neg A_5) \wedge A_6))$$

we write

$$\Box A_1 \wedge A_2 \rightarrow A_3 \ \leftrightarrow\ \Diamond(\bigcirc A_4 \vee \neg A_5) \wedge A_6. \qquad \triangle$$

Semantical interpretations in classical propositional logic are given by boolean valuations. For LTL we have to extend this concept according to our informal idea that formulas are evaluated over sequences of states ("time scales").

Let $\mathbf{V}$ be a set of propositional constants. A *temporal* (or *Kripke*) *structure* for $\mathbf{V}$ is an infinite sequence $\mathsf{K} = (\eta_0, \eta_1, \eta_2, \ldots)$ of mappings

$$\eta_i : \mathbf{V} \rightarrow \{\mathsf{ff}, \mathsf{tt}\}$$

called *states*. η_0 is called *initial state* of K. Observe that states are just valuations in the classical logic sense. For K and $i \in \mathbb{N}$ we define $\mathsf{K}_i(F) \in \{\mathsf{ff}, \mathsf{tt}\}$ (informally meaning the "truth value of F in the ith state of K") for every formula F inductively as follows:

1. $\mathsf{K}_i(v) = \eta_i(v)$ for $v \in \mathbf{V}$.
2. $\mathsf{K}_i(\mathbf{false}) = \mathsf{ff}$.
3. $\mathsf{K}_i(A \rightarrow B) = \mathsf{tt} \Leftrightarrow \mathsf{K}_i(A) = \mathsf{ff}$ or $\mathsf{K}_i(B) = \mathsf{tt}$.
4. $\mathsf{K}_i(\bigcirc A) = \mathsf{K}_{i+1}(A)$.
5. $\mathsf{K}_i(\Box A) = \mathsf{tt} \Leftrightarrow \mathsf{K}_j(A) = \mathsf{tt}$ for every $j \geq i$.

Obviously, the formula **false** and the operator $\rightarrow$ behave classically in each state. The definitions for $\bigcirc$ and $\Box$ make these operators formalize the phrases *in the next state* and *in all states* mentioned above. More precisely now, a formula $\Box A$ informally means "A holds in all forthcoming states including the present one".

The definitions induce the following truth values for the formula abbreviations:

6. $\mathsf{K}_i(\neg A) = \mathsf{tt} \Leftrightarrow \mathsf{K}_i(A) = \mathsf{ff}$.
7. $\mathsf{K}_i(A \vee B) = \mathsf{tt} \Leftrightarrow \mathsf{K}_i(A) = \mathsf{tt}$ or $\mathsf{K}_i(B) = \mathsf{tt}$.
8. $\mathsf{K}_i(A \wedge B) = \mathsf{tt} \Leftrightarrow \mathsf{K}_i(A) = \mathsf{tt}$ and $\mathsf{K}_i(B) = \mathsf{tt}$.
9. $\mathsf{K}_i(A \leftrightarrow B) = \mathsf{tt} \Leftrightarrow \mathsf{K}_i(A) = \mathsf{K}_i(B)$.
10. $\mathsf{K}_i(\mathbf{true}) = \mathsf{tt}$.
11. $\mathsf{K}_i(\Diamond A) = \mathsf{tt} \Leftrightarrow \mathsf{K}_j(A) = \mathsf{tt}$ for some $j \geq i$.

The clauses 6–10 are as in classical propositional logic. They particularly imply that $\vee$ and $\wedge$ are *associative* in the sense that

$$\mathsf{K}_i((A \vee B) \vee C) = \mathsf{K}_i(A \vee (B \vee C))$$

and analogously for $\wedge$. The syntactic bracketing of such formulas is therefore unimportant, and we will use (as in Chap. 1) notation like

$$A_1 \vee A_2 \vee \ldots \vee A_n \qquad \text{and} \qquad A_1 \wedge A_2 \wedge \ldots \wedge A_n$$

also abbreviated by

$$\bigvee_{i=1}^{n} A_i \qquad \text{and} \qquad \bigwedge_{i=1}^{n} A_i$$

(or similarly displaying the index range).

The clause 11 in the above list (saying that $\Diamond A$ informally means that "A will hold sometime in the present or a forthcoming state") can easily be proved:

$$\begin{aligned} \mathsf{K}_i(\Diamond A) = \mathsf{tt} &\Leftrightarrow \mathsf{K}_i(\neg\Box\neg A) = \mathsf{tt} \\ &\Leftrightarrow \mathsf{K}_i(\Box\neg A) = \mathsf{ff} \\ &\Leftrightarrow \mathsf{K}_j(\neg A) = \mathsf{ff} \text{ for some } j \geq i \\ &\Leftrightarrow \mathsf{K}_j(A) = \mathsf{tt} \text{ for some } j \geq i. \end{aligned}$$

Example. Let $A \equiv \Diamond\neg v_1 \wedge \bigcirc v_1 \rightarrow \Box v_2$ where $v_1, v_2 \in \mathbf{V}$, and let K be given as indicated by the following matrix:

	η_0	η_1	η_2	η_3	η_4	$\ldots$
v_1	ff	ff	tt	tt	ff	... (arbitrary) ...
v_2	tt	tt	ff	tt	tt	... (tt forever) ...

The entries define the values of $\eta_0, \eta_1, \ldots$ for v_1 and v_2. The values for other $v \in \mathbf{V}$ are of no relevance. We can compute:

$$\begin{aligned} &\mathsf{K}_0(\bigcirc v_1) = \mathsf{ff} \Rightarrow \mathsf{K}_0(\Diamond\neg v_1 \wedge \bigcirc v_1) = \mathsf{ff} \Rightarrow \mathsf{K}_0(A) = \mathsf{tt}, \\ &\mathsf{K}_1(\Diamond\neg v_1) = \mathsf{K}_1(\bigcirc v_1) = \mathsf{tt}, \mathsf{K}_1(\Box v_2) = \mathsf{ff} \Rightarrow \mathsf{K}_1(A) = \mathsf{ff}, \\ &\mathsf{K}_2(\Diamond\neg v_1) = \mathsf{K}_2(\bigcirc v_1) = \mathsf{tt}, \mathsf{K}_2(\Box v_2) = \mathsf{ff} \Rightarrow \mathsf{K}_2(A) = \mathsf{ff}, \\ &\mathsf{K}_3(\Box v_2) = \mathsf{K}_4(\Box v_2) = \ldots = \mathsf{tt} \Rightarrow \mathsf{K}_3(A) = \mathsf{K}_4(A) = \ldots = \mathsf{tt}. \end{aligned}$$ △

Definition. A formula A of $\mathcal{L}_{\mathrm{LTL}}(\mathbf{V})$ is called *valid in the temporal structure* K for $\mathbf{V}$ (or K *satisfies* A), denoted by $\models_{\mathsf{K}} A$, if $\mathsf{K}_i(A) = \mathsf{tt}$ for every $i \in \mathbb{N}$. A is called a *consequence of* a set $\mathcal{F}$ of formulas ($\mathcal{F} \models A$) if $\models_{\mathsf{K}} A$ holds for every K such that $\models_{\mathsf{K}} B$ for all $B \in \mathcal{F}$. A is called (*universally*) *valid* ($\models A$) if $\emptyset \models A$.

These definitions are a natural extension of the classical validity and consequence concepts. We remark, however, that often another version (called *initial* or *anchored*) of these notions is used. This semantics will be discussed in Sect. 2.6. For distinction, we call the present approach *normal* or *floating semantics*.

As we will see subsequently, many interesting valid formulas will be of the syntactical form $A \leftrightarrow B$. We distinguish this case with a particular notion.

Definition. Two formulas A and B of $\mathcal{L}_{\mathrm{LTL}}$ are called *logically equivalent* (denoted by $A \cong B$) if the formula $A \leftrightarrow B$ is valid.

Example. The formula $\neg \bigcirc A \leftrightarrow \bigcirc \neg A$ is valid, i.e., $\neg \bigcirc A$ and $\bigcirc \neg A$ are logically equivalent. To prove this we have to show that $\mathsf{K}_i(\neg \bigcirc A) = \mathsf{K}_i(\bigcirc \neg A)$ for every K and $i \in \mathbb{N}$:

$$\begin{aligned}\mathsf{K}_i(\neg \bigcirc A) = \mathsf{tt} &\Leftrightarrow \mathsf{K}_i(\bigcirc A) = \mathsf{ff}\\ &\Leftrightarrow \mathsf{K}_{i+1}(A) = \mathsf{ff}\\ &\Leftrightarrow \mathsf{K}_{i+1}(\neg A) = \mathsf{tt}\\ &\Leftrightarrow \mathsf{K}_i(\bigcirc \neg A) = \mathsf{tt}.\end{aligned}$$ △

We now collect some facts about the semantical notions.

Lemma 2.1.1. *Let* $\mathsf{K} = (\eta_0, \eta_1, \eta_2, \ldots)$ *be some temporal structure and* $i \in \mathbb{N}$. *If* $\mathsf{K}_i(A) = \mathsf{tt}$ *and* $\mathsf{K}_i(A \rightarrow B) = \mathsf{tt}$ *then* $\mathsf{K}_i(B) = \mathsf{tt}$.

Proof. $\mathsf{K}_i(A \rightarrow B)$ means $\mathsf{K}_i(A) = \mathsf{ff}$ or $\mathsf{K}_i(B) = \mathsf{tt}$, and together with the assumption $\mathsf{K}_i(A) = \mathsf{tt}$ it must be the case that $\mathsf{K}_i(B) = \mathsf{tt}$. △

Theorem 2.1.2. *If* $\mathcal{F} \models A$ *and* $\mathcal{F} \models A \rightarrow B$ *then* $\mathcal{F} \models B$.

Proof. Let K be some temporal structure such that $\models_{\mathsf{K}} C$ for every $C \in \mathcal{F}$, and $i \in \mathbb{N}$. Then $\mathsf{K}_i(A) = \mathsf{K}_i(A \rightarrow B) = \mathsf{tt}$, implying $\mathsf{K}_i(B) = \mathsf{tt}$ by Lemma 2.1.1. This means that $\mathcal{F} \models B$. △

Theorem 2.1.3. *If* $\mathcal{F} \models A$ *then* $\mathcal{F} \models \bigcirc A$ *and* $\mathcal{F} \models \Box A$. *In particular:* $A \models \bigcirc A$ *and* $A \models \Box A$.

Proof. Let K be some temporal structure such that $\models_{\mathsf{K}} C$ for every $C \in \mathcal{F}$, and $i \in \mathbb{N}$. Then $\mathsf{K}_j(A) = \mathsf{tt}$ for every $j \in \mathbb{N}$; in particular $\mathsf{K}_{i+1}(A) = \mathsf{tt}$ and $\mathsf{K}_j(A) = \mathsf{tt}$ for every $j \geq i$. This means that $\mathcal{F} \models \bigcirc A$ and $\mathcal{F} \models \Box A$. △

Theorem 2.1.4. *If* $\mathcal{F} \models A \rightarrow B$ *and* $\mathcal{F} \models A \rightarrow \bigcirc A$ *then* $\mathcal{F} \models A \rightarrow \Box B$.

Proof. Let K be some temporal structure such that $\models_{\mathsf{K}} C$ for every $C \in \mathcal{F}$, and $i \in \mathbb{N}$. We must show that $\mathsf{K}_i(A \rightarrow \Box B) = \mathsf{tt}$. This holds trivially if $\mathsf{K}_i(A) = \mathsf{ff}$, so assume that $\mathsf{K}_i(A) = \mathsf{tt}$. Inductively, we show that $\mathsf{K}_j(A) = \mathsf{tt}$ holds for all $j \geq i$. The base case (where $j = i$) holds by assumption. For the induction step, fix some $j \geq i$ and assume that $\mathsf{K}_j(A) = \mathsf{tt}$. Now, the assumption $\mathcal{F} \models A \rightarrow \bigcirc A$ implies that $\mathsf{K}_j(A \rightarrow \bigcirc A) = \mathsf{tt}$, and therefore $\mathsf{K}_j(\bigcirc A) = \mathsf{tt}$ by Lemma 2.1.1, i.e., $\mathsf{K}_{j+1}(A) = \mathsf{tt}$.

The assumption $\mathcal{F} \models A \rightarrow B$ implies $\mathsf{K}_j(A \rightarrow B) = \mathsf{tt}$ for all $j \in \mathbb{N}$, and in particular $\mathsf{K}_j(A \rightarrow B) = \mathsf{tt}$ for all $j \geq i$. But since $\mathsf{K}_j(A) = \mathsf{tt}$ for all $j \geq i$ it follows, again by Lemma 2.1.1, that $\mathsf{K}_j(B) = \mathsf{tt}$ for all $j \geq i$, i.e., $\mathsf{K}_i(\Box B) = \mathsf{tt}$. Altogether, we obtain $\mathsf{K}_i(A \rightarrow \Box B) = \mathsf{tt}$, which completes the proof. △

For any temporal structure $\mathsf{K} = (\eta_0, \eta_1, \eta_2, \ldots)$ (for some $\mathbf{V}$) and $i \in \mathbb{N}$, let $\mathsf{K}^i = (\eta'_0, \eta'_1, \eta'_2, \ldots)$ be defined by $\eta'_j = \eta_{i+j}$ for every $j \in \mathbb{N}$, i.e., $\mathsf{K}^i = (\eta_i, \eta_{i+1}, \eta_{i+2}, \ldots)$. K^i is also a temporal structure for $\mathbf{V}$.

Lemma 2.1.5. *Let* K *be a temporal structure,* $i \in \mathbb{N}$. *Then* $\mathsf{K}^i_j(A) = \mathsf{K}_{i+j}(A)$ *for every* $j \in \mathbb{N}$ *and every formula* A.

Proof. The proof runs by structural induction (i.e., induction on the syntactical structure according to the inductive definition of formulas) on A, simultaneously for all $j \in \mathbb{N}$. We will indicate the application of the respective induction hypothesis by "ind.hyp.". Let $\mathsf{K} = (\eta_0, \eta_1, \eta_2, \ldots)$ and $\mathsf{K}^i = (\eta'_0, \eta'_1, \eta'_2, \ldots)$.

1. $A \equiv v \in \mathbf{V}$: $\mathsf{K}^i_j(v) = \eta'_j(v) = \eta_{i+j}(v) = \mathsf{K}_{i+j}(v)$.
2. $A \equiv$ **false**: $\mathsf{K}^i_j(\mathbf{false}) = \mathsf{ff} = \mathsf{K}_{i+j}(\mathbf{false})$.
3. $A \equiv B \to C$:

$$\begin{aligned} \mathsf{K}^i_j(B \to C) = \mathsf{tt} &\Leftrightarrow \mathsf{K}^i_j(B) = \mathsf{ff} \text{ or } \mathsf{K}^i_j(C) = \mathsf{tt} \\ &\Leftrightarrow \mathsf{K}_{i+j}(B) = \mathsf{ff} \text{ or } \mathsf{K}_{i+j}(C) = \mathsf{tt} \quad \text{(ind.hyp.)} \\ &\Leftrightarrow \mathsf{K}_{i+j}(B \to C) = \mathsf{tt}. \end{aligned}$$

4. $A \equiv \bigcirc B$:

$$\begin{aligned} \mathsf{K}^i_j(\bigcirc B) &= \mathsf{K}^i_{j+1}(B) \\ &= \mathsf{K}_{i+j+1}(B) \quad \text{(ind.hyp.)} \\ &= \mathsf{K}_{i+j}(\bigcirc B). \end{aligned}$$

5. $A \equiv \Box B$:

$$\begin{aligned} \mathsf{K}^i_j(\Box B) = \mathsf{tt} &\Leftrightarrow \mathsf{K}^i_l(B) = \mathsf{tt} \text{ for all } l \geq j \\ &\Leftrightarrow \mathsf{K}_{i+l}(B) = \mathsf{tt} \text{ for all } l \geq j \quad \text{(ind.hyp.)} \\ &\Leftrightarrow \mathsf{K}_{i+j}(\Box B) = \mathsf{tt}. \end{aligned}$$

△

Theorem 2.1.6. $\mathcal{F} \cup \{A\} \models B$ *if and only if* $\mathcal{F} \models \Box A \to B$.

Proof. For the "only if" part, assume that $\mathcal{F} \cup \{A\} \models B$ and let $\mathsf{K} = (\eta_0, \eta_1, \eta_2, \ldots)$ be some temporal structure such that $\models_{\mathsf{K}} C$ for every $C \in \mathcal{F}$, and $i \in \mathbb{N}$. Then $\mathsf{K}_j(C) = \mathsf{tt}$ for every $C \in \mathcal{F}$ and every $j \in \mathbb{N}$. We must show $\mathsf{K}_i(\Box A \to B) = \mathsf{tt}$. If $\mathsf{K}_i(\Box A) = \mathsf{ff}$ this holds trivially, so assume that $\mathsf{K}_i(\Box A) = \mathsf{tt}$, i.e., $\mathsf{K}_j(A) = \mathsf{tt}$ for every $j \geq i$. Now let K^i be the temporal structure defined as above. By Lemma 2.1.5 we get $\mathsf{K}^i_j(A) = \mathsf{K}^i_j(C) = \mathsf{tt}$ for every $j \in \mathbb{N}$ and every $C \in \mathcal{F}$, and by assumption it follows that $\models_{\mathsf{K}^i} B$. In particular, $\mathsf{K}^i_0(B) = \mathsf{tt}$, which again by Lemma 2.1.5 implies that $\mathsf{K}_i(B) = \mathsf{tt}$.

The converse direction is shown as follows: assume that $\mathcal{F} \models \Box A \to B$ and let K be a temporal structure such that $\models_{\mathsf{K}} C$ for every $C \in \mathcal{F} \cup \{A\}$, and $i \in \mathbb{N}$. Then $\mathsf{K}_j(\Box A \to B) = \mathsf{K}_j(A) = \mathsf{tt}$ for every $j \in \mathbb{N}$, so particularly $\mathsf{K}_i(\Box A \to B) = \mathsf{tt}$ and $\mathsf{K}_j(A) = \mathsf{tt}$ for every $j \geq i$, i.e., $\mathsf{K}_i(\Box A) = \mathsf{tt}$. By Lemma 2.1.1 we obtain $\mathsf{K}_i(B) = \mathsf{tt}$. This means $\models_{\mathsf{K}} B$, and so we have $\mathcal{F} \cup \{A\} \models B$. △

Theorem 2.1.6 is the temporal logic analogy of the classical

$$\mathcal{F} \cup \{A\} \models B \;\Leftrightarrow\; \mathcal{F} \models A \rightarrow B.$$

It should be noted that the latter does no longer hold in LTL. A simple counterexample (with $\mathcal{F} = \emptyset$) is given by $A \models \Box A$ which holds according to Theorem 2.1.3, but $A \rightarrow \Box A$ is clearly not valid. It is the only if part of the equivalence which fails; the other direction still holds:

Theorem 2.1.7. *If $\mathcal{F} \models A \rightarrow B$ then $\mathcal{F} \cup \{A\} \models B$.*

Proof. If $\mathcal{F} \models A \rightarrow B$ then also $\mathcal{F} \cup \{A\} \models A \rightarrow B$. Furthermore, $\mathcal{F} \cup \{A\} \models A$, and hence $\mathcal{F} \cup \{A\} \models B$ by Theorem 2.1.2. △

Theorem 2.1.8. *If $\mathcal{F} \models A$ and $\models B$ for every $B \in \mathcal{F}$ then $\models A$.*

Proof. Let K be a temporal structure. Then $\models_{\mathsf{K}} B$ for every $B \in \mathcal{F}$ and hence $\models_{\mathsf{K}} A$. This holds for every K, so we have $\models A$. △

We define still another semantical notion which will be needed in Sect. 2.4.

Definition. A formula A is called (*locally*) *satisfiable* if there is a temporal structure K and $i \in \mathbb{N}$ such that $\mathsf{K}_i(A) = \mathsf{tt}$.

Example. Consider the formulas $A \equiv \Box\neg v_1 \wedge \neg v_2 \rightarrow \bigcirc v_1$ and $B \equiv \Box\neg v_1 \wedge \bigcirc v_1$ where $v_1, v_2 \in \mathbf{V}$. For a temporal structure K with $\mathsf{K}_i(v_1) = \mathsf{ff}$ for all $i \in \mathbb{N}$ and $\mathsf{K}_0(v_2) = \mathsf{tt}$ we obtain $\mathsf{K}_0(A) = \mathsf{tt}$, which shows that A is satisfiable. The formula B, however, is not satisfiable since, for any K and $i \in \mathbb{N}$, $\mathsf{K}_i(B) = \mathsf{tt}$ would imply $\mathsf{K}_{i+1}(v_1) = \mathsf{ff}$ as well as $\mathsf{K}_{i+1}(v_1) = \mathsf{tt}$ which is impossible. △

Validity and satisfiability are "dual" notions in the following sense:

Theorem 2.1.9. *$\models A$ if and only if $\neg A$ is not satisfiable.*

Proof. $\models A$ if and only if $\mathsf{K}_i(A) = \mathsf{tt}$ and hence $\mathsf{K}_i(\neg A) = \mathsf{ff}$ for every temporal structure K and every $i \in \mathbb{N}$. This just holds if and only if $\neg A$ is not satisfiable. △

We conclude this section by listing some (forms of) temporal logic formulas that typically occur in applications together with their informal meanings.

$A \rightarrow \bigcirc B$:	"If A then B in the next state",
$A \rightarrow \Box B$:	"If A then (now and) henceforth B",
$A \rightarrow \Diamond B$:	"If A then sometime (now or in the future) B",
$\Box(A \rightarrow B)$:	"Whenever (now or) henceforth A then B in that state",
$\Box\Diamond A$:	"For all following states, A will hold in some later state", i.e., "A holds infinitely often from now on",
$\Diamond\Box A$:	"Sometime A will hold permanently", i.e., "A is false only finitely often from now on" or "A is almost always true from now on".

2.2 Temporal Logical Laws

In any logic, the valid formulas and consequence relationships express "logical laws". An example from classical logic is the tautology

$$(A \rightarrow B) \wedge (B \rightarrow C) \rightarrow (A \rightarrow C)$$

mentioned in Sect. 1.1. According to the semantical definitions in the previous section we should expect that such tautologies remain valid in temporal logic where we may substitute formulas of $\mathcal{L}_{\text{LTL}}$ for A and B, e.g.,

$$(\bigcirc C \rightarrow \Box D) \wedge (\Box D \rightarrow \Diamond E) \rightarrow (\bigcirc C \rightarrow \Diamond E).$$

Let us confirm this expectation formally:

Definition. A formula of $\mathcal{L}_{\text{LTL}}$ is called *tautologically valid* if it results from a tautology A of $\mathcal{L}_{\text{PL}}$ by consistently replacing the propositional constants of A by formulas of $\mathcal{L}_{\text{LTL}}$.

Theorem 2.2.1. *Every tautologically valid formula is valid.*

Proof. Let $\mathbf{V}' = \{v_1, \dots, v_n\}$ be a set of propositional constants, and let $A_1, \dots, A_n$ be formulas of $\mathcal{L}_{\text{LTL}}$. For any formula A of $\mathcal{L}_{\text{PL}}(\mathbf{V}')$, let A^* denote the formula of $\mathcal{L}_{\text{LTL}}$ which results from A by replacing every occurrence of a propositional constant $v_j \in \mathbf{V}'$ in A by A_j. Let K be a temporal structure (for the propositional constants of $\mathcal{L}_{\text{LTL}}$) and $i \in \mathbb{N}$. We define a (classical) valuation B for $\mathbf{V}'$ by $\mathsf{B}(v_j) = \mathsf{K}_i(A_j)$ for $j = 1, \dots, n$ and claim that

$$\mathsf{B}(A) = \mathsf{K}_i(A^*),$$

which proves the theorem. Indeed, if B is tautologically valid, and therefore $B \equiv A^*$ for some classical tautology A, then $\mathsf{K}_i(B) = \mathsf{B}(A) = \mathsf{tt}$. The proof of the claim runs by structural induction on A.

1. $A \equiv v_j \in \mathbf{V}'$: Then $A^* \equiv A_j$; hence $\mathsf{B}(A) = \mathsf{B}(v_j) = \mathsf{K}_i(A_j) = \mathsf{K}_i(A^*)$.
2. $A \equiv$ **false**: Then $A^* \equiv$ **false** and $\mathsf{B}(A) = \mathsf{ff} = \mathsf{K}_i(A^*)$.
3. $A \equiv B \rightarrow C$: Then $A^* \equiv B^* \rightarrow C^*$, and with the induction hypothesis we get

$$\begin{aligned} \mathsf{B}(A) = \mathsf{tt} &\Leftrightarrow \mathsf{B}(B) = \mathsf{ff} \text{ or } \mathsf{B}(C) = \mathsf{tt} \\ &\Leftrightarrow \mathsf{K}_i(B^*) = \mathsf{ff} \text{ or } \mathsf{K}_i(C^*) = \mathsf{tt} \\ &\Leftrightarrow \mathsf{K}_i(B^* \rightarrow C^*) = \mathsf{K}_i(A^*) = \mathsf{tt}. \end{aligned}$$

△

Clearly, the transfer of classical logical laws to LTL can be extended to the relation $\vDash$. Suppose a formula B is a consequence of some set $\mathcal{F}$ of formulas in PL. Again, if we (consistently) substitute formulas of LTL in the formulas of $\mathcal{F}$ and B, we should not destroy the logical relationship. For example,

$$\bigcirc C \rightarrow \Box D, \Box D \rightarrow \Diamond E \vDash \bigcirc C \rightarrow \Diamond E$$

should hold because of the classical

$$A \to B, B \to C \vDash A \to C.$$

For a simple formulation of this fact (restricted to finite sets $\mathcal{F}$) we remember that

$$A_1, \dots, A_n \vDash B \;\Leftrightarrow\; \vDash A_1 \to (A_2 \to \dots \to (A_n \to B)\dots)$$

in PL, and so we may define:

Definition. Let $A_1, \dots, A_n, B$ (where $n \geq 1$) be formulas of $\mathcal{L}_{\mathrm{LTL}}$. B is called a *tautological consequence* of $A_1, \dots, A_n$ if $A_1 \to (A_2 \to \dots \to (A_n \to B)\dots)$ is tautologically valid.

Theorem 2.2.2. *$A_1, \dots, A_n \vDash B$ whenever B is a tautological consequence of $A_1, \dots, A_n$.*

Proof. Let B be a tautological consequence of $A_1, \dots, A_n$. Then, by Theorem 2.2.1, $\vDash A_1 \to (A_2 \to \dots \to (A_n \to B)\dots)$. Applying Theorem 2.1.7 n times (starting with $\mathcal{F} = \emptyset$) we get $A_1, \dots, A_n \vDash B$. △

Example. As a simple application of theorems 2.2.1 and 2.2.2 we may show that logical equivalence $\cong$ of formulas of $\mathcal{L}_{\mathrm{LTL}}$ is an equivalence relation (i.e., a reflexive, symmetrical, and transitive relation): since $A \leftrightarrow A$ is tautologically valid we have the reflexivity assertion $A \cong A$, i.e.,

$$\vDash A \leftrightarrow A$$

with Theorem 2.2.1. Second, $A \leftrightarrow B$ is a tautological consequence of $B \leftrightarrow A$, so we have $A \leftrightarrow B \vDash B \leftrightarrow A$ by Theorem 2.2.2, and this implies the symmetry $A \cong B \Rightarrow B \cong A$, i.e.,

$$\vDash A \leftrightarrow B \;\Rightarrow\; \vDash B \leftrightarrow A$$

with Theorem 2.1.8. An analogous argument establishes

$$\vDash A \leftrightarrow B \text{ and } \vDash B \leftrightarrow C \;\Rightarrow\; \vDash A \leftrightarrow C$$

expressing the transitivity of $\cong$. △

With the Theorems 2.2.1 and 2.2.2 we know of logical laws in LTL coming from the "classical basis" of the new logic. Let us now turn to proper temporal logical laws concerning the temporal operators. We give quite an extensive list of valid formulas, proving the validity only for a few examples. Many of these laws describe logical equivalences.

Duality laws

(T1) $\neg \bigcirc A \leftrightarrow \bigcirc \neg A$,
(T2) $\neg \Box A \leftrightarrow \Diamond \neg A$,

(T3) $\neg\Diamond A \leftrightarrow \Box\neg A$.

(T2) and (T3) express the *duality* of the operators $\Box$ and $\Diamond$. (T1) asserts that $\bigcirc$ is *self-dual* and was proved in the previous section.

Reflexivity laws

(T4) $\Box A \rightarrow A$,
(T5) $A \rightarrow \Diamond A$.

These formulas express the fact that "henceforth" and "sometime" include the "present".

Laws about the "strength" of the operators

(T6) $\Box A \rightarrow \bigcirc A$,
(T7) $\bigcirc A \rightarrow \Diamond A$,
(T8) $\Box A \rightarrow \Diamond A$,
(T9) $\Diamond\Box A \rightarrow \Box\Diamond A$.

Proof of (T9). We have to show that, for arbitrary K and $i \in \mathbb{N}$, $\mathsf{K}_i(\Diamond\Box A) = \mathsf{tt}$ implies $\mathsf{K}_i(\Box\Diamond A) = \mathsf{tt}$:

$$\begin{aligned}
\mathsf{K}_i(\Diamond\Box A) = \mathsf{tt} &\Rightarrow \mathsf{K}_j(\Box A) = \mathsf{tt} \text{ for some } j \geq i \\
&\Rightarrow \mathsf{K}_k(A) = \mathsf{tt} \text{ for some } j \geq i \text{ and every } k \geq j \\
&\Rightarrow \mathsf{K}_k(A) = \mathsf{tt} \text{ for some } k \geq j \text{ with arbitrary } j \geq i \\
&\Rightarrow \mathsf{K}_j(\Diamond A) = \mathsf{tt} \text{ for every } j \geq i \\
&\Rightarrow \mathsf{K}_i(\Box\Diamond A) = \mathsf{tt}.
\end{aligned}$$

△

Idempotency laws

(T10) $\Box\Box A \leftrightarrow \Box A$,
(T11) $\Diamond\Diamond A \leftrightarrow \Diamond A$.

Proof of (T10). Here we have to show that $\mathsf{K}_i(\Box\Box A) = \mathsf{K}_i(\Box A)$ for arbitrary K and $i \in \mathbb{N}$:

$$\begin{aligned}
\mathsf{K}_i(\Box\Box A) = \mathsf{tt} &\Leftrightarrow \mathsf{K}_j(\Box A) = \mathsf{tt} \text{ for every } j \geq i \\
&\Leftrightarrow \mathsf{K}_k(A) = \mathsf{tt} \text{ for every } j \geq i \text{ and every } k \geq j \\
&\Leftrightarrow \mathsf{K}_k(A) = \mathsf{tt} \text{ for every } k \geq i \\
&\Leftrightarrow \mathsf{K}_i(\Box A) = \mathsf{tt}.
\end{aligned}$$

△

Commutativity laws

(T12) $\Box\bigcirc A \leftrightarrow \bigcirc\Box A$,
(T13) $\Diamond\bigcirc A \leftrightarrow \bigcirc\Diamond A$.

These logical equivalences state the *commutativity* of $\bigcirc$ with $\Box$ and $\Diamond$.

Proof of (T12). For arbitrary K and $i \in \mathbb{N}$:

$$\begin{aligned}
\mathsf{K}_i(\Box \bigcirc A) = \mathsf{tt} &\Leftrightarrow \mathsf{K}_j(\bigcirc A) = \mathsf{tt} \text{ for every } j \geq i \\
&\Leftrightarrow \mathsf{K}_{j+1}(A) = \mathsf{tt} \text{ for every } j \geq i \\
&\Leftrightarrow \mathsf{K}_j(A) = \mathsf{tt} \text{ for every } j \geq i+1 \\
&\Leftrightarrow \mathsf{K}_{i+1}(\Box A) = \mathsf{tt} \\
&\Leftrightarrow \mathsf{K}_i(\bigcirc \Box A) = \mathsf{tt}.
\end{aligned}$$

△

Distributivity laws

(T14) $\bigcirc(A \rightarrow B) \leftrightarrow \bigcirc A \rightarrow \bigcirc B$,
(T15) $\bigcirc(A \land B) \leftrightarrow \bigcirc A \land \bigcirc B$,
(T16) $\bigcirc(A \lor B) \leftrightarrow \bigcirc A \lor \bigcirc B$,
(T17) $\bigcirc(A \leftrightarrow B) \leftrightarrow (\bigcirc A \leftrightarrow \bigcirc B)$,
(T18) $\Box(A \land B) \leftrightarrow \Box A \land \Box B$,
(T19) $\Diamond(A \lor B) \leftrightarrow \Diamond A \lor \Diamond B$,
(T20) $\Box\Diamond(A \lor B) \leftrightarrow \Box\Diamond A \lor \Box\Diamond B$,
(T21) $\Diamond\Box(A \land B) \leftrightarrow \Diamond\Box A \land \Diamond\Box B$.

(T14)–(T17) express the *distributivity* of $\bigcirc$ over all (binary) classical operators. According to (T18) and (T19), $\Box$ is distributive over $\land$ and $\Diamond$ is distributive over $\lor$. Finally, (T20) and (T21) assert that "infinitely often" distributes over $\lor$ and "almost always" distributes over $\land$.

Proof of (T14). For arbitrary K and $i \in \mathbb{N}$:

$$\begin{aligned}
\mathsf{K}_i(\bigcirc(A \rightarrow B)) = \mathsf{tt} &\Leftrightarrow \mathsf{K}_{i+1}(A \rightarrow B) = \mathsf{tt} \\
&\Leftrightarrow \mathsf{K}_{i+1}(A) = \mathsf{ff} \text{ or } \mathsf{K}_{i+1}(B) = \mathsf{tt} \\
&\Leftrightarrow \mathsf{K}_i(\bigcirc A) = \mathsf{ff} \text{ or } \mathsf{K}_i(\bigcirc B) = \mathsf{tt} \\
&\Leftrightarrow \mathsf{K}_i(\bigcirc A \rightarrow \bigcirc B) = \mathsf{tt}.
\end{aligned}$$

△

Weak distributivity laws

(T22) $\Box(A \rightarrow B) \rightarrow (\Box A \rightarrow \Box B)$,
(T23) $\Box A \lor \Box B \rightarrow \Box(A \lor B)$,
(T24) $(\Diamond A \rightarrow \Diamond B) \rightarrow \Diamond(A \rightarrow B)$,
(T25) $\Diamond(A \land B) \rightarrow \Diamond A \land \Diamond B$,
(T26) $\Box\Diamond(A \land B) \rightarrow \Box\Diamond A \land \Box\Diamond B$,
(T27) $\Diamond\Box A \lor \Diamond\Box B \rightarrow \Diamond\Box(A \lor B)$.

These formulas state that at least "some direction" of further distributivities of $\Box$, $\Diamond$, $\Box\Diamond$, and $\Diamond\Box$ hold.

Proof of (T23). For arbitrary K and $i \in \mathbb{N}$:

$$\begin{aligned}
\mathsf{K}_i(\Box A \vee \Box B) = \mathsf{tt} &\Rightarrow \mathsf{K}_i(\Box A) = \mathsf{tt} \text{ or } \mathsf{K}_i(\Box B) = \mathsf{tt}\\
&\Rightarrow \mathsf{K}_j(A) = \mathsf{tt} \text{ for every } j \geq i \text{ or}\\
&\quad\; \mathsf{K}_j(B) = \mathsf{tt} \text{ for every } j \geq i\\
&\Rightarrow \mathsf{K}_j(A) = \mathsf{tt} \text{ or } \mathsf{K}_j(B) = \mathsf{tt} \text{ for every } j \geq i\\
&\Rightarrow \mathsf{K}_j(A \vee B) = \mathsf{tt} \text{ for every } j \geq i\\
&\Rightarrow \mathsf{K}_i(\Box(A \vee B)) = \mathsf{tt}. \qquad \triangle
\end{aligned}$$

Fixpoint characterizations of $\Box$ *and* $\Diamond$

(T28) $\Box A \leftrightarrow A \wedge \bigcirc\Box A$,
(T29) $\Diamond A \leftrightarrow A \vee \bigcirc\Diamond A$.

(T28) is a recursive formulation of the informal characterization of $\Box A$ as an "infinite conjunction":

$$\Box A \;\leftrightarrow\; A \wedge \bigcirc A \wedge \bigcirc\bigcirc A \wedge \bigcirc\bigcirc\bigcirc A \wedge \ldots,$$

and (T29) is analogous for $\Diamond A$. These formulas are therefore also called *recursive characterizations*. The relationship with "fixpoints" will be reconsidered in a more general context in Sect. 3.2.

Proof of (T28). For arbitrary K and $i \in \mathbb{N}$:

$$\begin{aligned}
\mathsf{K}_i(A \wedge \bigcirc\Box A) = \mathsf{tt} &\Leftrightarrow \mathsf{K}_i(A) = \mathsf{tt} \text{ and } \mathsf{K}_i(\bigcirc\Box A) = \mathsf{tt}\\
&\Leftrightarrow \mathsf{K}_i(A) = \mathsf{tt} \text{ and } \mathsf{K}_j(A) = \mathsf{tt} \text{ for every } j \geq i+1\\
&\Leftrightarrow \mathsf{K}_j(A) = \mathsf{tt} \text{ for every } j \geq i\\
&\Leftrightarrow \mathsf{K}_i(\Box A) = \mathsf{tt}. \qquad \triangle
\end{aligned}$$

Monotonicity laws

(T30) $\Box(A \rightarrow B) \rightarrow (\bigcirc A \rightarrow \bigcirc B)$,
(T31) $\Box(A \rightarrow B) \rightarrow (\Diamond A \rightarrow \Diamond B)$.

It may be observed that this list of laws is (deliberately) redundant. For example, (T30) can be established as a consequence of the laws (T6) and (T14). We now give a direct proof.

Proof of (T30). For arbitrary K and $i \in \mathbb{N}$:

$$\begin{aligned}
\mathsf{K}_i(\Box(A \rightarrow B)) = \mathsf{tt} &\Rightarrow \mathsf{K}_j(A \rightarrow B) = \mathsf{tt} \text{ for every } j \geq i\\
&\Rightarrow \mathsf{K}_j(A) = \mathsf{ff} \text{ or } \mathsf{K}_j(B) = \mathsf{tt} \text{ for every } j \geq i\\
&\Rightarrow \mathsf{K}_{i+1}(A) = \mathsf{ff} \text{ or } \mathsf{K}_{i+1}(B) = \mathsf{tt}\\
&\Rightarrow \mathsf{K}_i(\bigcirc A) = \mathsf{ff} \text{ or } \mathsf{K}_i(\bigcirc B) = \mathsf{tt}\\
&\Rightarrow \mathsf{K}_i(\bigcirc A \rightarrow \bigcirc B) = \mathsf{tt}. \qquad \triangle
\end{aligned}$$

Frame laws

(T32) $\Box A \rightarrow (\bigcirc B \rightarrow \bigcirc(A \wedge B))$,

(T33) $\Box A \rightarrow (\Box B \rightarrow \Box(A \wedge B))$,
(T34) $\Box A \rightarrow (\Diamond B \rightarrow \Diamond(A \wedge B))$.

These formulas mean that if A holds forever then it may be "added" (by conjunction) under each temporal operator.

Proof of (T32). For arbitrary K and $i \in \mathbb{N}$:

$$\begin{aligned}
\mathsf{K}_i(\Box A) = \mathsf{tt} \Rightarrow\ & \mathsf{K}_{i+1}(A) = \mathsf{tt} \\
\Rightarrow\ & \mathsf{K}_{i+1}(B) = \mathsf{ff} \\
& \text{or} \\
& \mathsf{K}_{i+1}(B) = \mathsf{tt} \text{ and } \mathsf{K}_{i+1}(A) = \mathsf{tt} \\
\Rightarrow\ & \mathsf{K}_i(\bigcirc B) = \mathsf{ff} \text{ or } \mathsf{K}_i(\bigcirc(A \wedge B)) = \mathsf{tt} \\
\Rightarrow\ & \mathsf{K}_i(\bigcirc B \rightarrow \bigcirc(A \wedge B)) = \mathsf{tt}.
\end{aligned}$$

△

Temporal generalization and particularization laws

(T35) $\Box(\Box A \rightarrow B) \rightarrow (\Box A \rightarrow \Box B)$,
(T36) $\Box(A \rightarrow \Diamond B) \rightarrow (\Diamond A \rightarrow \Diamond B)$.

Proof of (T35). For arbitrary K and $i \in \mathbb{N}$, assume that $\mathsf{K}_i(\Box(\Box A \rightarrow B)) = \mathsf{tt}$, i.e., $\mathsf{K}_j(\Box A \rightarrow B) = \mathsf{tt}$ for every $j \geq i$. To prove $\mathsf{K}_i(\Box A \rightarrow \Box B) = \mathsf{tt}$, assume also that $\mathsf{K}_i(\Box A) = \mathsf{tt}$. This means $\mathsf{K}_k(A) = \mathsf{tt}$ for every $k \geq i$; hence $\mathsf{K}_k(A) = \mathsf{tt}$ for every $k \geq j$ and every $j \geq i$ and therefore $\mathsf{K}_j(\Box A) = \mathsf{tt}$ for every $j \geq i$. With Lemma 2.1.1 we obtain $\mathsf{K}_j(B) = \mathsf{tt}$ for every $j \geq i$, which means $\mathsf{K}_i(\Box B) = \mathsf{tt}$ and proves the claim. △

In Theorem 2.1.6 we stated the fundamental relationship between implication and consequence in LTL. In the presence of this theorem, laws of the form

$$\Box A \rightarrow B$$

can also be written as a consequence relationship in the form

$$A \vDash B,$$

for example:

(T22) $A \rightarrow B \vDash \Box A \rightarrow \Box B$,
(T30) $A \rightarrow B \vDash \bigcirc A \rightarrow \bigcirc B$,
(T32) $A \vDash \bigcirc B \rightarrow \bigcirc(A \wedge B)$,
(T35) $\Box A \rightarrow B \vDash \Box A \rightarrow \Box B$,
(T36) $A \rightarrow \Diamond B \vDash \Diamond A \rightarrow \Diamond B$.

This notation also explains why (T30) and (T31) are called monotonicity laws: they express a kind of monotonicity of $\bigcirc$ and $\Diamond$ with respect to $\rightarrow$ (viewed as an order relation). The same property of $\Box$ is noted as a weak distributivity law in (T22) but could also occur here.

The reformulations of (T35) and (T36) show their correspondence to the generalization and particularization rules of classical first-order logic (cf. Sect. 1.2) according to the informal meaning of $\Box$ and $\Diamond$ as a kind of "for all" and "for some" relating these temporal operators to the classical quantifiers $\forall$ and $\exists$, respectively. According to this relationship we call – following the notion of universal closure – a formula $\Box A$ the *temporal closure* of A.

We end this section with some examples of how to use this collection of temporal logical laws. Firstly, assume that two formulas A and B are logically equivalent. Then so are $\bigcirc A$ and $\bigcirc B$, in symbols:

$$A \cong B \;\Rightarrow\; \bigcirc A \cong \bigcirc B.$$

The detailed arguments for this fact could be as follows: assume $\models A \leftrightarrow B$. Both $A \rightarrow B$ and $B \rightarrow A$ are tautological consequences of $A \leftrightarrow B$, and so we obtain both $\models A \rightarrow B$ and $\models B \rightarrow A$ by the Theorems 2.2.2 and 2.1.8. Applying (T30) and again Theorem 2.1.8, we conclude $\models \bigcirc A \rightarrow \bigcirc B$ and $\models \bigcirc B \rightarrow \bigcirc A$. Finally, the formula $\bigcirc A \leftrightarrow \bigcirc B$ is a tautological consequence of $\bigcirc A \rightarrow \bigcirc B$ and $\bigcirc B \rightarrow \bigcirc A$, and another application of Theorems 2.2.2 and 2.1.8 yields $\models \bigcirc A \leftrightarrow \bigcirc B$.

In analogous ways we could use (T22) and (T31) to show

$$A \cong B \;\Rightarrow\; \Box A \cong \Box B$$

and

$$A \cong B \;\Rightarrow\; \Diamond A \cong \Diamond B$$

which altogether mean a kind of substitutivity of logically equivalent formulas under the temporal operators $\bigcirc$, $\Box$, and $\Diamond$.

As another application of the logical laws we finally show a remarkable consequence and generalization of the idempotency laws (T10) and (T11). These seem to imply that, e.g., the formula

$$\Box\Box\Box\Diamond\Box\Diamond\Diamond A$$

is logically equivalent to

$$\Box\Diamond\Box\Diamond A,$$

informally: the $\Box$-$\Diamond$-*prefix* $\Box\Box\Box\Diamond\Box\Diamond\Diamond$ can be reduced to the shorter $\Box\Diamond\Box\Diamond$. In fact, we will show that the formula is actually logically equivalent to

$$\Box\Diamond A.$$

and, more generally, any $\Box$-$\Diamond$-prefix is reducible to one of the four cases $\Box$, $\Diamond$, $\Diamond\Box$, or $\Box\Diamond$. In preparation, we state two more laws of temporal logic.

Absorption laws

(T37) $\Diamond\Box\Diamond A \leftrightarrow \Box\Diamond A$,

(T38) $\Box\Diamond\Box A \leftrightarrow \Diamond\Box A$.

These laws assert that in a series of three alternating operators $\Box$ and $\Diamond$, the first is "absorbed" by the remaining two operators.

Proof. First, $\vDash \Box\Diamond A \rightarrow \Diamond\Box\Diamond A$ is just an instance of (T5). On the other hand, (T9) yields $\vDash \Diamond\Box\Diamond A \rightarrow \Box\Diamond\Diamond A$, and $\vDash \Diamond\Box\Diamond A \rightarrow \Box\Diamond A$ then follows from (T11) and the substitutivity principle mentioned above. Taken together, we obtain (T37).

For the proof of (T38) we observe the following chain of logical equivalences:

$$\begin{aligned}
\Box\Diamond\Box A &\equiv \Box\neg\Box\neg\Box A && \text{(by definition of } \Diamond\text{)}\\
&\cong \neg\Diamond\Box\Diamond\neg A && \text{(by substitutivity from (T2) and (T3))}\\
&\cong \neg\Box\Diamond\neg A && \text{(by substitutivity from (T37))}\\
&\cong \Diamond\Box A && \text{(by substitutivity from (T2) and (T3)).}
\end{aligned}$$
△

Theorem 2.2.3. *Let $A \equiv \boxtimes_1 \boxtimes_2 \dots \boxtimes_n B$, $n \geq 1$, be a formula of $\mathcal{L}_{\mathrm{LTL}}$ where every $\boxtimes_i$, $1 \leq i \leq n$, is either $\Box$ or $\Diamond$. Then*

$$A \cong \mathbf{pref}\, B$$

where **pref** *is one of the four $\Box$-$\Diamond$-prefixes $\Box$, $\Diamond$, $\Diamond\Box$, or $\Box\Diamond$.*

Proof. The theorem is proved by induction on n. The case $n = 1$ is trivial since then $A \equiv \Box B$ or $A \equiv \Diamond B$. If $n > 1$ then we have by induction hypothesis that

$$\boxtimes_1 \dots \boxtimes_{n-1} \boxtimes_n B \cong \mathbf{pref}'\, \boxtimes_n B$$

with $\mathbf{pref}'$ being as described. If $\mathbf{pref}'$ is $\Box$ or $\Diamond$ then $\mathbf{pref}'\, \boxtimes_n B \cong \mathbf{pref}\, B$, for some $\Box$-$\Diamond$-prefix **pref** of admissible form, can be established with the help of (T10) and (T11). Otherwise, we distinguish four different combinations of $\mathbf{pref}'$, which can be $\Diamond\Box$ or $\Box\Diamond$, and $\boxtimes_n$, which can be $\Box$ or $\Diamond$. Any of these combinations can be reduced to an admissible prefix with the help of (T10), (T11), (T37), and (T38), and the substitutivity principle. △

2.3 Axiomatization

We now give a formal system Σ_{LTL} for the formal derivation of consequence relationships between formulas:

Axioms

(taut) All tautologically valid formulas,
(ltl1) $\neg\bigcirc A \leftrightarrow \bigcirc\neg A$,
(ltl2) $\bigcirc(A \rightarrow B) \rightarrow (\bigcirc A \rightarrow \bigcirc B)$,
(ltl3) $\Box A \rightarrow A \wedge \bigcirc\Box A$.

Rules

(mp) $A, A \to B \vdash B$,
(nex) $A \vdash \circ A$,
(ind) $A \to B, A \to \circ A \vdash A \to \Box B$.

The "axiom" (taut) may seem somewhat strange. We could instead have taken some axioms for classical propositional logic such as those shown in Sect. 1.1. We are, however, not interested here in how tautologically valid formulas can be derived (which would proceed completely within the "classical part" of the formal system). In order to abbreviate derivations we simply take all such formulas (the set of which is decidable) as axioms. In fact, we will use (taut) extensively without really verifying the tautological validity of the formula in question explicitly. In the axioms (ltl2) and (ltl3) one should notice that these are only implications and not equivalences although the latter are also valid according to the laws (T14) and (T28) proven in the previous section. The rule (ind) is the proof-theoretical counterpart to Theorem 2.1.4; it is an *induction rule* informally stating:

> "If A (always) implies B and A is invariant from any state to the next then A implies B forever".

Let us now show the soundness of Σ_{LTL} with respect to the semantics of LTL.

Theorem 2.3.1 (Soundness Theorem for Σ_{LTL}). *Let A be a formula and $\mathcal{F}$ a set of formulas. If $\mathcal{F} \vdash A$ then $\mathcal{F} \vDash A$. In particular: if $\vdash A$ then $\vDash A$.*

Proof. The proof runs by induction on the assumed derivation of A from $\mathcal{F}$ which is inductively defined as explained in Sect. 1.1.

1. A is an axiom of Σ_{LTL}: All axioms (taut), (ltl1), (ltl2), (ltl3) are valid according to Theorem 2.2.1 and the laws (T1), (T14), and (T28) which were proved in Sect. 2.2. Of course, then also $\mathcal{F} \vDash A$.
2. $A \in \mathcal{F}$: In this case $\mathcal{F} \vDash A$ holds trivially.
3. The rule applied last is (mp) with premises B and $B \to A$: This means that $\mathcal{F} \vdash B$ as well as $\mathcal{F} \vdash B \to A$. By the induction hypothesis we get $\mathcal{F} \vDash B$ and $\mathcal{F} \vDash B \to A$ and hence $\mathcal{F} \vDash A$ by Theorem 2.1.2.
4. The rule applied last is (nex) with premise B: Therefore, $A \equiv \circ B$ such that $\mathcal{F} \vdash B$. By the induction hypothesis we get $\mathcal{F} \vDash B$, and $\mathcal{F} \vDash \circ B$ then follows by Theorem 2.1.3.
5. The rule applied last is (ind) with premises $B \to C$ and $B \to \circ B$: Therefore, $A \equiv B \to \Box C$, and we have $\mathcal{F} \vdash B \to C$ and $\mathcal{F} \vdash B \to \circ B$. By the induction hypothesis we get $\mathcal{F} \vDash B \to C$ and $\mathcal{F} \vDash B \to \circ B$, and hence $\mathcal{F} \vDash B \to \Box C$; so $\mathcal{F} \vDash A$ follows by Theorem 2.1.4. △

We argued above that in derivations within Σ_{LTL} we do not want to bother with how to derive tautologically valid formulas; we will simply use them as axioms. Nevertheless, there will still occur purely classical derivation parts where only (taut) and (mp) are used. We will abbreviate such parts by using – often again without really proving the respective presupposition – the following derived rule:

(prop) $A_1, \ldots, A_n \vdash B$ if B is a tautological consequence of $A_1, \ldots, A_n$.

As an example we note again the chaining rule

$$A \to B, B \to C \vdash A \to C$$

which we will apply from now on in derivations, together with many others, as a rule of the kind (prop). This shortcut is justified by the following theorem.

Theorem 2.3.2. *$A_1, \ldots, A_n \vdash B$ whenever B is a tautological consequence of $A_1, \ldots, A_n$.*

Proof. We prove only the case $n = 2$. The general case is analogous. If B is a tautological consequence of A_1 and A_2 then the formula $A_1 \to (A_2 \to B)$ is tautologically valid and we can give the following derivation of B from A_1 and A_2:

(1)	A_1	assumption
(2)	A_2	assumption
(3)	$A_1 \to (A_2 \to B)$	(taut)
(4)	$A_2 \to B$	(mp),(1),(3)
(5)	B	(mp),(2),(4) △

In the following we give some examples of derivations of proper temporal formulas and rules. We begin with the "opposite directions" of the axioms (ltl2) and (ltl3):

(ltl2') $(\circ A \to \circ B) \to \circ(A \to B)$,
(ltl3') $A \land \circ\Box A \to \Box A$.

Derivation of (ltl2').

(1)	$\neg(A \to B) \to A$	(taut)
(2)	$\circ(\neg(A \to B) \to A)$	(nex),(1)
(3)	$\circ(\neg(A \to B) \to A) \to (\circ\neg(A \to B) \to \circ A)$	(ltl2)
(4)	$\circ\neg(A \to B) \to \circ A$	(mp),(2),(3)
(5)	$\neg\circ(A \to B) \leftrightarrow \circ\neg(A \to B)$	(ltl1)
(6)	$\neg\circ(A \to B) \to \circ A$	(prop),(4),(5)
(7)	$\neg(A \to B) \to \neg B$	(taut)
(8)	$\neg\circ(A \to B) \to \circ\neg B$	from (7) in the same way as (6) from (1)
(9)	$\circ\neg B \to \neg\circ B$	(prop),(ltl1)
(10)	$\neg\circ(A \to B) \to \neg\circ B$	(prop),(8),(9)
(11)	$\neg\circ(A \to B) \to \neg(\circ A \to \circ B)$	(prop),(6),(10)
(12)	$(\circ A \to \circ B) \to \circ(A \to B)$	(prop),(11) △

Derivation of (ltl3').

(1)	$A \land \circ\Box A \to A$	(taut)
(2)	$\Box A \to A \land \circ\Box A$	(ltl3)

(3) $\bigcirc(\Box A \to A \land \bigcirc\Box A)$	(nex),(2)	
(4) $\bigcirc\Box A \to \bigcirc(A \land \bigcirc\Box A)$	(mp),(ltl2),(3)	
(5) $A \land \bigcirc\Box A \to \bigcirc(A \land \bigcirc\Box A)$	(prop),(4)	
(6) $A \land \bigcirc\Box A \to \Box A$	(ind),(1),(5)	$\triangle$

The following two rules are simple but useful variants of the induction rule (ind):

(ind1) $A \to \bigcirc A \vdash A \to \Box A$,
(ind2) $A \to B, B \to \bigcirc B \vdash A \to \Box B$.

Derivation of (ind1).

(1) $A \to \bigcirc A$	assumption	
(2) $A \to A$	(taut)	
(3) $A \to \Box A$	(ind),(1),(2)	$\triangle$

Derivation of (ind2).

(1) $A \to B$	assumption	
(2) $B \to \bigcirc B$	assumption	
(3) $B \to \Box B$	(ind1),(1)	
(4) $A \to \Box B$	(prop),(1),(3)	$\triangle$

Next we show two rules the first of which is the analogy of (nex) for $\Box$:

(alw) $A \vdash \Box A$,
(som) $A \to \bigcirc B \vdash A \to \Diamond B$.

Derivation of (alw).

(1) A	assumption	
(2) $\bigcirc A$	(nex),(1)	
(3) $A \to \bigcirc A$	(prop),(2)	
(4) $A \to \Box A$	(ind1),(3)	
(5) $\Box A$	(mp),(1),(4)	$\triangle$

Derivation of (som).

(1) $A \to \bigcirc B$	assumption	
(2) $\Box\neg B \to \neg B \land \bigcirc\Box\neg B$	(ltl3)	
(3) $\Box\neg B \to \bigcirc\Box\neg B$	(prop),(2)	
(4) $\Box\neg B \to \neg B$	(prop),(2)	
(5) $\bigcirc(\Box\neg B \to \neg B)$	(nex),(4)	
(6) $\bigcirc(\Box\neg B \to \neg B) \to (\bigcirc\Box\neg B \to \bigcirc\neg B)$	(ltl2)	
(7) $\bigcirc\Box\neg B \to \bigcirc\neg B$	(mp),(5),(6)	
(8) $\Box\neg B \to \bigcirc\neg B$	(prop),(3),(7)	
(9) $\neg\bigcirc B \leftrightarrow \bigcirc\neg B$	(ltl1)	
(10) $\Box\neg B \to \neg\bigcirc B$	(prop),(8),(9)	
(11) $\bigcirc B \to \neg\Box\neg B$	(prop),(10)	
(12) $A \to \Diamond B$	(prop),(1),(11)	$\triangle$

We finish these exercises with a derivation of one direction of the law (T15) which will be needed subsequently:

(T15') $\quad \circ A \land \circ B \to \circ(A \land B)$.

Derivation of (T15'). We derive $\neg(\circ A \to \neg\circ B) \to \circ\neg(A \to \neg B)$ which is (T15') in its strict syntactical form:

(1)	$\circ(A \to \neg B) \to (\circ A \to \circ\neg B)$	(ltl2)
(2)	$\circ(A \to \neg B) \to (\circ A \to \neg\circ B)$	(prop),(ltl1),(1)
(3)	$\neg(\circ A \to \neg\circ B) \to \neg\circ(A \to \neg B)$	(prop),(2)
(4)	$\neg(\circ A \to \neg\circ B) \to \circ\neg(A \to \neg B)$	(prop),(ltl1),(3) $\triangle$

In Theorem 2.1.6 we observed a connection between implication and the consequence relation. There is an analogous relationship between implication and derivability.

Theorem 2.3.3 (Deduction Theorem of LTL). *Let A, B be formulas, $\mathcal{F}$ a set of formulas. If $\mathcal{F} \cup \{A\} \vdash B$ then $\mathcal{F} \vdash \Box A \to B$.*

Proof. The proof runs by induction on the assumed derivation of B from $\mathcal{F} \cup \{A\}$.

1. B is an axiom of Σ_{LTL} or $B \in \mathcal{F}$: Then $\mathcal{F} \vdash B$, and $\mathcal{F} \vdash \Box A \to B$ follows with (prop).
2. $B \equiv A$: Then $\mathcal{F} \vdash \Box A \to A \land \circ\Box A$ by (ltl3), and $\mathcal{F} \vdash \Box A \to A$ follows with (prop).
3. B is a conclusion of (mp) with premises C and $C \to B$: We then have both $\mathcal{F} \cup \{A\} \vdash C$ and $\mathcal{F} \cup \{A\} \vdash C \to B$. Applying the induction hypothesis, we get $\mathcal{F} \vdash \Box A \to C$ and $\mathcal{F} \vdash \Box A \to (C \to B)$, from which $\mathcal{F} \vdash \Box A \to B$ follows with (prop).
4. $B \equiv \circ C$ is a conclusion of (nex) with premise C: Then $\mathcal{F} \cup \{A\} \vdash C$, and therefore $\mathcal{F} \vdash \Box A \to C$ by induction hypothesis. We continue the derivation of $\Box A \to C$ to a derivation of $\Box A \to \circ C$:

(1)	$\Box A \to C$	derivable
(2)	$\circ(\Box A \to C)$	(nex),(1)
(3)	$\circ(\Box A \to C) \to (\circ\Box A \to \circ C)$	(ltl2)
(4)	$\circ\Box A \to \circ C$	(mp),(2),(3)
(5)	$\Box A \to A \land \circ\Box A$	(ltl3)
(6)	$\Box A \to \circ\Box A$	(prop),(5)
(7)	$\Box A \to \circ C$	(prop),(4),(6)

5. $B \equiv C \to \Box D$ is a conclusion of (ind) with premises $C \to D$ and $C \to \circ C$: As above we get with the induction hypothesis that $\Box A \to (C \to D)$ and $\Box A \to (C \to \circ C)$ are derivable from $\mathcal{F}$, and their derivations can be continued to derive $\Box A \to (C \to \Box D)$ as follows (using (T15') derived above):

(1)	$\Box A \to (C \to D)$	derivable
(2)	$\Box A \to (C \to \circ C)$	derivable

(3)	$\Box A \land C \to D$	(prop),(1)
(4)	$\Box A \land C \to \circ C$	(prop),(2)
(5)	$\Box A \to \circ\Box A$	(prop),(ltl3)
(6)	$\Box A \land C \to \circ\Box A \land \circ C$	(prop),(4),(5)
(7)	$\circ\Box A \land \circ C \to \circ(\Box A \land C)$	(T15')
(8)	$\Box A \land C \to \circ(\Box A \land C)$	(prop),(6),(7)
(9)	$\Box A \land C \to \Box D$	(ind),(3),(8)
(10)	$\Box A \to (C \to \Box D)$	(prop),(9) △

The Deduction Theorem can be used to abbreviate derivations, as illustrated by the following example: in order to derive the valid formula

(T22) $\Box(A \to B) \to (\Box A \to \Box B)$

it suffices, according to the theorem (with $\mathcal{F} = \emptyset$), to show $A \to B \vdash \Box A \to \Box B$. Applying the theorem once more, it suffices to prove $A \to B, A \vdash \Box B$, which is very easy using the derived rule (alw):

(1)	$A \to B$	assumption
(2)	A	assumption
(3)	B	(mp),(1),(2)
(4)	$\Box B$	(alw),(3)

According to the semantical considerations in Sect. 2.1 and the soundness of Σ_{LTL}, the Deduction Theorem of classical propositional logic

If $\mathcal{F} \cup \{A\} \vdash B$ then $\mathcal{F} \vdash A \to B$

does not hold generally in LTL. The converse direction of this relationship, however, holds trivially because it is nothing but an application of (mp), and the converse of Theorem 2.3.3 can be shown in a similar way:

Theorem 2.3.4. *Let A, B be formulas, and let $\mathcal{F}$ be a set of formulas. If $\mathcal{F} \vdash \Box A \to B$ then $\mathcal{F} \cup \{A\} \vdash B$.*

Proof. If $\mathcal{F} \vdash \Box A \to B$ then also $\mathcal{F} \cup \{A\} \vdash \Box A \to B$. With $\mathcal{F} \cup \{A\} \vdash A$ we get $\mathcal{F} \cup \{A\} \vdash \Box A$ by (alw) and finally $\mathcal{F} \cup \{A\} \vdash B$ by applying (mp). △

Second Reading

Temporal logic is a branch of *modal logic*. In its basic (propositional) form, modal logic extends classical PL by one *modal operator* $\Box$ which allows for building formulas of the form $\Box A$ and, as an abbreviation, $\Diamond A \equiv \neg\Box\neg A$ as in LTL. In modal logic these formulas are read *necessarily* A and *possibly* A, respectively.

A *Kripke structure* $\mathfrak{K} = (\{\eta_\iota\}_{\iota \in K}, \lhd)$ for a set $\mathbf{V}$ of propositional constants underlying a modal logic language consists of

- a set $K \neq \emptyset$,

- a binary *accessibility relation* $\lhd$ on K,
- a valuation $\eta_\iota : \mathbf{V} \to \{\mathsf{ff}, \mathsf{tt}\}$ for every $\iota \in K$.

The η_ι (or sometimes only the elements of the index set K) are called *possible worlds* in this context, and truth values $\mathfrak{K}_\iota(F)$ can be defined for all formulas F in an analogous way to that in LTL. For the classical part the inductive formation rules are just the same:

1. $\mathfrak{K}_\iota(v) = \eta_\iota(v) \quad$ for $v \in \mathbf{V}$,
2. $\mathfrak{K}_\iota(\mathbf{false}) = \mathsf{ff}$,
3. $\mathfrak{K}_\iota(A \to B) = \mathsf{tt} \Leftrightarrow \mathfrak{K}_\iota(A) = \mathsf{ff}$ or $\mathfrak{K}_\iota(B) = \mathsf{tt}$,

and for formulas $\Box A$ the definition reads:

4. $\mathfrak{K}_\iota(\Box A) = \mathsf{tt} \Leftrightarrow \mathfrak{K}_\kappa(A) = \mathsf{tt}$ for every κ with $\iota \lhd \kappa$.

For $\Diamond A$ this clearly provides:

5. $\mathfrak{K}_\iota(\Diamond A) = \mathsf{tt} \Leftrightarrow \mathfrak{K}_\kappa(A) = \mathsf{tt}$ for some κ with $\iota \lhd \kappa$.

A modal logic formula A is called *valid in the Kripke structure* $\mathfrak{K}$ if $\mathfrak{K}_\iota(A) = \mathsf{tt}$ for every $\iota \in K$. *Consequence* and *(universal) validity* are defined according to the usual pattern.

It is easy to see how LTL fits into this general modal framework. The language of LTL contains two operators $\circ$ and $\Box$ (instead of one) with corresponding accessibility relations $\lhd_\circ$ and $\lhd_\Box$. (In a more general setting of *multimodal logic* with $n \geq 1$ modal operators $\Box_1, \ldots, \Box_n$, LTL would be a *bimodal logic*.) Temporal structures for LTL can be understood as a special case of Kripke structures where $K = \mathbb{N}$ and, for $i, j \in \mathbb{N}$,

$$i \lhd_\circ j \Leftrightarrow i + 1 = j,$$
$$i \lhd_\Box j \Leftrightarrow i \leq j.$$

Taking these definitions in clause 4 above (with $\lhd_\circ$ and $\lhd_\Box$, respectively) we indeed get back the LTL definitions for $\mathsf{K}_i(\circ A)$ and $\mathsf{K}_i(\Box A)$.

As long as no restrictions are put on the relation $\lhd \subseteq K \times K$, modal logic can be axiomatized by a sound and complete formal system with the axioms

- all tautologically valid formulas (defined as in LTL),
- $\Box(A \to B) \to (\Box A \to \Box B)$

and the rules

- $A, A \to B \vdash B$,
- $A \vdash \Box A$.

A large variety of modal logics is obtained by requiring particular properties of accessibility. Many of these can be characterized by (additional) axioms. For example, reflexivity of $\lhd$ can be described by adding

$$\Box A \to A$$

to the basic system, and transitivity of $\lhd$ is characterized by

$$\Box A \to \Box\Box A.$$

The modal logic with both additional axioms is usually denoted by S4. An extension of S4, often denoted by S4.3*Dum*, is obtained by adding the *Lemmon formula*

$$\Box(\Box A \to B) \lor \Box(\Box B \to A)$$

and the *Dummett formula*

$$\Box(\Box(A \rightarrow \Box A) \rightarrow A) \rightarrow (\Diamond\Box A \rightarrow \Box A)$$

to the axioms of S4. These additional axioms force $\lhd$ to be linear and discrete, respectively. This logic is "very close" to LTL: a formula A is derivable in the resulting formal system if and only if A is valid in all Kripke structures $(\{\eta_i\}_{i \in \mathbb{N}}, \leq)$. However, formulas of S4.3*Dum* do not contain the "nexttime" operator, and in particular it is impossible to formulate an induction rule in that logic.

2.4 Completeness

We want to address now the question of whether the formal system Σ_{LTL} is complete. This has to be treated quite carefully. Consider the infinite set

$$\mathcal{F} = \{A \rightarrow B, A \rightarrow \bigcirc B, A \rightarrow \bigcirc\bigcirc B, A \rightarrow \bigcirc\bigcirc\bigcirc B, \ldots\}$$

of formulas. It is easy to calculate that

$$\mathcal{F} \vDash A \rightarrow \Box B.$$

Within a (sound and) complete formal system, $A \rightarrow \Box B$ would then be derivable from $\mathcal{F}$. This, however, cannot be the case in general. Any derivation in such a system can only use finitely many of the assumptions of $\mathcal{F}$. So, assuming a derivation of $A \rightarrow \Box B$ from $\mathcal{F}$, the soundness of the system would imply that $A \rightarrow \Box B$ is a consequence of a finite subset of $\mathcal{F}$ (the subset of assumptions from $\mathcal{F}$ used in the derivation). Again it is easy to see that this is not the case. This consideration shows that

$$\mathcal{F} \vDash A \;\Rightarrow\; \mathcal{F} \vdash A$$

does not hold for the formal system Σ_{LTL} (for arbitrary $\mathcal{F}$ and A) and, moreover, that no sound formal system can achieve this kind of completeness at all. The above example shows in particular that in LTL, one may have $\mathcal{F} \vDash A$ but not $\mathcal{F}' \vDash A$ for any finite subset $\mathcal{F}' \subseteq \mathcal{F}$. In other words, the consequence relation of LTL is not *compact*, unlike that of classical propositional or first-order logic.

The above incompleteness argument mainly relied on the set $\mathcal{F}$ being infinite. This leads us to consider a weaker notion of completeness: we call a formal system *weakly complete* if

$$\mathcal{F} \vDash A \;\Rightarrow\; \mathcal{F} \vdash A \quad \text{for finite } \mathcal{F}.$$

In this section we will show that Σ_{LTL} is indeed weakly complete. Our proof will roughly follow the proof idea in the classical logic case, often called the *Henkin-Hasenjäger method*, modified in many details for the present situation. Because we have already restricted ourselves to finite sets $\mathcal{F}$ of assumptions, Theorems 2.1.6 and 2.3.4 can be seen to imply that it suffices to consider the case where $\mathcal{F} = \emptyset$ and to prove that $\models A$ implies $\vdash A$ or, equivalently, that A is not valid whenever it is not derivable. Since $A \cong \neg\neg A$, we may assume without loss of generality that A is of the form $\neg B$, and we will show that A is satisfiable (by constructing a suitable temporal structure) whenever $\neg A$ cannot be derived in Σ_{LTL}.

Let us begin with introducing some notation. A *positive-negative pair* (shortly: PNP) is a pair $\mathcal{P} = (\mathcal{F}^+, \mathcal{F}^-)$ of two finite sets $\mathcal{F}^+$ and $\mathcal{F}^-$ of formulas. We denote the set $\mathcal{F}^+ \cup \mathcal{F}^-$ by $\mathcal{F}_\mathcal{P}$. Furthermore, we will sometimes denote $\mathcal{F}^+$ by $pos(\mathcal{P})$ and $\mathcal{F}^-$ by $neg(\mathcal{P})$. Finally, the formula $\widehat{\mathcal{P}}$ will be the abbreviation

$$\widehat{\mathcal{P}} \equiv \bigwedge_{A \in \mathcal{F}^+} A \wedge \bigwedge_{B \in \mathcal{F}^-} \neg B$$

where empty conjunctions are identified with the formula **true**. PNPs will be used to represent (possibly incomplete) information about the temporal structure under construction; the intuition is that the formulas in $\mathcal{F}^+$ should be true and those in $\mathcal{F}^-$ should be false at the current state.

A PNP $\mathcal{P}$ is called *inconsistent* if $\vdash \neg\widehat{\mathcal{P}}$. Otherwise, $\mathcal{P}$ is called *consistent.*

Lemma 2.4.1. *Let $\mathcal{P} = (\mathcal{F}^+, \mathcal{F}^-)$ be a consistent PNP and A a formula.*

a) $\mathcal{F}^+$ and $\mathcal{F}^-$ are disjoint.
b) $(\mathcal{F}^+ \cup \{A\}, \mathcal{F}^-)$ or $(\mathcal{F}^+, \mathcal{F}^- \cup \{A\})$ is a consistent PNP.

Proof. a) Assume that $\mathcal{F}^+$ and $\mathcal{F}^-$ are not disjoint and pick some $A \in \mathcal{F}^+ \cap \mathcal{F}^-$. Then $\widehat{\mathcal{P}}$ is of the form $\ldots \wedge A \wedge \ldots \wedge \neg A \wedge \ldots$ which implies that $\neg\widehat{\mathcal{P}}$ is tautologically valid. So $\vdash \neg\widehat{\mathcal{P}}$, which means that $\mathcal{P}$ is inconsistent and a contradiction is reached. Hence, $\mathcal{F}^+$ and $\mathcal{F}^-$ must be disjoint.

b) If $A \in \mathcal{F}^+$ or $A \in \mathcal{F}^-$ then we have $(\mathcal{F}^+ \cup \{A\}, \mathcal{F}^-) = (\mathcal{F}^+, \mathcal{F}^-)$ or $(\mathcal{F}^+, \mathcal{F}^- \cup \{A\}) = (\mathcal{F}^+, \mathcal{F}^-)$, respectively, and the assertion follows by the assumed consistency of $(\mathcal{F}^+, \mathcal{F}^-)$. Otherwise, assuming both pairs under consideration are inconsistent implies $\vdash \neg(\widehat{\mathcal{P}} \wedge A)$ and $\vdash \neg(\widehat{\mathcal{P}} \wedge \neg A)$. With (prop) we obtain $\vdash \neg\widehat{\mathcal{P}}$, which again contradicts the consistency of $\mathcal{P}$. Hence, (at least) one of the pairs must be consistent. △

Lemma 2.4.2. *Let $\mathcal{P} = (\mathcal{F}^+, \mathcal{F}^-)$ be a consistent PNP and A and B formulas.*

a) **false** $\notin \mathcal{F}^+$.
b) If $A, B, A \to B \in \mathcal{F}_\mathcal{P}$ then $A \to B \in \mathcal{F}^+ \Leftrightarrow A \in \mathcal{F}^-$ or $B \in \mathcal{F}^+$.
c) If $\vdash A \to B, A \in \mathcal{F}^+, B \in \mathcal{F}_\mathcal{P}$ then $B \in \mathcal{F}^+$.

Proof. a) Assume **false** $\in \mathcal{F}^+$. Then $\vdash \widehat{\mathcal{P}} \to$ **false** by (taut) which is just $\vdash \neg\widehat{\mathcal{P}}$, and a contradiction is reached. This proves **false** $\notin \mathcal{F}^+$.

b) Assume that $A \to B \in \mathcal{F}^+$ but $A \notin \mathcal{F}^-$ and $B \notin \mathcal{F}^+$. Since $A, B \in \mathcal{F}_\mathcal{P}$ we get $A \in \mathcal{F}^+$ and $B \in \mathcal{F}^-$. Then $\vdash \widehat{\mathcal{P}} \to (A \to B) \wedge A \wedge \neg B$ and this yields $\vdash \neg\widehat{\mathcal{P}}$ with (prop) which is a contradiction. Hence $A \in \mathcal{F}^-$ or $B \in \mathcal{F}^+$. On the other hand, assume that $A \in \mathcal{F}^-$ or $B \in \mathcal{F}^+$. If $A \to B \notin \mathcal{F}^+$ we must have $A \to B \in \mathcal{F}^-$, and we get $\vdash \widehat{\mathcal{P}} \to \neg(A \to B) \wedge \neg A$ or $\vdash \widehat{\mathcal{P}} \to \neg(A \to B) \wedge B$. In both cases we again obtain the contradiction $\vdash \neg\widehat{\mathcal{P}}$; hence $A \to B \in \mathcal{F}^+$.

c) Assume that $B \notin \mathcal{F}^+$. Then $B \in \mathcal{F}^-$ because of $B \in \mathcal{F}_{\mathcal{P}}$, and with $A \in \mathcal{F}^+$ we get $\vdash \widehat{\mathcal{P}} \to A \land \neg B$, and furthermore $\vdash \neg\widehat{\mathcal{P}}$ with $\vdash A \to B$ and (prop). This is in contradiction to the consistency of $\mathcal{P}$; hence $B \in \mathcal{F}^+$. △

Let F be a formula. With F we associate a set $\tau(F)$ of formulas, inductively defined as follows:

1. $\tau(v) = \{v\}$ for $v \in \mathbf{V}$.
2. $\tau(\mathbf{false}) = \{\mathbf{false}\}$.
3. $\tau(A \to B) = \{A \to B\} \cup \tau(A) \cup \tau(B)$.
4. $\tau(\bigcirc A) = \{\bigcirc A\}$.
5. $\tau(\Box A) = \{\Box A\} \cup \tau(A)$.

Informally, $\tau(F)$ is the set of "subformulas" of F where, however, formulas $\bigcirc A$ are treated as "indivisible". For a set $\mathcal{F}$ of formulas we let

$$\tau(\mathcal{F}) = \{A \mid A \in \tau(F), F \in \mathcal{F}\}.$$

Obviously, $\tau(\tau(\mathcal{F})) = \tau(\mathcal{F})$ and $\tau(\mathcal{F}_{\mathcal{P}})$ is finite for every PNP $\mathcal{P}$ (since $\mathcal{F}_{\mathcal{P}}$ is finite). We call a PNP $\mathcal{P}$ *complete* if $\tau(\mathcal{F}_{\mathcal{P}}) = \mathcal{F}_{\mathcal{P}}$.

Lemma 2.4.3. *Let $\mathcal{P}$ be a consistent PNP. There is a consistent and complete PNP $\mathcal{P}^*$ with $pos(\mathcal{P}) \subseteq pos(\mathcal{P}^*)$ and $neg(\mathcal{P}) \subseteq neg(\mathcal{P}^*)$.*

Proof. Starting from $\mathcal{P}$, $\mathcal{P}^*$ is constructed by successively adding A to $pos(\mathcal{P})$ or to $neg(\mathcal{P})$ for every $A \in \tau(\mathcal{F}_{\mathcal{P}})$ depending on which of these extensions is consistent. By Lemma 2.4.1 b) this is always possible and it evidently yields some consistent and complete PNP $\mathcal{P}^*$. △

Given a consistent PNP $\mathcal{P}$, we call any PNP $\mathcal{P}^*$ that satisfies the conditions of Lemma 2.4.3 a *completion* of $\mathcal{P}$. In general, different completions of a given $\mathcal{P}$ are possible, but obviously only finitely many.

Lemma 2.4.4. *Let $\mathcal{P}_1^*, \dots, \mathcal{P}_n^*$ be all different completions of a consistent PNP $\mathcal{P}$. Then $\vdash \widehat{\mathcal{P}} \to \widehat{\mathcal{P}_1^*} \lor \dots \lor \widehat{\mathcal{P}_n^*}$.*

Proof. We first prove an auxiliary assertion: let $\mathcal{F}$ be some finite set of formulas and let $\mathcal{Q}_1, \dots, \mathcal{Q}_m$ be all the different PNP $\mathcal{Q}$ with $\mathcal{F}_{\mathcal{Q}} = \tau(\mathcal{F})$ and such that $pos(\mathcal{Q})$ and $neg(\mathcal{Q})$ are disjoint. Because $\tau(\mathcal{F}_{\mathcal{Q}}) = \tau(\tau(\mathcal{F})) = \tau(\mathcal{F}) = \mathcal{F}_{\mathcal{Q}}$ holds for any such $\mathcal{Q}$, all $\mathcal{Q}_1, \dots, \mathcal{Q}_m$ are complete and we show by induction on the number of formulas in $\tau(\mathcal{F})$ that

$$(*) \qquad \vdash \bigvee_{i=1}^{m} \widehat{\mathcal{Q}_i}\,.$$

If $\tau(\mathcal{F}) = \emptyset$ then $m = 1$, $\mathcal{Q}_1 = (\emptyset, \emptyset)$, and $\widehat{\mathcal{Q}_1} \equiv \mathbf{true}$, so $(*)$ holds by (taut). Assume now that $\tau(\mathcal{F}) = \{A_1, \dots, A_k\}$ for some $k \geq 1$. Clearly there must be some j (where $1 \leq j \leq k$) such that $A_j \notin \tau(\{A_1, \dots, A_{j-1}, A_{j+1}, \dots, A_k\})$, i.e., A_j is a "most complex" formula in $\tau(\mathcal{F})$; let $\mathcal{F}' = \tau(\mathcal{F}) \setminus \{A_j\}$. In particular, it follows that $\tau(\mathcal{F}') = \mathcal{F}'$. Let $\mathcal{Q}_1', \dots, \mathcal{Q}_l'$ be all PNP constructed for $\mathcal{F}'$ as described. Then $m = 2l$ and the PNP $\mathcal{Q}_1, \dots, \mathcal{Q}_m$ are obtained from $\mathcal{Q}_1', \dots, \mathcal{Q}_l'$ as follows:

$$\mathcal{Q}_1 = (pos(\mathcal{Q}'_1) \cup \{A_j\}, neg(\mathcal{Q}'_1)),$$
$$\vdots$$
$$\mathcal{Q}_l = (pos(\mathcal{Q}'_l) \cup \{A_j\}, neg(\mathcal{Q}'_l)),$$
$$\mathcal{Q}_{l+1} = (pos(\mathcal{Q}'_1), neg(\mathcal{Q}'_1) \cup \{A_j\}),$$
$$\vdots$$
$$\mathcal{Q}_m = (pos(\mathcal{Q}'_l), neg(\mathcal{Q}'_l) \cup \{A_j\}).$$

By the induction hypothesis we have $\vdash \bigvee_{i=1}^{l} \widehat{\mathcal{Q}'_i}$ which yields

$$\vdash \bigvee_{i=1}^{l} (\widehat{\mathcal{Q}'_i} \wedge A_j) \vee \bigvee_{i=1}^{l} (\widehat{\mathcal{Q}'_i} \wedge \neg A_j),$$

i.e., $(*)$ by (prop).

Let now $\mathcal{P}$ be a consistent PNP, and let $\mathcal{P}'_1, \dots, \mathcal{P}'_m$ be all different PNP $\mathcal{P}'$ with $\mathcal{F}_{\mathcal{P}'} = \tau(\mathcal{F}_\mathcal{P})$ and such that $pos(\mathcal{P}')$ and $neg(\mathcal{P}')$ are disjoint. The completions $\mathcal{P}^*_1, \dots, \mathcal{P}^*_n$ are just those $\mathcal{P}'_i$ which are consistent and for which $pos(\mathcal{P}) \subseteq pos(\mathcal{P}'_i)$ and $neg(\mathcal{P}) \subseteq neg(\mathcal{P}'_i)$. Without loss of generality, we may suppose that these are $\mathcal{P}'_1, \dots, \mathcal{P}'_n$, which means that for $i > n$,

(i) $\mathcal{P}'_i$ is inconsistent

or

(ii) $pos(\mathcal{P}) \not\subseteq pos(\mathcal{P}'_i)$ or $neg(\mathcal{P}) \not\subseteq neg(\mathcal{P}'_i)$.

We obtain $\vdash \neg\widehat{\mathcal{P}_i}$ in case (i) and $pos(\mathcal{P}) \cap neg(\mathcal{P}'_i) \neq \emptyset$ or $neg(\mathcal{P}) \cap pos(\mathcal{P}'_i) \neq \emptyset$ and therefore $\vdash \neg(\widehat{\mathcal{P}} \wedge \widehat{\mathcal{P}'_i})$ by (taut) in case (ii). In either case, we may conclude $\vdash \widehat{\mathcal{P}} \to \neg\widehat{\mathcal{P}'_i}$ with (prop), and this holds for every $i > n$. With $(*)$ we obtain $\vdash \bigvee_{i=1}^{m} \widehat{\mathcal{P}'_i}$ and with (prop) we then get $\vdash \widehat{\mathcal{P}} \to \bigvee_{i=1}^{n} \widehat{\mathcal{P}'_i}$ which is just the desired assertion. △

The informal meaning of a completion $\mathcal{P}^*$ of a consistent PNP $\mathcal{P}$ is that those subformulas of formulas appearing in $\mathcal{F}_\mathcal{P}$ that should be true or false in some state are collected in $pos(\mathcal{P}^*)$ and $neg(\mathcal{P}^*)$, respectively, ensuring that all formulas of $pos(\mathcal{P})$ are true and all formulas of $neg(\mathcal{P})$ false in that state. Let us illustrate this idea with a little example. Suppose $A \equiv (v_1 \to v_2) \to \Box v_3$, $B \equiv v_3 \to \bigcirc v_2$ (with $v_1, v_2, v_3 \in \mathbf{V}$), and $\mathcal{P} = (\{A\}, \{B\})$. One possible completion of $\mathcal{P}$ is

$$\mathcal{P}^* = (\{A, v_1 \to v_2, \Box v_3, v_2, v_3\}, \{B, v_1, \bigcirc v_2\}).$$

If all the (proper) parts of A and B in $pos(\mathcal{P}^*)$ evaluate to tt and those in $neg(\mathcal{P}^*)$ to ff then A becomes tt and B becomes ff and, moreover, such a valuation is in fact possible because of the consistency of $\mathcal{P}^*$. However, some of this information focussed on one state may also have implications for other states. In our example, $\Box v_3$ becomes true in a state only if v_3 is true in that state which is already noted by

v_3 belonging to $pos(\mathcal{P}^*)$ and v_3 is also true in every future state or, equivalently, $\Box v_3$ is true in the next state. To make $\bigcirc v_2$ false requires v_2 to be false in the next state. The "transfer" of such information from one state to the next is the purpose of our next construction.

For a PNP $\mathcal{P} = (\mathcal{F}^+, \mathcal{F}^-)$ we define the following four sets of formulas

$$\begin{aligned}
\sigma_1(\mathcal{P}) &= \{A \mid \bigcirc A \in \mathcal{F}^+\},\\
\sigma_2(\mathcal{P}) &= \{\Box A \mid \Box A \in \mathcal{F}^+\},\\
\sigma_3(\mathcal{P}) &= \{A \mid \bigcirc A \in \mathcal{F}^-\},\\
\sigma_4(\mathcal{P}) &= \{\Box A \mid \Box A \in \mathcal{F}^- \text{ and } A \in \mathcal{F}^+\}
\end{aligned}$$

and the PNP

$$\sigma(\mathcal{P}) = \big(\sigma_1(\mathcal{P}) \cup \sigma_2(\mathcal{P}), \sigma_3(\mathcal{P}) \cup \sigma_4(\mathcal{P})\big).$$

For the example above we have

$$\sigma(\mathcal{P}^*) = (\{\Box v_3\}, \{v_2\})$$

comprehending the information about what has to become true or false in the next state to "fulfill" $\mathcal{P}^*$ in the way described above.

Lemma 2.4.5. *Let $\mathcal{P}$ be a PNP.*

a) $\vdash \widehat{\mathcal{P}} \to \bigcirc \widehat{\sigma(\mathcal{P})}$.
b) If $\mathcal{P}$ is consistent then $\sigma(\mathcal{P})$ is consistent.

Proof. a) We show that $\vdash \widehat{\mathcal{P}} \to \bigcirc C$ if $C \in \sigma_1(\mathcal{P}) \cup \sigma_2(\mathcal{P})$ and that $\vdash \widehat{\mathcal{P}} \to \bigcirc \neg C$ if $C \in \sigma_3(\mathcal{P}) \cup \sigma_4(\mathcal{P})$. The assertion a) then follows immediately with (prop) and (T15'), which was formally derived in the previous section. We distinguish the four cases of $C \in \sigma_i$, $i = 1, \ldots, 4$:

1. If $C \in \sigma_1(\mathcal{P})$ then $\bigcirc C \in pos(\mathcal{P})$ and therefore $\vdash \widehat{\mathcal{P}} \to \bigcirc C$ by (prop).
2. If $C \equiv \Box A \in \sigma_2(\mathcal{P})$ then $\Box A \in pos(\mathcal{P})$ and therefore $\vdash \widehat{\mathcal{P}} \to \Box A$ by (prop), from which we get $\vdash \widehat{\mathcal{P}} \to \bigcirc\Box A$ with (ltl3) and (prop).
3. If $C \in \sigma_3(\mathcal{P})$ then $\bigcirc C \in neg(\mathcal{P})$ and therefore $\vdash \widehat{\mathcal{P}} \to \neg\bigcirc C$ by (prop) from which we get $\vdash \widehat{\mathcal{P}} \to \bigcirc\neg C$ with (ltl1) and (prop).
4. If $C \equiv \Box A \in \sigma_4(\mathcal{P})$ then $\Box A \in neg(\mathcal{P})$ and $A \in pos(\mathcal{P})$ and therefore $\vdash \widehat{\mathcal{P}} \to A \land \neg\Box A$ by (prop) from which we get $\vdash \widehat{\mathcal{P}} \to \neg\bigcirc\Box A$ with (ltl3') and (prop) and finally $\vdash \widehat{\mathcal{P}} \to \bigcirc\neg\Box A$ with (ltl1) and (prop).

b) Assume that $\sigma(\mathcal{P})$ is inconsistent, i.e., $\vdash \neg\widehat{\sigma(\mathcal{P})}$. Using (nex) it follows that $\vdash \bigcirc\neg\widehat{\sigma(\mathcal{P})}$; hence also $\vdash \neg\bigcirc\widehat{\sigma(\mathcal{P})}$ with (ltl1) and (prop). Together with a) we infer $\vdash \neg\widehat{\mathcal{P}}$ by (prop), implying that $\mathcal{P}$ would be inconsistent. △

According to our explanation of the proof idea above, in order to satisfy the formulas of $pos(\mathcal{P})$ and falsify those of $neg(\mathcal{P})$ of a given consistent PNP $\mathcal{P}$, respectively, in a state, the infinite sequence

$$\mathcal{P}^*, \sigma(\mathcal{P}^*)^*, \sigma(\sigma(\mathcal{P}^*)^*)^*, \ldots$$

should now carry the complete information about how the parts of those formulas should evaluate in that state and all subsequent ones. There is, however, one remaining problem: for some element $\mathcal{P}_i$ of this sequence there could be $\Box A \in neg(\mathcal{P}_i)$ which means that A should become false in the corresponding state or in a subsequent state. But, either forced by the consistency constraint or just by having chosen a "bad" completion, $A \in pos(\mathcal{P}_j)$ could hold for all elements $\mathcal{P}_j$, $j \geq i$, of the sequence. In order to overcome this last difficulty we consider all possible completions in every step "from one state to the next".

Formally, let $\mathcal{P}$ be a consistent and complete PNP. We define an infinite tree $\mathcal{K}_\mathcal{P}$:

- The root of $\mathcal{K}_\mathcal{P}$ is $\mathcal{P}$.
- If $\mathcal{Q}$ is a node of $\mathcal{K}_\mathcal{P}$ then the successor nodes of $\mathcal{Q}$ are all different completions of $\sigma(\mathcal{Q})$.

According to our remarks and results above, every node of $\mathcal{K}_\mathcal{P}$ is a consistent and complete PNP. If $\mathcal{Q}$ is a node then the subtree of $\mathcal{K}_\mathcal{P}$ with root $\mathcal{Q}$ is just $\mathcal{K}_\mathcal{Q}$.

Lemma 2.4.6. *Let $\mathcal{P}$ be a consistent and complete PNP.*

a) $\mathcal{K}_\mathcal{P}$ has only finitely many different nodes $\mathcal{Q}_1, \ldots, \mathcal{Q}_n$.
b) $\vdash \bigvee_{i=1}^{n} \widehat{\mathcal{Q}_i} \to \bigcirc \bigvee_{i=1}^{n} \widehat{\mathcal{Q}_i}$.

Proof. a) From the definitions of the σ and τ operations it follows immediately that all formulas that occur in some node of $\mathcal{K}_\mathcal{P}$ are subformulas of the formulas contained in $\mathcal{F}_\mathcal{P}$, of which there are only finitely many. This implies that there can be only finitely many different nodes in $\mathcal{K}_\mathcal{P}$.

b) Lemma 2.4.5 a) shows that we have $\vdash \widehat{\mathcal{Q}_i} \to \bigcirc\widehat{\sigma(\mathcal{Q}_i)}$ for every $i = 1, \ldots, n$. Let $\mathcal{Q}'_{i_1}, \ldots, \mathcal{Q}'_{i_m}$ be all different completions of $\sigma(\mathcal{Q}_i)$; then Lemma 2.4.4 proves $\vdash \widehat{\sigma(\mathcal{Q}_i)} \to \bigvee_{j=1}^{m} \widehat{\mathcal{Q}'_{i_j}}$. The definition of $\mathcal{K}_\mathcal{P}$ implies $\mathcal{Q}'_{i_j} \in \{\mathcal{Q}_1, \ldots, \mathcal{Q}_n\}$; hence $\vdash \widehat{\mathcal{Q}'_{i_j}} \to \bigvee_{k=1}^{n} \widehat{\mathcal{Q}_k}$, for every $j = 1, \ldots, m$. So we get $\vdash \widehat{\sigma(\mathcal{Q}_i)} \to \bigvee_{k=1}^{n} \widehat{\mathcal{Q}_k}$ with (prop); furthermore $\vdash \bigcirc\widehat{\sigma(\mathcal{Q}_i)} \to \bigcirc\bigvee_{k=1}^{n} \widehat{\mathcal{Q}_k}$ with (nex) and (ltl2) and hence $\vdash \widehat{\mathcal{Q}_i} \to \bigcirc\bigvee_{k=1}^{n} \widehat{\mathcal{Q}_k}$ for $i = 1, \ldots, n$. From this, assertion b) follows with (prop). △

A finite path (from $\mathcal{P}_1$ to $\mathcal{P}_k$) in $\mathcal{K}_\mathcal{P}$ is a sequence $\mathcal{P}_1, \ldots, \mathcal{P}_k$ of nodes such that $\mathcal{P}_{i+1}$ is a successor node of $\mathcal{P}_i$ for every $i = 1, \ldots, k-1$. An infinite path is defined analogously.

Lemma 2.4.7. *Let $\mathcal{P}$ be a consistent and complete PNP, $\mathcal{P}_0, \mathcal{P}_1, \mathcal{P}_2, \ldots$ an infinite path in $\mathcal{K}_\mathcal{P}$, $i \in \mathbb{N}$, and A a formula.*

a) If $\bigcirc A \in \mathcal{F}_{\mathcal{P}_i}$ then: $\bigcirc A \in pos(\mathcal{P}_i) \Leftrightarrow A \in pos(\mathcal{P}_{i+1})$.
b) $\Box A \in pos(\mathcal{P}_i) \Rightarrow A \in pos(\mathcal{P}_j)$ for every $j \geq i$.

Proof. a) Assume that $\bigcirc A \in \mathcal{F}_{\mathcal{P}_i}$. If $\bigcirc A \in pos(\mathcal{P}_i)$ then $A \in pos(\sigma(\mathcal{P}_i))$; hence $A \in pos(\mathcal{P}_{i+1})$. If $\bigcirc A \notin pos(\mathcal{P}_i)$ then $\bigcirc A \in neg(\mathcal{P}_i)$; hence $A \in neg(\sigma(\mathcal{P}_i))$, and therefore $A \in neg(\mathcal{P}_{i+1})$ and $A \notin pos(\mathcal{P}_{i+1})$ with Lemma 2.4.1 a).

b) Assume that $\Box A \in pos(\mathcal{P}_i)$. Then $A \in \mathcal{F}_{\mathcal{P}_i}$ because of $A \in \tau(\Box A)$ and the completeness of $\mathcal{P}_i$. We get $A \in pos(\mathcal{P}_i)$ with Lemma 2.4.2 c) and $\vdash \Box A \rightarrow A$, which follows from (ltl3). Moreover, $\Box A \in pos(\sigma(\mathcal{P}_i))$; hence $\Box A \in pos(\mathcal{P}_{i+1})$. By induction we may conclude that $A \in pos(\mathcal{P}_j)$ for every $j \geq i$. △

An infinite path in $\mathcal{K}_{\mathcal{P}}$ is just a sequence of PNPs as in our informal explanation above. However, as explained there, we have to find such a path where every ("negative") occurrence of some formula $\Box A$ in some $neg(\mathcal{P}_i)$ is eventually followed by a negative occurrence of A. Formally, let us call an infinite path $\mathcal{P}_0, \mathcal{P}_1, \mathcal{P}_2, \ldots$ in $\mathcal{K}_{\mathcal{P}}$ *complete* if $\mathcal{P}_0 = \mathcal{P}$ and the following condition holds for every $i \in \mathbb{N}$:

If $\Box A \in neg(\mathcal{P}_i)$ then $A \in neg(\mathcal{P}_j)$ for some $j \geq i$.

Lemma 2.4.7 and this definition will be seen to ensure the existence of a temporal structure satisfying $\widehat{\mathcal{P}}$. It remains to guarantee that a complete path really exists whenever $\mathcal{P}$ is consistent and complete.

Lemma 2.4.8. *Let $\mathcal{P}$ be a consistent and complete PNP. There is a complete path in $\mathcal{K}_{\mathcal{P}}$.*

Proof. We first show:

(∗) If $\mathcal{Q}$ is some node of $\mathcal{K}_{\mathcal{P}}$ and A is some formula such that $\Box A \in neg(\mathcal{Q})$ then there is a node $\mathcal{Q}'$ of $\mathcal{K}_{\mathcal{Q}}$ such that $A \in neg(\mathcal{Q}')$.

Assume that $A \notin neg(\mathcal{Q}')$ for every node $\mathcal{Q}'$ of $\mathcal{K}_{\mathcal{Q}}$. Because of $A \in \tau(\Box A)$ we then have $A \in pos(\mathcal{Q})$ and therefore $\Box A \in neg(\mathcal{Q}')$ for all successor nodes $\mathcal{Q}'$ of $\mathcal{Q}$ according to the construction σ. Continuing inductively, we find that $\Box A \in neg(\mathcal{Q}')$, $A \in pos(\mathcal{Q}')$, and hence $\vdash \widehat{\mathcal{Q}'} \rightarrow A$ for every node $\mathcal{Q}'$ of $\mathcal{K}_{\mathcal{Q}}$. Let $\mathcal{Q}'_1, \ldots, \mathcal{Q}'_n$ be all nodes of $\mathcal{K}_{\mathcal{Q}}$. Then $\vdash \bigvee_{i=1}^{n} \widehat{\mathcal{Q}'_i} \rightarrow A$. Furthermore, by Lemma 2.4.6 b) we have $\vdash \bigvee_{i=1}^{n} \widehat{\mathcal{Q}'_i} \rightarrow \bigcirc \bigvee_{i=1}^{n} \widehat{\mathcal{Q}'_i}$; so with (ind) we obtain $\vdash \bigvee_{i=1}^{n} \widehat{\mathcal{Q}'_i} \rightarrow \Box A$. Because of $\mathcal{Q} \in \{\mathcal{Q}'_1, \ldots, \mathcal{Q}'_n\}$ we also have $\vdash \widehat{\mathcal{Q}} \rightarrow \bigvee_{i=1}^{n} \widehat{\mathcal{Q}'_i}$ and so we get $\vdash \widehat{\mathcal{Q}} \rightarrow \Box A$ by (prop). Because of $\Box A \in neg(\mathcal{Q})$, i.e., $\vdash \widehat{\mathcal{Q}} \rightarrow \neg\Box A$, this implies $\vdash \neg\widehat{\mathcal{Q}}$ by (prop) which means that $\mathcal{Q}$ is inconsistent. This is a contradiction; thus (∗) is proved.

From Lemma 2.4.6 a) we know that $\mathcal{K}_{\mathcal{P}}$ contains only finitely many different nodes. Since $neg(\mathcal{Q})$ is a finite set of formulas for every node $\mathcal{Q}$, there can only be finitely many formulas A such that $\Box A \in neg(\mathcal{Q})$ for some node $\mathcal{Q}$ of $\mathcal{K}_{\mathcal{P}}$. Choose some fixed enumeration $A_0, \ldots, A_{m-1}$ of all such formulas. In order to construct a complete path in $\mathcal{K}_{\mathcal{P}}$ we now define a succession $\pi_0, \pi_1, \ldots$ of finite and non-empty paths in $\mathcal{K}_{\mathcal{P}}$ such that π_i is a proper prefix of π_{i+1}:

- Let $\pi_0 = \mathcal{P}$ consist only of the root $\mathcal{P}$ of $\mathcal{K}_{\mathcal{P}}$.

- Inductively, assume that $\pi_i = \mathcal{Q}_0, \mathcal{Q}_1, \ldots, \mathcal{Q}_k$ has already been defined. We distinguish two cases: if $\Box A_{i \bmod m} \notin neg(\mathcal{Q}_k)$ or $A_{i \bmod m} \in neg(\mathcal{Q}_k)$ then π_{i+1} is obtained from π_i by appending some successor node $\mathcal{Q}'$ of $\mathcal{Q}_k$ in $\mathcal{K}_{\mathcal{P}}$. (Lemmas 2.4.5 and 2.4.3 imply that $\mathcal{Q}_k$ has at least one successor node.)
  If $\Box A_{i \bmod m} \in neg(\mathcal{Q}_k)$ and $A_{i \bmod m} \notin neg(\mathcal{Q}_k)$ then, by (∗), $\mathcal{K}_{\mathcal{Q}_k}$ contains some node $\mathcal{Q}'$ such that $A_{i \bmod m} \in neg(\mathcal{Q}')$. Choose such a $\mathcal{Q}'$ (which must obviously be different from $\mathcal{Q}_k$), and let π_{i+1} be obtained by appending the path from $\mathcal{Q}_k$ to $\mathcal{Q}'$ to the path π_i.

The succession $\pi_0, \pi_1, \ldots$ uniquely determines an infinite path $\pi = \mathcal{Q}_0, \mathcal{Q}_1, \ldots$ with $\mathcal{Q}_0 = \mathcal{P}$ in $\mathcal{K}_{\mathcal{P}}$. To see that π is complete, assume that $\Box A \in neg(\mathcal{Q}_i)$ for some i but that $A \notin neg(\mathcal{Q}_{i'})$ for all $i' \geq i$. As in the proof of (∗), it follows that $\Box A \in neg(\mathcal{Q}_{i'})$ for every $i' \geq i$. The formula A occurs in the enumeration of all formulas of this kind fixed above, say, as A_l. Now choose $j \in \mathbb{N}$ such that $\pi_{j \cdot m+l} = \mathcal{Q}_0, \ldots, \mathcal{Q}_k$ where $k \geq i$; in particular it follows that $\Box A_l \in neg(\mathcal{Q}_k)$. But the construction of π_{i+1} ensures that π_{i+1}, which is a finite prefix of π, ends with some node $\mathcal{Q}'$ such that $A \equiv A_l \in neg(\mathcal{Q}')$, and a contradiction is reached. We have thus found a complete path $\pi = \mathcal{Q}_0, \mathcal{Q}_1, \ldots$ in $\mathcal{K}_{\mathcal{P}}$. △

Now we have in fact all means for proving a theorem which is a rather trivial transcription of the desired completeness result.

Theorem 2.4.9 (Satisfiability Theorem for Σ_{LTL}). *For every consistent PNP $\mathcal{P}$, the formula $\widehat{\mathcal{P}}$ is satisfiable.*

Proof. Let $\mathcal{P}$ be a consistent PNP, $\mathcal{P}^*$ be a completion of $\mathcal{P}$, and $\mathcal{P}_0, \mathcal{P}_1, \mathcal{P}_2, \ldots$ a complete path in $\mathcal{K}_{\mathcal{P}^*}$ according to Lemma 2.4.8. We define a temporal structure $\mathsf{K} = (\eta_0, \eta_1, \eta_2, \ldots)$ by:

$$\eta_i(v) = \mathsf{tt} \Leftrightarrow v \in pos(\mathcal{P}_i) \quad \text{for every } v \in \mathbf{V}, i \in \mathbb{N}.$$

We will prove below that for every formula F and every $i \in \mathbb{N}$:

(∗) If $F \in \mathcal{F}_{\mathcal{P}_i}$ then: $\mathsf{K}_i(F) = \mathsf{tt} \Leftrightarrow F \in pos(\mathcal{P}_i)$.

Before we prove this, let us show that (∗) implies the satisfiability of $\widehat{\mathcal{P}}$: because of $pos(\mathcal{P}) \subseteq pos(\mathcal{P}_0)$, $neg(\mathcal{P}) \subseteq neg(\mathcal{P}_0)$, and $pos(\mathcal{P}_0) \cap neg(\mathcal{P}_0) = \emptyset$ we get

$$\mathsf{K}_0(\widehat{\mathcal{P}}) = \mathsf{K}_0\Bigg(\bigwedge_{A \in pos(\mathcal{P})} A \wedge \bigwedge_{B \in neg(\mathcal{P})} \neg B\Bigg) = \mathsf{tt}$$

from (∗). In particular, $\widehat{\mathcal{P}}$ is satisfiable.

The proof of (∗) runs by structural induction on the formula F.

1. $F \equiv v \in \mathbf{V}$: $\mathsf{K}_i(v) = \eta_i(v) = \mathsf{tt} \Leftrightarrow v \in pos(\mathcal{P}_i)$ by definition.
2. $F \equiv$ **false**: We have $\mathsf{K}_i(\mathbf{false}) = \mathsf{ff}$ and **false** $\notin pos(\mathcal{P}_i)$ by Lemma 2.4.2 a) and this implies (∗).

3. $F \equiv A \to B$: If $A \to B \in \mathcal{F}_{\mathcal{P}_i}$ then also $A \in \mathcal{F}_{\mathcal{P}_i}$ and $B \in \mathcal{F}_{\mathcal{P}_i}$ because $\mathcal{P}_i$ is a complete PNP, and therefore:

$$\begin{aligned} \mathsf{K}_i(A \to B) = \mathsf{tt} &\Leftrightarrow \mathsf{K}_i(A) = \mathsf{ff} \text{ or } \mathsf{K}_i(B) = \mathsf{tt} \\ &\Leftrightarrow A \notin pos(\mathcal{P}_i) \text{ or } B \in pos(\mathcal{P}_i) \quad \text{(ind.hyp.)} \\ &\Leftrightarrow A \in neg(\mathcal{P}_i) \text{ or } B \in pos(\mathcal{P}_i) \quad (\text{since } A \in \mathcal{F}_{\mathcal{P}_i}) \\ &\Leftrightarrow A \to B \in pos(\mathcal{P}_i) \quad \text{(by Lemma 2.4.2 b).} \end{aligned}$$

4. $F \equiv \bigcirc A$: From $\bigcirc A \in \mathcal{F}_{\mathcal{P}_i}$ we obtain $A \in \mathcal{F}_{\mathcal{P}_{i+1}}$ and therefore:

$$\begin{aligned} \mathsf{K}_i(\bigcirc A) = \mathsf{tt} &\Leftrightarrow \mathsf{K}_{i+1}(A) = \mathsf{tt} \\ &\Leftrightarrow A \in pos(\mathcal{P}_{i+1}) \quad \text{(ind.hyp.)} \\ &\Leftrightarrow \bigcirc A \in pos(\mathcal{P}_i) \quad \text{(by Lemma 2.4.7 a).} \end{aligned}$$

5. $F \equiv \Box A$: If $\Box A \in pos(\mathcal{P}_i)$ it follows that $A \in pos(\mathcal{P}_j)$ for every $j \geq i$ by Lemma 2.4.7 b) and we get $A \in \mathcal{F}_{\mathcal{P}_j}$ and therefore $\mathsf{K}_j(A) = \mathsf{tt}$ for every $j \geq i$ by the induction hypothesis; hence $\mathsf{K}_i(\Box A) = \mathsf{tt}$.
Assume, on the other hand, that $\Box A \in \mathcal{F}_{\mathcal{P}_i}$ and $\Box A \notin pos(\mathcal{P}_i)$. Therefore $\Box A \in neg(\mathcal{P}_i)$, and the definition of a complete path and Lemma 2.4.1 a) ensure $A \in neg(\mathcal{P}_j)$ and thus $A \notin pos(\mathcal{P}_j)$ and $A \in \mathcal{F}_{\mathcal{P}_j}$ for some $j \geq i$. By the induction hypothesis we get $\mathsf{K}_j(A) = \mathsf{ff}$ for this j, which implies $\mathsf{K}_i(\Box A) \neq \mathsf{tt}$. △

Before we finally deduce our main result from this theorem we still mention that a close look at its proof provides another interesting corollary called *finite model property* (of LTL):

- Every satisfiable formula is satisfiable by a temporal structure which has only finitely many different states.

To see this fact, assume that a formula A is satisfiable. From the definition it follows immediately that $\neg\neg A$ is satisfiable; hence $\neg A$ is not valid by Theorem 2.1.9 and not derivable in Σ_{LTL} by Theorem 2.3.1. So, by definition, the PNP $(\{A\}, \emptyset)$ is consistent and therefore A is satisfiable by a temporal structure K according to (the proof of) Theorem 2.4.9. By construction and Lemma 2.4.6 a), K has only finitely many different states.

Theorem 2.4.10 (Weak Completeness Theorem for Σ_{LTL}). *Σ_{LTL} is weakly complete, i.e., for every finite set $\mathcal{F}$ of formulas and formula A, if $\mathcal{F} \vDash A$ then $\mathcal{F} \vdash A$. In particular: if $\vDash A$ then $\vdash A$.*

Proof. We prove the claim first for $\mathcal{F} = \emptyset$: if $\vDash A$ then $\neg A$ is not satisfiable by Theorem 2.1.9 and hence the PNP $(\emptyset, \{A\})$ is inconsistent by Theorem 2.4.9. This means $\vdash \neg\neg A$ by definition and implies $\vdash A$ using (prop).

Let now $\mathcal{F} = \{A_1, \ldots, A_n\} \neq \emptyset$. We then have

$$\mathcal{F} \models A \Rightarrow A_1 \ldots A_{n-1} \models \Box A_n \to A \qquad \text{(Theorem 2.1.6)}$$

$$\vdots$$

$$\Rightarrow \models \Box A_1 \to (\Box A_2 \to \ldots \to (\Box A_n \to A) \ldots) \qquad \text{(Theorem 2.1.6)}$$
$$\Rightarrow \vdash \Box A_1 \to (\Box A_2 \to \ldots \to (\Box A_n \to A) \ldots) \qquad \text{(proved above)}$$
$$\Rightarrow A_1 \vdash \Box A_2 \to (\Box A_3 \to \ldots \to (\Box A_n \to A) \ldots) \qquad \text{(Theorem 2.3.4)}$$

$$\vdots$$

$$\Rightarrow \mathcal{F} \vdash A \qquad \text{(Theorem 2.3.4).}$$

△

Let us summarize. We now know from the Soundness and the Weak Completeness Theorems that

$$\mathcal{F} \models A \;\Leftrightarrow\; \mathcal{F} \vdash A \quad \text{for finite } \mathcal{F},$$

in particular that

$$\models A \;\Leftrightarrow\; \vdash A.$$

This also means that we can view all logical laws (T1)–(T38) considered in Sect. 2.2 as derivable. For example, the law (T31) can be considered as the derived rule

$$A \to B \vdash \Diamond A \to \Diamond B.$$

We will take advantage of this and freely use the laws in subsequent derivations.

Example. $\Box A \to \Diamond B, B \to \bigcirc C \vdash \Box A \to \bigcirc\Box\Diamond C$ can be derived using (T12), (T13), (T31), and (T35) as follows:

(1)	$\Box A \to \Diamond B$	assumption
(2)	$B \to \bigcirc C$	assumption
(3)	$\Diamond B \to \Diamond\bigcirc C$	(T31),(2)
(4)	$\Diamond B \to \bigcirc\Diamond C$	(T13),(prop),(3)
(5)	$\Box A \to \bigcirc\Diamond C$	(prop),(1),(4)
(6)	$\Box A \to \Box\bigcirc\Diamond C$	(T35),(5)
(7)	$\Box A \to \bigcirc\Box\Diamond C$	(T12),(prop),(6) △

As another example, we derive the rule

(chain) $\quad A \to \Diamond B, B \to \Diamond C \vdash A \to \Diamond C$

which will be needed later.

Derivation of (chain).

(1)	$A \to \Diamond B$	assumption
(2)	$B \to \Diamond C$	assumption
(3)	$\Diamond B \to \Diamond C$	(T36),(2)
(4)	$A \to \Diamond C$	(prop),(1),(3) △

At the beginning of this section we argued that the non-derivability of

$$\mathcal{F} \vdash A \rightarrow \Box B$$

for $\mathcal{F} = \{A \rightarrow \bigcirc^i B \mid i \in \mathbb{N}\}$ ($\bigcirc^i$ denotes the sequence $\bigcirc \ldots \bigcirc$ of i subsequently applied $\bigcirc$-operators) shows that there is no sound formal system which is complete in the full sense. Another view of this situation together with the proven weak completeness is given by the fact that full completeness could be achieved by weakening the concept of formal systems: a *semi-formal system* is like a formal system but may contain *ω-rules*, i.e., rules of the form

$$A_1, A_2, A_3, \ldots \vdash B$$

with an infinite sequence $A_1, A_2, A_3, \ldots$ of premises.

We conclude this section with the remark that the semi-formal system which results from Σ_{LTL} by replacing the induction rule (ind) by the ω-rule

$$(\omega\text{-ind}) \quad A \rightarrow \bigcirc^i B,\ i \in \mathbb{N} \ \vdash A \rightarrow \Box B$$

is indeed (sound and) complete in the full sense that

$$\mathcal{F} \vDash A \ \Rightarrow \ \mathcal{F} \vdash A$$

then holds for arbitrary $\mathcal{F}$ and A.

Of course, a derivation in a semi-formal system is no longer a purely "mechanical" process. In order to apply an ω-rule the derivation of their infinitely many premises needs some argument "outside" the system, typically an inductive one. For example, a derivation of (ind) with (ω-ind) is given as follows:

(1)	$A \rightarrow B$	assumption
(2)	$A \rightarrow \bigcirc A$	assumption
(3)	$A \rightarrow \bigcirc^i B$ for all $i \in \mathbb{N}$	from (1) and (2) by induction on i
(4)	$A \rightarrow \Box B$	(ω-ind),(3)

Line (3) is achieved by the fact that for $i = 0$ it is just the assumption (1) and with

(3a)	$A \rightarrow \bigcirc^i B$	induction hypothesis
(3b)	$\bigcirc(A \rightarrow \bigcirc^i B)$	(nex),(3a)
(3c)	$\bigcirc A \rightarrow \bigcirc^{i+1} B$	(mp),(ltl2),(3b)
(3d)	$A \rightarrow \bigcirc^{i+1} B$	(prop),(2),(3c)

we obtain the necessary induction step.

2.5 Decidability

The Weak Completeness Theorem 2.4.10 implies that every valid LTL formula can be derived in Σ_{LTL}. Coupled with a method to enumerate all instances of classical tautologies, Σ_{LTL} therefore systematically generates all valid LTL formulas.

We will now show that the validity of LTL formulas is even decidable. In fact, we will present a method to decide the *satisfiability problem*, i.e., whether a formula is satisfiable or not. Applying Theorem 2.1.9, validity of formula F (the *validity problem*) can then be decided by determining whether $\neg F$ is unsatisfiable.

The decision procedure for satisfiability is based on the same ideas as the proof of the Weak Completeness Theorem 2.4.10; recall that its essence was to construct a satisfying temporal structure for any finite and consistent set of formulas. In fact, the definitions of the τ and σ operations were carefully chosen to ensure that the tree of PNPs contained only finitely many different nodes. The information contained in the infinite tree can therefore be more succinctly represented in a finite graph if identical nodes are identified. The resulting graph encodes all temporal structures that satisfy the initially given consistent set of formulas. On the other hand, if the given set of formulas is inconsistent, we will see that the construction fails for one of two possible reasons: first, **false** $\in pos(\mathcal{P})$ or $pos(\mathcal{P}) \cap neg(\mathcal{P}) \neq \emptyset$ may hold for all leaf nodes $\mathcal{P}$, implying that they are immediately contradictory. Second, the resulting graph may contain no "appropriate" path because for some node $\mathcal{P}$ and some formula $\Box A \in neg(\mathcal{P})$ there is no node $\mathcal{Q}$ reachable from $\mathcal{P}$ such that $A \in neg(\mathcal{Q})$; cf. the proof of Lemma 2.4.8.

Let us make these ideas more formal. Given a PNP $\mathcal{P}$, we define a *tableau* for $\mathcal{P}$ to be any rooted directed graph $\mathcal{T}$ of pairwise distinct PNPs whose root is $\mathcal{P}$ and such that for every node $\mathcal{Q} = (\mathcal{F}^+, \mathcal{F}^-)$ of $\mathcal{T}$, one of the following conditions hold:

($\bot$) **false** $\in \mathcal{F}^+$ or $\mathcal{F}^+ \cap \mathcal{F}^- \neq \emptyset$, and $\mathcal{Q}$ has no successor node.

($\rightarrow^+$) $A \rightarrow B \in \mathcal{F}^+$ for some formulas A, B, and $\mathcal{Q}$ has precisely two successor nodes: the left-hand successor $(\mathcal{F}^+ \setminus \{A \rightarrow B\}, \mathcal{F}^- \cup \{A\})$ and the right-hand successor $((\mathcal{F}^+ \setminus \{A \rightarrow B\}) \cup \{B\}, \mathcal{F}^-)$.

($\rightarrow^-$) $A \rightarrow B \in \mathcal{F}^-$ for some formulas A, B, and $\mathcal{Q}$ has precisely the successor node $(\mathcal{F}^+ \cup \{A\}, (\mathcal{F}^- \setminus \{A \rightarrow B\}) \cup \{B\})$.

($\Box^+$) $\Box A \in \mathcal{F}^+$ for some formula A, and $\mathcal{Q}$ has precisely the successor node $((\mathcal{F}^+ \setminus \{\Box A\}) \cup \{A, \bigcirc\Box A\}, \mathcal{F}^-)$.

($\Box^-$) $\Box A \in \mathcal{F}^-$ for some formula A, and $\mathcal{Q}$ has precisely two successor nodes: the left-hand successor $(\mathcal{F}^+, (\mathcal{F}^- \setminus \{\Box A\}) \cup \{A\})$ and the right-hand successor $(\mathcal{F}^+, (\mathcal{F}^- \setminus \{\Box A\}) \cup \{\bigcirc\Box A\})$.

($\bigcirc$) All formulas in $\mathcal{F}_\mathcal{Q}$ are of the form **false**, v (where $v \in \mathbf{V}$), or $\bigcirc A$ for some formula A, node $\mathcal{Q}$ does not satisfy ($\bot$), and $\mathcal{Q}$ has precisely the successor node $(\sigma_1(\mathcal{Q}), \sigma_3(\mathcal{Q}))$.

(σ_1 and σ_3 are the functions defined in Sect. 2.4.) The "rules" ($\rightarrow^+$) through ($\bigcirc$) propagate information to the successor nodes. In fact, they construct completions in the sense of Sect. 2.4 in a systematic way. The nodes of the tableau that satisfy condition ($\bigcirc$) are called *tableau states*. Paths in $\mathcal{T}$ are defined like paths in the tree $\mathcal{K}_\mathcal{P}$ in Sect. 2.4.

As in that tree construction (cf. Lemma 2.4.6) it follows that the construction of a tableau $\mathcal{T}$ according to the above rules can give rise to only finitely many different nodes, so any tableau for a given PNP is finite. Moreover, the rules ($\rightarrow^+$) through ($\Box^-$) decompose complex operators and can therefore hold only finitely often until

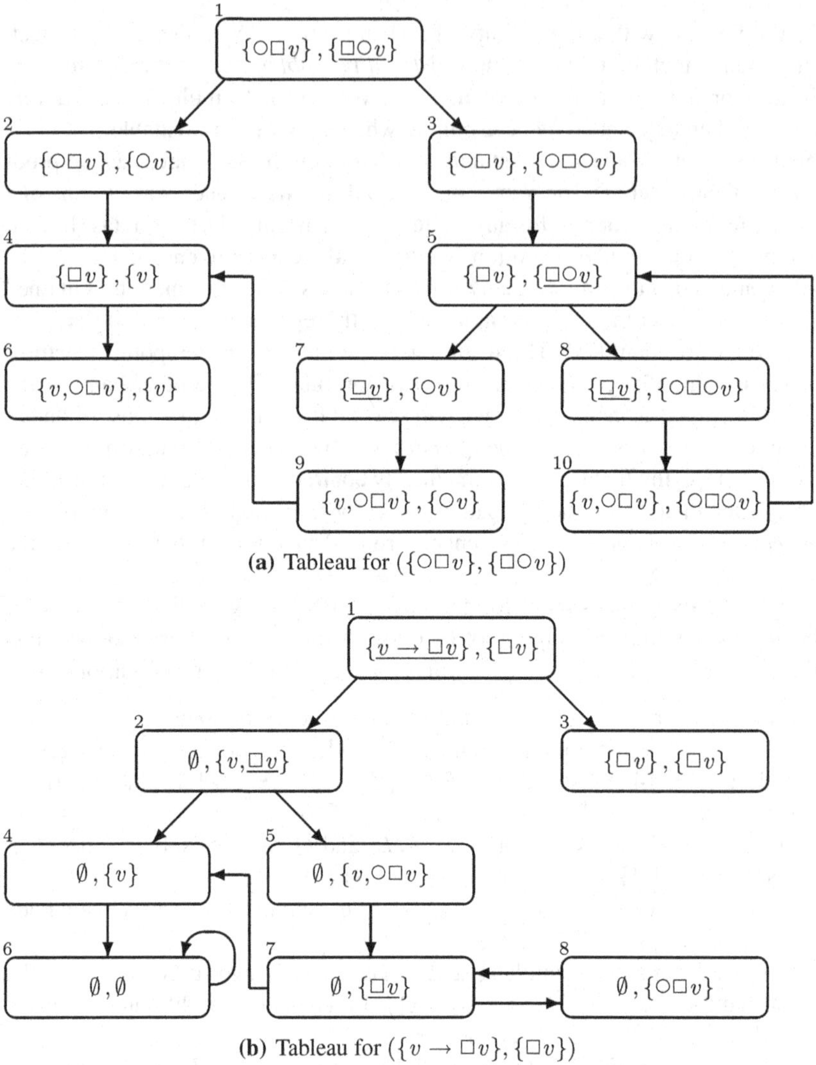
1
{○□v} , {□○v}
2
{○□v} , {○v}
3
{○□v} , {○□○v}
4
{□v} , {v}
5
{□v} , {□○v}
6
{v,○□v} , {v}
7
{□v} , {○v}
8
{□v} , {○□○v}
9
{v,○□v} , {○v}
10
{v,○□v} , {○□○v}
(a) Tableau for ({○□v}, {□○v})
1
{v → □v} , {□v}
2
∅ , {v,□v}
3
{□v} , {□v}
4
∅ , {v}
5
∅ , {v,○□v}
6
∅ , ∅
7
∅ , {□v}
8
∅ , {○□v}
(b) Tableau for ({v → □v}, {□v})

Fig. 2.1. Example tableaux

either $(\perp)$ or $(\bigcirc)$ must be applied. In particular, any infinite path in the tableau must contain infinitely many tableau states.

Finally, observe that propositional constants and formulas of the form **false** or $\bigcirc A$ that appear in some node $\mathcal{Q}$ that is not a tableau state are copied to all successor nodes of $\mathcal{Q}$. Therefore, if $\mathcal{Q}_1, \ldots, \mathcal{Q}_k$ is a path in a tableau such that none of $\mathcal{Q}_1, \ldots, \mathcal{Q}_{k-1}$ is a tableau state then $\mathcal{Q}_k$ contains all of the formulas of these forms that $\mathcal{Q}_1$ contains.

Figures 2.1(a) and 2.1(b) illustrate the tableau construction at the hand of the PNPs $(\{\bigcirc\Box v\}, \{\Box\bigcirc v\})$ and $(\{v \rightarrow \Box v\}, \{\Box v\})$ where $v \in \mathbf{V}$. The nodes (denoting

PNPs without surrounding parentheses) are marked by numbers for easy reference. Those marked 2, 3, 9, and 10 in Fig. 2.1(a) and 4, 5, 6, and 8 in Fig. 2.1(b) are tableau states. In the other nodes, the formula to which a decomposing rule is applied is shown underlined.

It remains to define the unsatisfiable nodes or subgraphs of a tableau. Given a tableau $\mathcal{T}$, the set of *closed nodes* of $\mathcal{T}$ is inductively defined as follows:

$(C1)$ All nodes $\mathcal{Q}$ of $\mathcal{T}$ that satisfy condition $(\bot)$ are closed.
$(C2)$ Every node $\mathcal{Q}$ of $\mathcal{T}$ all of whose successors are closed is closed.
$(C3)$ If $\mathcal{Q}$ is a node and A is a formula such that $\Box A \in neg(\mathcal{Q})$ and every path from $\mathcal{Q}$ to nodes $\mathcal{Q}'$ with $A \in neg(\mathcal{Q}')$ contains some closed node then $\mathcal{Q}$ is closed.

A tableau is called *unsuccessful* if its root is closed; otherwise it is called *successful*.

Let us apply these rules to the tableau shown in Fig. 2.1(a): the node 6 is closed by condition $(C1)$; therefore node 4, whose only successor node is node 6, is closed by condition $(C2)$, and nodes 2, 9, and 7 are closed applying $(C2)$ two times more. Now consider node 5: the formula $\Box \bigcirc v$ is contained negatively and the only nodes in paths from node 5 that contain $\bigcirc v$ negatively are nodes 7 and 9 which are closed. Therefore, node 5 is also closed by condition $(C3)$, implying by $(C2)$ that node 3 is closed and finally, again by $(C2)$, node 1 (the root of the tableau) is closed, so the tableau is unsuccessful. In fact, the PNP $(\{\bigcirc\Box v\}, \{\Box\bigcirc v\})$ represents the unsatisfiable formula $\bigcirc\Box v \land \neg\Box\bigcirc v$.

In the tableau of Fig. 2.1(b) the node 3 is closed by condition $(C1)$, but no other node is found closed. For example, node 2 is not closed since nodes 4 and 6 are not closed. So, the root of the tableau is also not closed and the tableau is successful; observe that the PNP $(\{v \to \Box v\}, \{\Box v\})$ corresponds to the satisfiable formula $(v \to \Box v) \land \neg\Box v$.

We now set out to prove in a series of lemmas that a tableau for a given PNP $\mathcal{P}$ is successful if and only if $\widehat{\mathcal{P}}$ is satisfiable.

Lemma 2.5.1. *Let $\mathcal{T}$ be a tableau and $\mathcal{Q}$ some node of $\mathcal{T}$. For all temporal structures K and all $i \in \mathbb{N}$:*

a) If $\mathcal{Q}$ is not a tableau state of $\mathcal{T}$ then $\mathsf{K}_i(\widehat{\mathcal{Q}}) = \mathsf{tt}$ if and only if $\mathsf{K}_i(\widehat{\mathcal{Q}'}) = \mathsf{tt}$ for some successor node $\mathcal{Q}'$ of $\mathcal{Q}$ in $\mathcal{T}$.

b) If $\mathcal{Q}$ is a tableau state of $\mathcal{T}$ then $\mathsf{K}_i(\widehat{\mathcal{Q}}) = \mathsf{tt}$ implies that $\mathsf{K}_{i+1}(\widehat{\mathcal{Q}'}) = \mathsf{tt}$ for the unique successor node $\mathcal{Q}'$ of $\mathcal{Q}$ in $\mathcal{T}$. Moreover, $\widehat{\mathcal{Q}'}$ is satisfiable only if $\widehat{\mathcal{Q}}$ is satisfiable.

Proof. a) It suffices to distinguish the possible conditions $(\bot)$ to $(\Box^-)$ that tableau nodes which are not tableau states must satisfy. We only give two illustrative cases; the other ones are equally obvious.

1. $\mathcal{Q}$ is a node satisfying $(\bot)$. Then **false** $\in pos(\mathcal{Q})$ or $pos(\mathcal{Q}) \cap neg(\mathcal{Q}) = \emptyset$; hence $\mathsf{K}_i(\widehat{\mathcal{Q}}) = \mathsf{tt}$ for no K and i, and $\mathcal{Q}$ has no successor node.
2. $\mathcal{Q}$ is a node according to $(\Box^+)$. Then $\Box A \in pos(\mathcal{Q})$ for some formula A. Now, $\mathsf{K}_i(\Box A) = \mathsf{tt}$ if and only if both $\mathsf{K}_i(A) = \mathsf{tt}$ and $\mathsf{K}_i(\bigcirc\Box A) = \mathsf{tt}$ by (T28), which implies the assertion.

b) Suppose that $\mathcal{Q}$ is a tableau state of $\mathcal{T}$, i.e., it satisfies ($\bigcirc$), and that $\mathsf{K}_i(\widehat{\mathcal{Q}}) = \mathsf{tt}$. In particular, $\mathsf{K}_i(\bigcirc A) = \mathsf{tt}$ for every $\bigcirc A \in pos(\mathcal{Q})$ and $\mathsf{K}_i(\bigcirc A) = \mathsf{ff}$ for every $\bigcirc A \in neg(\mathcal{Q})$ and therefore $\mathsf{K}_{i+1}(A) = \mathsf{tt}$ for every $A \in pos(\mathcal{Q}')$ and $\mathsf{K}_{i+1}(A) = \mathsf{ff}$ for every $A \in neg(\mathcal{Q}')$. It follows that $\mathsf{K}_{i+1}(\widehat{\mathcal{Q}'}) = \mathsf{tt}$.

Furthermore, suppose that $\mathcal{Q}'$ is satisfiable, and choose $\mathsf{K} = (\eta_0, \eta_1, \ldots)$ and $i \in \mathbb{N}$ such that $\mathsf{K}_i(\widehat{\mathcal{Q}'}) = \mathsf{tt}$. For $\mathsf{K}^i = (\eta_i, \eta_{i+1}, \ldots)$ we have $\mathsf{K}^i_0(\widehat{\mathcal{Q}'}) = \mathsf{tt}$ by Lemma 2.1.5. Now let $\mathsf{K}' = (\eta, \eta_i, \eta_{i+1}, \ldots)$ where η is defined by $\eta(v) = \mathsf{tt}$ if and only if $v \in pos(\mathcal{Q})$. Again by Lemma 2.1.5 it follows that $\mathsf{K}'_1(\widehat{\mathcal{Q}'}) = \mathsf{tt}$. Moreover, because $pos(\mathcal{Q}) \cap neg(\mathcal{Q}) = \emptyset$ we have $\mathsf{K}'_0(A) = \mathsf{tt}$ for all $A \in pos(\mathcal{Q}) \cap \mathbf{V}$ and $\mathsf{K}'_0(A) = \mathsf{ff}$ for all $A \in neg(\mathcal{Q}) \cap \mathbf{V}$. Since all formulas in $\mathcal{Q}$ are either **false**, $v \in \mathbf{V}$ or of the form $\bigcirc A$ and because **false** $\notin pos(\mathcal{Q})$ it follows, together with the definition of $\mathcal{Q}'$, that $\mathsf{K}'_0(\widehat{\mathcal{Q}}) = \mathsf{tt}$; hence $\widehat{\mathcal{Q}}$ is satisfiable. △

Intuitively, a successful tableau represents all temporal structures that satisfy the root PNP. Consecutive nodes not of type ($\bigcirc$) in tableau paths gather information about formulas to be satisfied at the same state of the temporal structure. Formally, given an infinite path $\mathcal{Q}_0, \mathcal{Q}_1, \ldots$ in a tableau we define the function $cnt : \mathbb{N} \to \mathbb{N}$ by letting

$$cnt(i) \;=\; |\{j < i \mid \mathcal{Q}_j \text{ is a tableau state}\}|$$

which maps i to the number of nodes of type ($\bigcirc$) in the prefix $\mathcal{Q}_0, \ldots, \mathcal{Q}_i$ of the path. The function cnt is clearly monotonic; it is also surjective because any infinite path must contain infinitely many tableau states. We may therefore define the following "inverse" function $st : \mathbb{N} \to \mathbb{N}$ by

$$st(k) \;=\; \max\{i \in \mathbb{N} \mid cnt(i) = k\}$$

which is again monotonic and determines the index of the kth tableau state (counting from 0) along the path $\mathcal{Q}_0, \mathcal{Q}_1, \ldots$. Observe that these definitions ensure that $st(cnt(i)) \geq i$, that $cnt(st(k)) = k$, and that $cnt(st(k) + 1) = cnt(k) + 1$.

Given some temporal structure K and some node $\mathcal{Q}$ in a tableau we inductively define the (finite or infinite) path $\pi^{\mathsf{K}}_{\mathcal{Q}} = \mathcal{Q}_0, \mathcal{Q}_1, \ldots$ as follows:

- $\mathcal{Q}_0 = \mathcal{Q}$.
- If $\mathcal{Q}_i$ has no successor node in the tableau then $\pi^{\mathsf{K}}_{\mathcal{Q}}$ ends in node $\mathcal{Q}_i$.
- If $\mathcal{Q}_i$ has precisely one successor node $\mathcal{Q}'$ then $\mathcal{Q}_{i+1} = \mathcal{Q}'$.
- If $\mathcal{Q}_i$ has a left-hand successor node $\mathcal{Q}'$ and a right-hand successor node $\mathcal{Q}''$ then $\mathcal{Q}_{i+1} = \mathcal{Q}'$ if $\mathsf{K}_{cnt(i)}(\widehat{\mathcal{Q}'}) = \mathsf{tt}$, else $\mathcal{Q}_{i+1} = \mathcal{Q}''$.

Note that this definition of $\pi^{\mathsf{K}}_{\mathcal{Q}}$ is such that for any formula $\Box A \in neg(\mathcal{Q}_i)$ the successor $\mathcal{Q}'$ containing $A \in neg(\mathcal{Q}')$ is "preferred" in the sense that this node is chosen to continue the path "if possible".

Lemma 2.5.2. *Let $\mathcal{Q}$ be a node in a tableau and K a temporal structure such that $\mathsf{K}_0(\widehat{\mathcal{Q}}) = \mathsf{tt}$. Then $\pi^{\mathsf{K}}_{\mathcal{Q}} = \mathcal{Q}_0, \mathcal{Q}_1, \ldots$ is infinite and does not contain any closed tableau node. Moreover, $\mathsf{K}_{cnt(i)}(\widehat{\mathcal{Q}_i}) = \mathsf{tt}$ for all $i \in \mathbb{N}$.*

Proof. a) We first prove by induction on the definition of $\pi_{\mathcal{Q}}^{\mathsf{K}}$ that $\mathsf{K}_{cnt(i)}(\widehat{\mathcal{Q}_i}) = \mathsf{tt}$ for all nodes $\mathcal{Q}_i$ of $\pi_{\mathcal{Q}}^{\mathsf{K}}$.

1. With $cnt(0) = 0$ we have $\mathsf{K}_{cnt(0)}(\widehat{\mathcal{Q}_0}) = \mathsf{K}_0(\widehat{\mathcal{Q}_0}) = \mathsf{tt}$ from the assumption.
2. Consider the node $\mathcal{Q}_{i+1}$. By induction hypothesis we have $\mathsf{K}_{cnt(i)}(\widehat{\mathcal{Q}_i}) = \mathsf{tt}$. If $\mathcal{Q}_i$ is not a tableau state then $cnt(i+1) = cnt(i)$. According to the definition of $\pi_{\mathcal{Q}}^{\mathsf{K}}$ we then get $\mathsf{K}_{cnt(i+1)}(\widehat{\mathcal{Q}_{i+1}}) = \mathsf{K}_{cnt(i)}(\widehat{\mathcal{Q}_{i+1}}) = \mathsf{tt}$ with Lemma 2.5.1 a). If $\mathcal{Q}_i$ is a tableau state then $cnt(i+1) = cnt(i) + 1$ and $\mathcal{Q}_{i+1}$ is the unique successor of $\mathcal{Q}_i$ in $\mathcal{T}$. So we obtain $\mathsf{K}_{cnt(i+1)}(\widehat{\mathcal{Q}_{i+1}}) = \mathsf{K}_{cnt(i)+1}(\widehat{\mathcal{Q}_{i+1}}) = \mathsf{tt}$ with Lemma 2.5.1 b).

This observation also implies that $\pi_{\mathcal{Q}}^{\mathsf{K}}$ must be infinite for otherwise condition $(\bot)$ would have to hold for the final node $\mathcal{Q}_k$, contradicting $\mathsf{K}_{cnt(k)}(\widehat{\mathcal{Q}_k}) = \mathsf{tt}$.

b) It remains to prove that no node $\mathcal{Q}_i$ is closed, which is shown by induction on the definition of the set of closed nodes (simultaneously for all $i \in \mathbb{N}$):

1. We have already observed above that condition $(\bot)$ can hold for no node $\mathcal{Q}_i$, so no $\mathcal{Q}_i$ is closed because of $(C1)$.
2. Assume that node $\mathcal{Q}_i$ was closed according to $(C2)$, i.e., because all its successor nodes had already been established as being closed. This implies that $\mathcal{Q}_{i+1}$ is also closed, which is impossible according to the induction hypothesis.
3. Assume that node $\mathcal{Q}_i$ was closed because of a formula $\Box A \in neg(\mathcal{Q}_i)$ such that all paths from $\mathcal{Q}_i$ to nodes $\mathcal{Q}'$ of the tableau with $A \in neg(\mathcal{Q}')$ contain a node that had already been found to be closed. Because of $\mathsf{K}_{cnt(i)}(\widehat{\mathcal{Q}_i}) = \mathsf{tt}$ there is some smallest $j \geq cnt(i)$ such that $\mathsf{K}_j(A) = \mathsf{ff}$. Now consider the subpath $\mathcal{Q}_i, \mathcal{Q}_{i+1}, \ldots, \mathcal{Q}_{st(j)}$ from $\mathcal{Q}_i$ up to (and including) the jth tableau state of the path. Observe that $st(j)$ is well defined because the path is known to be infinite; moreover, $st(j) \geq st(cnt(i)) \geq i$.
   We prove that for all k such that $i \leq k \leq st(j)$, either $\Box A \in neg(\mathcal{Q}_k)$ or $\bigcirc\Box A \in neg(\mathcal{Q}_k)$: for $k = i$, we know by assumption that $\Box A \in neg(\mathcal{Q}_k)$. Following any edge other than according to $(\bigcirc)$ or $(\Box^-)$, applied to $\Box A$, preserves the assertion. If $\mathcal{Q}_k$ satisfies condition $(\Box^-)$, applied to $\Box A$, it has two successor nodes $\mathcal{Q}'$ and $\mathcal{Q}''$ such that $A \in neg(\mathcal{Q}')$ and $\bigcirc\Box A \in neg(\mathcal{Q}'')$. Now, by assumption we know that $\mathcal{Q}'$ is closed; therefore $\mathcal{Q}_{k+1}$ must be $\mathcal{Q}''$, and thus we have $\bigcirc\Box A \in neg(\mathcal{Q}_{k+1})$. Finally, if $\mathcal{Q}_k$ satisfies condition $(\bigcirc)$, we cannot have $\Box A \in \mathcal{Q}_k$, so we have $\bigcirc\Box A \in \mathcal{Q}_k$ and thus $\Box A \in \mathcal{Q}_{k+1}$.
   Now let l denote the least index such that $i \leq l \leq st(j)$ and $cnt(l) = j$; observe that either $l = i$ or $\mathcal{Q}_l$ is the successor of a tableau state, and therefore we must have $\Box A \in neg(\mathcal{Q}_l)$. It follows from the definition of a tableau that at some node $\mathcal{Q}_m$ where $l \leq m \leq st(j)$, and thus $cnt(m) = j$, rule $(\Box^-)$ must be applied to $\Box A$. Moreover, $\mathsf{K}_j(\widehat{\mathcal{Q}_m}) = \mathsf{tt}$ and $\mathsf{K}_j(A) = \mathsf{ff}$, so $\mathcal{Q}_{m+1}$ is the left-hand successor of node $\mathcal{Q}_m$, and $A \in neg(\mathcal{Q}_{m+1})$. We have thus found a path $\mathcal{Q}_i, \ldots, \mathcal{Q}_{m+1}$ from $\mathcal{Q}_i$ to a node where $A \in neg(\mathcal{Q}_{m+1})$ such that no node along the path has already been found to be closed, and a contradiction is reached. Therefore, $\mathcal{Q}_i$ cannot be closed because of $(C3)$. △

Lemma 2.5.3. *If $\mathcal{T}$ is a tableau for a PNP $\mathcal{P}$ and $\widehat{\mathcal{P}}$ is satisfiable then $\mathcal{T}$ is successful.*

Proof. Assume that $\widehat{\mathcal{P}}$ is satisfiable and let $\mathsf{K} = (\eta_0, \eta_1, \ldots)$ be a temporal structure and $i \in \mathbb{N}$ such that $\mathsf{K}_i(\widehat{\mathcal{P}}) = \mathsf{tt}$. For $\mathsf{K}^i = (\eta_i, \eta_{i+1}, \ldots)$ Lemma 2.1.5 implies that $\mathsf{K}^i_0(\widehat{\mathcal{P}}) = \mathsf{tt}$. By Lemma 2.5.2 the path $\pi^{\mathsf{K}^i}_{\mathcal{P}}$ through $\mathcal{T}$ does not contain any closed tableau node. In particular, the root $\mathcal{P}$ is not closed, i.e., the tableau is successful. △

We will now prove that, conversely, any successful tableau $\mathcal{T}$ for $\mathcal{P}$ contains some path that represents a temporal structure satisfying $\widehat{\mathcal{P}}$. As in Sect. 2.4 we say that an infinite path $\mathcal{Q}_0, \mathcal{Q}_1, \ldots$ in $\mathcal{T}$ is *complete* if $\mathcal{Q}_0 = \mathcal{P}$, if it does not contain any closed node, and if for all formulas A and all $i \in \mathbb{N}$ such that $\Box A \in neg(\mathcal{Q}_i)$ there exists some $j \geq i$ such that $A \in neg(\mathcal{Q}_j)$.

Lemma 2.5.4. *Every successful tableau for a PNP $\mathcal{P}$ contains some complete path.*

Proof. The proof is similar to that of Lemma 2.4.8: Assume that $\mathcal{T}$ is a successful tableau for a PNP $\mathcal{P}$. Since $\mathcal{T}$ is a finite graph of PNPs there are only finitely many formulas A such that $\Box A \in neg(\mathcal{Q})$ for some node $\mathcal{Q}$ of $\mathcal{T}$. Choose some fixed enumeration $A_0, \ldots, A_{m-1}$ of all such formulas A. We define a succession $\pi_0, \pi_1, \ldots$ of finite, non-empty paths in $\mathcal{T}$ that do not contain any closed nodes and such that π_i is a proper prefix of π_{i+1} as follows:

- Let $\pi_0 = \mathcal{P}$ be the path that contains only the root of $\mathcal{T}$. Since $\mathcal{T}$ is successful, $\mathcal{P}$ is not closed.
- Inductively, assume that $\pi_i = \mathcal{Q}_0, \ldots, \mathcal{Q}_k$ has already been defined. We distinguish two cases: if $\Box A_{i \bmod m} \notin neg(\mathcal{Q}_k)$ or $A_{i \bmod m} \in neg(\mathcal{Q}_k)$ then π_{i+1} is obtained from π_i by appending some non-closed successor node of $\mathcal{Q}_k$. (Observe that $\mathcal{Q}_k$ has some such successor since otherwise it were closed by condition $(C2)$.) If, on the other hand, $\Box A_{i \bmod m} \in neg(\mathcal{Q}_k)$ and $A_{i \bmod m} \notin neg(\mathcal{Q}_k)$ then condition $(C3)$ ensures that there exists some path π' from $\mathcal{Q}$ to some node $\mathcal{Q}'$ with $A_{i \bmod m} \in neg(\mathcal{Q}')$ such that π' does not contain any closed node (and obviously, π' must be non-empty). Let π_{i+1} be the concatenation of π_i and π'.

The succession $\pi_0, \pi_1, \ldots$ uniquely determines an infinite path π in $\mathcal{T}$, which is complete by construction. △

Lemma 2.5.5. *If $\mathcal{T}$ is a successful tableau for a PNP $\mathcal{P}$ then $\widehat{\mathcal{P}}$ is satisfiable.*

Proof. Assume that $\mathcal{T}$ is successful, and choose some complete path $\mathcal{Q}_0, \mathcal{Q}_1, \ldots$ in $\mathcal{T}$, which is possible by Lemma 2.5.4. Now let $\mathcal{K} = (\eta_0, \eta_1, \ldots)$ be any temporal structure such that, for all $v \in \mathbf{V}$ and $i \in \mathbb{N}$,

$$v \in pos(\mathcal{Q}_{st(i)}) \Rightarrow \eta_i(v) = \mathsf{tt},$$
$$v \in neg(\mathcal{Q}_{st(i)}) \Rightarrow \eta_i(v) = \mathsf{ff}.$$

Such structures exist because no node $\mathcal{Q}_j$ is closed, and in particular one cannot have $v \in pos(\mathcal{Q}_{st(i)}) \cap neg(\mathcal{Q}_{st(i)})$ for any v and i. For example, one can define K by stipulating that $\eta_i(v) = \mathsf{tt}$ if and only if $v \in pos(\mathcal{Q}_{st(i)})$, for all v and i.

We will prove that the above condition ensures

$$(*) \quad \begin{array}{l} A \in pos(\mathcal{Q}_i) \Rightarrow \mathsf{K}_{cnt(i)}(A) = \mathrm{tt}, \\ A \in neg(\mathcal{Q}_i) \Rightarrow \mathsf{K}_{cnt(i)}(A) = \mathrm{ff} \end{array}$$

for all formulas A and all $i \in \mathbb{N}$. In particular, $(*)$ implies $\mathsf{K}_{cnt(0)}(\widehat{\mathcal{Q}_0}) = \mathrm{tt}$, that is, $\mathsf{K}_0(\widehat{\mathcal{P}}) = \mathrm{tt}$ since $\mathcal{Q}_0 = \mathcal{P}$ and $cnt(0) = 0$, proving the lemma.

Assertion $(*)$ is proven by structural induction on A.

1. $A \equiv v \in \mathbf{V}$: If $v \in pos(\mathcal{Q}_i)$ then $v \in pos(\mathcal{Q}_{st(cnt(i))})$ by the tableau construction and thus $\mathsf{K}_{cnt(i)}(v) = \mathsf{K}_{cnt(st(cnt(i)))}(v) = \mathrm{tt}$.
   If $v \in neg(\mathcal{Q}_i)$ then again we have $v \in neg(\mathcal{Q}_{st(cnt(i))})$, and the assertion $\mathsf{K}_{cnt(i)}(v) = \mathrm{ff}$ follows as above from the assumption on K.
2. $A \equiv$ **false**: Since $\mathcal{Q}_i$ is not closed, we know that **false** $\notin pos(\mathcal{Q}_i)$; moreover, $\mathsf{K}_{cnt(i)}(\mathbf{false}) = \mathrm{ff}$. This suffices.
3. $A \equiv B \to C$: Assume that $B \to C \in pos(\mathcal{Q}_i)$ and consider the path $\mathcal{Q}_i, \ldots, \mathcal{Q}_{st(cnt(i))}$. By the tableau construction there exists some j where $i \le j < st(cnt(i))$ such that rule $(\to^+)$ is applied to A at node $\mathcal{Q}_j$; observe that $cnt(j) = cnt(i)$. It follows that $B \in neg(\mathcal{Q}_{j+1})$ or $C \in pos(\mathcal{Q}_{j+1})$, and thus by induction hypothesis $\mathsf{K}_{cnt(j)}(B) = \mathrm{ff}$ or $\mathsf{K}_{cnt(j)}(C) = \mathrm{tt}$. In either case, we obtain $\mathsf{K}_{cnt(i)}(B \to C) = \mathrm{tt}$.
   If $B \to C \in neg(\mathcal{Q}_i)$ the argument is analogous with $B \in pos(\mathcal{Q}_{j+1})$ and $C \in neg(\mathcal{Q}_{j+1})$ because of rule $(\to^-)$.
4. $A \equiv \bigcirc B$: If $\bigcirc B \in pos(\mathcal{Q}_i)$ then $\bigcirc B \in pos(\mathcal{Q}_{st(cnt(i))})$ by the tableau construction and $B \in pos(\mathcal{Q}_{st(cnt(i))+1})$ since rule $(\bigcirc)$ is applied at node $\mathcal{Q}_{st(cnt(i))}$. Applying the induction hypothesis it follows that

   $$\mathsf{K}_{cnt(i)}(\bigcirc B) = \mathsf{K}_{cnt(i)+1}(B) = \mathsf{K}_{cnt(st(cnt(i))+1)}(B) = \mathrm{tt}.$$

   The case $\bigcirc B \in neg(\mathcal{Q}_i)$ is argued analogously with $B \in neg(\mathcal{Q}_{st(cnt(i))+1})$ because of rule $(\bigcirc)$.
5. $A \equiv \Box B$: Assume $\Box B \in pos(\mathcal{Q}_i)$, and consider the path $\mathcal{Q}_i, \ldots, \mathcal{Q}_{st(cnt(i))}$: by the tableau construction there exists some j where $i \le j < st(cnt(i))$ such that rule $(\Box^+)$ is applied to formula $\Box B$ at node $\mathcal{Q}_j$, and therefore we have $\{B, \bigcirc\Box B\} \subseteq pos(\mathcal{Q}_{j+1})$. Moreover, it follows that $\bigcirc\Box B \in pos(\mathcal{Q}_{st(cnt(i))})$; thus $\Box B \in pos(\mathcal{Q}_{st(cnt(i))+1})$. Continuing inductively, for all $k \ge cnt(i)$ we find some j such that $cnt(j) = k$ and $B \in pos(\mathcal{Q}_j)$. The induction hypothesis implies that $\mathsf{K}_k(B) = \mathrm{tt}$ holds for all $k \ge cnt(i)$, that is, $\mathsf{K}_{cnt(i)}(\Box B) = \mathrm{tt}$.
   Now suppose that $\Box B \in neg(\mathcal{Q}_i)$. The definition of a complete path ensures that $B \in neg(\mathcal{Q}_j)$ for some $j \ge i$. By the induction hypothesis it follows that $\mathsf{K}_{cnt(j)}(B) = \mathrm{ff}$, and the monotonicity of cnt implies $\mathsf{K}_{cnt(i)}(\Box B) = \mathrm{ff}$. △

The previous results provide now the desired algorithmic decision procedure for satisfiability. Given a PNP $\mathcal{P}$, a tableau $\mathcal{T}$ for $\mathcal{P}$ can be constructed by *expansion* steps according to the rules $(\to^+)$ through $(\bigcirc)$ and terminating according to rule $(\perp)$. Rules $(C1)$–$(C3)$ can be used to remove unsatisfiable nodes or subgraphs in $\mathcal{T}$ (*pruning* steps) providing the decision whether $\mathcal{T}$ is successful or unsuccessful, i.e., by the Lemmas 2.5.3 and 2.5.5, whether $\widehat{\mathcal{P}}$ is satisfiable or not. We summarize this investigation in the following theorem.

Theorem 2.5.6 (Decidability Theorem for LTL). *The satisfiability and validity problems for $\mathcal{L}_{\rm LTL}$ are decidable.*

Proof. In order to decide the satisfiability problem for a given formula F of $\mathcal{L}_{\rm LTL}$, the decision procedure is applied to the PNP $(\{F\}, \emptyset)$. Since F is valid if and only if $\neg F$ is unsatisfiable, the validity problem for F can be decided with the PNP $(\emptyset, \{F\})$. △

The given tableau definitions refer to the basic logical operators of LTL. Of course, for practical use one could add also "direct" rules for the derived operators, e.g., conditions

($\vee^+$) $A \vee B \in \mathcal{F}^+$ for some formulas A, B, and $\mathcal{Q}$ has precisely two successor nodes: the left-hand successor $((\mathcal{F}^+ \setminus \{A \vee B\}) \cup \{A\}, \mathcal{F}^-)$ and the right-hand successor $((\mathcal{F}^+ \setminus \{A \vee B\}) \cup \{B\}, \mathcal{F}^-)$,

($\vee^-$) $A \vee B \in \mathcal{F}^-$ for some formulas A, B, and $\mathcal{Q}$ has precisely the successor node $(\mathcal{F}^+, (\mathcal{F}^- \setminus \{A \vee B\}) \cup \{A, B\})$

for tableau nodes $\mathcal{Q} = (\mathcal{F}^+, \mathcal{F}^-)$, providing expansion steps with respect to $\vee$, or

$(C4)$ If $\mathcal{Q}$ is a node and A is a formula such that $\Diamond A \in pos(\mathcal{Q})$ and every path from $\mathcal{Q}$ to some node $\mathcal{Q}'$ with $A \in pos(\mathcal{Q}')$ contains some closed node then $\mathcal{Q}$ is itself closed

as another rule for pruning steps.

Moreover, the description of the decision procedure above seems to suggest that pruning steps are applied only after all nodes have been fully expanded. However, actual implementations would be likely to interleave expansion and pruning steps in order to avoid unnecessary expansions. So, the closure conditions $(C1)$ and $(C2)$ can be implemented at the time of construction of $\mathcal{T}$. Condition $(C3)$ can be checked by inspecting the strongly connected components (SCC) of the tableau: an SCC is said to *promise* A if $\Box A \in neg(\mathcal{Q})$ holds for some node $\mathcal{Q}$ of the SCC. It is said to *fulfill* A if $A \in neg(\mathcal{Q})$ holds for some node $\mathcal{Q}$ of the SCC. Finally, we call an SCC *honest* if it fulfills all formulas A that it promises. A tableau $\mathcal{T}$ is successful if and only if it contains some honest SCC that is reachable on a path from the root of $\mathcal{T}$. The existence of honest SCCs can be decided, for example using *Tarjan's algorithm*, in time linear in the size of $\mathcal{T}$.

Formulas that occur in nodes of a tableau $\mathcal{T}$ for a PNP $\mathcal{P}$ are either subformulas of formulas in $\mathcal{F}_\mathcal{P}$ or formulas of the form $\bigcirc A$ where A is a subformula of some formula in $\mathcal{F}_\mathcal{P}$. Because the number of subformulas of a formula is linear in the length of the formula (measured as the number of symbols), it follows that the number of nodes of $\mathcal{T}$ is at most exponential in the size of $\mathcal{P}$, measured as the sum of the lengths of the formulas in $\mathcal{P}$. Altogether we find that the tableau method can be implemented in time exponential in the size of $\mathcal{P}$.

2.6 Initial Validity Semantics

We mentioned in Sect. 2.1 that LTL is sometimes introduced with a notion of validity different from the "normal" one defined there. Specifically, whereas the concepts of a temporal structure and the evaluation of formulas remain unchanged, validity and consequence are defined as follows.

Definition. A formula A of $\mathcal{L}_{\mathrm{LTL}}(\mathbf{V})$ is called *initially valid in the temporal structure* K for $\mathbf{V}$, denoted by $\overset{0}{\vDash}_{\mathsf{K}} A$, if $\mathsf{K}_0(A) = \mathrm{tt}$. A is called an *initial consequence of* a set $\mathcal{F}$ of formulas ($\mathcal{F} \overset{0}{\vDash} A$) if $\overset{0}{\vDash}_{\mathsf{K}} A$ holds for every K such that $\overset{0}{\vDash}_{\mathsf{K}} B$ for all $B \in \mathcal{F}$. A is called *(universally) initially valid* ($\overset{0}{\vDash} A$) if $\emptyset \overset{0}{\vDash} A$.

We denote LTL equipped with this *initial validity semantics* by LTL_0. This semantics and LTL_0 are also called *anchored semantics* and *anchored* LTL. (In some presentations of LTL_0 the notion of initial validity is defined in a technically somewhat different way. We will come back to this in another context in Sect. 10.2.)

Temporal logic can be used to "specify" temporal structures, as we will see in Chap. 6, similar to the description of first-order structures by theories in Sect. 1.3. For such applications, it is often desirable to express that some formula A holds in the initial state of some temporal structure. This is clearly possible in the framework of LTL_0, just by asserting A, whereas the same effect cannot be achieved in LTL where A would then have to hold in all states of the structure (we will come back to this issue, however, in Sects. 3.4 and 3.5). In LTL_0 the latter condition can obviously be expressed by asserting $\Box A$.

More technically, the connections between LTL and LTL_0 are rendered by the following lemma.

Lemma 2.6.1. *Let A be a formula, and let K be a temporal structure.*

a) If $\vDash_{\mathsf{K}} A$ then $\overset{0}{\vDash}_{\mathsf{K}} A$.
b) $\vDash_{\mathsf{K}} A$ if and only if $\overset{0}{\vDash}_{\mathsf{K}} \Box A$.

Proof. $\vDash_{\mathsf{K}} A$ means $\mathsf{K}_i(A) = \mathrm{tt}$ for every $i \in \mathbb{N}$, and this implies $\mathsf{K}_0(A) = \mathrm{tt}$; hence $\overset{0}{\vDash}_{\mathsf{K}} A$ which proves a), and it is, moreover, equivalent to $\mathsf{K}_0(\Box A) = \mathrm{tt}$, i.e., $\overset{0}{\vDash}_{\mathsf{K}} \Box A$, thus proving also b). △

With the help of this lemma we are now able to state the precise connections on the level of the different consequence relations.

Theorem 2.6.2. *Let A be a formula, $\mathcal{F}$ be a set of formulas, and let $\Box\mathcal{F}$ denote the set $\{\Box B \mid B \in \mathcal{F}\}$.*

a) If $\mathcal{F} \overset{0}{\vDash} A$ then $\mathcal{F} \vDash A$.
b) $\mathcal{F} \vDash A$ if and only if $\Box\mathcal{F} \overset{0}{\vDash} A$.

Proof. a) Assume that $\mathcal{F} \overset{0}{\vDash} A$, let K be a temporal structure such that $\vDash_{\mathsf{K}} B$ for all $B \in \mathcal{F}$, and let $i \in \mathbb{N}$. For $\mathsf{K}^i = (\eta_i, \eta_{i+1}, \eta_{i+2}, \ldots)$ we have, by Lemma 2.1.5, $\mathsf{K}^i_0(B) = \mathsf{K}_i(B) = \mathrm{tt}$, i.e., $\overset{0}{\vDash}_{\mathsf{K}^i} B$ for all $B \in \mathcal{F}$. Because of the assumption that $\mathcal{F} \overset{0}{\vDash} A$, this implies $\overset{0}{\vDash}_{\mathsf{K}^i} A$; hence again by Lemma 2.1.5, $\mathsf{K}_i(A) = \mathsf{K}^i_0(A) = \mathrm{tt}$, and shows that $\mathcal{F} \vDash A$.

b) Assume that $\mathcal{F} \vDash A$ and let K be a temporal structure such that $\overset{0}{\vDash}_{\mathsf{K}} \Box B$ for all $B \in \mathcal{F}$. Then $\vDash_{\mathsf{K}} B$ for all $B \in \mathcal{F}$ by Lemma 2.6.1 b); hence $\vDash_{\mathsf{K}} A$, and therefore $\overset{0}{\vDash}_{\mathsf{K}} A$ by Lemma 2.6.1 a). This means that $\Box\mathcal{F} \overset{0}{\vDash} A$. Conversely, assume that $\Box\mathcal{F} \overset{0}{\vDash} A$, let K be a temporal structure such that $\vDash_{\mathsf{K}} B$ for all $B \in \mathcal{F}$, and let $i \in \mathbb{N}$. Then, for all $B \in \mathcal{F}$, $\mathsf{K}_j(B) = \mathsf{tt}$ for every $j \in \mathbb{N}$. This implies, for K^i as in a) and again for all $B \in \mathcal{F}$, $\mathsf{K}^i_j(B) = \mathsf{K}_{i+j}(B) = \mathsf{tt}$ for every $j \in \mathbb{N}$ by Lemma 2.1.5; hence $\vDash_{\mathsf{K}^i} B$, and therefore $\overset{0}{\vDash}_{\mathsf{K}^i} \Box B$ by Lemma 2.6.1 b). From this we get $\overset{0}{\vDash}_{\mathsf{K}^i} A$, which shows as in a) that $\mathcal{F} \vDash A$. △

The converse of part a) of Theorem 2.6.2 does not hold in general. For example, we have $A \vDash \bigcirc A$, but $\bigcirc A$ is not an initial consequence of A. This is easy to see by taking A to be some $v \in \mathbf{V}$ and $\mathsf{K} = (\eta_0, \eta_1, \eta_2, \ldots)$ with $\eta_0(v) = \mathsf{tt}$ and $\eta_1(v) = \mathsf{ff}$. Then $\overset{0}{\vDash}_{\mathsf{K}} v$ but not $\overset{0}{\vDash}_{\mathsf{K}} \bigcirc v$. From Theorem 2.6.2 b) we only learn that $\Box A \overset{0}{\vDash} \bigcirc A$ holds.

The relationship between implication and initial consequence also has to be reconsidered. The characteristic (if part of the) equivalence

$$\mathcal{F} \cup \{A\} \vDash B \;\Leftrightarrow\; \mathcal{F} \vDash \Box A \to B$$

of LTL (cf. Theorem 2.1.6) does not hold in general for LTL_0. For example (with $\mathcal{F} = \emptyset$), $\overset{0}{\vDash} \Box A \to \bigcirc A$ since $\mathsf{K}_0(\Box A) = \mathsf{tt} \Rightarrow \mathsf{K}_1(A) = \mathsf{K}_0(\bigcirc A) = \mathsf{tt}$, but $A \overset{0}{\vDash} \bigcirc A$ does not hold as we just saw. Instead, we get back the relationship of classical logic for LTL_0:

Theorem 2.6.3. *$\mathcal{F} \cup \{A\} \overset{0}{\vDash} B$ if and only if $\mathcal{F} \overset{0}{\vDash} A \to B$.*

Proof. Assume that $\mathcal{F} \cup \{A\} \overset{0}{\vDash} B$ and let K be a temporal structure such that $\overset{0}{\vDash}_{\mathsf{K}} C$ for all $C \in \mathcal{F}$. To see that $\overset{0}{\vDash}_{\mathsf{K}} A \to B$, assume that $\mathsf{K}_0(A) = \mathsf{tt}$. Then $\overset{0}{\vDash}_{\mathsf{K}} A$ and therefore $\overset{0}{\vDash}_{\mathsf{K}} B$, i.e., $\mathsf{K}_0(B) = \mathsf{tt}$. This shows that $\mathcal{F} \overset{0}{\vDash} A \to B$. If, conversely, the latter holds and K is a temporal structure with $\overset{0}{\vDash}_{\mathsf{K}} C$ for all $C \in \mathcal{F} \cup \{A\}$ then we have $\mathsf{K}_0(A) = \mathsf{tt}$ and $\mathsf{K}_0(A \to B) = \mathsf{tt}$, and by Lemma 2.1.1 we obtain $\mathsf{K}_0(B) = \mathsf{tt}$ which shows that $\mathcal{F} \cup \{A\} \overset{0}{\vDash} B$. △

Despite all these differences between LTL and LTL_0 it is remarkable, however, that the two (universal) validity concepts still coincide:

Theorem 2.6.4. *$\vDash A$ if and only if $\overset{0}{\vDash} A$.*

Proof. The assertion follows directly from Theorem 2.6.2 b), choosing $\mathcal{F} = \emptyset$ which, of course, implies $\Box\mathcal{F} = \emptyset$. △

This observation generalizes to another connection: a consequence relationship of LTL like $A \vDash \bigcirc A$ can be "weakened" to

$$\overset{0}{\vDash} A \;\Rightarrow\; \overset{0}{\vDash} \bigcirc A$$

in LTL_0. In general, we have:

Theorem 2.6.5. *If $\mathcal{F} \models A$ and $\overset{0}{\models} B$ for all $B \in \mathcal{F}$ then $\overset{0}{\models} A$.*

Proof. From $\overset{0}{\models} B$ we get $\models B$ for all $B \in \mathcal{F}$ with Theorem 2.6.4. Using $\mathcal{F} \models A$ and Theorem 2.1.8, we obtain $\models A$; hence $\overset{0}{\models} A$ again with Theorem 2.6.4. △

To sum up, we realize that LTL and LTL_0 coincide with respect to (universal) validity, but differ in their consequence relations. In particular, all laws (T1), (T2), etc. (expressed by formulas) also hold in LTL_0. Any consequence relationship

$$\mathcal{F} \models A$$

of LTL is changed to

$$\Box\mathcal{F} \overset{0}{\models} A$$

and can also be "rewritten" as

$$\overset{0}{\models} B \text{ for all } B \in \mathcal{F} \;\Rightarrow\; \overset{0}{\models} A$$

in LTL_0.

These semantical observations carry over to axiomatizations of LTL_0. If we are interested only in deriving valid formulas (without any assumptions) then Σ_{LTL} would obviously be an adequate formal system for LTL_0, too. Rules of Σ_{LTL} (and derived rules) have then to be understood in a new way, semantically indicated by Theorem 2.6.5. For example, the rule

$$A \vdash \bigcirc A$$

should be read as asserting

"if A is derivable then $\bigcirc A$ is derivable"

whereas in LTL it reads

"for any $\mathcal{F}$, if A is derivable from $\mathcal{F}$ then $\bigcirc A$ is derivable from $\mathcal{F}$".

If we want, however, to axiomatize LTL_0 such that the relation $\mathcal{F} \vdash A$ mirrors the relation $\mathcal{F} \overset{0}{\models} A$ of initial consequence then Σ_{LTL} is no longer appropriate. For example, the rule $A \vdash \bigcirc A$ would not be sound any more with respect to this reading. One possible formal system Σ_{LTL_0} for LTL_0 in this sense is given as follows:

Axioms

(taut$_0$) $\Box A$ for all tautologically valid formulas,
(ltl1$_0$) $\Box(\neg\bigcirc A \leftrightarrow \bigcirc\neg A)$,
(ltl2$_0$) $\Box(\bigcirc(A \rightarrow B) \rightarrow (\bigcirc A \rightarrow \bigcirc B))$,
(ltl3$_0$) $\Box(\Box A \rightarrow A \land \bigcirc\Box A)$.

Rules

(mp) $A, A \rightarrow B \vdash B$,
(mp$_0$) $\Box A, \Box(A \rightarrow B) \vdash \Box B$,
(refl$_0$) $\Box A \vdash A$,
(nex$_0$) $\Box A \vdash \Box\circ A$,
(ind$_0$) $\Box(A \rightarrow B), \Box(A \rightarrow \circ A) \vdash \Box(A \rightarrow \Box B)$.

The axioms (taut$_0$), (ltl1$_0$), (ltl2$_0$), and (ltl3$_0$) are obvious transcriptions from the axioms of Σ_{LTL}. Modus ponens occurs in the usual form (mp) and in a transcribed version (mp$_0$). The rules (nex$_0$) and (ind$_0$) are adjustments of (nex) and (ind) of Σ_{LTL}. The additional rule (refl$_0$) reminds us of the reflexivity law (T4).

Theorem 2.6.6 (Soundness Theorem for Σ_{LTL_0}). *Let A be a formula and $\mathcal{F}$ a set of formulas. If $\mathcal{F} \vdash_{\Sigma_{\mathrm{LTL}_0}} A$ then $\mathcal{F} \overset{0}{\vDash} A$. In particular: if $\vdash_{\Sigma_{\mathrm{LTL}_0}} A$ then $\overset{0}{\vDash} A$.*

Proof. The proof runs by induction on the assumed derivation of A from $\mathcal{F}$.

1. All axioms of Σ_{LTL_0} are of the form $\Box A$ where A is an axiom of Σ_{LTL}. Together with rule (alw) we get $\vdash_{\Sigma_{\mathrm{LTL}}} \Box A$, which implies $\vDash \Box A$ by Theorem 2.3.1, and hence $\overset{0}{\vDash} \Box A$ by Theorem 2.6.4. This implies $\mathcal{F} \overset{0}{\vDash} \Box A$ for all axioms $\Box A$ of Σ_{LTL_0}.
2. If $A \in \mathcal{F}$ then $\mathcal{F} \overset{0}{\vDash} A$ holds trivially.
3. If A is concluded by a rule of Σ_{LTL_0} then, by induction hypothesis, we have $\mathcal{F} \overset{0}{\vDash} C$ for the premises C of that rule. So, for a temporal structure K with $\overset{0}{\vDash}_{\mathsf{K}} B$ for all $B \in \mathcal{F}$ we have $\overset{0}{\vDash}_{\mathsf{K}} C$, i.e., $\mathsf{K}_0(C) = \mathrm{tt}$ for these C. It remains to show that, for each rule, this implies $\mathsf{K}_0(A) = \mathrm{tt}$. For the rule (mp) the claim follows directly using Lemma 2.1.1. For (mp$_0$), $\mathsf{K}_0(\Box B) = \mathsf{K}_0(\Box(B \rightarrow A)) = \mathrm{tt}$ means $\mathsf{K}_i(B) = \mathsf{K}_i(B \rightarrow A) = \mathrm{tt}$ for every $i \in \mathbb{N}$ and yields $\mathsf{K}_i(A) = \mathrm{tt}$ for every $i \in \mathbb{N}$ by Lemma 2.1.1, and therefore we obtain $\mathsf{K}_0(\Box A) = \mathrm{tt}$. For (refl$_0$), $\mathsf{K}_0(\Box A) = \mathrm{tt}$ clearly implies $\mathsf{K}_0(A) = \mathrm{tt}$. If $A \equiv \Box\circ B$ is the conclusion of (nex$_0$), the premise C is of the form $\Box B$, and $\mathsf{K}_0(\Box B) = \mathrm{tt}$ implies $\mathsf{K}_i(B) = \mathrm{tt}$ for every $i \geq 1$, which means $\mathsf{K}_0(\Box\circ B) = \mathrm{tt}$. Finally, in the case of (ind$_0$), $\mathsf{K}_0(\Box(D \rightarrow E)) = \mathrm{tt}$ and $\mathsf{K}_0(\Box(D \rightarrow \circ D)) = \mathrm{tt}$ imply $\mathsf{K}_i(D \rightarrow E) = \mathrm{tt}$ and $\mathsf{K}_i(D \rightarrow \circ D) = \mathrm{tt}$ for every $i \in \mathbb{N}$. Let $j \in \mathbb{N}$ and assume that $\mathsf{K}_j(D) = \mathrm{tt}$. As in the proof of Theorem 2.3.1 we obtain $\mathsf{K}_k(E) = \mathrm{tt}$ for every $k \geq j$, hence $\mathsf{K}_j(D \rightarrow \Box E) = \mathrm{tt}$. Since j is arbitrary this implies $\mathsf{K}_0(\Box(D \rightarrow \Box E)) = \mathrm{tt}$. △

The (weak) completeness of Σ_{LTL_0} can be reduced to that of Σ_{LTL} proved in Sect. 2.4. (In fact, we have stated Σ_{LTL_0} in just such a form that this reduction is directly possible.) The crucial step is the following proof-theoretical counterpart of (the "only if" part of) Theorem 2.6.4:

Lemma 2.6.7. *Let A be a formula. If $\vdash_{\Sigma_{\mathrm{LTL}}} A$ then $\vdash_{\Sigma_{\mathrm{LTL}_0}} A$.*

Proof. Assume that $\vdash_{\Sigma_{\mathrm{LTL}}} A$. We show $\vdash_{\Sigma_{\mathrm{LTL}_0}} \Box A$ by induction on the presumed derivation of A in Σ_{LTL} from which the assertion of the lemma follows immediately with an application of the rule (refl$_0$).

If A is an axiom of Σ_{LTL} then $\Box A$ is an axiom of Σ_{LTL_0} and therefore derivable in the latter. If A is concluded from premises B and $B \to A$ by (mp) then we have $\vdash_{\Sigma_{\mathrm{LTL}_0}} \Box B$ and $\vdash_{\Sigma_{\mathrm{LTL}_0}} \Box(B \to A)$ by induction hypothesis and therefore $\vdash_{\Sigma_{\mathrm{LTL}_0}} \Box A$ with (mp_0). If $A \equiv \bigcirc B$ is concluded from B with (nex) then, by induction hypothesis, $\Box B$ is derivable in Σ_{LTL_0} and so is $\Box\bigcirc B$, i.e., $\Box A$ with (nex_0). Finally, if $A \equiv B \to \Box C$ is the conclusion of applying (ind) to $B \to C$ and $B \to \bigcirc B$ then $\Box(B \to C)$ and $\Box(B \to \bigcirc B)$ are derivable in Σ_{LTL_0} by induction hypothesis, and $\Box(B \to \Box C)$ is obtained by (ind_0). △

With this lemma we are able to establish the weak completeness of Σ_{LTL_0}:

Theorem 2.6.8 (Weak Completeness Theorem for Σ_{LTL_0}). Σ_{LTL_0} *is weakly complete, i.e., for every finite set $\mathcal{F}$ of formulas and formula A, if $\mathcal{F} \overset{0}{\vDash} A$ then $\mathcal{F} \vdash_{\Sigma_{\mathrm{LTL}_0}} A$. In particular: if $\overset{0}{\vDash} A$ then $\vdash_{\Sigma_{\mathrm{LTL}_0}} A$.*

Proof. Let $\mathcal{F} = \{A_1, \ldots, A_n\}$ where $n \geq 0$. We then have

$$\begin{aligned}
\mathcal{F} \overset{0}{\vDash} A &\Rightarrow \overset{0}{\vDash} A_1 \to (A_2 \to \ldots \to (A_n \to A)\ldots) \\
&\qquad\qquad \text{(by Theorem 2.6.3, applied } n \text{ times)} \\
&\Rightarrow \vDash A_1 \to (A_2 \to \ldots \to (A_n \to A)\ldots) \\
&\qquad\qquad \text{(by Theorem 2.6.4)} \\
&\Rightarrow \vdash_{\Sigma_{\mathrm{LTL}}} A_1 \to (A_2 \to \ldots \to (A_n \to A)\ldots) \\
&\qquad\qquad \text{(by Theorem 2.4.10)} \\
&\Rightarrow \vdash_{\Sigma_{\mathrm{LTL}_0}} A_1 \to (A_2 \to \ldots \to (A_n \to A)\ldots) \\
&\qquad\qquad \text{(by Lemma 2.6.7)} \\
&\Rightarrow \mathcal{F} \vdash_{\Sigma_{\mathrm{LTL}_0}} A \qquad \text{(by (mp), applied } n \text{ times).}
\end{aligned}$$

△

We do not want to develop the proof theory of LTL_0 in further detail. We only remark that the Deduction Theorem (and its converse) for Σ_{LTL_0} holds in the classical form

$$\mathcal{F} \cup \{A\} \vdash_{\Sigma_{\mathrm{LTL}_0}} B \;\Leftrightarrow\; \mathcal{F} \vdash_{\Sigma_{\mathrm{LTL}_0}} A \to B$$

which obviously corresponds to the semantical considerations above.

Bibliographical Notes

As mentioned in the Second Reading paragraph in Sect. 2.3, temporal logic is a branch of modal logic, a detailed presentation of which can be found, e.g., in [21, 66]. The "possible worlds" semantics (here adapted to the notion of temporal structures) was introduced by Kripke [76]. Prior [125] was the first to suggest a "temporal" interpretation of the modal operators $\Box$ and $\Diamond$ as "always" and "sometime". An overview of different subsequent developments can be found in [130].

In the framework of a discrete and linearly ordered time structure, v. Wright [156] developed a logic with the operators "always" and "next" which was axiomatized by Prior [126] who also suggested using the logical formalism for proofs of the "working of digital computers". Prior attributes the axiomatization to Lemmon. Probably it should appear in [90] but Lemmon died before finishing this book. Other similar formal systems were given by Scott (reported in [126]), Clifford [36], and Segerberg [136].

A first concrete mention of how the modal operators "always" and "sometime" could be used in program verification was given by Burstall [25]. This idea was elaborated by Pnueli [120]. Kröger [77, 78] developed logics with "next" and used the operators "next", "always", and "sometime" in the field of verification of (sequential) programs in [79]. Pnueli [121] introduced the (normal) semantical apparatus for this logic as described in this book and applied it to concurrent programs.

From that time on, a large number of investigations arose. We will cite extracts from the relevant literature in the following chapters. Here we only add some remarks with respect to the contents of Sects. 2.4–2.6. The completeness proof presented in Sect. 2.4 is based on proofs given in [79] and [132]. The tableau method is a very general approach to show the decidability of logics. A survey of its application in the area of temporal logics is given in [160]. Initial validity semantics was introduced in [100], some other semantical aspects are discussed in [44].

3

Extensions of LTL

We have so far considered the temporal operators $\bigcirc$ and $\Box$, which are the basic equipment of (propositional) linear temporal logic. In this chapter we present some extensions by additional propositional operators that have been found useful for different applications. These extensions are introduced as separate "modules" on top of the basic logic LTL. Of course, appropriate combinations of the extensions are possible as we will indicate in Sect. 3.6.

The following discussions will show that some of the results that have been developed for LTL have to be modified for certain extensions. Important changes (mainly concerning the Deduction Theorem, which already had to be modified for LTL_0 in Sect. 2.6) will be mentioned explicitly. However, most of the previous results – particularly the validity of the temporal logic laws (T1)–(T38) – carry over to the extensions as well and will be used without justifying them anew. In fact, their proofs would go through unmodified except for the obvious extensions.

3.1 Binary Temporal Operators

As a first extension of LTL we introduce binary temporal operators. In contrast to the unary operators $\bigcirc$ and $\Box$ that can be used to express that the argument formula holds in states somehow related to the present state, binary operators have two arguments A and B and express statements about truth or falsity of these argument formulas in states related to each other as well as to the present state. Some popular examples of such statements are informally given by the following phrases:

"A will hold in all subsequent states until B holds",
"A will hold in the next state in which B holds",
"A will hold before B holds".

These informal statements leave some choices on how to interpret them precisely, as we will illustrate with the first of the phrases. We know already from the always operator that "in all subsequent" states may include the present state, but we can interpret it also more strictly counting only states after the present one. Furthermore, the informal wording does not state whether B will actually hold in the future. In a "strong" version this is the case; in a "weak" version B need not become true, and A should therefore hold "forever".

We thus get four possible readings that are represented by four different binary operators denoted by **until**, **unt**, **unless**, and **unl** with the following informal interpretations:

A **until** B:	"There is a (strictly) subsequent state in which B holds, and A holds until that state",
A **unt** B:	"There is a subsequent state (possibly the present one) in which B holds, and A holds until that state",
A **unless** B:	"If there is a (strictly) subsequent state in which B holds then A holds until that state or else A holds permanently",
A **unl** B:	"If there is a subsequent state (possibly the present one) in which B holds then A holds until that state or else A holds permanently".

The operators **until** and **unt** are called *strict* and *non-strict* (or *reflexive*) *until operator*, respectively. They are *strong* operators because they demand that B will hold sometime. In contrast, **unless** and **unl** are the *weak* versions of **until** and **unt** and are called *strict* and *non-strict* (*reflexive*) *unless* or *waiting-for operators*.

Actually, there are still some more choices when interpreting the informal phrase "A holds until that state". Clearly, A should hold over an interval of states, determined by the present state and "that state", but the formulation is ambiguous about whether the end points of this interval are included or not. Instead of introducing even more operators to distinguish these possibilities, we choose to include the present state in the non-strict versions and to exclude it in the strict ones; the other end point is not included in either case.

To make these considerations precise, we define the semantics of the four operators in the framework introduced in Sect. 2.1. Given a temporal structure K and $i \in \mathbb{N}$, these definitions are as follows.

- $\mathsf{K}_i(A \textbf{ until } B) = \mathsf{tt} \Leftrightarrow \mathsf{K}_j(B) = \mathsf{tt}$ for some $j > i$ and
  $\mathsf{K}_k(A) = \mathsf{tt}$ for every k, $i < k < j$.
- $\mathsf{K}_i(A \textbf{ unt } B) = \mathsf{tt} \Leftrightarrow \mathsf{K}_j(B) = \mathsf{tt}$ for some $j \geq i$ and
  $\mathsf{K}_k(A) = \mathsf{tt}$ for every k, $i \leq k < j$.
- $\mathsf{K}_i(A \textbf{ unless } B) = \mathsf{tt} \Leftrightarrow \mathsf{K}_j(B) = \mathsf{tt}$ for some $j > i$ and
  $\mathsf{K}_k(A) = \mathsf{tt}$ for every k, $i < k < j$
  or
  $\mathsf{K}_k(A) = \mathsf{tt}$ for every $k > i$.
- $\mathsf{K}_i(A \textbf{ unl } B) = \mathsf{tt} \Leftrightarrow \mathsf{K}_j(B) = \mathsf{tt}$ for some $j \geq i$ and
  $\mathsf{K}_k(A) = \mathsf{tt}$ for every k, $i \leq k < j$
  or
  $\mathsf{K}_k(A) = \mathsf{tt}$ for every $k \geq i$.

(We should remark that the designations of the binary operators of temporal logic are not universally agreed upon, and this can be a source of confusion. For example, many authors write **until** for the operator that we denote by **unt**.)

Example. Consider, for $v_1, v_2 \in \mathbf{V}$, the four formulas $A_1 \equiv v_1 \,\mathbf{until}\, \Box v_2$, $A_2 \equiv v_1 \,\mathbf{unt}\, \Box v_2$, $B_1 \equiv v_2 \,\mathbf{unless}\, \Box v_1$, $B_2 \equiv v_2 \,\mathbf{unl}\, \Box v_1$, and let K be given by:

	η_0	η_1	η_2	η_3	η_4	$\dots$
v_1	ff	tt	tt	ff	ff	...(ff forever)...
v_2	tt	tt	ff	tt	tt	...(tt forever)...

Then $\mathsf{K}_i(\Box v_2) = \mathrm{ff}$ for $i < 3$ and $\mathsf{K}_i(\Box v_2) = \mathrm{tt}$ for $i \geq 3$ and therefore:

$$\begin{aligned}
&\mathsf{K}_0(A_1) = \mathrm{tt}, \mathsf{K}_0(A_2) = \mathrm{ff},\\
&\mathsf{K}_1(A_1) = \mathsf{K}_1(A_2) = \mathrm{tt},\\
&\mathsf{K}_i(A_1) = \mathrm{tt} \;\text{ for } i \geq 2\\
&\qquad\qquad\qquad (\text{since } \mathsf{K}_{i+1}(\Box v_2) = \mathrm{tt} \text{ and there is no } k \text{ with } i < k < i+1),\\
&\mathsf{K}_2(A_2) = \mathrm{tt},\\
&\mathsf{K}_i(A_2) = \mathrm{tt} \;\text{ for } i \geq 3\\
&\qquad\qquad\qquad (\text{since } \mathsf{K}_i(\Box v_2) = \mathrm{tt} \text{ and there is no } k \text{ with } i \leq k < i).
\end{aligned}$$

Furthermore, because of $\mathsf{K}_j(\Box v_1) = \mathrm{ff}$ for every $j \in \mathbb{N}$ we have:

$$\begin{aligned}
&\mathsf{K}_i(B_1) = \mathsf{K}_i(B_2) = \mathrm{ff} \;\text{ for } i \leq 1,\\
&\mathsf{K}_2(B_1) = \mathrm{tt}, \mathsf{K}_2(B_2) = \mathrm{ff},\\
&\mathsf{K}_i(B_1) = \mathsf{K}_i(B_2) = \mathrm{tt} \;\text{ for } i \geq 3.
\end{aligned}$$

△

From the formal definitions, it should be clear that there are simple relationships between the operators. We note some of them as valid formulas:

(Tb1) $A \,\mathbf{until}\, B \leftrightarrow \bigcirc\Diamond B \land A \,\mathbf{unless}\, B$,
(Tb2) $A \,\mathbf{unless}\, B \leftrightarrow \bigcirc(A \,\mathbf{unl}\, B)$,
(Tb3) $A \,\mathbf{unl}\, B \leftrightarrow A \,\mathbf{unt}\, B \lor \Box A$,
(Tb4) $A \,\mathbf{unt}\, B \leftrightarrow B \lor (A \land A \,\mathbf{until}\, B)$.

(We save parentheses by assigning all binary temporal operators introduced in this section higher priority than the classical binary operators.) These laws show in fact that all the versions can be expressed by each other (and $\bigcirc$ and $\Box$). The validity proofs are easy calculations:

Proof of (Tb1)–(Tb4). For any temporal structure K and $i \in \mathbb{N}$ we have:

$$\begin{aligned}
\mathsf{K}_i(A \,\mathbf{until}\, B) = \mathrm{tt} &\Leftrightarrow \mathsf{K}_j(B) = \mathrm{tt} \;\text{ for some } j > i \text{ and}\\
&\; \mathsf{K}_k(A) = \mathrm{tt} \;\text{ for every } k,\, i < k < j\\
&\Leftrightarrow \mathsf{K}_{i+1}(\Diamond B) = \mathrm{tt} \text{ and } \mathsf{K}_i(A \,\mathbf{unless}\, B) = \mathrm{tt}\\
&\Leftrightarrow \mathsf{K}_i(\bigcirc\Diamond B \land A \,\mathbf{unless}\, B) = \mathrm{tt}.
\end{aligned}$$

$$\begin{aligned}
\mathsf{K}_i(A\ \textbf{unless}\ B) = \mathsf{tt} \Leftrightarrow\ & \mathsf{K}_j(B) = \mathsf{tt} \text{ for some } j > i \text{ and} \\
& \mathsf{K}_k(A) = \mathsf{tt} \text{ for every } k,\ i < k < j \\
& \text{or} \\
& \mathsf{K}_k(A) = \mathsf{tt} \text{ for every } k > i \\
\Leftrightarrow\ & \mathsf{K}_j(B) = \mathsf{tt} \text{ for some } j \geq i+1 \text{ and} \\
& \mathsf{K}_k(A) = \mathsf{tt} \text{ for every } k,\ i+1 < k < j \\
& \text{or} \\
& \mathsf{K}_k(A) = \mathsf{tt} \text{ for every } k \geq i+1 \\
\Leftrightarrow\ & \mathsf{K}_{i+1}(A\ \textbf{unl}\ B) = \mathsf{tt} \\
\Leftrightarrow\ & \mathsf{K}_i(\bigcirc(A\ \textbf{unl}\ B)) = \mathsf{tt}.
\end{aligned}$$

$$\begin{aligned}
\mathsf{K}_i(A\ \textbf{unl}\ B) = \mathsf{tt} \Leftrightarrow\ & \mathsf{K}_j(B) = \mathsf{tt} \text{ for some } j \geq i \text{ and} \\
& \mathsf{K}_k(A) = \mathsf{tt} \text{ for every } k,\ i \leq k < j \\
& \text{or} \\
& \mathsf{K}_k(A) = \mathsf{tt} \text{ for every } k \geq i \\
\Leftrightarrow\ & \mathsf{K}_i(A\ \textbf{unt}\ B) = \mathsf{tt} \text{ or } \mathsf{K}_i(\Box A) = \mathsf{tt} \\
\Leftrightarrow\ & \mathsf{K}_i(A\ \textbf{unt}\ B \vee \Box A) = \mathsf{tt}.
\end{aligned}$$

$$\begin{aligned}
\mathsf{K}_i(A\ \textbf{unt}\ B) = \mathsf{tt} \Leftrightarrow\ & \mathsf{K}_j(B) = \mathsf{tt} \text{ for some } j \geq i \text{ and} \\
& \mathsf{K}_k(A) = \mathsf{tt} \text{ for every } k,\ i \leq k < j \\
\Leftrightarrow\ & \mathsf{K}_i(B) = \mathsf{tt} \\
& \text{or} \\
& \mathsf{K}_j(B) = \mathsf{tt} \text{ for some } j > i \text{ and} \\
& \mathsf{K}_k(A) = \mathsf{tt} \text{ for every } k,\ i \leq k < j \\
\Leftrightarrow\ & \mathsf{K}_i(B) = \mathsf{tt} \\
& \text{or} \\
& \mathsf{K}_i(A) = \mathsf{tt} \text{ and } \mathsf{K}_j(B) = \mathsf{tt} \text{ for some } j > i \text{ and} \\
& \mathsf{K}_k(A) = \mathsf{tt} \text{ for every } k,\ i < k < j \\
\Leftrightarrow\ & \mathsf{K}_i(B \vee (A \wedge A\ \textbf{until}\ B)) = \mathsf{tt}.
\end{aligned}$$

△

Similarly, we could introduce various versions of binary operators as formal counterparts to the two other informal phrases at the beginning of this section. We restrict ourselves, however, to defining only the strict and weak operators **atnext** (*atnext* or *first time operator*) and **before** (*before* or *precedence operator*) with the semantical definitions

- $\mathsf{K}_i(A\ \textbf{atnext}\ B) = \mathsf{tt} \Leftrightarrow \mathsf{K}_j(B) = \mathsf{ff}$ for every $j > i$ or
  $\mathsf{K}_k(A) = \mathsf{tt}$ for the smallest $k > i$ with $\mathsf{K}_k(B) = \mathsf{tt}$,
- $\mathsf{K}_i(A\ \textbf{before}\ B) = \mathsf{tt} \Leftrightarrow$ for every $j > i$ with $\mathsf{K}_j(B) = \mathsf{tt}$
  there is some k, $i < k < j$, with $\mathsf{K}_k(A) = \mathsf{tt}$.

Definitions for the reflexive and/or strong versions of these operators would be obvious and as above, the different versions would be mutually expressible. It is more interesting to observe that all binary operators introduced so far can be expressed by each other. Having already established the mutual expressibility of the different "until" operators as laws (Tb1)–(Tb4), this fact follows from the validity of the following laws.

(Tb5) A **unless** $B \leftrightarrow B$ **atnext** $(A \rightarrow B)$,
(Tb6) A **atnext** $B \leftrightarrow B$ **before** $(\neg A \wedge B)$,
(Tb7) A **before** $B \leftrightarrow \neg(A \vee B)$ **unless** $(A \wedge \neg B)$.

Again the proofs are simple calculations; we only give one example.

Proof of (Tb5). For any temporal structure K and $i \in \mathbb{N}$ we have:

$$\begin{aligned}
\mathsf{K}_i(A\ \textbf{unless}\ B) = \mathrm{tt} \Leftrightarrow\ & \mathsf{K}_j(B) = \mathrm{tt} \text{ for some } j > i \text{ and} \\
& \mathsf{K}_k(A) = \mathrm{tt} \text{ for every } k,\ i < k < j \\
& \text{or} \\
& \mathsf{K}_k(A) = \mathrm{tt} \text{ for every } k > i \\
\Leftrightarrow\ & \text{there is a smallest } j > i \text{ with } \mathsf{K}_j(B) = \mathrm{tt} \text{ and} \\
& \mathsf{K}_k(A) = \mathrm{tt} \text{ for every } k,\ i < k < j \\
& \text{or} \\
& \mathsf{K}_k(A) = \mathrm{tt} \text{ and } \mathsf{K}_k(B) = \mathrm{ff} \text{ for every } k > i \\
\Leftrightarrow\ & \mathsf{K}_j(B) = \mathrm{tt} \text{ for the smallest } j > i \text{ with} \\
& \mathsf{K}_j(A \rightarrow B) = \mathrm{tt} \\
& \text{or} \\
& \mathsf{K}_k(A \rightarrow B) = \mathrm{ff} \text{ for every } k > i \\
\Leftrightarrow\ & \mathsf{K}_i(B\ \textbf{atnext}\ (A \rightarrow B)) = \mathrm{tt}.
\end{aligned}$$

△

To conclude the discussion about the linguistic power of all these operators we still note that the basic operators $\bigcirc$ and $\Box$ can also be expressed by each of the strict operators (using no other operator), e.g.:

(Tb8) $\bigcirc A \leftrightarrow A$ **atnext true**,
(Tb9) $\Box A \leftrightarrow A \wedge A$ **unless false**.

For $\Box$ (but not for $\bigcirc$) similar equivalences hold for the non-strict operators, e.g.:

(Tb10) $\Box A \leftrightarrow A$ **unl false**.

The proofs are quite trivial, e.g.:

Proof of (Tb9). For any temporal structure K and $i \in \mathbb{N}$ we have:

$$\begin{aligned}
\mathsf{K}_i(\Box A) = \mathrm{tt} \Leftrightarrow\ & \mathsf{K}_j(A) = \mathrm{tt} \text{ for every } j \geq i \\
\Leftrightarrow\ & \mathsf{K}_i(A) = \mathrm{tt} \text{ and } \mathsf{K}_k(A) = \mathrm{tt} \text{ for every } k > i \\
\Leftrightarrow\ & \mathsf{K}_i(A) = \mathrm{tt} \\
& \text{and} \\
& \quad \mathsf{K}_j(\textbf{false}) = \mathrm{tt} \text{ for some } j > i \text{ and} \\
& \quad \mathsf{K}_k(A) = \mathrm{tt} \text{ for every } k,\ i < k < j \\
& \quad \text{or} \\
& \quad \mathsf{K}_k(A) = \mathrm{tt} \text{ for every } k > i \\
\Leftrightarrow\ & \mathsf{K}_i(A \wedge A\ \textbf{unless false}) = \mathrm{tt}.
\end{aligned}$$

△

On the other hand, we will prove in Sect. 4.1 that none of the binary operators can be defined just from $\circ$ and $\Box$.

In Sect. 2.2 we mentioned fixpoint characterizations for $\Box$ and $\Diamond$. Such characterizations also exist for the new operators and are given by the following laws:

(Tb11) $A\ \mathbf{until}\ B \leftrightarrow \circ B \lor \circ(A \land A\ \mathbf{until}\ B)$,
(Tb12) $A\ \mathbf{unless}\ B \leftrightarrow \circ B \lor \circ(A \land A\ \mathbf{unless}\ B)$,
(Tb13) $A\ \mathbf{unt}\ B \leftrightarrow B \lor (A \land \circ(A\ \mathbf{unt}\ B))$,
(Tb14) $A\ \mathbf{unl}\ B \leftrightarrow B \lor (A \land \circ(A\ \mathbf{unl}\ B))$,
(Tb15) $A\ \mathbf{atnext}\ B \leftrightarrow \circ(B \rightarrow A) \land \circ(\neg B \rightarrow A\ \mathbf{atnext}\ B)$,
(Tb16) $A\ \mathbf{before}\ B \leftrightarrow \circ\neg B \land \circ(A \lor A\ \mathbf{before}\ B)$.

It is worth noting that the recursive equivalences for the strong and weak versions of an operator are of the same shape. The strict and non-strict versions differ only by the scope of operators $\circ$. Again we show only one proof, the others being analogous.

Proof of (Tb15). For any temporal structure K and $i \in \mathbb{N}$ we have:

$$
\begin{aligned}
\mathsf{K}_i(A\ \mathbf{atnext}\ B) = \mathrm{tt} \Leftrightarrow\ & \mathsf{K}_j(B) = \mathrm{ff} \text{ for every } j > i \text{ or} \\
& \mathsf{K}_k(A) = \mathrm{tt} \text{ for the smallest } k > i \text{ with } \mathsf{K}_k(B) = \mathrm{tt} \\
\Leftrightarrow\ & \mathsf{K}_{i+1}(A) = \mathsf{K}_{i+1}(B) = \mathrm{tt} \\
& \text{or} \\
& \mathsf{K}_j(B) = \mathrm{ff} \text{ for every } j > i \\
& \text{or} \\
& \mathsf{K}_{i+1}(B) = \mathrm{ff} \text{ and } \mathsf{K}_k(A) = \mathrm{tt} \\
& \text{for the smallest } k > i+1 \text{ with } \mathsf{K}_k(B) = \mathrm{tt} \\
\Leftrightarrow\ & \mathsf{K}_{i+1}(A) = \mathsf{K}_{i+1}(B) = \mathrm{tt} \\
& \text{or} \\
& \mathsf{K}_{i+1}(B) = \mathrm{ff} \text{ and } \mathsf{K}_{i+1}(A\ \mathbf{atnext}\ B) = \mathrm{tt} \\
\Leftrightarrow\ & \text{if } \mathsf{K}_{i+1}(B) = \mathrm{tt} \text{ then } \mathsf{K}_{i+1}(A) = \mathrm{tt} \\
& \text{and} \\
& \text{if } \mathsf{K}_{i+1}(B) = \mathrm{ff} \text{ then } \mathsf{K}_{i+1}(A\ \mathbf{atnext}\ B) = \mathrm{tt} \\
\Leftrightarrow\ & \mathsf{K}_i(\circ(B \rightarrow A) \land \circ(\neg B \rightarrow A\ \mathbf{atnext}\ B)) = \mathrm{tt}. \qquad \triangle
\end{aligned}
$$

Let us now summarize our discussion for the extension of the basic language $\mathcal{L}_{\mathrm{LTL}}$ with binary operators. We call the extended language $\mathcal{L}_{\mathrm{LTL}}^{\mathrm{b}}$ and define it to be obtained from $\mathcal{L}_{\mathrm{LTL}}$ by adding the symbol **op**, among the above binary operators, to the alphabet and the formation rule

- If A and B are formulas then $(A\ \mathbf{op}\ B)$ is a formula

to its syntax (with the notational convention that **op** has higher priority than the binary operators of propositional logic).

We leave it at this "parametric" definition instead of fixing an actual choice for **op**. As we have seen, any one of the operators can be taken for **op**, and all the others can then be introduced as abbreviations. If **op** is a strict binary operator, it could even serve as the sole basic temporal operator of $\mathcal{L}_{\mathrm{LTL}}^{\mathrm{b}}$ because $\circ$ and $\Box$ are then expressible. If **op** is non-strict, $\circ$ still needs to be present but $\Box$ could be introduced as an abbreviation.

The semantics of the new operators of $\mathcal{L}_{\mathrm{LTL}}^{\mathrm{b}}$ has already been defined above, and the proof theory for the extended logic (which we will denote by LTL+b) can be given quite uniformly. For any choice of the operator **op**, the formal system Σ_{LTL} needs to be extended by two additional axioms to obtain a sound and weakly complete formal system $\Sigma_{\mathrm{LTL}}^{\mathrm{b}}$ for LTL+b. One of these axioms is the fixpoint characterization of the operator **op** and the other one indicates whether **op** is strong or weak (remember that the fixpoint characterizations of the strong and weak versions of the operators are "equal"). So, e.g., if we choose **until** as the basic operator, the additional axioms are

(until1) $A\ \mathbf{until}\ B \leftrightarrow \circ B \vee \circ(A \wedge A\ \mathbf{until}\ B)$,
(until2) $A\ \mathbf{until}\ B \rightarrow \circ\Diamond B$.

The axiom (until1) is just (Tb11), whereas (until2) expresses that **until** is a strong operator because the formula A **until** B implies that B must hold sometime in the (strict) future.

In the case of **unless** we take

(unless1) $A\ \mathbf{unless}\ B \leftrightarrow \circ B \vee \circ(A \wedge A\ \mathbf{unless}\ B)$,
(unless2) $\circ\Box A \rightarrow A\ \mathbf{unless}\ B$.

The axiom (unless2) expresses that **unless** is a weak operator because the formula A **unless** B holds if A will always hold in the (strict) future, irrespective of B.

For the non-strict operators **unt** and **unl**, we have to replace the axioms (until1) and (unless1) by (Tb13) or (Tb14) and the axioms (until2) and (unless2) by the obvious versions

(unt2) $A\ \mathbf{unt}\ B \rightarrow \Diamond B$

or

(unl2) $\Box A \rightarrow A\ \mathbf{unl}\ B$,

respectively. If we choose the atnext operator then

(atnext1) $A\ \mathbf{atnext}\ B \leftrightarrow \circ(B \rightarrow A) \wedge \circ(\neg B \rightarrow A\ \mathbf{atnext}\ B)$,
(atnext2) $\circ\Box\neg B \rightarrow A\ \mathbf{atnext}\ B$

are appropriate and, finally, for the before operator the axioms are

(before1) $A\ \mathbf{before}\ B \leftrightarrow \circ\neg B \wedge \circ(A \vee A\ \mathbf{before}\ B)$,
(before2) $\circ\Box\neg B \rightarrow A\ \mathbf{before}\ B$.

Again we give a formal validity proof only for one of these cases:

Proof of (before2). For any temporal structure K and $i \in \mathbb{N}$ we have:

$$\begin{aligned} \mathsf{K}_i(\circ\Box\neg B) = \mathsf{tt} &\Leftrightarrow \mathsf{K}_j(B) = \mathsf{ff} \text{ for every } j > i \\ &\Rightarrow \text{for every } j > i \text{ with } \mathsf{K}_j(B) = \mathsf{tt} \\ &\quad\ \ \text{there is some } k, i < k < j \text{ with } \mathsf{K}_k(A) = \mathsf{tt} \\ &\Leftrightarrow \mathsf{K}_i(A\ \mathbf{before}\ B) = \mathsf{tt}. \end{aligned}$$

△

As a simple example of application, we derive a formula within $\Sigma_{\mathrm{LTL}}^{\mathrm{b}}$ (with (unless1) and (unless2)) that can be considered as a fixpoint characterization of $\neg(A\ \mathbf{unless}\ B)$:

(Tb17) $\neg(A\ \mathbf{unless}\ B) \leftrightarrow \bigcirc\neg B \wedge \bigcirc(\neg A \vee \neg(A\ \mathbf{unless}\ B))$.

Derivation of (Tb17).

(1)	$A\ \mathbf{unless}\ B \leftrightarrow \bigcirc B \vee \bigcirc(A \wedge A\ \mathbf{unless}\ B)$	(unless1)
(2)	$\neg(A\ \mathbf{unless}\ B) \leftrightarrow \neg\bigcirc B \wedge \neg\bigcirc(A \wedge A\ \mathbf{unless}\ B)$	(prop),(1)
(3)	$\neg(A\ \mathbf{unless}\ B) \leftrightarrow \bigcirc\neg B \wedge \bigcirc\neg(A \wedge A\ \mathbf{unless}\ B)$	(prop),(ltl1),(2)
(4)	$\bigcirc\neg(A \wedge A\ \mathbf{unless}\ B) \leftrightarrow \bigcirc(\neg A \vee \neg(A\ \mathbf{unless}\ B))$	(taut),(T30)
(5)	$\neg(A\ \mathbf{unless}\ B) \leftrightarrow \bigcirc\neg B \wedge \bigcirc(\neg A \vee \neg(A\ \mathbf{unless}\ B))$	(prop),(3),(4) △

We have seen the importance of the fixpoint characterizations for these binary operators to express their interplay with the nexttime operator $\bigcirc$. Whereas (T28) provides a similar characterization for the unary always operator $\Box$, its axiomatic characterization required one more fundamental principle, namely the induction rule (ind). Analogous induction principles can also be formulated for the weak binary operators:

(indunless) $A \rightarrow \bigcirc C \vee \bigcirc(A \wedge B) \vdash A \rightarrow B\ \mathbf{unless}\ C$,
(indunl) $A \rightarrow C \vee (B \wedge \bigcirc A) \vdash A \rightarrow B\ \mathbf{unl}\ C$,
(indatnext) $A \rightarrow \bigcirc(C \rightarrow B) \wedge \bigcirc(\neg C \rightarrow A) \vdash A \rightarrow B\ \mathbf{atnext}\ C$,
(indbefore) $A \rightarrow \bigcirc\neg C \wedge \bigcirc(A \vee B) \vdash A \rightarrow B\ \mathbf{before}\ C$.

These rules need not be included in $\Sigma_{\mathrm{LTL}}^{\mathrm{b}}$ because they can already be derived with the help of rule (ind), as we show for one of them:

Derivation of (indunless).

(1)	$A \rightarrow \bigcirc C \vee \bigcirc(A \wedge B)$	assumption
(2)	$\neg(B\ \mathbf{unless}\ C) \rightarrow \neg\bigcirc C \wedge \bigcirc(\neg B \vee \neg(B\ \mathbf{unless}\ C))$	(prop),(Tb17),(ltl1)
(3)	$A \wedge \neg(B\ \mathbf{unless}\ C) \rightarrow \bigcirc B$	(prop),(T15),(1),(2)
(4)	$\neg(B\ \mathbf{unless}\ C) \rightarrow \neg\bigcirc B \vee \bigcirc\neg(B\ \mathbf{unless}\ C)$	(prop),(T16),(ltl1),(2)
(5)	$A \wedge \neg(B\ \mathbf{unless}\ C) \rightarrow \bigcirc(A \wedge \neg(B\ \mathbf{unless}\ C))$	(prop),(T15),(1),(4)
(6)	$A \wedge \neg(B\ \mathbf{unless}\ C) \rightarrow \Box\bigcirc B$	(ind),(3),(5)
(7)	$\bigcirc\Box B \rightarrow B\ \mathbf{unless}\ C$	(unless2)
(8)	$A \wedge \neg(B\ \mathbf{unless}\ C) \rightarrow B\ \mathbf{unless}\ C$	(prop),(T12),(6),(7)
(9)	$A \rightarrow B\ \mathbf{unless}\ C$	(prop),(8) △

The common characteristic feature of the above rules (including the induction rules for $\Box$) is that they all express some form of *computational induction* over state sequences. There is no such induction principle for the operator $\Diamond$ or for the strong binary operators like **until** or **unt**, which imply a formula of the form $\Diamond B$. Only in Chap. 5 will we become able to formulate induction principles of a different nature for this kind of assertion.

We still remark that each of the above induction rules could be used for an alternative axiomatization of LTL+b. The systematic pattern of the axiomatization described above was to take as axioms the fixpoint characterization of a binary operator and a formula expressing whether it is chosen in its strong or weak version, respectively. Another possibility would be to take the fixpoint characterization or, what is actually sufficient, even only "one direction" of it together with the respective rule. For example, with the operator **unless** this would be the axiom

(unless1') $A \textbf{ unless } B \rightarrow \circ B \vee \circ(A \wedge A \textbf{ unless } B)$

and the rule (indunless). In the next section we will see that there is also an intuitive pattern which underlies this form of axiomatization.

We conclude this section by illustrating the new operators with the help of some more logical laws. We restrict ourselves to formulas involving the non-strict unless and the strict atnext operator. Analogous laws can easily be stated for the other operators.

(Tb18) $\Box(\neg B \rightarrow A) \rightarrow A \textbf{ unl } B$,
(Tb19) $\circ(A \textbf{ unl } B) \leftrightarrow \circ A \textbf{ unl } \circ B$,
(Tb20) $(A \wedge B) \textbf{ unl } C \leftrightarrow A \textbf{ unl } C \wedge B \textbf{ unl } C$,
(Tb21) $A \textbf{ unl } (B \vee C) \leftrightarrow A \textbf{ unl } B \vee A \textbf{ unl } C$,
(Tb22) $A \textbf{ unl } (B \wedge C) \rightarrow A \textbf{ unl } B \wedge A \textbf{ unl } C$,
(Tb23) $A \textbf{ unl } (A \textbf{ unl } B) \leftrightarrow A \textbf{ unl } B$,
(Tb24) $(A \textbf{ unl } B) \textbf{ unl } B \leftrightarrow A \textbf{ unl } B$,
(Tb25) $\Box(B \rightarrow A) \rightarrow A \textbf{ atnext } B$,
(Tb26) $\circ(A \textbf{ atnext } B) \leftrightarrow \circ A \textbf{ atnext } \circ B$,
(Tb27) $(A \wedge B) \textbf{ atnext } C \leftrightarrow A \textbf{ atnext } C \wedge B \textbf{ atnext } C$,
(Tb28) $(A \vee B) \textbf{ atnext } C \leftrightarrow A \textbf{ atnext } C \vee B \textbf{ atnext } C$,
(Tb29) $A \textbf{ atnext } (B \vee C) \rightarrow A \textbf{ atnext } B \vee A \textbf{ atnext } C$.

Note that "idempotency" laws like (Tb23) and (Tb24) hold only for non-strict operators but not for the strict ones.

The laws can easily be verified semantically or by a derivation within $\Sigma_{\mathrm{LTL}}^{\mathrm{b}}$. As an example, we show how to derive (Tb25):

Derivation of (Tb25).

(1)	$\Box(B \rightarrow A) \rightarrow \circ(B \rightarrow A)$	(T6)
(2)	$\Box(B \rightarrow A) \rightarrow \circ\Box(B \rightarrow A)$	(prop),(ltl3)
(3)	$\Box(B \rightarrow A) \rightarrow \circ(\neg B \rightarrow \Box(B \rightarrow A))$	(prop),(T14),(2)
(4)	$\Box(B \rightarrow A) \rightarrow \circ(B \rightarrow A) \wedge \circ(\neg B \rightarrow \Box(B \rightarrow A))$	(prop),(1),(3)
(5)	$\Box(B \rightarrow A) \rightarrow A \textbf{ atnext } B$	(indatnext),(4) △

3.2 Fixpoint Operators

The operators $\Box$ and $\Diamond$, as well as the binary operators discussed in the previous section, all satisfy some fixpoint laws. Consider, e.g., the law (T28) concerning the always operator:

$$\Box A \leftrightarrow A \wedge \bigcirc\Box A.$$

This logical equivalence means, in a sense which will be made more precise shortly, that the formula $\Box A$ can be viewed as a "solution" of the "equality"

(i) $\quad u \leftrightarrow A \wedge \bigcirc u$

with the "unknown" u. In the same way, $\Diamond A$ and A **unless** B can be viewed as "solutions" of

(ii) $\quad u \leftrightarrow A \vee \bigcirc u,$
(iii) $\quad u \leftrightarrow \bigcirc B \vee \bigcirc(A \wedge u),$

and similarly for the other connectives. However, given such an equivalence, the corresponding temporal operator may not be determined uniquely. For example, (iii) is also solved by $u \equiv A$ **until** B, while (ii) admits the solution $u \equiv$ **true**.

In order to analyse the situation more formally, let us provisionally extend the underlying alphabet by a set $\mathcal{V}$ of (propositional) variables and allow formulas to contain such variables. For example, the equivalences (i)–(iii) are then formulas containing the variable u. The semantical notions are extended by valuations $\Xi = (\xi_0, \xi_1, \xi_2, \ldots)$ which are infinite sequences of mappings

$$\xi_i : \mathcal{V} \to \{\mathsf{ff}, \mathsf{tt}\},$$

and the value $\mathsf{K}_i^{(\Xi)}(F) \in \{\mathsf{tt}, \mathsf{ff}\}$ is inductively defined as $\mathsf{K}_i(F)$ before, with the provision that

$$\mathsf{K}_i^{(\Xi)}(u) = \xi_i(u) \quad \text{for } u \in \mathcal{V}.$$

We also write $[\![F]\!]_{\mathsf{K}}^{\Xi}$ to denote the set of (indexes of) states of K in which formula F "is true":

$$[\![F]\!]_{\mathsf{K}}^{\Xi} = \{i \in \mathbb{N} \mid \mathsf{K}_i^{(\Xi)}(F) = \mathsf{tt}\}.$$

$[\![F]\!]_{\mathsf{K}}^{\Xi}$ is a subset of $\mathbb{N}$, i.e., an element of the powerset $2^{\mathbb{N}}$ of $\mathbb{N}$.

Consider now, e.g., the equivalence (ii), assume that A does not contain the variable u, and fix some arbitrary K and Ξ. With the "right-hand side" $A \vee \bigcirc u$ we associate the mapping $\Upsilon_{A \vee \bigcirc u} : 2^{\mathbb{N}} \to 2^{\mathbb{N}}$ with

$$\Upsilon_{A \vee \bigcirc u} : \mathbb{M} \mapsto [\![A \vee \bigcirc u]\!]_{\mathsf{K}}^{\Xi[u:\mathbb{M}]}$$

where $\Xi[u\!:\!\mathbb{M}]$ denotes the valuation $(\xi'_0, \xi'_1, \xi'_2, \ldots)$ that agrees with Ξ for all variables except for u, for which it is given by $\xi'_i(u) = \mathsf{tt} \Leftrightarrow i \in \mathbb{M}$. The formulas **true** and $\Diamond A$ are solutions of the equivalence. For **true** we have

$$[\![\mathbf{true}]\!]_{\mathsf{K}}^{\Xi} = \mathbb{N}.$$

With $\Xi[u:\mathbb{M}] = (\xi'_0, \xi'_1, \xi'_2, \ldots)$ such that $\xi'_i(u) = \mathsf{tt} \Leftrightarrow i \in [\![\mathbf{true}]\!]^{\Xi}_{\mathsf{K}}$, i.e., $\xi'_i(u) = \mathsf{tt}$ for every $i \in \mathbb{N}$, we obtain $\mathsf{K}_i^{(\Xi[u:\mathbb{M}])}(A \lor \circ u) = \mathsf{tt}$ for every $i \in \mathbb{N}$ and therefore

$$[\![A \lor \circ u]\!]^{\Xi[u:\mathbb{M}]}_{\mathsf{K}} = \mathbb{N}.$$

This means that

$$\Upsilon_{A \lor \circ u}([\![\mathbf{true}]\!]^{\Xi}_{\mathsf{K}}) = [\![\mathbf{true}]\!]^{\Xi}_{\mathsf{K}}$$

and similarly one can find that

$$\Upsilon_{A \lor \circ u}([\![\Diamond A]\!]^{\Xi}_{\mathsf{K}}) = [\![\Diamond A]\!]^{\Xi}_{\mathsf{K}}.$$

Generally, for a solution C of the equivalence, $[\![C]\!]^{\Xi}_{\mathsf{K}}$ is a fixpoint of $\Upsilon_{A \lor \circ u}$, i.e., a set $\mathbb{M} \subseteq \mathbb{N}$ such that $\Upsilon_{A \lor \circ u}(\mathbb{M}) = \mathbb{M}$. Moreover, the representations $[\![C]\!]^{\Xi}_{\mathsf{K}}$ of solutions can be compared by set inclusion. For example, $[\![\Diamond A]\!]^{\Xi}_{\mathsf{K}} \subseteq [\![\mathbf{true}]\!]^{\Xi}_{\mathsf{K}}$ holds for any K and Ξ, and we summarize all this by simply saying that **true** and $\Diamond A$ are fixpoints of (ii) and $\Diamond A$ is a smaller fixpoint than **true**.

An equivalence may have many fixpoints, and extremal (least or greatest) fixpoints among them are usually of particular interest. In case of (ii), $[\![\mathbf{true}]\!]^{\Xi}_{\mathsf{K}} = \mathbb{N}$, so **true** is obviously the greatest fixpoint (for any K and Ξ) and, in fact, $\Diamond A$ is the least one. To see this, assume that $\mathbb{M} \subseteq \mathbb{N}$ is some set such that

$$(*) \qquad [\![A \lor \circ u]\!]^{\Xi[u:\mathbb{M}]}_{\mathsf{K}} = \mathbb{M}$$

holds. It then suffices to prove that $[\![\Diamond A]\!]^{\Xi}_{\mathsf{K}} \subseteq \mathbb{M}$. To this end, assume that $i \notin \mathbb{M}$ for some $i \in \mathbb{N}$. Inductively, we show that $j \notin \mathbb{M}$ holds for all $j \geq i$: the base case holds by assumption, and if $j \notin \mathbb{M}$ then equation $(*)$ implies that $\mathsf{K}_j^{(\Xi[u:\mathbb{M}])}(A \lor \circ u) = \mathsf{ff}$, which means $\xi'_{j+1}(u) = \mathsf{K}_j^{(\Xi[u:\mathbb{M}])}(\circ u) = \mathsf{ff}$; hence $j \notin [\![\circ u]\!]^{\Xi[u:\mathbb{M}]}_{\mathsf{K}}$ and therefore $j+1 \notin \mathbb{M}$. Moreover, equation $(*)$ analogously implies that, for every $j \notin \mathbb{M}$, $\mathsf{K}_j^{(\Xi)}(A) = \mathsf{K}_j^{(\Xi[u:\mathbb{M}])}(A) = \mathsf{ff}$; hence $j \notin [\![A]\!]^{\Xi}_{\mathsf{K}}$. Together we obtain that $j \notin [\![A]\!]^{\Xi}_{\mathsf{K}}$ for all $j \geq i$, which means $\mathsf{K}_i^{(\Xi)}(\Diamond A) = \mathsf{ff}$, i.e., $i \notin [\![\Diamond A]\!]^{\Xi}_{\mathsf{K}}$ and so concludes the proof of $[\![\Diamond A]\!]^{\Xi}_{\mathsf{K}} \subseteq \mathbb{M}$.

Similarly, it can be shown that **false** and $\Box A$ are the least and greatest fixpoints of the equivalence (i) above, and that A **until** B and A **unless** B are the least and greatest fixpoints of (iii).

We now generalize these considerations to an extension of LTL. We want to introduce new (unary) logical operators which, applied to a formula F (generally containing a variable u), provide formulas which are the least and the greatest fixpoints of the equivalence

$$u \leftrightarrow F;$$

more precisely: the semantical evaluation $\mathsf{K}_i^{(\Xi)}$ of the formulas is determined by the least and greatest fixpoints of the mapping $\Upsilon_F : 2^{\mathbb{N}} \to 2^{\mathbb{N}}$ (i.e., the least and greatest subsets $\mathbb{M} \subseteq \mathbb{N}$ with $\Upsilon_F(\mathbb{M}) = \mathbb{M}$) where

$$\Upsilon_F : \mathbb{M} \mapsto [\![F]\!]_{\mathsf{K}}^{\Xi[u:\mathbb{M}]},$$

as exemplified above for $F \equiv A \vee \circ u$.

However, we must take some care: not all equivalences need have solutions. A simple example is the equivalence $u \leftrightarrow \neg u$ which obviously does not admit any solutions. But, as shown by the following example, even if fixpoints exist there need not be least and greatest ones.

Example. For a propositional constant $v \in \mathbf{V}$, consider the formula

$$F \equiv v \leftrightarrow \circ u$$

and let $\mathsf{K} = (\eta_0, \eta_1, \eta_2, \ldots)$ be a temporal structure such that $\eta_i(v) = \mathsf{tt}$ if and only if i is even. We will show that the function Υ_F has precisely two incomparable fixpoints with respect to K. In fact, $\mathbb{M}$ is a fixpoint if and only if, for arbitrary Ξ,

$$\begin{aligned} \mathbb{M} &= \Upsilon_F(\mathbb{M}) \\ &= [\![v \leftrightarrow \circ u]\!]_{\mathsf{K}}^{\Xi[u:\mathbb{M}]} \\ &= \{i \in \mathbb{N} \mid \eta_i(v) = \mathsf{tt} \Leftrightarrow i+1 \in \mathbb{M}\} \\ &= \{2j \mid 2j+1 \in \mathbb{M}\} \cup \{2j+1 \mid 2j+2 \notin \mathbb{M}\}. \end{aligned}$$

This means that, for every $j \in \mathbb{N}$,

$$2j \in \mathbb{M} \Leftrightarrow 2j+1 \in \mathbb{M} \qquad \text{and} \qquad 2j+1 \in \mathbb{M} \Leftrightarrow 2j+2 \notin \mathbb{M}$$

which is obviously the case if and only if either

$$\mathbb{M} = \{0,1,4,5,8,9,\ldots\} = \{n \in \mathbb{N} \mid n \bmod 4 \in \{0,1\}\}$$

or

$$\mathbb{M} = \{2,3,6,7,10,11,\ldots\} = \{n \in \mathbb{N} \mid n \bmod 4 \in \{2,3\}\}.$$

So these two sets are the only fixpoints of Υ_F. One is the complement of the other; in particular, they are incomparable. △

To pursue our approach, let us now first note the trivial fact that, if a least fixpoint exists then it is unique, and the same holds for the greatest fixpoint. Furthermore, a well-known sufficient condition that least and greatest fixpoints exist at all in situations like the one given here is that of monotonicity: for any set $\mathbb{D}$, a function $\Upsilon : 2^{\mathbb{D}} \to 2^{\mathbb{D}}$ is called *monotone* if $\Upsilon(\mathbb{E}_1) \subseteq \Upsilon(\mathbb{E}_2)$ holds whenever $\mathbb{E}_1 \subseteq \mathbb{E}_2$, for arbitrary $\mathbb{E}_1, \mathbb{E}_2 \subseteq \mathbb{D}$. It is called *anti-monotone* if $\mathbb{E}_1 \subseteq \mathbb{E}_2$ implies $\Upsilon(\mathbb{E}_1) \supseteq \Upsilon(\mathbb{E}_2)$.

Theorem 3.2.1 (Fixpoint Theorem of Tarski). *Assume that $\mathbb{D}$ is some set and that $\Upsilon : 2^{\mathbb{D}} \to 2^{\mathbb{D}}$ is a monotone function. Then*

a) $\mu\Upsilon = \bigcap\{\mathbb{E} \subseteq \mathbb{D} \mid \Upsilon(\mathbb{E}) \subseteq \mathbb{E}\}$ *is the least fixpoint of* Υ.
b) $\nu\Upsilon = \bigcup\{\mathbb{E} \subseteq \mathbb{D} \mid \mathbb{E} \subseteq \Upsilon(\mathbb{E})\}$ *is the greatest fixpoint of* Υ.

Proof. a) We write $\overline{\Upsilon}$ for the set $\{\mathbb{E} \subseteq \mathbb{D} \mid \Upsilon(\mathbb{E}) \subseteq \mathbb{E}\}$. Let $\mathbb{E} \in \overline{\Upsilon}$. Because $\mu\Upsilon = \bigcap\overline{\Upsilon}$, we certainly have $\mu\Upsilon \subseteq \mathbb{E}$, and by monotonicity of Υ it follows that $\Upsilon(\mu\Upsilon) \subseteq \Upsilon(\mathbb{E})$. By definition of $\overline{\Upsilon}$, we know that $\Upsilon(\mathbb{E}) \subseteq \mathbb{E}$. Thus, $\Upsilon(\mu\Upsilon) \subseteq \mathbb{E}$ holds for all $\mathbb{E} \in \overline{\Upsilon}$, which implies that $\Upsilon(\mu\Upsilon) \subseteq \bigcap\overline{\Upsilon} = \mu\Upsilon$.

Again by monotonicity of Υ, we obtain that $\Upsilon(\Upsilon(\mu\Upsilon)) \subseteq \Upsilon(\mu\Upsilon)$, and therefore $\Upsilon(\mu\Upsilon) \in \overline{\Upsilon}$. This implies $\mu\Upsilon = \bigcap\overline{\Upsilon} \subseteq \Upsilon(\mu\Upsilon)$, so altogether we have shown that $\Upsilon(\mu\Upsilon) = \mu\Upsilon$, and thus $\mu\Upsilon$ is a fixpoint of Υ.

To see that $\mu\Upsilon$ is the least fixpoint of Υ, assume that $\mathbb{E} \subseteq \mathbb{D}$ is some arbitrary fixpoint, i.e., $\Upsilon(\mathbb{E}) = \mathbb{E}$. In particular, $\Upsilon(\mathbb{E}) \subseteq \mathbb{E}$, and thus $\mathbb{E} \in \overline{\Upsilon}$. By definition of $\mu\Upsilon$, it follows that $\mu\Upsilon \subseteq \mathbb{E}$, which completes the proof.

b) The proof of this part is dual, exchanging $\subseteq$ and $\bigcap$ by $\supseteq$ and $\bigcup$. △

In the present context, we can apply Theorem 3.2.1 to functions Υ_F, and it is easy to see that the *polarity* of (the occurrences of) the variable u in the formula F helps us determine the monotonicity of Υ_F. Roughly speaking, u occurs with *positive* or *negative* polarity depending on which side of an implication u occurs. Formally, polarity is inductively defined as follows:

- u occurs with positive polarity in the formula u.
- An occurrence of u in a formula $A \to B$ is of positive polarity if it is of positive polarity in B or of negative polarity in A; otherwise it is an occurrence of negative polarity.
- The operators $\bigcirc$ and $\Box$ preserve the polarity of variable occurrences.

For the derived operators, it follows that $\wedge$, $\vee$, and $\Diamond$ preserve the polarity, whereas $\neg$ reverses the polarity of occurrences. As for formulas $A \leftrightarrow B$, every occurrence of u is both of positive and negative polarity because it appears on both sides of an implication. For example, the variable u has a positive polarity in the formula $v \to \bigcirc u$, a negative polarity in $v \to \neg\bigcirc u$ and occurrences of both positive and negative polarity in the formula $v \leftrightarrow \bigcirc u$ of the above example ($v \in \mathbf{V}$ in each case).

Lemma 3.2.2. *Let F be a formula, $u \in \mathcal{V}$ be a propositional variable, and the function $\Upsilon_F : 2^{\mathbb{N}} \to 2^{\mathbb{N}}$ be given by*

$$\Upsilon_F(\mathbb{M}) = [\![F]\!]_{\mathsf{K}}^{\Xi[u:\mathbb{M}]}.$$

a) Υ_F is monotone if every occurrence of u in F has positive polarity.
b) Υ_F is anti-monotone if every occurrence of u in F has negative polarity.

Proof. Both parts a) and b) are proved simultaneously by structural induction on the formula F.

1. $F \equiv v \in \mathbf{V}$, $F \equiv \mathbf{false}$ or $F \equiv \bar{u} \in \mathcal{V}$, $\bar{u} \not\equiv u$: Then u does not occur in F. This implies $\Upsilon_F(\mathbb{M}) = \Upsilon_F(\mathbb{M}')$ for arbitrary $\mathbb{M}$ and $\mathbb{M}'$; so Υ_F is both monotone and anti-monotone.
2. $F \equiv u$: Then the only occurrence of u in F is of positive polarity. So, part b) is trivial, and part a) follows since we have

$$\Upsilon_F(\mathbb{M}) = \{i \in \mathbb{N} \mid \mathsf{K}_i^{(\Xi[u:\mathbb{M}])}(u) = \mathsf{tt}\} = \mathbb{M}$$

for every $\mathbb{M}$; so Υ_F is monotone.

3. $F \equiv A \to B$: Then

$$\begin{aligned}\Upsilon_F(\mathbb{M}) &= [\![A \to B]\!]_{\mathsf{K}}^{\Xi[u:\mathbb{M}]} \\ &= \{i \in \mathbb{N} \mid \mathsf{K}_i^{(\Xi[u:\mathbb{M}])}(A \to B) = \mathsf{tt}\} \\ &= \{i \in \mathbb{N} \mid \mathsf{K}_i^{(\Xi[u:\mathbb{M}])}(A) = \mathsf{ff}\} \cup \{i \in \mathbb{N} \mid \mathsf{K}_i^{(\Xi[u:\mathbb{M}])}(B) = \mathsf{tt}\} \\ &= (\mathbb{N} \setminus \Upsilon_A(\mathbb{M})) \cup \Upsilon_B(\mathbb{M})\end{aligned}$$

for every $\mathbb{M}$. Let now $\mathbb{M}_1 \subseteq \mathbb{M}_2$. If every occurrence of u in F is of positive polarity then every occurrence of u in A is of negative polarity and every occurrence of u in B is of positive polarity. By induction hypothesis, Υ_A is anti-monotone and Υ_B is monotone; thus we have $\Upsilon_A(\mathbb{M}_1) \supseteq \Upsilon_A(\mathbb{M}_2)$ and $\Upsilon_B(\mathbb{M}_1) \subseteq \Upsilon_B(\mathbb{M}_2)$ and therefore obtain $\Upsilon_F(\mathbb{M}_1) \subseteq \Upsilon_F(\mathbb{M}_2)$ which proves part a). If every occurrence of u in F is of negative polarity then we conclude analogously that Υ_A is monotone and Υ_B is anti-monotone which provides part b).

4. $F \equiv \bigcirc A$: Then

$$\Upsilon_F(\mathbb{M}) = [\![\bigcirc A]\!]_{\mathsf{K}}^{\Xi[u:\mathbb{M}]} = \{i \in \mathbb{N} \mid i+1 \in \Upsilon_A(\mathbb{M})\}$$

for every $\mathbb{M}$. Let $\mathbb{M}_1 \subseteq \mathbb{M}_2$. If every occurrence of u in F is of positive polarity then so it is in A. By induction hypothesis, $\Upsilon_B(\mathbb{M}_1) \subseteq \Upsilon_B(\mathbb{M}_2)$; so we obtain part a) because of

$$\{i \in \mathbb{N} \mid i+1 \in \Upsilon_A(\mathbb{M}_1)\} \subseteq \{i \in \mathbb{N} \mid i+1 \in \Upsilon_A(\mathbb{M}_2)\},$$

and the argument for part b) is analogous.

5. $F \equiv \Box A$: Then

$$\Upsilon_F(\mathbb{M}) = \{i \in \mathbb{N} \mid j \in \Upsilon_A(\mathbb{M}) \text{ for every } j \geq i\}$$

for every $\mathbb{M}$, and the assertions a) and b) are found analogously as in the previous case. △

These observations now suggest how to define the extension of LTL announced above: we introduce a new operator μ with the informal meaning that $\mu u A$ denotes the least fixpoint of the equivalence $u \leftrightarrow A$. (A second operator ν for the greatest fixpoint can be derived from μ.) In order to ensure the existence of the fixpoints, we restrict the application of μ to A by requiring that all occurrences of u in A must be of positive polarity.

The propositional variable u becomes bound by the new (*fixpoint*) operator, just as quantifiers bind variables of first-order logic: an occurrence of a propositional variable u in a formula A is called *bound* if it appears in some subformula $\mu u B$ of A; otherwise it is called *free*. A formula is *closed* if it does not contain any free propositional variables. The formula $A_u(B)$ results from A by substituting the formula B for all free occurrences of the propositional variable u. When carrying out this substitution, we tacitly assume that no free occurrences of propositional variables in B become bound by this substitution. (As in first-order logic, this can be achieved by renaming the bound propositional variables of A if necessary.)

We denote this extension of LTL by LTL+μ. Its language $\mathcal{L}_{\mathrm{LTL}}^{\mu}$ is formally obtained from $\mathcal{L}_{\mathrm{LTL}}$ by adding a denumerable set $\mathcal{V}$ of *propositional variables* to the alphabet, extending the syntax rules of $\mathcal{L}_{\mathrm{LTL}}$ by the two clauses

- Every propositional variable of $\mathcal{V}$ is a formula,
- If A is a formula and $u \in \mathcal{V}$ is a propositional variable all of whose free occurrences in A are of positive polarity then $\mu u A$ is a formula,

and extending the polarity definition by fixing that the polarity of every free occurrence of a propositional variable in $\mu u A$ is the same as the polarity of the occurrence in A.

The ν operator is introduced as the abbreviation

$$\nu u A \equiv \neg \mu u \neg A_u(\neg u);$$

we will see below that $\nu u A$ denotes the greatest fixpoint of the equivalence $u \leftrightarrow A$. The substitution of $\neg u$ for the free occurrences of u ensures that all occurrences of u are of positive polarity in the formula to which the fixpoint operator is applied. Clearly, the polarities of all free occurrences of propositional variables in $\nu u A$ are as in A.

The semantics of LTL+μ has to take into account the valuation of propositional variables. As indicated already, the earlier $\mathsf{K}_i(F)$ therefore takes now the form $\mathsf{K}_i^{(\Xi)}(F)$ where $\Xi = (\xi_0, \xi_1, \xi_2, \ldots)$ is a sequence of valuations $\xi_i : \mathcal{V} \to \{\mathsf{ff}, \mathsf{tt}\}$ of the propositional variables. The clauses of the inductive definition for $\mathsf{K}_i^{(\Xi)}(F)$ are as for $\mathsf{K}_i(F)$ before, extended by

- $\mathsf{K}_i^{(\Xi)}(u) = \xi_i(u)$ for $u \in \mathcal{V}$,
- $\mathsf{K}_i^{(\Xi)}(\mu u A) = \mathsf{tt} \Leftrightarrow i \in \mu \Upsilon_A$

and the definition of validity in K is adapted accordingly: $\models_{\mathsf{K}} F$ if $\mathsf{K}_i^{(\Xi)}(F) = \mathsf{tt}$ for every i and Ξ. Expanding the representation of $\mu \Upsilon_A$ given in Theorem 3.2.1 and the definition of Υ_A, the semantic clause for $\mu u A$ can be restated more explicitly as

- $\mathsf{K}_i^{(\Xi)}(\mu u A) = \mathsf{tt} \Leftrightarrow i \in \mathbb{M}$ for all $\mathbb{M} \subseteq \mathbb{N}$ such that $[\![A]\!]_{\mathsf{K}}^{\Xi[u:\mathbb{M}]} \subseteq \mathbb{M}$.

In order to be sure that this definition really corresponds to our intention of defining the least fixpoint of the mapping Υ_A, even for nested fixpoints, we have to extend the proof of Lemma 3.2.2 for the case where $F \equiv \mu \bar{u} A$. If $u \equiv \bar{u}$ then u has no free occurrence in F, and therefore Υ_F is both monotone and anti-monotone. So let $u \not\equiv \bar{u}$, assume for part a) that every free occurrence of u in F, hence in A, is of positive polarity, and let $\mathbb{M}_1, \mathbb{M}_2, \mathbb{M} \subseteq \mathbb{N}$ where $\mathbb{M}_1 \subseteq \mathbb{M}_2$. The assertions of the lemma are to be understood for arbitrary K and Ξ. So the induction hypothesis, applied for the valuation $\Xi[\bar{u}:\mathbb{M}]$, implies that

$$[\![A]\!]_{\mathsf{K}}^{\Xi[\bar{u}:\mathbb{M}][u:\mathbb{M}_1]} \subseteq [\![A]\!]_{\mathsf{K}}^{\Xi[\bar{u}:\mathbb{M}][u:\mathbb{M}_2]}.$$

We have to show that $\Upsilon_F(\mathbb{M}_1) \subseteq \Upsilon_F(\mathbb{M}_2)$ where

$$\Upsilon_F(\mathbb{M}_i) = \bigcap\{\mathbb{M} \subseteq \mathbb{N} \mid [\![A]\!]_{\mathsf{K}}^{\Xi[u:\mathbb{M}_i][\bar{u}:\mathbb{M}]} \subseteq \mathbb{M}\}.$$

Assume that $i \notin \Upsilon_F(\mathbb{M}_2)$ for some $i \in \mathbb{N}$; then there exists some $\mathbb{M} \subseteq \mathbb{N}$ such that $[\![A]\!]_{\mathsf{K}}^{\Xi[u:\mathbb{M}_2][\bar{u}:\mathbb{M}]} \subseteq \mathbb{M}$ and $i \notin \mathbb{M}$. Because u and $\bar{u}$ are different propositional variables, $\Xi[u:\mathbb{M}_2][\bar{u}:\mathbb{M}] = \Xi[\bar{u}:\mathbb{M}][u:\mathbb{M}_2]$, and the induction hypothesis yields $[\![A]\!]_{\mathsf{K}}^{\Xi[\bar{u}:\mathbb{M}][u:\mathbb{M}_1]} \subseteq [\![A]\!]_{\mathsf{K}}^{\Xi[\bar{u}:\mathbb{M}][u:\mathbb{M}_2]} \subseteq \mathbb{M}$, and therefore we find $i \notin \Upsilon_F(\mathbb{M}_1)$. Because i was chosen arbitrarily, this proves $\Upsilon_F(\mathbb{M}_1) \subseteq \Upsilon_F(\mathbb{M}_2)$, completing the proof of part a) of the lemma. The arguments for part b) are similar.

From this completed proof of Lemma 3.2.2 and Theorem 3.2.1 we have shown that $[\![\mu u A]\!]_{\mathsf{K}}^{\Xi}$ defines the least fixpoint of the mapping Υ_A as intended.

For the derived ν operator, the semantics is given by

- $\mathsf{K}_i^{(\Xi)}(\nu u A) = \mathsf{tt} \Leftrightarrow i \in \nu\Upsilon_A$

or, again somewhat more explicitly, by

- $\mathsf{K}_i^{(\Xi)}(\nu u A) = \mathsf{tt} \Leftrightarrow \mathbb{M} \subseteq [\![A]\!]_{\mathsf{K}}^{\Xi[u:\mathbb{M}]}$ for some $\mathbb{M} \subseteq \mathbb{N}$ such that $i \in \mathbb{M}$.

This can be seen by observing that with $\mathbb{M}' = \mathbb{N} \setminus \mathbb{M}$ we obviously have

$$[\![\neg A_u(\neg u)]\!]_{\mathsf{K}}^{\Xi[u:\mathbb{M}]} = \mathbb{N} \setminus [\![A]\!]_{\mathsf{K}}^{\Xi[u:\mathbb{M}']}$$

and therefore

$$[\![\neg A_u(\neg u)]\!]_{\mathsf{K}}^{\Xi[u:\mathbb{M}]} \subseteq \mathbb{M} \text{ and } i \notin \mathbb{M} \quad \Leftrightarrow \quad \mathbb{M}' \subseteq [\![A]\!]_{\mathsf{K}}^{\Xi[u:\mathbb{M}']} \text{ and } i \in \mathbb{M}'.$$

So we obtain in fact

$$\begin{aligned} \mathsf{K}_i^{(\Xi)}(\nu u A) = \mathsf{tt} &\Leftrightarrow \mathsf{K}_i^{(\Xi)}(\neg \mu u \neg A_u(\neg u)) = \mathsf{tt} \\ &\Leftrightarrow [\![\neg A_u(\neg u)]\!]_{\mathsf{K}}^{\Xi[u:\mathbb{M}]} \subseteq \mathbb{M} \text{ and } i \notin \mathbb{M} \text{ for some } \mathbb{M} \subseteq \mathbb{N} \\ &\Leftrightarrow \mathbb{M}' \subseteq [\![A]\!]_{\mathsf{K}}^{\Xi[u:\mathbb{M}']} \text{ for some } \mathbb{M}' \subseteq \mathbb{N} \text{ such that } i \in \mathbb{M}'. \end{aligned}$$

Example. Assuming that u does not occur in A, let us verify that the formula $\Box A \leftrightarrow \nu u(A \land \bigcirc u)$ is valid. This claim can obviously be proved by showing that

$$[\![\Box A]\!]_{\mathsf{K}}^{\Xi} = [\![\nu u(A \land \bigcirc u)]\!]_{\mathsf{K}}^{\Xi}$$

holds for any K and Ξ. For the direction "$\subseteq$" of this set equation, assume that $i \in [\![\Box A]\!]_{\mathsf{K}}^{\Xi}$. Writing $\mathbb{M}$ for $[\![\Box A]\!]_{\mathsf{K}}^{\Xi}$, we will prove $\mathbb{M} \subseteq [\![A \land \bigcirc u]\!]_{\mathsf{K}}^{\Xi[u:\mathbb{M}]}$ in order to obtain $i \in [\![\nu u(A \land \bigcirc u)]\!]_{\mathsf{K}}^{\Xi}$ by the above semantic clause. Indeed, for any

$j \in \mathbb{M}$, we find that $j \in [\![A]\!]_{\mathsf{K}}^{\Xi}$ and that $j+1 \in \mathbb{M}$. Because u does not occur in A, we may conclude that $j \in [\![A]\!]_{\mathsf{K}}^{\Xi[u:\mathbb{M}]} \cap [\![\bigcirc u]\!]_{\mathsf{K}}^{\Xi[u:\mathbb{M}]}$, and thus $j \in [\![A \wedge \bigcirc u]\!]_{\mathsf{K}}^{\Xi[u:\mathbb{M}]}$.

For "$\supseteq$" we show that $\mathbb{M} \subseteq [\![\Box A]\!]_{\mathsf{K}}^{\Xi}$ holds for any $\mathbb{M}$ with $\mathbb{M} \subseteq [\![A \wedge \bigcirc u]\!]_{\mathsf{K}}^{\Xi[u:\mathbb{M}]}$. Since $[\![\nu u(A \wedge \bigcirc u)]\!]_{\mathsf{K}}^{\Xi}$ is defined as the union of all such sets $\mathbb{M}$, the assertion then follows. So assume that $\mathbb{M} \subseteq [\![A \wedge \bigcirc u]\!]_{\mathsf{K}}^{\Xi[u:\mathbb{M}]}$ and that $i \in \mathbb{M}$. Clearly, we obtain that $i \in [\![A]\!]_{\mathsf{K}}^{\Xi[u:\mathbb{M}]}$; hence also $i \in [\![A]\!]_{\mathsf{K}}^{\Xi}$, because u does not occur in A. Moreover, we have $i+1 \in \mathbb{M}$. Continuing inductively, we find that $j \in [\![A]\!]_{\mathsf{K}}^{\Xi}$ for all $j \geq i$, that is, $i \in [\![\Box A]\!]_{\mathsf{K}}^{\Xi}$. △

Similarly, we find that the other temporal operators of LTL+b can be expressed in LTL+μ by noting the following equivalences, where the propositional variable u is again assumed not to occur in A or B. (Writing down these formulas we presuppose a suitable language which results from extending LTL by both "b" and "μ".)

(Tμ1) $\Box A \leftrightarrow \nu u(A \wedge \bigcirc u)$,
(Tμ2) $\Diamond A \leftrightarrow \mu u(A \vee \bigcirc u)$,
(Tμ3) A **until** $B \leftrightarrow \mu u(\bigcirc B \vee \bigcirc(A \wedge u))$,
(Tμ4) A **unless** $B \leftrightarrow \nu u(\bigcirc B \vee \bigcirc(A \wedge u))$,
(Tμ5) A **unt** $B \leftrightarrow \mu u(B \vee (A \wedge \bigcirc u))$,
(Tμ6) A **unl** $B \leftrightarrow \nu u(B \vee (A \wedge \bigcirc u))$,
(Tμ7) A **atnext** $B \leftrightarrow \nu u(\bigcirc(B \rightarrow A) \wedge \bigcirc(\neg B \rightarrow u))$,
(Tμ8) A **before** $B \leftrightarrow \nu u(\bigcirc\neg B \wedge \bigcirc(A \vee u))$.

The shape of these laws follows the fixpoint characterizations (T28), (T29), and (Tb11)–(Tb16). The difference between strong and weak binary operators is precisely reflected by the choice of the least or greatest fixpoint.

We thus find that the logic LTL+μ provides uniform syntactic means for the definition of all the temporal operators that we have encountered so far, although formulas written in that language may quickly become difficult to read: compare the formulas $\Box(A \rightarrow \Diamond B)$ and

$$\nu u_1((A \rightarrow \mu u_2(B \vee \bigcirc u_2)) \wedge \bigcirc u_1).$$

We will study in more depth the expressiveness of LTL+μ in Chap. 4 where we show that LTL+μ can express many more temporal relations than the logics LTL or LTL+b.

The uniform definition of the language $\mathcal{L}_{\mathrm{LTL}}^{\mu}$ is mirrored by a simple and uniform axiomatization of LTL+μ. A sound and weakly complete formal system $\Sigma_{\mathrm{LTL}}^{\mu}$ is obtained as an extension of Σ_{LTL} by the following axiom and rule:

(μ-rec) $A_u(\mu u A) \rightarrow \mu u A$,
(μ-ind) $A_u(B) \rightarrow B \vdash \mu u A \rightarrow B$ if there is no free occurrence of u in B.

The axiom (μ-rec) is "one direction" of the equivalence $\mu u A \leftrightarrow A_u(\mu u A)$ which asserts that $\mu u A$ is a fixpoint. The rule (μ-ind) expresses that $\mu u A$ is smaller than any other fixpoint B. For formulas involving greatest fixpoints, the following formula and rule can be derived:

(ν-rec) $\nu uA \to A_u(\nu uA)$,
(ν-ind) $B \to A_u(B) \vdash B \to \nu uA$ if there is no free occurrence of u in B.

As in first-order logic, the formulation of the deduction theorem requires some care. Still, we have

$$\mathcal{F} \cup \{A\} \vdash B \;\Rightarrow\; \mathcal{F} \vdash \Box A \to B$$

if A is a closed formula.

We illustrate the use of $\Sigma^{\mu}_{\mathrm{LTL}}$ (together with laws from LTL+b) by deriving (Tμ8):

Derivation of (Tμ8). Let $F \equiv \nu u(\bigcirc\neg B \wedge \bigcirc(A \vee u))$ and u not be free in A, B.

(1)	A **before** $B \to \bigcirc\neg B \wedge \bigcirc(A \vee A$ **before** $B)$	(prop), (Tb16)
(2)	A **before** $B \to F$	(ν-ind),(1)
(3)	$F \to \bigcirc\neg B \wedge \bigcirc(A \vee F)$	(ν-rec)
(4)	$F \to \bigcirc\neg B \wedge \bigcirc(F \vee A)$	(prop),(3)
(5)	$F \to A$ **before** B	(indbefore),(4)
(6)	A **before** $B \leftrightarrow \nu u(\bigcirc\neg B \wedge \bigcirc(A \vee u))$	(prop),(2),(5) △

It is instructive to observe the special cases of the axioms and rules for the $\Box$ operator: by law (Tμ1), $\Box A$ is just $\nu u(A \wedge \bigcirc u)$, and therefore ($\nu$-rec) and ($\nu$-ind) can be rewritten as

$$\Box A \to A \wedge \bigcirc\Box A \qquad \text{and} \qquad B \to A \wedge \bigcirc B \vdash B \to \Box A,$$

the first of which is (ltl3) whereas the second one is just a reformulation of the induction rule (ind) of Σ_{LTL}. We could therefore drop (ltl3) and (ind) from the system $\Sigma^{\mu}_{\mathrm{LTL}}$ if $\Box$ were understood as a derived operator in $\mathcal{L}^{\mu}_{\mathrm{LTL}}$.

Similarly, the special cases for the binary operators show that the systematic pattern of the alternative axiomatization of LTL+b indicated at the end of the previous section is just the pattern described here. For example, (Tμ4) shows that A **unless** B is $\nu(\bigcirc B \vee \bigcirc(A \wedge u))$; so ($\nu$-rec) becomes the axiom

(unless1') A **unless** $B \to \bigcirc B \vee \bigcirc(A \wedge A$ **unless** $B)$

of Sect. 3.1, and (ν-ind) becomes the rule

$$C \to \bigcirc B \vee \bigcirc(A \wedge C) \vdash C \to A \textbf{ unless } B$$

which is a reformulation of (indunless). So this latter rule determines A **unless** B to be a greatest fixpoint.

Second Reading

In a Second Reading paragraph in Sect. 2.3 we mentioned some relationships between temporal and modal logic. The idea of introducing fixpoint operators may also be applied to "normal" modal logic; the result is known as *modal μ-calculus* MμC.

This logic contains a (unary) modal operator $\Box$ together with the fixpoint operator μ. Formulas are built analogously as in LTL+μ, including the constraint concerning polarity. The operators $\Diamond$ and ν are introduced as before. As indicated in Sect. 2.3, a *Kripke structure* $\mathfrak{K} = (\{\eta_\iota\}_{\iota \in K}, \lhd)$ for an underlying set $\mathbf{V}$ of propositional constants consists of a non-empty set K, valuations $\eta_\iota : \mathbf{V} \to \{\mathsf{ff}, \mathsf{tt}\}$ for all $\iota \in K$, and a binary *accessibility relation* $\lhd$. Using an analogous notation as in the above main text with a valuation $\Xi = (\xi_\iota)_{\iota \in K}$ (where $\xi_\iota : \mathbf{V} \to \{\mathsf{ff}, \mathsf{tt}\}$ for $\iota \in K$), the semantics of the operator $\Box$ is given by

$$\mathfrak{K}_\iota(\Box A) = \mathsf{tt} \Leftrightarrow \mathfrak{K}_\kappa(A) = \mathsf{tt} \text{ for every } \kappa \text{ with } \iota \lhd \kappa$$

which provides

$$\mathfrak{K}_\iota(\Diamond A) = \mathsf{tt} \Leftrightarrow \mathfrak{K}_\kappa(A) = \mathsf{tt} \text{ for some } \kappa \text{ with } \iota \lhd \kappa$$

for the dual operator $\Diamond$. For the semantics of μ one defines, for any formula F, the mapping

$$\Upsilon_F : 2^K \to 2^K,$$
$$\Upsilon_F : \mathbb{E} \mapsto [\![F]\!]_{\mathfrak{K}}^{\Xi[u:\mathbb{E}]}$$

where $[\![F]\!]_{\mathfrak{K}}^{\Xi} = \{\iota \in K \mid \mathfrak{K}_\iota^{(\Xi)}(F) = \mathsf{tt}\}$ and $\Xi[u:\mathbb{E}]$ denotes the valuation $(\xi'_\iota)_{\iota \in K}$ with $\xi'_\iota(u) = \mathsf{tt} \Leftrightarrow \iota \in \mathbb{E}$ and $\xi'_\iota(u') = \xi_\iota(u')$ for all variables u' other than u. Then

$$\mathfrak{K}_\iota^{(\Xi)}(\mu u A) = \mathsf{tt} \Leftrightarrow \iota \in \mu\Upsilon_A$$

and

$$\mathfrak{K}_\iota^{(\Xi)}(\nu u A) = \mathsf{tt} \Leftrightarrow \iota \in \nu\Upsilon_A$$

where $\mu\Upsilon_A$ and $\nu\Upsilon_A$ are the least and greatest fixpoints of Υ_A, respectively (which can be shown to exist as in the case of LTL+μ).

From these definitions, the fixpoint characterization (Tμ1) for the temporal always operator, and recalling the discussion in the above-mentioned Second Reading paragraph, it is evident that LTL+μ can be viewed as a special instant of MμC based on the operator $\bigcirc$ (with distinguished Kripke structures). However, there is also another more general relationship between MμC and temporal logics (including even others outside the "LTL family") that can all be "embedded" into MμC. This makes MμC a simple common "framework" for all such logics. We will briefly come back to this aspect in Sect. 10.4.

3.3 Propositional Quantification

The language $\mathcal{L}_{\mathrm{LTL}}^{\mu}$ of the "fixpoint logic" studied in Sect. 3.2 introduced propositional variables and "binders". Alternatively, LTL can be extended by standard existential or universal quantification over propositional variables to obtain the logic LTL+q. Its language $\mathcal{L}_{\mathrm{LTL}}^{\mathrm{q}}$ is formally obtained from $\mathcal{L}_{\mathrm{LTL}}$ by adding a denumerable set $\mathcal{V}$ of *propositional variables* to the alphabet and by extending the syntax rules of $\mathcal{L}_{\mathrm{LTL}}$ by the following clauses:

- Every propositional variable of $\mathcal{V}$ is a formula.
- If A is a formula and u is a propositional variable then $\exists u A$ is a formula.

The notions of free and bound occurrences of variables, closed formula, substitution of formulas for free variables, etc. carry over from $\mathcal{L}^{\mu}_{\mathrm{LTL}}$ to $\mathcal{L}^{\mathrm{q}}_{\mathrm{LTL}}$ in the obvious way. We write

$$\forall u A \equiv \neg\exists u \neg A$$

for the dual, universally quantified formula.

As in Sect. 3.2, the semantics of LTL+q is defined with respect to a valuation $\Xi = (\xi_0, \xi_1, \xi_2, \ldots)$, $\xi_i : \mathcal{V} \to \{\mathsf{ff}, \mathsf{tt}\}$ of the propositional variables. $\mathsf{K}_i^{(\Xi)}$ replaces K_i again (with validity in K being defined as for LTL+μ), and the semantic clauses corresponding to the extended syntax are

- $\mathsf{K}_i^{(\Xi)}(u) = \xi_i(u)$ for $u \in \mathcal{V}$.
- $\mathsf{K}_i^{(\Xi)}(\exists u A) = \mathsf{tt} \Leftrightarrow$ there is a Ξ' such that $\Xi \sim_u \Xi'$ and $\mathsf{K}_i^{(\Xi')}(A) = \mathsf{tt}$.

The relation $\sim_u$ between valuations $\Xi = (\xi_0, \xi_1, \xi_2, \ldots)$ and $\Xi' = (\xi'_0, \xi'_1, \xi'_2, \ldots)$ is adapted from classical FOL:

$$\Xi \sim_u \Xi' \Leftrightarrow \xi_i(\bar{u}) = \xi'_i(\bar{u}) \text{ for all } \bar{u} \in \mathcal{V} \text{ other than } u \text{ and all } i \in \mathbb{N}.$$

For $\forall u A$ we clearly obtain

- $\mathsf{K}_i^{(\Xi)}(\forall u A) = \mathsf{tt} \Leftrightarrow \mathsf{K}_i^{(\Xi')}(A) = \mathsf{tt}$ for all Ξ' with $\Xi \sim_u \Xi'$.

Intuitively, the formula $\exists u A$ asserts that one can find a *sequence* of truth values for u satisfying the formula A, and not just a single truth value. This is why quantification over propositional variables cannot simply be reduced to ordinary propositional LTL (which is the case in classical propositional logic PL). Indeed, the following example shows that in $\mathcal{L}^{\mathrm{q}}_{\mathrm{LTL}}$, as in $\mathcal{L}^{\mu}_{\mathrm{LTL}}$, one can define the binary temporal operators.

Example. Consider, for $v_1, v_2 \in \mathbf{V}$, the formula

$$F \equiv \exists u(u \wedge \Box(u \to v_2 \vee (v_1 \wedge \bigcirc u)))$$

of $\mathcal{L}^{\mathrm{q}}_{\mathrm{LTL}}$. We claim that the following formula is valid:

$$F \leftrightarrow v_1 \ \mathbf{unl} \ v_2.$$

(As in the similar situation in the previous section, we presuppose a corresponding language for which the semantical clause defining $\mathsf{K}_i(v_1 \ \mathbf{unl} \ v_2)$ in LTL+b is transferred to $\mathsf{K}_i^{(\Xi)}(v_1 \ \mathbf{unl} \ v_2)$ for every temporal structure K, $i \in \mathbb{N}$, and arbitrary Ξ).

To show the "$\to$" part, let $\mathsf{K}_i^{(\Xi)}(F) = \mathsf{tt}$, and $\Xi' = (\xi'_0, \xi'_1, \xi'_2, \ldots)$ such that $\Xi' \sim_u \Xi$ and

$$(*) \qquad \mathsf{K}_i^{(\Xi')}(u \wedge \Box(u \to v_2 \vee (v_1 \wedge \bigcirc u))) = \mathsf{tt}.$$

For a contradiction, assume moreover that $\mathsf{K}_i^{(\Xi)}(v_1 \,\mathbf{unl}\, v_2) = \mathsf{ff}$. Using the law (Tb14), it follows that $\mathsf{K}_i^{(\Xi')}(v_2) = \mathsf{K}_i^{(\Xi)}(v_2) = \mathsf{ff}$; therefore we must have $\mathsf{K}_i^{(\Xi')}(v_1 \wedge \circ u) = \mathsf{tt}$ by (*), hence $\mathsf{K}_i^{(\Xi)}(v_1) = \mathsf{K}_i^{(\Xi')}(v_1) = \mathsf{tt}$. Again law (Tb14) then implies that $\mathsf{K}_{i+1}^{(\Xi)}(v_1 \,\mathbf{unl}\, v_2) = \mathsf{ff}$. Continuing inductively, we find that $\mathsf{K}_j^{(\Xi)}(v_1) = \mathsf{tt}$ and $\mathsf{K}_j^{(\Xi)}(v_1 \,\mathbf{unl}\, v_2) = \mathsf{ff}$ for all $j \geq i$. In particular, we obtain $\mathsf{K}_i^{(\Xi)}(\Box v_1) = \mathsf{tt}$. This implies $\mathsf{K}_i^{(\Xi)}(v_1 \,\mathbf{unl}\, v_2) = \mathsf{tt}$ by (Tb3), and a contradiction is reached.

For the opposite direction, let $\mathsf{K}_i^{(\Xi)}(v_1 \,\mathbf{unl}\, v_2) = \mathsf{tt}$ and $\Xi' = (\xi'_0, \xi'_1, \xi'_2, \ldots)$ such that $\xi'_k(u) = \mathsf{K}_k^{(\Xi)}(v_1 \,\mathbf{unl}\, v_2)$ for every $k \in \mathbb{N}$ and $\Xi' \sim_u \Xi$. Then we have $\mathsf{K}_i^{(\Xi')}(u) = \mathsf{tt}$ and $\mathsf{K}_j^{(\Xi')}(v_1 \,\mathbf{unl}\, v_2) = \mathsf{tt}$ for every $j \geq i$ with $\mathsf{K}_j^{(\Xi')}(u) = \mathsf{tt}$. By law (Tb14) it follows that $\mathsf{K}_j^{(\Xi')}(v_2 \vee (v_1 \wedge \circ(v_1 \,\mathbf{unl}\, v_2))) = \mathsf{tt}$ which, by the definition of Ξ', implies that $\mathsf{K}_j^{(\Xi')}(v_2 \vee (v_1 \wedge \circ u)) = \mathsf{tt}$ for every $j \geq i$. Together we thus have $\mathsf{K}_i^{(\Xi)}(F) = \mathsf{tt}$. △

The semantic definitions for LTL+μ and LTL+q have a "global" flavor in the sense that the valuation Ξ is used in its entirety for the definition of $\mathsf{K}_i^{(\Xi)}(A)$, and not just its suffix $\Xi^i = (\xi_i, \xi_{i+1}, \ldots)$. Nevertheless, a natural generalization of Lemma 2.1.5 holds for these logics, as we now show for the logic LTL+q. (An analogous proof holds for LTL+μ.)

Lemma 3.3.1. *Let* K *be a temporal structure and* Ξ *be a propositional valuation. Then* $(\mathsf{K}^i)_j^{(\Xi^i)}(A) = \mathsf{K}_{i+j}^{(\Xi)}(A)$ *for every* $j \in \mathbb{N}$ *and every formula* A *of* $\mathcal{L}_{\mathrm{LTL}}^{\mathrm{q}}$.

Proof. Adapting the proof of Lemma 2.1.5, we only need to prove the case of a quantified formula $\exists u A$. From the definition we see that $(\mathsf{K}^i)_j^{(\Xi^i)}(\exists u A) = \mathsf{tt}$ if and only if $(\mathsf{K}^i)_j^{(\Xi')}(A) = \mathsf{tt}$ for some valuation $\Xi' \sim_u \Xi^i$. Now, any such valuation Ξ' can be extended to a valuation $\Xi'' \sim_u \Xi$ such that $\Xi' = (\Xi'')^i$, and vice versa. The preceding condition is therefore equivalent to requiring that $(\mathsf{K}^i)_j^{(\Xi'')^i}(A) = \mathsf{tt}$ holds for some $\Xi'' \sim_u \Xi$, and by the induction hypothesis (applied to the valuation Ξ''), the latter is equivalent to $\mathsf{K}_{i+j}^{(\Xi'')}(A) = \mathsf{tt}$ for some $\Xi'' \sim_u \Xi$, which just means $\mathsf{K}_{i+j}^{(\Xi)}(\exists u A) = \mathsf{tt}$. △

As a particular consequence of Lemma 3.3.1 it follows that the two notions of validity that we have considered in Chap. 2 also coincide for LTL+q (and LTL+μ), that is, we again have $\models A$ if and only if $\overset{0}{\models} A$ for these logics. This equivalence is implied by Lemma 3.3.1 in the same way that Theorems 2.6.2 and 2.6.4 follow from Lemma 2.1.5.

A sound and weakly complete formal system $\Sigma_{\mathrm{LTL}}^{\mathrm{q}}$ for LTL+q is obtained by extending Σ_{LTL} by the following axioms and rules. For the formulation of rule (qltl-ind) we introduce some short notation: if $\mathbf{u} = (u_1, u_2, \ldots, u_n)$ is a tuple of propositional variables then $\exists \mathbf{u} F$ denotes $\exists u_1 \exists u_2 \ldots \exists u_n F$. The notation $\Xi' \sim_{\mathbf{u}} \Xi$ is extended to tuples of variables in the obvious way. Furthermore, for two such tuples $\mathbf{u}_1$ and $\mathbf{u}_2$

of equal length, $F_{\mathbf{u}_1}(\mathbf{u}_2)$ denotes the result of simultaneously substituting the variables of $\mathbf{u}_2$ for the free occurrences of the variables (with the same index) of $\mathbf{u}_1$ in F. If $\mathbf{u}_1 = (u_1^1, \ldots, u_1^n)$ and $\mathbf{u}_2 = (u_2^1, \ldots, u_2^n)$ are two such tuples, we also write $\mathbf{u}_2 \leftrightarrow \mathbf{u}_1$ as an abbreviation for $(u_2^1 \leftrightarrow u_1^1) \wedge \ldots \wedge (u_2^n \leftrightarrow u_1^n)$.

Additional axioms

(qltl1) $A_u(B) \rightarrow \exists u A$,
(qltl2) $\exists u \bigcirc A \leftrightarrow \bigcirc \exists u A$,
(qltl3) $\exists u(u \wedge \bigcirc \Box \neg u)$.

Additional rules

(qltl-part) $A \rightarrow B \vdash \exists u A \rightarrow B$ if there is no free occurrence of u in B,
(qltl-ind) $F \rightarrow \exists \mathbf{u}_2 \bigcirc ((\mathbf{u}_2 \leftrightarrow \mathbf{u}_1) \wedge F_{\mathbf{u}_1}(\mathbf{u}_2))$
$\vdash F \rightarrow \exists \mathbf{u}_2((\mathbf{u}_2 \leftrightarrow \mathbf{u}_1) \wedge \Box F_{\mathbf{u}_1}(\mathbf{u}_2))$
if every occurrence of variables u_1^i in F is in the scope of at most one $\bigcirc$ operator and no other temporal operator.

The axiom (qltl1) and the rule (qltl-part) are rather obvious counterparts of the standard quantifier axiom and the particularization rule of classical first-order logic as introduced in Sect. 1.2. The generalization rule of FOL can also be adapted providing the derived rule

(qltl-gen) $A \rightarrow B \vdash A \rightarrow \forall u B$ if there is no free occurrence of u in A.

Similarly, we obtain the derived law

(Tq1) $\forall u A \rightarrow A_u(B)$.

The axiom (qltl2) asserts that existential quantification and the next-time operator commute. Its validity is easy to see:

$$
\begin{aligned}
\mathsf{K}_i^{(\Xi)}(\exists u \bigcirc A) = \mathsf{tt} &\Leftrightarrow \text{there is a } \Xi' \text{ such that } \Xi \sim_u \Xi' \text{ and } \mathsf{K}_i^{(\Xi')}(\bigcirc A) = \mathsf{tt} \\
&\Leftrightarrow \text{there is a } \Xi' \text{ such that } \Xi \sim_u \Xi' \text{ and } \mathsf{K}_{i+1}^{(\Xi')}(A) = \mathsf{tt} \\
&\Leftrightarrow \mathsf{K}_{i+1}^{(\Xi)}(\exists u A) = \mathsf{tt} \\
&\Leftrightarrow \mathsf{K}_i^{(\Xi)}(\bigcirc \exists u A) = \mathsf{tt}.
\end{aligned}
$$

Axiom (qltl3) can be used to introduce a fresh propositional variable that marks the current state; its validity is obvious.

The rule (qltl-ind) formalizes a principle for defining a proposition by induction. By the assumption that the variables in $\mathbf{u}_1$ occur in F under the scope of at most one operator $\bigcirc$ and no other temporal operator, the value of $\mathsf{K}_i^{(\Xi)}(F)$, where $\Xi = (\xi_0, \xi_1, \xi_2, \ldots)$, does not depend on any $\xi_j(u_1^k)$ for $j \geq i + 2$. To understand the "correctness" of the rule, assume now that

(∗) $\models_{\mathsf{K}} F \rightarrow \exists \mathbf{u}_2 \bigcirc ((\mathbf{u}_2 \leftrightarrow \mathbf{u}_1) \wedge F_{\mathbf{u}_1}(\mathbf{u}_2))$

and that $\mathsf{K}_i^{(\Xi)}(F) = \mathsf{tt}$ where $\Xi = (\xi_0, \xi_1, \xi_2, \ldots)$. By assumption (∗), there exists $\Xi' = (\xi'_0, \xi'_1, \xi'_2, \ldots)$ where $\Xi' \sim_{\mathbf{u}_2} \Xi$ such that $\xi'_{i+1}(u_2^k) = \xi_{i+1}(u_1^k)$ for all k, and $\mathsf{K}_{i+1}^{(\Xi')}(F_{\mathbf{u}_1}(\mathbf{u}_2)) = \mathsf{tt}$. Defining the valuation $\Xi'' = (\xi''_0, \xi''_1, \xi''_2, \ldots)$ by

$$\xi''_j(u) = \begin{cases} \xi'_j(u_2^k) & \text{if } u \equiv u_2^k \text{ and } j \geq i+2, \\ \xi_j(u) & \text{otherwise,} \end{cases}$$

the above remark implies that $\mathsf{K}_{i+1}^{(\Xi'')}(F) = \mathsf{tt}$. Continuing in the same way, we find a valuation $\widehat{\Xi} = (\hat{\xi}_0, \hat{\xi}_1, \hat{\xi}_2, \ldots)$ such that $\mathsf{K}_i^{(\widehat{\Xi})}(F) = \mathsf{tt}$ and $\hat{\xi}_j = \xi_j$ for all $j \leq i$. This is just a transcription of the conclusion of the rule (qltl-ind).

The statement of a Deduction Theorem for the formal system $\Sigma_{\mathrm{LTL}}^{\mathrm{q}}$ again requires some care. The restricted version mentioned in the previous section is also correct for $\Sigma_{\mathrm{LTL}}^{\mathrm{q}}$.

Example. We will demonstrate the use of $\Sigma_{\mathrm{LTL}}^{\mathrm{q}}$ by deriving the existence of an "oscillating" sequence of truth values beginning with "true" and changing at every instant. More precisely, we derive the formula

$$\exists u(u \land \Box(\bigcirc u \leftrightarrow \neg u))$$

in $\Sigma_{\mathrm{LTL}}^{\mathrm{q}}$. In this derivation we sometimes write (ltl) to denote valid LTL formulas, without deriving them formally.

(1)	$\exists u_1(u_1 \land \bigcirc\Box\neg u_1)$	(qltl3)
(2)	$u_1 \land \bigcirc\Box\neg u_1 \rightarrow \neg\neg u_1 \land \bigcirc\Box\neg u_1$	(taut)
(3)	$\neg\neg u_1 \land \bigcirc\Box\neg u_1 \rightarrow \exists u_2(\neg u_2 \land \bigcirc\Box u_2)$	(qltl1)
(4)	$u_1 \land \bigcirc\Box\neg u_1 \rightarrow \exists u_2(\neg u_2 \land \bigcirc\Box u_2)$	(prop),(2),(3)
(5)	$\exists u_1(u_1 \land \bigcirc\Box\neg u_1) \rightarrow \exists u_2(\neg u_2 \land \bigcirc\Box u_2)$	(qltl-part),(4)
(6)	$\exists u_2(\neg u_2 \land \bigcirc\Box u_2)$	(mp),(1),(5)
(7)	$\bigcirc\exists u_2(\neg u_2 \land \bigcirc\Box u_2)$	(nex),(6)
(8)	$\exists u_2\bigcirc(\neg u_2 \land \bigcirc\Box u_2)$	(prop),(7),(qltl2)
(9)	$\bigcirc(\neg u_2 \land \bigcirc\Box u_2) \rightarrow \bigcirc\neg u_2 \land \bigcirc\bigcirc\Box u_2$	(prop),(T15)
(10)	$\bigcirc(\neg u_2 \land \bigcirc\Box u_2) \rightarrow \exists u_2(\bigcirc\neg u_2 \land \bigcirc\bigcirc\Box u_2)$	(qltl1)
(11)	$\exists u_2\bigcirc(\neg u_2 \land \bigcirc\Box u_2) \rightarrow \exists u_2\bigcirc\neg u_2 \land \bigcirc\bigcirc\Box u_2$	(qltl-part),(10)
(12)	$\exists u_2\bigcirc\neg u_2 \land \bigcirc\bigcirc\Box u_2$	(mp),(8),(11)
(13)	$\bigcirc\neg u_2 \land \bigcirc\bigcirc\Box u_2 \rightarrow$ $(\bar{u} \land (\bigcirc\bar{u} \leftrightarrow \neg\bar{u}) \rightarrow \bigcirc((u_2 \leftrightarrow \bar{u}) \land (\bigcirc u_2 \leftrightarrow \neg u_2)))$	(ltl)
(14)	$\bigcirc((u_2 \leftrightarrow \bar{u}) \land (\bigcirc u_2 \leftrightarrow \neg u_2)) \rightarrow$ $\exists u\bigcirc((u \leftrightarrow \bar{u}) \land (\bigcirc u \leftrightarrow \neg u))$	(qltl1)
(15)	$\bigcirc\neg u_2 \land \bigcirc\bigcirc\Box u_2 \rightarrow$ $(\bar{u} \land (\bigcirc\bar{u} \leftrightarrow \neg\bar{u}) \rightarrow \exists u\bigcirc((u \leftrightarrow \bar{u}) \land (\bigcirc u \leftrightarrow \neg u)))$	(prop),(13,(14)
(16)	$\exists u_2(\bigcirc\neg u_2 \land \bigcirc\bigcirc\Box u_2) \rightarrow$ $(\bar{u} \land (\bigcirc\bar{u} \leftrightarrow \neg\bar{u}) \rightarrow \exists u\bigcirc((u \leftrightarrow \bar{u}) \land (\bigcirc u \leftrightarrow \neg u)))$	(qltl-part),(15)
(17)	$\bar{u} \land (\bigcirc\bar{u} \leftrightarrow \neg\bar{u}) \rightarrow \exists u\bigcirc((u \leftrightarrow \bar{u}) \land (\bigcirc u \leftrightarrow \neg u))$	(mp),(12),(16)
(18)	$\bigcirc\exists u_1(u_1 \land \bigcirc\Box\neg u_1)$	(nex),(1)

(19) $\exists u_1 \circ(u_1 \wedge \circ\Box\neg u_1)$ (prop),(18),(qltl2)
(20) $\circ(u_1 \wedge \circ\Box\neg u_1) \rightarrow \circ u_1 \wedge \circ\circ\Box\neg u_1$ (prop),(T15)
(21) $\circ u_1 \wedge \circ\circ\Box\neg u_1 \rightarrow \exists u_1(\circ u_1 \wedge \circ\circ\Box\neg u_1)$ (qltl1)
(22) $\circ(u_1 \wedge \circ\Box\neg u_1) \rightarrow \exists u_1(\circ u_1 \wedge \circ\circ\Box\neg u_1)$ (prop),(20),(21)
(23) $\exists u_1 \circ(u_1 \wedge \circ\Box\neg u_1) \rightarrow \exists u_1(\circ u_1 \wedge \circ\circ\Box\neg u_1)$ (qltl-part),(22)
(24) $\exists u_1(\circ u_1 \wedge \circ\circ\Box\neg u_1)$ (mp),(19),(23)
(25) $\circ u_1 \wedge \circ\circ\Box\neg u_1 \rightarrow$
$(\neg\bar{u} \wedge (\circ\bar{u} \leftrightarrow \neg\bar{u}) \rightarrow \circ((u_1 \leftrightarrow \bar{u}) \wedge (\circ u_1 \leftrightarrow \neg u_1)))$ (ltl)
(26) $\neg\bar{u} \wedge (\circ\bar{u} \leftrightarrow \neg\bar{u}) \rightarrow \exists u \circ((u \leftrightarrow \bar{u}) \wedge (\circ u \leftrightarrow \neg u))$ from (24),(25) in the same way as (17) from (12),(13)
(27) $(\circ\bar{u} \leftrightarrow \neg\bar{u}) \rightarrow \exists u \circ((u \leftrightarrow \bar{u}) \wedge (\circ u \leftrightarrow \neg u))$ (prop),(17),(26)
(28) $(\circ\bar{u} \leftrightarrow \neg\bar{u}) \rightarrow \exists u((u \leftrightarrow \bar{u}) \wedge \Box(\circ u \leftrightarrow \neg u))$ (qltl-ind),(27)
(29) $\forall\bar{u}((\circ\bar{u} \leftrightarrow \neg\bar{u}) \rightarrow \exists u((u \leftrightarrow \bar{u}) \wedge \Box(\circ u \leftrightarrow \neg u)))$ (qltl-gen),(28)
(30) $u_1 \wedge \circ\Box\neg u_1 \rightarrow (\circ u_1 \leftrightarrow \neg u_1)$ (ltl)
(31) $u_1 \wedge \circ\Box\neg u_1 \rightarrow \exists u((u \leftrightarrow u_1) \wedge \Box(\circ u \leftrightarrow \neg u))$ (prop),(29),(Tq1)
(32) $(u \leftrightarrow u_1) \wedge \Box(\circ u \leftrightarrow \neg u) \rightarrow (u_1 \rightarrow u \wedge \Box(\circ u \leftrightarrow \neg u))$ (taut)
(33) $u \wedge \Box(\circ u \leftrightarrow \neg u) \rightarrow \exists u(u \wedge \Box(\circ u \leftrightarrow \neg u))$ (qltl1)
(34) $(u \leftrightarrow u_1) \wedge \Box(\circ u \leftrightarrow \neg u) \rightarrow$
$(u_1 \rightarrow \exists u(u \wedge \Box(\circ u \leftrightarrow \neg u)))$ (prop),(32),(33)
(35) $\exists u((u \leftrightarrow u_1) \wedge \Box(\circ u \leftrightarrow \neg u)) \rightarrow$
$(u_1 \rightarrow \exists u(u \wedge \Box(\circ u \leftrightarrow \neg u)))$ (qltl-part),(34)
(36) $u_1 \wedge \circ\Box\neg u_1 \rightarrow \exists u(u \wedge \Box(\circ u \leftrightarrow \neg u))$ (prop),(31),(35)
(37) $\exists u_1(u_1 \wedge \circ\Box\neg u_1) \rightarrow \exists u(u \wedge \Box(\circ u \leftrightarrow \neg u))$ (qltl-part),(36)
(38) $\exists u(u \wedge \Box(\circ u \leftrightarrow \neg u))$ (mp),(1),(37) △

We conclude by listing some further laws that are not hard to derive in $\Sigma^{\mathrm{q}}_{\mathrm{LTL}}$. We will revisit this extension of LTL in Chap. 4 where its expressive power will be related with the fixpoint logic LTL+μ considered in Sect. 3.2.

(Tq2) $\forall u \circ A \leftrightarrow \circ\forall u A$,
(Tq3) $\forall u \Box A \leftrightarrow \Box\forall u A$,
(Tq4) $\exists u \Diamond A \leftrightarrow \Diamond\exists u A$,
(Tq5) $\Box(A \vee B) \rightarrow \exists u \Box((A \wedge u) \vee (B \wedge \neg u))$.

3.4 Past Operators

Our next extension starts from the observation that in LTL and its versions investigated so far it is only possible to "speak about the future". The temporal operators $\circ$, $\Box$, **until**, etc. (in this context also called *future operators*) relate assertions on future states (including possibly the present one) to the reference state. It is very natural to extend the general idea of temporal logic by *past operators* which allow for "looking into the past".

To do this, starting again from LTL, we introduce the "symmetrical" versions of the basic operators $\circ$ and $\Box$. The new operators are denoted by $\ominus$ and $\boxminus$ and called *weak previous operator* and *has-always-been operator*, respectively. Their informal meaning is as follows.

$\ominus A$: "A held in the previous state",
$\boxminus A$: "A held in all past states (including the present one)".

More formally, we obtain an extended logic LTL+p the language $\mathcal{L}_{\mathrm{LTL}}^{\mathrm{p}}$ of which results from $\mathcal{L}_{\mathrm{LTL}}$ by adding the symbols $\ominus$ and $\boxminus$ to the alphabet and the clause

- If A is a formula then $\ominus A$ and $\boxminus A$ are formulas

to the inductive definition of formulas. The semantics is given by extending the inductive definition of $\mathsf{K}_i(F)$ for a temporal structure K, $i \in \mathbb{N}$, and formula F given in Sect. 2.1 by

- $\mathsf{K}_i(\ominus A) = \mathsf{tt} \;\Leftrightarrow\;$ if $i > 0$ then $\mathsf{K}_{i-1}(A) = \mathsf{tt}$.
- $\mathsf{K}_i(\boxminus A) = \mathsf{tt} \;\Leftrightarrow\; \mathsf{K}_j(A) = \mathsf{tt}$ for every $j \le i$.

Example. Let $v \in \mathbf{V}$, $A \equiv \Box\ominus v$, $B \equiv \boxminus\bigcirc\neg v$, and K be given by:

	η_0	η_1	η_2	η_3	...
v	ff	ff	tt	tt	... (tt forever) ...

Then we get $\mathsf{K}_0(\ominus v) = \mathsf{tt}$, $\mathsf{K}_1(\ominus v) = \mathsf{K}_2(\ominus v) = \mathsf{ff}$, $\mathsf{K}_i(\ominus v) = \mathsf{tt}$ for $i \ge 3$, $\mathsf{K}_0(\bigcirc\neg v) = \mathsf{tt}$, $\mathsf{K}_1(\bigcirc\neg v) = \mathsf{ff}$, and therefore

$$\mathsf{K}_i(A) = \mathsf{ff} \text{ for } i \le 2,$$
$$\mathsf{K}_i(A) = \mathsf{tt} \text{ for } i \ge 3,$$
$$\mathsf{K}_0(B) = \mathsf{tt},$$
$$\mathsf{K}_i(B) = \mathsf{ff} \text{ for } i \ge 1.$$

△

The symmetry between the pairs of operators $\bigcirc$ and $\Box$ on the one hand and $\ominus$ and $\boxminus$ on the other hand is not "exact" since in any state, there are infinitely many future states but the past is limited by the initial state. The particularity of this state is expressed by the fact that, for any temporal structure K,

$$\mathsf{K}_0(\ominus A) = \mathsf{tt},$$
$$\mathsf{K}_0(\boxminus A) = \mathsf{K}_0(A)$$

hold for arbitrary A. The first of these equalities comes from the "weak" semantical definition for $\ominus$. A dual ("strong") version is obtained by introducing the *strong previous operator* $\circleddash$ through the abbreviation

$$\circleddash A \equiv \neg\ominus\neg A$$

which obviously provides

$$\mathsf{K}_i(\circleddash A) = \mathsf{tt} \;\Leftrightarrow\; i > 0 \text{ and } \mathsf{K}_{i-1}(A) = \mathsf{tt}$$

and

$$\mathsf{K}_0(\circledequal A) = \mathsf{ff},$$
$$\mathsf{K}_i(\circledequal A) = \mathsf{K}_i(\ominus A) \quad \text{for } i > 0$$

for arbitrary A.

Finally we may introduce a counterpart $\diamondminus$, called *once operator*, of $\Diamond$ by the abbreviation

$$\diamondminus A \;\equiv\; \neg\boxminus\neg A$$

which implies

$$\mathsf{K}_i(\diamondminus A) = \mathsf{tt} \;\Leftrightarrow\; \mathsf{K}_j(A) = \mathsf{tt} \text{ for some } j \leq i$$

and

$$\mathsf{K}_0(\diamondminus A) = \mathsf{K}_0(A)$$

for every formula A.

For more illustration, we give again a short list of valid formulas of LTL+p and prove some few of them.

(Tp1) $\circledequal A \rightarrow \neg\ominus\,\mathbf{false}$,
(Tp2) $\ominus\neg A \rightarrow \neg\circledequal A$,
(Tp3) $\neg\ominus A \leftrightarrow \circledequal\neg A$,
(Tp4) $A \rightarrow \ominus\bigcirc A$,
(Tp5) $A \rightarrow \bigcirc\circledequal A$,
(Tp6) $\ominus(A \rightarrow B) \leftrightarrow \ominus A \rightarrow \ominus B$,
(Tp7) $\ominus(A \land B) \leftrightarrow \ominus A \land \ominus B$,
(Tp8) $\circledequal(A \land B) \leftrightarrow \circledequal A \land \circledequal B$.

Proof of (Tp2), (Tp4), *and* (Tp8). For any temporal structure K and $i \in \mathbb{N}$ we have:

$$\begin{aligned}\mathsf{K}_i(\ominus\neg A) = \mathsf{tt} &\Rightarrow i > 0 \text{ and } \mathsf{K}_{i-1}(A) = \mathsf{ff}\\ &\Rightarrow \mathsf{K}_i(\circledequal A) = \mathsf{ff}\\ &\Rightarrow \mathsf{K}_i(\neg\circledequal A) = \mathsf{tt}.\end{aligned}$$

$$\begin{aligned}\mathsf{K}_i(A) = \mathsf{tt} &\Rightarrow \text{if } i > 0 \text{ then } \mathsf{K}_i(A) = \mathsf{tt}\\ &\Rightarrow \text{if } i > 0 \text{ then } \mathsf{K}_{i-1}(\bigcirc A) = \mathsf{tt}\\ &\Rightarrow \mathsf{K}_i(\ominus\bigcirc A) = \mathsf{tt}.\end{aligned}$$

$$\begin{aligned}\mathsf{K}_i(\circledequal(A \land B)) = \mathsf{tt} &\Leftrightarrow i > 0 \text{ and } \mathsf{K}_{i-1}(A \land B) = \mathsf{tt}\\ &\Leftrightarrow i > 0 \text{ and } \mathsf{K}_{i-1}(A) = \mathsf{K}_{i-1}(B) = \mathsf{tt}\\ &\Leftrightarrow \mathsf{K}_i(\circledequal A \land \circledequal B) = \mathsf{tt}.\end{aligned}$$
△

LTL+p is more expressive than LTL. Consider the formula $\ominus\,\mathbf{false}$. According to the arguments from above we have

$$\mathsf{K}_0(\ominus\,\mathbf{false}) = \mathsf{tt}$$

and since

$$\mathsf{K}_i(\ominus \mathbf{false}) = \mathsf{ff} \quad \text{for } i > 0$$

is obvious, we obtain

$$\mathsf{K}_i(\ominus \mathbf{false}) = \mathsf{tt} \Leftrightarrow i > 0.$$

We will see in the next section that this has some connections to initial validity discussed in Sect. 2.6 and indeed, like in the logic LTL_0 introduced there, we have to face the fact that the typical LTL relationship

$$\mathcal{F} \cup \{A\} \models B \;\Leftrightarrow\; \mathcal{F} \models \Box A \to B$$

between implication and consequence does not hold in general in LTL+p but has to be modified in the following manner.

Theorem 3.4.1. *In* LTL+p, $\mathcal{F} \cup \{A\} \models B$ *if and only if* $\mathcal{F} \models \Box A \land \boxminus A \to B$.

Proof. We first note that for every temporal structure K and $i \in \mathbb{N}$ we have

$$\begin{aligned} \models_{\mathsf{K}} A &\Leftrightarrow \mathsf{K}_j(A) = \mathsf{tt} \text{ for every } j \in \mathbb{N} \\ &\Leftrightarrow \mathsf{K}_j(A) = \mathsf{tt} \text{ for every } j \leq i \text{ and } \mathsf{K}_j(A) = \mathsf{tt} \text{ for every } j \geq i \\ &\Leftrightarrow \mathsf{K}_i(\Box A \land \boxminus A) = \mathsf{tt}. \end{aligned}$$

So, if $\mathcal{F} \cup \{A\} \models B$, let K be a temporal structure with $\models_{\mathsf{K}} F$ for every $F \in \mathcal{F}$ and $i \in \mathbb{N}$. Then $\mathsf{K}_i(\Box A \land \boxminus A) = \mathsf{tt}$ implies $\models_{\mathsf{K}} A$ from which we get $\models_{\mathsf{K}} B$ and, hence, $\mathsf{K}_i(B) = \mathsf{tt}$. This proves the only if part of the theorem.

For the converse, let $\mathcal{F} \models \Box A \land \boxminus A \to B$, K be a temporal structure with $\models_{\mathsf{K}} F$ for every $F \in \mathcal{F} \cup \{A\}$, and $i \in \mathbb{N}$. Then $\models_{\mathsf{K}} A$ and therefore $\mathsf{K}_i(\Box A \land \boxminus A) = \mathsf{tt}$. From the presupposition we get $\mathsf{K}_i(\Box A \land \boxminus A \to B) = \mathsf{tt}$ and, by Lemma 2.1.1, $\mathsf{K}_i(B) = \mathsf{tt}$ which proves the assertion. △

(A close look at this proof shows that the if part of the LTL relationship still holds in LTL+p.)

Finally, LTL+p can be axiomatized by a sound and weakly complete formal system $\Sigma_{\mathrm{LTL}}^{\mathrm{p}}$ which results from Σ_{LTL} by the following extensions.

Additional axioms

(pltl1) $\circleddash \neg A \to \neg \circleddash A$,
(pltl2) $\ominus(A \to B) \to (\ominus A \to \ominus B)$,
(pltl3) $\boxminus A \to A \land \ominus \boxminus A$,
(pltl4) $\diamondminus \ominus \mathbf{false}$,
(pltl5) $A \to \ominus \bigcirc A$,
(pltl6) $A \to \bigcirc \circleddash A$.

Additional rules

(prev) $A \vdash \ominus A$,
(indpast) $A \to B, A \to \ominus A \vdash A \to \boxminus B$.

The axioms (pltl1), (pltl2), (pltl3), and both rules are counterparts of the ("proper temporal") axioms and rules of Σ_{LTL}. Axiom (pltl4) expresses the existence of an initial state. Finally, axioms (pltl5) and (pltl6) connect past and future.

As an example of application, we show how to derive the law (Tp1) noted above.

Derivation of (Tp1).

(1) $\textbf{false} \to \neg A$ (taut)
(2) $\ominus(\textbf{false} \to \neg A)$ (prev),(1)
(3) $\ominus\,\textbf{false} \to \ominus\neg A$ (prop),(pltl2),(2)
(4) $\circleddash A \to \neg\ominus\,\textbf{false}$ (prop),(3) △

We conclude with the obvious remark that the Deduction Theorem does not hold in LTL+p in the form of Theorem 2.3.3 but has to be modified to

$$\mathcal{F} \cup \{A\} \vdash_{\Sigma^{\text{p}}_{\text{LTL}}} B \Rightarrow \mathcal{F} \vdash_{\Sigma^{\text{p}}_{\text{LTL}}} \Box A \land \boxminus A \to B$$

which directly mirrors the semantical considerations above. The converse of this relationship holds as well as the LTL version formulated in Theorem 2.3.4.

3.5 Syntactic Anchoring

In the previous section we already indicated a connection between the expressibility of past operators and initial validity semantics discussed in Sect. 2.6. If we want to describe that a formula A holds in the initial state of some temporal structure this can be achieved by taking LTL with that semantics, i.e., LTL_0, or, alternatively, by choosing LTL+p. As we have seen in Sect. 3.4, a particular feature of the latter extension is that

$$\mathsf{K}_i(\ominus\,\textbf{false}) = \mathsf{tt} \Leftrightarrow i = 0$$

for every temporal structure K. For the formula

$$B \equiv \ominus\,\textbf{false} \to A$$

we then obviously obtain

$$\mathsf{K}_0(B) = \mathsf{K}_0(A),$$
$$\mathsf{K}_i(B) = \mathsf{tt} \text{ for every } i > 0$$

and therefore

$$\models_{\mathsf{K}} B \Leftrightarrow \mathsf{K}_0(A) = \mathsf{tt}.$$

So, $\ominus\,\mathbf{false} \rightarrow A$ in fact describes that "A holds in the initial state (of K)".

We may take this observation to introduce a simpler extension of LTL than by past operators which allows this "syntactic anchoring" as well. We only enrich the alphabet of $\mathcal{L}_{\mathrm{LTL}}$ by an additional symbol **init** and extend the inductive definition of formulas of $\mathcal{L}_{\mathrm{LTL}}$ by the clause

- **init** is a formula.

We denote the resulting logic by LTL+i and its language by $\mathcal{L}^{\mathrm{i}}_{\mathrm{LTL}}$.

The informal meaning of **init** is to behave like $\ominus\,\mathbf{false}$ in LTL+p, i.e., to hold exactly in the initial state of a temporal structure. This is formalized by extending the inductive definition of $\mathsf{K}_i(F)$ for a temporal structure K, $i \in \mathbb{N}$, and formula F to the new formula in the following evident way:

- $\mathsf{K}_i(\mathbf{init}) = \mathsf{tt} \;\Leftrightarrow\; i = 0.$

Then, as above, the formula

$$\mathbf{init} \rightarrow A$$

describes the initial validity of A (in some K).

There are two characteristic laws for the new formula. The first one is given by the formula

$$\bigcirc\neg\mathbf{init}$$

which expresses that **init** does not hold in non-initial states. Its validity is clear because of

$$\mathsf{K}_i(\bigcirc\neg\mathbf{init}) = \mathsf{K}_{i+1}(\neg\mathbf{init}) = \mathsf{tt}$$

for every temporal structure K and $i \in \mathbb{N}$. The second law is the consequence relationship

$$\mathbf{init} \rightarrow \Box A \models A$$

which captures the property that **init** holds in initial states. For its proof, let K be a temporal structure with $\models_{\mathsf{K}} \mathbf{init} \rightarrow \Box A$ and $i \in \mathbb{N}$. Then $\mathsf{K}_0(\mathbf{init} \rightarrow \Box A) = \mathsf{tt}$ which means $\mathsf{K}_j(A) = \mathsf{tt}$ for all $j \geq 0$. This implies $\mathsf{K}_i(A) = \mathsf{tt}$ and shows that $\models_{\mathsf{K}} A$.

The expressibility of initial validity in LTL+i induces the same remarkable fact about the relationship between implication and consequence as in LTL_0 and in LTL+p: the equivalence

$$\mathcal{F} \cup \{A\} \models B \;\Leftrightarrow\; \mathcal{F} \models \Box A \rightarrow B$$

does not hold in general in LTL+i. A simple counterexample (with $\mathcal{F} = \emptyset$) is given by

$$\mathbf{init} \to \Box\mathbf{init} \vDash \mathbf{init}$$

which is an instance of the general law just mentioned. However, the formula

$$\Box(\mathbf{init} \to \Box\mathbf{init}) \to \mathbf{init}$$

is not valid. Otherwise we would get, e.g.,

$$\mathsf{K}_1(\Box(\mathbf{init} \to \Box\mathbf{init}) \to \mathbf{init}) = \mathsf{tt}.$$

As in the example at the beginning of the section we have $\mathsf{K}_i(\mathbf{init} \to \Box\mathbf{init}) = \mathsf{tt}$ for every $i > 0$ and therefore

$$\mathsf{K}_1(\Box(\mathbf{init} \to \Box\mathbf{init})) = \mathsf{tt}.$$

Lemma 2.1.1 may be applied here as in LTL, so together we would get $\mathsf{K}_1(\mathbf{init}) = \mathsf{tt}$ which is an obvious contradiction.

The general relationship above can be saved in LTL+i only with some restrictions. One possible modification is

$$\mathcal{F} \cup \{A\} \vDash B \;\Leftrightarrow\; \mathcal{F} \vDash \Box A \to B \quad \text{if } A, B \text{ and all formulas of } \mathcal{F} \text{ do not contain the formula } \mathbf{init}.$$

With this restriction, the proof of Theorem 2.1.6 can be transferred verbally. The crucial point is that Lemma 2.1.5 still holds for formulas without **init** (but is violated by **init**) which can easily be seen from its proof. Clearly, the proof of Theorem 2.1.6 also shows that the "if" part of the relationship still holds without any restriction.

An axiomatization of LTL+i is given by extending the formal system Σ_{LTL} by the two characteristic laws introduced above, i.e., the additional axiom

(iltl) $\bigcirc\neg\mathbf{init}$

and the additional rule

(init) $\mathbf{init} \to \Box A \vdash A$.

We denote the extended system by $\Sigma^{\mathrm{i}}_{\mathrm{LTL}}$. It is sound as proved by the semantical arguments above, and it can also be shown to be weakly complete.

A useful derived rule of $\Sigma^{\mathrm{i}}_{\mathrm{LTL}}$ is the following additional version of the basic induction rule (ind) of Σ_{LTL}:

(indinit) $\mathbf{init} \to A, A \to \bigcirc A \vdash A$.

Derivation of (indinit).

(1)	$\mathbf{init} \to A$	assumption
(2)	$A \to \bigcirc A$	assumption
(3)	$\mathbf{init} \to \Box A$	(ind2),(1),(2)
(4)	A	(init),(3)

△

As in Sects. 2.6 and 3.4 we conclude with a remark on the Deduction Theorem. According to the semantical considerations above this no longer holds in LTL+i in the general form of LTL. A possible modification could be formulated with the restriction as in the semantical case. Another, more precise one is given as follows:

$\mathcal{F} \cup \{A\} \vdash B \;\Rightarrow\; \mathcal{F} \vdash \Box A \rightarrow B$ if the derivation of B from $\mathcal{F} \cup \{A\}$ contains no application of the rule (init).

Its justification can be taken verbally from the proof of Theorem 2.3.3. The converse of the general form (i.e., without any restriction) still holds in LTL+i.

3.6 Combinations of Extensions

As indicated already in Sects. 3.2 and 3.3, the extensions presented separately in the preceding sections can also be combined, and various of such combinations are quite reasonable. For example, the extension by the formula **init** can be combined with binary or fixpoint operators. Propositional quantification could be added to an extension with binary or past operators. A combination of **init** with past operators, on the other hand, would not make much sense, since **init** is expressible in LTL+p.

In any such combination, a proper formal system is given by adding the respective axioms and rules introduced in the preceding sections to Σ_{LTL}. For example, the logic LTL+b+i obtained by extending LTL by the extensions "b" and "i" has the following sound and weakly complete formal system $\Sigma^{\mathrm{bi}}_{\mathrm{LTL}}$ (based, e.g., on the operator **atnext**).

Axioms

(taut) All tautologically valid formulas,
(ltl1) $\neg\bigcirc A \leftrightarrow \bigcirc\neg A$,
(ltl2) $\bigcirc(A \rightarrow B) \rightarrow (\bigcirc A \rightarrow \bigcirc B)$,
(ltl3) $\Box A \rightarrow A \wedge \bigcirc\Box A$,
(atnext1) $A\ \mathbf{atnext}\ B \leftrightarrow \bigcirc(B \rightarrow A) \wedge \bigcirc(\neg B \rightarrow A\ \mathbf{atnext}\ B)$,
(atnext2) $\bigcirc\Box\neg B \rightarrow A\ \mathbf{atnext}\ B$,
(iltl) $\bigcirc\neg\mathbf{init}$.

Rules

(mp) $A, A \rightarrow B \vdash B$,
(nex) $A \vdash \bigcirc A$,
(ind) $A \rightarrow B, A \rightarrow \bigcirc A \vdash A \rightarrow \Box B$,
(init) $\mathbf{init} \rightarrow \Box A \vdash A$.

Furthermore, all temporal logic laws and derived rules of LTL and the respective extensions hold in the combination. For example, in LTL+b+i the laws (T1)–(T38), (Tb1)–(Tb29) and the derived rules (prop), (ind1), (ind2), (alw), (som), and (indinit) are available.

If past operators are combined with binary or fixpoint operators it would be reasonable to extend the "past aspect" to these operators. For example, enriching LTL+b by past operators (yielding a logic LTL+b+p) should not only introduce $\ominus$ and $\boxminus$ as discussed in Sect. 3.4 but also the "past analogies" of the binary operators. Such *binary past operators* can be introduced, e.g., for the informal phrase

"A held in all preceding states since the last state in which B held".

Again strict or non-strict, strong or weak interpretations are possible. We consider only strict versions and fix the following formal definitions.

- $\mathsf{K}_i(A\ \mathbf{since}\ B) = \mathsf{tt} \Leftrightarrow \mathsf{K}_j(B) = \mathsf{tt}$ for some $j < i$ and $\mathsf{K}_k(A) = \mathsf{tt}$ for every $k, j < k < i$.
- $\mathsf{K}_i(A\ \mathbf{backto}\ B) = \mathsf{tt} \Leftrightarrow \mathsf{K}_j(B) = \mathsf{tt}$ for some $j < i$ and $\mathsf{K}_k(A) = \mathsf{tt}$ for every $k, j < k < i$ or $\mathsf{K}_k(A) = \mathsf{tt}$ for every $k < i$.

The operators **since** and **backto** are obvious past analogies of **until** and **unless**. In the same way operators **atlast** ("A held in the last state in which B held") and **after** ("A held after B held") reflecting **atnext** and **before** can be defined as follows.

- $\mathsf{K}_i(A\ \mathbf{atlast}\ B) = \mathsf{tt} \Leftrightarrow \mathsf{K}_j(B) = \mathsf{ff}$ for every $j < i$ or $\mathsf{K}_k(A) = \mathsf{tt}$ for the greatest $k < i$ with $\mathsf{K}_k(B) = \mathsf{tt}$.
- $\mathsf{K}_i(A\ \mathbf{after}\ B) = \mathsf{tt} \Leftrightarrow$ for every $j < i$ with $\mathsf{K}_j(B) = \mathsf{tt}$ there is some $k, j < k < i$, with $\mathsf{K}_k(A) = \mathsf{tt}$.

The various relationships between the (future) binary operators and their connections to $\bigcirc$, $\Box$, and $\Diamond$ can be systematically transferred to these new operators and $\ominus$, $\circleddash$, $\boxminus$, and $\diamondminus$. We give only a few examples which should be compared with (Tb1) and (Tb5)–(Tb9).

- $A\ \mathbf{since}\ B \leftrightarrow \circleddash\diamondminus B \land A\ \mathbf{backto}\ B$,
- $A\ \mathbf{backto}\ B \leftrightarrow B\ \mathbf{atlast}\ (A \rightarrow B)$,
- $A\ \mathbf{atlast}\ B \leftrightarrow B\ \mathbf{after}\ (\neg A \land B)$,
- $A\ \mathbf{after}\ B \leftrightarrow \neg(A \lor B)\ \mathbf{backto}\ (A \land \neg B)$,
- $\ominus A \leftrightarrow A\ \mathbf{atlast\ true}$,
- $\boxminus A \leftrightarrow A \land A\ \mathbf{backto\ false}$.

A sound and weakly complete axiomatization could be based on one of the operators. Depending on this choice, one of the axioms

(since)	$A\ \mathbf{since}\ B \leftrightarrow \circleddash B \lor \circleddash(A \land A\ \mathbf{since}\ B)$,
(backto)	$A\ \mathbf{backto}\ B \leftrightarrow \ominus B \lor \ominus(A \land A\ \mathbf{backto}\ B)$,
(atlast)	$A\ \mathbf{atlast}\ B \leftrightarrow \ominus(B \rightarrow A) \land \ominus(\neg B \rightarrow A\ \mathbf{atlast}\ B)$,
(after)	$A\ \mathbf{after}\ B \leftrightarrow \ominus\neg B \land \ominus(A \lor A\ \mathbf{after}\ B)$

being the analogies of (until1), (unless1), (atnext1), and (before1), respectively, should be added to the other extending axioms. These are again fixpoint characterizations and it should be noted that the strong and weak versions **since** and **backto** of "since" now have different characterizations with respect to the involved previous operators.

Another remarkable fact is that none of the analogies of the respective axioms (until2), (unless2), (atnext2), and (before2) needs to be taken as a further axiom here. They can be derived in the formal system $\Sigma_{\mathrm{LTL}}^{\mathrm{p}}$ augmented with one of the above axioms. Observe that for the binary future operators those additional axioms characterized strong and weak operator versions, i.e., as mentioned in Sect. 3.2, least or greatest fixpoints, of certain corresponding equivalences. So the derivability of their analogies also indicates that, in fact, the least and greatest fixpoints in the case of past operators coincide.

As an example we derive the formula

$$\ominus\boxminus\neg B \rightarrow A\ \mathbf{atlast}\ B$$

which corresponds to (atnext2). The derivation also makes use of the laws (Tp1), (Tp7), and (Tp8) listed in Sect. 3.4:

(1)	$\neg(A\ \mathbf{atlast}\ B) \rightarrow$ $\neg\ominus(B \rightarrow A) \vee \neg\ominus(\neg B \rightarrow A\ \mathbf{atlast}\ B)$	(prop),(atlast)
(2)	$\neg(A\ \mathbf{atlast}\ B) \rightarrow$ $\boldsymbol{\ominus}(B \wedge \neg A) \vee \boldsymbol{\ominus}(\neg B \wedge \neg(A\ \mathbf{atlast}\ B))$	(prop),(prev),(pltl2),(1)
(3)	$\neg(A\ \mathbf{atlast}\ B) \rightarrow \neg\ominus\ \mathbf{false}$	(prop),(Tp1),(2)
(4)	$\neg(A\ \mathbf{atlast}\ B) \wedge \ominus\boxminus\neg B \rightarrow \neg\ominus\ \mathbf{false}$	(prop),(3)
(5)	$\neg(A\ \mathbf{atlast}\ B) \rightarrow$ $(\boldsymbol{\ominus}B \wedge \boldsymbol{\ominus}\neg A) \vee (\boldsymbol{\ominus}\neg B \wedge \boldsymbol{\ominus}\neg(A\ \mathbf{atlast}\ B))$	(prop),(Tp8),(2)
(6)	$\boxminus\neg B \rightarrow \neg B \wedge \ominus\boxminus\neg B$	(pltl3)
(7)	$\ominus(\boxminus\neg B \rightarrow \neg B \wedge \ominus\boxminus\neg B)$	(prev),(6)
(8)	$\ominus\boxminus\neg B \rightarrow \ominus(\neg B \wedge \ominus\boxminus\neg B)$	(prop),(pltl2),(7)
(9)	$\ominus\boxminus\neg B \rightarrow \neg\boldsymbol{\ominus}B \wedge \ominus\ominus\boxminus\neg B$	(prop),(Tp7),(8)
(10)	$\neg(A\ \mathbf{atlast}\ B) \wedge \ominus\boxminus\neg B \rightarrow$ $\boldsymbol{\ominus}\neg(A\ \mathbf{atlast}\ B) \wedge \ominus\ominus\boxminus\neg B$	(prop),(5),(9)
(11)	$\boldsymbol{\ominus}\neg(A\ \mathbf{atlast}\ B) \rightarrow \ominus\neg(A\ \mathbf{atlast}\ B)$	(prop),(pltl1)
(12)	$\neg(A\ \mathbf{atlast}\ B) \wedge \ominus\boxminus\neg B \rightarrow$ $\ominus(\neg(A\ \mathbf{atlast}\ B) \wedge \ominus\boxminus\neg B)$	(prop),(Tp7),(10),(11)
(13)	$\neg(A\ \mathbf{atlast}\ B) \wedge \ominus\boxminus\neg B \rightarrow \boxminus\neg\ominus\ \mathbf{false}$	(indpast),(4),(12)
(14)	$\diamondminus\ominus\ \mathbf{false} \rightarrow (\ominus\boxminus\neg B \rightarrow A\ \mathbf{atlast}\ B)$	(prop),(13)
(15)	$\ominus\boxminus\neg B \rightarrow A\ \mathbf{atlast}\ B$	(mp),(pltl4),(14) △

Finally we note that the extensions may also be combined with initial validity semantics. In this case the axiomatizations have to be adjusted in a similar way to the one in which Σ_{LTL_0} results from Σ_{LTL}.

Second Reading

As sketched out in the Second Reading paragraph in Sect. 2.3, temporal logic is a special branch of modal logic. Its intention is to formalize reasoning about statements "in the flow of time" and it is particularly designed for applications in computer science.

Capturing aspects of time is quite generally of interest in logics, and another field of possible applications is encountered by the relationship between logic and (natural) languages. In fact, there is also a "modal approach" to this topic, called *tense logic*, which is very close to temporal logic as described here.

"Basic" tense logic is an extension of classical propositional logic by unary *tense operators* for building formulas of the form

$\Box A$ ("It will always be the case that A"),
$\boxminus A$ ("It has always been the case that A")

(we use, because of the close relationship, the operator symbols of temporal logic) and

$\Diamond A$ ("It will be the case that A"),
$\diamondminus A$ ("It has been the case that A")

with the duality relationship that $\Diamond A$ can be identified as $\neg\Box\neg A$ and $\diamondminus A$ as $\neg\boxminus\neg A$.

An extended version adds the binary tense operators **until** and **since**, i.e., formulas of the kind

A **until** B ("It will be the case that B, and A up to then"),
A **since** B ("It has been the case that B, and A since then")

to the basic equipment.

As to the language, this tense logic is "LTL+b+p without nexttime and previous operators". The semantics, however, is a "most general one" in the lines of modal logic (and many investigations then again address the questions of whether and how particular restrictions can be characterized by formulas of the logic). Adopting the notion of a Kripke structure $\mathfrak{K} = (\{\eta_\iota\}_{\iota \in K}, \lhd)$ as defined for modal logic in the Second Reading paragraph of Sect. 2.3 (and informally understanding now K as a set of "time points" and $\lhd$ as the relation "earlier than") the semantics of the tense operators is given by the clauses

$$\mathfrak{K}_\iota(\Box A) = \mathsf{tt} \Leftrightarrow \mathfrak{K}_\kappa(A) = \mathsf{tt} \text{ for every } \kappa \text{ with } \iota \lhd \kappa,$$
$$\mathfrak{K}_\iota(\boxminus A) = \mathsf{tt} \Leftrightarrow \mathfrak{K}_\kappa(A) = \mathsf{tt} \text{ for every } \kappa \text{ with } \kappa \lhd \iota,$$
$$\mathfrak{K}_\iota(A \textbf{ until } B) = \mathsf{tt} \Leftrightarrow \mathfrak{K}_\kappa(B) = \mathsf{tt} \text{ for some } \kappa \text{ with } \iota \lhd \kappa \text{ and } \mathfrak{K}_k(A) = \mathsf{tt} \text{ for every } k \text{ with } \iota \lhd k \text{ and } k \lhd \kappa$$

and analogously for the other operators.

The definition for $\Box A$ is just as in modal logic and taken together, the clauses show that the semantical difference to temporal logic (as introduced so far) is given by the fact that in the latter K is fixed to be the set $\mathbb{N}$ of natural numbers and $\lhd$ is $<$ (which also means that $\Box$ and $\boxminus$ are here defined in a "non-reflexive" version).

Bibliographical Notes

The until operator was originally investigated in tense logic (cf. the above Second Reading paragraph of Sect. 3.6) by Kamp [70] and introduced into the context of program analysis in [53]. The before operator can be found in [96], the atnext operator was introduced in [82].

The logic LTL+μ was introduced in [11], based on the modal μ-calculus, which was studied in depth by Pratt [124] and Kozen [75]. Walukiewicz [157] proved the completeness of Kozen's axiomatization of the μ-calculus, on which that of LTL+μ is based.

Quantification over propositional constants was investigated, e.g., in [138]. The first axiomatization of quantified propositional temporal logic (with future and past operators) is due to Kesten and Pnueli [73]; our presentation follows French and Reynolds [51]. The since operator was already used in [70]. Past operators in the form presented here were reintroduced in [92]. Our account of syntactic anchoring in Sect. 3.5 is related to [145].

4

Expressiveness of Propositional Linear Temporal Logics

As for every logical language, it is interesting to investigate the "expressive power" of temporal logic(s). There are various aspects of this notion raising different questions about, e.g, which temporal operators are expressible by others, how the various temporal logics compare with each other in their expressive power, how temporal logic descriptions compare with descriptions in other formalisms, and the like.

In some previous sections we already argued rather casually about "expressibilities". In this chapter we want to address these questions more systematically. In particular, we want to compare temporal logics with classical predicate logic and with certain automata. Both formalisms can serve as "yardsticks" for measuring the expressiveness of temporal logics.

4.1 LTL and Its Extensions

Temporal logic formulas describe assertions about temporal relationships in state sequences like the phrase

"If A holds then B holds in all forthcoming states including the present one"

that is formally mirrored by the semantics of the formula $A \rightarrow \Box B$. The basis for this kind of description is given by the temporal operators, and which relationships can be described depends on the "expressive power" of the operators. In Chap. 3 we already noted, among others, the following simple facts concerning this aspect:

- the binary operators of LTL+b are mutually expressible by each other,
- the operator $\Box$ is expressible by each of these binary operators,
- the operator $\bigcirc$ is expressible by each of the strict binary operators,
- The operators of LTL+b are expressible by fixpoint operators and by propositional quantification.

We will, throughout this book, compare the expressiveness of formalisms in various ways. Actually, the notion of "being expressible by" is not defined in a uniform way; it will be determined by different concrete relationships between the formalisms. Assertions of the kind recalled here compare various temporal logical operators and refer to the same "logical framework". In this particular case we will define in the following a first adequate formal setting of expressivity notions for such comparisons. Later we will extend or modify the notions or even use them for other "similar" relationships.

Let TL_1 and TL_2 be two temporal logics (with normal semantics) as discussed in Chaps. 2 und 3. We write $\mathrm{TL}_1 \subseteq \mathrm{TL}_2$, if every formula of TL_1 (more precisely: of any language of TL_1) is also a formula of TL_2, i.e., if TL_2 is an *extension* of TL_1 in the sense in which this notion was introduced in Sect. 1.4.

A formula A of a temporal logic TL_1 is called *expressible in* the logic TL_2 if there is a formula B in TL_2 such that

$$\models A \leftrightarrow B$$

holds in a logic TL which is a common extension of both TL_1 and TL_2 (so $A \leftrightarrow B$ is a formula of TL); in other words, A and B are logically equivalent (in TL). In general this means that

$$\mathsf{K}_i^{(\Xi)}(A) = \mathsf{K}_i^{(\Xi)}(B)$$

holds for every temporal structure K, valuation Ξ, and $i \in \mathbb{N}$, and reduces to

$$\mathsf{K}_i(A) = \mathsf{K}_i(B)$$

in the case that TL does not contain propositional variables. We now write

$$\mathrm{TL}_1 \leq \mathrm{TL}_2$$

if every formula A of TL_1 is expressible in TL_2. Obviously we have $\mathrm{TL}_1 \leq \mathrm{TL}_2$ if $\mathrm{TL}_1 \subseteq \mathrm{TL}_2$. TL_1 and TL_2 are called *equally expressive*, denoted by

$$\mathrm{TL}_1 = \mathrm{TL}_2$$

if $\mathrm{TL}_1 \leq \mathrm{TL}_2$ and $\mathrm{TL}_2 \leq \mathrm{TL}_1$. TL_1 is called *less expressive* than TL_2 (or TL_2 *more expressive* than TL_1), denoted by

$$\mathrm{TL}_1 < \mathrm{TL}_2,$$

if $\mathrm{TL}_1 \leq \mathrm{TL}_2$ and not $\mathrm{TL}_1 = \mathrm{TL}_2$.

In this terminology the facts from Chap. 3 repeated above can be stated as follows. For any versions LTL+b and LTL+b′ extending LTL by different binary operators we have

$$\mathrm{LTL{+}b} = \mathrm{LTL{+}b}'.$$

If we denote the sublogic of LTL+b not containing the operator $\Box$ by $\mathrm{LTL{+}b}^-$ then

$$\mathrm{LTL{+}b}^- = \mathrm{LTL{+}b},$$

and analogously in the case of a logic with a strict binary operator and without $\bigcirc$ and $\Box$. Moreover, we have

$$\text{LTL+b} \leq \text{LTL+}\mu \qquad \text{and} \qquad \text{LTL+b} \leq \text{LTL+q}.$$

Additionally, we note that these relationships can be transferred to LTL+b+p. For example we have

$$\text{LTLbp} = \text{LTL+b+p}$$

where LTLbp denotes the temporal logic with one strict binary future and one strict binary past operator, but without $\bigcirc$ and $\Box$.

We now will show some more expressiveness results of this kind about the various extensions of LTL. For some of the proofs, we recall a notation introduced in Sect. 2.1: for any temporal structure $\mathsf{K} = (\eta_0, \eta_1, \eta_2, \dots)$, the "suffix structure" $(\eta_i, \eta_{i+1}, \eta_{i+2}, \dots)$ is denoted by K^i.

In Sect. 3.1 we remarked already that the binary operators of LTL+b cannot be expressed in LTL. To show this formally, let $\mathbf{V}$ be some set of propositional constants. We define, for three arbitrary states η, η', η'' (with respect to $\mathbf{V}$) and $m, n \in \mathbb{N}$, the two temporal structures

$$\mathsf{K}^{(m,n,1)} = (\underbrace{\eta, \dots, \eta}_{m+1}, \eta', \underbrace{\eta, \dots, \eta}_{n}, \eta'', \underbrace{\eta, \dots, \eta}_{n}, \eta', \underbrace{\eta, \dots, \eta}_{n}, \eta'', \dots),$$

$$\mathsf{K}^{(m,n,2)} = (\underbrace{\eta, \dots, \eta}_{m+1}, \eta'', \underbrace{\eta, \dots, \eta}_{n}, \eta', \underbrace{\eta, \dots, \eta}_{n}, \eta'', \underbrace{\eta, \dots, \eta}_{n}, \eta', \dots)$$

for $\mathbf{V}$. Observe in particular that if $n \geq m+1$ then

$$(\mathsf{K}^{(m,n,1)})^i = (\mathsf{K}^{(m,n,2)})^{i+n+1} \qquad \text{and} \qquad (\mathsf{K}^{(m,n,2)})^i = (\mathsf{K}^{(m,n,1)})^{i+n+1}$$

hold for every $i \in \mathbb{N}$.

Lemma 4.1.1. *Let $m, n \in \mathbb{N}$ with $n \geq m+1$ and let A be formula of $\mathcal{L}_{\mathrm{LTL}}(\mathbf{V})$ containing at most m occurrences of the operator $\bigcirc$. Then $\mathsf{K}_0^{(m,n,1)}(A) = \mathsf{K}_0^{(m,n,2)}(A)$.*

Proof. Let m, n, and A be as described. The proof runs by structural induction on A. (We write $\mathsf{K}^{(1)}$ for $\mathsf{K}^{(m,n,1)}$ and $\mathsf{K}^{(2)}$ for $\mathsf{K}^{(m,n,2)}$.)

1. $A \equiv v \in \mathbf{V}$: $\mathsf{K}_0^{(1)}(v) = \eta(v) = \mathsf{K}_0^{(2)}(v)$.
2. $A \equiv$ **false**: $\mathsf{K}_0^{(1)}(\mathbf{false}) = \mathsf{ff} = \mathsf{K}_0^{(2)}(\mathbf{false})$.
3. $A \equiv B \to C$: Applying the induction hypothesis we have

$$\begin{aligned} \mathsf{K}_0^{(1)}(B \to C) = \mathsf{tt} &\Leftrightarrow \mathsf{K}_0^{(1)}(B) = \mathsf{ff} \text{ or } \mathsf{K}_0^{(1)}(C) = \mathsf{tt} \\ &\Leftrightarrow \mathsf{K}_0^{(2)}(B) = \mathsf{ff} \text{ or } \mathsf{K}_0^{(2)}(C) = \mathsf{tt} \\ &\Leftrightarrow \mathsf{K}_0^{(2)}(B \to C) = \mathsf{tt}. \end{aligned}$$

4. $A \equiv \bigcirc B$: Then $m \geq 1$, and the induction hypothesis can be applied to $(\mathsf{K}^{(1)})^1$, $(\mathsf{K}^{(2)})^1$, and B. With Lemma 2.1.5 we obtain

$$\begin{aligned}\mathsf{K}_0^{(1)}(\bigcirc B) &= \mathsf{K}_1^{(1)}(B)\\ &= (\mathsf{K}^{(1)})_0^1(B)\\ &= (\mathsf{K}^{(2)})_0^1(B)\\ &= \mathsf{K}_1^{(2)}(B)\\ &= \mathsf{K}_0^{(2)}(\bigcirc B).\end{aligned}$$

5. $A \equiv \Box B$: Using the above remark and applying again Lemma 2.1.5 we have

$$\begin{aligned}\mathsf{K}_0^{(1)}(\Box B) = \mathrm{ff} &\Rightarrow \mathsf{K}_i^{(1)}(B) = \mathrm{ff} \text{ for some } i \in \mathbb{N}\\ &\Rightarrow (\mathsf{K}^{(1)})_0^i(B) = \mathrm{ff} \text{ for some } i \in \mathbb{N}\\ &\Rightarrow (\mathsf{K}^{(2)})_0^{i+n+1}(B) = \mathrm{ff} \text{ for some } i \in \mathbb{N}\\ &\Rightarrow \mathsf{K}_0^{(2)}(\Box B) = \mathrm{ff}\end{aligned}$$

and the opposite direction is obtained analogously. △

Lemma 4.1.1 informally means that an LTL formula cannot "distinguish" two suitably chosen temporal structures of the above shape. Binary operators can do this; so we obtain the desired result.

Theorem 4.1.2. *LTL < LTL+b.*

Proof. Since LTL $\leq$ LTL+b is trivial it suffices to show that there is no LTL formula A over some $\mathbf{V}$ with $v_1, v_2 \in \mathbf{V}$ such that $\mathsf{K}_i(A) = \mathsf{K}_i(v_1 \textbf{ atnext } v_2)$ for every temporal structure K for $\mathbf{V}$ and $i \in \mathbb{N}$. Assume, on the contrary, that such an A exists and let m be the number of occurrences of the operator $\bigcirc$ in A. Consider the temporal structures $\mathsf{K}^{(1)} = \mathsf{K}^{(m,m+1,1)}$ and $\mathsf{K}^{(2)} = \mathsf{K}^{(m,m+1,2)}$ with states η, η', η'' such that

$$\begin{aligned}&\eta(v_2) = \mathrm{ff},\\ &\eta'(v_1) = \eta'(v_2) = \mathrm{tt},\\ &\eta''(v_1) = \mathrm{ff}, \eta''(v_2) = \mathrm{tt}.\end{aligned}$$

Then we have

$$\mathsf{K}_0^{(1)}(v_1 \textbf{ atnext } v_2) = \mathrm{tt} \quad \text{and} \quad \mathsf{K}_0^{(2)}(v_1 \textbf{ atnext } v_2) = \mathrm{ff},$$

and since $\mathsf{K}_0^{(1)}(A) = \mathsf{K}_0^{(2)}(A)$ by Lemma 4.1.1, we obtain the contradiction that

$$\mathsf{K}_0^{(i)}(A) \neq \mathsf{K}_0^{(i)}(v_1 \textbf{ atnext } v_2)$$

for one of the temporal structures $\mathsf{K}^{(i)}$, $i = 1, 2$. △

In another remark in Sect. 3.2 we announced that we will prove that LTL+μ is more expressive than LTL+b (and, hence, LTL). To show this consider the formula

$$\nu u(A \land \circ\circ u)$$

of LTL+μ (where u does not occur in A). We abbreviate this formula by

$$\textbf{even}\, A$$

using a new temporal operator **even** with the informal meaning "at all states with even distance". In fact, an immediate transfer of the proof of the equality $[\![\Box A]\!]^{\Xi}_{\mathsf{K}} = [\![\nu u(A \land \circ u)]\!]^{\Xi}_{\mathsf{K}}$ in an example in Sect. 3.2 shows that

$$[\![\nu u(A \land \circ\circ u)]\!]^{\Xi}_{\mathsf{K}} = \{i \in \mathbb{N} \mid \mathsf{K}^{(\Xi)}_{i+2k}(A) = \mathsf{tt} \text{ for every } k \in \mathbb{N}\}$$

for any K and Ξ, and this means

$$\mathsf{K}^{(\Xi)}_i(\textbf{even}\, A) = \mathsf{tt} \;\Leftrightarrow\; \mathsf{K}^{(\Xi)}_{i+2k}(A) = \mathsf{tt} \text{ for every } k \in \mathbb{N}.$$

At a first glance the formula **even** A might appear to be expressible in LTL (if A is an LTL formula), e.g., by

$$A \land \Box(A \leftrightarrow \circ\neg A).$$

This formula, however, asserts that A is true precisely at the states with even distance, and is false at the remaining states; it is therefore stronger than **even** A. Another candidate could be

$$A \land \Box(A \rightarrow \circ\circ A)$$

asserting that A is true at all states with even distance. However, if A also happens to be true at some state with odd distance, it will have to be true at all future states with odd distance, too, which is again stronger than what **even** A asserts.

In fact, **even** cannot be expressed in LTL+b. To show this, let $\mathbf{V}$ be a set of propositional constants and $v \in \mathbf{V}$. For every $k \in \mathbb{N}$ we define the temporal structure $\mathsf{K}^{(k)} = (\eta^{(k)}_0, \eta^{(k)}_1, \eta^{(k)}_2, \ldots)$ for $\mathbf{V}$ by

$$\eta^{(k)}_i(v) = \mathsf{ff} \;\Leftrightarrow\; i = k,$$
$$\eta^{(k)}_i(v') = \mathsf{ff} \quad \text{for all } v' \in \mathbf{V} \text{ other than } v$$

(for every $i \in \mathbb{N}$).

Lemma 4.1.3. *For every formula A of $\mathcal{L}^{\mathrm{b}}_{\mathrm{LTL}}(\mathbf{V})$ there is some $l \in \mathbb{N}$ such that $\mathsf{K}^{(k)}_0(A) = \mathsf{K}^{(l)}_0(A)$ for every $k \geq l$.*

Proof. Observe first that for all $n \in \mathbb{N}$, we have $\mathsf{K}^{(n)} = (\mathsf{K}^{(n+1)})^1$ by definition of the structure K. Using Lemma 2.1.5 it follows that

$$\mathsf{K}_1^{(n+1)}(A) = (\mathsf{K}^{(n+1)})_0^1(A) = \mathsf{K}_0^{(n)}(A)$$

for every formula A of $\mathcal{L}_{\mathrm{LTL}}^{\mathrm{b}}(\mathbf{V})$.

The proof of the lemma proceeds by structural induction on A. We adopt **unless** as binary operator; since the operators $\Box$ and $\bigcirc$ can be expressed in this logic, we need not include them in the inductive proof.

1. $A \in \mathbf{V}$: If $A \equiv v$ then $\mathsf{K}_0^{(k)}(A) = \mathsf{tt}$ for every $k \geq 1$ and if $A \not\equiv v$ then $\mathsf{K}_0^{(k)}(A) = \mathsf{ff}$ for every $k \in \mathbb{N}$. Thus, with $l = 1$ we have in both cases that $\mathsf{K}_0^{(k)}(A) = \mathsf{K}_0^{(l)}(A)$ for $k \geq l$.
2. $A \equiv$ **false**: Because of $\mathsf{K}_0^{(k)}(\mathbf{false}) = \mathsf{ff}$ for every $k \in \mathbb{N}$, we may choose $l = 0$.
3. $A \equiv B \to C$: By the induction hypothesis the property to be proved holds for B and C with numbers l_B and l_C, respectively. Let $l = \max(l_B, l_C)$. For every $k \geq l$ we then have

$$\begin{aligned} \mathsf{K}_0^{(k)}(B \to C) = \mathsf{tt} &\Leftrightarrow \mathsf{K}_0^{(k)}(B) = \mathsf{ff} \text{ or } \mathsf{K}_0^{(k)}(C) = \mathsf{tt} \\ &\Leftrightarrow \mathsf{K}_0^{(l)}(B) = \mathsf{ff} \text{ or } \mathsf{K}_0^{(l)}(C) = \mathsf{tt} \\ &\Leftrightarrow \mathsf{K}_0^{(l)}(B \to C) = \mathsf{tt}. \end{aligned}$$

4. $A \equiv B$ **unless** C: Let $l = \max(l_B, l_C)$ where l_B and l_C are given by the induction hypothesis for B and C, respectively. We show that $\mathsf{K}_0^{(k)}(A) = \mathsf{K}_0^{(l)}(A)$ for every $k \geq l+1$ by induction on k.
The case $k = l+1$ is trivial. For the inductive step, we observe the following chain equivalences:

$$\begin{aligned} &\mathsf{K}_0^{(k+1)}(B \textbf{ unless } C) = \mathsf{tt} \\ &\quad\Leftrightarrow \mathsf{K}_1^{(k+1)}(C) = \mathsf{tt} \text{ or} \\ &\qquad \mathsf{K}_1^{(k+1)}(B) = \mathsf{K}_1^{(k+1)}(B \textbf{ unless } C) = \mathsf{tt} && \text{(law (Tb14))} \\ &\quad\Leftrightarrow \mathsf{K}_0^{(k)}(C) = \mathsf{tt} \text{ or} \\ &\qquad \mathsf{K}_0^{(k)}(B) = \mathsf{K}_0^{(k)}(B \textbf{ unless } C) = \mathsf{tt} && \text{(above observation)} \\ &\quad\Leftrightarrow \mathsf{K}_0^{(l)}(C) = \mathsf{tt} \text{ or} \\ &\qquad \mathsf{K}_0^{(l)}(B) = \mathsf{K}_0^{(k)}(B \textbf{ unless } C) = \mathsf{tt} && \text{(major ind. hyp.)} \\ &\quad\Leftrightarrow \mathsf{K}_0^{(l)}(C) = \mathsf{tt} \text{ or} \\ &\qquad \mathsf{K}_0^{(l)}(B) = \mathsf{K}_0^{(l)}(B \textbf{ unless } C) = \mathsf{tt} && \text{(minor ind. hyp.)} \\ &\quad\Leftrightarrow \mathsf{K}_1^{(l+1)}(C) = \mathsf{tt} \text{ or} \\ &\qquad \mathsf{K}_1^{(l+1)}(B) = \mathsf{K}_1^{(l+1)}(B \textbf{ unless } C) = \mathsf{tt} && \text{(above observation)} \\ &\quad\Leftrightarrow \mathsf{K}_0^{(l)}(B \textbf{ unless } C) = \mathsf{tt} && \text{(law (Tb14))} \quad \triangle \end{aligned}$$

Lemma 4.1.3 informally means that any formula of $\mathcal{L}_{\mathrm{LTL}}^{\mathrm{b}}(\mathbf{V})$ can distinguish only finitely many of the temporal structures $\mathsf{K}^{(k)}$ and this is the key argument for the desired non-expressibility result.

Theorem 4.1.4. *LTL+b < LTL+μ.*

Proof. Assume that there is a formula A of $\mathcal{L}_{\mathrm{LTL}}^{\mathrm{b}}(\mathbf{V})$ (for some $\mathbf{V}$ with $v \in \mathbf{V}$) such that $\mathsf{K}_i(A) = \mathsf{K}_i(\mathbf{even}\, v)$ for every temporal structure K for $\mathbf{V}$ and $i \in \mathbb{N}$. (We understand LTL+b as a sublogic of LTL+μ and write K_i instead of $\mathsf{K}_i^{(\Xi)}$ since neither A nor **even** v contain free propositional variables.) This assumption implies $\mathsf{K}_0^{(k)}(A) = \mathsf{K}_0^{(k)}(\mathbf{even}\, v)$ for every $k \in \mathbb{N}$. Then by Lemma 4.1.3 there is an $l \in \mathbb{N}$ such that

$$\mathsf{K}_0^{(k)}(\mathbf{even}\, v) = \mathsf{K}_0^{(k)}(A) = \mathsf{K}_0^{(l)}(A)$$

holds for every $k \geq l$. This means

$$\mathsf{K}_0^{(k)}(\mathbf{even}\, v) = \mathsf{K}_0^{(k')}(\mathbf{even}\, v)$$

for all $k, k' \geq l$ and is a contradiction to the fact that, according to the definition of the temporal structures $\mathsf{K}^{(k)}$, we have

$$\mathsf{K}_0^{(k)}(\mathbf{even}\, v) = \mathsf{tt} \Leftrightarrow k \text{ is an odd number.}$$

Thus, **even** v is not expressible in LTL+b; together with the trivial observation that LTL+b $\leq$ LTL+μ we obtain LTL+b $<$ LTL+μ. △

The operator **even** is also expressible in LTL+q: it is easy to see that the formula **even** A can be expressed by

$$\exists u(u \wedge \Box(u \leftrightarrow \bigcirc\neg u) \wedge \Box(u \rightarrow A))$$

(where u is a propositional variable that does not occur free in A). In this formulation, the "auxiliary" propositional variable u is constrained to hold precisely at the instants with even distance from the point of evaluation; hence A has to be true at all these instants. Another, more concise but perhaps less intuitive expression of **even** A in LTL+q is given by the formula

$$\exists u(u \wedge \Box(u \rightarrow A \wedge \bigcirc\bigcirc u)).$$

More generally, the extensions LTL+μ and LTL+q are equally expressive. We now show that LTL+$\mu \leq$ LTL+q and leave the proof of the other direction for Sect. 4.4. As in previous proofs of this kind, we show that the μ operator can be expressed by a formula of LTL+q.

Lemma 4.1.5. *Assume that A is a formula of $\mathcal{L}_{\mathrm{LTL}}^{\mathrm{q}}$ and $u \in \mathcal{V}$ a propositional variable all of whose occurrences in A are of positive polarity. Then*

$$\mu u A \leftrightarrow \forall u(\Box(A \rightarrow u) \rightarrow u)$$

is valid in LTL+q+μ.

Proof. For an arbitrary temporal structure K and valuation Ξ, recall from Sect. 3.2 that $[\![\mu u A]\!]_{\mathsf{K}}^{\Xi} = \mu\Upsilon_A$ for the mapping

$$\Upsilon_A : \begin{cases} 2^{\mathbb{N}} \to 2^{\mathbb{N}} \\ \mathbb{M} \mapsto [\![A]\!]_{\mathsf{K}}^{\Xi[u:\mathbb{M}]}. \end{cases}$$

It is therefore enough to prove that

$$[\![\forall u(\Box(A \to u) \to u)]\!]_{\mathsf{K}}^{\Xi} = \mu\Upsilon_A.$$

For the inclusion "$\subseteq$", assume that $i \in [\![\forall u(\Box(A \to u) \to u)]\!]_{\mathsf{K}}^{\Xi}$. Considering the valuation $\Xi' = \Xi[u{:}\mu\Upsilon_A]$, we have in particular $i \in [\![\Box(A \to u) \to u]\!]_{\mathsf{K}}^{\Xi'}$. We claim that $i \in [\![\Box(A \to u)]\!]_{\mathsf{K}}^{\Xi'}$; hence $i \in [\![u]\!]_{\mathsf{K}}^{\Xi'} = \Xi'(u) = \mu\Upsilon_A$, and the inclusion follows.

To prove the claim, assume that $j \in [\![A]\!]_{\mathsf{K}}^{\Xi'}$ for some $j \geq i$. By definition of Υ_A and of Ξ', this means that $j \in \Upsilon_A(\mu\Upsilon_A)$. From the assumptions on the polarity of the occurrences of u in A, Lemma 3.2.2 and Theorem 3.2.1 imply $\Upsilon_A(\mu\Upsilon_A) = \mu\Upsilon_A$; hence $j \in \mu\Upsilon_A = [\![u]\!]_{\mathsf{K}}^{\Xi'}$, which completes the proof.

For the proof of the inclusion "$\supseteq$", assume that

$$i \in \mu\Upsilon_A = \bigcap\{\mathbb{M} \subseteq \mathbb{N} \mid \Upsilon_A(\mathbb{M}) \subseteq \mathbb{M}\}.$$

We must show that $i \in [\![\forall u(\Box(A \to u) \to u)]\!]_{\mathsf{K}}^{\Xi}$, i.e., $i \in [\![\Box(A \to u) \to u]\!]_{\mathsf{K}}^{\Xi[u:\mathbb{M}]}$ for all $\mathbb{M} \subseteq \mathbb{N}$. Assume therefore that $\mathbb{M} \subseteq \mathbb{N}$ is such that $i \in [\![\Box(A \to u)]\!]_{\mathsf{K}}^{\Xi[u:\mathbb{M}]}$; we need to prove that $i \in [\![u]\!]_{\mathsf{K}}^{\Xi[u:\mathbb{M}]} = \mathbb{M}$. From the assumption, we know that

$(*)$ for all $j \geq i$, if $j \in [\![A]\!]_{\mathsf{K}}^{\Xi[u:\mathbb{M}]}$ then $j \in \mathbb{M}$.

Consider now the set $\mathbb{M}' = \mathbb{M} \cup \{0, \ldots, i-1\}$. Because of Lemma 3.2.2 (which naturally extends to $\mathcal{L}_{\mathrm{LTL}}^{\mathrm{q}}$) and the assumption that all occurrences of u in A are of positive polarity, it follows that $[\![A]\!]_{\mathsf{K}}^{\Xi[u:\mathbb{M}]} \subseteq [\![A]\!]_{\mathsf{K}}^{\Xi[u:\mathbb{M}']}$. Also, for all $j \geq i$ we find that

$$\begin{aligned}
& j \in [\![A]\!]_{\mathsf{K}}^{\Xi[u:\mathbb{M}']} \\
& \quad \Leftrightarrow \mathsf{K}_j^{(\Xi[u:\mathbb{M}'])}(A) = \mathrm{tt} \\
& \quad \Leftrightarrow (\mathsf{K}^j)_0^{((\Xi[u:\mathbb{M}'])^j)}(A) = \mathrm{tt} \quad \text{(by Lemma 3.3.1)} \\
& \quad \Leftrightarrow (\mathsf{K}^j)_0^{((\Xi[u:\mathbb{M}])^j)}(A) = \mathrm{tt} \quad \text{(because } (\Xi[u:\mathbb{M}'])^j = (\Xi[u:\mathbb{M}])^j) \\
& \quad \Leftrightarrow \mathsf{K}_j^{(\Xi[u:\mathbb{M}])}(A) = \mathrm{tt} \quad \text{(by Lemma 3.3.1)} \\
& \quad \Leftrightarrow j \in [\![A]\!]_{\mathsf{K}}^{\Xi[u:\mathbb{M}]}.
\end{aligned}$$

Now, it is easy to see that $\Upsilon_A(\mathbb{M}') \subseteq \mathbb{M}'$: for $j < i$, we have $j \in \mathbb{M}'$ anyway, and for $j \geq i$, if $j \in \Upsilon_A(\mathbb{M}') = [\![A]\!]_{\mathsf{K}}^{\Xi[u:\mathbb{M}']}$ then we have just shown that $j \in [\![A]\!]_{\mathsf{K}}^{\Xi[u:\mathbb{M}]}$, and $(*)$ yields that $j \in \mathbb{M} \subseteq \mathbb{M}'$.

From the definition of $\mu\Upsilon_A$ it now follows immediately that $\mu\Upsilon_A \subseteq \mathbb{M}'$, and the assumption $i \in \mu\Upsilon_A$ shows that $i \in \mathbb{M}'$; hence also $i \in \mathbb{M}$ by definition of $\mathbb{M}'$, which completes the proof. △

Theorem 4.1.6. *LTL+$\mu \leq$ LTL+q.*

Proof. By Lemma 4.1.5, $\mu u A$ can be considered as an abbreviation for a formula of LTL+q whenever it is a legal formula of LTL+μ. △

Summarizing the above results we have so far established the following chain comparing the expressiveness of various propositional linear temporal logics:

LTL < LTL+b < LTL+μ $\leq$ LTL+q.

The logics in this chain do not contain past operators. Comparing past and future operators we have the following basic relationship.

Theorem 4.1.7. *LTL < LTL+p.*

Proof. Let $\mathbf{V}$ be a set of propositional constants, $v \in \mathbf{V}$. For the temporal structures $\mathsf{K} = (\eta_0, \eta_1, \eta_2, \ldots)$ and $\mathsf{K}' = (\eta'_0, \eta'_1, \eta'_2, \ldots)$ for $\mathbf{V}$ where $\eta_0(v) \neq \eta'_0(v)$, $\eta_i(v) = \eta'_i(v)$ for $i > 0$, and $\eta_i(v') = \eta'_i(v')$ for $i \in \mathbb{N}$ and all other $v' \in \mathbf{V}$ we have $\mathsf{K}_1(\ominus v) \neq \mathsf{K}'_1(\ominus v)$; but $\mathsf{K}_1(A) = \mathsf{K}'_1(A)$ for every formula A of $\mathcal{L}_{\mathrm{LTL}}(\mathbf{V})$ by Lemma 2.1.5. No such formula can therefore be logically equivalent to $\ominus v$, and together with the trivial LTL $\leq$ LTL+p this proves the claim. △

It is easy to see from the proof that this result extends also to LTL+b < LTL+b+p.

We said already at the beginning of this section that we will compare the expressiveness of formalisms in various ways. The expressibility notions defined there refer to normal semantics. Alternative measures are provided if the notions are based on initial validity semantics: for logics TL_1 and TL_2, a formula A of TL_1 is called *initially expressible in* TL_2 if there is a formula B in TL_2 such that

$$\overset{0}{\vDash} A \leftrightarrow B$$

holds in a logic TL which is a common extension of both TL_1 and TL_2. Because of Theorem 2.6.4 which we proved in Sect. 2.6 for LTL and which carries over to the extensions "b", "μ", and "q" as well, the new notions and the corresponding results for these logics are the same as before. For logics with past operators, however, Theorem 2.6.4 does not hold in general and different results may arise for "initial expressiveness". In fact, writing $=_0$ instead of $=$ to indicate the underlying initial validity semantics, we have

LTL+b $=_0$ LTL+b+p

which will follow immediately from considerations in the subsequent section. Many verification tools that implement temporal logic are based on initial validity, and the equal expressive power of LTL+b and LTL+b+p under this semantics has been considered as a justification for the omission of past operators from the temporal logics that these tools implement. On the other hand, past operators may still be useful because they often help to make formulas more readable and concise.

The expressiveness notions considered so far are based on logical equivalence. One particular aspect of logically equivalent ("mutually expressible") formulas is that they "describe the same temporal structures". (We used this phrase already a few times in previous discussions.) We call this relationship between formulas A and B *model equivalence*, defined by

$$\models_{\mathsf{K}} A \Leftrightarrow \models_{\mathsf{K}} B \qquad \text{or} \qquad \overset{0}{\models}_{\mathsf{K}} A \Leftrightarrow \overset{0}{\models}_{\mathsf{K}} B$$

for every temporal structure K, depending on the underlying semantics. In the case of initial validity semantics, logical and model equivalence are actually the same. With normal semantics, however, model equivalence is weaker than logical equivalence which can trivially be seen by means of the formulas A and $\Box A$: we have

$$\models_{\mathsf{K}} A \Leftrightarrow \models_{\mathsf{K}} \Box A$$

for every K, but A and $\Box A$ are clearly not logically equivalent.

So, in general, model equivalence is another notion for capturing the expressive power of temporal logics. It will be of special interest for our intended applications and we will come back to it in Sect. 6.1.

4.2 Temporal Logic and Classical First-Order Logic

Relationships between the truth of assertions along the "flow of time" can also be stated in a language of first-order logic. In such a representation, the present state (or "point in time") is expressed as a "time parameter". The propositional constants of temporal logic therefore become monadic predicate symbols, and time points can be compared using a "less-than" relation. For example, the formulas

$$\forall x(x_0 \le x \to v(x)),$$
$$\forall x(x_0 < x \to v_1(x) \lor \exists y(x_0 < y \land y \le x \land v_2(y)))$$

assert respectively that v holds at all states from the present state x_0 onwards and that v_1 holds in all future states unless v_2 becomes true; they intuitively correspond to the temporal logic formulas

$$\Box v \qquad \text{and} \qquad v_1 \ \mathbf{unless}\ v_2.$$

We will now make this correspondence more precise for the logic LTLbp that contains one strict binary future and one strict binary past operator, say **until** and **since**, but that does not contain $\bigcirc$, $\Box$, or their past-time counterparts as primitive operators; recall from Sect. 4.1 that this logic is as expressive as LTL+b+p. Thereafter, we will consider the fragment without past operators.

For a set $\mathbf{V}$ of propositional constants, we define the signature $SIG_{\mathbf{V}} = (\mathbf{S}, \mathbf{F}, \mathbf{P})$ where

- $\mathbf{S} = \{TIME\}$,

- $\mathbf{F} = \emptyset$,
- $\mathbf{P} = \{<^{(TIME\ TIME)}\} \cup \{v^{(TIME)} \mid v \in \mathbf{V}\}$.

With a given temporal structure $\mathsf{K} = (\eta_0, \eta_1, \eta_2, \ldots)$ for $\mathbf{V}$ we associate a (first-order) structure $\mathsf{S_K}$ for $SIG_\mathbf{V}$ where $|\mathsf{S_K}| = |\mathsf{S_K}|_{TIME} = \mathbb{N}$, the predicate symbol $<$ is interpreted as the "less than" relation on $\mathbb{N}$, and the interpretations of the unary predicate symbols v are obtained from the states η_i of K:

$$v^{\mathsf{S_K}}(i) = \eta_i(v) \qquad \text{for } i \in \mathbb{N}.$$

It is straightforward to define a translation

$$\mathbf{FOL} : \mathcal{L}_{\mathrm{LTLbp}}(\mathbf{V}) \to \mathcal{L}_{\mathrm{FOL}}(SIG_\mathbf{V})$$

that associates a formula in the first-order language $\mathcal{L}_{\mathrm{FOL}}(SIG_\mathbf{V})$ induced by the signature $SIG_\mathbf{V}$ with every formula of the language $\mathcal{L}_{\mathrm{LTLbp}}(\mathbf{V})$ of LTLbp. (For simplicity, we occasionally "abuse" in this chapter the denotations of languages to denote their sets of formulas.) The translation is defined by induction on the structure of temporal formulas as follows; it ensures that $\mathbf{FOL}(A)$ contains at most one free variable x_0 that represents the current state:

$$\begin{aligned}
&\mathbf{FOL}(v) = v(x_0) \qquad \text{for } v \in \mathbf{V},\\
&\mathbf{FOL}(\mathbf{false}) = \mathbf{false},\\
&\mathbf{FOL}(A \to B) = \mathbf{FOL}(A) \to \mathbf{FOL}(B),\\
&\mathbf{FOL}(A \ \mathbf{until}\ B) = \exists x(x_0 < x \land (\mathbf{FOL}(B))_{x_0}(x)\\
&\qquad\qquad \land \forall y(x_0 < y \land y < x \to (\mathbf{FOL}(A))_{x_0}(y))),\\
&\mathbf{FOL}(A \ \mathbf{since}\ B) = \exists x(x < x_0 \land (\mathbf{FOL}(B))_{x_0}(x)\\
&\qquad\qquad \land \forall y(x < y \land y < x_0 \to (\mathbf{FOL}(A))_{x_0}(y))).
\end{aligned}$$

The structure of this translation resembles the semantic definition of the temporal connectives. It preserves the meaning of formulas in the following sense.

Theorem 4.2.1. *Let* K *be a temporal structure for* $\mathbf{V}$ *and let* $\mathsf{S_K}$ *be the first-order structure corresponding to* K. *For any formula* A *of* $\mathcal{L}_{\mathrm{LTLbp}}(\mathbf{V})$, *any* $i \in \mathbb{N}$, *and any variable valuation* ξ *such that* $\xi(x_0) = i$:

$$\mathsf{K}_i(A) = \mathsf{S}_\mathsf{K}^{(\xi)}(\mathbf{FOL}(A)).$$

Proof. The assertion is proved by structural induction on the formula A.

1. $A \equiv v \in \mathbf{V}$: $\mathsf{K}_i(v) = \eta_i(v) = v^{\mathsf{S_K}}(i) = \mathsf{S}_\mathsf{K}^{(\xi)}(v(x_0)) = \mathsf{S}_\mathsf{K}^{(\xi)}(\mathbf{FOL}(v))$.
2. $A \equiv \mathbf{false}$: $\mathsf{K}_i(\mathbf{false}) = \mathsf{ff} = \mathsf{S}_\mathsf{K}^{(\xi)}(\mathbf{false}) = \mathsf{S}_\mathsf{K}^{(\xi)}(\mathbf{FOL}(\mathbf{false}))$.
3. $A \equiv B \to C$: Using the induction hypothesis we obtain

$$\begin{aligned}
\mathsf{K}_i(B \to C) = \mathsf{tt} &\Leftrightarrow \mathsf{K}_i(B) = \mathsf{ff} \text{ or } \mathsf{K}_i(C) = \mathsf{tt}\\
&\Leftrightarrow \mathsf{S}_\mathsf{K}^{(\xi)}(\mathbf{FOL}(B)) = \mathsf{ff} \text{ or } \mathsf{S}_\mathsf{K}^{(\xi)}(\mathbf{FOL}(C)) = \mathsf{tt}\\
&\Leftrightarrow \mathsf{S}_\mathsf{K}^{(\xi)}(\mathbf{FOL}(B \to C)) = \mathsf{tt}.
\end{aligned}$$

4. $A \equiv B$ **until** C: Assume that $\mathsf{K}_i(B$ **until** $C) = \mathsf{tt}$ and choose some $j > i$ such that $\mathsf{K}_j(C) = \mathsf{tt}$ and $\mathsf{K}_k(B) = \mathsf{tt}$ for all k where $i < k < j$. By the induction hypothesis we know that $\mathsf{S}_{\mathsf{K}}^{(\bar{\xi})}(\mathbf{FOL}(C)) = \mathsf{tt}$ for every variable valuation $\bar{\xi}$ such that $\bar{\xi}(x_0) = j$, and since x_0 is the only free variable in $\mathbf{FOL}(C)$, it also follows that $\mathsf{S}_{\mathsf{K}}^{(\xi')}((\mathbf{FOL}(C))_{x_0}(x)) = \mathsf{tt}$ for every valuation ξ' such that $\xi'(x) = j$. Similarly, it follows that $\mathsf{S}_{\mathsf{K}}^{(\xi'')}((\mathbf{FOL}(B))_{x_0}(y)) = \mathsf{tt}$ for every valuation ξ'' where $i < \xi''(y) < j$.
Thus, if ξ is a variable valuation such that $\xi(x_0) = i$, we may choose $\xi' \sim_x \xi$ where $\xi'(x) = j$. We then clearly have $\xi'(x_0) = i < j = \xi'(x)$, and the above arguments show that $\mathsf{S}_{\mathsf{K}}^{(\xi')}((\mathbf{FOL}(C))_{x_0}(x)) = \mathsf{tt}$ and that for all $\xi'' \sim_y \xi'$ where $i = \xi''(x_0) < \xi''(y) < \xi''(x) = j$, it holds that $\mathsf{S}_{\mathsf{K}}^{(\xi'')}((\mathbf{FOL}(B))_{x_0}(y)) = \mathsf{tt}$. Together we obtain $\mathsf{S}_{\mathsf{K}}^{(\xi)}(\mathbf{FOL}(B\ \mathbf{until}\ C)) = \mathsf{tt}$.
Conversely, assume that $\mathsf{S}_{\mathsf{K}}^{(\xi)}(\mathbf{FOL}(B\ \mathbf{until}\ C)) = \mathsf{tt}$, and so it follows that
$$\begin{aligned}\mathsf{S}_{\mathsf{K}}^{(\xi')}(&x_0 < x \wedge (\mathbf{FOL}(C))_{x_0}(x) \wedge \\ &\forall y(x_0 < y \wedge y < x \rightarrow (\mathbf{FOL}(B))_{x_0}(x))) = \mathsf{tt}\end{aligned}$$
for some ξ' such that $\xi' \sim_x \xi$. Again using the induction hypothesis and the fact that $\mathbf{FOL}(B)$ and $\mathbf{FOL}(C)$ contain at most the free variable x_0, we obtain that $\mathsf{K}_{\xi'(x)}(C) = \mathsf{tt}$, where $\xi'(x) > \xi'(x_0) = i$, and that $\mathsf{K}_k(B) = \mathsf{tt}$ for every k where $\xi'(x_0) < k < \xi'(x)$. This argument establishes $\mathsf{K}_i(B$ **until** $C) = \mathsf{tt}$.
5. $A \equiv B$ **since** C: This case runs "symmetrically" as for B **until** C. △

Adapting the notions from Sect 4.1 in an obvious way, Theorem 4.2.1 asserts that FOL (based on the signature $SIG_{\mathbf{V}}$) is at least as expressive as LTLbp, and *a fortiori* at least as expressive as LTL. On the other hand, it turns out that every formula of $\mathcal{L}_{\mathrm{FOL}}(SIG_{\mathbf{V}})$ with a single free variable can be expressed in temporal logic. Because of this result, temporal logic is often said to be *expressively complete* (with respect to first-order logic).

For the proof of expressive completeness, we introduce some additional concepts. A formula A of LTLbp is said to be

- a *pure future* formula if A is of the form B **until** C where neither B nor C contain an occurrence of **since**,
- a *pure past* formula if A is of the form B **since** C where neither B nor C contain an occurrence of **until**,
- a *present* formula if A contains no temporal operator,
- *separated* if A is a combination of pure future, pure past, and present formulas by the operator $\rightarrow$.

As the key result it turns out that LTLbp is *separable*: every formula is logically equivalent to some separated formula.

Example. We claim the equivalence

$$\models \bigcirc\Diamond(A \wedge \ominus\boxminus B) \;\leftrightarrow\; \ominus\boxminus B \wedge B \wedge (B\ \mathbf{until}\ A).$$

The right hand side of this equivalence is (the abbreviation of) a separated formula: its first conjunct is a pure past formula, its second conjunct is a present formula, and its third conjunct is a pure future formula. For the proof of the equivalence, consider an arbitrary temporal structure K and $i \in \mathbb{N}$. We then have

$$\begin{aligned}
&\mathsf{K}_i(\bigcirc\Diamond(A \wedge \ominus\boxminus B)) = \mathrm{tt}\\
&\quad\Leftrightarrow \text{ there is } j > i \text{ such that } \mathsf{K}_j(A) = \mathrm{tt} \text{ and } \mathsf{K}_k(B) = \mathrm{tt} \text{ for all } k < j\\
&\quad\Leftrightarrow \text{ there is } j > i \text{ such that } \mathsf{K}_j(A) = \mathrm{tt}\\
&\qquad\ \ \text{and } \mathsf{K}_k(B) = \mathrm{tt} \text{ for all } k \le i \text{ and } \mathsf{K}_k(B) = \mathrm{tt} \text{ for all } k \text{ where } i < k < j\\
&\quad\Leftrightarrow \mathsf{K}_k(B) = \mathrm{tt} \text{ for all } k < i \text{ and } \mathsf{K}_i(B) = \mathrm{tt} \text{ and there is } j > i \text{ such that}\\
&\qquad\ \ \mathsf{K}_j(A) = \mathrm{tt} \text{ and } \mathsf{K}_k(B) = \mathrm{tt} \text{ for all } k \text{ where } i < k < j\\
&\quad\Leftrightarrow \mathsf{K}_i(\ominus\boxminus B) = \mathrm{tt} \text{ and } \mathsf{K}_i(B) = \mathrm{tt} \text{ and } \mathsf{K}_i(B \textbf{ until } A) = \mathrm{tt}\\
&\quad\Leftrightarrow \mathsf{K}_i(\ominus\boxminus B \wedge B \wedge (B \textbf{ until } A)) = \mathrm{tt}.
\end{aligned}$$

△

A rather tedious enumeration of all possible cases establishes the general result.

Lemma 4.2.2. *For every formula A of $\mathcal{L}_{\mathrm{LTLbp}}(\mathbf{V})$ there is a separated formula B such that $\models A \leftrightarrow B$.*

Proof. Let us first consider a formula $F \equiv A$ **until** B where A or B contain a subformula $F' \equiv C$ **since** D that is not in the scope of a temporal operator. Let $A^{\perp}$ and $A^{\top}$ denote the formula that results from A by replacing all such occurrences of F' by **false** and **true**, respectively, and similarly define $B^{\perp}$ and $B^{\top}$. By propositional reasoning we have the valid equivalences

$$A \leftrightarrow ((F' \vee A^{\perp}) \wedge (\neg F' \vee A^{\top})) \quad \text{and} \quad B \leftrightarrow ((F' \wedge B^{\top}) \vee (\neg F' \wedge B^{\perp})).$$

Substituting in F, we find that

$$F \leftrightarrow ((F' \vee A^{\perp}) \wedge (\neg F' \vee A^{\top})) \textbf{ until } ((F' \wedge B^{\top}) \vee (\neg F' \wedge B^{\perp})),$$

is valid and applying distribution laws for the **until** operator we finally obtain the validity of

$$\begin{aligned}
F \leftrightarrow\ &((F' \vee A^{\perp}) \textbf{ until } (F' \wedge B^{\top}) \vee (F' \vee A^{\perp}) \textbf{ until } (\neg F' \wedge B^{\perp})) \wedge\\
&((\neg F' \vee A^{\top}) \textbf{ until } (F' \wedge B^{\top}) \vee (\neg F' \vee A^{\top}) \textbf{ until } (\neg F' \wedge B^{\perp})).
\end{aligned}$$

For each of the four main subformulas of the right-hand side, Fig. 4.1 gives an equivalent formula where F' no longer occurs in the scope of an **until** operator, and no additional nestings of **until** and **since** have been introduced. (To understand the long formulas in Fig. 4.1, recall that **until** and **since** bind stronger than $\wedge$ and $\vee$.)

An analogous transformation can be applied when **until** occurs in the scope of **since**. Indeed, the equivalences of Fig. 4.1 remain valid when **until** and **since** are exchanged.

Carrying out a single replacement along these lines eliminates one degree of nesting of **since** inside **until** or vice versa, and repeated transformations therefore produce an equivalent separated formula. △

$$\begin{aligned}
&(C\ \textbf{since}\ D \lor A)\ \textbf{until}\ (C\ \textbf{since}\ D \land B) \leftrightarrow \\
&\quad (C\ \textbf{until}\ B \land (D \lor (C \land C\ \textbf{since}\ D))) \lor \\
&\quad ((C \lor D \lor \neg(\neg D\ \textbf{until}\ \neg A))\ \textbf{until}\ (D \land C\ \textbf{until}\ B) \land \\
&\qquad (\neg(\neg D\ \textbf{until}\ \neg A) \lor D \lor (C \land C\ \textbf{since}\ D)))
\end{aligned}$$

$$\begin{aligned}
&(C\ \textbf{since}\ D \lor A)\ \textbf{until}\ (\neg(C\ \textbf{since}\ D) \land B) \leftrightarrow \\
&\quad ((A \land \neg D)\ \textbf{until}\ B \land \neg D \land (\neg C \lor \neg(C\ \textbf{since}\ D))) \lor \\
&\quad ((C \lor D \lor A\ \textbf{until}\ (B \lor (A \land D)))\ \textbf{until}\ (\neg C \land \neg D \land (A \land \neg D)\ \textbf{until}\ B) \land \\
&\qquad (A\ \textbf{until}\ (A \land D) \lor D \lor (C \land C\ \textbf{since}\ D)))
\end{aligned}$$

$$\begin{aligned}
&(\neg(C\ \textbf{since}\ D) \lor A)\ \textbf{until}\ (C\ \textbf{since}\ D \land B) \leftrightarrow \\
&\quad ((A \land C)\ \textbf{until}\ B \land (D \lor (C \land C\ \textbf{since}\ D))) \lor \\
&\quad ((\neg D \lor A\ \textbf{until}\ (B \lor (A \land \neg C \land \neg D)))\ \textbf{until}\ (D \land (A \land C)\ \textbf{until}\ B) \land \\
&\qquad (A\ \textbf{until}\ (A \land \neg C \land \neg D) \lor (\neg D \land (\neg C \lor \neg(C\ \textbf{since}\ D)))))
\end{aligned}$$

$$\begin{aligned}
&(\neg(C\ \textbf{since}\ D) \lor A)\ \textbf{until}\ (\neg(C\ \textbf{since}\ D) \land B) \leftrightarrow \\
&\quad (\neg(C\ \textbf{until}\ \neg A) \lor (\neg D \land (\neg C \lor \neg(C\ \textbf{since}\ D)))) \land \\
&\quad (\neg((C \lor D \lor \neg(\neg D\ \textbf{until}\ B))\ \textbf{until}\ (D \land C\ \textbf{until}\ \neg A)) \lor \\
&\qquad (\neg D\ \textbf{until}\ B \land \neg D \land \neg D \land (\neg C \lor \neg(C\ \textbf{since}\ D)))) \land \\
&\quad (\textbf{true}\ \textbf{until}\ (\neg C \land \neg D \land (\neg D\ \textbf{until}\ B)) \lor \\
&\qquad (\neg D\ \textbf{until}\ B \land \neg D \land (\neg C \lor \neg(C\ \textbf{since}\ D))))
\end{aligned}$$

Fig. 4.1. Separating **until** and **since**

Based on the separability of LTLbp, we can now show the announced expressive completeness result.

Theorem 4.2.3. *For every formula A of $\mathcal{L}_{\mathrm{FOL}}(SIG_{\mathbf{V}})$ with at most one free variable x_0 there is a formula B of $\mathcal{L}_{\mathrm{LTLbp}}(\mathbf{V})$ such that for any temporal structure K and $i \in \mathbb{N}$,*

$$\mathsf{K}_i(B) = \mathsf{S}_{\mathsf{K}}^{(\xi)}(A)$$

where S_{K} is the first-order structure corresponding to K and $\xi(x_0) = i$.

Proof. The theorem is proved by structural induction on the formula A. For A and x_0 we define a formula $\mathbf{LTL}(A, x_0)$ of $\mathcal{L}_{\mathrm{LTLbp}}(\mathbf{V})$ that satisfies the assertion of the theorem.

1. A is an atomic formula: If $A \equiv v(x_0)$ where v is a monadic predicate symbol corresponding to $v \in \mathbf{V}$, then the definition $\mathbf{LTL}(A, x_0) = v$ clearly suffices. For $A \equiv x_0 = x_0$ we take $\mathbf{LTL}(A, x_0) = \textbf{true}$, and if $A \equiv x_0 < x_0$ then we let $\mathbf{LTL}(A, x_0) = \textbf{false}$. The first-order language $\mathcal{L}_{\mathrm{FOL}}(SIG_{\mathbf{V}})$ does not admit any other atomic formulas with the single free variable x_0.
2. For $A \equiv \textbf{false}$, we take $\mathbf{LTL}(A, x_0) = \textbf{false}$.
3. If $A \equiv B \to C$, we define $\mathbf{LTL}(A, x_0) = \mathbf{LTL}(B, x_0) \to \mathbf{LTL}(C, x_0)$, and the assertion follows with the help of the induction hypothesis.
4. For $A \equiv \exists x B$, we may assume without loss of generality that $x_0 \not\equiv x$, that B does not contain subformulas of the form $x_0 = x_0$ or $x_0 < x_0$ (these can equivalently be replaced by **true** or **false**), and that x_0 does not occur in B as

a bound variable. We may further assume that B does not contain any atomic subformulas $v(x_0)$, for some $v \in \mathbf{V}$, because such formulas can be moved out of the scope of the quantifier using equivalences such as

$$\exists x(C \wedge v(x_0)) \leftrightarrow v(x_0) \wedge \exists x C.$$

Therefore, the only occurrences of x_0 in B are of the forms $x_0 < y$, $x_0 = y$ or $y < x_0$ where y is some variable (either x or a variable bound in some subformula of B). We temporarily introduce auxiliary unary predicate symbols FU_{x_0}, NO_{x_0}, and PA_{x_0} (for "future", "now", and "past"), and replace every occurrence of $x_0 < y$ by $FU_{x_0}(y)$, of $x_0 = y$ by $NO_{x_0}(y)$, and of $y < x_0$ by $PA_{x_0}(y)$. The resulting formula $\overline{B}$ contains the single free variable x, and by the induction hypothesis we find a formula $\mathbf{LTL}(\overline{B}, x)$ of $\mathcal{L}_{\mathrm{LTLbp}}(\mathbf{V} \cup \{FU_{x_0}, NO_{x_0}, PA_{x_0}\})$ such that for any temporal structure K' and any $j \in \mathbb{N}$,

$$\mathsf{K}'_j(\mathbf{LTL}(\overline{B}, x)) = \mathsf{S}^{(\xi')}_{\mathsf{K}'}(\overline{B})$$

where $\xi'(x) = j$. In particular, consider $\mathsf{K}' = (\eta'_0, \eta'_1, \eta'_2, \ldots)$ where

$$\begin{aligned} &\eta'_j(FU_{x_0}) = \mathsf{tt} \Leftrightarrow i < j \\ &\eta'_j(NO_{x_0}) = \mathsf{tt} \Leftrightarrow i = j \\ &\eta'_j(PA_{x_0}) = \mathsf{tt} \Leftrightarrow j < i \end{aligned}$$

and $\eta'_j(v) = \eta_j(v)$ for all $v \in \mathbf{V}$. Obviously, this choice of K' then ensures that

$$\mathsf{S}^{(\xi')}_{\mathsf{K}}(B) = \mathsf{S}^{(\xi')}_{\mathsf{K}'}(\overline{B}) = \mathsf{K}'_j(\mathbf{LTL}(\overline{B}, x))$$

whenever $\xi'(x) = j$. Observing moreover that $\exists x B$ can equivalently be replaced by

$$\exists x(x < x_0 \wedge B) \vee B_x(x_0) \vee \exists x(x_0 < x \wedge B),$$

it follows that

$$\mathsf{S}^{(\xi)}_{\mathsf{K}}(\exists x B) = \mathsf{K}'_i(C)$$

where

$$C \equiv \ominus\diamondminus\mathbf{LTL}(\overline{B}, x) \vee \mathbf{LTL}(\overline{B}, x) \vee \bigcirc\Diamond\mathbf{LTL}(\overline{B}, x).$$

Since LTLbp is separable by Lemma 4.2.2, there exists a separated formula $\overline{C}$ of LTLbp such that $\vDash \overline{C} \leftrightarrow C$; hence also

$$\mathsf{S}^{(\xi)}_{\mathsf{K}}(\exists x B) = \mathsf{K}'_i(\overline{C}).$$

$\overline{C}$ still contains the auxiliary propositional constants FU_{x_0}, NO_{x_0}, and PA_{x_0}. We define $\mathbf{LTL}(A, x_0)$ to be the formula that results from $\overline{C}$ by replacing

- FU_{x_0} by **true** in all pure future subformulas of $\overline{C}$,
- NO_{x_0} by **true** in all present subformulas of $\overline{C}$,
- PA_{x_0} by **true** in all pure past subformulas of $\overline{C}$,

and all other occurrences of FU_{x_0}, NO_{x_0}, and PA_{x_0} by **false**. With these replacements, we obtain that

$$\mathsf{K}_i(\mathbf{LTL}(A, x_0)) = \mathsf{K}'_i(\overline{C}) = \mathsf{S}_{\mathsf{K}}^{(\xi)}(\exists x B)$$

which completes the proof. △

Example. We illustrate the construction of the above proof at the hand of the FOL formula

$$\exists x(x_0 < x \wedge v_2(x) \wedge \neg\exists y(x_0 < y \wedge y < x \wedge \neg v_1(y))).$$

The first replacements of $x_0 < x$ result in the formula

$$\exists x(FU_{x_0}(x) \wedge v_2(x) \wedge \neg\exists y(B))$$

where

$$B \equiv FU_{x_0}(y) \wedge y < x \wedge \neg v_1(y)$$

and we continue with the construction of $\mathbf{LTL}(\exists yB, x)$. We first have to replace the subformula $y < x$, resulting in

$$\exists y(FU_{x_0}(y) \wedge PA_x(y) \wedge \neg v_1(y))$$

where the predicate symbol PA_x corresponds to the variable x. This formula can now be translated to temporal logic, yielding

$$\ominus\diamondminus(FU_{x_0} \wedge PA_x \wedge \neg v_1) \vee (FU_{x_0} \wedge PA_x \wedge \neg v_1) \vee \bigcirc\Diamond(FU_{x_0} \wedge PA_x \wedge \neg v_1)$$

which is already in separated form. It remains to eliminate the auxiliary propositional constant PA_x, from which we obtain

$$\ominus\diamondminus(FU_{x_0} \wedge \mathbf{true} \wedge \neg v_1) \vee (FU_{x_0} \wedge \mathbf{false} \wedge \neg v_1) \vee \bigcirc\Diamond(FU_{x_0} \wedge \mathbf{false} \wedge \neg v_1)$$

which can be further simplified to

$$\ominus\diamondminus(FU_{x_0} \wedge \neg v_1).$$

Continuing with the translation of the main formula, we obtain

$$\begin{aligned}&\ominus\diamondminus(FU_{x_0} \wedge v_2 \wedge \neg\ominus\diamondminus(FU_{x_0} \wedge \neg v_1)) \vee \\ &(FU_{x_0} \wedge v_2 \wedge \neg\ominus\diamondminus(FU_{x_0} \wedge \neg v_1)) \vee \\ &\bigcirc\Diamond(FU_{x_0} \wedge v_2 \wedge \neg\ominus\diamondminus(FU_{x_0} \wedge \neg v_1)).\end{aligned}$$

The first disjunct is a pure past formula, and the second disjunct is a combination of present and pure past formulas. It remains to separate the third disjunct, which (up to trivial transformations) is just of the shape of the left-hand side of the equivalence considered in a previous example. We thus obtain the separated form

$$\ominus\diamondminus(FU_{x_0} \wedge v_2 \wedge \neg\ominus\diamondminus(FU_{x_0} \wedge \neg v_1)) \vee$$
$$(FU_{x_0} \wedge v_2 \wedge \neg\ominus\diamondminus(FU_{x_0} \wedge \neg v_1)) \vee$$
$$\ominus\boxminus(FU_{x_0} \rightarrow v_1) \wedge (FU_{x_0} \rightarrow v_1) \wedge ((FU_{x_0} \rightarrow v_1) \textbf{ until } (FU_{x_0} \wedge v_2))$$

in which we now replace FU_{x_0} by **true** and **false** as appropriate, obtaining

$$\ominus\diamondminus(\textbf{false} \wedge v_2 \wedge \neg\ominus\diamondminus(\textbf{false} \wedge \neg v_1)) \vee$$
$$(\textbf{false} \wedge v_2 \wedge \neg\ominus\diamondminus(\textbf{false} \wedge \neg v_1)) \vee$$
$$\ominus\boxminus(\textbf{false} \rightarrow v_1) \wedge (\textbf{false} \rightarrow v_1) \wedge ((\textbf{true} \rightarrow v_1) \textbf{ until } (\textbf{true} \wedge v_2))$$

which can be finally simplified to the formula v_1 **until** v_2. △

In the preceding example, we obtained a temporal formula that was noticeably smaller than the original first-order formula. In general, however, the separation step that is part of the construction of Theorem 4.2.3 requires subformulas to be duplicated, and the resulting formula may in fact be nonelementarily larger than the original FOL formula.

Taken together, the Theorems 4.2.1 and 4.2.3 imply that first-order logic FOL^1 (over the signature $SIG_{\mathbf{V}}$ and over the class of interpretations where "time" is interpreted as natural numbers and where $<$ denotes "less than") with a single free variable and LTLbp are equally expressive. Adopting the notation of Sect. 4, this can be stated succinctly as

$$\mathrm{FOL}^1 = \mathrm{LTLbp}.$$

As a simple corollary, we obtain a similar result for the logic LTL+b without past operators: every FOL^1 formula A can be translated to a formula B of LTL+b such that the two formulas evaluate to the same truth value "with respect to initial validity semantics".

Theorem 4.2.4. *For every formula A of $\mathcal{L}_{\mathrm{FOL}}(SIG_{\mathbf{V}})$ with at most one free variable x_0 there is a formula B of $\mathcal{L}^{\mathrm{b}}_{\mathrm{LTL}}(\mathbf{V})$ such that for any temporal structure K,*

$$\mathsf{K}_0(B) = \mathsf{S}_{\mathsf{K}}^{(\xi)}(A)$$

where S_{K} is the first-order structure corresponding to K and $\xi(x_0) = 0$.

Proof. By Theorem 4.2.3, we may find a formula $\overline{B}$ of $\mathcal{L}_{\mathrm{LTLbp}}(\mathbf{V})$ such that A and $\overline{B}$ evaluate to the same value at all points. By Lemma 4.2.2, we may moreover assume that $\overline{B}$ is separated. The formula B results from $\overline{B}$ by replacing all pure past subformulas of $\overline{B}$ by **false**. △

Applying the argument used in the proof of Theorem 4.2.4, we may also observe that every formula of LTLbp is initially expressible in LTL+b. Since we trivially have LTLbp $=_0$ LTL+b+p and LTL+b $\leq_0$ LTL+b+p (where $\leq_0$ denotes the "initial validity variant" of $\leq$), we obtain the result

$$\text{LTL+b} =_0 \text{LTL+b+p}$$

which was already noted at the end of Sect. 4.1.

Expressive completeness of temporal logic refers to the first-order logic FOL[1] with a fixed interpretation of "time" by the set of natural numbers. Of course, this corresponds to the choice of $\mathbb{N}$ as the underlying "time model" in the semantics of LTL and its variants. In Sect. 10.1 we will briefly discuss other sets such as the integers $\mathbb{Z}$ or the reals $\mathbb{R}$ which could be chosen instead of $\mathbb{N}$. Remarkably, expressive completeness of temporal logic carries over (in an analogously defined way) to a number of such time domains including Dedekind-complete structures such as $\mathbb{R}$, but not for example the rational numbers $\mathbb{Q}$.

4.3 Non-deterministic ω-Automata

The expressiveness of temporal logics can also be measured with respect to formalisms other than logics. In this section, we will begin to examine a very fruitful connection that exists between temporal logics and automata theory. This connection has not only yielded another "yardstick" with which to measure the expressiveness of different temporal logics, explored in more detail in the subsequent sections, but it has also found applications in verification that will be discussed in Chap. 11. We begin by introducing elements of the theory of finite non-deterministic automata over ω-words.

A (finite) *ω-automaton* Ω is a mathematical device equipped with bounded memory that, in a *run* ρ, scans a temporal structure K and produces a verdict whether ρ is accepting or not. If there exists some accepting run of Ω over K, we say that Ω *accepts* K or that K belongs to the *language* of Ω. This description leaves open the precise details of the structure of Ω, of what constitutes a run, and when a run is accepting, and in fact there exist different kinds of ω-automata some of which we will study in this chapter. A remarkable fact about the theory of ω-automata is that quite different ways to fill in the details of the above description yield the same class of definable languages.

We will begin by studying Büchi automata, which are a straightforward variant of non-deterministic finite automata.

Definition. A *Büchi automaton* $\Omega = (\mathbf{V}, Q, Q_0, \delta, Q_f)$ for a finite set $\mathbf{V}$ of propositional constants is given by

- a finite set Q of *locations*,
- a finite set $Q_0 \subseteq Q$ of *initial locations*,
- a mapping $\delta : Q \times Q \to \mathcal{L}_{\mathrm{PL}}(\mathbf{V})$ that associates a propositional formula $\delta(q, q')$ with any pair of locations $q, q' \in Q$,
- and a finite set $Q_f \subseteq Q$ of *accepting locations*.

A *run* of Ω over a temporal structure $\mathsf{K} = (\eta_0, \eta_1, \eta_2, \ldots)$ for $\mathbf{V}$ is an infinite sequence $\varrho = (q_0, q_1, q_2 \ldots)$ of locations $q_i \in Q$ such that

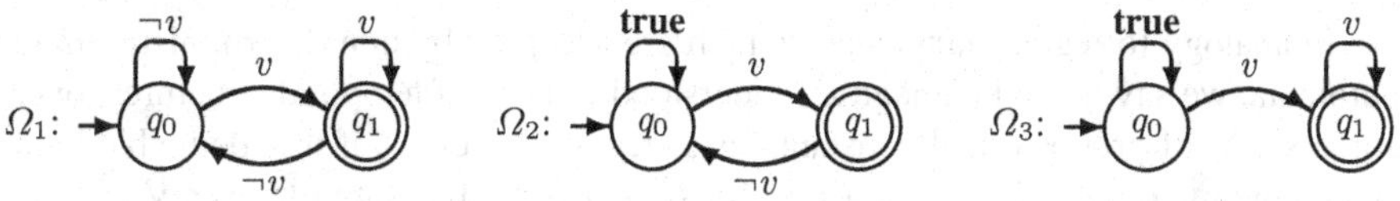

Fig. 4.2. Three Büchi automata

- $q_0 \in Q_0$ is an initial location and
- $\models_{\eta_i} \delta(q_i, q_{i+1})$ holds for all $i \in \mathbb{N}$ (in the sense of Sect. 1.1).

The run ϱ is *accepting* and K is *accepted* if $q_i \in Q_f$ holds for infinitely many $i \in \mathbb{N}$. The *language* $\mathcal{L}(\Omega)$ of Ω is the set of temporal structures for $\mathbf{V}$ which are accepted by Ω.

The structure of a Büchi automaton is that of an ordinary non-deterministic finite automaton (NFA). Locations of automata are often called (automaton) states, but we prefer to use a different word in order to distinguish them from the states of a temporal structure. The acceptance condition of a Büchi automaton adapts that of an NFA to ω-runs: a run is accepting if it visits an accepting location infinitely often. In the above definition, we have replaced the conventional notion of the alphabet over which the automaton operates by a set $\mathbf{V}$ of propositional constants, because we will use automata as acceptors of temporal structures.

Example. Figure 4.2 shows three Büchi automata Ω_1, Ω_2, and Ω_3, where we assume $\mathbf{V} = \{v\}$. When drawing Büchi automata, we indicate initial locations by incoming arrows without a source location. Accepting locations are marked by double circles. We omit transitions labeled by **false** from the diagrams: for example, we have $\delta(q_1, q_1) = \mathbf{false}$ for the middle automaton.

Automaton Ω_1 visits location q_1 upon reading a state satisfying v, and visits location q_0 otherwise. Since q_1 is accepting, the automaton accepts precisely those temporal structures that contain infinitely many states satisfying v. Observe also that Ω_1 is *deterministic*: it has only one initial location and for any location q and state η there is precisely one location q' such that $\models_{\eta} \delta(q, q')$. In particular, there is only one possible run over any temporal structure for $\mathbf{V}$.

Starting from location q_0, automaton Ω_2 may always choose to remain at q_0. However, when reading a state satisfying v it may choose to move to q_1; it then verifies that the following state satisfies $\neg v$ (otherwise, the run cannot be completed). The acceptance condition ensures that any structure accepted by Ω_2 contains infinitely many states satisfying v followed by a state satisfying $\neg v$. In other words, $\mathcal{L}(\Omega_2)$ consists of those temporal structures satisfying the formula $\Box\Diamond(v \wedge \bigcirc\neg v)$. Observe that this formula is equivalent to $\Box\Diamond v \wedge \Box\Diamond\neg v$. It is not hard to find a deterministic Büchi automaton defining the same language.

Automaton Ω_3 may similarly decide to move to location q_1 upon reading a state satisfying v. It can complete the run only if all subsequent states satisfy v: the language $\mathcal{L}(\Omega_3)$ consists of those structures that satisfy $\Diamond\Box v$. This language cannot be defined by a deterministic Büchi automaton. In fact, it can be shown that deterministic Büchi automata are strictly weaker than non-deterministic ones. △

In analogy to regular languages, which are accepted by non-deterministic finite automata, we say that a language $\mathcal{L}$, understood as a set of temporal structures, over some set $\mathbf{V}$ of propositional constants, is *ω-regular* (over $\mathbf{V}$) if it is definable by a Büchi automaton, that is, if $\mathcal{L} = \mathcal{L}(\Omega)$ for some Büchi automaton Ω over $\mathbf{V}$.

The class of ω-regular languages enjoys many of the closure properties known from regular languages. These are interesting in their own right, but are also at the basis of the characterizations of the expressiveness of the logics LTL+q and LTL+μ in Sect. 4.4, and they are related to decidability results that will be useful in Chap. 11.

Theorem 4.3.1. *If $\mathcal{L}_1$ and $\mathcal{L}_2$ are ω-regular over $\mathbf{V}$ then so are $\mathcal{L}_1 \cup \mathcal{L}_2$ and $\mathcal{L}_1 \cap \mathcal{L}_2$.*

Proof. Let $\Omega_1 = (\mathbf{V}, Q^{(1)}, Q_0^{(1)}, \delta^{(1)}, Q_f^{(1)})$ and $\Omega_2 = (\mathbf{V}, Q^{(2)}, Q_0^{(2)}, \delta^{(2)}, Q_f^{(2)})$ be Büchi automata characterizing $\mathcal{L}_1 = \mathcal{L}(\Omega_1)$ and $\mathcal{L}_2 = \mathcal{L}(\Omega_2)$. We will construct Büchi automata $\Omega^{\cup}$ and $\Omega^{\cap}$ such that $\mathcal{L}(\Omega^{\cup}) = \mathcal{L}_1 \cup \mathcal{L}_2$ and $\mathcal{L}(\Omega^{\cap}) = \mathcal{L}_1 \cap \mathcal{L}_2$.

For $\Omega^{\cup}$, we simply take the disjoint union of Ω_1 and Ω_2. More precisely, define $\Omega^{\cup} = (\mathbf{V}, Q^{\cup}, Q_0^{\cup}, \delta^{\cup}, Q_f^{\cup})$ where

- $Q^{\cup} = (Q^{(1)} \times \{1\}) \cup (Q^{(2)} \times \{2\})$,
- $Q_0^{\cup} = (Q_0^{(1)} \times \{1\}) \cup (Q_0^{(2)} \times \{2\})$,
- $\delta^{\cup}((q,i),(q',i')) = \begin{cases} \delta^{(i)}(q,q') & \text{if } i = i', \\ \mathbf{false} & \text{otherwise,} \end{cases}$
- $Q_f^{\cup} = (Q_f^{(1)} \times \{1\}) \cup (Q_f^{(2)} \times \{2\})$.

It follows immediately from this definition that, for $i \in \{1,2\}$, $\Omega^{\cup}$ has a run $\varrho = ((q_0,i),(q_1,i),(q_2,i),\ldots)$ over a temporal structure K for $\mathbf{V}$ if and only if Ω_i has a corresponding run $\varrho_i = (q_0, q_1, q_2, \ldots)$ over K. Moreover, ϱ is accepting for $\Omega^{\cup}$ if and only if ϱ_i is accepting for Ω_i, and all runs of $\Omega^{\cup}$ are of this form. Hence, $\Omega^{\cup}$ characterizes $\mathcal{L}_1 \cup \mathcal{L}_2$.

The automaton $\Omega^{\cap}$ is essentially defined as the product of Ω_1 and Ω_2, but we have to be a little careful about the definition of the acceptance condition: the product automaton has to visit accepting locations of both Ω_1 and Ω_2 infinitely often, and it is easy to find examples for which the naive definitions of the set of accepting locations as $Q_f^{(1)} \times Q_f^{(2)}$, or as $(Q_f^{(1)} \times Q^{(2)}) \cup (Q^{(1)} \times Q_f^{(2)})$, produce wrong results. Instead, we observe that requiring infinitely many visits to both $Q_f^{(1)}$ and $Q_f^{(2)}$ is equivalent to requiring that infinitely often the run visits $Q_f^{(1)}$, eventually followed by a visit of a location in $Q_f^{(2)}$.

Technically, the locations of $\Omega^{\cap}$ contain an extra component $l \in \{1,2\}$ that indicates whether we are waiting for a visit of an accepting location of Ω_1 or of Ω_2. The automaton is defined as $\Omega^{\cap} = (\mathbf{V}, Q^{\cap}, Q_0^{\cap}, \delta^{\cap}, Q_f^{\cap})$ where

- $Q^{\cap} = Q^{(1)} \times Q^{(2)} \times \{1,2\}$,
- $Q_0^{\cap} = Q_0^{(1)} \times Q_0^{(2)} \times \{1\}$,

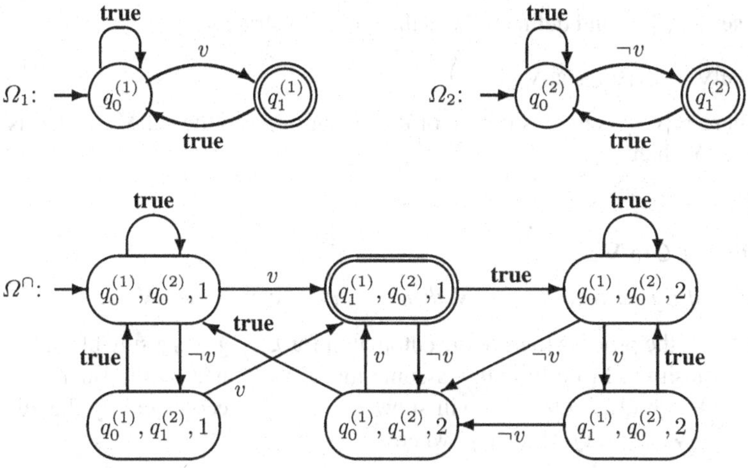

Fig. 4.3. Construction of a product

- $\delta^\cap((q^{(1)}, q^{(2)}, l), (\bar{q}^{(1)}, \bar{q}^{(2)}, \bar{l})) = \begin{cases} \delta^{(1)}(q^{(1)}, \bar{q}^{(1)}) \wedge \delta^{(2)}(q^{(2)}, \bar{q}^{(2)}) \\ \qquad \text{if } q^{(l)} \notin Q_f^{(l)} \text{ and } \bar{l} = l \\ \qquad \text{or } q^{(l)} \in Q_f^{(l)} \text{ and } \bar{l} \neq l, \\ \textbf{false} \quad \text{otherwise,} \end{cases}$
- $Q_f^\cap = Q_f^{(1)} \times Q^{(2)} \times \{1\}$.

Figure 4.3 illustrates this construction (locations that are only reachable via unsatisfiable transition labels have been omitted).

Assume that $\Omega^\cap$ has an accepting run $\varrho = ((q_0^{(1)}, q_0^{(2)}, l_0), (q_1^{(1)}, q_1^{(2)}, l_1), \ldots)$ over the temporal structure K. By the definitions of $Q_0^\cap$ and $\delta^\cap$, it follows immediately that $\varrho_1 = (q_0^{(1)}, q_1^{(1)}, \ldots)$ and $\varrho_2 = (q_0^{(2)}, q_1^{(2)}, \ldots)$ are runs of Ω_1 and Ω_2, respectively. Moreover, ϱ is accepting, and therefore we must have $q_k^{(1)} \in Q_f^{(1)}$ and $l_k = 1$ for infinitely many $k \in \mathbb{N}$. In particular, ϱ_1 is an accepting run of Ω_1 over K. We now show that for every k such that $q_k^{(1)} \in Q_f^{(1)}$ and $l_k = 1$ there exists some $j > k$ such that $q_j^{(2)} \in Q_f^{(2)}$. Since we already know that there are infinitely many positions such that $q_k^{(1)} \in Q_f^{(1)}$ and $l_k = 1$, it follows that $q_j^{(2)} \in Q_f^{(2)}$ also holds infinitely often; hence ϱ_2 is an accepting run of Ω_2. Indeed, assume that $q_k^{(1)} \in Q_f^{(1)}$ and $l_k = 1$. By the definition of $\delta^\cap$, we have $l_{k+1} = 2$. Now, if $q_j^{(2)} \notin Q_f^{(2)}$ for all $j > k$, it would follow that $l_j = 2$ for all $j > k$, contradicting the fact that $l_i = 1$ for infinitely many $i \in \mathbb{N}$.

Conversely, given runs ϱ_1 and ϱ_2 of Ω_1 and Ω_2 over K, it is straightforward to construct an accepting run of $\Omega^\cap$ over K. △

The ω-regular languages are also closed under projection: for a temporal structure $\mathsf{K} = (\eta_0, \eta_1, \eta_2, \ldots)$ for a set $\mathbf{V}$ of propositional constants and $v \in \mathbf{V}$, we write

$\mathbf{V}_{-v}$ for the set $\mathbf{V} \setminus \{v\}$ and define K_{-v} as the temporal structure

$$\mathsf{K}_{-v} = (\eta_0|_{\mathbf{V}_{-v}}, \eta_1|_{\mathbf{V}_{-v}}, \eta_2|_{\mathbf{V}_{-v}}, \ldots)$$

over $\mathbf{V}_{-v}$ where $\eta_i|_{\mathbf{V}_{-v}}$ is the restriction of the valuation η_i to the set $\mathbf{V}_{-v}$. If $\mathcal{L}$ is a language over $\mathbf{V}$ then

$$\mathcal{L}_{-v} = \{\mathsf{K}_{-v} \mid \mathsf{K} \in \mathcal{L}\}$$

is the *projection* of $\mathcal{L}$ to $\mathbf{V}_{-v}$.

Theorem 4.3.2. *If $\mathcal{L}$ is ω-regular over $\mathbf{V}$ then $\mathcal{L}_{-v}$ is ω-regular over $\mathbf{V}_{-v}$.*

Proof. The idea of the proof is to have the automaton for $\mathcal{L}_{-v}$ guess a suitable value for v at every transition. More formally, assume that $\mathcal{L}$ is defined by the Büchi automaton $\Omega = (\mathbf{V}, Q, Q_0, \delta, Q_f)$. We will show that $\mathcal{L}_{-v}$ is recognized by the automaton $\Omega_{-v} = (\mathbf{V}_{-v}, Q, Q_0, \delta_{-v}, Q_f)$ where

$$\delta_{-v}(q, q') = (\delta(q, q'))_v(\mathbf{true}) \vee (\delta(q, q'))_v(\mathbf{false})$$

($\delta(q, q')_v(\mathbf{true})$ and $\delta(q, q')_v(\mathbf{false})$ are obtained from $\delta(q, q')$ by replacing all occurrences of v by **true** or **false**, respectively). This definition ensures that

$$\models_{\eta} \delta(q, q') \Leftrightarrow \models_{\eta|_{\mathbf{V}_{-v}}} \delta_{-v}(q, q')$$

for any locations q, q' and any valuation η. Therefore, any run ϱ of Ω over some temporal structure K is also a run of Ω_{-v} over K_{-v}. Conversely, given a run ϱ of Ω_{-v} over a temporal structure K^- for $\mathbf{V}_{-v}$, one can find a structure K for $\mathbf{V}$ such that $\mathsf{K}^- = \mathsf{K}_{-v}$ and ϱ is a run of Ω over K. Because any run is accepting for Ω if and only if it is accepting for Ω_{-v}, this suffices to establish the assertion. △

Finally, we now set out to prove that ω-regular languages are closed under complement. For a regular language $\mathcal{L}$ (of finite words), the proof of the analogous result relies on determinization: one first constructs a deterministic finite automaton (DFA) that recognizes $\mathcal{L}$, and then obtains a DFA that accepts the complement of $\mathcal{L}$ by exchanging accepting and non-accepting locations. This proof idea does not carry over to Büchi automata: as we remarked earlier, one cannot always determinize a given Büchi automaton. Besides, exchanging accepting and non-accepting locations in a deterministic Büchi automaton does not necessarily result in an automaton accepting the complement language. For example, consider the leftmost automaton of Fig. 4.2, which is deterministic and recognizes those structures that satisfy $\Box\Diamond v$. Making q_0 the accepting location instead of q_1, we obtain an automaton that corresponds to the class of temporal structures satisfying $\Box\Diamond\neg v$, which is not the complement of those that satisfy $\Box\Diamond v$.

In the present case the result will be proved in several steps as follows. Firstly, we represent all possible runs of a Büchi automaton in a directed acyclic graph (dag): the *run dag* of a Büchi automaton $\Omega = (\mathbf{V}, Q, Q_0, \delta, Q_f)$ and a temporal structure $\mathsf{K} = (\eta_0, \eta_1, \eta_2 \ldots)$ for $\mathbf{V}$, denoted $dag(\Omega, \mathsf{K})$, is the rooted directed acyclic graph (with multiple roots) with elements from $Q \times \mathbb{N}$ as nodes given by the following inductive definition.

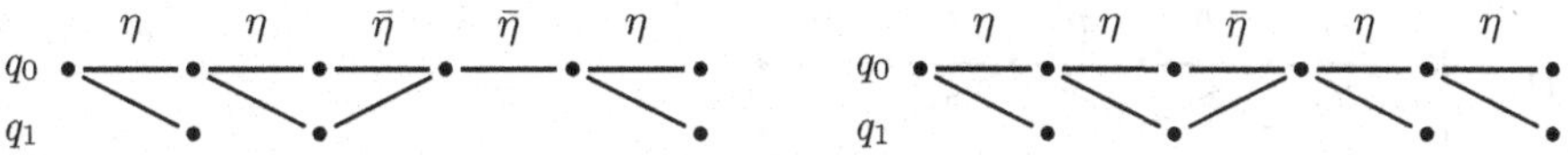

Fig. 4.4. Two run dags

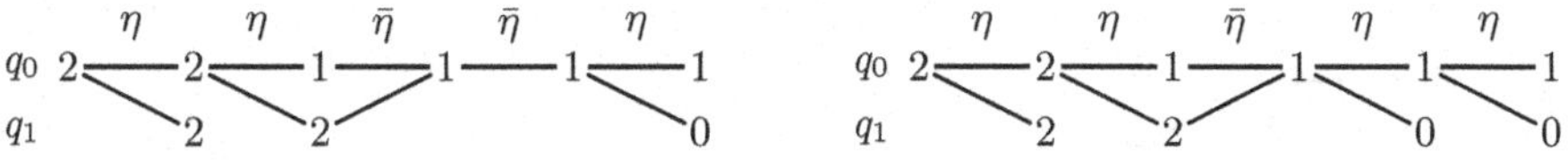

Fig. 4.5. Rankings of run dags

- The roots of $dag(\Omega, \mathsf{K})$ are the nodes $(q, 0)$ for every initial location q of Ω.
- The successor nodes of any node (q, i) are the possible successors $(q', i + 1)$ in a run of Ω over K. Formally, if (q, i) is a node of $dag(\Omega, \mathsf{K})$ and $q' \in Q$ is a location of Ω such that $\underset{\eta_i}{\models} \delta(q, q')$ then $dag(\Omega, \mathsf{K})$ contains a node $(q', i + 1)$ and an edge $((q, i), (q', i + 1))$.

Clearly, $(q_0, q_1, q_2, \ldots)$ is a run of Ω over K if and only if $dag(\Omega, \mathsf{K})$ contains a path $((q_0, 0), (q_1, 1), (q_2, 2), \ldots)$. Let us call a node (q, i) *accepting* if $q \in Q_f$ is an accepting location of Ω.

Figure 4.4 shows (prefixes of) run dags for the automaton Ω_2 from Fig. 4.2 and the two temporal structures $\mathsf{K}_1 = (\eta, \eta, \bar{\eta}, \bar{\eta}, \ldots)$ and $\mathsf{K}_2 = (\eta, \eta, \bar{\eta}, \eta, \eta, \ldots)$ where η (respectively, $\bar{\eta}$) is a state that satisfies (respectively, does not satisfy) v: K_1 alternates between two states satisfying v and two states that do not satisfy v whereas K_2 eventually always satisfies v. For conciseness, the figure only indicates the structure of the dag (together with the corresponding temporal structure) but does not show the precise designations of the nodes. Observe that K_1 is accepted by Ω_2 whereas K_2 is not.

Our next proof step is to define a labeling of any $dag(\Omega, \mathsf{K})$ by which the (non-)acceptance of K by Ω can be characterized. A *ranking* rk of $dag(\Omega, \mathsf{K})$ assigns a *rank* $rk(d)$ to every node d such that the two following conditions are satisfied:

- $rk(d') \leq rk(d)$ whenever d' is a successor node of d,
- ranks of accepting nodes are even.

Consider any infinite path $\pi = (d_0, d_1, d_2, \ldots)$ in the dag. The ranks of the nodes along π are non-increasing; hence they must eventually stabilize: there exists some n such that $rk(d_m) = rk(d_n)$ for all $m \geq n$, and we call $rk(d_n)$ the *stable rank* of path π (for the ranking rk). We say that the ranking rk is *odd* if the stable rank of all infinite paths is odd. Otherwise, i.e., if the run dag contains some infinite path whose stable rank is even, rk is *even*.

Possible rankings for the prefixes of the run dags of Fig.4.4 are shown in Fig. 4.5. Continuing the rankings in a similar manner, it is easy to see that the ranking for the left-hand dag is even, whereas the ranking for the right-hand dag is odd. In fact, one cannot find an odd ranking for the left-hand run dag, and we will now show that a Büchi automaton Ω does not accept the temporal structure K if and only if $dag(\Omega, \mathsf{K})$

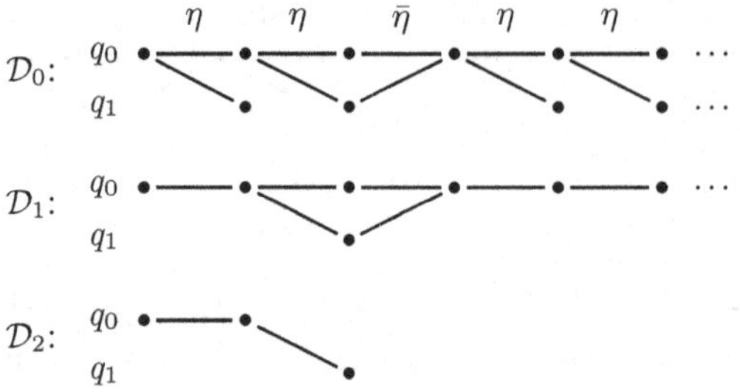

Fig. 4.6. A dag sequence

admits an odd ranking. (Observe in passing that any run dag trivially admits an even ranking, for example by assigning rank 0 to each node.) The "if" part of this theorem is quite obvious.

Lemma 4.3.3. *If rk is an odd ranking of $dag(\Omega, \mathsf{K})$ then $\mathsf{K} \notin \mathcal{L}(\Omega)$.*

Proof. We must show that no run of Ω over K is accepting. So let $\varrho = (q_0, q_1, q_2, \ldots)$ be some run of Ω over K. Then $\pi = ((q_0, 0), (q_1, 1), (q_2, 2), \ldots)$ is a path of $dag(\Omega, \mathsf{K})$. Because rk is an odd ranking for $dag(\Omega, \mathsf{K})$, the stable rank srk_π of π for rk must be odd; hence there exists some n such that $rk((q_m, m)) = srk_\pi$ for all $m \geq n$. Since rk must assign even ranks to accepting nodes, it follows that $q_m \notin Q_f$ holds for all $m \geq n$; so ϱ is not accepting, as we intended to prove. △

The proof of the "only if" part is more difficult: given some structure $\mathsf{K} \notin \mathcal{L}(\Omega)$, we must construct an odd ranking for $dag(\Omega, \mathsf{K})$. Let us call a node d *useless* in $dag(\Omega, \mathsf{K})$ if either no accepting node is reachable from d or only finitely many nodes are reachable from d. Obviously, if (q, n) is useless then q cannot occur at the nth position of any accepting run of Ω over K. Successively eliminating useless nodes will help us to construct an odd ranking. Given a (finite or infinite) dag $\mathcal{D}$ and some set $\mathcal{U}$ of nodes of $\mathcal{D}$, we write $\mathcal{D} \setminus \mathcal{U}$ for the dag from which all nodes in $\mathcal{U}$ and all edges adjacent to these nodes have been removed. The *width of a dag $\mathcal{D}$ at level k* is the number of nodes of $\mathcal{D}$ of the form (q, k).

Given the run dag $dag(\Omega, \mathsf{K})$ of Ω over K, we inductively define a sequence $\mathcal{D}_0, \mathcal{D}_1, \mathcal{D}_2, \ldots$ of dags as follows:

- $\mathcal{D}_0 = dag(\Omega, \mathsf{K})$,
- $\mathcal{D}_{2i+1} = \mathcal{D}_{2i} \setminus \{d \mid \text{only finitely many nodes are reachable from } d \text{ in } \mathcal{D}_{2i}\}$,
- $\mathcal{D}_{2i+2} = \mathcal{D}_{2i+1} \setminus \{d \mid \text{no node reachable from } d \text{ in } \mathcal{D}_{2i+1} \text{ is accepting}\}$.

Figure 4.6 illustrates this construction for the right-hand dag of Fig. 4.4 (we know that the temporal structure underlying this run dag is not accepted by the automaton). The dags $\mathcal{D}_3, \mathcal{D}_4, \ldots$ are all empty.

We say that node d is *useless at stage i* if it is eliminated in the construction of $\mathcal{D}_{i+1}$. That is, d is useless at stage i if it is a node of dag $\mathcal{D}_i$ and either i is even and only finitely many nodes are reachable from d in $\mathcal{D}_i$, or i is odd and no node reachable from d in $\mathcal{D}_i$ is accepting. Observe that if node d is useless at stage i and node d' is reachable from d in dag $\mathcal{D}_i$ then d' is also useless at stage i. Since all nodes of $\mathcal{D}_0$ are reachable from some root node by definition of $dag(\Omega, \mathsf{K})$, this continues to hold for all $\mathcal{D}_i$. The following lemma shows that if Ω does not accept K then each node of $dag(\Omega, \mathsf{K})$ becomes useless at some stage.

Lemma 4.3.4. *If $\mathsf{K} \notin \mathcal{L}(\Omega)$ where Ω is a Büchi automaton with n locations then each node of $dag(\Omega, \mathsf{K})$ is useless at some stage $i \leq 2n$.*

Proof. We will show inductively that for every $i \in \mathbb{N}$ there exists some level l_i such that the width of dag $\mathcal{D}_{2i}$ at any level $l \geq l_i$ is at most $n - i$. It then follows that the width of dag $\mathcal{D}_{2n}$ at all levels beyond l_n is 0, i.e., $\mathcal{D}_{2n}$ does not contain any nodes beyond level l_n. Therefore, all nodes of dag $\mathcal{D}_{2n}$ are useless at stage $2n$.

For $i = 0$, we may choose $l_0 = 0$ because the width of dag $\mathcal{D}_0 = dag(\Omega, \mathsf{K})$ at any level is bounded by the number n of locations of Ω.

For the induction step, assume that the assertion holds for i. We first observe that for each node d, the dag $\mathcal{D}_{2i+1}$ contains an infinite path starting at d: since d was already a node of $\mathcal{D}_{2i}$ and was not useless at stage $2i$, infinitely many nodes must have been reachable from d in $\mathcal{D}_{2i}$. Furthermore, each level of $\mathcal{D}_{2i}$ is of finite width, because $\mathcal{D}_{2i}$ is a subdag of $dag(\Omega, \mathsf{K})$. Therefore, by a general graph-theoretical argument, known as *König's lemma,* there must be an infinite path from d in $\mathcal{D}_{2i}$, none of whose nodes is useless at stage $2i$, and which therefore continues to exist in $\mathcal{D}_{2i+1}$. In particular, infinitely many nodes are reachable from any node d of $\mathcal{D}_{2i+1}$.

We now consider two cases. Either $\mathcal{D}_{2i+1}$ is empty; then so is $\mathcal{D}_{2i+2}$, and the assertion holds trivially. Otherwise, we now show that $\mathcal{D}_{2i+1}$ contains some node that is useless at stage $2i+1$: assume that this were not the case and pick some root node d_0 of $\mathcal{D}_{2i+1}$ (recall that all nodes in $\mathcal{D}_{2i+1}$ are reachable from some root so $\mathcal{D}_{2i+1}$ must contain a root node if it is non-empty). By assumption, d_0 is not useless at stage $2i+1$, and therefore there must be some accepting node d_0' that is reachable from d_0. Moreover, infinitely many nodes are reachable from d_0' in $\mathcal{D}_{2i+1}$, by the observation above. In particular, d_0' has some successor node d_1. By our assumption, d_1 is not useless at stage $2i+1$; hence there is some accepting node d_1' reachable from d_1. Continuing inductively, we find an infinite path $(d_0, \ldots, d_0', d_1, \ldots, d_1', d_2, \ldots, d_2', \ldots)$ in $\mathcal{D}_{2i+1}$ that contains infinitely many accepting nodes. However, this path must already have existed in $\mathcal{D}_0 = dag(\Omega, \mathsf{K})$, and it corresponds to an accepting run of Ω over K, contradicting the assumption that $\mathsf{K} \notin \mathcal{L}(\Omega)$.

Hence, $\mathcal{D}_{2i+1}$ contains some node, say, (q, l) that is useless at stage $2i+1$. Recall that $\mathcal{D}_{2i+1}$ contains an infinite path from node (q, l). By definition, all nodes along this path are useless at stage $2i+1$ and will therefore be removed in the construction of $\mathcal{D}_{2i+2}$. In particular, the width at all levels beyond l in $\mathcal{D}_{2i+2}$ must be strictly smaller than that of the corresponding levels in $\mathcal{D}_{2i+1}$, which is at most the width at these levels in $\mathcal{D}_{2i}$. Therefore, we may choose $l_{i+1} = \max(l_i, l)$ and conclude that the width at any level beyond l_{i+1} in dag $\mathcal{D}_{2i+1}$ is bounded by $n - (i+1)$, which completes the proof. △

We now define the (partial) function rk_{ul} that assigns to each node d of $dag(\Omega, \mathsf{K})$ the number i if d is useless at stage i. If $\mathsf{K} \notin \mathcal{L}(\Omega)$, then Lemma 4.3.4 shows that rk_{ul} is a total function, and we now prove that rk_{ul} is indeed an odd ranking.

Lemma 4.3.5. *If $\mathsf{K} \notin \mathcal{L}(\Omega)$ then rk_{ul} is an odd ranking of $dag(\Omega, \mathsf{K})$.*

Proof. Let d be any node of $dag(\Omega, \mathsf{K})$ and d' a successor node of d. If $rk_{ul}(d) = i$ then d is useless at stage i. If d' has already been eliminated at an earlier stage, we have $rk_{ul}(d') < i$ by definition. Otherwise, d' is still a successor node of d in dag $\mathcal{D}_i$ and is therefore also useless at stage i; hence $rk_{ul}(d') = i$. In either case we have $rk_{ul}(d') \leq rk_{ul}(d)$.

If d is an accepting node of $dag(\Omega, \mathsf{K})$ then $rk_{ul}(d)$ cannot be odd by definition. Since rk_{ul} is a total function, $rk_{ul}(d)$ must be even and, hence, rk_{ul} is a ranking of $dag(\Omega, \mathsf{K})$.

Finally, let $(d_0, d_1, d_2, \ldots)$ be an infinite path in $dag(\Omega, \mathsf{K})$, and assume that its stable rank i is even. Then we find some $n \in \mathbb{N}$ such that all d_m for $m \geq n$ are useless at stage i, which is impossible if i is even and proves the claim. △

Taking the preceding lemmas together, the non-acceptance of Büchi automata can be characterized as follows.

Theorem 4.3.6. *If Ω is a Büchi automaton with n locations and K is a temporal structure, then $\mathsf{K} \notin \mathcal{L}(\Omega)$ if and only if there exists an odd ranking rk of $dag(\Omega, \mathsf{K})$ that assigns to each node d a rank $rk(d) \leq 2n$.*

Proof. The claim follows immediately from the Lemmas 4.3.3, 4.3.4, and 4.3.5. △

We turn now to the final step of our proof of the claimed closure property. Given a Büchi automaton $\Omega = (\mathbf{V}, Q, Q_0, \delta, Q_f)$ with n locations, we construct the complement automaton $\overline{\Omega}$ that accepts a temporal structure K if and only if there exists an odd ranking of range $\{0, \ldots, 2n\}$ for $dag(\Omega, \mathsf{K})$. The idea is that $\overline{\Omega}$ "guesses" an odd ranking while it reads the temporal structure. We identify a ranking rk with an infinite sequence $(rk_0, rk_1, rk_2, \ldots)$ of assignments $rk_i : Q \to \{0, \ldots, 2n\} \cup \{\bot\}$ where $rk_i(q) = rk(q, i)$ if the node (q, i) appears in $dag(\Omega, \mathsf{K})$, and $rk_i(q) = \bot$ otherwise. For example, the ranking shown in the left-hand side of Fig. 4.5 is identified with the sequence

$$\left(\begin{bmatrix}2\\\bot\end{bmatrix}, \begin{bmatrix}2\\2\end{bmatrix}, \begin{bmatrix}1\\2\end{bmatrix}, \begin{bmatrix}1\\\bot\end{bmatrix}, \begin{bmatrix}1\\\bot\end{bmatrix}, \begin{bmatrix}1\\0\end{bmatrix}, \ldots\right).$$

Let us denote by $\mathcal{Z}$ the set of assignments $\psi : Q \to (\{0, \ldots, 2n\} \cup \{\bot\})$ such that $\psi(q)$ is even if $q \in Q_f'$. The transition relation of $\overline{\Omega}$ ensures that ranks do not increase along any path of the run dag. Formally, $\psi' \in \mathcal{Z}$ is a *successor assignment* of $\psi \in \mathcal{Z}$ for a state η if for all $q \in Q$ with $\psi(q) \neq \bot$ and all $q' \in Q$ with $\models_{\eta} \delta(q, q')$, we have $\psi'(q') \neq \bot$ and $\psi'(q') \leq \psi(q)$. The automaton $\overline{\Omega}$ verifies that the guessed ranking is odd by ensuring that each even-ranked node along any path is eventually followed by an odd-ranked node. For this reason, the locations of $\overline{\Omega}$ are pairs (ψ, Y)

where $\psi \in \mathcal{Z}$ and $Y \subseteq Q$ is a set of locations of Ω that, intuitively, need to traverse an odd-ranked node.

Formally, the automaton $\overline{\Omega} = (\mathbf{V}, \overline{Q}, \overline{Q}_0, \overline{\delta}, \overline{Q}_f)$ is defined by

- $\overline{Q} = \mathcal{Z} \times 2^Q$,
- $\overline{Q}_0 = \{(\psi, \emptyset) \mid \psi(q) \neq \bot \text{ for all } q \in Q_0\}$,
- $\overline{\delta}((\psi, Y), (\psi', Y')) = \begin{cases} \bigvee\{char_{\mathbf{V}}^{\eta} \mid \psi' \text{ is a successor assignment of } \psi \text{ for } \eta\} \\ \quad \text{if } Y = \emptyset \text{ and } Y' = \{q' \in Q \mid \psi'(q') \text{ even}\} \\ \quad \text{or } Y \neq \emptyset \text{ and } Y' = \{q' \in Q \mid \psi'(q') \text{ even and} \\ \qquad \models_{\eta} \delta(q, q') \text{ for some } q \in Y\}, \\ \textbf{false} \quad \text{otherwise,} \end{cases}$
- $\overline{Q}_f = \mathcal{Z} \times \{\emptyset\}$.

In this definition, the characteristic formula $char_{\mathbf{V}}^{\eta}$ of a valuation $\eta : \mathbf{V} \to \{\mathsf{ff}, \mathsf{tt}\}$ is defined as

$$char_{\mathbf{V}}^{\eta} \equiv \bigwedge\{v \mid v \in \mathbf{V} \text{ and } \eta(v) = \mathsf{tt}\} \wedge \bigwedge\{\neg v \mid v \in \mathbf{V} \text{ and } \eta(v) = \mathsf{ff}\}.$$

Because $\mathbf{V}$ is a finite set, there are only finitely many valuations to consider for the definition of the formulas $\overline{\delta}((\psi, Y), (\psi', Y'))$.

Theorem 4.3.7. *If $\mathcal{L}$ is ω-regular over $\mathbf{V}$ then so is $\overline{\mathcal{L}}$.*

Proof. Let Ω be a Büchi automaton such that $\mathcal{L} = \mathcal{L}(\Omega)$ and K be any temporal structure. We show that $\mathsf{K} \in \mathcal{L}(\overline{\Omega})$ if and only if $dag(\Omega, \mathsf{K})$ admits an odd ranking with ranks in $\{0, \ldots, 2n\}$. The assertion of the theorem then follows immediately by Theorem 4.3.6.

To show the "if" part, assume that rk is an odd ranking of $dag(\Omega, \mathsf{K})$ and define rk_i and Y_i, for $i \in \mathbb{N}$ as follows:

$$rk_i(q) = \begin{cases} rk(q, i) & \text{if } (q, i) \text{ is a node of } dag(\Omega, \mathsf{K}), \\ \bot & \text{otherwise,} \end{cases}$$

$$Y_0 = \emptyset,$$

$$Y_{i+1} = \begin{cases} \{q' \in Q \mid rk_{i+1}(q') \text{ even}\} & \text{if } Y_i = \emptyset, \\ \{q' \in Q \mid rk_{i+1}(q') \text{ even and} \\ \quad \models_{\eta_i} \delta(q, q') \text{ for some } q \in Y_i\} & \text{otherwise.} \end{cases}$$

It is not hard to see that $\varrho = ((rk_0, Y_0), (rk_1, Y_1), \ldots)$ is a run of $\overline{\Omega}$ over K: the initial assignment rk_0 satisfies $rk_0(q) \neq \bot$ for all $q \in Q_0$ because $(q, 0)$ is clearly a node of $dag(\Omega, \mathsf{K})$ for every location $q \in Q_0$; hence $(rk_0, \emptyset) \in \overline{Q}_0$. Because rk is a ranking, the ranks along any path are non-increasing, and rk_{i+1} is a successor assignment of rk_i. Moreover, the definition of Y_{i+1} mirrors the transition relation $\overline{\delta}$. It remains to show that ϱ is an accepting run of $\overline{\Omega}$, that is, $Y_i = \emptyset$ for infinitely many $i \in \mathbb{N}$. Assume to the contrary that there is some $n \in \mathbb{N}$ such that $Y_m \neq \emptyset$ holds for all $m \geq n$. We claim that there exists a path in $dag(\Omega, \mathsf{K})$ whose stable rank is even; this contradicts the assumption that rk is an odd ranking.

To show this claim, we observe that for all $i \in \mathbb{N}$, $rk_i(q)$ is even for all locations $q \in Y_i$; in particular, the run dag $dag(\Omega, \mathsf{K})$ contains the nodes (q, i). Moreover, from any location $q_k \in Y_{n+k}$ we can find a finite path $(q_0, q_1, \ldots, q_k)$ such that $q_i \in Y_{n+i}$ and $\models_{\eta_i} \delta(q_i, q_{i+1})$ for all i. Applying again König's lemma, it follows that there exists an infinite path $((q_0, 0), (q_1, 1), \ldots, (q_n, n), (q_{n+1}, n+1), \ldots)$ in $dag(\Omega, \mathsf{K})$ that contains only nodes that correspond to locations in Y_i for $i \geq n$, and the stable rank of this path is even.

For the "only if" part, assume that $\varrho = ((\psi_0, Y_0), (\psi_1, Y_1), \ldots)$ is an accepting run of $\overline{\Omega}$ over K, and define the function rk by

$$rk(q, i) = \psi_i(q) \quad \text{for all nodes } (q, i) \text{ of } dag(\Omega, \mathsf{K}).$$

Observe that $rk(q, i) \neq \perp$ for all nodes (q, i) of $dag(\Omega, \mathsf{K})$: for the initial nodes this follows from the definition of $\overline{Q}_0$, and the definition of a successor assignment ensures the induction step. Also, ranks are non-increasing along paths. Therefore, rk is a ranking of $dag(\Omega, \mathsf{K})$; it remains to show that it is an odd ranking. Assume, to the contrary, that $((q_0, 0), (q_1, 1), \ldots)$ is a path in $dag(\Omega, \mathsf{K})$ whose stable rank under rk is even, and let $((q_m, m), (q_{m+1}, m+1), \ldots)$ be a suffix of this path such that $rk(q_i, i) = r$ equals the stable rank for all $i \geq m$. Because ϱ is an accepting run of $\overline{\Omega}$, we know that $Y_i = \emptyset$ for infinitely many $i \in \mathbb{N}$. Let $n \geq m$ be such that $Y_n = \emptyset$, so by definition of the transition relation $\overline{\delta}$ we must have $q_{n+1} \in Y_{n+1}$, and by the definition of $\overline{\delta}$ it follows indeed that $q_i \in Y_i$ holds for all $i \geq n+1$, and a contradiction is reached, which completes the proof. △

Automata are especially useful to resolve decision problems on languages. Again, many of the standard results known from the theory of finite automata carry over to Büchi automata. We introduce some additional notation. Given two locations q and q' of a Büchi automaton Ω, we say that q' is a one-step successor of q, written $q \rightarrow_\Omega q'$, if $\models_\eta \delta(q, q')$ holds for some state η. The reflexive transitive closure of the one-step successor relation $\rightarrow_\Omega$ is denoted by $\rightarrow_\Omega^*$, and we say that q' is *reachable* from q if $q \rightarrow_\Omega^* q'$. The transitive closure of $\rightarrow_\Omega$ is denoted by $\rightarrow_\Omega^+$. The following theorem gives a criterion to decide the *emptiness problem* about whether the language accepted by a Büchi automaton is empty or not.

Theorem 4.3.8. *Given a Büchi automaton $\Omega = (\mathbf{V}, Q, Q_0, \delta, Q_f)$, the language $\mathcal{L}(\Omega)$ is non-empty if and only if there exist locations $q \in Q_0$ and $q' \in Q_f$ such that $q \rightarrow_\Omega^* q'$ and $q' \rightarrow_\Omega^+ q'$.*

Proof. Assume that there exist q and q' as indicated. Since $q \rightarrow_\Omega^* q'$, we can find a finite (possibly empty) sequence $(\eta_0, \ldots, \eta_{k-1})$ of states and a corresponding sequence $(q_0, \ldots, q_k)$ of automata locations such that $q_0 = q$, $q_k = q'$, and where $\models_{\eta_i} \delta(q_i, q_{i+1})$ holds for all i, $0 \leq i < k$. Similarly, from the assumption $q' \rightarrow_\Omega^+ q'$ we obtain finite and non-empty sequences $(\eta_k, \ldots, \eta_{l-1})$ of states and $(q_k, \ldots, q_l)$ of locations where $q_k = q_l = q'$ and $\models_{\eta_i} \delta(q_i, q_{i+1})$ for $k \leq i < l$. Now consider the temporal structure K and sequence ϱ defined by

$$\mathsf{K} = (\eta_0, \ldots, \eta_{k-1}, \underbrace{\eta_k, \ldots, \eta_{l-1}}_{\text{repeating forever}}, \ldots), \quad \varrho = (q_0, \ldots, q_{k-1}, \underbrace{q_k, \ldots, q_{l-1}}_{\text{repeating forever}}, \ldots).$$

The conditions above ensure that ϱ is a run of Ω over K, which contains infinitely many occurrences of location q' and is therefore accepting. In particular, $\mathcal{L}(\Omega) \neq \emptyset$.

Conversely, assume that $\mathcal{L}(\Omega) \neq \emptyset$, and let $\varrho = (q_0, q_1, q_2, \ldots)$ be an accepting run of Ω over some structure $\mathsf{K} \in \mathcal{L}(\Omega)$. Thus, $q_0 \in Q_0$ is an initial location of Ω, and there is some accepting location $q' \in Q_f$ that appears infinitely often. Choose some $i < j$ such that $q_i = q_j = q'$, and it follows that $q_0 \rightarrow^*_\Omega q'$ and $q' \rightarrow^+_\Omega q'$, which completes the proof. △

Theorem 4.3.8 reduces the problem of deciding whether the language of a Büchi automaton is empty or not to that of searching cycles in a graph. Assuming that the satisfiability of edge labels has been precomputed, this search can be performed in time linear in the size of the automaton.

Other decision problems can be reduced to the emptiness problem. In particular, a Büchi Ω automaton is *universal*, that is, accepts every temporal structure, if and only if its complement $\overline{\Omega}$ defines the empty language. Similarly, given two Büchi automata Ω_1 and Ω_2 we can decide the *inclusion problem* whether $\mathcal{L}(\Omega_1) \subseteq \mathcal{L}(\Omega_2)$ by checking if $\mathcal{L}(\Omega_1) \cap \mathcal{L}(\overline{\Omega_2}) = \emptyset$. Observe, however, that the solutions to the universality and the inclusion problems both rely on complementation, and are therefore of exponential complexity.

Büchi automata can naturally express the requirement that some state occurs infinitely often in a temporal structure. Because "infinitely often A and infinitely often B" is not the same as "infinitely often A and B", the construction of a Büchi automaton accepting the intersection of two languages is a little more complicated than the standard product construction, as could already be observed in the proof of Theorem 4.3.1. A generalization of Büchi automata overcomes this problem by allowing for several acceptance sets.

Definition. A *generalized Büchi automaton* $\Omega = (\mathbf{V}, Q, Q_0, \delta, Acc)$ for a finite set $\mathbf{V}$ of propositional constants has the same structure as a Büchi automaton, except that the acceptance condition is given by a finite set $Acc = \{Q_f^{(1)}, \ldots, Q_f^{(m)}\}$ of sets $Q_f^{(i)} \subseteq Q$ of accepting locations.

Runs of generalized Büchi automata are defined as for standard Büchi automata. A run $\varrho = (q_0, q_1, q_2, \ldots)$ is *accepting* if for every $Q_f^{(k)} \in Acc$, there exist infinitely many $i \in \mathbb{N}$ such that $q_i \in Q_f^{(k)}$. The language of a generalized Büchi automaton Ω is again the set of temporal structures for $\mathbf{V}$ for which Ω has some accepting run.

Clearly, every Büchi automaton can be viewed as a generalized Büchi automaton with a single set of accepting locations. The closure of ω-regular languages under intersection, proven in Theorem 4.3.1, lets us expect that generalized Büchi automata are just as expressive as ordinary Büchi automata, an expectation that is confirmed by the following theorem.

Theorem 4.3.9. *For every generalized Büchi automaton Ω there is a Büchi automaton Ω^* such that $\mathcal{L}(\Omega^*) = \mathcal{L}(\Omega)$.*

Proof. Let $\Omega = (\mathbf{V}, Q, Q_0, \delta, Acc)$ where $Acc = \{Q_f^{(1)}, \dots, Q_f^{(m)}\}$. If $m = 0$, i.e., if $Acc = \emptyset$, then Ω imposes no acceptance condition and Ω^* can be defined as $(\mathbf{V}, Q, Q_0, \delta, Q)$. Otherwise, the construction is similar to the proof of Theorem 4.3.1 and uses an additional counter that indicates the accepting set that should be visited next. Formally, we define $\Omega^* = (\mathbf{V}, Q^*, Q_0^*, \delta^*, Q_f^*)$ where

- $Q^* = Q \times \{1, \dots, m\}$,
- $Q_0^* = Q_0 \times \{1\}$,
- $\delta((q,k),(q',k')) = \begin{cases} \delta(q,q') & \text{if either } q \in Q_f^{(k)} \text{ and } k' = (k \bmod m) + 1 \\ & \quad\text{or } q \notin Q_f^{(k)} \text{ and } k' = k, \\ \mathbf{false} & \text{otherwise,} \end{cases}$
- $Q_f^* = Q_f^{(1)} \times \{1\}$.

The proof that $\mathcal{L}(\Omega^*) = \mathcal{L}(\Omega)$ runs analogously to the proof of Theorem 4.3.1. △

Generalized Büchi automata are defined in precisely such a way that they admit a simpler product construction: given two generalized Büchi automata Ω_1 and Ω_2 where $\Omega_i = (\mathbf{V}, Q^{(i)}, Q_0^{(i)}, \delta^{(i)}, \{Q_f^{(i,1)}, \dots, Q_f^{(i,m_i)}\})$ for $i = 1, 2$, the intersection of $\mathcal{L}(\Omega_1)$ and $\mathcal{L}(\Omega_2)$ is characterized by the generalized Büchi automaton $\Omega^\cap = (\mathbf{V}, Q^{(1)} \times Q^{(2)}, Q_0^{(1)} \times Q_0^{(2)}, \delta^\cap, Acc^\cap)$ where

$$\begin{aligned} &\delta^\cap((q_0,q_1),(q_0',q_1')) = \delta^{(1)}(q_0,q_0') \wedge \delta^{(2)}(q_1,q_1'), \\ &Acc^\cap = \{Q_f^{(1,1)} \times Q^{(2)}, \dots, Q_f^{(1,m_1)} \times Q^{(2)}, \\ &\qquad\quad Q^{(1)} \times Q_f^{(2,1)}, \dots, Q^{(1)} \times Q_f^{(2,m_2)}\}. \end{aligned}$$

The ability of generalized Büchi automata to represent several acceptance conditions will also be helpful for the construction of Büchi automata that correspond to LTL formulas in the next section.

4.4 LTL and Büchi Automata

Temporal logic and automata provide different means to describe sets of temporal structures: LTL formulas are more "declarative" whereas automata are more "operational" in nature. We will now characterize their expressiveness, and in particular describe a construction that associates a generalized Büchi automaton Ω_F with any given LTL formula F such that Ω_F accepts precisely those temporal structures K for which $\mathsf{K}_0(F) = \mathsf{tt}$. Based on this construction and Theorem 4.3.8, we obtain a second decision algorithm for the satisfiability of LTL formulas, after the tableau construction described in Sect. 2.5. In fact, Ω_F can quite easily be obtained from a tableau $\mathcal{T}$ for the PNP $(\{F\}, \emptyset)$. The idea is that the locations of Ω_F are the (tableau) states of $\mathcal{T}$, the initial locations are the states reachable from the root of $\mathcal{T}$, and the transitions of Ω_F are determined from the successor relation of $\mathcal{T}$ and the literals that appear in the tableau states. The acceptance condition of Ω_F reflects the honest SCCs of $\mathcal{T}$.

More formally, for a PNP $\mathcal{P}$, we define the corresponding generalized Büchi automaton $\Omega_{\mathcal{P}} = (\mathbf{V}, Q, Q_0, \delta, Acc)$ as follows.

- $\mathbf{V}$ is the set of propositional constants that appear in the formulas of $\mathcal{P}$.
- Q is the set of states of the tableau $\mathcal{T}$ for $\mathcal{P}$ that are not closed.
- $Q_0 \subseteq Q$ is the set of states reachable from the root of $\mathcal{T}$ without crossing an application of rule ($\bigcirc$).
- If $\mathcal{Q}$ and $\mathcal{Q}'$ are states of $\mathcal{T}$ such that $\mathcal{Q}'$ is reachable from $\mathcal{Q}$ in $\mathcal{T}$ by crossing precisely one application of rule ($\bigcirc$) then

$$\delta(\mathcal{Q}, \mathcal{Q}') \equiv \bigwedge_{v \in pos(\mathcal{Q})} v \;\wedge\; \bigwedge_{v \in neg(\mathcal{Q})} \neg v,$$

  otherwise $\delta(\mathcal{Q}, \mathcal{Q}') \equiv$ **false**.
- Let $\Box A_1, \ldots, \Box A_n$ be all formulas of this form that occur in $neg(\mathcal{N})$, for some tableau node $\mathcal{N}$; then the acceptance condition $Acc = \{Q_f^{(1)}, \ldots, Q_f^{(n)}\}$ of Ω contains n sets $Q_f^{(i)}$ where $\mathcal{Q} \in Q_f^{(i)}$ if for every node $\mathcal{N}$ of $\mathcal{T}$ for which $\Box A_i \in neg(\mathcal{N})$ and from which $\mathcal{Q}$ can be reached without crossing any application of rule ($\bigcirc$), we have $A_i \in neg(\mathcal{N}')$ for some node $\mathcal{N}'$ along every path from $\mathcal{N}$ to $\mathcal{Q}$.

This construction is illustrated in Fig. 4.7 for the PNP $\mathcal{P} = (\{\Box\Diamond v, \Box\Diamond\neg v\}, \emptyset)$. Figure 4.7(a) contains a tableau for $\mathcal{P}$: applications of the rule ($\bigcirc$) are explicitly indicated; for the other transitions the formulas to which tableau rules are applied are underlined; we sometimes apply rules to several formulas at once and also use a derived rule for the $\Diamond$-operator such that a formula $\Diamond A \in pos(\mathcal{N})$ is expanded like a formula $\Box\neg A \in neg(\mathcal{N})$. Node 5 is a closed tableau state; the remaining tableau states 6, 7, and 8 are the locations of the generalized Büchi automaton $\Omega_{\mathcal{P}}$, shown in Fig. 4.7(b). Because all three states are reachable from the root of the tableau without crossing an application of rule ($\bigcirc$), they are initial locations of the automaton. Similarly, each state in this example is reachable from every other state, and itself, by crossing a single edge corresponding to rule ($\bigcirc$). The transition formulas are determined by the propositional constants in the source PNPs: for example, all edges leaving location 6 are labeled by v. It remains to determine the acceptance conditions of $\Omega_{\mathcal{P}}$. The "eventualities" promised by tableau nodes are $\Diamond v$ and $\Diamond\neg v$; so $\Omega_{\mathcal{P}}$ has two acceptance sets $Q_f^{(1)}$ and $Q_f^{(2)}$. Both eventualities occur in the tableau node 2, from which all three states are reachable without crossing an edge of type ($\bigcirc$). The paths from node 2 to states 6 and 7 fulfill the promise v and $\neg v$, respectively, and therefore $Q_f^{(1)} = \{6\}$, whereas $Q_f^{(2)} = \{7\}$. In particular, any accepting run of $\Omega_{\mathcal{P}}$ must pass infinitely often through both locations, and the underlying temporal structure must therefore satisfy infinitely often v and infinitely often $\neg v$, which is just what the original PNP asserts.

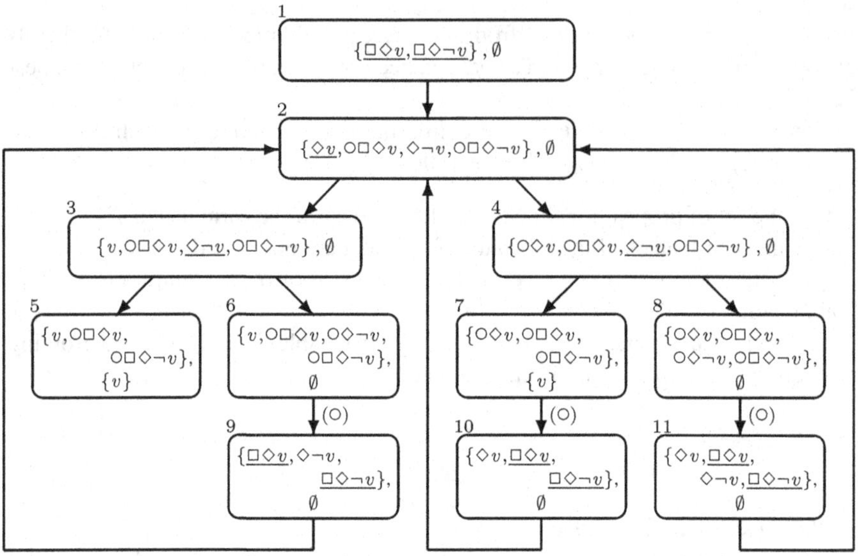

(a) Tableau for $(\{\Box\Diamond v, \Box\Diamond\neg v\}, \emptyset)$

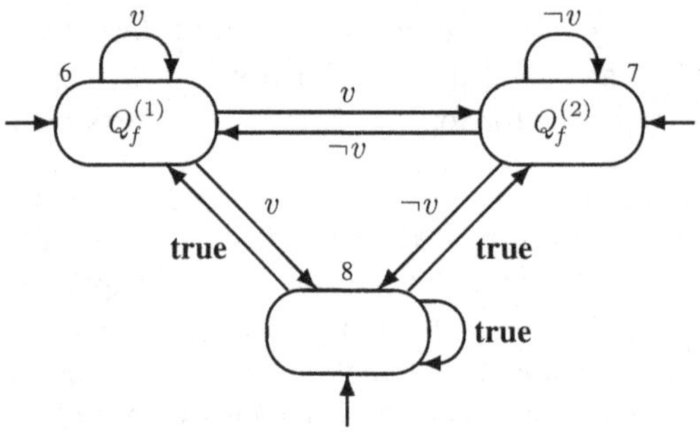

(b) Corresponding generalized Büchi automaton

Fig. 4.7. Construction of a Büchi automaton from a tableau

More generally, the correctness proof of the construction of $\Omega_{\mathcal{P}}$ is based on (the proofs of) the lemmas about the tableau construction in Sect. 2.5.

Theorem 4.4.1. *For any PNP $\mathcal{P}$, the generalized Büchi automaton $\Omega_{\mathcal{P}}$ accepts precisely the temporal structures K such that $\mathsf{K}_0(\widehat{\mathcal{P}}) = \mathsf{tt}$.*

Proof. Assume that $\Omega_{\mathcal{P}}$ accepts the temporal structure $\mathsf{K} = (\eta_0, \eta_1, \eta_2, \ldots)$, via an accepting run $\varrho = (q_0, q_1, q_2, \ldots)$. To this run corresponds an infinite path $(\mathcal{N}_0, \mathcal{N}_1, \mathcal{N}_2, \ldots)$ through the tableau such that $q_i = \mathcal{N}_{st(i)}$ for all $i \in \mathbb{N}$, that is, the q_i are precisely the tableau states that appear among the $\mathcal{N}_j$ (see Sect. 2.5 for the definition of this notation). The definition of the acceptance condition of $\Omega_{\mathcal{P}}$ ensures that this path is complete. Moreover, the transition relation of $\Omega_{\mathcal{P}}$ is defined such that $\eta_i(v) = \mathsf{tt}$ if $v \in pos(q_i)$ and $\eta_i(v) = \mathsf{ff}$ if $v \in neg(q_i)$. Now, (the proof

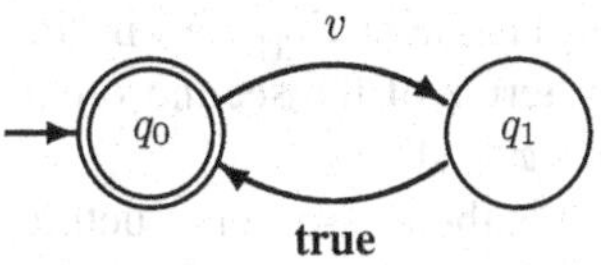

Fig. 4.8. Büchi automaton characterizing **even** v

of) Lemma 2.5.5 ensures that $\mathsf{K}_0(A) = \mathsf{tt}$ for all $A \in pos(\mathcal{N}_0)$ and $\mathsf{K}_0(A) = \mathsf{ff}$ for all $A \in neg(\mathcal{N}_0)$, which just means $\mathsf{K}_0(\widehat{\mathcal{P}}) = \mathsf{tt}$.

Conversely, assume that $\mathsf{K}_0(\widehat{\mathcal{P}}) = \mathsf{tt}$. Then Lemma 2.5.2 ensures that the path $\pi_{\mathcal{Q}}^{\mathsf{K}} = (\mathcal{Q}_0, \mathcal{Q}_1, \mathcal{Q}_2, \ldots)$ is infinite and that $\mathsf{K}_{cnt(i)}(\widehat{\mathcal{Q}_i}) = \mathsf{tt}$ for all $i \in \mathbb{N}$. In fact, the subsequence $\varrho = (\mathcal{Q}_{st(0)}, \mathcal{Q}_{st(1)}, \mathcal{Q}_{st(2)}, \ldots)$ of $\pi_{\mathcal{Q}}^{\mathsf{K}}$ is an accepting run of the automaton $\Omega_{\mathcal{P}}$ over K. Indeed, $\mathcal{Q}_{st(0)}$ is reachable from the root $\mathcal{P}$ without crossing an application of rule ($\bigcirc$) and $(\mathcal{Q}_{st(i)}, \mathcal{Q}_{st(i+1)}) \in \delta$ holds by definition of δ and because of $\mathsf{K}_i(\widehat{\mathcal{Q}_{st(i)}}) = \mathsf{tt}$. As for the acceptance condition, the proof of Lemma 2.5.2 shows that whenever $\Box A \in neg(\mathcal{Q}_i)$ for some $i \in \mathbb{N}$ then $A \in neg(\mathcal{Q}_j)$ for some $j \geq i$, and this implies that ϱ contains infinitely many accepting locations for each of the acceptance conditions of $\Omega_{\mathcal{P}}$. △

Because tableau nodes are labeled with sets of subformulas (possibly prefixed by an additional $\bigcirc$-operator) of the original PNP, the size of the tableau, and therefore also of the resulting generalized Büchi automaton, may in general be exponential in the size of the PNP. The translation into a (standard) Büchi automaton according to Theorem 4.3.9 is polynomial, so we can construct a Büchi automaton of exponential size for a PNP (or an LTL formula). Because deciding language emptiness is of linear complexity for Büchi automata, we again find an overall exponential complexity for deciding satisfiability or validity of LTL formulas, as observed in Sect. 2.5. The translation into Büchi automata will be useful for other purposes, and we will take this up again in Chap. 11.

Theorem 4.4.1 shows that Büchi automata are at least as expressive as LTL (with respect to initial validity semantics), and this result can easily be extended to LTL+b. The converse is not true: a simple counterexample is provided by the temporal operator **even** introduced in Sect. 4.1. We already showed in the proof of Theorem 4.1.4 that LTL cannot express the formula **even** v of LTL+μ. However, the temporal structures K with $\mathsf{K}_0(\mathbf{even}\, v) = \mathsf{tt}$ are clearly characterized by the Büchi automaton shown in Fig. 4.8.

Section 4.2 has shown that LTL+b with respect to initial validity semantics corresponds precisely to a monadic first-order logic. In order to classify the expressive power of Büchi automata more precisely we now show that, in the same spirit, ω-regular languages correspond to monadic second-order logic.

For a set $\mathbf{V}$ of propositional constants, we consider the second-order language over the signature $SIG_{\mathbf{V}} = (\mathbf{S}, \mathbf{F}, \mathbf{P})$ defined in Sect. 4.2, i.e., where $\mathbf{S} = \{TIME\}$, $\mathbf{F} = \emptyset$, and $\mathbf{P} = \{<^{(TIME\ TIME)}\} \cup \{v^{(TIME)} \mid v \in \mathbf{V}\}$. Because we are interested in a monadic language, we only consider unary predicate variables $u \in \mathcal{R}_{TIME}$

corresponding to the propositional variables $u \in \mathcal{V}$ of a language $\mathcal{L}^{q}_{\mathrm{LTL}}$. As in the corresponding first-order language of Sect. 4.2, the only terms of the second-order language defined by this signature are individual variables $x \in \mathcal{X}$.

As in Sect. 4.2, we associate with a temporal structure K the first-order structure S_{K} for $SIG_{\mathbf{V}}$ described there. A sequence $\Xi = (\xi_o, \xi_1, \xi_2)$ of valuations of the propositional variables $\mathcal{V}$ determines the valuation of the predicate variables

$$\xi(u)(j) = \xi_j(u) \qquad \text{for } j \in \mathbb{N}.$$

In the same spirit as that of the translation **FOL** of Sect. 4.2, we define the translation $\mathbf{SOL} : \mathcal{L}^{q}_{\mathrm{LTL}}(\mathbf{V}) \to \mathcal{L}_{\mathrm{SOL}}(SIG_{\mathbf{V}})$:

$$\begin{aligned}
&\mathbf{SOL}(v) = v(x_0) && \text{for } v \in \mathbf{V},\\
&\mathbf{SOL}(u) = u(x_0) && \text{for } u \in \mathcal{V},\\
&\mathbf{SOL}(\mathbf{false}) = \mathbf{false},\\
&\mathbf{SOL}(A \to B) = \mathbf{SOL}(A) \to \mathbf{SOL}(B),\\
&\mathbf{SOL}(\bigcirc A) = \exists y_1(x_0 < y_1 \land \neg\exists y_2(x_0 < y_2 \land y_2 < y_1) \land (\mathbf{SOL}(A))_{x_0}(y_1)),\\
&\mathbf{SOL}(\Box A) = \forall y(x_0 = y \lor x_0 < y \;\to\; (\mathbf{SOL}(A))_{x_0}(y)),\\
&\mathbf{SOL}(\exists u A) = \exists u\, \mathbf{SOL}(A)
\end{aligned}$$

Again, $\mathbf{SOL}(A)$ contains at most one free variable x_0 that represents the current state. Observe also that free and bound occurrences of predicate variables in $\mathbf{SOL}(A)$ correspond precisely to free and bound occurrences of the corresponding propositional variables in A. The structure of this translation reflects the semantic definition of the connectives of $\mathcal{L}^{q}_{\mathrm{LTL}}(\mathbf{V})$. As in Sect. 4.2 we therefore obtain the correctness of the translation.

Theorem 4.4.2. *Let* K *be a temporal structure for* $\mathbf{V}$, $\Xi = (\xi_0, \xi_1, \xi_2, \ldots)$ *be a propositional valuation for* $\mathcal{V}$, S_{K} *be the structure corresponding to* K, *and* ξ *be a valuation such that* $\xi(u)(j) = \xi_j(u)$ *for all* $u \in \mathcal{V}$ *and* $j \in \mathbb{N}$. *For any formula* A *of* $\mathcal{L}^{q}_{\mathrm{LTL}}(\mathbf{V})$*:*

$$\mathsf{K}^{(\Xi)}_{\xi(x_0)}(A) = \mathsf{S}^{(\xi)}_{\mathsf{K}}(\mathbf{SOL}(A)).$$

Proof. The proof parallels the one of Theorem 4.2.1 and runs by structural induction on the formula A, simultaneously for all valuations Ξ and ξ. The clauses corresponding to the temporal connectives $\bigcirc$ and $\Box$ in the definition of **SOL** reflect their semantics in the same sense as the clauses for **until** and **since** in the definition of **FOL**, and their correctness proof is completely analogous. This leaves us with the two clauses concerning propositional variables and quantification:

- $A \equiv u \in \mathcal{V}$: $\mathsf{K}^{(\Xi)}_{\xi(x_0)}(u) = \xi_{\xi(x_0)}(u) = \xi(u)(\xi(x_0)) = \mathsf{S}^{(\xi)}_{\mathsf{K}}(\mathbf{SOL}(u))$.
- $A \equiv \exists u B$: Using the induction hypothesis we obtain

$$\begin{aligned}
\mathsf{K}^{(\Xi)}_{\xi(x_0)}(\exists u B) = \mathsf{tt} &\Leftrightarrow \mathsf{K}^{(\Xi')}_{\xi(x_0)}(B) = \mathsf{tt} \text{ for some } \Xi' \text{ such that } \Xi' \sim_u \Xi\\
&\Leftrightarrow \mathsf{S}^{(\xi')}_{\mathsf{K}}(\mathbf{SOL}(B)) = \mathsf{tt} \text{ for some } \xi' \text{ such that } \xi' \sim_u \xi\\
&\Leftrightarrow \mathsf{S}^{(\xi)}_{\mathsf{K}}(\mathbf{SOL}(\exists u B)) = \mathsf{tt}.
\end{aligned}$$

△

In the sense of Sections 4.1 and 4.2, Theorem 4.4.2 asserts that monadic second-order logic (based on the signature $SIG_{\mathbf{V}}$) is at least as expressive as LTL+q. We will now set out to show that monadic second-order logic, Büchi automata, and the logics LTL+q and LTL+μ are actually of the same expressive power in the sense that they define the same classes of temporal structures. In the terms of the discussion at the end of Sect. 4.1, our measure of expressiveness is model equivalence with respect to initial validity semantics, which is clearly the appropriate "yardstick" for definability by Büchi automata, but also (cf. Theorem 4.2.4) for comparing predicate logic and temporal logics without past operators.

We will base that proof on an intermediate first-order language over a signature with a single sort representing sets of time points. Instead of using (quantifiers over) variables representing time points as in the language considered so far, we will use (quantifiers over) singleton sets, and the signature contains a predicate to characterize such sets. More precisely, given a set $\mathbf{V}$ of propositional constants, we define the signature $SIG_{\mathbf{V}}^{-} = (\mathbf{S}^{-}, \mathbf{F}^{-}, \mathbf{P}^{-})$ where

- $\mathbf{S}^{-} = \{SET\}$,
- $\mathbf{F}^{-} = \{v^{(\varepsilon, SET)} \mid v \in \mathbf{V}\}$,
- $\mathbf{P}^{-} = \{\subseteq^{(SET\ SET)}, SING^{(SET)}, SUCS^{(SET\ SET)}\}$.

We will interpret the formulas of $\mathcal{L}_{\mathrm{FOL}}(SIG_{\mathbf{V}}^{-})$ over structures S where $|\mathsf{S}| = |\mathsf{S}|_{SET} = 2^{\mathbb{N}}$, $\subseteq$ is interpreted as the subset relation over sets of natural numbers, $SING^{\mathsf{S}}$ as the predicate that holds precisely of singleton sets, and $SUCS^{\mathsf{S}}(\mathrm{M}_1, \mathrm{M}_2)$ holds if and only if $\mathrm{M}_1 = \{n\}$ and $\mathrm{M}_2 = \{m\}$ are two singleton sets with $m = n+1$. We will call any such structure a $SIG_{\mathbf{V}}^{-}$-structure, and we call a structure S for $\mathcal{L}_{\mathrm{FOL}}(SIG_{\mathbf{V}})$ where $|\mathsf{S}| = \mathbb{N}$ and that interprets $<$ as the "less than" relation over $\mathbb{N}$ a $SIG_{\mathbf{V}}$-structure.

The language $\mathcal{L}_{\mathrm{SOL}}(SIG_{\mathbf{V}})$ has both (individual) variables x (of sort $TIME$) and predicate variables u. In $\mathcal{L}_{\mathrm{FOL}}(SIG_{\mathbf{V}}^{-})$, both types of variables will be represented by (individual) variables of sort SET. Formally, we say that a $SIG_{\mathbf{V}}^{-}$-structure S^{-} and valuation ξ^{-} and a $SIG_{\mathbf{V}}$-structure S and valuation ξ correspond to each other, written $(\mathsf{S}^{-}, \xi^{-}) \rightleftharpoons (\mathsf{S}, \xi)$, if all of the following conditions hold:

- $v^{\mathsf{S}^{-}} = \{i \in \mathbb{N} \mid v^{\mathsf{S}}(i) = \mathrm{tt}\}$,
- $\xi^{-}(u) = \{i \in \mathbb{N} \mid \xi(u)(i) = \mathrm{tt}\}$ for predicate variables u of $\mathcal{L}_{\mathrm{SOL}}(SIG_{\mathbf{V}})$,
- $\xi^{-}(x) = \{\xi(x)\}$ for (individual) variables x of $\mathcal{L}_{\mathrm{SOL}}(SIG_{\mathbf{V}})$.

Lemma 4.4.3. *For every formula A of $\mathcal{L}_{\mathrm{FOL}}(SIG_{\mathbf{V}}^{-})$ there exists a formula A^{+} of $\mathcal{L}_{\mathrm{SOL}}(SIG_{\mathbf{V}})$ such that*

$$\mathsf{S}^{(\xi)}(A^{+}) = (\mathsf{S}^{-})^{(\xi^{-})}(A)$$

whenever $(\mathsf{S}^{-}, \xi^{-}) \rightleftharpoons (\mathsf{S}, \xi)$.

Proof. The proof runs by structural induction on the formula A.

1. $A \equiv \mathbf{false}$: The assertion obviously holds for $A^{+} \equiv \mathbf{false}$.

2. $A \equiv B \to C$ or $A \equiv \exists u B$: Then the assertion follows from the induction hypothesis for $A^+ \equiv B^+ \to C^+$ or $A^+ \equiv \exists u B^+$ (in the latter case, u is a predicate variable in A^+).
3. $A \equiv t \subseteq t'$ for terms t and t' of $\mathcal{L}_{\mathrm{FOL}}(SIG_{\mathbf{V}}^-)$: Then t and t' are either constants v or variables u, and we distinguish the different cases. For example, the formula $(u \subseteq v)^+$ is defined as $\forall x(u(x) \to v(x))$, and the remaining cases are similar. With a slight abuse of notation, we will from now on write $(t \subseteq t')^+ \equiv \forall x(t(x) \to t'(x))$, and analogously for similar formulas.
4. $A \equiv t = t'$: Then $A^+ \equiv \forall x(t(x) \leftrightarrow t'(x))$.
5. $A \equiv SING(t)$ for a term t: Then we define

$$A^+ \equiv \exists x\, t(x) \land \forall x \forall y(t(x) \land t(y) \to x = y),$$

and this obviously proves the assertion.
6. $A \equiv SUCS(t, t')$: Then

$$\begin{aligned} A^+ \equiv\ & \exists x \exists y_1(t(x) \land t'(y_1) \land \neg \exists y_2(x < y_2 \land y_2 < y_1)) \land \\ & \forall x \forall y(t(x) \land t(y) \to x = y) \land \\ & \forall x \forall y(t'(x) \land t'(y) \to x = y). \end{aligned}$$

The first conjunct ensures that t and t' hold for some values i and j such that $j = i + 1$, and the second and third conjuncts ensure that t and t' hold for a single value. △

Similarly, for every formula of $\mathcal{L}_{\mathrm{SOL}}(SIG_{\mathbf{V}})$ we can find a corresponding formula of $\mathcal{L}_{\mathrm{FOL}}(SIG_{\mathbf{V}}^-)$. In this translation, the third condition in the definition of $\rightleftharpoons$ becomes important, and we will ensure that quantifiers over (individual) variables in the second-order language are translated into quantifiers over singleton sets in the first-order language.

Lemma 4.4.4. *For every formula A of $\mathcal{L}_{\mathrm{SOL}}(SIG_{\mathbf{V}})$ there exists a formula A^- of $\mathcal{L}_{\mathrm{FOL}}(SIG_{\mathbf{V}}^-)$ such that*

$$(\mathsf{S}^-)^{(\xi^-)}(A^-) = \mathsf{S}^{(\xi)}(A)$$

whenever $(\mathsf{S}^-, \xi^-) \rightleftharpoons (\mathsf{S}, \xi)$.

Proof. Performing again an inductive proof, the cases of $A \equiv$ **false**, $A \equiv B \to C$, and $A \equiv \exists u B$ (for a predicate variable u) are trivial or follow immediately from the induction hypothesis. For the remainder of the proof, remember that the only terms of $\mathcal{L}_{\mathrm{SOL}}(SIG_{\mathbf{V}})$ are (individual) variables x.

1. $A \equiv x = y$: Then the assertion clearly holds for $A^- \equiv x = y$.

2. $A \equiv v(x)$: Then $A^- \equiv x \subseteq v$. Now, using the definition of $\rightleftharpoons$, we find that

$$\begin{aligned} \mathsf{S}^{\xi}(A) = \mathrm{tt} &\Leftrightarrow v^{\mathsf{S}}(\xi(x)) = \mathrm{tt} \\ &\Leftrightarrow \xi(x) \in v^{\mathsf{S}^-} \\ &\Leftrightarrow \{\xi(x)\} \subseteq v^{\mathsf{S}^-} \\ &\Leftrightarrow \xi^-(x) \subseteq v^{\mathsf{S}^-} \\ &\Leftrightarrow (\mathsf{S}^-)^{(\xi^-)}(A^-) = \mathrm{tt}. \end{aligned}$$

3. $A \equiv u(x)$ for a predicate variable u: Then we similarly prove the assertion for $A^- \equiv x \subseteq u$.
4. $A \equiv x < y$: Then we define

$$\begin{aligned} A^- \equiv \neg(x = y) \land \forall u(x \subseteq u \land &\\ &\forall y_1 \forall y_2 (y_1 \subseteq u \land SUCS(y_1, y_2) \to y_2 \subseteq u) \to \\ &y \subseteq u). \end{aligned}$$

Assume that $\mathsf{S}^{\xi}(A) = \mathrm{tt}$, that is, $\xi(x) < \xi(y)$, and that $(\mathsf{S}^-, \xi^-) \rightleftharpoons (\mathsf{S}, \xi)$. Clearly, we find that $\xi^-(x) = \{\xi(x)\} \neq \{\xi(y)\} = \xi^-(y)$. Let now $\xi' \sim_u \xi^-$ and assume that $\xi'(x) \subseteq \xi'(u)$ and that for all singleton sets $\{n\}, \{n'\}$ such that $n = n' + 1$, if $\{n\} \subseteq \xi'(u)$ then $\{n'\} \subseteq \xi'(u)$. Inductively, the latter assumption ensures that whenever $n \in \xi'(u)$ for some $n \in \mathbb{N}$ then $m \in \xi'(u)$ for all $m \geq n$. Together with the assumptions that $\xi'(x) = \{\xi(x)\} \subseteq \xi'(u)$ and that $\xi(x) < \xi(y)$ this ensures that $\xi(y) \in \xi'(u)$, which completes the proof. Conversely, assume that $(\mathsf{S}^-)^{(\xi^-)}(A^-) = \mathrm{tt}$. This implies $\{\xi(x)\} \neq \{\xi(y)\}$, and therefore $\xi(x) \neq \xi(y)$. Moreover, let the valuation $\xi' \sim_u \xi^-$ be defined by $\xi'(u) = \{n \in \mathbb{N} \mid \xi(x) \leq n\}$. Obviously, $\xi'(x) = \{\xi(x)\} \subseteq \xi'(u)$. Moreover, $\{i + 1\} \subseteq \xi'(u)$ holds whenever $\{i\} \subseteq \xi'(u)$. Because $(\mathsf{S}^-)^{(\xi^-)}(A^-) = \mathrm{tt}$, it follows that $\xi'(y) = \{\xi(y)\} \subseteq \xi'(u)$ and therefore $\xi(x) \leq \xi(y)$, and the assertion follows.
5. $A \equiv \exists x B$ for an (individual) variable x: Then we let $A^- \equiv \exists x(SING(x) \land B^-)$, and the assertion follows using the induction hypothesis and the definition of $\rightleftharpoons$.

△

Lemmas 4.4.3 and 4.4.4 show that the second-order monadic logic $\mathcal{L}_{\mathrm{SOL}}(SIG_{\mathbf{V}})$ and the first-order logic $\mathcal{L}_{\mathrm{FOL}}(SIG_{\mathbf{V}}^-)$ are equally expressive, over the intended interpretations. Pursuing our goal of establishing a correspondence between Büchi automata and $\mathcal{L}_{\mathrm{FOL}}(SIG_{\mathbf{V}}^-)$, we now define a $SIG_{\mathbf{V}}^-$-structure S_{K} for a temporal structure K, similar to the corresponding definition in Sect. 4.2 for $\mathcal{L}_{\mathrm{FOL}}(SIG_{\mathbf{V}})$. Given $\mathsf{K} = (\eta_0, \eta_1, \eta_2, \ldots)$, the structure S_{K} has $|\mathsf{S}_{\mathsf{K}}| = |\mathsf{S}_{\mathsf{K}}|_{Set} = 2^{\mathbb{N}}$, the predicate symbols $\subseteq$, $SING$, and $SUCS$ are interpreted as the subset relation, the characteristic predicate of singleton sets, and the set-theoretic version of the successor relation, as required for $SIG_{\mathbf{V}}^-$-structures. The interpretations of the constant symbols v are obtained from the states η_i of K:

$$v^{\mathsf{S}_{\mathsf{K}}} = \{i \in \mathbb{N} \mid \eta_i(v) = \mathrm{tt}\}.$$

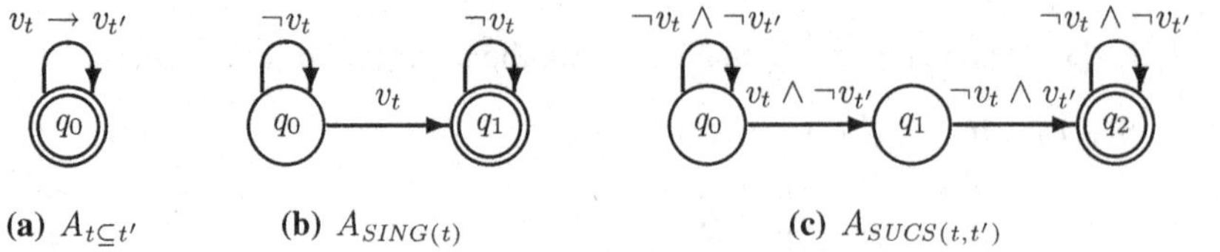

Fig. 4.9. Automata for the proof of Theorem 4.4.5

The following theorem, originally established by Büchi, associates a Büchi automaton Ω_A with every closed formula A of $\mathcal{L}_{\text{FOL}}(SIG^-_{\mathbf{V}})$ such that Ω_A accepts K if and only if $\mathsf{S}^{(\xi)}_{\mathsf{K}}(A) = \mathrm{tt}$, for an arbitrary variable valuation ξ. In this sense, it demonstrates that Büchi automata and $\mathcal{L}_{\text{FOL}}(SIG^-_{\mathbf{V}})$ are equally expressive.

Theorem 4.4.5 (Büchi). *For every closed formula A of $\mathcal{L}_{\text{FOL}}(SIG^-_{\mathbf{V}})$ there is a Büchi automaton Ω_A such that Ω_A accepts temporal structure K if and only if $\mathsf{S}^{(\xi)}_{\mathsf{K}}(A) = \mathrm{tt}$.*

Proof. For the inductive proof, the assertion has to be generalized for formulas of $\mathcal{L}_{\text{FOL}}(SIG^-_{\mathbf{V}})$ that may contain variables x (of sort SET). The automata Ω_A will operate over temporal structures K for the set of propositional constants

$$\mathbf{V}_A = \mathbf{V} \cup \{v_x \mid x \text{ has a free occurrence in } A\},$$

i.e., $\mathbf{V}$ augmented by new propositional constants v_x corresponding to the variables that are free in A. Recall from the definition of $SIG^-_{\mathbf{V}}$ that the only terms of $\mathcal{L}_{\text{FOL}}(SIG^-_{\mathbf{V}})$ are either constants $v \in \mathbf{V}$ or variables x, which are represented in $\mathbf{V}_A$ by either v or v_x. In the following, we write v_t for the propositional constant that represents the term t of $\mathcal{L}_{\text{FOL}}(SIG^-_{\mathbf{V}})$. We prove that Ω_A accepts K if and only if $\mathsf{S}^{(\xi)}_{\mathsf{K}}(A) = \mathrm{tt}$ for any variable valuation ξ such that

$$\xi(x) = \{i \in \mathbb{N} \mid \eta_i(v_x) = \mathrm{tt}\}.$$

1. $A \equiv t \subseteq t'$ for terms t and t': The automaton accepts K if and only if for all $i \in \mathbb{N}$, if $\eta_i(v_t) = \mathrm{tt}$ then $\eta_i(t') = \mathrm{tt}$. Formally,

   $$\Omega_{t\subseteq t'} = (\mathbf{V}_{t\subseteq t'}, \{q_0\}, \{q_0\}, \delta, \{q_0\})$$

   where $\delta(q_0, q_0) = v_t \to v_{t'}$ (cf. Fig. 4.9(a)), and the assertion obviously holds.
2. $A \equiv t = t'$: The automaton is similar, except that $\delta(q_0, q_0) = v_t \leftrightarrow v_{t'}$.
3. $A \equiv SING(t)$: The automaton checks that the propositional constant v_t is true at precisely one state. Formally,

   $$\Omega_{SING(t)} = (\mathbf{V}_{SING(t)}, \{q_0, q_1\}, \{q_0\}, \delta, \{q_1\})$$

   where $\delta(q_0, q_0) = \delta(q_1, q_1) = \neg v_t$, $\delta(q_0, q_1) = v_t$, and $\delta(q_1, q_0) =$ **false**; cf. Fig. 4.9(b).

4. $A \equiv SUCS(t, t')$: The automaton verifies that the propositional constants v_t and $v_{t'}$ are true precisely once, and that the state where $v_{t'}$ is true is the successor position of the one where v_t is true. Formally,

$$\Omega_{SUCS(t,t')} = (\mathbf{V}_{SUCS(t,t')}, \{q_0, q_1, q_2\}, \{q_0\}, \delta, \{q_2\})$$

where $\delta(q_0, q_0) = \delta(q_2, q_2) = \neg v_t \wedge \neg v_{t'}$, $\delta(q_0, q_1) = v_t \wedge \neg v_{t'}$, $\delta(q_1, q_2) = \neg v_t \wedge v_{t'}$, and $\delta(q, q') = \mathbf{false}$ otherwise; cf. Fig. 4.9(c).

5. $A \equiv B \to C$: Then $\mathsf{S}_{\mathsf{K}}^{(\xi)}(A) = \mathsf{tt}$ if and only if $\mathsf{S}_{\mathsf{K}}^{(\xi)}(B) = \mathsf{ff}$ or $\mathsf{S}_{\mathsf{K}}^{(\xi)}(C) = \mathsf{tt}$. By the induction hypothesis there exist automata Ω_B and Ω_C for $\mathbf{V}_B$ and $\mathbf{V}_C$ corresponding to B and C. Both automata can also be understood as automata for $\mathbf{V}_A$, and by Theorems 4.3.7 and 4.3.1 the automaton Ω_A can be constructed such that it accepts a structure K if and only if K is not accepted by Ω_B or accepted by Ω_C.
6. $A \equiv \exists x B$: Without loss of generality, we assume that x has no free occurrences in A. By the induction hypothesis there exists Ω_B for $\mathbf{V}_B = \mathbf{V}_A \cup \{v_x\}$ that corresponds to B. The automaton Ω_A for $\mathbf{V}_A$ is defined so that it accepts the projection $(\mathcal{L}(\Omega_B))_{-v_x}$; see Theorem 4.3.2. △

The final step in proving the expressiveness results announced previously is to show that the fixpoint logic LTL+μ of Sect. 3.2 is expressive enough to represent definability of temporal structures by Büchi automata. The proof idea is to encode the structure and the acceptance condition of a Büchi automaton Ω as a (closed) formula A_Ω which is initially true if and only if Ω accepts K. In order to define A_Ω we need some preparation and assume that $\Omega = (\mathbf{V}, Q, Q_0, \delta, Q_f)$ where $Q = \{q_0, q_1, \dots, q_{nloc}\}$. We define two formula transformers

$$\Phi_{ij}, \Phi_{ij}^{+} : \mathcal{L}_{\mathrm{LTL}}^{\mu}(\mathbf{V}) \to \mathcal{L}_{\mathrm{LTL}}^{\mu}(\mathbf{V}) \qquad (\text{for } i, j \in \{0, \dots, nloc\})$$

inductively with the help of auxiliary functions ${}_k\Phi_{ij}^{(+)}$ for $k \in \{-1, 0, \dots, nloc\}$, as follows:

- For $k = -1$:

$$\begin{aligned} {}_{-1}\Phi_{ii}(F) &= F \vee (\delta(q_i, q_i) \wedge \bigcirc F), \\ {}_{-1}\Phi_{ij}(F) &= \delta(q_i, q_j) \wedge \bigcirc F \quad \text{for } i \neq j, \\ {}_{-1}\Phi_{ij}^{+}(F) &= \delta(q_i, q_j) \wedge \bigcirc F. \end{aligned}$$

- For $k = 0, \dots, nloc$:

$$\begin{aligned} {}_k\Phi_{kk}(F) &= \mu u (F \vee {}_{k-1}\Phi_{kk}^{+}(u)) \\ &\qquad \text{where } u \text{ is chosen such that it has no free occurrences in } F, \\ {}_k\Phi_{kk}^{+}(F) &= {}_{k-1}\Phi_{kk}^{+}({}_k\Phi_{kk}(F)), \\ {}_k\Phi_{ij}^{(+)}(F) &= {}_{k-1}\Phi_{ij}^{(+)}(F) \vee {}_{k-1}\Phi_{ik}({}_k\Phi_{kk}({}_{k-1}\Phi_{kj}(F))) \\ &\qquad \text{for } i \neq k \text{ or } j \neq k. \end{aligned}$$

- Finally:

$$\Phi_{ij}(F) = {}_{nloc}\Phi_{ij}(F),$$
$$\Phi^+_{ij}(F) = {}_{nloc}\Phi^+_{ij}(F).$$

Observe that the propositional variables free in ${}_k\Phi^{(+)}_{ij}(F)$ are just those that are free in F. The idea is that $\Phi_{ij}(F)$ and $\Phi^+_{ij}(F)$ characterize those temporal structures where F becomes true "after following a path (respectively, non-empty path) from q_i to q_j". The following lemma makes this intuition precise.

Lemma 4.4.6. *Let* $\mathsf{K} = (\eta_0, \eta_1, \eta_2 \ldots)$ *be a temporal structure,* Ξ *be a valuation of the propositional variables,* F *be a formula of* $\mathcal{L}^{\mu}_{\mathrm{LTL}}(\mathbf{V})$*, and* $m \in \mathbb{N}$.

a) $\mathsf{K}^{(\Xi)}_m(\Phi_{ij}(F)) = \mathrm{tt}$ *if and only if there exists a finite sequence* $(\bar{q}_0, \ldots, \bar{q}_n) \in Q^*$ *where* $n \geq 0$ *such that* $\bar{q}_0 = q_i$, $\bar{q}_n = q_j$, $\models_{\eta_{m+l}} \delta(\bar{q}_l, \bar{q}_{l+1})$ *holds for* $0 \leq l < n$, *and* $\mathsf{K}^{(\Xi)}_{m+n}(F) = \mathrm{tt}$.

b) The assertion holds similarly for $\Phi^+_{ij}(F)$*, but with* $n > 0$.

Proof. The two assertions are proved simultaneously for ${}_k\Phi^{(+)}_{ij}(F)$ by induction on k, for arbitrary F, Ξ, and $m \in \mathbb{N}$, with the restriction that the sequence of intermediate locations contains only locations between q_0 and q_k. We call a finite sequence $(\bar{q}_0, \ldots, \bar{q}_n)$ with $\bar{q}_0 = q_i$, $\bar{q}_n = q_j$, $(\bar{q}_1, \ldots, \bar{q}_{n-1}) \in \{q_0, \ldots, q_k\}^*$, $\models_{\eta_{m+l}} \delta(\bar{q}_l, \bar{q}_{l+1})$ for $0 \leq l < n$, and $\mathsf{K}^{(\Xi)}_{m+n}(F) = \mathrm{tt}$ an (i, j, k, F, Ξ)*-path* from state m (of length n), and an $(i, j, k, F, \Xi)^+$*-path* if $n > 0$.

For $k = -1$, the only $(i, j, -1, F, \Xi)^+$-paths from state m are of the form (q_i, q_j), and such a path exists if and only if $\models_{\eta_m} \delta(q_i, q_j)$ and $\mathsf{K}^{(\Xi)}_{m+1}(F) = \mathrm{tt}$. For $i = j$, the additional $(i, i, -1, F, \Xi)$-path (q_i) exists in case $\mathsf{K}^{(\Xi)}_m(F) = \mathrm{tt}$. The definitions of ${}_{-1}\Phi^{(+)}_{ij}(F)$ clearly correspond to these situations.

For the induction step ($k = 0, \ldots, nloc$) we first consider (i, j, k, F, Ξ)-paths where $i = j = k$. Assume that there exists a (k, k, k, F, Ξ)-path from state m of length $n \geq 0$, we will show that $\mathsf{K}^{(\Xi)}_m({}_k\Phi_{kk}(F)) = \mathrm{tt}$, by induction on n.

1. Case $n = 0$: By definition we have $\mathsf{K}^{(\Xi)}_m(F) = \mathrm{tt}$. This trivially implies that $\mathsf{K}^{(\Xi)}_m(F \vee {}_{k-1}\Phi_{kk}({}_k\Phi_{kk}(F))) = \mathrm{tt}$ and therefore $\mathsf{K}^{(\Xi)}_m({}_k\Phi_{kk}(F)) = \mathrm{tt}$ by definition of ${}_k\Phi_{kk}(F)$ as fixpoint.
2. Case $n > 0$: Because $\bar{q}_0 = \bar{q}_n = q_k$ and $n > 0$ there exists some smallest $0 < l \leq n$ such that $\bar{q}_l = q_k$, and $(\bar{q}_l, \bar{q}_{l+1}, \ldots, \bar{q}_n)$ is a (k, k, k, F, Ξ)-path from state $m + l$ of shorter length. By induction hypothesis it follows that $\mathsf{K}^{(\Xi)}_{m+l}({}_k\Phi_{kk}(F)) = \mathrm{tt}$. Since l was chosen minimally, we find that $(\bar{q}_0, \ldots, \bar{q}_l)$ is a $(k, k, k-1, {}_k\Phi_{kk}(F), \Xi)^+$-path from state m, and we may invoke the (main) induction hypothesis to infer $\mathsf{K}^{(\Xi)}_m({}_{k-1}\Phi_{kk}({}_k\Phi_{kk}(F))) = \mathrm{tt}$, from which the assertion $\mathsf{K}^{(\Xi)}_m({}_k\Phi_{kk}(F)) = \mathrm{tt}$ follows as in the preceding case.

Conversely, assume that $\mathsf{K}^{(\Xi)}_m({}_k\Phi_{kk}(F)) = \mathrm{tt}$; we have to show that there exists a (k, k, k, F, Ξ)-path from state m. Defining

$$\mathbb{M} = \{i \in \mathbb{N} \mid \text{there exists a } (k,k,k,F,\Xi)\text{-path from state } i\},$$

we will prove that

$$(*) \qquad [\![F \vee {}_{k-1}\Phi^+_{kk}(u)]\!]_{\mathsf{K}}^{\Xi[u:\mathbb{M}]} \subseteq \mathbb{M}.$$

The definition of ${}_k\Phi_{kk}(F)$ as the smallest fixpoint implies that $[\![{}_k\Phi_{kk}(F)]\!]_{\mathsf{K}} \subseteq \mathbb{M}$, and in particular $m \in \mathbb{M}$, from which the assertion follows by the definition of $\mathbb{M}$.

For the proof of $(*)$, assume that $i \in [\![F \vee {}_{k-1}\Phi^+_{kk}(u)]\!]_{\mathsf{K}}^{\Xi[u:\mathbb{M}]}$.

- If $i \in [\![F]\!]_{\mathsf{K}}^{\Xi[u:\mathbb{M}]}$ then we also have $i \in [\![F]\!]_{\mathsf{K}}^{\Xi}$ because u has no free occurrences in F, and (q_k) is a (k,k,k,F,Ξ)-path from state i; hence $i \in \mathbb{M}$.
- If $i \in [\![{}_{k-1}\Phi^+_{kk}(u)]\!]_{\mathsf{K}}^{\Xi[u:\mathbb{M}]}$ then by the induction hypothesis there exists a $(k,k,k-1,u,\Xi[u:\mathbb{M}])^+$-path $(\bar{q}_0,\ldots,\bar{q}_n)$ from state i, and in particular $\mathsf{K}_{i+n}^{(\Xi[u:\mathbb{M}])}(u) = \mathsf{tt}$; hence $i+n \in \mathbb{M}$. By definition of $\mathbb{M}$, there exists a (k,k,k,F,Ξ)-path $(\bar{q}'_0,\ldots,\bar{q}'_{n'})$ from state $i+n$, and therefore the sequence $(\bar{q}_0,\ldots,\bar{q}_n,\bar{q}'_1,\ldots,\bar{q}'_{n'})$ is a (k,k,k,F,Ξ)-path from state i, which proves that $i \in \mathbb{M}$.

We have now shown that ${}_k\Phi_{kk}(F)$ characterizes (k,k,k,F,Ξ)-paths. Clearly, $(k,k,k,F,\Xi)^+$-paths are just those sequences $(\bar{q}_0,\ldots,\bar{q}_n)$ that can be decomposed into a $(k,k,k-1,{}_k\Phi_{kk}(F))^+$-path $(\bar{q}_0,\ldots,\bar{q}_l)$ and a (k,k,k,F)-path $(\bar{q}_l,\ldots,\bar{q}_n)$, for some $0 < l \leq n$. With the help of the induction hypothesis and the assertion that we have just proved, this shows that ${}_k\Phi^+_{kk}(F)$ characterizes those paths.

Finally, if $i \neq k$ or $j \neq k$, then an $(i,j,k,F,\Xi)^{(+)}$-path exists from state m if and only if either there exists an $(i,j,k-1,F,\Xi)^{(+)}$-path, or if there exist paths $(q_i,\ldots,q_k)$ and $(q_k,\ldots,q_j)$ (with intermediate locations among $q_0,\ldots,q_{k-1}$) and $(q_k,\ldots,q_k)$ (with intermediate locations among $q_0,\ldots,q_k$) that can be concatenated to form an $(i,j,k,F,\Xi)^+$-path. (Observe that at least one of these constituent paths has to be of non-zero length.) These two cases are precisely reflected in the definition of ${}_k\Phi^{(+)}_{kk}(F)$, and the assertion follows with the help of the respective induction hypotheses. △

From the encoding of finite paths by formulas of LTL+μ it is not hard to prove the desired characterization of Büchi-definable languages by fixpoint temporal logic.

Theorem 4.4.7. *Let Ω be a Büchi automaton over* $\mathbf{V}$. *There is a closed formula A_Ω of $\mathcal{L}^{\mu}_{\mathrm{LTL}}(\mathbf{V})$ such that for any temporal structure* K *for* $\mathbf{V}$ *and valuation* Ξ, $\mathsf{K}_0^{(\Xi)}(A_\Omega) = \mathsf{tt}$ *if and only if the automaton* Ω *accepts* K.

Proof. Let $\Omega = (\mathbf{V}, Q, Q_0, \delta, Q_f)$ as above and define

$$A_\Omega = \bigvee_{\substack{q_i \in Q_0 \\ q_j \in Q_f}} \Phi_{ij}(\nu\bar{u}\,\Phi^+_{jj}(\bar{u})).$$

Assume that $\mathsf{K}_0(A_\Omega) = \mathsf{tt}$ where $\mathsf{K} = (\eta_0,\eta_1,\eta_2,\ldots)$. (For simplicity, we write K_0 instead of $\mathsf{K}_0^{(\Xi)}$ since the evaluation does not depend on Ξ for closed formulas.) There exist $q_i \in Q_0$ and $q_j \in Q_f$ such that $\mathsf{K}_0(\Phi_{ij}(\nu\bar{u}\,\Phi^+_{jj}(\bar{u}))) = \mathsf{tt}$. By

k	i	j	${}_k\Phi_{ij}(F)$	simplified	${}_k\Phi^+_{ij}(F)$
-1	0	0	$F \vee (\textbf{true} \wedge \circ F)$	$F \vee \circ F$	$\circ F$
	0	1	$v \wedge \circ F$	$v \wedge \circ F$	$v \wedge \circ F$
	1	0	$\textbf{false} \wedge \circ F$	**false**	**false**
	1	1	$F \vee (v \wedge \circ F)$	$F \vee (v \wedge \circ F)$	$v \wedge \circ F$
0	0	0	$\mu u(F \vee \circ u)$	$\diamond F$	$\circ\diamond F$
	0	1	$(v \wedge \circ F) \vee \diamond(v \wedge \circ F) \vee \circ\diamond(v \wedge \circ F)$	$\diamond(v \wedge \circ F)$	$\diamond(v \wedge \circ F)$
	1	0	$\textbf{false} \vee \textbf{false}$	**false**	**false**
	1	1	$F \vee (v \wedge \circ F) \vee \textbf{false}$	$F \vee (v \wedge \circ F)$	$v \wedge \circ F$
1	1	1	$\mu u(F \vee (v \wedge \circ u))$	$v \ \textbf{unt}\ F$	$v \wedge \circ(v \ \textbf{unt}\ F)$
	0	0	$\diamond F \vee \diamond(v \wedge \circ(v \ \textbf{unt false}))$	$\diamond F$	$\circ\diamond F$
	0	1	$\diamond(v \wedge \circ F) \vee \diamond(v \wedge \circ(v \ \textbf{unt}\ (v \wedge \circ F)))$	$\diamond(v \wedge \circ F)$	$\diamond(v \wedge \circ F)$
	1	0	$\textbf{false} \vee v \ \textbf{unt false} \vee (v \wedge \circ(v \ \textbf{unt false}))$	**false**	**false**

Table 4.1. Construction of ${}_k\Phi_{ij}(F)$ for Ω_3 (see Fig. 4.2)

Lemma 4.4.6 a) there exists a sequence $(\bar{q}_0, \ldots, \bar{q}_n) \in Q^*$ such that $\bar{q}_0 = q_i$, $\bar{q}_n = q_j$, $\underset{\eta_l}{\vDash} \delta(\bar{q}_l, \bar{q}_{l+1})$ for all $0 \le l < n$, and $\mathsf{K}_n(\nu \bar{u}\, \Phi^+_{jj}(\bar{u})) = \mathsf{tt}$. Applying the fixpoint law (ν-rec), it follows that $\mathsf{K}_n(\Phi^+_{jj}(\nu \bar{u}\, \Phi^+_{jj}(\bar{u}))) = \mathsf{tt}$, and Lemma 4.4.6 b) ensures that there exists a sequence $(\bar{q}'_0, \ldots, \bar{q}'_{n'}) \in Q^+$ with $\bar{q}'_0 = \bar{q}'_{n'} = q_j$, $\underset{\eta_{n+l}}{\vDash} \delta(\bar{q}'_l, \bar{q}'_{l+1})$ for all $0 \le l < n'$, and again $\mathsf{K}_{n+n'}(\nu \bar{u}\, \Phi^+_{jj}(\bar{u})) = \mathsf{tt}$. Continuing inductively, we obtain an accepting run of Ω over K.

Conversely, assume that Ω accepts K, via an accepting run $\varrho = (\bar{q}_0, \bar{q}_1, \bar{q}_2, \ldots)$ where $\bar{q}_0 \in Q_0$. By definition, $\bar{q}_k \in Q_f$ holds for infinitely many $k \in \mathbb{N}$, and because Q_f is finite there exists some $q_j \in Q_f$ such that $\bar{q}_k = q_j$ for infinitely many $k \in \mathbb{N}$. Defining

$$\mathbb{M} = \{k \in \mathbb{N} \mid \bar{q}_k = q_j\},$$

it is easy to show from the corresponding segments of ϱ and Lemma 4.4.6 b) that

$$(*) \qquad \mathbb{M} \subseteq [\![\Phi^+_{jj}(\bar{u})]\!]_{\mathsf{K}}^{\Xi[\bar{u}:\mathbb{M}]}$$

for an arbitrary valuation Ξ. This entails $\mathbb{M} \subseteq [\![\nu \bar{u}\, \Phi^+_{jj}(\bar{u})]\!]_{\mathsf{K}}$. Choosing some $k \in \mathbb{M}$ (among the infinitely many elements of that set), we have $\mathsf{K}_k(\nu \bar{u}\, \Phi^+_{jj}(\bar{u})) = \mathsf{tt}$, and the desired conclusion $\mathsf{K}_0(A_\Omega) = \mathsf{tt}$ follows using Lemma 4.4.6 a), taking the prefix $(\bar{q}_0, \bar{q}_1, \ldots, \bar{q}_k)$ of the run ϱ as the finite sequence of automaton locations. $\triangle$

We illustrate the construction of the formula A_Ω for the Büchi automaton Ω_3 of Fig. 4.2. Table 4.1 shows the different formulas ${}_k\Phi^{(+)}_{ij}(F)$. The column ${}_k\Phi_{ij}(F)$ contains the formulas according to the inductive definition. The column to the right contains an equivalent formula after simplification by laws of propositional and temporal logic; this simplified version is used for the construction of subsequent formulas. Similarly simplified versions of the formulas ${}_k\Phi^+_{ij}(F)$ appear in the rightmost column.

The locations q_0 and q_1 are respectively the only initial and accepting locations of Ω_3. The encoding of the Büchi automaton in LTL+μ is therefore given by the formula

$$\Phi_{01}(\nu\bar{u}\,\Phi_{11}^{+}(\bar{u})) \;=\; \Diamond(v \wedge \bigcirc(\nu\bar{u}(v \wedge \bigcirc(v \;\textbf{unt}\; \bar{u})))),$$

which in this case is equivalent to the LTL formula $\Diamond\Box v$.

Summing up the preceding expressiveness results, we have established the following chain, adapting the notation introduced in Sects. 4.1 and 4.2:

$$\begin{aligned}\mathcal{L}_{\mathrm{SOL}}(SIG_{\mathbf{V}}) \leq\; & \mathcal{L}_{\mathrm{FOL}}(SIG_{\mathbf{V}}^{-}) \leq_0 BA(\mathbf{V}) \\ & \leq_0 \mathcal{L}_{\mathrm{LTL}}^{\mu}(\mathbf{V}) \leq \mathcal{L}_{\mathrm{LTL}}^{\mathrm{q}}(\mathbf{V}) \leq \mathcal{L}_{\mathrm{SOL}}(SIG_{\mathbf{V}})\end{aligned}$$

where $BA(\mathbf{V})$ represents the class of temporal structures that are accepted by Büchi automata over $\mathbf{V}$. (The relation between LTL+μ and LTL+q was already established by Theorem 4.1.6.) It follows that all these formalisms are actually equally expressive with respect to model equivalence, based on initial validity semantics. In particular, this holds for LTL+μ and LTL+q and means that LTL+μ $=_0$ LTL+q. Because of Theorem 2.6.4, which we have already remarked to also hold for these two logics, this actually implies that LTL+μ = LTL+q, as was already announced in Sect. 4.1.

Second Reading

A simple consequence of the results described in this section is that Büchi automata can also be encoded in the logic LTL+q. In fact, the following direct encoding yields a more succinct formula characterizing the existence of a successful run of a Büchi automaton over a temporal structure:

$$A_\Omega \;=\; \exists u_0 \cdots \exists u_{nloc} \left(\bigwedge_{\substack{i,j=0\\ i\neq j}}^{nloc} \Box\neg(u_i \wedge u_j) \;\wedge\; \bigvee_{q_i \in Q_0} u_i \;\wedge\; \Box \bigvee_{i,j=0}^{nloc} (u_i \wedge \delta(u_i,u_j) \wedge \bigcirc u_j) \;\wedge\; \bigvee_{q_j \in Q_f} \Box\Diamond u_j \right)$$

with a propositional variable u_i per automaton location q_i. This formula A_Ω asserts that there exists a valuation of the propositional variables $u_0, \ldots, u_{nloc}$ that simulates a run: no two variables are simultaneously true; initially a variable corresponding to an initial location is true, the transition formulas of the automaton are consistent with the variables true before and after the transition, and some variable representing an accepting location is true infinitely often.

Because we also know that every formula of LTL+q can be represented by a Büchi automaton, it follows that the "pure existential fragment" of $\mathcal{L}_{\mathrm{LTL}}^{\mathrm{q}}(\mathbf{V})$ in which a series of outermost existential quantifiers is applied to a quantifier-free formula is as expressive as the full logic. A similar remark holds for $\mathcal{L}_{\mathrm{SOL}}(SIG_{\mathbf{V}})$ in the sense that every formula of that logic can effectively be transformed into one where a series of existential second-order quantifiers are applied to a first-order formula.

4.5 Weak Alternating Automata

Büchi automata and their variants are non-deterministic: every automaton location q may admit several possible successor locations for a given state η, as there may exist several locations q' such that $\models_{\eta} \delta(q, q')$. A temporal structure is accepted if, starting from an initial location, at every state some successor can be chosen in such a way that the resulting run (a sequence of locations) satisfies the acceptance condition.

We conclude these considerations by sketching another class of ω-automata, called alternating automata, where every location admits a non-deterministic choice between *sets* of successor locations, which will then be active simultaneously. Consequently, a run of an alternating automaton over a temporal structure is no longer a sequence, but a tree or a dag of locations. The acceptance condition is defined in terms of the sets of paths through this tree or dag. Alternating automata thus combine the familiar "disjunctive" branching mode of non-deterministic automata with a dual "conjunctive" branching mode, empowering the automaton to verify several conditions in parallel. This does not necessarily make alternating automata more powerful with respect to expressiveness: with suitable acceptance conditions, they again accept precisely the class of ω-regular languages. However, they can be exponentially more succinct than non-deterministic automata, and this succinctness can yield interesting trade-offs. In particular, the translation from LTL formulas to alternating automata is of linear complexity, whereas checking emptiness of alternating automata is an exponentially hard problem.

As in the definition of Büchi automata, we represent the transition relation of an alternating automaton via propositional formulas. However, these formulas are now formed from propositional constants as well as from automaton locations, with the restriction that all occurrences of the latter are of positive polarity; this property is defined in the same way as for propositional variables in Sect. 3.2. For example, for $v_1, v_2 \in \mathbf{V}$, $q_0, q_1, q_2 \in Q$, $\mathbf{V}$ and Q as before,

$$\delta(q_0) = (v_1 \wedge v_2 \wedge q_1 \wedge q_2) \vee ((\neg v_1 \vee v_2) \wedge (q_0 \vee q_1)) \vee v_2$$

defines the possible transitions from an automaton location q_0: the automaton can simultaneously activate locations q_1 and q_2 upon reading a state satisfying $v_1 \wedge v_2$. It can choose between activating q_0 or q_1 upon reading a state satisfying $\neg v_1 \vee v_2$, and need not activate any location for a state satisfying v_2. Implicitly, no transition is possible for a state satisfying $v_1 \wedge \neg v_2$. For a valuation η of $\mathbf{V}$ and a set $Y \subseteq Q$ of automaton locations, we define the joint valuation η^Y of $\mathbf{V} \cup Q$ by $\eta^Y(v) = \eta(v)$ for $v \in \mathbf{V}$ and $\eta^Y(q) = \mathsf{tt}$ if and only if $q \in Y$. A location q that is active at some point in a run of the automaton may thus activate a set Y of successor locations upon reading a state η of a temporal structure if and only if $\models_{\eta^Y} \delta(q)$ holds.

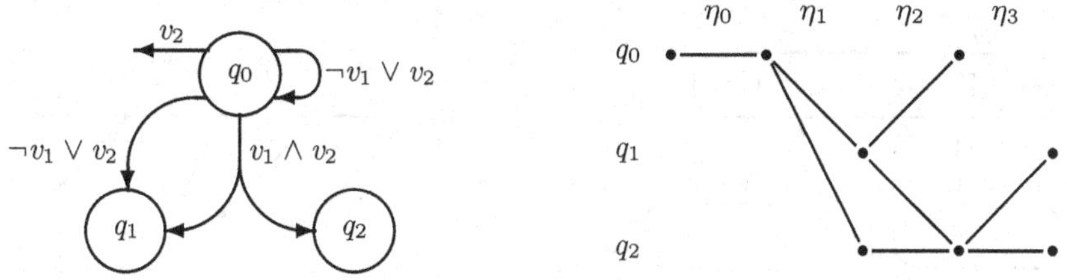

(a) Transitions from location q_0 **(b)** Prefix of a run dag

Fig. 4.10. Alternating automata: transitions and run dag

Transitions of alternating automata can be visualized using hyperedges, as shown in Fig. 4.10(a) for the example.

We will represent automaton runs as dags labeled with automaton locations. For example, Fig. 4.10(b) illustrates an initial prefix of a hypothetical run dag: initially, just location q_0 is active, and it is reactivated by the first transition of the automaton. The state η_1 triggers a transition that activates the locations q_1 and q_2, which then both react to state η_2. In our example, q_1 activates locations q_0 and q_2, while q_2 activates just q_2. Observe that since we record only which locations are active at a given instant, we obtain a single successor node labeled by q_2. Also, a run dag may contain finite paths; for example, we have assumed that q_0 activates no successor locations in the transition for η_3.

It remains to define when a run dag is accepting. This condition is given in terms of the infinite paths through the run dag. For example, an alternating Büchi automaton would require each infinite path to contain infinitely many accepting locations. We consider here *weak alternating automata* whose acceptance condition is defined in terms of a ranking of locations with natural numbers. This ranking is required to stratify the set of automaton locations in the sense that if q' occurs in $\delta(q)$ then the rank of q' is at most the rank of q. Therefore, if run dags are drawn as in Fig. 4.10(b), but such that locations are topologically ordered according to their rank, the dag does not contain any rising edges, and ranks along any path can never increase. Consequently, every (infinite) path in a run dag defines a *stable* rank such that after some finite prefix, all locations along the path are of the same rank. A run dag is accepting if and only if the stable rank of every infinite path is even.

Because locations may occur only positively in transition formulas, it is easy to see that taking more successor locations cannot invalidate a transition formula: if $\models_{\eta}^{Y} \delta(q)$ holds, then so does $\models_{\eta}^{Y'} \delta(q)$ for every superset Y' of Y. However, taking more successors increases the number of paths through the dag, making the acceptance condition harder to satisfy. We therefore assume that for every active location q, the set of successors is chosen minimally such that $\delta(q)$ is satisfied.

Definition. A *weak alternating automaton* $\Omega = (\mathbf{V}, Q, q_0, rk, \delta)$ for a finite set $\mathbf{V}$ of propositional constants is given by

- a finite set Q of *locations* (where $\mathbf{V} \cap Q = \emptyset$),
- an *initial location* $q_0 \in Q$,

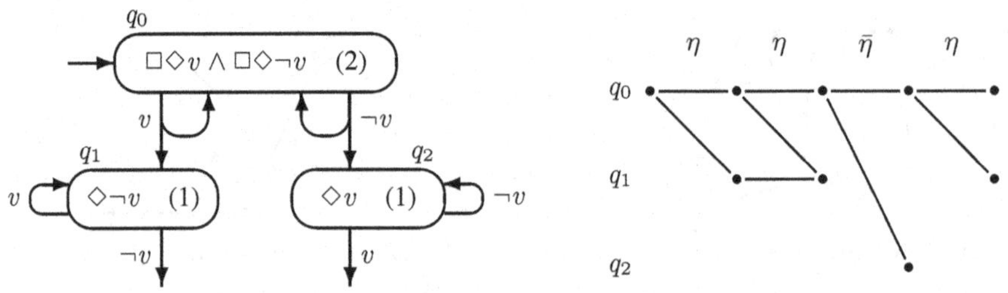

Fig. 4.11. A weak alternating automaton and a prefix of a run dag

- a mapping $rk : Q \to \mathbb{N}$ that assigns a rank to every location,
- a mapping $\delta : Q \to \mathcal{L}_{\mathrm{PL}}(\mathbf{V} \cup Q)$ that associates a propositional formula $\delta(q)$ with any location $q \in Q$, where locations $q' \in Q$ occur only positively in $\delta(q)$ and such that $rk(q') \leq rk(q)$ whenever q' appears in $\delta(q)$.

A *run* of Ω over a temporal structure $\mathsf{K} = (\eta_0, \eta_1, \eta_2, \ldots)$ for $\mathbf{V}$ is a dag $\varrho = (Y_0, \vec{Y}_0, Y_1, \vec{Y}_1, Y_2, \vec{Y}_2, \ldots)$ consisting of *configurations* $Y_i \subseteq Q$ and sets $\vec{Y}_i \subseteq Y_i \times Y_{i+1}$ of edges leading from locations of Y_i to those of Y_{i+1} where

- $Y_0 = \{q_0\}$,
- for every $i \in \mathbb{N}$ and all $q \in Y_i$, the set $Y = \{q' \mid (q, q') \in \vec{Y}_i\}$ is minimal such that $\models^{Y}_{\eta_i} \delta(q)$ holds,
- $Y_{i+1} = \{q' \mid (q, q') \in \vec{Y}_i$ for some $q \in Y_i\}$ is the range of $\vec{Y}_i$.

The run ϱ is *accepting* and K is *accepted* if for every infinite path $(q_0, q_1, q_2, \ldots)$ through ϱ (i.e., every infinite sequence such that $q_0 \in Y_0$ and $(q_i, q_{i+1}) \in \vec{Y}_i$ for all $i \in \mathbb{N}$) the minimum rank assumed along that path,

$$rk_{\min} = \min\{rk(q_i) \mid i \in \mathbb{N}\},$$

is even. The *language* $\mathcal{L}(\Omega)$ of Ω is the set of temporal structures for $\mathbf{V}$ which are accepted by Ω.

Figure 4.11 shows an example of a weak alternating automaton over $\mathbf{V} = \{v\}$ and a prefix of a run dag belonging to it, where the states η and $\bar{\eta}$ satisfy v and $\neg v$, respectively. The automaton accepts precisely those temporal structures that contain infinitely many states satisfying v and infinitely many states satisfying $\neg v$. For better readability, we have labeled every automaton location with the temporal formula it is intended to enforce. (The relationship between temporal logic and weak alternating automata will be made more precise subsequently.) Thus, the initial location q_0 is labeled with the formula $\Box\Diamond v \wedge \Box\Diamond\neg v$. Upon reading a state satisfying v, the automaton reactivates the initial location because the original formula also has to be true in the remainder of the temporal structure. Moreover, it activates the location q_1 labeled by $\Diamond\neg v$; this can intuitively be understood as starting a new thread waiting for v to become false. In fact, the automaton loops at q_1 as long as v is true, and the thread "dies" (by activating the empty set of successors) as soon as v is false. Similarly, the initial location activates itself and the location q_2 labeled by $\Diamond v$ upon reading a state satisfying $\neg v$, and location q_2 waits for v to become true. The numbers written in parentheses indicate the rank assigned to the respective location. In particular, the locations q_1 and q_2 have odd rank, enforcing that no accepting run dag contains a path that remains in those locations forever. However, the initial location has rank 2 because that location is allowed to remain active.

For the analysis of alternating automata and their languages, it is useful to introduce elementary notions of the theory of logical games. The paths through a run dag of a weak alternating automaton Ω over a temporal structure K can be understood as the outcomes of the following game $G(\Omega, \mathsf{K})$, played by two players that are traditionally called AUTOMATON and PATHFINDER. Intuitively, AUTOMATON tries to demonstrate that K is accepted by Ω; it makes use of the disjunctive non-determinism of the transition relation. Dually, PATHFINDER challenges the acceptance of K by Ω and tries to exhibit a path whose stable rank is odd; it chooses some location among those proposed by AUTOMATON. Continuing in this way, both players construct a sequence of "positions". Either one of the players has no move and therefore loses after a finite number of moves, or the winner is determined by the parity of the minimal rank of locations that appear in the sequence.

Formally, the positions of $G(\Omega, \mathsf{K})$ are of the form (i, q) when AUTOMATON draws where $i \in \mathbb{N}$ and $q \in Q$. They are of the form (i, q, Y) when PATHFINDER has to draw where i and q are as before and $Y \subseteq Q$ is a set of locations. The initial position is $(0, q_0)$ where q_0 is the initial location of Ω; therefore, player AUTOMATON makes the first move. Whenever AUTOMATON draws from some position (i, q), it chooses some minimal set $Y \subseteq Q$ such that $\models_{\eta_i^Y} \delta(q)$ holds for the joint valuation η_i^Y, provided some such set exists, producing the position (i, q, Y). A move of PATHFINDER from any such position consists in choosing some $q' \in Y$, provided $Y \neq \emptyset$, and yields the position $(i+1, q')$, and the play continues from there. Let us remark that from any position in $G(\Omega, \mathsf{K})$, the player who has to make a move has only finitely many moves because the set Q of automaton locations is assumed to be finite.

Any infinite play determines a sequence $(q_0, q_1, q_2, \ldots)$, called the *outcome* of the play, of locations determined from AUTOMATON's positions $(0, q_0)$, $(1, q_1)$, $\ldots$ encountered during the play. A play is won by AUTOMATON if either some position $(i, q, \emptyset)$ is reached from where PATHFINDER has no move, or if it is infinite and the minimal rank of the locations in the outcome is even. Otherwise, the play is won by PATHFINDER.

We are now interested in the question of whether one of the players can force a win, assuming optimal play. For the games considered here, it suffices to consider particularly simple strategies that determine the next move from the current position alone, without regard to the history of the play. A *memoryless strategy* (for either player AUTOMATON or PATHFINDER) is a partial function that, given a position for that player, determines the next draw, respecting the rules of the game. It is a *winning strategy* for the player from a game position if for any play starting from that position such that his moves are determined by the strategy is won by him (for arbitrary moves of his opponent); in particular, the strategy must always be defined in such a play. It is a winning strategy for the game $G(\Omega, \mathsf{K})$ if it is a winning strategy from the initial position. Because the rules of the game mirror the definition of a run, player AUTOMATON has a winning strategy if and only if K is accepted by Ω.

Lemma 4.5.1. *A temporal structure* K *is accepted by the weak alternating automaton* Ω *if and only if player* AUTOMATON *has a memoryless winning strategy for the game* $G(\Omega, \mathsf{K})$.

Proof. Assume first that $\mathsf{K} \in \mathcal{L}(\Omega)$, and let $\varrho = (Y_0, \vec{Y}_0, Y_1, \vec{Y}_1, \ldots)$ be an accepting run dag of Ω over K. Define a strategy *str* for player AUTOMATON that, given a position (i, q), returns the successors of the node labeled q at the ith configuration of the dag, i.e.,

$$str(i, q) = \{q' \mid (q, q') \in \vec{Y}_i\}$$

so that $(i, q, str(i, q))$ will be the next position in the play. By applying this strategy starting at the initial position $(0, q_0)$, AUTOMATON thus forces the play to follow a path through the run dag ϱ, i.e., $q \in Y_i$ holds whenever the strategy *str* is applied to position (i, q). Because ϱ is a run dag, $Y = str(i, q)$ is therefore a minimal set such that $\models^{Y}_{\eta_i} \delta(q)$ holds, and thus *str* determines a valid move for AUTOMATON. Either the strategy computes the empty set at some point, and PATHFINDER loses immediately, or the outcome of the play is an infinite path through ϱ, and therefore the minimal rank assumed along that path must be even; hence AUTOMATON wins in this case, too.

Conversely, assume that AUTOMATON has a memoryless winning strategy *str* for $G(\Omega, \mathsf{K})$, and inductively construct a dag $\varrho = (Y_0, \vec{Y}_0, Y_1, \vec{Y}_1, \ldots)$ as follows:

- $Y_0 = \{q_0\}$.
- If Y_i has been constructed, define $\vec{Y}_i = \{(q, q') \mid q \in Y_i \text{ and } q' \in str(i, q)\}$ and let $Y_{i+1} = \{q' \mid (q, q') \in \vec{Y}_i \text{ for some } q \in Y_i\}$ be the range of $\vec{Y}_i$.

As before, the paths in the resulting dag correspond exactly to the plays in $G(\Omega, \mathsf{K})$, and therefore ϱ is an accepting run dag of Ω over K. △

We will now define a translation that associates a weak alternating automaton Ω_F to any formula F of LTL such that $\mathcal{L}(\Omega_F) = \{\mathsf{K} \mid \mathsf{K}_0(F) = \mathrm{tt}\}$. It follows that weak alternating automata are at least as expressive as LTL.

The basic idea of the translation is to have locations of Ω_F enforce the truth of subformulas of F, as was already indicated in the example automaton of Fig. 4.11 corresponding to the formula $\Box\Diamond v \wedge \Box\Diamond\neg v$. The transition formulas of Ω_F are defined by induction on the structure of the temporal formulas: propositional connectives are directly provided by the combinational structure of alternating automata, and temporal connectives are decomposed according to their recursive characterizations.

location q	$\delta(q)$	$rk(q)$
$q_{\mathbf{true}}$	**true**	0
$q_{\mathbf{false}}$	**false**	0
q_v $(v \in \mathbf{V})$	v	0
$q_{\neg v}$ $(v \in \mathbf{V})$	$\neg v$	0
$q_{A \wedge B}$	$\delta(q_A) \wedge \delta(q_B)$	$\max\{rk(q_A), rk(q_B)\}$
$q_{A \vee B}$	$\delta(q_A) \vee \delta(q_B)$	$\max\{rk(q_A), rk(q_B)\}$
$q_{\circ A}$	q_A	$rk(q_A)$
$q_{\Box A}$	$q_{\Box A} \wedge \delta(q_A)$	$\lceil rk(q_A) \rceil_{\text{even}}$
$q_{\Diamond A}$	$q_{\Diamond A} \vee \delta(q_A)$	$\lceil rk(q_A) \rceil_{\text{odd}}$

Fig. 4.12. Transition and ranking functions for automaton Ω_F

More formally, we assume F to be given in positive normal form, that is, built from propositional constants or their negations by applying the connectives $\wedge$, $\vee$, $\circ$, $\Box$, and $\Diamond$. Every formula of LTL can be rewritten in this form by eliminating implication and negation (other than applied to propositional constants) using standard laws of propositional logic and the laws (T1), (T2), and (T3). The weak alternating automaton Ω_F contains a location q_A for every subformula A of F, with q_F being the initial location. The transition formulas $\delta(q_A)$ and the ranks $rk(q_A)$ are inductively defined as shown in Fig. 4.12 where $\lceil n \rceil_{\text{odd}}$ and $\lceil n \rceil_{\text{even}}$ denote respectively the smallest odd and even number greater or equal than n. Observe that the ranks of successors are non-increasing, so Ω_F is a well-formed weak alternating automaton.

Theorem 4.5.2. *For any formula F of LTL, the weak alternating automaton Ω_F accepts precisely the temporal structures K such that $\mathsf{K}_0(F) = \mathsf{tt}$.*

Proof. Let $\Omega_F = (\mathbf{V}, Q, q_F, \delta, rk)$ be the weak alternating automaton associated with F and K be some temporal structure for $\mathbf{V}$. We show by induction on the subformula A of F that for any $q_A \in Q$ and any $i \in \mathbb{N}$, player AUTOMATON has a (memoryless) winning strategy from the position (i, q_A) in the game $G(\Omega_F, \mathsf{K})$ if and only if $\mathsf{K}_i(A) = \mathsf{tt}$. From this, the claim follows with Lemma 4.5.1.

1. $A \in \{\mathbf{true}, \mathbf{false}\}$ or $A \in \{v, \neg v\}$ for some $v \in \mathbf{V}$: In these cases, $\delta(q_A) = A$. If $\mathsf{K}_i(A) = \mathsf{tt}$, the trivial strategy that returns $\emptyset$ for the position (i, q_A) and is undefined otherwise determines a valid move in $G(\Omega_F, \mathsf{K})$, and AUTOMATON wins at the successor position $(i, q_A, \emptyset)$ because PATHFINDER has no move. If $\mathsf{K}_i(A) = \mathsf{ff}$, player AUTOMATON has no move in $G(\Omega_F, \mathsf{K})$, so PATHFINDER wins immediately. In particular, AUTOMATON does not have a winning strategy.
2. $A \equiv B \wedge C$: Then $\delta(q_A) \equiv \delta(q_B) \wedge \delta(q_C)$. Assume that $\mathsf{K}_i(A) = \mathsf{tt}$; thus $\mathsf{K}_i(B) = \mathsf{K}_i(C) = \mathsf{tt}$. By the induction hypothesis, AUTOMATON has winning strategies str_B and str_C from the positions (i, q_B) and (i, q_C). Then the strategy

$$str(j,q) = \begin{cases} str_B(i,q_B) \cup str_C(i,q_C) & \text{if } (j,q) = (i,q_A), \\ str_B(j,q) & \text{else if } str_B \text{ is defined for } (j,q), \\ str_C(j,q) & \text{otherwise} \end{cases}$$

obviously defines a winning strategy for AUTOMATON from position (i, q_A). Conversely, a winning strategy str for position (i, q_A) gives rise to strategies str_B and str_C for positions (i, q_B) and (i, q_C) since all minimal sets Y such that $\models_{\eta}^{Y} \delta(q_A)$ are of the form $Y_B \cup Y_C$ where $\models_{\eta}^{Y_B} \delta(q_B)$ and $\models_{\eta}^{Y_C} \delta(q_C)$. Therefore, say, str_B is defined to produce a minimal set $Y_1 \subseteq str(q_A, i)$ such that $\models_{\eta}^{Y_1} \delta(q_B)$, and equals str_A on all other positions, and similarly for str_C. In this way, str_B and str_C become winning strategies for positions (i, q_B) and (i, q_C), so by the induction hypothesis we have $\mathsf{K}_i(B) = \mathsf{K}_i(C) = \mathsf{tt}$, implying $\mathsf{K}_i(A) = \mathsf{tt}$.

3. The case $A \equiv B \vee C$ is analogous.
4. $A \equiv \bigcirc B$: Then AUTOMATON has no choice but to move to $(i, q_A, \{q_B\})$, from where PATHFINDER must move to position $(i+1, q_B)$. By induction hypothesis, AUTOMATON has a winning strategy for $(i+1, q_B)$ if and only if $\mathsf{K}_{i+1}(B) = \mathsf{tt}$, which implies the assertion for position (i, q_A).
5. $A \equiv \Box B$: Then $\delta(q_A) = q_A \wedge \delta(q_B)$. Assume that $\mathsf{K}_i(A) = \mathsf{tt}$, and therefore $\mathsf{K}_j(B) = \mathsf{tt}$ for all $j \geq i$, and by induction hypothesis AUTOMATON has winning strategies str_B^j for (j, q_B), for all $j \geq i$. Define the strategy

$$str(j,q) = \begin{cases} \{q_A\} \cup str_B^j(j,q_B) & \text{if } q = q_A, \\ str_B^k(j,q) & \text{otherwise, where } k \geq i \text{ is the largest} \\ & \text{index of a position } (k, q_A). \end{cases}$$

A straighforward induction on the positions of the game shows that str produces legal moves for player AUTOMATON from position (i, q_A) onwards. If player PATHFINDER chooses positions (j, q_A) for all $j \geq i$ then AUTOMATON wins because the rank of q_A is even. Otherwise, AUTOMATON follows the strategy str_B^k from the last position (k, q_A) of that form onwards, which by induction hypothesis is a winning strategy for AUTOMATON.
Conversely, assume that $\mathsf{K}_i(A) = \mathsf{ff}$, that is, $\mathsf{K}_j(B) = \mathsf{ff}$ for some $j \geq i$. By induction hypothesis, AUTOMATON has no winning strategy from position (j, q_B). Now, PATHFINDER can force the play to reach position (j, q_A) by choosing positions (k, q_A) for all $i \leq k \leq j$, since any (minimal) model of $\delta(q_A)$ must obviously contain q_A. At position (j, q_A), AUTOMATON must produce the position $(j, q_A, \{q_A\} \cup Y)$ where Y is a (minimal) non-empty set such that $\models_{\eta_j}^{Y} \delta(q_B)$, and PATHFINDER will choose some $q \in Y$ to reach the position $(j+1, q)$. Clearly, any winning strategy from that position would determine a winning strategy from (j, q_B), so we find that AUTOMATON does not have a winning strategy from (i, q_A).
6. The case of $A \equiv \Diamond B$ is similar. △

location q	$\delta(q)$	$rk(q)$
$q_{A\,\mathbf{until}\,B}$	$q_B \vee (q_A \wedge q_{A\,\mathbf{until}\,B})$	$\lceil \max\{rk(q_A), rk(q_B)\} \rceil_{\mathrm{odd}}$
$q_{A\,\mathbf{unless}\,B}$	$q_B \vee (q_A \wedge q_{A\,\mathbf{unless}\,B})$	$\lceil \max\{rk(q_A), rk(q_B)\} \rceil_{\mathrm{even}}$

Fig. 4.13. Automaton construction for LTL+b

The construction of Ω_F ensures that its size is linear in the size of F. The construction extends in the canonical way to LTL+b. For example, Fig. 4.13 shows the definitions of $\delta(q)$ and $rk(q)$ for the binary operators **until** and **unless**.

In order to decide emptiness of a weak alternating automaton Ω, one can construct a Büchi automaton that accepts the same language. Because this conversion relies on a subset construction, the Büchi automaton will in general be exponentially larger than Ω. However, minimizations can be performed on Ω as well as during the construction of the Büchi automaton, and this approach to computing Büchi automata in practice outperforms direct techniques based on the tableau construction as described in Sect. 4.4.

Bibliographical Notes

The expressive completeness of LTL+b+p (in the setting of tense logic) was already proved by Kamp [70]. The proof based on separability is due to Gabbay et al. and is presented in depth (and also for more general situations than our semantics) in [52].

Wolper [159] observed that the operator **even** cannot be expressed in LTL+b and proposed an extension by grammar operators corresponding to regular languages.

Büchi automata were introduced in [24] for the proof of decidability of the monadic second-order theory of one successor. Connections between non-deterministic automata and temporal logic were studied in great depth by Vardi et al., see, e.g., [139, 152, 155]. In particular, the proof of equi-expressiveness of the monadic second-order theory of one successor, Büchi automata, LTL+μ, and LTL+b combines results due to Büchi, Sistla, Vardi, and Wolper. Schneider [134] also presents these results and further connections with topology.

Other types of non-deterministic ω-automata include Muller, Rabin, and Streett automata, and Thomas [147, 148] gives an excellent account of this theory. Büchi [24] proved the closure of ω-regular languages under complementation, albeit non-constructively, and Safra [131] gave a first optimal construction. The proof using run dags was introduced by Kupferman and Vardi [84]; it was shown in [85] to extend across a wide range of ω-automata. That proof is related to constructions for weak alternating automata, which were first studied in connection with temporal logics by Muller et al. [112]; see also [149, 153].

Gerth et al. [55] gave an efficient algorithm to construct a generalized Büchi automaton corresponding to a formula of LTL+b, related to our construction in

Sect. 4.4. An alternative method, using weak alternating automata as an intermediate representation, was proposed by Gastin and Oddoux [54].

5

First-Order Linear Temporal Logic

Temporal logic – studied so far in its propositional form – can be developed to a predicate logic in a way analogous to how this is performed in classical logic.

We present temporal predicate logic only in a first-order version and in a first step with the basic temporal concepts of LTL (as an extension of both LTL and FOL). This basic *first-order linear temporal logic* FOLTL can easily be augmented with the propositional extensions introduced in Chap. 3, and we will also discuss in Sects. 5.4–5.6 some more predicate logic additions.

When passing from propositional to first-order logic in the classical framework, decidability gets lost. As the main theoretical result of this chapter we will show that this "gap" is even more essential in temporal logics: FOLTL turns out to be incomplete.

5.1 Basic Language and Semantics

In propositional temporal logic the propositional constants (which are the only basic building blocks) are "time-dependent". In a predicate logic, formulas are built from function and predicate symbols (and variables), and there is a free choice of which of these basic atoms are to be interpreted differently in different states. The symbols which are chosen for this to establish the temporal aspect are called *flexible*; the others are interpreted "time-independently" and are called *rigid*.

The most widely used choice is to take particular individual and propositional constants as the flexible symbols called *flexible individual constants* and *flexible propositional constants*, respectively. (Alternatives will be sketched in Sect. 10.1.) To put it formally, a *temporal signature* $TSIG = (SIG, \mathbf{X}, \mathbf{V})$ is given by

- a signature $SIG = (\mathbf{S}, \mathbf{F}, \mathbf{P})$,
- $\mathbf{X} = \bigcup_{s \in \mathbf{S}} \mathbf{X}_s$ where $\mathbf{X}_s$, for every $s \in \mathbf{S}$, is a set of *flexible individual constants*,
- a set $\mathbf{V}$ of *flexible propositional constants*.

For $TSIG = (SIG, \mathbf{X}, \mathbf{V})$ let SIG^+ be the (classical) signature resulting from $SIG = (\mathbf{S}, \mathbf{F}, \mathbf{P})$ by joining $\mathbf{X}_s$ to $\mathbf{F}^{(\varepsilon,s)}$ for every $s \in \mathbf{S}$ and $\mathbf{V}$ to $\mathbf{P}^{(\varepsilon)}$. In SIG^+ the view of the flexible symbols of $\mathbf{X}$ and $\mathbf{V}$ as individual and propositional constants is established. As we will see shortly from the semantical definitions, the flexible propositional constants will play the role of the propositional constants of LTL while rigid propositional constants in the sense of classical PL are, as in FOL, available as elements of $\mathbf{P}^{(\varepsilon)}$. Note moreover, that $TSIG$ is just another form of SIG^+ displaying $\mathbf{X}$ and $\mathbf{V}$ explicitly.

Given a temporal signature $TSIG = (SIG, \mathbf{X}, \mathbf{V})$, $SIG = (\mathbf{S}, \mathbf{F}, \mathbf{P})$, let $\mathcal{L}_{\mathrm{FOL}}(SIG^+)$ be a first-order language in the sense of Sect. 1.2 (over the signature SIG^+ defined above) with $\mathcal{X} = \bigcup_{s \in \mathbf{S}} \mathcal{X}_s$ being its set of variables. The alphabet of a *(basic) language* $\mathcal{L}_{\mathrm{FOLTL}}(TSIG)$ (also shortly: $\mathcal{L}_{\mathrm{FOLTL}}$) *of first-order linear temporal logic* is given by

- all symbols of $\mathcal{L}_{\mathrm{FOL}}(SIG^+)$,
- the symbols $\bigcirc$ and $\Box$.

Terms (with *their sorts*) and *atomic formulas* of $\mathcal{L}_{\mathrm{FOLTL}}(TSIG)$ are the terms and atomic formulas of $\mathcal{L}_{\mathrm{FOL}}(SIG^+)$. In particular this means that every $a \in \mathbf{X}$ is a term and every $v \in \mathbf{V}$ is an atomic formula.

Inductive Definition of *formulas* (of $\mathcal{L}_{\mathrm{FOLTL}}(TSIG)$).

1. Every atomic formula is a formula.
2. **false** is a formula, and if A and B are formulas then $(A \to B)$, $\bigcirc A$, and $\Box A$ are formulas.
3. If A is a formula and x is a variable then $\exists x A$ is a formula.

It is obvious that every formula of the classical language $\mathcal{L}_{\mathrm{FOL}}(SIG^+)$ is a formula of $\mathcal{L}_{\mathrm{FOLTL}}(TSIG)$ as well. These formulas contain no temporal operators and are called *non-temporal*. Terms and formulas containing no flexible symbols are called *rigid*. The rigid and non-temporal formulas are just the formulas of $\mathcal{L}_{\mathrm{FOL}}(SIG)$.

All abbreviations, the notions of free and bound variables and of closed formulas, and the conventions about notation introduced in Sects. 1.2 and 2.1 are carried over to $\mathcal{L}_{\mathrm{FOLTL}}$. For better readability we will additionally bracket atomic formulas in formulas of the form $\bigcirc(a < b)$, $\exists x(x = a)$ and the like.

For the definition of semantics for $\mathcal{L}_{\mathrm{FOLTL}}$, the notion of temporal structures (serving again as interpretations) has to be adjusted to the first-order situation. A *temporal structure* $\mathsf{K} = (\mathsf{S}, \mathsf{W})$ for a temporal signature $TSIG = (SIG, \mathbf{X}, \mathbf{V})$ consists of

- a structure S for SIG (in the sense of Sect. 1.2), called the *data component* of K,
- an infinite sequence $\mathsf{W} = (\eta_0, \eta_1, \eta_2, \ldots)$ of mappings

  $$\eta_i : \mathbf{X} \cup \mathbf{V} \to |\mathsf{S}| \cup \{\mathsf{ff}, \mathsf{tt}\}$$

  with $\eta_i(a) \in |\mathsf{S}|_s$ for $a \in \mathbf{X}_s$, $s \in \mathsf{S}$, and $\eta_i(v) \in \{\mathsf{ff}, \mathsf{tt}\}$ for $v \in \mathbf{V}$ for every $i \in \mathbb{N}$. (The η_i are again called *states*; η_0 is the *initial state* of K.)

A temporal structure $\mathsf{K} = (\mathsf{S}, \mathsf{W})$ together with a variable valuation ξ with respect to S (which is a mapping $\xi : \mathcal{X} \to |\mathsf{S}|$ as in Sect. 1.2) defines, for every state η_i of W, mappings $\mathsf{S}^{(\xi,\eta_i)}$ which associate values $\mathsf{S}^{(\xi,\eta_i)}(t) \in |\mathsf{S}|$ for every term t and $\mathsf{S}^{(\xi,\eta_i)}(A) \in \{\mathsf{ff}, \mathsf{tt}\}$ for every atomic formula A. The inductive definition runs quite analogously as in FOL:

1. $\mathsf{S}^{(\xi,\eta_i)}(x) = \xi(x)$ for $x \in \mathcal{X}$.
2. $\mathsf{S}^{(\xi,\eta_i)}(a) = \eta_i(a)$ for $a \in \mathbf{X}$.
3. $\mathsf{S}^{(\xi,\eta_i)}(v) = \eta_i(v)$ for $v \in \mathbf{V}$.
4. $\mathsf{S}^{(\xi,\eta_i)}(f(t_1,\dots,t_n)) = f^{\mathsf{S}}(\mathsf{S}^{(\xi,\eta_i)}(t_1),\dots,\mathsf{S}^{(\xi,\eta_i)}(t_n))$ for $f \in \mathbf{F}$.
5. $\mathsf{S}^{(\xi,\eta_i)}(p(t_1,\dots,t_n)) = p^{\mathsf{S}}(\mathsf{S}^{(\xi,\eta_i)}(t_1),\dots,\mathsf{S}^{(\xi,\eta_i)}(t_n))$ for $p \in \mathbf{P}$.
6. $\mathsf{S}^{(\xi,\eta_i)}(t_1 = t_2) = \mathsf{tt} \Leftrightarrow \mathsf{S}^{(\xi,\eta_i)}(t_1)$ and $\mathsf{S}^{(\xi,\eta_i)}(t_2)$ are equal values in $|\mathsf{S}|$.

$\mathsf{S}^{(\xi,\eta_i)}$ plays the combined role of $\mathsf{S}^{(\xi)}$ in FOL and η_i in LTL and can now be inductively extended to the definition of $\mathsf{K}_i^{(\xi)}(F) \in \{\mathsf{ff}, \mathsf{tt}\}$ for every formula F (the "truth value of F in η_i under ξ") transferring the according clauses from FOL and LTL:

1. $\mathsf{K}_i^{(\xi)}(A) = \mathsf{S}^{(\xi,\eta_i)}(A)$ for every atomic formula A.
2. $\mathsf{K}_i^{(\xi)}(\mathbf{false}) = \mathsf{ff}$.
3. $\mathsf{K}_i^{(\xi)}(A \to B) = \mathsf{tt} \Leftrightarrow \mathsf{K}_i^{(\xi)}(A) = \mathsf{ff}$ or $\mathsf{K}_i^{(\xi)}(B) = \mathsf{tt}$.
4. $\mathsf{K}_i^{(\xi)}(\bigcirc A) = \mathsf{K}_{i+1}^{(\xi)}(A)$.
5. $\mathsf{K}_i^{(\xi)}(\Box A) = \mathsf{tt} \Leftrightarrow \mathsf{K}_j^{(\xi)}(A) = \mathsf{tt}$ for every $j \geq i$.
6. $\mathsf{K}_i^{(\xi)}(\exists x A) = \mathsf{tt} \Leftrightarrow$ there is a ξ' with $\xi \sim_x \xi'$ and $\mathsf{K}_i^{(\xi')}(A) = \mathsf{tt}$.

For the other logical operators (in particular $\Diamond$ and $\forall$) the definitions carry over as in FOL and LTL, i.e.,

7. $\mathsf{K}_i^{(\xi)}(\Diamond A) = \mathsf{tt} \Leftrightarrow \mathsf{K}_j^{(\xi)}(A) = \mathsf{tt}$ for some $j \geq i$.
8. $\mathsf{K}_i^{(\xi)}(\forall x A) = \mathsf{tt} \Leftrightarrow \mathsf{K}_i^{(\xi')}(A) = \mathsf{tt}$ for all ξ' with $\xi \sim_x \xi'$.

Note that for rigid terms t and rigid formulas A these evaluations do not depend on η_i, so we have in such cases $\mathsf{S}^{(\xi,\eta_i)}(t) = \mathsf{S}^{(\xi,\eta_j)}(t)$ and $\mathsf{K}_i^{(\xi)}(A) = \mathsf{K}_j^{(\xi)}(A)$ for arbitrary $i, j \in \mathbb{N}$. If A is a rigid and non-temporal formula then, viewing A as a formula of $\mathcal{L}_{\mathrm{FOL}}(SIG)$, we can also evaluate $\mathsf{S}^{(\xi)}(A)$ in the sense of classical FOL, and comparing the respective clauses in Sect. 1.2 with those for $\mathsf{K}_i^{(\xi)}(A)$ above, it follows immediately that $\mathsf{K}_i^{(\xi)}(A) = \mathsf{S}^{(\xi)}(A)$ then holds for every $\mathsf{K} = (\mathsf{S}, \mathsf{W})$, ξ, and $i \in \mathbb{N}$.

Example. Let $TSIG = (SIG_{Nat}, \{a, b\}, \{v\})$ be a temporal signature with SIG_{Nat} being a natural number signature and let x, y be variables (of sort NAT). Then

$$A \equiv \exists x(a = x + y) \land \bigcirc v \to \Box(b \leq 7)$$

is a formula of $\mathcal{L}_{\mathrm{FOLTL}}(TSIG)$. Furthermore, let $\mathsf{K} = (\mathsf{N}, \mathsf{W})$ be a temporal structure with the standard model N of natural numbers and W given by

	η_0	η_1	η_2	η_3	η_4	...
a	2	8	5	7	3	...(arbitrary)...
b	4	7	9	5	5	...(5 forever)...
v	tt	tt	ff	tt	tt	...(arbitrary)...

and let ξ be a variable valuation with $\xi(y) = 3$. Then

$$\mathsf{K}_i^{(\xi)}(\exists x(a = x + y)) = \mathsf{tt} \Leftrightarrow \text{there is a } \xi' \text{ with } \xi \sim_x \xi' \text{ and } \eta_i(a) = \xi'(x) + 3.$$

This means $\mathsf{K}_0^{(\xi)}(\exists x(a = x + y)) = \mathsf{ff}$ and $\mathsf{K}_2^{(\xi)}(\exists x(a = x + y)) = \mathsf{tt}$ (with $\xi'(x) = 2$). So we get

$$\begin{aligned}
&\mathsf{K}_0^{(\xi)}(A) = \mathsf{tt},\\
&\mathsf{K}_1^{(\xi)}(\bigcirc v) = \eta_2(v) = \mathsf{ff} \Rightarrow \mathsf{K}_1^{(\xi)}(A) = \mathsf{tt},\\
&\mathsf{K}_2^{(\xi)}(\bigcirc v) = \eta_3(v) = \mathsf{tt}, \mathsf{K}_2^{(\xi)}(b \le 7) = \mathsf{ff}, \mathsf{K}_2^{(\xi)}(\Box(b \le 7)) = \mathsf{ff}\\
&\quad \Rightarrow \mathsf{K}_2^{(\xi)}(A) = \mathsf{ff},\\
&\mathsf{K}_i^{(\xi)}(\Box(b \le 7)) = \mathsf{tt} \Rightarrow \mathsf{K}_i^{(\xi)}(A) = \mathsf{tt} \text{ for } i \ge 3.
\end{aligned}$$

△

Definition. A formula A of $\mathcal{L}_{\mathrm{FOLTL}}(TSIG)$ is called *valid in the temporal structure* K for $TSIG$ (or K *satisfies* A), denoted by $\models_{\mathsf{K}} A$, if $\mathsf{K}_i^{(\xi)}(A) = \mathsf{tt}$ for every $i \in \mathbb{N}$ and every variable valuation ξ. A is called a *consequence of* a set $\mathcal{F}$ of formulas ($\mathcal{F} \models A$) if $\models_{\mathsf{K}} A$ holds for every K with $\models_{\mathsf{K}} B$ for all $B \in \mathcal{F}$. A is called *(universally) valid* ($\models A$) if $\emptyset \models A$.

These definitions are the obvious adaptations from FOL and the (normal) validity concept of LTL. Clearly, FOLTL can alternatively be equipped with initial validity semantics as well by modifying the notion of validity in a temporal structure according to Sect. 2.6.

Example. The formula $\exists x \bigcirc A \leftrightarrow \bigcirc \exists x A$ is valid since for every K, $i \in \mathbb{N}$ and ξ we have

$$\begin{aligned}
\mathsf{K}_i^{(\xi)}(\exists x \bigcirc A) = \mathsf{tt} &\Leftrightarrow \text{there is a } \xi' \text{ with } \xi \sim_x \xi' \text{ and } \mathsf{K}_i^{(\xi')}(\bigcirc A) = \mathsf{tt}\\
&\Leftrightarrow \text{there is a } \xi' \text{ with } \xi \sim_x \xi' \text{ and } \mathsf{K}_{i+1}^{(\xi')}(A) = \mathsf{tt}\\
&\Leftrightarrow \mathsf{K}_{i+1}^{(\xi)}(\exists x A) = \mathsf{tt}\\
&\Leftrightarrow \mathsf{K}_i^{(\xi)}(\bigcirc \exists x A) = \mathsf{tt}.
\end{aligned}$$

(Observe that in this calculation we have just rephrased the validity proof of the axiom (qltl2) of LTL+q in Sect. 3.3.) △

Formulas A and B with $\models A \leftrightarrow B$ (like $\exists x \bigcirc A$ and $\bigcirc \exists x A$ in the example) are again called *logically equivalent*, denoted by $A \cong B$.

Validity of a formula A means that A "holds for all data interpretations and all state sequences". We still introduce as a weaker notion that A "holds for all state sequences for a fixed data component".

Definition. Let $TSIG = (SIG, \mathbf{X}, \mathbf{V})$ be a temporal signature, S a structure for SIG. A formula A of $\mathcal{L}_{\mathrm{FOLTL}}(TSIG)$ is called S-*valid* if $\models_{\mathsf{K}} A$ holds for every temporal structure K for $TSIG$ with data component S.

Example. The formula $A \equiv \bigcirc(a + x = a) \rightarrow x = 0$ over a natural number signature with $a \in \mathbf{X}_{NAT}$ and $x \in \mathcal{X}_{NAT}$ is N-valid (N being the standard model of natural numbers) since, for every $\mathsf{K} = (\mathsf{N}, (\eta_0, \eta_1, \eta_2, \ldots))$, ξ, and $i \in \mathbb{N}$, we have

$$\begin{aligned} \mathsf{K}_i^{(\xi)}(\bigcirc(a + x = a)) = \mathsf{tt} &\Rightarrow \eta_{i+1}(a) + \xi(x) = \eta_{i+1}(a) \\ &\Rightarrow \xi(x) = 0 \\ &\Rightarrow \mathsf{K}_i^{(\xi)}(x = 0) = \mathsf{tt} \end{aligned}$$

which means $\models_{\mathsf{K}} A$. △

In case A is a rigid and non-temporal formula, S-validity is already given by validity in a single temporal structure with data component S. Moreover, such a formula is a classical first-order formula over the underlying signature SIG. So, for A we have also the notion of being valid in S as defined in Sect. 1.2, and it is quite trivial to compare this classical validity with S-validity in the present context.

Lemma 5.1.1. *Let $TSIG = (SIG, \mathbf{X}, \mathbf{V})$ be a temporal signature, S be a structure for SIG, $\mathsf{K} = (\mathsf{S}, \mathsf{W})$ be a temporal structure for $TSIG$, and A be a rigid and non-temporal formula of $\mathcal{L}_{\mathrm{FOLTL}}(TSIG)$. Then*

$$\models_{\mathsf{K}} A \;\Leftrightarrow\; A \textit{ is } \mathsf{S}\textit{-valid} \;\Leftrightarrow\; A \textit{ is valid in } \mathsf{S} \textit{ (in the classical first-order sense).}$$

Proof. As already noted above, $\mathsf{K}_i^{(\xi)}(A) = \mathsf{S}^{(\xi)}(A)$ holds for every ξ and arbitrary $\mathsf{K} = (\mathsf{S}, \mathsf{W})$ and $i \in \mathbb{N}$ if A is rigid and non-temporal. So we have

$$\begin{aligned} \models_{\mathsf{K}} A &\Leftrightarrow \mathsf{K}_i^{(\xi)}(A) = \mathsf{tt} \text{ for every } \xi, i \\ &\Leftrightarrow \mathsf{S}^{(\xi)}(A) = \mathsf{tt} \text{ for every } \xi \end{aligned}$$

and from this we obtain

$$\models_{\mathsf{K}} A \Leftrightarrow A \text{ is valid in } \mathsf{S}$$

and

$$\begin{aligned} \models_{\mathsf{K}} A &\Leftrightarrow \models_{\mathsf{K}'} A \text{ for every temporal structure } \mathsf{K}' = (\mathsf{S}, \mathsf{W}') \text{ for } TSIG \\ &\Leftrightarrow A \text{ is } \mathsf{S}\text{-valid.} \end{aligned}$$

Together, this proves the claim. △

The formula $A_x(t) \rightarrow \exists x A$ is a typical classically valid formula as seen in Sect. 1.2. In general, it is no longer valid in FOLTL. Consider, e.g., the formula

$$A \equiv x = a \wedge \bigcirc(x \neq a)$$

with $a \in \mathbf{X}$. Let $b \in \mathbf{X}$ and K be such that $\eta_0(a) = \eta_0(b) = \eta_1(a) \neq \eta_1(b)$. Then $A_x(b) \equiv b = a \wedge \bigcirc(b \neq a)$ and, for arbitrary ξ,

$$\mathsf{K}_0^{(\xi)}(A_x(b)) = \mathsf{tt}$$

but

$$\mathsf{K}_0^{(\xi)}(\exists x A) = \mathsf{ff}$$

since otherwise there would be a ξ' with $\xi'(x) = \eta_0(a)$ and $\xi'(x) \neq \eta_1(a)$ which contradicts $\eta_0(a) = \eta_1(a)$.

The problem illustrated here arises from the too liberal substitution of the flexible constant b for the rigid variable x in A. In order to avoid it, a reasonable restriction could be formulated as follows.

Definition. Let A be a formula of $\mathcal{L}_{\mathrm{FOLTL}}$. A term t is called *substitutable for x in A* if $A_x(t)$ has no new occurrences of flexible individual constants in the scope of a temporal operator as compared with A.

Example. In the situation above, the term b is not substitutable for x in A since in $A_x(b)$ there is a new occurrence of b in the scope of $\bigcirc$. However, for

$$B \equiv x = a \wedge \bigcirc(y \neq a)$$

we get

$$B_x(b) \equiv b = a \wedge \bigcirc(y \neq a),$$

so b is substitutable for x in B. It is easy to compute that $B_x(b) \rightarrow \exists x B$ is valid. More generally, if a term t is substitutable for x in a formula A of $\mathcal{L}_{\mathrm{FOLTL}}$ then the formula

$$A_x(t) \rightarrow \exists x A$$

is valid. In fact we have for arbitrary K, $i \in \mathbb{N}$, and ξ:

$$\begin{aligned} \mathsf{K}_i^{(\xi)}(A_x(t)) = \mathsf{tt} &\Rightarrow \mathsf{K}_i^{(\xi')}(A) = \mathsf{K}_i^{(\xi)}(A_x(t)) = \mathsf{tt} \\ &\quad\ \text{for } \xi' \sim_x \xi,\ \xi'(x) = \mathsf{S}^{(\xi,\eta_i)}(t) \\ &\Rightarrow \mathsf{K}_i^{(\xi)}(\exists x A) = \mathsf{tt}. \end{aligned}$$

△

We still note that the LTL relationship

$$\mathcal{F} \cup \{A\} \vDash B \Leftrightarrow \mathcal{F} \vDash \Box A \rightarrow B$$

has to be modified as in Sect. 1.2 (it holds if A does not contain free variables), and extend the list of laws (T1)–(T38) carried over from LTL by some more valid formulas as "typical" laws of FOLTL (also repeating the one proved in an example above).

(T39) $\exists x \bigcirc A \leftrightarrow \bigcirc \exists x A$,
(T40) $\forall x \bigcirc A \leftrightarrow \bigcirc \forall x A$,
(T41) $\exists x \Diamond A \leftrightarrow \Diamond \exists x A$,
(T42) $\forall x \Box A \leftrightarrow \Box \forall x A$.

We mentioned already that FOLTL can be augmented with the propositional extensions of Chap. 3 in the same way as LTL. For example, the logic FOLTL+b is FOLTL with the addition of binary operators described in Sect. 3.1 and contains formulas like

$$\exists x(A \textbf{ unless } B),\ A \textbf{ atnext } (\forall x B).$$

With such extensions, new temporal logical laws arise. We only give some examples in the line of (T39)–(T42) and conclude this section by proving one of them.

(Tb30) $\exists x(A \textbf{ unl } B) \leftrightarrow A \textbf{ unl } (\exists x B)$
if there is no free occurrence of x in A,
(Tb31) $\forall x(A \textbf{ unl } B) \leftrightarrow (\forall x A) \textbf{ unl } B$
if there is no free occurrence of x in B,
(Tb32) $\exists x(A \textbf{ atnext } B) \leftrightarrow (\exists x A) \textbf{ atnext } B$
if there is no free occurrence of x in B,
(Tb33) $\forall x(A \textbf{ atnext } B) \leftrightarrow (\forall x A) \textbf{ atnext } B$
if there is no free occurrence of x in B.

Proof of (Tb32). If there is no free occurrence of x in B then for any temporal structure K, $i \in \mathbb{N}$, and variable valuation ξ we have:

$\mathsf{K}_i^{(\xi)}(\exists x(A \textbf{ atnext } B)) = \mathsf{tt}$

$\Leftrightarrow$ there is a ξ' with $\xi \sim_x \xi'$ and $\mathsf{K}_i^{(\xi')}(A \textbf{ atnext } B) = \mathsf{tt}$

$\Leftrightarrow$ there is a ξ' with $\xi \sim_x \xi'$ and
$\mathsf{K}_j^{(\xi')}(B) = \mathsf{ff}$ for every $j > i$ or
$\mathsf{K}_k^{(\xi')}(A) = \mathsf{tt}$ for the smallest $k > i$ with $\mathsf{K}_k^{(\xi')}(B) = \mathsf{tt}$

$\Leftrightarrow$ there is a ξ' with $\xi \sim_x \xi'$ and
$\mathsf{K}_j^{(\xi)}(B) = \mathsf{ff}$ for every $j > i$ or
$\mathsf{K}_k^{(\xi')}(A) = \mathsf{tt}$ for the smallest $k > i$ with $\mathsf{K}_k^{(\xi)}(B) = \mathsf{tt}$

$\Leftrightarrow$ $\mathsf{K}_j^{(\xi)}(B) = \mathsf{ff}$ for every $j > i$ or
there is a ξ' with $\xi \sim_x \xi'$ and
$\mathsf{K}_k^{(\xi')}(A) = \mathsf{tt}$ for the smallest $k > i$ with $\mathsf{K}_k^{(\xi)}(B) = \mathsf{tt}$

$\Leftrightarrow$ $\mathsf{K}_j^{(\xi)}(B) = \mathsf{ff}$ for every $j > i$ or
$\mathsf{K}_k^{(\xi)}(\exists x A) = \mathsf{tt}$ for the smallest $k > i$ with $\mathsf{K}_k^{(\xi)}(B) = \mathsf{tt}$

$\Leftrightarrow$ $\mathsf{K}_i^{(\xi)}((\exists x A) \textbf{ atnext } B) = \mathsf{tt}$. △

5.2 A Formal System

A reasonable formal system Σ_{FOLTL} for FOLTL can be given as an extension of Σ_{LTL} in the following way.

Axioms

(taut) All tautologically valid formulas,
(ltl1) $\neg\bigcirc A \leftrightarrow \bigcirc\neg A$,
(ltl2) $\bigcirc(A \rightarrow B) \rightarrow (\bigcirc A \rightarrow \bigcirc B)$,
(ltl3) $\Box A \rightarrow A \wedge \bigcirc\Box A$,
(ltl4) $A_x(t) \rightarrow \exists x A$ if t is substitutable for x in A,
(ltl5) $\bigcirc\exists x A \rightarrow \exists x \bigcirc A$,
(ltl6) $A \rightarrow \bigcirc A$ if A is rigid,
(eq1) $x = x$,
(eq2) $x = y \rightarrow (A \rightarrow A_x(y))$ if A is non-temporal.

Rules

(mp) $A, A \rightarrow B \vdash B$,
(nex) $A \vdash \bigcirc A$,
(ind) $A \rightarrow B, A \rightarrow \bigcirc A \vdash A \rightarrow \Box B$,
(par) $A \rightarrow B \vdash \exists x A \rightarrow B$ if there is no free occurrence of x in B.

Σ_{FOLTL} is essentially a conglomeration of Σ_{LTL} and the classical first-order system Σ_{FOL} shown in Sect. 1.2. The only new items are (ltl5), combining temporal and first-order operators, and (ltl6), expressing the fact that all symbols except the flexible ones are equally interpreted in all states.

Theorem 5.2.1 (Soundness Theorem for Σ_{FOLTL}). *Let A be a formula and $\mathcal{F}$ a set of formulas. If $\mathcal{F} \vdash_{\Sigma_{\text{FOLTL}}} A$ then $\mathcal{F} \models A$.*

Proof. The proof runs again by induction on the assumed derivation of A from $\mathcal{F}$.

1. A is an axiom of Σ_{FOLTL}: It suffices to show that A is valid. For the axioms (taut), (ltl1), (ltl2), (ltl3) of Σ_{LTL} this can be taken from Sect. 2.2 and for (ltl4) and (ltl5) this was shown in Sect. 5.1. For (ltl6) it is clear since if A is rigid then $\mathsf{K}_i^{(\xi)}(A) = \mathsf{K}_{i+1}^{(\xi)}(A) = \mathsf{K}_i^{(\xi)}(\bigcirc A)$. The validity of the equality axioms (eq1) and (eq2) is also obvious according to the semantical definition for $=$.
2. $A \in \mathcal{F}$: In this case $\mathcal{F} \models A$ holds trivially.
3. A is a conclusion of a rule of Σ_{FOLTL}: The rules (mp), (nex), and (ind) of Σ_{LTL} are treated exactly as in the proof of Theorem 2.3.1. For the rule (par) we may assume the induction hypothesis $\mathcal{F} \models A \rightarrow B$. To show $\mathcal{F} \models \exists x A \rightarrow B$, let K be a temporal structure, $\models_{\mathsf{K}} C$ for all $C \in \mathcal{F}$. Then $\models_{\mathsf{K}} A \rightarrow B$. Assume $\mathsf{K}_i^{(\xi)}(\exists x A \rightarrow B) = \mathsf{ff}$, i.e., $\mathsf{K}_i^{(\xi)}(\exists x A) = \mathsf{tt}$ and $\mathsf{K}_i^{(\xi)}(B) = \mathsf{ff}$ for some $i \in \mathbb{N}$ and variable valuation ξ. Then there is some ξ' with $\xi \sim_x \xi'$ and $\mathsf{K}_i^{(\xi')}(A) = \mathsf{tt}$. Since B does not contain free occurrences of x we get $\mathsf{K}_i^{(\xi')}(B) = \mathsf{K}_i^{(\xi)}(B) = \mathsf{ff}$ and therefore $\mathsf{K}_i^{(\xi')}(A \rightarrow B) = \mathsf{ff}$, which is a contradiction to $\models_{\mathsf{K}} A \rightarrow B$.

Thus, $\mathsf{K}_i^{(\xi)}(\exists x A \to B) = \mathrm{tt}$ for every i and ξ, i.e., $\vDash_{\mathsf{K}} \exists x A \to B$ and hence $\mathcal{F} \vDash \exists x A \to B$. △

We can transfer all logical laws and derived rules from LTL to Σ_{FOLTL} since Σ_{LTL} is a part of Σ_{FOLTL}. Moreover, we may incorporate classical first-order reasoning into derivations within Σ_{FOLTL} because of the first-order axioms and the rule (par). So, analogously to the derived rule (prop) we may use an additional rule

(pred) $A_1, \ldots, A_n \vdash B$ if B is a "first-order consequence" of $A_1, \ldots, A_n$.

A formal definition of the notion "first-order consequence", however, is not as easy as it was for the "tautological consequence" in (prop). In particular, due to the restriction in (ltl4) we have to be somewhat careful in the case when flexible symbols are involved. The simplest precise meaning of (pred) is taking its application as a shortcut of a derivation of B within Σ_{FOLTL}, which uses the assumptions $A_1, \ldots, A_n$ and only (taut), (ltl4), (eq1), (eq2), (mp), and (par). Examples for (pred) are the following rules, which can easily be verified in this sense:

- $A \to B \vdash A \to \forall x B$ if there is no free occurrence of x in A,
- $A \vdash \forall x A$,
- $t_1 = t_2 \vdash t_2 = t_1$,
- $t_1 = t_2, t_2 = t_3 \vdash t_1 = t_3$.

The laws (T39)–(T42) introduced in the previous section (and others of this kind) can also be derived in Σ_{FOLTL}. As a sample derivation we show this for (T42).

Derivation of (T42).

(1)	$\neg\Box A \to \exists x \neg\Box A$	(ltl4)
(2)	$\Box A \to \circ\Box A$	(prop),(ltl3)
(3)	$\forall x \Box A \to \circ\Box A$	(prop),(1),(2)
(4)	$\forall x \Box A \to \forall x \circ\Box A$	(pred),(3)
(5)	$\circ\exists x \neg\Box A \to \exists x \circ\neg\Box A$	(ltl5)
(6)	$\circ\exists x \neg\Box A \to \exists x \neg\circ\Box A$	(pred),(ltl1),(5)
(7)	$\forall x \circ\Box A \to \circ\forall x \Box A$	(prop),(ltl1),(6)
(8)	$\forall x \Box A \to \circ\forall x \Box A$	(prop),(4),(7)
(9)	$\forall x \Box A \to A$	(prop),(ltl3),(1)
(10)	$\forall x \Box A \to \forall x A$	(pred),(9)
(11)	$\forall x \Box A \to \Box\forall x A$	(ind),(8),(10)
(12)	$\neg A \to \exists x \neg A$	(ltl4)
(13)	$\Box\forall x A \to \Box A$	(prop),(T19),(12)
(14)	$\Box\forall x A \to \forall x \Box A$	(pred),(13)
(15)	$\forall x \Box A \leftrightarrow \Box\forall x A$	(prop),(11),(14) △

The Deduction Theorem 2.3.3 of LTL can be transferred to Σ_{FOLTL} with some restriction, as discussed in Sect. 1.2.

Theorem 5.2.2. *Let A, B be formulas, $\mathcal{F}$ a set of formulas. If $\mathcal{F} \cup \{A\} \vdash B$ and this derivation of B contains no application of the rule* (par) *for a variable occurring free in A, then $\mathcal{F} \vdash \Box A \to B$.*

Proof. Performing an induction on the presupposed derivation of B from $\mathcal{F} \cup \{A\}$, the cases that B is an axiom or $B \in \mathcal{F} \cup \{A\}$ or B is the conclusion of (mp), (nex), or (ind) can be taken word for word from the proof of Theorem 2.3.3. It remains to consider rule (par). Let $\mathcal{F} \cup \{A\} \vdash C \to D$, x not free in D, such that $\exists x C \to D$ is derived by (par) and there is no free occurrence of x in A. By the induction hypothesis we know that $\mathcal{F} \vdash \Box A \to (C \to D)$; hence $\mathcal{F} \vdash C \to (\Box A \to D)$ by (prop). From this we obtain $\mathcal{F} \vdash \exists x C \to (\Box A \to D)$ by (par) and finally $\mathcal{F} \vdash \Box A \to (\exists x C \to D)$ by (prop). △

As before, the variable condition in this theorem is trivially fulfilled if A is closed and, of course, the converse assertion

$$\mathcal{F} \vdash \Box A \to B \;\Rightarrow\; \mathcal{F} \cup \{A\} \vdash B$$

holds again without any restrictions and can be proved exactly as in Theorem 2.3.4.

5.3 Incompleteness

Propositional linear temporal logic LTL and classical propositional logic PL are both decidable. PL can be completely axiomatized and for LTL this is possible at least in the weak form described in Sect. 2.4. Comparing linear temporal and classical logics in their first-order versions, FOL is undecidable and hence FOLTL is undecidable as well. The main difference appears with respect to axiomatizations. In contrast to FOL, FOLTL can not be completely axiomatized, not even in the weak form. More precisely: FOLTL is incomplete in the sense defined in Sect. 1.4. We may show this following the pattern given there by proving that, roughly speaking, the standard model of natural numbers can be "characterized" in FOLTL.

To make this argument precise, let SIG_{Nat} be the natural number signature with the function symbols $0, SUCC, +, *$ and $TSIG_{Nat} = (SIG_{Nat}, \{num\}, \emptyset)$ with the flexible individual constant num (of sort NAT). We consider the following formulas of $\mathcal{L}_{\mathrm{FOLTL}}(TSIG_{Nat})$:

$$\begin{aligned}
P_1 &\equiv SUCC(x) \neq 0,\\
P_2 &\equiv SUCC(x) = SUCC(y) \to x = y,\\
P_3 &\equiv x + 0 = x,\\
P_4 &\equiv x + SUCC(y) = SUCC(x + y),\\
P_5 &\equiv x * 0 = 0,\\
P_6 &\equiv x * SUCC(y) = (x * y) + x,\\
P_7 &\equiv \Diamond(num = x),\\
P_8 &\equiv num = x \to \bigcirc(num = 0 \lor num = SUCC(x)).
\end{aligned}$$

Note that P_1–P_6 are axioms of the first-order theory *Nat* considered in Sect. 1.3 and are (as classical FOL formulas) valid in the standard model N of natural numbers.

Furthermore, let $i_j = j(j+1)/2$ for every $j \in \mathbb{N}$ and $\mathsf{P} = (\mathsf{N}, \mathsf{W}_{Nat})$ be the temporal structure for $TSIG_{Nat}$ with $\mathsf{W}_{Nat} = (\eta_0, \eta_1, \eta_2, \ldots)$ such that

$$\begin{aligned}&\eta_{i_j}(num) = 0 \quad \text{for every } j,\\ &\eta_{i_j+k}(num) = k \quad \text{for } i_j < i_j + k < i_{j+1}.\end{aligned}$$

More intuitively, $i_0 = 0$, $i_1 = 1$, $i_2 = 3$, $i_3 = 6$, ..., so W_{Nat} may be depicted by

	η_0	η_1	η_2	η_3	η_4	η_5	η_6	η_7	η_8	η_9	η_{10}	...
num	0	0	1	0	1	2	0	1	2	3	0	...

Lemma 5.3.1. *The formulas P_1–P_8 are valid in* P.

Proof. P_1–P_6 are rigid and non-temporal, valid in N and hence in P by Lemma 5.1.1. The validity of P_7 and P_8 in P follows from the definition of W_{Nat}: if $\xi(x) = n$ then $\eta_{i_{n+1}+n}(num) = n$ and if $\eta_i(num) = n$ and $\eta_{i+1}(num) \neq 0$ then $i = i_j + n$ for some j and $i + 1 = i_j + n + 1 \neq i_{j+1}$; hence $\eta_{i+1}(num) = n + 1$. So we get $\mathsf{P}_i^{(\xi)}(P_7) = \mathsf{tt}$ and $\mathsf{P}_i^{(\xi)}(P_8) = \mathsf{tt}$ for every i and ξ. △

The temporal structure P has N as its data component. Let now $\mathsf{K} = (\mathsf{S}, \mathsf{W})$ be any temporal structure for $TSIG_{Nat}$. We define the mapping $\chi : |\mathsf{N}| \to |\mathsf{S}|$ by

$$\begin{aligned}&\chi(0) = 0^{\mathsf{S}},\\ &\chi(n+1) = SUCC^{\mathsf{S}}(\chi(n)).\end{aligned}$$

Lemma 5.3.2. *If the formulas P_7 and P_8 are valid in K then there is $k \in \mathbb{N}$ such that*

a) $\eta_k(num) = 0^{\mathsf{S}}$,
b) for every $i \geq k$, $\eta_i(num) = \chi(n)$ for some $n \in \mathbb{N}$.

Proof. Let P_7 and P_8 be valid in K. Then $\mathsf{K}_0^{\xi}(P_7) = \mathsf{tt}$ for ξ with $\xi(x) = 0$ and this implies $\eta_k(num) = 0^{\mathsf{S}}$ for some $k \in \mathbb{N}$. So this k has the property a), and b) is shown by induction on i.

1. For $i = k$ we have $\eta_i(num) = \eta_k(num) = 0^{\mathsf{S}} = \chi(0)$ from a).
2. For $i > k$ we have $\eta_{i-1}(num) = \chi(m)$ for some $m \in \mathbb{N}$ by the induction hypothesis. Since $\vDash_{\mathsf{K}} P_8$, we have $\mathsf{K}_{i-1}^{\xi}(P_8) = \mathsf{tt}$ for ξ with $\xi(x) = \chi(m)$; so $\eta_i(num) = 0^{\mathsf{S}} = \chi(0)$ or $\eta_i(num) = SUCC^{\mathsf{S}}(\chi(m)) = \chi(m+1)$. △

Lemma 5.3.3. *If the formulas P_1, P_2, P_7, and P_8 are valid in K then:*

a) $m \neq n \Rightarrow \chi(m) \neq \chi(n)$ for every $m, n \in \mathbb{N}$.
b) For every $d \in |\mathsf{S}|$ there is an $m \in \mathbb{N}$ with $\chi(m) = d$.

Proof. a) Let $n \neq m$. We show $\chi(n) \neq \chi(m)$ by induction on $n + m$.

1. If $n = 0$, $m \neq 0$, and P_1 is valid in K then $\chi(n) = 0^{\mathsf{S}} \neq SUCC^{\mathsf{S}}(\chi(m-1)) = \chi(m)$. The case $m = 0$, $n \neq 0$ is symmetrical.

2. If $n \neq 0$ and $m \neq 0$ then $\chi(n-1) \neq \chi(m-1)$ by the induction hypothesis and if P_2 is valid in K then we get $\chi(n) = SUCC^{\mathsf{S}}(\chi(n-1)) \neq SUCC^{\mathsf{S}}(\chi(m-1)) = \chi(m)$.

b) Assume that there is some $d \in |\mathsf{S}|$ such that $\chi(m) \neq d$ for every $m \in \mathbb{N}$. If P_7 and P_8 are valid in K then by Lemma 5.3.2 b) there are $k, n \in \mathbb{N}$ such that $\eta_i(num) = \eta(n)$ for $i \geq k$. This means that $\eta_i(num) \neq d$ for $i \geq k$. Moreover, because of P_7, $\mathsf{K}_k^{(\xi)}(\Diamond(num = x)) = \mathsf{tt}$ for ξ with $\xi(x) = d$; hence $\eta_i(num) = d$ for some $i \geq k$ and this is a contradiction. △

Lemma 5.3.3 says that χ is a *bijective* mapping and by the next lemma it is, in the terminology of classical logic, even an "isomorphism" (if K satisfies the respective formulas).

Lemma 5.3.4. *If the formulas P_3–P_6 are valid in K then for every $m, n \in \mathbb{N}$:*

a) $\chi(m + n) = \chi(m) +^{\mathsf{S}} \chi(n)$.
b) $\chi(m * n) = \chi(m) *^{\mathsf{S}} \chi(n)$.

Proof. a) The assertion is proved by induction on n.

1. If P_3 is valid in K then we have $d +^{\mathsf{S}} 0^{\mathsf{S}} = d$ for arbitrary $d \in |\mathsf{S}|$; so we get $\chi(m + 0) = \chi(m) = \chi(m) +^{\mathsf{S}} 0^{\mathsf{S}} = \chi(m) +^{\mathsf{S}} \chi(n)$.
2. Utilizing the validity of P_4 and the induction hypothesis we get

$$\begin{aligned}
\chi(m + (n + 1)) &= \chi((m + n) + 1) \\
&= SUCC^{\mathsf{S}}(\chi(m + n)) \\
&= SUCC^{\mathsf{S}}(\chi(m) +^{\mathsf{S}} \chi(n)) \\
&= \chi(m) +^{\mathsf{S}} SUCC^{\mathsf{S}}(\chi(m)) \\
&= \chi(m) +^{\mathsf{S}} \chi(m + 1).
\end{aligned}$$

b) The proof of this part runs analogously, using the validity of P_5 and P_6. △

In isomorphic structures the same (closed) formulas are valid (in the FOL sense). We transfer this property to the present situation.

Lemma 5.3.5. *Let $\mathsf{K} = (\mathsf{S}, \mathsf{W})$ be a temporal structure for $TSIG_{Nat}$ in which the formulas P_1–P_8 are valid and A a closed formula of $\mathcal{L}_{\mathrm{FOL}}(SIG_{Nat})$. Then*

$$\models_{\mathsf{N}} A \Leftrightarrow \models_{\mathsf{S}} A.$$

Proof. For any variable valuation ξ with respect to N let $\chi\circ\xi$ be the variable valuation $\chi\circ\xi(x) = \chi(\xi(x))$ with respect to S. (Note that all notations in the assertion of the lemma and in the following proof are from classical first-order logic.)

a) We first show by induction on t that

$$\chi(\mathsf{N}^{(\xi)}(t)) = \mathsf{S}^{(\chi\circ\xi)}(t)$$

holds for every term of $\mathcal{L}_{\mathrm{FOL}}(SIG_{Nat})$ and for every ξ.

1. If t is a variable x then $\chi(\mathsf{N}^{(\xi)}(t)) = \chi(\xi(x)) = \mathsf{S}^{(\chi\circ\xi)}(t)$.
2. $t \equiv 0$: $\chi(\mathsf{N}^{(\xi)}(t)) = \chi(0) = 0^{\mathsf{S}} = \mathsf{S}^{(\chi\circ\xi)}(t)$ by definition of χ.
3. $t \equiv SUCC(t_1)$: Then by definition of χ and the induction hypothesis we have

$$\begin{aligned}\chi(\mathsf{N}^{(\xi)}(t)) &= \chi(\mathsf{N}^{(\xi)}(t_1)+1)\\ &= SUCC^{\mathsf{S}}(\chi(\mathsf{N}^{(\xi)}(t_1)))\\ &= SUCC^{\mathsf{S}}(\mathsf{S}^{(\chi\circ\xi)}(t_1))\\ &= \mathsf{S}^{(\chi\circ\xi)}(t).\end{aligned}$$

4. $t \equiv t_1 + t_2$ or $t \equiv t_1 * t_2$: Then, in the first case,

$$\begin{aligned}\chi(\mathsf{N}^{(\xi)}(t)) &= \chi(\mathsf{N}^{(\xi)}(t_1)+\mathsf{N}^{(\xi)}(t_2))\\ &= \chi(\mathsf{N}^{(\xi)}(t_1)) +^{\mathsf{S}} \chi(\mathsf{N}^{(\xi)}(t_2))\\ &= \mathsf{S}^{(\chi\circ\xi)}(t_1) +^{\mathsf{S}} \mathsf{S}^{(\chi\circ\xi)}(t_2)\\ &= \mathsf{S}^{(\chi\circ\xi)}(t)\end{aligned}$$

with Lemma 5.3.4 a) and the induction hypothesis. The second case runs analogously with Lemma 5.3.4 b).

b) Let now A be a formula of $\mathcal{L}_{\mathrm{FOL}}(SIG_{Nat})$. We show by induction on A that

$$\mathsf{N}^{(\xi)}(A) = \mathsf{S}^{(\chi\circ\xi)}(A)$$

holds for every ξ.

1. $A \equiv t_1 = t_2$: Then with Lemma 5.3.3 a) and a) we have

$$\begin{aligned}\mathsf{N}^{(\xi)}(A) = \mathsf{tt} &\Leftrightarrow \mathsf{N}^{(\xi)}(t_1) = \mathsf{N}^{(\xi)}(t_2)\\ &\Leftrightarrow \chi(\mathsf{N}^{(\xi)}(t_1)) = \chi(\mathsf{N}^{(\xi)}(t_2))\\ &\Leftrightarrow \mathsf{S}^{(\chi\circ\xi)}(t_1) = \mathsf{S}^{(\chi\circ\xi)}(t_2)\\ &\Leftrightarrow \mathsf{S}^{(\chi\circ\xi)}(A) = \mathsf{tt}.\end{aligned}$$

2. $A \equiv$ **false**: $\mathsf{N}^{(\xi)}(A) = \mathsf{ff} = \mathsf{S}^{(\chi\circ\xi)}(A)$.
3. $A \equiv B \to C$: Then with the induction hypothesis we have

$$\begin{aligned}\mathsf{N}^{(\xi)}(A) = \mathsf{tt} &\Leftrightarrow \mathsf{N}^{(\xi)}(B) = \mathsf{ff} \text{ or } \mathsf{N}^{(\xi)}(C) = \mathsf{tt}\\ &\Leftrightarrow \mathsf{S}^{(\chi\circ\xi)}(B) = \mathsf{ff} \text{ or } \mathsf{S}^{(\chi\circ\xi)}(C) = \mathsf{tt}\\ &\Leftrightarrow \mathsf{S}^{(\chi\circ\xi)}(A) = \mathsf{tt}.\end{aligned}$$

4. $A \equiv \exists x B$: If $\xi \sim_x \xi'$ then $\chi\circ\xi(y) = \chi(\xi(y)) = \chi(\xi'(y)) = \chi\circ\xi'(y)$ for every variable y other than x; so $\chi\circ\xi \sim_x \chi\circ\xi'$. On the other hand, for any variable valuation ξ'' with respect to S, let ξ' be the variable valuation with respect to N with $\chi(\xi'(y)) = \xi''(y)$ for every y, i.e., $\xi'' = \chi\circ\xi'$. ξ' is well defined because of Lemma 5.3.3 b). Then, for $\chi\circ\xi \sim_x \xi''$ and y different from x, we have

$\chi(\xi'(x)) = \chi(\xi(y))$ which implies $\xi(y) = \xi'(y)$ by Lemma 5.3.3 a); hence $\xi \sim_x \xi'$. Altogether we get with the induction hypothesis

$$\begin{aligned}
\mathsf{N}^{(\xi)}(A) = \mathsf{tt} &\Leftrightarrow \text{there is a } \xi' \text{ with } \xi \sim_x \xi' \text{ and } \mathsf{N}^{(\xi')}(B) = \mathsf{tt} \\
&\Leftrightarrow \text{there is a } \xi' \text{ with } \xi \sim_x \xi' \text{ and } \mathsf{S}^{(\chi\circ\xi')}(B) = \mathsf{tt} \\
&\Leftrightarrow \text{there is a } \xi'' \text{ with } \chi\circ\xi \sim_x \xi'' \text{ and } \mathsf{S}^{(\xi'')}(B) = \mathsf{tt} \\
&\Leftrightarrow \mathsf{S}^{(\chi\circ\xi)}(A) = \mathsf{tt}.
\end{aligned}$$

c) With b) we finally get the assertion of the lemma: if A is closed then $\mathsf{N}^{(\xi)}(A)$ and $\mathsf{S}^{(\chi\circ\xi)}(A)$ do not depend on ξ and $\chi\circ\xi$, respectively; so we have

$$\begin{aligned}
\models_{\mathsf{N}} A &\Leftrightarrow \mathsf{N}^{(\xi)}(A) = \mathsf{tt} \text{ for every } \xi \\
&\Leftrightarrow \mathsf{S}^{(\chi\circ\xi)}(A) = \mathsf{tt} \text{ for every } \xi \\
&\Leftrightarrow \models_{\mathsf{S}} A.
\end{aligned}$$

△

Recalling the discussion in Sect. 1.3, Lemma 5.3.5 informally says that the formulas P_1–P_8 "characterize" the standard model N of natural numbers (up to isomorphism). This provides the key argument to the desired incompleteness result which can now easily be formalized.

Theorem 5.3.6 (Incompleteness Theorem for FOLTL). *The logic FOLTL is incomplete.*

Proof. The result follows from the Gödel Incompleteness Principle pointed out in Sect. 1.4 if we can find a (decidable) set $\mathcal{F}$ of formulas of $\mathcal{L}_{\mathrm{FOLTL}}(TSIG_{Nat})$ such that

$$\mathcal{F} \models A \Leftrightarrow \models_{\mathsf{N}} A$$

holds for every closed formula A of $\mathcal{L}_{\mathrm{FOL}}(SIG_{Nat})$. In fact this works with $\mathcal{F}$ being the set of formulas P_1–P_8: A is a rigid and non-temporal formula of the language $\mathcal{L}_{\mathrm{FOLTL}}(TSIG_{NAT})$; so if $\mathcal{F} \models A$ then $\models_{\mathsf{P}} A$ by Lemma 5.3.1 which implies $\models_{\mathsf{N}} A$ by Lemma 5.1.1. If, on the other hand, $\models_{\mathsf{N}} A$ and $\mathsf{K} = (\mathsf{S}, \mathsf{W})$ is a temporal structure for $TSIG_{Nat}$ which satisfies the formulas of $\mathcal{F}$ then $\models_{\mathsf{S}} A$ by Lemma 5.3.5; hence $\models_{\mathsf{K}} A$ by Lemma 5.1.1, and this means $\mathcal{F} \models A$. △

The preceding discussion shows that FOLTL is a bit comparable with classical second-order logic. We remark, however, that FOLTL is still "weaker" than SOL: there are properties of structures which can be characterized in SOL but not in FOLTL.

A proof-theoretical indication of the difference between FOLTL and SOL is the following observation. In Sect. 2.4 we remarked that weakening the concept of formal systems to semi-formal ones may bridge the gap between weak and full completeness in LTL. In fact, the "much bigger" step from incompleteness to (full) completeness in FOLTL (but not in SOL) can be achieved in the same way. Interestingly, it is even the same ω-rule (ω-ind) $A \to \circ^i B,\ i \in \mathbb{N} \ \vdash\ A \to \Box B$

(appropriate in the LTL case) which works here. Replacing (ind) by (ω-ind) in Σ_{FOLTL} provides a (sound) semi-formal system which is complete in the sense that

$$\mathcal{F} \models A \ \Rightarrow\ \mathcal{F} \vdash A$$

then holds for arbitrary $\mathcal{F}$ and A.

Second Reading

Besides the consideration of semi-formal systems, there is another concept of weakening completeness called *relative completeness*. Originally introduced for *Hoare logic*, this modification can also be defined in the present context.

Focusing on weak completeness, the question of whether some formal system Σ is weakly complete can be reduced to the question of whether any valid formula A is derivable in Σ (cf. the proof of Theorem 2.4.10). The basic idea of relative completeness is induced by the observation that in applications one often does not want to derive universally valid formulas, but formulas which hold in the context of concrete data types. For example, if A is a formula expressing some property of temporal structures with the natural numbers as underlying data, i.e., a formula of some language $\mathcal{L}_{\mathrm{FOLTL}}(TSIG_{Nat})$, then the relative completeness question for Σ is as follows:

- Provided A is valid in every temporal structure for $TSIG_{Nat}$ which has the standard model N of natural numbers as its data component, is A derivable in Σ if every non-temporal formula of this kind may be taken as assumption?

In other (informal) words: can we derive any formula which holds for arbitrary state sequences and data from N if we need not care about how to derive classical first-order formulas valid in N, but may use these just as assumptions in the derivation?

In general, and using the terminology introduced in Sect. 5.1, let $TSIG = (SIG, \mathbf{X}, \mathbf{V})$ be a temporal signature and $\mathcal{C}$ be a class of structures for SIG. For $\mathsf{S} \in \mathcal{C}$ we denote the set of all non-temporal S-valid formulas of $\mathcal{L}_{\mathrm{FOLTL}}(TSIG)$ by $Th(\mathsf{S})$. Then a formal system Σ for FOLTL is called *relatively complete* with respect to $\mathcal{C}$ if

$$Th(\mathsf{S}) \vdash_{\Sigma} A$$

holds for every S-valid formula A and every $\mathsf{S} \in \mathcal{C}$.

In Hoare logic it turns out that (an analogously defined) relative completeness can be achieved – apart from other trivial cases – for the class of *arithmetical* structures. Such a structure presupposes that the signature SIG contains the sort NAT and the usual symbols $0, SUCC, +, *$ of SIG_{Nat}, and S restricted to this part of SIG is the standard model N. For FOLTL we call a formal system *arithmetically complete* if it is relatively complete with respect to the class of arithmetical structures.

In fact it is possible to give a sound and arithmetically complete axiomatization for FOLTL. Informally this means that an axiomatization with the property

$$A \text{ is } \mathsf{S}\text{-valid} \ \Rightarrow\ Th(\mathsf{S}) \vdash A$$

is possible if the temporal logic language is rich enough to contain formulas which express statements about natural numbers and the interpretation of these formulas by S is the "standard" one.

As in the case of a semi-formal axiomatization briefly mentioned in the main text above, the induction rule (ind) of temporal logic plays the crucial role in an approach to an arithmetically complete formal system. One essential part of the modification of Σ_{FOLTL} could be to replace (ind) by the rule

(ar-ind) $\quad A_y(0) \rightarrow B, A_y(SUCC(y)) \rightarrow \circ A \ \vdash \forall y A \rightarrow \Box B$

in which y is a variable from $\mathcal{X}_{Nat}$ and B does not contain y. This rule describes just another inductive argumentation ("over the natural numbers") which is easy to understand informally. It obviously corresponds to the basic semantical fact that the states in a state sequence $\mathsf{W} = (\eta_0, \eta_1, \eta_2, \ldots)$ are indexed by the natural numbers. (Examining the considerations of this section, it is easy to see that this fact is, on the other hand, essentially responsible for the incompleteness of FOLTL.) Interestingly, we will encounter a similar line of argumentation (for another purpose) in Sect. 5.5.

Observe finally that the rule (ind) is just a trivial case of (ar-ind): if A does not contain the variable y then (ar-ind) reduces to

$$A \rightarrow B, A \rightarrow \circ A \ \vdash A \rightarrow \Box B$$

which is in fact (ind).

5.4 Primed Individual Constants

We now want to introduce some (predicate logic) extensions of FOLTL and we begin in this section with the observation that there is a special difference between the two kinds of flexible constants of FOLTL. A flexible propositional constant $v \in \mathbf{V}$ allows a direct access to "its value in the next state". Since v is a formula we may write

$$\bigcirc v$$

to describe this. A simple (but typical) application is a formula like

$$\bigcirc v \leftrightarrow \neg v$$

expressing that

"moving from the present to the next state the value of v will be negated".

For a flexible individual constant $a \in \mathbf{X}$ such a direct denotation of a's next state value is not possible, its usage has to be encoded into an appropriate formula with $\bigcirc$. For example, a phrase like

"moving from the present to the next state will increase the value of a by 1"

can be expressed by

$$\exists x(\bigcirc(a = x) \wedge x = a + 1).$$

Assertions of this kind occur frequently in applications and in order to make their formal description more convenient we extend FOLTL by a linguistic feature allowing the direct application of the next time operator to flexible individual constants.

We write a' (instead of the direct transcription $\bigcirc a$) for such new syntactic entities and call them *primed (flexible) individual constants*. With this extension the sample phrase is simply expressible by

$$a' = a + 1.$$

Note that the next time operator is not really transferred in its full power. We allow only "one priming", so there is no analogy to $\bigcirc\bigcirc v$. Our approach will be sufficient for the usual applications.

Formally we extend FOLTL to a logic FOLTL$'$ the language $\mathcal{L}_{\text{FOLTL}'}$ of which results from $\mathcal{L}_{\text{FOLTL}}$ by adding the prime symbol $'$ to the alphabet and the clause

- If $a \in \mathbf{X}$ then a' is a term of the same sort as a

to the syntactical definition of terms.

For defining the semantics of $\mathcal{L}_{\text{FOLTL}'}$ we slightly modify our technical apparatus. Up to now terms and atomic formulas were evaluated in states (and with respect to some variable valuation ξ) whereas general formulas were interpreted over state sequences. This conceptual difference is emphasized by the different "interpretation functions" $\mathsf{S}^{(\xi,\eta_i)}$ and $\mathsf{K}_i^{(\xi)}$, respectively. Primed individual constants and, hence, terms and atomic formulas of $\mathcal{L}_{\text{FOLTL}'}$ contain a temporal aspect as well referring not only to one but also to the next state in a state sequence. Accordingly, we omit here the separate mapping $\mathsf{S}^{(\xi,\eta_i)}$ and use $\mathsf{K}_i^{(\xi)}$ instead from the very beginning of the inductive definition.

So, given a temporal structure $\mathsf{K} = (\mathsf{S}, \mathsf{W})$ for the underlying temporal signature $TSIG = ((\mathbf{S}, \mathbf{F}, \mathbf{P}), \mathbf{X}, \mathbf{V})$, a variable valuation ξ for the set $\mathcal{X}$ of variables, and $i \in \mathbb{N}$, we define $\mathsf{K}_i^{(\xi)}(t) \in |\mathsf{S}|$ for terms t inductively by the clauses

1. $\mathsf{K}_i^{(\xi)}(x) = \xi(x)$ for $x \in \mathcal{X}$.
2. $\mathsf{K}_i^{(\xi)}(a) = \eta_i(a)$ for $a \in \mathbf{X}$.
3. $\mathsf{K}_i^{(\xi)}(a') = \eta_{i+1}(a)$ for $a \in \mathbf{X}$.
4. $\mathsf{K}_i^{(\xi)}(f(t_1, \ldots, t_n)) = f^{\mathsf{S}}(\mathsf{K}_i^{(\xi)}(t_1), \ldots, \mathsf{K}_i^{(\xi)}(t_n))$ for $f \in \mathbf{F}$.

For atomic formulas A, $\mathsf{K}_i^{(\xi)}(A) \in \{\mathsf{ff}, \mathsf{tt}\}$ is defined by

1. $\mathsf{K}_i^{(\xi)}(v) = \eta_i(v)$ for $v \in \mathbf{V}$.
2. $\mathsf{K}_i^{(\xi)}(p(t_1, \ldots, t_n)) = p^{\mathsf{S}}(\mathsf{K}_i^{(\xi)}(t_1), \ldots, \mathsf{K}_i^{(\xi)}(t_n))$ for $p \in \mathbf{P}$.
3. $\mathsf{K}_i^{(\xi)}(t_1 = t_2) = \mathsf{tt} \Leftrightarrow \mathsf{K}_i^{(\xi)}(t_1)$ and $\mathsf{K}_i^{(\xi)}(t_2)$ are equal values in $|\mathsf{S}|$.

Finally, the additional clauses defining $\mathsf{K}_i^{(\xi)}(F)$ for general formulas F and the notions of validity and consequence are adopted from FOLTL.

It is evident that for formulas F without primed individual constants, $\mathsf{K}_i^{(\xi)}(F)$ according to this definition coincides with $\mathsf{K}_i^{(\xi)}(F)$ when F is viewed as a formula of FOLTL and evaluated as before.

Example. For $a \in \mathbf{X}$ and $x \in \mathcal{X}$, $A \equiv a' = a + 1$ and $B \equiv x * a < a + a'$ are formulas of $\mathcal{L}_{\mathrm{FOLTL'}}$ (with an obvious signature). Assuming N to be the underlying structure, we get

$$\mathsf{K}_i^{(\xi)}(A) = \mathsf{tt} \Leftrightarrow \eta_{i+1}(a) = \eta_i(a) + 1,$$
$$\mathsf{K}_i^{(\xi)}(B) = \mathsf{tt} \Leftrightarrow \xi(x) * \eta_i(a) < \eta_i(a) + \eta_{i+1}(a).$$

So, if $\xi(x) = 3$ and K is given by

	η_0	η_1	η_2	η_3	...
a	2	5	6	3	...

then we obtain

$$\mathsf{K}_0^{(\xi)}(A) = \mathsf{ff},\ \mathsf{K}_1^{(\xi)}(A) = \mathsf{tt},\ \mathsf{K}_2^{(\xi)}(A) = \mathsf{ff},$$
$$\mathsf{K}_0^{(\xi)}(B) = \mathsf{tt},\ \mathsf{K}_1^{(\xi)}(B) = \mathsf{ff},\ \mathsf{K}_2^{(\xi)}(B) = \mathsf{ff}. \qquad \triangle$$

Above we discussed already that the new formula $a' = a + 1$ can also be expressed in FOLTL by $\exists x(\bigcirc(a = x) \land x = a+1)$. Actually it turns out quite generally that FOLTL$'$ does not really produce more expressibility than FOLTL.

Theorem 5.4.1. *In any $\mathcal{L}_{\mathrm{FOLTL'}}$, for every formula A there is a formula A^* such that A and A^* are logically equivalent and A^* does not contain primed individual constants.*

Proof. a) We define A^* inductively according to the syntactic structure of A.

1. A is atomic: Then $A \equiv p(t_1, \ldots, t_n)$ or $A \equiv t_1 = t_2$. If A does not contain primed individual constants then $A^* \equiv A$. Otherwise, let $a_1', \ldots, a_m'$, $m \geq 1$, be the primed individual constants occurring in $t_1, \ldots, t_n$ (or t_1, t_2, respectively) and $x_1, \ldots, x_m$ be variables not occurring in A. Then
$$A^* \equiv \exists x_1 \ldots \exists x_m(\bigcirc(a_1 = x_1 \land \ldots \land a_m = x_m) \land \overline{A})$$
where $\overline{A}$ results from A by replacing a_i' by x_i for $1 \leq i \leq m$.
2. $A \equiv$ **false**: Then $A^* \equiv$ **false**.
3. $A \equiv B \to C$ or $A \equiv \bigcirc B$ or $A \equiv \Box B$: Then $A^* \equiv B^* \to C^*$ or $A^* \equiv \bigcirc B^*$ or $A^* \equiv \Box B^*$, respectively, where B^* and C^* are the results of this construction for B and C.
4. $A \equiv \exists x B$: Then $A^* \equiv \exists x B^*$ where B^* is the constructed formula for B (and this construction does not use the variable x in step 1).

Obviously, A^* does not contain primed individual constants.

b) Let now $\mathsf{K} = (\mathsf{S}, \mathsf{W})$, $\mathsf{W} = (\eta_0, \eta_1, \eta_2, \ldots)$, be a temporal structure, ξ a variable valuation, and $i \in \mathbb{N}$. For the formula A^* defined in a) we show by the same induction that

$$\mathsf{K}_i^{(\xi)}(A^*) = \mathsf{K}_i^{(\xi)}(A)$$

from which the assertion of the theorem follows immediately.

1. A is atomic: We treat only the case $A \equiv p(t_1, \ldots, t_n)$. The case $A \equiv t_1 = t_2$ runs in quite the same way. If A does not contain primed individual constants then the assertion is trivial. Otherwise, $\overline{A}$ in the above construction is of the form $p(t_1^*, \ldots, t_n^*)$ where, for $1 \leq i \leq n$, t_i results from t_i by the replacement of the $a_1', \ldots, a_m'$ by $x_1, \ldots, x_m$. So, abbreviating $B \equiv a_1 = x_1 \wedge \ldots \wedge a_m = x_m$ we have

$$
\begin{aligned}
\mathsf{K}_i^{(\xi)}(A^*) = \mathsf{tt} &\Leftrightarrow \text{there is a } \xi' \text{ with } \xi \sim_{x_1} \xi' \text{ and} \\
&\ \mathsf{K}_i^{(\xi')}(\exists x_2 \ldots \exists x_m(\bigcirc B \wedge \overline{A})) = \mathsf{tt} \\
&\Leftrightarrow \text{there are } \xi', \xi'' \text{ with } \xi \sim_{x_1} \xi', \xi' \sim_{x_2} \xi'' \text{ and} \\
&\ \mathsf{K}_i^{(\xi'')}(\exists x_3 \ldots \exists x_m(\bigcirc B \wedge \overline{A})) = \mathsf{tt} \\
&\ \vdots \\
&\Leftrightarrow \text{there are } \xi', \xi'', \ldots, \xi^{(m)} \text{ with} \\
&\ \xi \sim_{x_1} \xi', \xi' \sim_{x_2} \xi'', \ldots, \xi^{(m-1)} \sim_{x_m} \xi^{(m)} \text{ and} \\
&\ \mathsf{K}_i^{(\xi^{(m)})}(\bigcirc B \wedge \overline{A}) = \mathsf{tt} \\
&\Leftrightarrow \text{there are } \xi', \xi'', \ldots, \xi^{(m)} \text{ with} \\
&\ \xi \sim_{x_1} \xi', \xi' \sim_{x_2} \xi'', \ldots, \xi^{(m-1)} \sim_{x_m} \xi^{(m)} \text{ and} \\
&\ \mathsf{K}_i^{(\xi^{(m)})}(p(t_1^*, \ldots, t_n^*)) = \mathsf{tt} \text{ and} \\
&\ \xi^{(m)}(x_j) = \eta_{i+1}(a_j) = \eta_i(a_j') \text{ for } 1 \leq j \leq m \\
&\Leftrightarrow \text{there are } \xi', \xi'', \ldots, \xi^{(m)} \text{ with} \\
&\ \xi \sim_{x_1} \xi', \xi' \sim_{x_2} \xi'', \ldots, \xi^{(m-1)} \sim_{x_m} \xi^{(m)} \text{ and} \\
&\ p^{\mathsf{S}}(\mathsf{K}_i^{(\xi)}(t_1), \ldots, \mathsf{K}_i^{(\xi)}(t_n)) = \mathsf{tt} \\
&\Leftrightarrow \mathsf{K}_i^{(\xi)}(A) = \mathsf{tt}.
\end{aligned}
$$

2. $A \equiv$ **false**: In this case the assertion is trivial.
3. $A \equiv B \to C$, $A \equiv \bigcirc B$, or $A \equiv \Box B$: Using the respective induction hypothesis in each case, we have

$$
\begin{aligned}
\mathsf{K}_i^{(\xi)}(A^*) = \mathsf{tt} &\Leftrightarrow \mathsf{K}_i^{(\xi)}(B^*) = \mathsf{ff} \text{ or } \mathsf{K}_i^{(\xi)}(C^*) = \mathsf{tt} \\
&\Leftrightarrow \mathsf{K}_i^{(\xi)}(B) = \mathsf{ff} \text{ or } \mathsf{K}_i^{(\xi)}(C) = \mathsf{tt} \\
&\Leftrightarrow \mathsf{K}_i^{(\xi)}(A) = \mathsf{tt}
\end{aligned}
$$

for $A \equiv B \to C$,

$$\mathsf{K}_i^{(\xi)}(A^*) = \mathsf{K}_{i+1}^{(\xi)}(B^*) = \mathsf{K}_{i+1}^{(\xi)}(B) = \mathsf{K}_i^{(\xi)}(A)$$

for $A \equiv \bigcirc B$, and

$$
\begin{aligned}
\mathsf{K}_i^{(\xi)}(A^*) = \mathsf{tt} &\Leftrightarrow \mathsf{K}_j^{(\xi)}(B^*) = \mathsf{tt} \text{ for every } j \geq i \\
&\Leftrightarrow \mathsf{K}_j^{(\xi)}(B) = \mathsf{tt} \text{ for every } j \geq i \\
&\Leftrightarrow \mathsf{K}_i^{(\xi)}(A) = \mathsf{tt}
\end{aligned}
$$

for $A \equiv \Box B$.

4. $A \equiv \exists x B$: Using the induction hypothesis, we have:

$$\begin{aligned}
\mathsf{K}_i^{(\xi)}(A^*) = \mathrm{tt} &\Leftrightarrow \text{there is a } \xi' \text{ with } \xi \sim_x \xi' \text{ and } \mathsf{K}_i^{(\xi')}(B^*) = \mathrm{tt} \\
&\Leftrightarrow \text{there is a } \xi' \text{ with } \xi \sim_x \xi' \text{ and } \mathsf{K}_i^{(\xi')}(B) = \mathrm{tt} \\
&\Leftrightarrow \mathsf{K}_i^{(\xi)}(A) = \mathrm{tt}.
\end{aligned}$$

△

Example. Let $A \equiv a' = a + 1$ and $B \equiv y * a < a + a'$ be the formulas from the previous example. The construction of Theorem 5.4.1 yields

$$A^* \equiv \exists x(\bigcirc(a = x) \land x = a + 1)$$

which is just the formula from the beginning of our discussion and

$$B^* \equiv \exists x(\bigcirc(a = x) \land y * a < a + x).$$

Note that the result of the general construction can often be simplified. For example, for $C \equiv \Box(a' > 1)$ we obtain

$$C^* \equiv \exists x(\bigcirc(a = x) \land \Box(x > 1)),$$

and this is logically equivalent to $\Box\bigcirc(a > 1)$. △

If we now transfer the expressivity notions from Sect. 4.1 to the present logics then an immediate corollary of Theorem 5.4.1 is that FOLTL$'$ is not really more expressive than FOLTL.

Theorem 5.4.2. FOLTL *and* FOLTL$'$ *are equally expressive.*

Proof. FOLTL $\leq$ FOLTL$'$ is trivial since FOLTL $\subseteq$ FOLTL$'$ (defined analogously as in Sect 4.1). Theorem 5.4.1 shows that FOLTL$'$ $\leq$ FOLTL; so together we obtain FOLTL $=$ FOLTL$'$. △

This fact means that we can view FOLTL$'$ as "the same" as FOLTL and formulas A with primed individual constants as abbreviations for the corresponding A^*. Formal derivations with such "primed" formulas can use

$$A \leftrightarrow A^*$$

as an additional axiom. Consider, for example, the formula

$$A \equiv a = y \land a' = a \rightarrow a' = y.$$

Forgetting for a moment that we deal with temporal logic, A looks like a simple FOL formula (with variables or individual constants y, a, and a') which should be derivable within Σ_{FOL}. Now

$$A^* \equiv a = y \land \exists x(\bigcirc(x = a) \land x = a) \rightarrow \exists x(\bigcirc(x = a) \land x = y)$$

and therefore a derivation of A as a FOLTL$'$ formula could consist of the two steps

(1) $a = y \land \exists x(\bigcirc(x = a) \land x = a) \rightarrow$
$\exists x(\bigcirc(x = a) \land x = y)$ (pred)
(2) $a = y \land a' = a \rightarrow a' = y$ axiom $A \leftrightarrow A^*$,(prop),(1)

To summarize, we will freely use in the following primed individual constants within FOLTL without explicitly considering this as a change of the logic (from FOLTL to FOLTL$'$) and we will directly use formulas like the above-derived A in derivations as applications of (pred). Clearly, non-temporal formulas of a respective language do not contain primed individual constants.

Furthermore, for sake of uniformity we will frequently extend the priming notation to flexible propositional constants $v \in \mathbf{V}$ using v' as a synonym for $\bigcirc v$:

$$v' \equiv \bigcirc v.$$

5.5 Well-Founded Relations

In certain applications one is interested in proving formulas of the form

$$A \rightarrow \Diamond B.$$

Looking into the repertory developed so far we find only rules like

(som) $A \rightarrow \bigcirc B \vdash A \rightarrow \Diamond B$,
(chain) $A \rightarrow \Diamond B, B \rightarrow \Diamond C \vdash A \rightarrow \Diamond C$

(see Sects. 2.3 and 2.4) which are rather weak, and we mentioned already in Sect. 3.1 that in propositional temporal logic there is no induction rule like the ones for formulas $A \rightarrow \Box B$, $A \rightarrow B$ **unless** C, etc. A vague informal argument for this fact is that the formula $A \rightarrow \Diamond B$ is logically equivalent to $\Box\neg B \rightarrow \neg A$ and therefore, by the Deduction Theorem and its converse, the problem of deriving $A \rightarrow \Diamond B$ amounts to the problem of proving $\neg B \vdash \neg A$ or, say,

$$C \vdash D.$$

We cannot expect to be able to formulate a single proof principle as a rule (within one of the propositional temporal logics) for deriving D from C for arbitrary C and D.

However, there is a general device for proofs of $A \rightarrow \Diamond B$ which lies "outside" the propositional proof systems but can be formulated within the linguistic means of FOLTL by a special extension. In order to illustrate the intention of this proof method let A be a formula of the particular form

$$A \equiv A_1 \land a = y$$

where $a \in \mathbf{X}_{NAT}$ and $y \in \mathcal{X}_{NAT}$. Suppose we know that

$$A_1 \land a = y \land y \neq 0 \to \bigcirc(A_1 \land a = y - 1)$$

and

$$A_1 \land a = 0 \to B$$

hold in every state. Then it is intuitively clear that whenever A holds in some state η_i (with $\xi(y) = n$) then the formulas $A_1 \land a = y-1$, $A_1 \land a = y-2, \dots, A_1 \land a = 0$ hold in the states $\eta_{i+1}, \eta_{i+2}, \dots, \eta_{i+n}$, respectively, and therefore B holds in η_{i+n}. This means that $A \to \Diamond B$ holds indeed in every state.

The main principle in this argumentation is a sort of induction "over the value of the variable y" expressed by arguing that successively decreasing an arbitrary natural number will sometimes lead to the number 0. (Note that there is some similarity with the situation in the Second Reading paragraph of Sect. 5.3.) We formally develop this basic idea now in a very general setting.

Definition. Let $\mathbb{D}$ be a set. A binary relation R on $\mathbb{D}$ is called *well-founded* if there is no infinite subset $\{d_0, d_1, d_2, \dots\} \subseteq \mathbb{D}$ such that $(d_{i+1}, d_i) \in R$ for every $i \in \mathbb{N}$.

As an example, the order relation $<$ on $\mathbb{N}$ is well-founded. The usual mathematical induction on natural numbers (with respect to $<$) is generalized for well-founded relations as follows.

General Induction Principle. Let R be a well-founded relation on a set $\mathbb{D}$ and $\mathbb{D}' \subseteq \mathbb{D}$. If, for every $d \in \mathbb{D}$, $d \in \mathbb{D}'$ can be concluded from the assumption that $d' \in \mathbb{D}'$ for every d' with $(d', d) \in R$ then $\mathbb{D}' = \mathbb{D}$.

Proof. Assume $\mathbb{D}' \neq \mathbb{D}$, i.e., there is some $d_0 \in \mathbb{D}$ with $d_0 \notin \mathbb{D}'$. Then there must be some d_1 with $(d_1, d_0) \in R$ and $d_1 \notin \mathbb{D}'$ since otherwise $d_0 \in \mathbb{D}'$ could be concluded. This argument can be applied infinitely often yielding infinitely many elements $d_0, d_1, d_2, \dots$ of $\mathbb{D}$ with $(d_{i+1}, d_i) \in R$ for every $i \in \mathbb{N}$ and contradicting the well-foundedness of R. △

Let now $\mathcal{L}^{\mathrm{w}}_{\mathrm{FOLTL}}(TSIG)$ be an FOLTL language such that the signature SIG of $TSIG$ contains a particular sort WF and a predicate symbol $\prec^{(WF\ WF)}$. The logic FOLTL+w is defined by such a language and the additional condition that in every temporal structure $\mathsf{K} = (\mathsf{S}, \mathsf{W})$ for $TSIG$, $\prec^{\mathsf{S}}$ is a well-founded relation on $|\mathsf{S}|_{WF}$. Note that, given some $\mathcal{L}_{\mathrm{FOLTL}}$, this language may already contain WF and $\prec$ with the requested interpretation and is then (without any extension) already an FOLTL+w language, or it has really to be extended to obtain an $\mathcal{L}^{\mathrm{w}}_{\mathrm{FOLTL}}$ by adding some appropriate sort and predicate symbol.

In FOLTL+w we can postulate an additional axiom reflecting the semantical requirements. The consideration above implies that the formula

(gip) $\quad \forall y(\forall \bar{y}(\bar{y} \prec y \to A_y(\bar{y})) \to A) \to A \quad$ for $y, \bar{y} \in \mathcal{X}_{WF}$

which formalizes the general induction principle is sound. The extension of the formal system Σ_{FOLTL} by the axiom (gip) will be denoted by $\Sigma^{\mathrm{w}}_{\mathrm{FOLTL}}$.

In a logic FOLTL+w we are now able to formalize and prove the announced proof principle as a derived rule in the following general form:

(wfr) $A \to \Diamond(B \lor \exists \bar{y}(\bar{y} \prec y \land A_y(\bar{y}))) \vdash \exists y A \to \Diamond B$
if B does not contain y,
for $y, \bar{y} \in \mathcal{X}_{WF}$.

Derivation of (wfr).

(1)	$A \to \Diamond(B \lor \exists \bar{y}(\bar{y} \prec y \land A_y(\bar{y})))$	assumption
(2)	$\Diamond A \to \Diamond(B \lor \exists \bar{y}(\bar{y} \prec y \land A_y(\bar{y})))$	(T36),(1)
(3)	$\Diamond A \to \Diamond B \lor \exists \bar{y}(\Diamond(\bar{y} \prec y) \land \Diamond A_y(\bar{y}))$	(T19),(T25),(T41),(2)
(4)	$\neg(\bar{y} \prec y) \to \bigcirc\neg(\bar{y} \prec y)$	(ltl6)
(5)	$\neg(\bar{y} \prec y) \to \Box\neg(\bar{y} \prec y)$	(ind1),(4)
(6)	$\Diamond(\bar{y} \prec y) \to \bar{y} \prec y$	(prop),(T2),(5)
(7)	$\Diamond A \to \Diamond B \lor \exists \bar{y}(\bar{y} \prec y \land \Diamond A_y(\bar{y}))$	(pred),(3),(6)
(8)	$\exists \bar{y}(\bar{y} \prec y \land \Diamond A_y(\bar{y})) \land$ $\forall \bar{y}(\bar{y} \prec y \to (\Diamond A_y(\bar{y}) \to \Diamond B)) \to \Diamond B$	(pred)
(9)	$\Diamond A \land \forall \bar{y}(\bar{y} \prec y \to (\Diamond A_y(\bar{y}) \to \Diamond B)) \to \Diamond B$	(prop),(7),(8)
(10)	$\forall \bar{y}(\bar{y} \prec y \to (\Diamond A_y(\bar{y}) \to \Diamond B)) \to (\Diamond A \to \Diamond B)$	(prop),(9)
(11)	$\Diamond A \to \Diamond B$	(mp),(gip),(10)
(12)	$A \to \Diamond B$	(prop),(T5),(11)
(13)	$\exists y A \to \Diamond B$	(par),(12) △

It should be noted that the premise in (wfr) is a formula of the form $C \to \Diamond D$ itself; so this rule still needs other means like (som) or (chain) for its application. In line (12) of the derivation of (wfr) the conclusion $A \to \Diamond B$ is achieved which was the starting point of our discussion. We prefer to take $\exists y A \to \Diamond B$ as the conclusion of the rule since in this latter formula the "auxiliary technical variable" y is "hidden" by the existential quantification, i.e., there is no free occurrence of y in it.

As a simple application we want to show that repeated application of the rule (chain) can be encoded into one application of (wfr). Suppose we are able to prove

$$B_0 \to \Diamond B_1, B_1 \to \Diamond B_2, \ldots, B_{k-1} \to \Diamond B_k$$

for formulas $B_0, \ldots, B_k$, $k \geq 1$, of some language $\mathcal{L}_{\text{FOLTL}}$. Applying (chain) $k-1$ times we get $B_0 \to \Diamond B_k$. Let now $\mathcal{L}^{\text{w}}_{\text{FOLTL}}$ be the language $\mathcal{L}_{\text{FOLTL}}$ extended (if necessary) by NAT as the sort WF and by $<$ which is taken for $\prec$. Consider the formula

$$A \equiv (y = k \land B_0) \lor \ldots \lor (y = 1 \land B_{k-1})$$

($y \in \mathcal{X}_{WF}$). Obviously, $A_y(i)$ is logically equivalent to B_{k-i} for $1 \leq i \leq k$; the assumptions $B_j \to \Diamond B_{j+1}$, $0 \leq j \leq k-1$, translate to

$$A_y(i) \to \Diamond A_y(i-1)$$

for $2 \leq i \leq k$ and

$$A_y(1) \to \Diamond B_k$$

and the conclusion $B_0 \to \Diamond B_k$ becomes $A_y(k) \to \Diamond B_k$. This formula can be derived with (wfr) as follows:

(1)	$A_y(i) \to \Diamond A_y(i-1)$ for $2 \le i \le k$	assumption
(2)	$A_y(1) \to \Diamond B_k$	assumption
(3)	$A \to y = k \vee \ldots \vee y = 1$	(taut)
(4)	$A \to A_y(k) \vee \ldots \vee A_y(1)$	(pred),(3)
(5)	$A \to \Diamond(B_k \vee \exists \bar{y}(\bar{y} < y \wedge A_y(\bar{y})))$	(pred),(1),(2),(4)
(6)	$\exists y A \to \Diamond B_k$	(wfr),(5)
(7)	$A_y(k) \to \exists y A$	(ltl4)
(8)	$A_y(k) \to \Diamond B_k$	(prop),(6),(7)

As can be seen, (wfr) is in fact the only proper temporal logic rule occurring in this derivation.

5.6 Flexible Quantification

In Sect. 3.3 we described quantification over ("flexible") propositional variables. This extension can be transferred to FOLTL providing a logic FOLTL+q. Consequently, however, quantification should then also be allowed over "flexible" individual variables. We do not repeat the details of Sect. 3.3 but describe only this latter extension.

Let $TSIG = (SIG, \mathbf{X}, \mathbf{V})$ be some temporal signature, where $SIG = (\mathbf{S}, \mathbf{F}, \mathbf{P})$. A language $\mathcal{L}^{q}_{\mathrm{FOLTL}}(TSIG)$ of FOLTL+q extends $\mathcal{L}_{\mathrm{FOLTL}}(TSIG)$ by additional sets $\mathcal{X}^{fl}_s$ of *flexible individual variables* for every $s \in \mathbf{S}$ and two additional syntax clauses (with $\mathcal{X}^{fl} = \bigcup_{s \in \mathbf{S}} \mathcal{X}^{fl}_s$):

- Every flexible individual variable of $\mathcal{X}^{fl}$ is a term.
- If A is a formula and z is a flexible individual variable then $\exists z A$ is a formula.

Again we write $\forall z A$ for $\neg \exists z \neg A$ and adopt notions like free and bound (flexible) variables and notations like $A_z(t)$ from FOLTL.

Given a temporal structure $\mathsf{K} = (\mathsf{S}, \mathsf{W})$ for $TSIG$, we define (analogously to the notions in Sect. 3.3) a *flexible (individual) variable valuation* (with respect to S) to be an infinite sequence $\Xi = (\xi_0, \xi_1, \xi_2, \ldots)$ of mappings

$$\xi_i : \mathcal{X}^{fl} \to |\mathsf{S}|$$

with $\xi_i(z) \in |\mathsf{S}|_s$ for $z \in \mathcal{X}^{fl}_s$, $i \in \mathbb{N}$. For two such valuations $\Xi = (\xi_0, \xi_1, \xi_2, \ldots)$ and $\Xi' = (\xi'_0, \xi'_1, \xi'_2, \ldots)$ and $z \in \mathcal{X}^{fl}$ let

$$\Xi \sim_z \Xi' \;\Leftrightarrow\; \xi_i(\bar{z}) = \xi'_i(\bar{z}) \text{ for all } \bar{z} \in \mathcal{X}^{fl} \text{ other than } z \text{ and all } i \in \mathbb{N}.$$

With a given $\Xi = (\xi_0, \xi_1, \xi_2, \ldots)$, the evaluation mappings $\mathsf{S}^{(\xi,\eta_i)}$ and $\mathsf{K}_i^{(\xi)}$ of FOLTL are now replaced by mappings $\mathsf{S}^{(\xi,\xi_i,\eta_i)}$ and $\mathsf{K}_i^{(\xi,\Xi)}$ with, adapting the earlier definitions and the additional clauses,

- $\mathsf{S}^{(\xi,\xi_i,\eta_i)}(z) = \xi_i(z)$ for $z \in \mathcal{X}^{fl}$,
- $\mathsf{K}_i^{(\xi,\Xi)}(\exists z A) = \mathsf{tt} \Leftrightarrow$ there is a Ξ' such that $\Xi \sim_z \Xi'$ and $\mathsf{K}_i^{(\xi,\Xi')}(A) = \mathsf{tt}$.

For $\forall z A$ we clearly obtain

- $\mathsf{K}_i^{(\xi,\Xi)}(\forall z A) = \mathsf{tt} \Leftrightarrow \mathsf{K}_i^{(\xi,\Xi')}(A) = \mathsf{tt}$ for all Ξ' with $\Xi \sim_z \Xi'$.

The definition of validity in K is adapted accordingly: $\vDash_{\mathsf{K}} A$ if $\mathsf{K}_i^{(\xi,\Xi)}(A) = \mathsf{tt}$ for every i, ξ, and Ξ.

Analogously to the propositional quantification described in Sect. 3.3, a formula $\exists z A$ informally means a quantification over a sequence of values (from $|\mathsf{S}|$) instead of the "normal" quantification $\exists x A$ over single values.

Example. For $z \in \mathcal{X}^{fl}$, $x \in \mathcal{X}$, and $a \in \mathbf{X}$, $A \equiv \exists z(z > x \wedge \Box(z < a))$ is a formula of $\mathcal{L}^{\mathrm{q}}_{\mathrm{FOLTL}}$ (with some natural number signature). Let K be such that

	η_0	η_1	η_2	η_3	η_4	$\dots$
a	8	3	9	7	7	...(7 forever)...

and $\xi(x) = 3$. Then (for arbitrary Ξ)

$$\mathsf{K}_0^{(\xi,\Xi)}(A) = \mathsf{K}_1^{(\xi,\Xi)}(A) = \mathsf{ff}$$

since for Ξ' with $\Xi \sim_z \Xi'$ and $i = 1, 2$, $\xi_i'(z) > \xi(x) = 3$ implies $\xi_i'(z) > \eta_1(a)$; hence $\mathsf{K}_i^{(\xi,\Xi')}(z > x \wedge \Box(z < a)) = \mathsf{ff}$. For $i \geq 2$ we get

$$\mathsf{K}_i^{(\xi,\Xi)}(A) = \mathsf{tt}$$

since, for such i, $\mathsf{K}_i^{(\xi,\Xi')}(z > x \wedge \Box(z < a)) = \mathsf{tt}$ for Ξ' with $3 < \xi'(z) < 7$. △

In many respects this form of quantification behaves like "normal" quantification in FOLTL. In particular, the formulas

- $A_z(t) \to \exists z A$
- $\exists z \bigcirc A \leftrightarrow \bigcirc \exists z A$

($z \in \mathcal{X}^{fl}$) are valid in FOLTL+q (we even need here no restriction on t in the first formula), and the particularization rule holds as consequence relationship in the form

- $A \to B \vDash \exists z A \to B \quad (z \in \mathcal{X}^{fl}$, z not free in B).

So, a (necessarily incomplete) axiomatization of FOLTL+q could contain these formulas as axioms and ("flexible") particularization as a rule. We do not pursue this aspect in more detail; instead we want to illustrate the expressive power of flexible quantification by an example which continues the observations made in Sect. 5.3.

We found there that the (standard model N of) natural numbers can be characterized in FOLTL. Recall, e.g., that the formulas P_3–P_6 described laws about addition and multiplication. Let now F_{add} be the FOLTL+q formula

$$\begin{aligned}F_{add} \equiv \exists z_1 \exists z_2 (z_1 = x_1 \wedge z_2 = 0 \wedge &\\ \Box((z_2 = x_2 \rightarrow z_1 = x_3) \wedge &\\ (z_2 \neq x_2 \rightarrow \forall y_1 \forall y_2 (z_1 = y_1 \wedge z_2 = y_2 \rightarrow &\\ \bigcirc(z_1 = SUCC(y_1) \wedge &\\ z_2 = SUCC(y_2))))))).\end{aligned}$$

This formula "defines" addition within a language based on a signature containing only 0 and $SUCC$ in the sense that

$$F_{add} \text{ "expresses" } x_1 + x_2 = x_3,$$

or, formally:

$$\mathsf{K}_i^{(\xi,\Xi)}(F_{add}) = \mathsf{tt} \Leftrightarrow \xi(x_1) + \xi(x_2) = \xi(x_3)$$

for arbitrary $\mathsf{K} = (\mathbb{N}, \mathsf{W})$, ξ, Ξ, and $i \in \mathbb{N}$. In fact, it is easy to see that with $\xi(x_1) = m$ and $\xi(x_2) = n$ we have

$$\begin{aligned}\mathsf{K}_i^{(\xi,\Xi)}(F_{add}) = \mathsf{tt} \Leftrightarrow\ & \text{there is a } \Xi' = (\xi'_0, \xi'_1, \xi'_2, \ldots) \text{ such that}\\ & \xi'_i(z_1) = m,\ \xi'_i(z_2) = 0,\\ & \xi'_{i+1}(z_1) = m+1,\ \xi'_{i+1}(z_2) = 1,\\ & \vdots\\ & \xi'_{i+n}(z_1) = m+n,\ \xi'_{i+n}(z_2) = n,\ \xi'_{i+n}(z_1) = \xi(x_3)\\ \Leftrightarrow\ & \xi(x_1) + \xi(x_2) = \xi(x_3).\end{aligned}$$

The "satisfying" Ξ' can be depicted by

	...	ξ'_i	ξ'_{i+1}	ξ'_{i+2}	...	ξ'_{i+n}	...
z_1	...	m	$m+1$	$m+2$	...	$m+n$	...
z_2	...	0	1	2	...	n	...

and the analogous matrix

	...	ξ'_i	ξ'_{i+1}	ξ'_{i+2}	...	ξ'_{i+n}	...
z_1	...	0	m	$m+m$	...	$m*n$	...
z_2	...	0	1	2	...	n	...

shows that multiplication can obviously be defined according to the same pattern by the formula

$$\begin{aligned}F_{add} \equiv \exists z_1 \exists z_2 (z_1 = 0 \wedge z_2 = 0 \wedge &\\ \Box((z_2 = x_2 \rightarrow z_1 = x_3) \wedge &\\ (z_2 \neq x_2 \rightarrow \forall y_1 \forall y_2 (z_1 = y_1 \wedge z_2 = y_2 \rightarrow &\\ \bigcirc(F_{add}(y_1, x_1, z_1) \wedge &\\ z_2 = SUCC(y_2))))))).\end{aligned}$$

Actually, even 0 and $SUCC$ can be expressed (even by FOLTL formulas) which results in the fact that in FOLTL+q the natural numbers (with 0, $SUCC$, $+$, $*$) can be (uniquely) characterized in a language $\mathcal{L}^{\mathrm{q}}_{\mathrm{FOLTL}}(TSIG)$ where $TSIG$ is based on the "empty" signature $SIG = (\{NAT\}, \emptyset, \emptyset)$.

In applications mainly pursued in this book, this result is only a side remark and quantification over flexible (individual or propositional) variables does not play an important role in the form described here. However, we will come back to it in a modified version in Sect. 9.5 where it will turn out to be a very useful tool.

Bibliographical Notes

From the very beginning, temporal logic was also given in first-order versions and attempts were made for their axiomatizations, starting even with semi-formal systems in [78, 79]. A formal system analogous to Σ_{FOLTL} can be found in [99].

First-order temporal logic was proved incomplete in [141, 146]. The result was sharpened in [107]: FOLTL is decidable over a signature that contains no function symbols and only unary predicate symbols (and no equality); the addition of a single binary predicate symbol leads to incompleteness. Complete axiomatizations, either using ω-rules or via arithmetical completeness, were proposed in [1, 142, 143]. More recently, a decidable, so-called monodic fragment of first-order temporal logic was proposed [63].

Well-founded relations have been used in program verification for a long time. The first formulations of temporal proof principles embodying induction based on well-founded relations appear in [80, 97].

The use of flexible quantification for the specification of reactive systems in computer science was first proposed by Lamport [88] who also popularized the use of primed individual constants. The characterization of natural numbers in FOLTL+q is due to [81]. This result can be generalized to obtain precise specifications of inductive data types [91, 144]; cf. also the Second Reading paragraph of Sect. 6.1.

6

State Systems

Temporal logic languages as described in the preceding chapters provide general linguistic and deductive frameworks for *state systems* in the same manner as classical logics do for mathematical systems. The notion of state systems – or state-based systems – is used here not as a technical term but only informally, referring to "systems" which characteristically involve "states" and exhibit "behaviours" by "running" through sequences of such states. Many computer science systems such as software modules, transmission protocols, database systems, circuits, and computing machines are of this kind, and we could also call them *dynamic* or *imperative systems*, contrasting them with the more *static* or *functional* mathematical systems.

We represent state systems formally by (*state*) *transition systems* and address in this chapter their specification with temporal logic.

6.1 Temporal Theories and Models

Following the patterns of classical logic outlined in Sect. 1.3, the concrete temporal logic language for dealing with a particular state system is obtained by (choosing an appropriate language version and) fixing its linguistic parameters. In the case of a (possibly extended) propositional language $\mathcal{L}_{\mathrm{LTL}}(\mathbf{V})$ these parameters are the propositional constant of $\mathbf{V}$, and in a first-order language $\mathcal{L}_{\mathrm{FOLTL}}(TSIG)$ they are comprehended in the temporal signature $TSIG$.

Consider, e.g., the Towers of Hanoi system mentioned already in Sect. 2.1. An appropriate temporal logic language for this system could be some (possibly extended) $\mathcal{L}_{\mathrm{FOLTL}}(TSIG_{ToH})$ with

$$
\begin{aligned}
&TSIG_{ToH} = (SIG_{ToH}, \mathbf{X}, \emptyset),\\
&SIG_{ToH} = (\{STONE, PILE\}, \mathbf{F}, \{<^{(STONE\ STONE)}, DECR^{(PILE)}\}),\\
&\mathbf{F} = \{TOWER^{(\varepsilon, PILE)}, EMPTY^{(\varepsilon, PILE)},\\
&\qquad PUSH^{(PILE\ STONE, PILE)}, POP^{(PILE, PILE)}, TOP^{(PILE, STONE)}\},\\
&\mathbf{X} = \mathbf{X}_{PILE} = \{pl_1, pl_2, pl_3\}.
\end{aligned}
$$

The flexible individual constants pl_1, pl_2, pl_3 represent the three places. Their possible values during a sequence of moves are piles – represented by the sort $PILE$ – of stones of sort $STONE$. The "less than" symbol $<$ is taken for the size comparison of stones; $DECR$ stands for the property of piles to be decreasing in the size of the stones from bottom to top. $TOWER$ is for the pile which stands on one of the places at the beginning and has to be moved to another place, $EMPTY$ is for the empty pile, and $PUSH$, POP, and TOP stand for the obvious operations of placing a new stone on the top of a pile, taking away the top stone of a pile, and selecting a top stone, respectively. The latter operations are the same as the usual operations of a stack.

These informal interpretations are formalized by giving a structure H for the first-order signature SIG_{ToH}. Let n be the number of stones. Representing them by the natural numbers $1, 2, \ldots, n-1, n$ and piles by finite sequences of such numbers we could fix

$$\begin{aligned}
&|\mathsf{H}|_{STONE} = \{1, \ldots, n\}, \\
&|\mathsf{H}|_{PILE} = \{1, \ldots, n\}^*, \\
&TOWER^{\mathsf{H}} = (n, n-1, \ldots, 2, 1), \\
&EMPTY^{\mathsf{H}} = \varepsilon, \\
&PUSH^{\mathsf{H}} = push, \\
&POP^{\mathsf{H}} = pop, \\
&TOP^{\mathsf{H}} = top, \\
&<^{\mathsf{H}}(i, j) = \mathsf{tt} \Leftrightarrow i < j, \\
&DECR^{\mathsf{H}}(i_1, \ldots, i_m) = \mathsf{tt} \Leftrightarrow i_m < i_{m-1} < \ldots < i_1
\end{aligned}$$

where $\varepsilon \in \{1, \ldots, n\}^*$ is the empty sequence and $push$, pop, and top are defined as usual (as for a stack), e.g.,

$$push((i_1, \ldots, i_m), l) = (i_1, \ldots, i_m, l).$$

(Note that the symbol $<$ on the right-hand sides of the last two clauses denotes the usual "less than" relation on the natural numbers $1, \ldots, n$.)

Any first-order structure S for SIG_{ToH} (e.g., H) extends to a temporal structure $\mathsf{K} = (\mathsf{S}, \mathsf{W})$ for $TSIG_{ToH}$ with W being an infinite sequence $(\eta_0, \eta_1, \eta_2, \ldots)$ of mappings

$$\eta_i : \{pl_1, pl_2, pl_3\} \to \{1, \ldots, n\}^*.$$

Each η_i (being a state in the technical sense of the formal definitions) obviously formalizes the informal notion of "state of the puzzle" determined by what piles are standing on the three places. The sequence W represents a "run" of the system. (Note that these runs are infinite, i.e., we consider the system as "never ending". We do not pay regard at this moment to the proper goal of the puzzle and the fact that a run can be ended when this goal is reached. We will come back to this aspect later.)

Within $\mathcal{L}_{\text{FOLTL}}(TSIG_{ToH})$ we are able to formulate assertions about such runs. For example, the formulas

$$pl_i \neq EMPTY \wedge pl_j \neq EMPTY \wedge TOP(pl_i) < TOP(pl_j) \rightarrow$$
$$(pl_i' \neq EMPTY \rightarrow TOP(pl_i') \neq TOP(pl_j))$$

for $i, j \in \{1, 2, 3\}$, $i \neq j$, (using the priming notation introduced in Sect. 5.4) formalize the phrase

> "if the top stone ts on some (non-empty) place is bigger than the top stone on another (non-empty) place then in the next state ts cannot be the top stone (if this exists) on this latter place"

mentioned in the introduction of Sect. 2.1. The phrase

> "in all states, on each of the three places the stones will be piled up with decreasing size"

from there is formally described by

$$\Box(DECR(pl_1) \wedge DECR(pl_2) \wedge DECR(pl_3)).$$

Not every temporal structure $\mathsf{K} = (\mathsf{S}, \mathsf{W})$ for $TSIG_{ToH}$ is a proper interpretation of the Towers of Hanoi system: of course, the data component S has to be a "correct data type" for the stones and piles and, moreover, W has to represent a run according to the rules of the puzzle. The desired distinction, i.e., the *specification* of the system, is performed – as in classical logic theories – by particular non-logical axioms. Typically, one part of such axioms would deal with the data types involving no temporal aspects, e.g., axioms like

$DECR(TOWER)$,
$POP(PUSH(x, y)) = x$,
etc.

which can be formulated in classical FOL. The second part of the axioms should distinguish the possible state sequences W and really use the proper temporal logic means.

Before we treat this in more detail, let us first generalize the discussion. We write $\mathcal{L}_{\mathrm{TL}}$ for any language $\mathcal{L}_{\mathrm{FOLTL}}$ with or without one or more of the extensions discussed in the preceding chapters. If not stated differently, we always assume $\mathcal{L}_{\mathrm{TL}}$ to be equipped with normal semantics. Theorems, logical laws, etc. which hold for all the respective logics (or for particular ones in restricted contexts) will freely be used as required.

Definition. An *FOLTL-theory* $Th = (\mathcal{L}_{\mathrm{TL}}(TSIG), \mathcal{A})$ is given by a language $\mathcal{L}_{\mathrm{TL}}(TSIG)$ and a set $\mathcal{A}$ of formulas of $\mathcal{L}_{\mathrm{TL}}(TSIG)$ called *non-logical axioms*. A temporal structure K for $TSIG$ is called a *model* of Th if every formula of $\mathcal{A}$ is valid in K.

If $\mathcal{C}$ is a class of temporal structures for some $TSIG$ (such as H together with "all possible runs" in the Towers of Hanoi example) then we are interested in a specification of this class (making up the state system in question), i.e., in a theory $Th = (\mathcal{L}_{\mathrm{TL}}(TSIG), \mathcal{A})$ such that every temporal structure of $\mathcal{C}$ is a model of Th. Such a theory is called a *$\mathcal{C}$-FOLTL-theory*.

Example. Let $TSIG = (SIG_{Nat}, \{a\}, \emptyset)$ and $\mathcal{C} = \{\mathsf{K}_1, \mathsf{K}_2\}$ with

$$\mathsf{K}_1 = (\mathsf{N}, \mathsf{W}_1 = (\eta_0^{(1)}, \eta_1^{(1)}, \eta_2^{(1)}, \ldots)),\ \eta_j^{(1)}(a) = 2 * j \ \text{ for every } j \in \mathbb{N},$$
$$\mathsf{K}_2 = (\mathsf{N}, \mathsf{W}_2 = (\eta_0^{(2)}, \eta_1^{(2)}, \eta_2^{(2)}, \ldots)),\ \eta_j^{(2)}(a) = 2 * j + 1 \ \text{ for every } j \in \mathbb{N}.$$

Informally, W_1 and W_2 look like

	$\eta_0^{(1)}$	$\eta_1^{(1)}$	$\eta_2^{(1)}$	$\eta_3^{(1)}$	...
a	0	2	4	6	...

and

	$\eta_0^{(2)}$	$\eta_1^{(2)}$	$\eta_2^{(2)}$	$\eta_3^{(2)}$	...
a	1	3	5	7	...

i.e., a runs through all even or odd numbers, respectively. An appropriate $\mathcal{C}$-FOLTL-theory could take a language $\mathcal{L}^{\mathsf{i}}_{\mathrm{FOLTL}}(TSIG)$ and contain the following non-logical axioms:

- Axioms for N,
- $\textbf{init} \rightarrow a = 0 \lor a = 1$,
- $\Box(a' = a + 2)$.

The axioms for N are left open at the moment, we will come back to this issue more generally in the subsequent section. The two latter axioms describe the state sequences W_1 and W_2. It is obvious that K_1 and K_2 are models of this theory. △

As discussed in Sect. 1.3, axioms of first-order theories may contain free variables or – equivalently – one can take their universal closures instead, providing closed formulas as axioms. It is obvious that the same holds for axioms in FOLTL-theories, but even more, there is a direct analogy to this concerning temporal closures. For every formula A and every temporal structure K, we have

$$\models_{\mathsf{K}} A \ \Leftrightarrow\ \models_{\mathsf{K}} \Box A$$

by Theorem 2.1.3 and (T4) and this means that A and its temporal closure $\Box A$ are valid in the same temporal structures. So axioms may always be given in one of the two forms A or $\Box A$.

In the example above, the axiom in the second line could be given as

$$\Box(\textbf{init} \rightarrow a = 0 \lor a = 1).$$

The last axiom is the temporal closure of

$$a' = a + 2$$

which could be taken itself as an axiom. Subsequently, when writing axioms, we will throughout prefer the "non-closed" formulation.

The relationship between A and $\Box A$ discussed here may be put into a more general setting indicated already in Sect. 4.1. We say that two formulas A and B of the underlying language $\mathcal{L}_{\mathrm{TL}}(TSIG)$ are *model equivalent*, written

$$A \simeq B,$$

if

$$\models_{\mathsf{K}} A \Leftrightarrow \models_{\mathsf{K}} B$$

holds for every temporal structure K for $TSIG$, which means that A and B are valid in the same temporal structures and is obviously the same as saying that

$$A \models B \text{ and } B \models A.$$

So, if we replace an axiom A of a theory Th by a formula B with $A \simeq B$ then the resulting theory has the same models as Th.

Model equivalence is a slight generalization of logical equivalence. It is obvious that it is an equivalence relation and that logically equivalent formulas are model equivalent. The case of A and $\Box A$ shows that the converse does not necessarily hold. Moreover, the model equivalence of the latter two formulas is just a special case of the more general fact that for formulas A and B to be model equivalent it suffices that $\Box A$ and $\Box B$ are logically equivalent. This is easy to see by applying (T4), Theorem 2.1.2, and the "if" part of Theorem 2.1.6:

$$\begin{aligned} \models \Box A \leftrightarrow \Box B \ &\Rightarrow\ \models \Box A \rightarrow \Box B \text{ and } \models \Box B \rightarrow \Box A \\ &\Rightarrow\ A \models \Box B \text{ and } B \models \Box A \\ &\Rightarrow\ A \models B \text{ and } B \models A. \end{aligned}$$

(It should be noted that if we take $\mathcal{L}_{\mathrm{TL}}$ with initial validity semantics then the two notions of model and logical equivalence are the same (for closed formulas). On the other hand, if some A is to hold in every state of a temporal structure we then have to express this by $\Box A$. Another formula $\Box B$ (A and B closed) expresses the same if and only if $\Box A$ and $\Box B$ are logically equivalent.)

FOLTL-theories are *first-order temporal theories*. Of course, we can carry the definition over to the propositional case: an *LTL-theory* $Th = (\mathcal{L}_{\mathrm{TL}}(\mathbf{V}), \mathcal{A})$ is given by a language $\mathcal{L}_{\mathrm{TL}}(\mathbf{V})$ (denoting some possibly extended $\mathcal{L}_{\mathrm{LTL}}(\mathbf{V})$) and a set $\mathcal{A}$ of formulas of $\mathcal{L}_{\mathrm{TL}}(\mathbf{V})$ as non-logical axioms. A *model* of Th is a temporal structure for $\mathbf{V}$ in which all formulas of $\mathcal{A}$ are valid. A *$\mathcal{C}$-LTL-theory* for a class $\mathcal{C}$ of temporal structures for $\mathbf{V}$ is a theory which has all elements of $\mathcal{C}$ as models. Such *propositional temporal theories* are of great interest in computer science since they are tractable by algorithmic means. They arise by encoding "appropriate" first-order theories (cf. Sect. 1.3 for a first hint and Sect. 11.1) or even "directly" by the state system under investigation.

A typical example for the latter case is given by circuits. Consider the simple synchronous circuit in Fig. 6.1 which continuously oscillates between a 3-bit binary

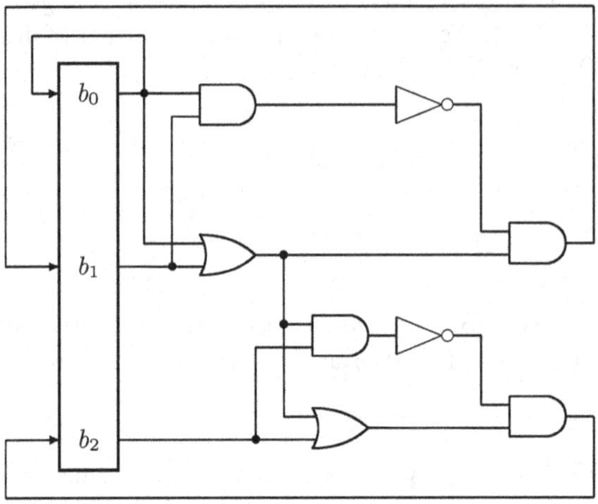

Fig. 6.1. An oscillator circuit

number and its two's complement. The "circuit variables" b_0, b_1, b_2 (representing the binary number $b_2 b_1 b_0$) are boolean valued, so an appropriate temporal logic language for this system is some $\mathcal{L}_{\mathrm{LTL}}(\mathbf{V})$ with $\mathbf{V} = \{b_0, b_1, b_2\}$.

A specification of the circuit (more precisely: a $\mathcal{C}$-LTL-theory for the class $\mathcal{C}$ of the temporal structures for $\mathbf{V}$ representing all possible runs of the circuit) is given by the non-logical axioms

- $b_0' \leftrightarrow b_0$,
- $b_1' \leftrightarrow (b_0 \vee b_1) \wedge \neg(b_0 \wedge b_1)$,
- $b_2' \leftrightarrow (b_0 \vee b_1 \vee b_2) \wedge \neg((b_0 \vee b_1) \wedge b_2)$

which describe the change of b_0, b_1, b_2 in "one step" and may be shortened to

- $b_0' \leftrightarrow b_0$,
- $b_1' \leftrightarrow \neg(b_0 \leftrightarrow b_1)$,
- $b_2' \leftrightarrow \neg(b_0 \vee b_1 \leftrightarrow b_2)$.

Of course, the above definition and the meaning of model equivalence of formulas can be literally transferred to the propositional case.

Second Reading

The intention of the usage of temporal logic is to specify state systems and the basic formal notion for this is that of an (FOLTL- or LTL-) theory: the non-logical axioms describe the "behaviour" of the system, formally given by the state sequences of temporal structures K. If FOLTL is to be applied then $\mathsf{K} = (\mathsf{S}, \mathsf{W})$, and the data component S of K describes the underlying data type of the system, the specification of which is the typical realm of classical logic as sketched out in Sect. 1.3.

In Sects. 5.3 and 5.6 we have indicated by means of the natural numbers that temporal logic could be used for such data type specifications as well (possibly achieving results which cannot be obtained by classical logic specifications). In fact, the considerations carried out there precisely fit into the concept of FOLTL-theories. For example, the set $\mathcal{A}_{\mathsf{N}}$ consisting of the formulas P_1–P_8 given in Sect. 5.3 constitute, together with an appropriate language $\mathcal{L}_{\mathrm{FOLTL}}$, an FOLTL-theory $Th_{\mathsf{N}} = (\mathcal{L}_{\mathrm{FOLTL}}, \mathcal{A}_{\mathsf{N}})$. According to the results of Sect. 5.3, Th_{N} specifies the standard model N of natural numbers in the sense that there exists a model (N, W) of Th_{N}, and even more: for any model $(\mathsf{S}, \mathsf{W}')$ of Th_{N}, S and N are "isomorphic".

So, while the FOLTL-specification of state systems mainly intends to describe the components W of models $\mathsf{K} = (\mathsf{S}, \mathsf{W})$, temporal logic specifications of data types would allow us also to address the data component S. For example, in the "even and odd number" system in the above main text the axioms for N could be given just by the formulas P_1–P_8.

The general notions for this approach are easy to define in the framework of this section. Let $TSIG = (SIG, \mathbf{X}, \mathbf{V})$ be a temporal signature, S be a structure for SIG, and Th be an FOLTL-theory. S is called a *model structure* of Th if there exists a model of Th which has S as its data component. (Observe that this definition includes the classical specifications of Sect. 1.3 since the non-logical axioms of Th could be only non-temporal formulas.)

Let us illustrate this method by a further example. In Sect. 1.3 we have specified stacks within classical FOL by the axioms

$$PUSH(x,y) \neq EMPTY,$$
$$POP(PUSH(x,y)) = x,$$
$$TOP(PUSH(x,y)) = y$$

formulated in a language $\mathcal{L}_{\mathrm{FOL}}(SIG_{st})$ where SIG_{st} contains the sorts OBJ and $STACK$. As with natural numbers, this specification has "non-standard" models. Using temporal logic, it is possible to specify stacks uniquely (up to isomorphism). Actually, there are several approaches to achieve this. One simple way is to choose the temporal signature $TSIG_{st}(SIG_{st}, \emptyset, \emptyset)$ and a language $\mathcal{L}^{\mathrm{q}}_{\mathrm{FOLTL}}(TSIG_{st})$ of the logic FOLTL+q with flexible quantification. Let then Th_{st} be the FOLTL-theory with the three axioms above and the additional axiom

$$\exists z(z = EMPTY \land \Diamond(z = x) \land (z \neq x \rightarrow \exists y(z' = PUSH(z,y))))$$

(where $z \in \mathcal{X}^{fl}_{STACK}$, $x \in \mathcal{X}_{STACK}$, $y \in \mathcal{X}_{OBJ}$ and the priming notation of Sect. 5.4 is extended to flexible variables in an obvious way). The "standard model" S of stacks (where elements of $|\mathsf{S}|_{STACK}$ are finite sequences of elements of $|\mathsf{S}|_{OBJ}$) is a model structure of Th_{st} and, in fact, all other model structures of Th_{st} are isomorphic to it. The idea of the additional axiom is quite simple: it says that every stack x is "generated" by subsequently "pushing" some finitely many elements from $|\mathsf{S}|_{OBJ}$ to the "empty stack".

6.2 State Transition Systems

The discussions in the previous section indicate a first main application area for temporal logic in computer science: the specification of state systems by temporal theories for (mainly) the class of all runs of such systems. A (possibly informally given) state system is formally described by such a specification. For a systematic approach to this application (and for applying particular techniques, cf. Chap. 11) it is helpful to represent state systems – besides the "descriptive" definitions through specifications (and other possible formal representations like the circuit example in the previous section) – also in a separate uniform formal way.

A very general and powerful concept for formally representing state systems is that of a (*state*) *transition system* which, roughly speaking, is a "generating mechanism" for the runs of a state system. Transition systems are used widely and in various different versions. We adjust the definition here in a way such that their relationship to temporal logic specifications becomes very close.

Definition. Let $SIG = (\mathbf{S}, \mathbf{F}, \mathbf{P})$ be a signature and S a structure for SIG. A *first-order* (*state*) *transition system* (briefly: STS) $\Gamma = (X, V, W, T)$ over SIG and S is given by

- $X = \bigcup_{s \in \mathbf{S}} X_s$ with sets X_s for every $s \in \mathbf{S}$,
- a set V,
- a set W of (*system*) *states*

$$\eta : X \cup V \to |\mathsf{S}| \cup \{\mathsf{ff}, \mathsf{tt}\}$$

  with $\eta(a) \in |\mathsf{S}|_s$ for $a \in X_s$, $s \in \mathbf{S}$ and $\eta(v) \in \{\mathsf{ff}, \mathsf{tt}\}$ for $v \in V$,
- a total binary relation $T \subseteq W \times W$, called *transition relation*.

(A binary relation R over some set $\mathbb{D}$ is called *total* if for every $d_1 \in \mathbb{D}$ there is a $d_2 \in \mathbb{D}$ with $(d_1, d_2) \in R$.) Elements of X and V are called (*individual* or *propositional*, respectively) *system* (or *state*) *variables*. An *execution sequence* of Γ is an infinite sequence $\mathsf{W} = (\eta_0, \eta_1, \eta_2, \ldots)$ of system states such that $(\eta_i, \eta_{i+1}) \in T$ for every $i \in \mathbb{N}$. For any $(\eta, \eta') \in T$, η' is called a *successor state* of η.

To indicate the basis of an STS Γ we will also write $\Gamma(SIG, \mathsf{S})$. Furthermore, we will often write $SIG_\Gamma, \mathbf{S}_\Gamma, \mathbf{F}_\Gamma, \mathbf{P}_\Gamma, \mathsf{S}_\Gamma, X_\Gamma, V_\Gamma, W_\Gamma, T_\Gamma, \mathsf{W}_\Gamma$ for the single constituents of a given $\Gamma(SIG, \mathsf{S})$ and depict an execution sequence $(\eta_0, \eta_1, \eta_2, \ldots)$ by

$$\eta_0 \longrightarrow \eta_1 \longrightarrow \eta_2 \longrightarrow \ldots.$$

Basing Γ on a signature and a structure informally means that Γ uses a fixed underlying data type. Notice, however, that in the definition of an STS Γ the sets $\mathbf{F}_\Gamma$ and $\mathbf{P}_\Gamma$ of SIG_Γ and the interpretations of their elements in S_Γ are not (yet) relevant. They will come into play subsequently and are included already here in order to provide a common framework. One first trivial outcome can be noted immediately: following patterns given in Sect. 5.1, the signature SIG_Γ induces a (classical) first-order language $\mathcal{L}_{\mathrm{FOL}}(SIG^+)$ where SIG^+ results from SIG_Γ by adding the elements of X and V to the individual and propositional constants, respectively. In order to meet our general assumption about countable languages in this definition we will assume throughout that the sets X and V are at most denumerable. (Actually, in applications X and V will usually even be finite, but we leave it with the more general assumption in order to maintain the close correspondence to the logical framework. This will particularly be used in the subsequent Theorem 6.2.1.)

We call $\mathcal{L}_{\mathrm{FOL}}(SIG^+)$ a *first-order language of* Γ and denote it by $\mathcal{L}_\Gamma$. Formulas of $\mathcal{L}_\Gamma$ are called *state formulas* (of Γ). Given a variable valuation ξ for the variables of $\mathcal{L}_\Gamma$, the structure S_Γ together with ξ and any state $\eta \in W_\Gamma$ defines a mapping $\mathsf{S}_\Gamma^{(\xi,\eta)}$ which associates a truth value $\mathsf{S}_\Gamma^{(\xi,\eta)}(A) \in \{\mathsf{ff}, \mathsf{tt}\}$ with every atomic formula A of $\mathcal{L}_\Gamma$ as in Sect. 5.1. As usual (cf. Sect. 1.2), $\mathsf{S}_\Gamma^{(\xi,\eta)}$ can be extended to all state formulas of $\mathcal{L}_\Gamma$. If A is a closed formula then $\mathsf{S}_\Gamma^{(\xi,\eta)}(A)$ does not depend on ξ and we will sometimes write $\mathsf{S}_\Gamma^{(\eta)}(A)$ instead.

An STS is called first-order in our definition because of the set X of individual system variables ranging over arbitrary sorts. If $X = \emptyset$ then the STS is called *propositional*. In this case, of course, SIG and S are completely irrelevant and can be omitted from the definition. We will also write $\Gamma(V)$ for a propositional STS Γ to indicate the underlying set V of state variables. For $\Gamma(V)$ the language $\mathcal{L}_\Gamma$ reduces to a language $\mathcal{L}_{\mathrm{PL}}(V)$ of (classical) propositional logic in an obvious way.

An STS Γ represents a state system in a formal way, the execution sequences of Γ are the runs of the state system. As a first simple example consider a natural number counter which can be switched on and off. As long as it is on its value increases by 1 in each step. Switching it off "freezes" the value which then remains unchanged until it is switched on again in which case the value is reset to 0. This informal description is formalized by the STS $\Gamma_{count}(SIG_{Nat}, \mathsf{N})$ consisting of

$$
\begin{aligned}
&X = X_{NAT} = \{c\},\\
&V = \{on\},\\
&W = \{\eta : X \cup V \to \mathbb{N} \cup \{\mathsf{ff}, \mathsf{tt}\} \mid \eta(c) \in \mathbb{N}, \eta(on) \in \{\mathsf{ff}, \mathsf{tt}\}\},\\
&T = \{([\mathsf{tt}, n], [\mathsf{tt}, n+1]), ([\mathsf{tt}, n], [\mathsf{ff}, n]), ([\mathsf{ff}, n], [\mathsf{ff}, n]), ([\mathsf{ff}, n], [\mathsf{tt}, 0]) \mid n \in \mathbb{N}\}
\end{aligned}
$$

where we represent in T a state η by the pair $[\eta(on), \eta(c)]$ so that, e.g., $[\mathsf{tt}, n]$ denotes the state η with $\eta(on) = \mathsf{tt}$ and $\eta(c) = n$. W comprises all possible values of c and on, and the four kinds of pairs of states (for every $n \in \mathbb{N}$) listed in T describe all possible *transitions* (one-step changes) of the system variables on and c: counting, switching off, pausing, and switching on, respectively. A possible execution sequence of Γ_{count} is

$$[\mathsf{ff}, 7] \longrightarrow [\mathsf{tt}, 0] \longrightarrow [\mathsf{tt}, 1] \longrightarrow [\mathsf{tt}, 2] \longrightarrow [\mathsf{tt}, 3] \longrightarrow [\mathsf{ff}, 3] \longrightarrow [\mathsf{ff}, 3] \longrightarrow \ldots$$

expressing that the counter starts switched off and with value 7, is switched on, counts up to 3, is switched off, remains off, and so on.

By definition, execution sequences of STSs are infinite (and for generating them, transition relations are total). In fact, many real systems, often called *reactive systems*, are intended for "running forever" ("reacting" with the environment). Other systems (usually calculating some input-output relation and called *transformational systems*) like the Towers of Hanoi, for which we indicated this discussion already in Sect. 6.1, are intended to *terminate*. They provide finite runs and seem, at a first glance, not to be covered by our formalization. However, such systems may be "encoded" very easily in the given framework: a finite run terminating with some state

η is represented by the infinite one which is obtained by repeating η forever when it is reached.

Consider, as a simple example, a modified counter Γ_{tcount} which terminates whenever it reaches some value, say, 100. (If it never reaches this value it still runs forever.) Reasonably, the states η are then restricted to those with $\eta(c) \leq 100$. A finite run could (informally) look like, e.g.,

$$[\mathsf{ff}, 32] \longrightarrow [\mathsf{tt}, 0] \longrightarrow [\mathsf{tt}, 1] \longrightarrow \ldots \longrightarrow [\mathsf{tt}, 99] \longrightarrow [\mathsf{tt}, 100]$$

where the counter, after being switched on, counts from 0 to 100 and then terminates. Such runs are generated by the (non-total) transition relation

$$\begin{aligned} T' = \{&([\mathsf{tt}, n], [\mathsf{tt}, n+1]), ([\mathsf{tt}, n], [\mathsf{ff}, n]), \\ &([\mathsf{ff}, n], [\mathsf{ff}, n]), ([\mathsf{ff}, n], [\mathsf{tt}, 0]) \mid n \in \mathbb{N}, n \leq 99\}. \end{aligned}$$

In order to cause infinite repetitions of the state in which the counter value 100 is reached, T' has to be enriched by the pair $([\mathsf{tt}, 100], [\mathsf{tt}, 100])$, and in order to make T' total, $([\mathsf{ff}, 100], [\mathsf{ff}, 100])$ has to be added as well. For subsequent, more general use we define the *total closure* $tot(R)$ of a binary relation R over a set $\mathbb{D}$ by

$$tot(R) = R \cup \{(d, d) \in \mathbb{D} \times \mathbb{D} \mid \text{there is no } d' \in \mathbb{D} \text{ such that } (d, d') \in R\}.$$

Then

$$\begin{aligned} W_{\Gamma_{tcount}} &= \{\eta \in W_{\Gamma_{count}} \mid \eta(c) \leq 100\}, \\ T_{\Gamma_{tcount}} &= tot(T') \end{aligned}$$

(with X and V as in Γ_{count}) obviously define Γ_{tcount} in the desired way. The above sample run is formally represented by the execution sequence

$$\begin{aligned} &[\mathsf{ff}, 32] \longrightarrow [\mathsf{tt}, 0] \longrightarrow [\mathsf{tt}, 1] \longrightarrow \ldots \longrightarrow \\ &\qquad [\mathsf{tt}, 99] \longrightarrow [\mathsf{tt}, 100] \longrightarrow [\mathsf{tt}, 100] \longrightarrow [\mathsf{tt}, 100] \longrightarrow \ldots \end{aligned}$$

generated by $T_{\Gamma_{tcount}}$.

It should be clear that the examples of Sect. 6.1 can also be formulated as STSs. While the Towers of Hanoi and the system with the even and odd number sequences have additional properties which will be addressed in the next section, the oscillator circuit can be reasonably represented in the uniform STS framework and according to the present definitions by a propositional STS $\Gamma_{osc}(V)$, $V = \{b_0, b_1, b_2\}$, with

$$W = \{\eta : V \to \{\mathsf{ff}, \mathsf{tt}\}\}$$

and

$$\begin{aligned} T = \{(\eta, \eta') \in W \times W \mid \\ &\eta'(b_0) = \eta(b_0), \\ &\eta'(b_1) = \mathsf{tt} \Leftrightarrow \eta(b_0) \neq \eta(b_1), \\ &\eta'(b_2) = \mathsf{tt} \Leftrightarrow \eta(b_2) = \mathsf{tt} \text{ if and only if } \eta(b_0) = \eta(b_1) = \mathsf{ff}\}. \end{aligned}$$

A possible execution sequence of Γ_{osc} is

$$011 \longrightarrow 101 \longrightarrow 011 \longrightarrow 101 \longrightarrow 011 \longrightarrow \ldots$$

where, with regard to the concrete background, we represent states by binary numbers: e.g., the entry 011 for η_0 means $\eta_0(b_0) = \mathsf{tt}$, $\eta_0(b_1) = \mathsf{tt}$, $\eta_0(b_2) = \mathsf{ff}$.

In preceding sections we have stressed several times a certain contrast between state systems and mathematical systems which are just data types in a functional setting. However, data types in computer science can be viewed and handled both in a functional and in an imperative way. In fact, the counters above are simple data types which could also be viewed (and algebraically specified) in a functional framework. The other way round, consider, e.g., the algebraic stack specification in Sect. 1.3 given by the (classical) first-order theory *Stack* with the characteristic signature SIG_{st}. Taking this data type in an imperative view as a "pushdown storing device" the "contents" of which may "change in time" by executing the typical stack operations we obtain a state system.

An STS Γ_{st} describing a stack in such a way is based on the signature SIG_{st} and some structure for SIG_{st}. To make it concrete here, let this structure U be given by

$$\begin{aligned}
&|\mathsf{U}|_{OBJ} = \mathbb{N},\\
&|\mathsf{U}|_{STACK} = \mathbb{N}^*,\\
&EMPTY^{\mathsf{U}} = \varepsilon,\\
&PUSH^{\mathsf{U}} = push,\\
&POP^{\mathsf{U}} = pop,\\
&TOP^{\mathsf{U}} = top,
\end{aligned}$$

where $\varepsilon \in \mathbb{N}^*$ is the empty sequence of natural numbers and *push*, *pop*, *top* are the usual stack operations on $\mathbb{N}^*$. Then we let $\Gamma_{st}(SIG_{st}, \mathsf{U})$ consist of

$$\begin{aligned}
&X = X_{STACK} = \{pd\},\\
&V = \emptyset,\\
&W = \{\eta : X \to \mathbb{N}^*\},\\
&T = \{(\eta, \eta') \in W \times W \mid \eta'(pd) = push(\eta(pd), m), m \in \mathbb{N}\} \cup\\
&\qquad \{(\eta, \eta') \in W \times W \mid \eta'(pd) \neq \varepsilon \text{ and } \eta'(pd) = pop(\eta(pd))\}.
\end{aligned}$$

The system variable *pd* represents the pushdown store which carries stacks of natural numbers as its value. The states of W map all such values to *pd*. T comprises all possible transitions: in a single step, some natural number m can be "pushed" on *pd*, or *pd* can be "popped".

An example of an execution sequence of Γ_{st} is

$$(7, 13) \longrightarrow (7, 13, 5) \longrightarrow (7, 13, 5, 21) \longrightarrow (7, 13, 5) \longrightarrow \ldots$$

where states are represented by their values of *pd*. In the initial state *pd* contains the numbers 7 and 13, then 5 and after that 21 are pushed to *pd*, then *pd* is popped, and so on.

As indicated already, the definition of STSs perfectly fits the temporal logic notions. Let $\Gamma = (X, V, W, T)$ be an STS over some *SIG* and S. A language $\mathcal{L}_{\mathrm{TL}}(TSIG_\Gamma)$ where $TSIG_\Gamma = (SIG, X, V)$ and $\mathcal{L}_{\mathrm{TL}}$ denotes a language as introduced in Sect. 6.1 is called *language of linear temporal logic of* Γ and denoted by $\mathcal{L}_{\mathrm{TL}\Gamma}$. Thus, $\mathcal{L}_{\mathrm{TL}\Gamma}$ takes over the signature *SIG* from Γ and identifies the flexible individual and propositional constants with the individual and propositional system variables from X and V, respectively. Clearly, the state formulas of Γ are just the non-temporal formulas of $\mathcal{L}_{\mathrm{TL}\Gamma}$.

It is obvious that, for every execution sequence W_Γ of Γ, $\mathsf{K} = (\mathsf{S}_\Gamma, \mathsf{W}_\Gamma)$ is a temporal structure for $TSIG_\Gamma$: S_Γ is a structure for the underlying *SIG* and W_Γ is just an infinite sequence of states in the sense of the semantical definitions in Sect. 5.1. The class

$$\mathcal{C}_\Gamma = \{\mathsf{K} = (\mathsf{S}_\Gamma, \mathsf{W}_\Gamma) \mid \mathsf{W}_\Gamma \text{ is an execution sequence of } \Gamma\}$$

then represents "all possible runs" of the state system formalized by Γ. Note that in $\mathcal{C}_\Gamma$, as in Γ itself, S_Γ is fixed.

As mentioned already, any state formula A of Γ can be evaluated by S_Γ, a variable valuation ξ, and $\eta \in W_\Gamma$ (denoted by $\mathsf{S}_\Gamma^{(\xi,\eta)}(A)$). So, if $\mathsf{K} \in \mathcal{C}_\Gamma$, this evaluation is possible for a state η_i of W_Γ and obviously coincides with evaluating "in K", i.e.,

$$\mathsf{K}_i^{(\xi)}(A) = \mathsf{S}_\Gamma^{(\xi,\eta_i)}(A)$$

holds for every ξ.

Definition. Let Γ be an STS. A formula A of $\mathcal{L}_{\mathrm{TL}\Gamma}$ is called Γ*-valid* (denoted by $\vDash_\Gamma A$) if A is valid in every $\mathsf{K} \in \mathcal{C}_\Gamma$.

Of course, all these notions can be transferred to the case that Γ is propositional. Then $\mathcal{L}_{\mathrm{TL}\Gamma}$ reduces to some $\mathcal{L}_{\mathrm{LTL}}(V)$ taking the system variables of Γ as the propositional constants of the language, $\mathcal{L}_\Gamma$ is the "sublanguage" of $\mathcal{L}_{\mathrm{TL}\Gamma}$ without temporal operators, every W_Γ is a temporal structure for V, and $\mathcal{C}_\Gamma$ is just the class of all such W_Γ.

A $\mathcal{C}_\Gamma$-FOLTL-theory (or $\mathcal{C}_\Gamma$-LTL-theory in the case of a propositional Γ) will be briefly called a Γ*-theory* and denoted by $Th(\Gamma) = (\mathcal{L}_{\mathrm{TL}\Gamma}, \mathcal{A}_\Gamma)$. As mentioned already, it can be understood as a *temporal logic specification* of (the state system represented by) Γ.

If we want to specify a state system given by an STS Γ in this sense we have to find an adequate language version $\mathcal{L}_{\mathrm{TL}\Gamma}$ and, more essential, appropriate non-logical axioms. We remark again (cf. Sect. 1.3) that a Γ-theory does not necessarily "characterize" Γ. The only requirement for $\mathcal{A}_\Gamma$ is that its formulas are Γ-valid, so even $\mathcal{A}_\Gamma = \emptyset$ would be a sound choice. It is clear, however, that we should try to make $\mathcal{A}_\Gamma$ as "powerful" and "close to distinguish" the system Γ as possible.

Looking for appropriate axioms, a first observation is that $\mathcal{A}_\Gamma$ should contain axioms for the data involved in Γ through the structure S_Γ (provided Γ is not propositional). Since the specification of (functional) data types is not the subject of this book and we therefore do not care (except for some remarks already made) about how this is possible, we help ourselves by simply taking every state formula of Γ which is S_Γ-valid as an axiom of $\mathcal{A}_\Gamma$ without any regard to how this formula could really be derived. So, any $\mathcal{A}_\Gamma$ will contain the axioms

(data$_\Gamma$) All S_Γ-valid state formulas of Γ

and we will freely use these axioms without explicitly justifying them. For example, if $\mathsf{S}_\Gamma = \mathsf{N}$ as in the counters above then (data$_\Gamma$) contains formulas like

$$x_1 + x_2 = x_2 + x_1,$$
$$x_1 * (x_2 + x_3) = x_1 * x_2 + x_1 * x_3,$$
etc.

Clearly, in the case of a propositional STS there is no need of such axioms.

The axioms in the proper focus of our investigations are those which specify the execution sequences W_Γ of Γ. We call them *temporal axioms* (of Γ), and they should reflect the sets W_Γ and T_Γ of states and transitions of Γ. We illustrate this for the four examples introduced in this section.

For the counter Γ_{count} the two obviously Γ_{count}-valid formulas

$$on \rightarrow (on' \wedge c' = c + 1) \vee (\neg on' \wedge c' = c),$$
$$\neg on \rightarrow (\neg on' \wedge c' = c) \vee (on' \wedge c' = 0)$$

could be taken as temporal axioms. They reflect the possible counting and switching off transitions if the counter is on and the possible pausing and switching on transitions if it is off.

For the terminating counter Γ_{tcount} these axioms can be easily modified and extended to

$$c \leq 100,$$
$$on \wedge c < 100 \rightarrow (on' \wedge c' = c + 1) \vee (\neg on' \wedge c' = c),$$
$$\neg on \wedge c < 100 \rightarrow (\neg on' \wedge c' = c) \vee (on' \wedge c' = 0),$$
$$c = 100 \rightarrow (on' \leftrightarrow on) \wedge c' = c.$$

Note that the first axiom reflects the restriction of the state set $W_{\Gamma_{tcount}}$.

Appropriate temporal axioms for the oscillator Γ_{osc} could be just the three formulas

$$b_0' \leftrightarrow b_0,$$
$$b_1' \leftrightarrow \neg(b_0 \leftrightarrow b_1),$$
$$b_2' \leftrightarrow \neg(b_0 \vee b_1 \leftrightarrow b_2)$$

already shown in Sect. 6.1. Their Γ_{osc}-validity is clear.

For the stack Γ_{st} a reasonable specification could be given by the single Γ_{st}-valid axiom

$$\exists y(pd' = PUSH(pd, y)) \vee (pd \neq EMPTY \wedge pd' = POP(pd))$$

describing the disjunction of the two possible kinds of transitions: pushing some y to pd or popping the (non-empty) pd.

Note that in the counter systems as well as in Γ_{st} the temporal axioms do not need all elements of the respective signatures. So for the exclusive use as a *specification language*, a less extensive signature would suffice for $\mathcal{L}_{\mathrm{TL}\Gamma}$. The full language, however, could be necessary for additional purposes such as the formal description of further "properties" (actually pursued in the following chapters). Instead of basing transition systems and their specification on a "minimal" signature which will then have to be enriched for other applications, we always will assume for simplicity that the signatures SIG_Γ are suitable for all intended investigations of Γ.

We conclude this section with a general discussion about the concept of transition systems. In fact, these could directly serve as the basic semantical vehicle for temporal logic insofar as the validity notions could be equivalently based on them instead of using the concept of temporal structures developed in our approach in the preceding chapters. To put this formally, consider a temporal signature $TSIG = (SIG, \mathbf{X}, \mathbf{V})$ and a language $\mathcal{L}_{\mathrm{TL}}(TSIG)$ of first-order linear temporal logic. We call any STS $\Gamma = (\mathbf{X}, \mathbf{V}, W, T)$ over SIG and some structure S for SIG (which takes $\mathbf{X}$ and $\mathbf{V}$ as its sets of individual and propositional system variables) a $TSIG$-STS. For every such STS, the language $\mathcal{L}_{\mathrm{TL}\Gamma}$ obviously coincides with $\mathcal{L}_{\mathrm{TL}}(TSIG)$ and every $\mathsf{K} \in \mathcal{C}_\Gamma$ is a temporal structure for $TSIG$.

Theorem 6.2.1. *Let $TSIG = (SIG, \mathbf{X}, \mathbf{V})$ be a temporal signature. A formula A of $\mathcal{L}_{\mathrm{TL}}(TSIG)$ is valid if and only if A, viewed as a formula of $\mathcal{L}_{\mathrm{TL}\Gamma}$, is Γ-valid for every $TSIG$-STS Γ.*

Proof. Let A be valid and Γ be a $TSIG$-STS. Then $\models_{\mathsf{K}} A$ for every temporal structure $\mathsf{K} = (\mathsf{S}, \mathsf{W})$ for $TSIG$; hence $\models_{\mathsf{K}} A$ for every $\mathsf{K} \in \mathcal{C}_\Gamma$ which means that A is Γ-valid. Let, conversely, A be Γ-valid for every $TSIG$-STS Γ and $\mathsf{K} = (\mathsf{S}, \mathsf{W})$ be a temporal structure for $TSIG$. We have to show that $\models_{\mathsf{K}} A$. To this end, we define the $TSIG$-STS $\Gamma^* = (\mathbf{X}, \mathbf{V}, W, T)$ over SIG and S with W being the set of all possible states (with respect to $\mathbf{X}$ and $\mathbf{V}$) and $T = W \times W$. Then $\mathsf{K} \in \mathcal{C}_{\Gamma^*}$ since W is obviously an execution sequence of Γ^*. From the assumption we get $\models_{\Gamma^*} A$ which means $\models_{\mathsf{K}^*} A$ for every $\mathsf{K}^* \in \mathcal{C}_{\Gamma^*}$ and implies $\models_{\mathsf{K}} A$. △

According to this theorem, validity of formulas of $\mathcal{L}_{\mathrm{TL}}(TSIG)$ (defined with respect to all possible temporal structures) is equivalent to Γ-validity for all STSs with fixed X, V, SIG taken from $TSIG$. Moreover, the proof shows that this could also be modified to the assertion that validity is equivalent to Γ^*-validity for all STSs Γ^* as defined in the proof (with "full" state set and transition relation and ranging over all structures S for SIG). In fact, $T = W \times W$ generates all possible state sequences W for temporal structures. Note that every Γ^* is specified only by $(\mathrm{data}_{\Gamma^*})$ but no temporal axioms.

Of course, Theorem 6.2.1 can be transferred to the propositional case in an obvious way: a formula A of some propositional temporal logic language $\mathcal{L}_{\mathrm{TL}}(\mathbf{V})$ is valid if and only if A is Γ-valid for every propositional STS $\Gamma = (\emptyset, \mathbf{V}, W, T)$ or, alternatively, if and only if A is Γ^*-valid for $\Gamma^* = (\emptyset, \mathbf{V}, W, T)$ where W is the set of all states $\eta : \mathbf{V} \to \{\mathsf{ff}, \mathsf{tt}\}$ and $T = W \times W$.

6.3 Rooted Transition Systems

Transition systems as defined in the previous section are our basic representations of state systems. In the following we investigate some variants and extensions of STSs which will enable us to model typical additional features of state systems.

A first very simple extension can be motivated by the Towers of Hanoi example. An execution sequence of an STS so far can start with an arbitrary initial state. In the puzzle, however, any sequence of moves is to start in a state where the full tower is piled up on one place and the other two places are empty.

Such restrictions on particular initial states occur very frequently in state systems and can be treated by the following version of STSs.

Definition. A *rooted (state) transition system* (briefly: rSTS)

$$\Gamma = (X, V, W, T, start)$$

(over some SIG and S) is an STS $\Gamma'(SIG, \mathsf{S}) = (X, V, W, T)$ together with a closed state formula $start$ of Γ' called *initial condition*. An *execution sequence* of Γ is an execution sequence $(\eta_0, \eta_1, \eta_2, \ldots)$ of Γ' with $\mathsf{S}^{(\eta_0)}(start) = \mathsf{tt}$.

Observe that an rSTS could also very easily (and maybe "more naturally") be defined to consist of an STS (X, V, W, T) together with a distinguished subset W_0 of W the elements of which are to be understood as the initial states. For a reasonable specification of the system, W_0 should then be "describable" by a formula. We have chosen here to provide the desired restriction directly by a (for simplicity: closed) state formula which must be "satisfied" by the initial state of any execution sequence.

Of course, the definition can easily be adjusted for propositional systems. We adopt all notational conventions introduced for STSs and extend them by fixing that we will write $start_\Gamma$ for the initial condition of some Γ and $\mathcal{L}_\Gamma$ for $\mathcal{L}_{\Gamma'}$.

The Towers of Hanoi puzzle can be represented as an rSTS $\Gamma_{ToH}(SIG_{ToH}, \mathsf{H})$ where we take SIG_{ToH} and H as defined in Sect. 6.1. The system variables (following the discussion in Sect. 6.1) and the initial condition of Γ_{ToH} are obvious:

$$X = X_{PILE} = \{pl_1, pl_2, pl_3\},$$
$$V = \emptyset,$$
$$start \equiv pl_1 = TOWER \wedge pl_2 = EMPTY \wedge pl_3 = EMPTY$$

(assuming that at the beginning the tower is standing on place pl_1). For the set of states the choice is not so clear since we could think of restricting W somehow to those states which will really occur in playing the puzzle. The easiest way, however, is to let W contain again all possible mappings from X to $|\mathsf{H}|_{PILE}$, i.e.,

$$W = \{\eta : X \to \{1, \ldots, n\}^*\},$$

and treat the non-accessible states appropriately in the transition relation T. A first approach to the latter is

$$\begin{aligned} T' = \{(\eta,\eta') \in W \times W \mid \\ & \eta \neq \eta_{fin}, \\ & \eta(pl_i) \neq \varepsilon, top(\eta(pl_i)) < top(\eta(pl_j)) \text{ if } \eta(pl_j) \neq \varepsilon, \\ & \eta'(pl_i) = pop(\eta(pl_i)), \eta'(pl_j) = push(\eta(pl_j), top(\eta(pl_i))), \\ & \eta'(pl_k) = \eta(pl_k), \\ & i,j,k \in \{1,2,3\} \text{ pairwise distinct}\}. \end{aligned}$$

where η_{fin} is the "final" state in which the tower is standing on the desired destination, say, place pl_2:

$$\eta_{fin}(pl_2) = (n, n-1, \ldots, 2, 1), \; \eta_{fin}(pl_1) = \eta_{fin}(pl_3) = \varepsilon.$$

Every $(\eta,\eta') \in T'$ represents a possible move according to the rules of the puzzle: the non-empty pile on some place pl_i is popped, its top stone is put on the pile of pl_j provided it is smaller than the top stone there, and the pile on the third place pl_k remains unchanged. By excluding pairs (η_{fin}, η) we express that when reaching η_{fin} no more moves are to be done. As illustrated in Sect. 6.2 the termination in η_{fin} is represented by adding the pair (η_{fin}, η_{fin}) to T' with the effect that whenever η_{fin} is reached in an execution sequence it has to be repeated forever. However, even with this addition, T' is not yet total because of the definition of W. For example, the state $\eta_\varepsilon \in W$ with $\eta_\varepsilon(pl_1) = \eta_\varepsilon(pl_2) = \eta_\varepsilon(pl_3) = \varepsilon$ has no successor state. This is a state which will obviously never occur in an execution sequence, so we solve this (purely technical) problem by simply adding the pair $(\eta_\varepsilon, \eta_\varepsilon)$ to the relation to make it total. Summarizing, T is built as the total closure of T', i.e.,

$$T = tot(T')$$

(and contains then also many other elements (η,η) with states (with "incorrect" piles) which will never be reached).

The execution sequences of this rSTS represent the possible runs and contain the reachable states of the system. An example of a (successful) execution sequence for $n = 3$ is

$$\begin{aligned} &[321,\varepsilon,\varepsilon] \longrightarrow [32,1,\varepsilon] \longrightarrow [3,1,2] \longrightarrow [3,\varepsilon,21] \longrightarrow \\ &\quad [\varepsilon,3,21] \longrightarrow [1,3,2] \longrightarrow [1,32,\varepsilon] \longrightarrow [\varepsilon,321,\varepsilon] \longrightarrow [\varepsilon,321,\varepsilon] \longrightarrow \ldots \end{aligned}$$

where, e.g., the shorthand $[3,\varepsilon,21]$ denotes the state η with $\eta(pl_1) = (3)$, $\eta(pl_2) = \varepsilon$, $\eta(pl_3) = (2,1)$.

Briefly examining the examples of Sect. 6.2, modified counter and stack systems with distinguished initial states could also be reasonable. In both counters one could require that at the beginning the counter is off and has value 0. This would be formalized by an rSTS which extends Γ_{count} (or Γ_{tcount}) by the initial condition

$$start \equiv \neg on \wedge c = 0.$$

For a stack, an analogous requirement could be that the stack is empty initially, expressed by

$$start \equiv pd = EMPTY.$$

Specifying an rSTS Γ, the additional initial condition $start_\Gamma$ restricts the set of execution sequences of the underlying STS. This restriction can be captured by a particular axiom uniformly given by

(root$_\Gamma$) $\quad$ **init** $\rightarrow start_\Gamma$.

Note that for this purpose $\mathcal{L}_{\mathrm{TL}\Gamma}$ has to contain at least the extension "i" and that $start_\Gamma$, as a formula of $\mathcal{L}_\Gamma$, is also a formula of $\mathcal{L}_{\mathrm{TL}\Gamma}$; hence, (root$_\Gamma$) is really a formula of $\mathcal{L}_{\mathrm{TL}\Gamma}$.

Theorem 6.3.1. *For every rSTS Γ the axiom* (root$_\Gamma$) *is Γ-valid.*

Proof. Let $\mathsf{K} \in \mathcal{C}_\Gamma$, ξ be a variable valuation, $i \in \mathbb{N}$. $start_\Gamma$ is a state formula; so, according to the remark about evaluation "in K" and "in S_Γ" in Sect. 6.2, we have $\mathsf{K}_0^{(\xi)}(start_\Gamma) = \mathsf{S}_\Gamma^{(\xi,\eta_0)}(start_\Gamma) = \mathrm{tt}$. Thus, $\mathsf{K}_0^{(\xi)}(\mathbf{init} \rightarrow start_\Gamma) = \mathrm{tt}$ and, for $i > 0$, $\mathsf{K}_i^{(\xi)}(\mathbf{init} \rightarrow start_\Gamma) = \mathrm{tt}$ because of $\mathsf{K}_i^{(\xi)}(\mathbf{init}) = \mathrm{ff}$. This shows that (root$_\Gamma$) is valid in K and proves the theorem. △

This theorem (the proof of which could easily be adjusted if Γ is propositional) means that (root$_\Gamma$) can be added to the set $\mathcal{A}_\Gamma$ of non-logical axioms of a specification of any rSTS Γ. For example, in the counter and stack rSTSs the specification given in the previous section could be enriched by the axioms

$$\mathbf{init} \rightarrow \neg on \wedge c = 0$$

and

$$\mathbf{init} \rightarrow pd = EMPTY,$$

respectively.

The Towers of Hanoi system can now be specified as follows: besides the axioms (data$_{\Gamma_{ToH}}$), the axiom (root$_{\Gamma_{ToH}}$) is taken to specify the initial condition. For describing the possible transitions let

$$\begin{aligned} A_{ijk} \equiv\ & pl_i \neq EMPTY \wedge (pl_j \neq EMPTY \rightarrow TOP(pl_i) < TOP(pl_j)) \wedge \\ & pl_i' = POP(pl_i) \wedge pl_j' = PUSH(pl_j, TOP(pl_i)) \wedge pl_k' = pl_k \end{aligned}$$

and

$$A_{fin} \equiv pl_1 = EMPTY \wedge pl_2 = TOWER \wedge pl_3 = EMPTY.$$

For pairwise distinct $i, j, k \in \{1, 2, 3\}$, A_{ijk} describes the move of putting a stone from pl_i to pl_j and A_{fin} describes the final state with the goal of the game. Together, therefore the axioms

$$\mathbf{init} \rightarrow pl_1 = TOWER \wedge pl_2 = EMPTY \wedge pl_3 = EMPTY,$$
$$\neg A_{fin} \rightarrow A_{123} \vee A_{132} \vee A_{213} \vee A_{231} \vee A_{312} \vee A_{321},$$
$$A_{fin} \rightarrow \bigcirc A_{fin}$$

are appropriate temporal axioms for Γ_{ToH}. The second formula describes all possible moves of the puzzle which can be performed when the goal is not yet reached. By the third formula, the repetition of the final state is expressed.

These axioms are directly drawn from the definition of the transition relation $T_{\Gamma_{ToH}}$. Note that, translating $T_{\Gamma_{ToH}}$ completely, one would expect additional axioms like

$$B \rightarrow \bigcirc B$$

with (e.g.) $B \equiv pl_1 = EMPTY \wedge pl_2 = EMPTY \wedge pl_3 = EMPTY$, expressing the full effect of the total closure operation in the construction of $T_{\Gamma_{ToH}}$. These formulas, however, have no influence on the execution sequences and can therefore be omitted in the specification.

6.4 Labeled Transition Systems

An execution sequence

$$\eta_0 \longrightarrow \eta_1 \longrightarrow \eta_2 \longrightarrow \ldots$$

of an (r)STS "records" the states which are visited during a run of the system. (The notation (r)STS means an STS which may be rooted or not.) In many applications the single transitions from η_i to η_{i+1} are caused by distinguished "actions" and it might be desirable to record the information about which actions are carried out in each step as well. This can informally be depicted by

$$\eta_0 \xrightarrow{\lambda_0} \eta_1 \xrightarrow{\lambda_1} \eta_2 \xrightarrow{\lambda_2} \ldots$$

where the labels λ_i denote the actions leading from η_i to η_{i+1}.

Again the Towers of Hanoi system is a good example: a single action is a move λ_{ij} putting a stone from pl_i to pl_j ($i \in \{1,2,3\}$). The execution sequence

$$[321, \varepsilon, \varepsilon] \longrightarrow [32, 1, \varepsilon] \longrightarrow [3, 1, 2] \longrightarrow [3, \varepsilon, 21] \longrightarrow \ldots$$

exemplifying the rSTS Γ_{ToH} in the previous section is caused by the sequence of moves $\lambda_{12}, \lambda_{13}, \lambda_{23}, \lambda_{12}, \ldots$, depicted by

$$[321, \varepsilon, \varepsilon] \xrightarrow{\lambda_{12}} [32, 1, \varepsilon] \xrightarrow{\lambda_{13}} [3, 1, 2] \xrightarrow{\lambda_{23}} [3, \varepsilon, 21] \xrightarrow{\lambda_{12}} \ldots$$

and, in fact, the information about the moves might be even more interesting than the intermediate states.

A formalization of this concept of including actions into the execution sequences is usually performed by *labeled transition systems*. We investigate two slightly different variants of such systems and again we adjust their definition here such that they can easily be translated into the temporal logical framework. The discussion is carried out for first-order systems but, as before, everything can easily be transferred also to propositional systems.

Definition. A *simple labeled (state) transition system* (briefly: $\mathrm{l_sSTS}$)

$$\Gamma = (X, V, W, T, Act)$$

is given by a finite set Act of *actions* and an STS $\Gamma' = (X, V, W, T)$ with V containing elements $exec\,\lambda$ for every $\lambda \in Act$ and such that, if $(\eta, \eta') \in T$ and $\eta(exec\,\lambda) = \mathsf{ff}$ for every $\lambda \in Act$, then $\eta' = \eta$. An *execution sequence of* Γ is an execution sequence of Γ'.

The idea of this definition is that with every action λ of the system a particular propositional system variable $exec\,\lambda$ is associated and a transition

$$\eta \xrightarrow{\lambda} \eta'$$

is formalized by $(\eta, \eta') \in T$ (as before) and $\eta(exec\,\lambda) = \mathsf{tt}$. So the informal reading of $exec\,\lambda$ is

"the action λ is executed (in the present state)".

Having this in mind one would expect the additional requirement that, in every state, $\eta(exec\,\lambda) = \mathsf{tt}$ should hold for exactly one $\lambda \in Act$. For capturing terminating system runs, however, we allow that $\eta(exec\,\lambda) = \mathsf{ff}$ for every $\lambda \in Act$ (i.e., no action is carried out) and, as before, the state η has to be repeated then forever. More interestingly, we also allow that $\eta(exec\,\lambda) = \mathsf{tt}$ may hold for more than one λ, i.e., that more than one action may be executed in a state η. (In the usual concept of transition systems one would have to distinguish such joint executions of actions as additional actions of their own.)

Obviously, this definition can be transferred to rooted transition systems providing systems denoted by $\mathrm{rl_sSTS}$, and all notational conventions from before (including optional notations like $\mathrm{(r)l_sSTS}$ or $\mathrm{r(l_s)STS}$) can be reused.

Considering the Towers of Hanoi example we can model this as an $\mathrm{rl_sSTS}$ Γ^{l}_{ToH} by taking SIG_{ToH}, H, and

$$X = X_{PILE} = \{pl_1, pl_2, pl_3\},$$
$$start \equiv pl_1 = TOWER \wedge pl_2 = EMPTY \wedge pl_3 = EMPTY$$

as in the rSTS Γ_{ToH} of the previous section and defining the set of actions by

$$Act = \{\lambda_{12}, \lambda_{13}, \lambda_{21}, \lambda_{23}, \lambda_{31}, \lambda_{32}\}$$

where every λ_{ij} has the informal meaning introduced above. Furthermore, we let

$$
\begin{aligned}
V = \{ & exec\lambda_{ij} \mid \lambda_{ij} \in Act\}, \\
W = \{ & \eta : X \cup V \to \{1,\dots,n\}^* \cup \{\mathsf{ff},\mathsf{tt}\} \mid \\
& \quad \eta(pl_i) \in \{1,\dots,n\}^* \text{ for } pl_i \in X, \\
& \quad \eta(exec\lambda_{ij}) \in \{\mathsf{ff},\mathsf{tt}\} \text{ for } \lambda_{ij} \in Act, \\
& \quad \eta(exec\lambda_{ij}) = \mathsf{tt} \text{ for at most one } \lambda_{ij} \in Act, \\
& \quad \text{if } \eta(exec\lambda_{ij}) = \mathsf{ff} \text{ for all } \lambda_{ij} \in Act \text{ then } \eta = \eta_{fin}, \\
& \quad \text{if } \eta(exec\lambda_{ij}) = \mathsf{tt} \text{ then} \\
& \quad\quad \eta(pl_i) \neq \varepsilon, top(\eta(pl_i)) < top(\eta(pl_j)) \text{ if } \eta(pl_j) \neq \varepsilon \\
& \quad\quad\quad \text{for } \lambda_{ij} \in Act\}
\end{aligned}
$$

where η_{fin} is now defined by

$$
\begin{aligned}
& \eta_{fin}(pl_2) = (n, n-1, \dots, 2, 1),\ \eta_{fin}(pl_1) = \eta_{fin}(pl_3) = \varepsilon, \\
& \eta_{fin}(exec\lambda_{ij}) = \mathsf{ff} \text{ for every } \lambda_{ij} \in Act.
\end{aligned}
$$

Finally, for the definition of the transition relation T, consider the relation

$$
\begin{aligned}
T' = \{ & (\eta, \eta') \in W \times W \mid \\
& \quad \eta \neq \eta_{fin}, \\
& \quad \text{if } \eta(exec\lambda_{ij}) = \mathsf{tt} \text{ then} \\
& \quad\quad \eta'(pl_i) = pop(\eta(pl_i)), \eta'(pl_j) = push(\eta(pl_j), top(\eta(pl_i))), \\
& \quad\quad \eta'(pl_k) = \eta(pl_k) \text{ for } k \neq i, k \neq j\}.
\end{aligned}
$$

Together with the restrictions on states in W, the pairs of T' describe again all possible moves and as before we can define then

$$T = tot(T').$$

The successful sequence of moves for the tower of three stones shown in the previous section is now formalized by the execution sequence

$$
\begin{aligned}
& [321, \varepsilon, \varepsilon, \lambda_{12}] \longrightarrow [32, 1, \varepsilon, \lambda_{13}] \longrightarrow [3, 1, 2, \lambda_{23}] \longrightarrow \\
& \quad [3, \varepsilon, 21, \lambda_{12}] \longrightarrow [\varepsilon, 3, 21, \lambda_{31}] \longrightarrow [1, 3, 2, \lambda_{32}] \longrightarrow \\
& \quad\quad [1, 32, \varepsilon, \lambda_{12}] \longrightarrow [\varepsilon, 321, \varepsilon, -] \longrightarrow [\varepsilon, 321, \varepsilon, -] \longrightarrow \dots
\end{aligned}
$$

where the λ_{ij} in a state η denotes the action with $\eta(exec\lambda_{ij}) = \mathsf{tt}$ and the notation $[\varepsilon, 321, \varepsilon, -]$ describes that $\eta(exec\lambda_{ij}) = \mathsf{ff}$ for every $\lambda_{ij} \in Act$.

In the above definition of Γ^l_{ToH}, W is not the "full state space", but restricted according to the intuition of the system variables of V in an evident way. One of these restrictions, expressed in the clause

$$\text{if } \eta(exec\lambda_{ij}) = \mathsf{tt} \text{ then } \eta(pl_i) \neq \varepsilon, top(\eta(pl_i)) < top(\eta(pl_j)) \text{ if } \eta(pl_j) \neq \varepsilon,$$

states that any λ_{ij} is only "enabled" to be executed if the pile on pl_i is not empty and its top stone is smaller than the top stone of the pile on pl_j (if this is not empty). The existence of such "enabling conditions" for the actions is characteristic for many systems and leads to a second version of labeled transition systems where such conditions are explicitly displayed.

Definition. For an $\mathrm{l_sSTS}$ $\Gamma' = (X, V, W, T, Act)$ let $\mathcal{E} = \{enabled_\lambda \mid \lambda \in Act\}$ be a set of closed state formulas of Γ'. A state $\eta \in W$ is called *admissible* (with respect to Γ' and $\mathcal{E}$) if $\mathsf{S}_{\Gamma'}^{(\eta)}(exec\lambda \rightarrow enabled_\lambda) = \mathsf{tt}$ for every $\lambda \in Act$. Γ' together with $\mathcal{E}$ defines an *extended labeled (state) transition system* (briefly: $\mathrm{l_eSTS}$)

$$\Gamma = (X, V, W, T, Act, \mathcal{E})$$

if every $\eta \in W$ is admissible. Each formula $enabled_\lambda$ is called *enabling condition (of* λ*)*.

According to this definition the states of an $\mathrm{l_eSTS}$ are (at least) restricted such that, in every state, only "enabled actions" may be executed and the requirements for an action for being enabled are expressed by special formulas of $\mathcal{L}_{\Gamma'}$ (which will then also be denoted by $\mathcal{L}_\Gamma$). Like initial conditions in the case of rSTSs, these enabling conditions are directly suited for specifications. Of course, an $\mathrm{l_eSTS}$ could alternatively also be defined by displaying, for every action λ, a subset W_λ of W comprising those states in which λ is enabled.

The formalization of the Towers of Hanoi system as an $\mathrm{l_eSTS}$ is very similar to the $\mathrm{l_sSTS}$ Γ^l_{ToH} considered before; we only add the set

$$\mathcal{E} = \{enabled_{\lambda_{ij}} \mid \lambda_{ij} \in Act\}$$

where the enabling conditions are defined by

$$enabled_{\lambda_{ij}} \equiv pl_i \neq EMPTY \wedge (pl_j \neq EMPTY \rightarrow TOP(pl_i) < TOP(pl_j))$$

for $\lambda_{ij} \in Act$. The execution sequences are obviously the same in both formalizations.

(Of course, we could also define further variants of such systems distinguishing other restrictions on states, e.g., the "single action" condition that in every state at most one action may be executed. We leave it here with the restriction installed in $\mathrm{l_eSTSs}$ which will play a useful role in subsequent considerations.)

It should be clear that the other preceding examples could also be modeled as lSTSs (i.e., either $\mathrm{l_sSTSs}$ or $\mathrm{l_eSTSs}$). We still show this for the (non-terminating) counter and define an $\mathrm{l_eSTS}$ $\Gamma^l_{count}(SIG_{Nat}, \mathsf{N})$ with the set

$$Act = \{\lambda_{on}, \lambda_{off}, \lambda_c, \lambda_p\}$$

of four actions which represent switching on, switching off, counting, and pausing, respectively, and the enabling conditions

$$\begin{aligned} enabled_{\lambda_{on}} &\equiv \neg on, \\ enabled_{\lambda_{off}} &\equiv on, \\ enabled_{\lambda_c} &\equiv on, \\ enabled_{\lambda_p} &\equiv \neg on \end{aligned}$$

expressing for which truth values of on the actions may be executed. The proper STS is then given by

$$
\begin{aligned}
X &= X_{NAT} = \{c\},\\
V &= \{on, exec\lambda_{on}, exec\lambda_{off}, exec\lambda_c, exec\lambda_p\},\\
W &= \{\eta : X \cup V \to \mathbb{N} \cup \{\mathsf{ff}, \mathsf{tt}\} \mid\\
&\qquad \eta(c) \in \mathbb{N}, \eta(v) \in \{\mathsf{ff}, \mathsf{tt}\} \text{ for } v \in V,\\
&\qquad \eta \text{ admissible},\\
&\qquad \eta(exec\lambda) = \mathsf{tt} \text{ for exactly one } \lambda \in Act\},\\
T &= \{(\eta, \eta') \in W \times W \mid\\
&\qquad \text{if } \eta(exec\lambda_{on}) = \mathsf{tt} \text{ then } \eta'(c) = 0, \eta'(on) = \mathsf{tt},\\
&\qquad \text{if } \eta(exec\lambda_{off}) = \mathsf{tt} \text{ then } \eta'(c) = \eta(c), \eta'(on) = \mathsf{ff},\\
&\qquad \text{if } \eta(exec\lambda_c) = \mathsf{tt} \text{ then } \eta'(c) = \eta(c) + 1, \eta'(on) = \mathsf{tt},\\
&\qquad \text{if } \eta(exec\lambda_p) = \mathsf{tt} \text{ then } \eta'(c) = \eta(c), \eta'(on) = \mathsf{ff}\}.
\end{aligned}
$$

Note that in the definition of W we simply wrote "η admissible" instead of the respective explicit restrictions on the states. T collects the effects of the four actions in c and on. In a notation analogous to that above the execution sequence of Γ_{count} shown in Sect. 6.2 is represented by the execution sequence

$$
\begin{aligned}
&[\mathsf{ff}, 7, \lambda_{on}] \longrightarrow [\mathsf{tt}, 0, \lambda_c] \longrightarrow [\mathsf{tt}, 1, \lambda_c] \longrightarrow\\
&\qquad [\mathsf{tt}, 2, \lambda_c] \longrightarrow [\mathsf{tt}, 3, \lambda_{off}] \longrightarrow [\mathsf{ff}, 3, \lambda_p] \longrightarrow [\mathsf{ff}, 3, \ldots] \longrightarrow \ldots
\end{aligned}
$$

of Γ^l_{count} or

$$
[\mathsf{ff}, 7] \xrightarrow{\lambda_{on}} [\mathsf{tt}, 0] \xrightarrow{\lambda_c} [\mathsf{tt}, 1] \xrightarrow{\lambda_c} [\mathsf{tt}, 2] \xrightarrow{\lambda_c} [\mathsf{tt}, 3] \xrightarrow{\lambda_{off}} [\mathsf{ff}, 3] \xrightarrow{\lambda_p} [\mathsf{ff}, 3] \xrightarrow{\ldots} \ldots
$$

in another notation.

Let us turn now again generally to the specification of labeled transition systems. For any (r)lSTS Γ with $Act_\Gamma = \{\lambda_1, \ldots, \lambda_n\}$ we introduce the abbreviation

$$
nil_\Gamma \equiv \neg exec\lambda_1 \wedge \ldots \wedge \neg exec\lambda_n
$$

informally expressing that "no action is executed". Intuitively it should be clear that whenever nil_Γ holds in some state η then η is the only possible successor state of η. So every state formula of Γ which holds in η will also hold in "the next state". This characteristic feature is captured by the following axiom.

(nil$_\Gamma$) $\quad nil_\Gamma \wedge A \to \bigcirc A \quad$ if A is a state formula of Γ.

Theorem 6.4.1. *For every (r)lSTS Γ the axiom* (nil$_\Gamma$) *is Γ-valid.*

Proof. Let $\mathsf{K} = (\mathsf{S}_\Gamma, \mathsf{W}_\Gamma) \in \mathcal{C}_\Gamma$, $\mathsf{W}_\Gamma = (\eta_0, \eta_1, \eta_2, \ldots)$, ξ be a variable valuation, $i \in \mathbb{N}$, and $\mathsf{K}_i^{(\xi)}(nil_\Gamma \wedge A) = \mathsf{tt}$. Since nil_Γ and A are state formulas we obtain $\eta_i(exec\lambda) = \mathsf{S}_\Gamma^{(\xi,\eta_i)}(exec\lambda) = \mathsf{ff}$ for every $\lambda \in Act_\Gamma$ and $\mathsf{S}_\Gamma^{(\xi,\eta_i)}(A) = \mathsf{tt}$. Because of $(\eta_i, \eta_{i+1}) \in T_\Gamma$ we have $\eta_{i+1} = \eta_i$ from the definition of lSTSs and this implies $\mathsf{K}_{i+1}^{(\xi)}(A) = \mathsf{S}_\Gamma^{(\xi,\eta_{i+1})}(A) = \mathsf{S}_\Gamma^{(\xi,\eta_i)}(A) = \mathsf{tt}$. Thus, (nil$_\Gamma$) is valid in K which proves the theorem. △

The theorem implies that (nil$_\Gamma$) can be added to the set $\mathcal{A}_\Gamma$ of non-logical axioms of a specification of any (r)lSTS. It should be noted that (nil$_\Gamma$) could even be strengthened. It is Γ-valid not only for state formulas but for many other formulas A of $\mathcal{L}_{\mathrm{TL}\Gamma}$. A counterexample, however, is given by $A \equiv \mathbf{init}$. If $\eta_0(nil_\Gamma) = \mathsf{tt}$ then $nil_\Gamma \wedge A \to \bigcirc A$ would get the value ff in η_0 because of $\eta_0(\bigcirc\,\mathbf{init}) = \mathsf{ff}$. We have chosen the above simple form of (nil$_\Gamma$) since it will be sufficient for our applications.

If Γ is an l$_\mathrm{e}$STS then we get the further evident axiom

(action$_\Gamma$) $\quad exec\lambda \to enabled_\lambda \quad$ for every $\lambda \in Act_\Gamma$.

It can be added to a specification of any (r)l$_\mathrm{e}$STS according to the following quite trivial justification.

Theorem 6.4.2. *For every (r)l$_\mathrm{e}$STS Γ the axiom* (action$_\Gamma$) *is Γ-valid.*

Proof. For every $\mathsf{K} = (\mathsf{S}_\Gamma, \mathsf{W}_\Gamma) \in \mathcal{C}_\Gamma$, $\mathsf{W}_\Gamma = (\eta_0, \eta_1, \eta_2, \ldots)$, variable valuation ξ, and $i \in \mathbb{N}$ we have $\mathsf{K}_i^{(\xi)}(exec\lambda \to enabled_\lambda) = \mathsf{S}_\Gamma^{(\xi,\eta_i)}(exec\lambda \to enabled_\lambda) = \mathsf{tt}$ for every $\lambda \in Act_\Gamma$, which proves the assertion. △

We briefly show now specifications of the examples Γ^l_{ToH} and Γ^l_{count}. The temporal axioms for the (rooted) labeled Towers of Hanoi system could be

$$
\begin{aligned}
&\mathbf{init} \to pl_1 = TOWER \wedge pl_2 = EMPTY \wedge pl_3 = EMPTY,\\
&nil_{\Gamma^l_{ToH}} \wedge A \to \bigcirc A \quad \text{if } A \text{ is a state formula of } \Gamma^l_{ToH},\\
&nil_{\Gamma^l_{ToH}} \leftrightarrow pl_1 = EMPTY \wedge pl_2 = TOWER \wedge pl_3 = EMPTY,\\
&exec\lambda_{ij} \to pl_i \neq EMPTY \wedge (pl_j \neq EMPTY \to TOP(pl_i) < TOP(pl_j))\\
&\qquad\qquad \text{for } \lambda_{ij} \in Act_{\Gamma^l_{ToH}},\\
&exec\lambda_{ij} \to pl_i' = POP(pl_i) \wedge pl_j' = PUSH(pl_j, TOP(pl_i)) \wedge pl_k' = pl_k\\
&\qquad\qquad \text{for } \lambda_{ij} \in Act_{\Gamma^l_{ToH}}, k \neq i, k \neq j.
\end{aligned}
$$

The first two axioms are (root$_{\Gamma^l_{ToH}}$) and (nil$_{\Gamma^l_{ToH}}$), the next two (sets of) axioms reflect restrictions on $W_{\Gamma^l_{ToH}}$, and the last one is translated from $T_{\Gamma^l_{ToH}}$. The fourth axiom is just (action$_{\Gamma^l_{ToH}}$) if we consider Γ^l_{ToH} as an l$_\mathrm{e}$STS. One might miss axioms

$$exec\lambda_{ij} \to \neg exec\lambda_{kl}$$

for $\lambda_{ij}, \lambda_{kl} \in Act_{\Gamma^l_{ToH}}$, $\lambda_{ij} \neq \lambda_{kl}$, expressing that in every state at most one action is executed (which is included as a restriction in $W_{\Gamma^l_{ToH}}$). It is evident, however, that these formulas can be derived from the other axioms. Moreover, it is not necessary to include

$$A_{fin} \to \bigcirc A_{fin}$$

for $A_{fin} \equiv pl_1 = EMPTY \wedge pl_2 = TOWER \wedge pl_3 = EMPTY$ as an axiom since this formula can now be easily derived as well: $A_{fin} \to nil_{\Gamma^l_{ToH}} \wedge A_{fin}$ follows with (prop) from the third axiom and this implies $A_{fin} \to \bigcirc A_{fin}$ with (nil$_{\Gamma^l_{ToH}}$) and (prop).

The counter Γ^l_{count} is specified by

$$
\begin{aligned}
&exec\,\lambda_{on} \rightarrow \neg on,\\
&exec\,\lambda_{off} \rightarrow on,\\
&exec\,\lambda_{c} \rightarrow on,\\
&exec\,\lambda_{p} \rightarrow \neg on,\\
&\neg nil_{\Gamma^l_{count}},\\
&exec\,\lambda_{on} \rightarrow on' \wedge c' = 0,\\
&exec\,\lambda_{off} \rightarrow \neg on' \wedge c' = c,\\
&exec\,\lambda_{c} \rightarrow on' \wedge c' = c + 1,\\
&exec\,\lambda_{p} \rightarrow \neg on' \wedge c' = c.
\end{aligned}
$$

The first four axioms explicitly write out (action$_{\Gamma^l_{count}}$). The axiom (nil$_{\Gamma^l_{count}}$) is not necessary since it follows from the fifth axiom which reflects that in every state at least one action is executed, and the last four axioms are translated from $T_{\Gamma^l_{count}}$. Again, formulas of the form $exec\,\lambda \rightarrow \neg exec\,\overline{\lambda}$ for $\lambda \neq \overline{\lambda}$ can be derived.

Second Reading

State transition systems are formal representations of state systems. There are other formalizations of such systems; prominent examples are all kinds of automata (machines) and (Petri) nets. Although technically defined quite differently, these formal "systems" can be viewed as particular transition systems as well. They pursue, however, different goals (in contrast to what we do here) and possess their own powerful repertories of special methods for dealing with them so that we do not want to advocate their temporal logic treatment. But it is at least interesting to see how they fit into our general framework.

In Chap. 4 we have already discussed some relationship between temporal logic and a special version of finite automata. Let us now consider "ordinary" (non-deterministic) finite automata (NFA) as state systems.

Such an NFA $Aut = (\mathbf{A}, Q, q_0, \delta, Q_f)$ is given by a finite *alphabet* $\mathbf{A}$, a finite, non-empty set Q of *locations*, an *initial location* $q_0 \in Q$, an (*automaton*) *transition relation* $\delta \subseteq Q \times \mathbf{A} \times Q$, and a set $Q_f \subseteq Q$ of *accepting locations*.

The figure

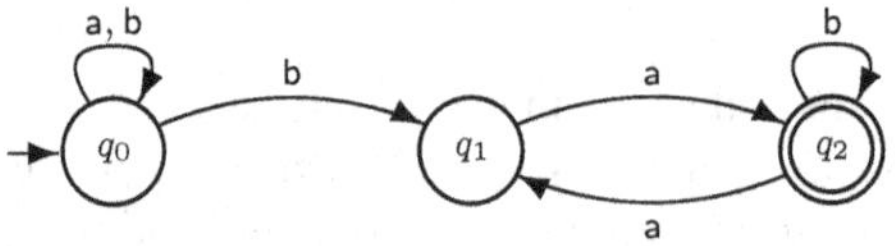

shows an NFA with

$$
\begin{aligned}
&\mathbf{A} = \{\mathsf{a}, \mathsf{b}\},\\
&Q = \{q_0, q_1, q_2\},\\
&\delta = \{(q_0, \mathsf{a}, q_0), (q_0, \mathsf{b}, q_0), (q_0, \mathsf{b}, q_1), (q_1, \mathsf{a}, q_2), (q_2, \mathsf{a}, q_1), (q_2, \mathsf{b}, q_2)\},\\
&Q_f = \{q_2\}
\end{aligned}
$$

in its usual graphical representation.

For any $q \in Q$ and $\mathsf{a} \in \mathbf{A}$, the set $\mathsf{a}(q)$ of *successor locations* of q *reading* the symbol a consists of all locations q' such that $(q, \mathsf{a}, q') \in \delta$. A *run* of Aut for a given *input word* $\mathsf{a}_1 \ldots \mathsf{a}_k \in \mathbf{A}^*$ is a finite sequence $(q_0, \ldots, q_l)$ of locations such that $q_{i+1} \in \mathsf{a}_{i+1}(q_i)$ for $0 \le i \le k-1$ and either $l = k$ or $\mathsf{a}_{l+1}(q_l) = \emptyset$. The word is *accepted* by Aut if there is a run $(q_0, \ldots, q_k)$ with $q_k \in Q_f$.

Let now $Aut = (\mathbf{A}, Q, q_0, \delta, Q_f)$ be an NFA. Let $SIG = (\mathbf{S}, \mathbf{F}, \emptyset)$ be the signature with

$$\begin{aligned}
&\mathbf{S} = \{SYMB, LOC, WORD\},\\
&\mathbf{F} = \{\mathsf{a}^{(\varepsilon, SYMB)}, q^{(\varepsilon, LOC)},\\
&\qquad EMPTY^{(\varepsilon, WORD)}, PREFIX^{(SYMB\ WORD, WORD)} \mid \mathsf{a} \in \mathbf{A}, q \in Q\}
\end{aligned}$$

and S be the structure for SIG with

$$\begin{aligned}
&|\mathsf{S}|_{SYMB} = \mathbf{A}, |\mathsf{S}|_{LOC} = Q, |\mathsf{S}|_{WORD} = \mathbf{A}^*,\\
&\mathsf{a}^{\mathsf{S}} = \mathsf{a} \quad \text{for } \mathsf{a} \in \mathbf{A},\\
&q^{\mathsf{S}} = q \quad \text{for } q \in Q,\\
&EMPTY^{\mathsf{S}} = \varepsilon,\\
&PREFIX^{\mathsf{S}}(\mathsf{a}, \mathsf{b}_1 \ldots \mathsf{b}_l) = \mathit{prefix}(\mathsf{a}, \mathsf{b}_1 \ldots \mathsf{b}_l)
\end{aligned}$$

where $\mathit{prefix}(\mathsf{a}, \mathsf{b}_1 \ldots \mathsf{b}_l) = \mathsf{a}\mathsf{b}_1 \ldots \mathsf{b}_l$. Aut (together with an input word $\mathsf{a}_1 \ldots \mathsf{a}_k \in \mathbf{A}^*$) can be viewed as an $\mathrm{rl_s}$STS $\Gamma_{Aut} = (X, V, W, T, start, Act)$ over SIG and S with

$$\begin{aligned}
&Act = \mathbf{A},\\
&X_{SYMB} = \emptyset, X_{LOC} = \{cs\}, X_{WORD} = \{rw\},\\
&V = \{exec\mathsf{a} \mid \mathsf{a} \in \mathbf{A}\},\\
&W = \{\eta : X \cup V \to Q \cup \mathbf{A}^* \cup \{\mathsf{ff}, \mathsf{tt}\} \mid\\
&\qquad \eta(cs) \in Q, \eta(rw) \in \mathbf{A}^*, \eta(exec\mathsf{a}) \in \{\mathsf{ff}, \mathsf{tt}\} \text{ for } \mathsf{a} \in \mathbf{A},\\
&\qquad \eta(exec\mathsf{a}) = \mathsf{tt} \text{ if and only if}\\
&\qquad\qquad \eta(rw) = \mathit{prefix}(\mathsf{a}, x) \text{ for some } x \in \mathbf{A}^* \text{ and } \mathsf{a}(\eta(cs)) \neq \emptyset\},\\
&T = \{(\eta, \eta') \in W \times W \mid\\
&\qquad \eta(exec\mathsf{a}) = \mathsf{tt} \text{ for } \mathsf{a} \in \mathbf{A} \text{ and}\\
&\qquad\qquad \eta(rw) = \mathit{prefix}(\mathsf{a}, \eta'(rw)) \text{ and } \eta'(cs) \in \mathsf{a}(\eta(cs))\\
&\qquad \text{or}\\
&\qquad \eta(exec\mathsf{a}) = \mathsf{ff} \text{ for every } \mathsf{a} \in \mathbf{A} \text{ and } \eta' = \eta\},\\
&start \equiv cs = q_0 \land rw = PREFIX(\mathsf{a}_1, \ldots PREFIX(\mathsf{a}_k, EMPTY) \ldots).
\end{aligned}$$

The system variables cs and rw carry the current automaton location and the rest of the input word (still to be read), respectively. Note that, as in preceding examples, the finite runs of the automaton are represented as infinite execution sequences repeating the "last state" forever.

It is easy to translate these definitions into a general form of temporal logic specifications. We only show appropriate temporal axioms (besides ($\mathrm{root}_{\Gamma_{Aut}}$) and ($\mathrm{nil}_{\Gamma_{Aut}}$)) for the example:

$$\begin{aligned}
&exec\mathsf{a} \leftrightarrow \exists x(rw = PREFIX(\mathsf{a}, x)),\\
&exec\mathsf{a} \to (cs = q_0 \to cs' = q_0) \land (cs = q_1 \to cs' = q_1) \land (cs = q_2 \to cs' = q_1),\\
&exec\mathsf{b} \leftrightarrow \exists x(rw = PREFIX(\mathsf{b}, x)) \land cs \neq q_1,\\
&exec\mathsf{b} \to (cs = q_0 \to cs' = q_0 \lor cs' = q_1) \land (cs = q_2 \to cs' = q_2).
\end{aligned}$$

The acceptance of the input word w by Aut can be expressed by a formula of $\mathcal{L}_{\mathrm{TL}\Gamma_{Aut}}$, in the example by

$$start \to \Diamond(cs = q_2 \land rw = EMPTY).$$

Petri nets exist in various versions. We consider *place-transition nets* (briefly: PTNs) $Net = (Pl, Tr, \delta)$ which are usually defined to consist of a finite, non-empty set Pl of *places*, a finite, non-empty set Tr of *net transitions*, and a (*net*) *transition relation* $\delta \subseteq (Pl \times Tr) \cup (Tr \times Pl)$. A *marking* of Net is a mapping $M : Pl \to \mathbb{N}$.

The figure

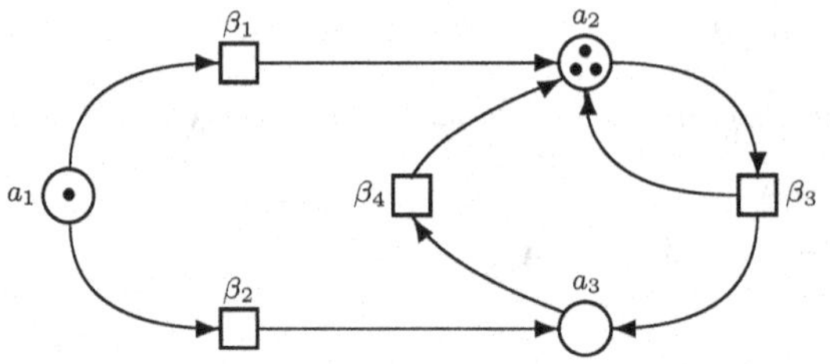

shows a typical graphical representation of a PTN with

$$\begin{aligned}
&Pl = \{a_1, a_2, a_3\},\\
&Tr = \{\beta_1, \beta_2, \beta_3, \beta_4\},\\
&\delta = \{(a_1, \beta_1), (a_1, \beta_2), (a_2, \beta_3), (a_3, \beta_4), (\beta_1, a_2), (\beta_2, a_3), (\beta_3, a_2),\\
&\qquad (\beta_3, a_3), (\beta_4, a_2)\}
\end{aligned}$$

together with a marking M (indicated by the bullets associated with the places) with

$$M(a_1) = 1, M(a_2) = 3, M(a_3) = 0.$$

For $\beta \in Tr$, the sets $\bullet\beta = \{a \in Pl \mid (a, \beta) \in \delta\}$ and $\beta\bullet = \{a \in Pl \mid (\beta, a) \in \delta\}$ are the *pre-set* and *post-set* of β, respectively. For a marking M, β is called *fireable* under M if $M(a) > 0$ for every $a \in \bullet\beta$. If β is fireable under M then the *firing* of β transforms M to its *successor marking* $\beta(M)$ defined by

$$\beta(M)(a) = \begin{cases} M(a) - 1 & \text{if } a \in \bullet\beta \setminus \beta\bullet \\ M(a) + 1 & \text{if } a \in \beta\bullet \setminus \bullet\beta \\ M(a) & \text{otherwise.} \end{cases}$$

In the example, β_1, β_2, and β_3, but not β_4 are fireable (under the given M). Firing of β_3 transforms M to M' with $M'(a_1) = 1$, $M'(a_2) = 3$, $M'(a_3) = 1$.

A *run* of a PTN Net is a sequence $(M_0, M_1, M_2, \ldots)$ of markings such that for every $i \in \mathbb{N}$, M_{i+1} is a successor marking of M_i if there is a fireable net transition under M_i, and $M_{i+1} = M_i$ otherwise.

Let now $SIG = (\mathbf{S}, \mathbf{F}, \mathbf{P})$ be the signature with

$$\begin{aligned}
&\mathbf{S} = \{NAT\},\\
&\mathbf{F} = \{0^{(\varepsilon, NAT)}, SUCC^{(NAT,NAT)}, PRED^{(NAT,NAT)}\},\\
&\mathbf{P} = \{POS^{(NAT)}\}
\end{aligned}$$

and S be the structure for SIG with

$$\begin{aligned}
&|\mathsf{S}| = |\mathsf{S}|_{NAT} = \mathbb{N},\\
&0^{\mathsf{S}} = 0,\\
&SUCC^{\mathsf{S}}(n) = n + 1,\\
&PRED^{\mathsf{S}}(n) = n - 1 \text{ if } n > 0,\ PRED^{\mathsf{S}}(0) = 0,\\
&POS^{\mathsf{S}}(n) = \mathsf{tt} \Leftrightarrow n > 0.
\end{aligned}$$

A PTN $Net = (Pl, Tr, \delta)$ can be viewed as an $\mathrm{l_eSTS}$ $\Gamma_{Net} = (X, V, W, T, Act, \mathcal{E})$ over SIG and S with

$$\begin{aligned}
&Act = Tr,\\
&X = X_{NAT} = Pl,\\
&V = \{exec\beta \mid \beta \in Tr\},\\
&enabled_\beta \;\equiv\; POS(a_1) \wedge \ldots \wedge POS(a_k) \quad \text{for every } \beta \in Tr, \bullet\beta = \{a_1, \ldots, a_k\},\\
&W = \{\eta : X \cup V \to \mathbb{N} \cup \{\mathsf{ff}, \mathsf{tt}\} \mid\\
&\qquad \eta(a) \in \mathbb{N} \text{ for } a \in Pl, \eta(exec\beta) \in \{\mathsf{ff}, \mathsf{tt}\} \text{ for } \beta \in Tr,\\
&\qquad \eta \text{ admissible},\\
&\qquad \eta(exec\beta) = \mathsf{tt} \text{ for at most one } \beta \in Tr,\\
&\qquad \text{if } \eta(exec\beta) = \mathsf{ff} \text{ for every } \beta \in Tr \text{ then}\\
&\qquad\quad \text{for every } \beta \in Tr \text{ there is some } a \in \bullet\beta \text{ with } \eta(a) = 0\},\\
&T = \{(\eta, \eta') \in W \times W \mid\\
&\qquad \eta(exec\beta) = \mathsf{tt} \text{ for } \beta \in Tr \text{ and } \eta'(a) = \beta(\eta|_{Pl})(a) \text{ for every } a \in Pl\\
&\qquad \text{or}\\
&\qquad \eta(exec\beta) = \mathsf{ff} \text{ for every } \beta \in Tr \text{ and } \eta' = \eta\}.
\end{aligned}$$

($\eta|_{Pl}$ denotes the restriction of η on Pl and is just a marking of Net.)

Again it is easy to translate these definitions into a general form of temporal logic specifications of such systems. Appropriate temporal axioms (besides ($\mathrm{nil}_{\Gamma_{Net}}$) and ($\mathrm{action}_{\Gamma_{Net}}$)) for the example could be:

$$\begin{aligned}
&exec\beta_1 \to a_1' = PRED(a_1) \wedge a_2' = SUCC(a_2) \wedge a_3' = a_3,\\
&exec\beta_2 \to a_1' = PRED(a_1) \wedge a_2' = a_2 \wedge a_3' = SUCC(a_3),\\
&exec\beta_3 \to a_1' = a_1 \wedge a_2' = a_2 \wedge a_3' = SUCC(a_3),\\
&exec\beta_4 \to a_1' = a_1 \wedge a_2' = SUCC(a_2) \wedge a_3' = PRED(a_3).
\end{aligned}$$

6.5 Fairness

The definition of (all the variants of) state transition systems accomodates *non-determinism*: in general, any state of the system may have more than one possible successor state according to the transition relation and runs may "branch" in such states following different successors. In fact, most of the examples of state systems so far are of this nature.

In a non-deterministic system the choice of the "next step" is free by definition. Sometimes the particular real-world application, however, imposes some restrictions upon this freedom. For example, in the Towers of Hanoi system most of the possible runs do not lead to the proper goal of the puzzle, so the choice of a real player would be goal-oriented in every step, trying to leave all useless transitions aside.

An important kind of restriction in many state systems is subsumed under the notion of *fairness*. Consider, as a simple example, the following propositional $\mathrm{l_eSTS}$ $\Gamma_{printer}$ formalizing a printer which, requested from two "users" U_1 and U_2, periodically executes printing jobs for U_1 and U_2. $\Gamma_{printer}$ is given by

$$\begin{aligned}
&Act = \{\alpha_1, \alpha_2, \beta_1, \beta_2, \gamma\},\\
&X = \emptyset,
\end{aligned}$$

$$
\begin{aligned}
&V = \{exec\lambda \mid \lambda \in Act\} \cup \{req_1, req_2\},\\
&enabled_{\alpha_1} \equiv \neg req_1,\\
&enabled_{\alpha_2} \equiv \neg req_2,\\
&enabled_{\beta_1} \equiv req_1,\\
&enabled_{\beta_2} \equiv req_2,\\
&enabled_{\gamma} \equiv \textbf{true},\\
&W = \{\eta : V \to \{\text{ff}, \text{tt}\} \mid \eta \text{ admissible},\\
&\qquad\qquad\qquad\qquad \eta(exec\lambda) = \text{tt for exactly one } \lambda \in Act\},\\
&T = \{(\eta, \eta') \in W \times W \mid\\
&\qquad\qquad \text{if } \eta(exec\alpha_1) = \text{tt then } \eta'(req_1) = \text{tt}, \eta'(req_2) = \eta(req_2),\\
&\qquad\qquad \text{if } \eta(exec\alpha_2) = \text{tt then } \eta'(req_1) = \eta(req_1), \eta'(req_2) = \text{tt},\\
&\qquad\qquad \text{if } \eta(exec\beta_1) = \text{tt then } \eta'(req_1) = \text{ff}, \eta'(req_2) = \eta(req_2),\\
&\qquad\qquad \text{if } \eta(exec\beta_2) = \text{tt then } \eta'(req_1) = \eta(req_1), \eta'(req_2) = \text{ff},\\
&\qquad\qquad \text{if } \eta(exec\gamma) = \text{tt then } \eta'(req_1) = \eta(req_1), \eta'(req_2) = \eta(req_2)\}.
\end{aligned}
$$

The actions α_i $(i = 1, 2)$ have the informal meaning "the printer is requested by user U_i", the β_i stand for "the printer is printing for U_i", and γ means "the printer does nothing". The system variables req_i informally read "there is a request from U_i". With this in mind, the other definitions can easily be understood. Note that the definition of $enabled_\gamma$ means that there is no restriction for the execution of γ.

$\Gamma_{printer}$ is non-deterministic since in T it is not fixed which action is executed in a next state. A possible execution sequence could be

$$\emptyset \xrightarrow{\gamma} \emptyset \xrightarrow{\alpha_1} \{1\} \xrightarrow{\alpha_2} \{1,2\} \xrightarrow{\beta_1} \{2\} \xrightarrow{\alpha_1} \{1,2\} \xrightarrow{\beta_2} \{1\} \xrightarrow{\beta_1} \ldots$$

where the states $\eta_0, \eta_1, \eta_2, \ldots$ are represented by sets containing those $i \in \{1,2\}$ with $\eta_j(req_i) = \text{tt}$. At the beginning of this run there is no request and the printer is not printing. Then U_1 and U_2 request the printer successively, the printer prints for U_1, another request from U_1 arrives, the printer prints for U_2, then for U_1, and so on. This is a quite reasonable behaviour of the printer. Consider, however, the execution sequence

$$
\begin{aligned}
&\emptyset \xrightarrow{\gamma} \emptyset \xrightarrow{\alpha_1} \{1\} \xrightarrow{\alpha_2} \{1,2\} \xrightarrow{\beta_1}\\
&\qquad \{2\} \xrightarrow{\alpha_1} \{1,2\} \xrightarrow{\beta_1} \{2\} \xrightarrow{\alpha_1} \{1,2\} \xrightarrow{\beta_1} \{2\} \xrightarrow{\alpha_1} \ldots
\end{aligned}
$$

where U_2 has requested the printer but only the permanently arriving requests of U_1 are served forever. This execution sequence describes an "unfair" behaviour of the printer since U_2 will never be served. An even "worse" behaviour would be given by

$$\emptyset \xrightarrow{\gamma} \emptyset \xrightarrow{\alpha_1} \{1\} \xrightarrow{\alpha_2} \{1,2\} \xrightarrow{\gamma} \{1,2\} \xrightarrow{\gamma} \{1,2\} \xrightarrow{\gamma} \ldots$$

never executing the requested jobs of U_1 and U_2 at all. Of course, it might be desirable to exclude such behaviours.

In general, restrictions in this sense are called *fairness* requirements and are expressed by connections between the enabledness of actions and their actual execution. They can be treated easily in the framework of labeled transition systems (in the extended version) since there the enabledness of actions is explicitly given by the enabling conditions. Among the several possibilities of how to reasonably fix the requirement we choose the following. (Again everything is treated in the first-order framework and can easily be adjusted for the propositional case.)

Definition. Let Γ be an (r)l$_e$STS. An execution sequence $\mathsf{W}_\Gamma = (\eta_0, \eta_1, \eta_2, \ldots)$ of Γ is called *fair* if it has the property that, for every $\lambda \in Act_\Gamma$, if $\mathsf{S}_\Gamma^{(\eta_j)}(enabled_\lambda) = \mathsf{tt}$ for infinitely many j then $\eta_k(exec\,\lambda) = \mathsf{tt}$ for infinitely many k. A *fair* (r)l$_e$STS (briefly: f(r)l$_e$STS) is an (r)l$_e$STS Γ where the execution sequences are restricted to the fair execution sequences of Γ.

Informally this fairness definition requires that, in every run, actions which are enabled infinitely often will be executed infinitely often, and it is easy to see that it excludes in fact the undesired execution sequences of the printer we showed above: in both runs, β_2 is enabled infinitely often but never executed.

The restriction of the set of execution sequences of an f(r)l$_e$STS Γ can be captured by the particular axiom

(fair$_\Gamma$) $\quad \Box\Diamond enabled_\lambda \rightarrow \Diamond exec\,\lambda \quad$ for every $\lambda \in Act_\Gamma$

which informally reads (for every $\lambda \in Act_\Gamma$)

"if λ is enabled infinitely often then it will eventually be executed".

This is not the direct transliteration of the above definition which would be given by the seemingly stronger

$$\Box\Diamond enabled_\lambda \rightarrow \Box\Diamond exec\,\lambda \quad \text{for every } \lambda \in Act_\Gamma$$

but these formulas can trivially be derived from (fair$_\Gamma$) with (T35), and are therefore model equivalent to those in (fair$_\Gamma$).

Theorem 6.5.1. *For every f(r)l$_e$STS Γ the axiom* (fair$_\Gamma$) *is Γ-valid.*

Proof. For every $\mathsf{K} = (\mathsf{S}_\Gamma, \mathsf{W}_\Gamma) \in \mathcal{C}_\Gamma$, $\mathsf{W}_\Gamma = (\eta_0, \eta_1, \eta_2, \ldots)$, variable valuation ξ, $i \in \mathbb{N}$, and $\lambda \in Act_\Gamma$ we have:

$$\begin{aligned}
\mathsf{K}_i^{(\xi)}(\Box\Diamond enabled_\lambda) = \mathsf{tt} &\Rightarrow \mathsf{K}_j^{(\xi)}(enabled_\lambda) = \mathsf{tt} \text{ for infinitely many } j \geq i \\
&\Rightarrow \mathsf{S}_\Gamma^{(\eta_j)}(enabled_\lambda) = \mathsf{tt} \text{ for infinitely many } j \\
&\Rightarrow \mathsf{K}_k^{(\xi)}(exec\,\lambda) = \eta_k(exec\,\lambda) = \mathsf{tt} \\
&\qquad\qquad \text{for infinitely many } k \\
&\Rightarrow \mathsf{K}_k^{(\xi)}(exec\,\lambda) = \mathsf{tt} \text{ for some } k \geq i \\
&\Rightarrow \mathsf{K}_i^{(\xi)}(\Diamond exec\,\lambda) = \mathsf{tt}. \qquad \triangle
\end{aligned}$$

According to this theorem, (fair$_\Gamma$) can be added to the specification of Γ. As an example, the specification of the above printer as a fair system could contain the following temporal axioms:

$$
\begin{aligned}
&exec\,\alpha_1 \to \neg req_1,\\
&exec\,\alpha_2 \to \neg req_2,\\
&exec\,\beta_1 \to req_1,\\
&exec\,\beta_2 \to req_2,\\
&\Box\Diamond enabled_\lambda \to \Diamond exec\,\lambda \quad \text{for } \lambda \in \{\alpha_1, \alpha_2, \beta_1, \beta_2, \gamma\},\\
&exec\,\alpha_1 \to req_1' \land (req_2' \leftrightarrow req_2),\\
&exec\,\alpha_2 \to (req_1' \leftrightarrow req_1) \land req_2',\\
&exec\,\beta_1 \to \neg req_1' \land (req_2' \leftrightarrow req_2),\\
&exec\,\beta_2 \to (req_1' \leftrightarrow req_1) \land \neg req_2',\\
&exec\,\gamma \to (req_1' \leftrightarrow req_1) \land (req_2' \leftrightarrow req_2).
\end{aligned}
$$

The first four axioms are (action$_{\Gamma_{printer}}$) for $\alpha_1, \alpha_2, \beta_1, \beta_2$. (action$_{\Gamma_{printer}}$) for γ reads $enabled_\gamma \to$ **true** and can be omitted since this is tautologically valid. The next axiom is (fair$_{\Gamma_{printer}}$) and the remaining ones are directly translated from the definition of $T_{\Gamma_{printer}}$. As in the examples in Sect. 6.4, formulas $exec\,\lambda \to \neg exec\,\overline{\lambda}$ can be derived. One would still expect the axiom

$$(*) \qquad \neg nil_{\Gamma_{printer}}$$

to describe that at least one action is executed in every state (which also implies (nil$_{\Gamma_{printer}}$)). However, $(*)$ can be omitted if fairness is presupposed: it can be derived from (fair$_{\Gamma_{printer}}$). More generally, and for further usage we derive the formula

$$(\text{progress}_\Gamma) \qquad enabled_\lambda \to \neg nil_\Gamma \qquad \text{for every } \lambda \in Act_\Gamma$$

from (fair$_\Gamma$). This formula expresses that the system "may not stop executing actions if there are still enabled actions". In the printer example, $(*)$ follows immediately applying (progress$_{\Gamma_{printer}}$) with $\lambda = \gamma$.

Derivation of (progress$_\Gamma$).

(1)	$nil_\Gamma \land enabled_\lambda \to \bigcirc(nil_\Gamma \land enabled_\lambda)$	(prop),(nil$_\Gamma$)
(2)	$nil_\Gamma \land enabled_\lambda \to \Box(nil_\Gamma \land enabled_\lambda)$	(ind1),(1)
(3)	$\Box(nil_\Gamma \land enabled_\lambda) \to \Box nil_\Gamma \land \Box enabled_\lambda$	(prop),(T18)
(4)	$\Box enabled_\lambda \to \Box\Diamond enabled_\lambda$	(T5),(T22)
(5)	$\Box enabled_\lambda \to \Diamond exec\,\lambda$	(prop),(fair$_\Gamma$),(4)
(6)	$nil_\Gamma \land enabled_\lambda \to \Box nil_\Gamma \land \Diamond exec\,\lambda$	(prop),(2),(3),(5)
(7)	$\Box nil_\Gamma \land \Diamond exec\,\lambda \to \Diamond(nil_\Gamma \land exec\,\lambda)$	(prop),(T34)
(8)	$\Box\neg(nil_\Gamma \land exec\,\lambda) \to (enabled_\lambda \to \neg nil_\Gamma)$	(prop),(T2),(6),(7)
(9)	$\neg(nil_\Gamma \land exec\,\lambda)$	(taut)
(10)	$\Box\neg(nil_\Gamma \land exec\,\lambda)$	(alw),(9)
(11)	$enabled_\lambda \to \neg nil_\Gamma$	(prop),(8),(10) △

The fairness restriction defined above and axiomatized by (fair$_\Gamma$) is also called *strong fairness*. As remarked already, other notions of fairness might be chosen in particular applications. We briefly indicate one different approach called *weak fairness*.

An execution sequence $\mathsf{W}_\Gamma = (\eta_0, \eta_1, \eta_2, \ldots)$ of an (r)l$_e$STS Γ is called *weakly fair* if it has the property that, for every $\lambda \in Act_\Gamma$, if there is a $j_0 \in \mathbb{N}$ such that $\mathsf{S}_\Gamma^{(\eta_j)}(enabled_\lambda) = \mathsf{tt}$ for every $j \geq j_0$ then $\eta_k(exec\,\lambda) = \mathsf{tt}$ for infinitely many k. A *weakly fair* (r)l$_e$STS is an (r)l$_e$STS Γ restricting the execution sequences to the weakly fair ones.

This fairness notion can be captured by the axiom

(wfair$_\Gamma$) $\quad \Box enabled_\lambda \to \Diamond exec\,\lambda \quad$ for every $\lambda \in Act_\Gamma$

(these formulas and the more direct formalizations $\Diamond\Box enabled_\lambda \to \Diamond exec\,\lambda$ are model equivalent) the correctness of which is shown as follows:

$$
\begin{aligned}
\mathsf{K}_i^{(\xi)}(\Box enabled_\lambda) = \mathsf{tt} &\Rightarrow \mathsf{K}_j^{(\xi)}(enabled_\lambda) = \mathsf{tt} \text{ for } j \geq i \\
&\Rightarrow \mathsf{S}_\Gamma^{(\eta_j)}(enabled_\lambda) = \mathsf{tt} \text{ for } j \geq i \\
&\Rightarrow \mathsf{K}_k^{(\xi)}(exec\,\lambda) = \eta_k(exec\,\lambda) = \mathsf{tt} \\
&\qquad\qquad\qquad\qquad \text{for infinitely many } k \\
&\Rightarrow \mathsf{K}_k^{(\xi)}(exec\,\lambda) = \mathsf{tt} \text{ for some } k \geq i \\
&\Rightarrow \mathsf{K}_i^{(\xi)}(\Diamond exec\,\lambda) = \mathsf{tt}.
\end{aligned}
$$

Every (strongly) fair system is weakly fair, which may easily be seen from the definition or, alternatively, by deriving (wfair$_\Gamma$) from (fair$_\Gamma$):

(1)	$\Box\Diamond enabled_\lambda \to \Diamond exec\,\lambda$	(fair$_\Gamma$)
(2)	$\Box enabled_\lambda \to \Box\Diamond enabled_\lambda$	(T5),(T22)
(3)	$\Box enabled_\lambda \to \Diamond exec\,\lambda$	(prop),(1),(2)

It should also be clear that weak fairness is really weaker than strong fairness. A trivial example to show this is a system with a system variable $a \in \mathcal{X}$ of sort NAT, and two actions α and β with $enabled_\alpha \equiv$ **true** and $enabled_\beta \equiv EVEN(a)$ such that the effect of α is increasing a by 1 (the predicate symbol $EVEN$ means "to be an even number"). In any execution sequence

$$\eta_0 \xrightarrow{\alpha} \eta_1 \xrightarrow{\alpha} \eta_2 \xrightarrow{\alpha} \eta_3 \xrightarrow{\alpha} \ldots$$

where $\eta_0(a)$ is an even number, β is enabled in states η_i with even i (and no others), so these execution sequences are obviously weakly fair but not (strongly) fair.

In the printer system, however, weak fairness would be sufficient to exclude undesired execution sequences as those noted above. Furthermore, a close look to the derivation of (progress$_\Gamma$) shows that weak fairness is also sufficient to derive this formula. Line (6) in the derivation is directly found from lines (2) and (3) by applying (prop) and (wfair$_\Gamma$). The lines (4) and (5) can be omitted.

The two concepts of fairness considered here are uniform in the sense that the axioms (fair$_\Gamma$) and (wfair$_\Gamma$) apply to all actions $\lambda \in Act_\Gamma$. For the printer example, they imply that the printer idles (i.e., executes the action γ) infinitely often because idling is always enabled. It is a natural generalization to indicate for each action whether weak or strong fairness is assumed for it. We will consider an example in Sect. 9.2.

Bibliographical Notes

The use of FOLTL for specifying the data components of models was proposed in [91, 144].

State transition systems were introduced by Keller [71] for modeling concurrent programs. Nowadays they are used in manifold forms for the formal representation of systems in general and also as alternative semantical basis for temporal logics, see, e.g., [67, 102]. An alternative approach is followed by Stirling [140] who interprets modal and temporal logics over process expressions.

Our special form of labeled transition systems is a generalization of the approach to the operational semantics of programs elaborated in [83].

Fair transition systems were considered by Queille and Sifakis [128]. A detailed overview of fairness issues can be found in [49].

Non-deterministic finite automata are described in many undergraduate textbooks on theoretical computer science. Petri nets were introduced by Petri [119], a detailed presentation of their theory is, e.g., given in [129]. Further formal system models can be found in [102].

7

Verification of State Systems

The non-logical axioms of a system specification as studied in the preceding chapter describe distinguished "characteristic" assertions about the "behaviour" of the runs of the system, i.e., "properties" of state sequences which hold for every run. As mentioned already several times it is one of the very aims of temporal logic to express, quite generally, such properties in a formal way.

Together with the logical ("reasoning") means this leads immediately to a next major area of application: the *verification* of state systems, i.e., the formal proof that certain (further) properties hold for (every run of) the system. One natural approach to perform this is to use the proof-theoretical means of the logic and derive the formula which describes the property from the specification axioms within the available axiomatization.

We study in the present chapter this kind of *deductive* verification for some typical classes of system properties. Another approach will be treated in Chap. 11.

7.1 System Properties

Some examples of system properties (beyond specification axioms) were already given in Sects. 2.1 and 6.1 for the Towers of Hanoi system; we only repeat the phrase

> "in all states, on each of the three places the stones will be piled up with decreasing size"

expressed by the formula

$$\Box(DECR(pl_1) \wedge DECR(pl_2) \wedge DECR(pl_3)).$$

Another property is

> "proceeding from a state in which the tower is on place 1, it will eventually be moved to place 2"

describing that the proper goal of the puzzle is reached sometime. This can be expressed by

$$start_{\Gamma_{ToH}} \rightarrow \Diamond A_{fin}$$

(with $A_{fin} \equiv pl_1 = EMPTY \wedge pl_2 = TOWER \wedge pl_3 = EMPTY$) but, as opposed to the former one, it does not hold for every run of the system but only for the "successful" ones leading to the desired state.

In general, given (a state system represented by) a transition system Γ (with or without extensions), a system property describes a behaviour of Γ satisfied by certain (possibly not all) of its runs. More formally, the property can be identified with the subset of the set of all execution sequences of Γ for which it is satisfied. Every formula F of $\mathcal{L}_{\mathrm{TL}\Gamma}$ *specifies* such a property: the property identified with the set of those execution sequences W_Γ of Γ for which F is valid in $\mathsf{K} = (\mathsf{S}_\Gamma, \mathsf{W}_\Gamma)$.

A property specified by the formula F (briefly: the property F) is a *valid property of* Γ (or: Γ *has the property* F) if it comprehends all execution sequences of Γ, i.e., if F is Γ-valid. In this general setting the non-logical axioms of Γ are valid properties of Γ. Note that, by the definition given in Sect. 6.1, model equivalent formulas specify the same property.

In this formal wording the Towers of Hanoi system Γ_{ToH} has the property

$$\Box(DECR(pl_1) \wedge DECR(pl_2) \wedge DECR(pl_3))$$

but it does not have the property

$$start_{\Gamma_{ToH}} \rightarrow \Diamond A_{fin}.$$

Every formula of $\mathcal{L}_{\mathrm{TL}\Gamma}$ specifies some property for a system Γ, but in general – if Γ has infinitely many execution sequences – the number of properties (i.e., sets of execution sequences) is uncountable and not all of them are expressed by formulas the number of which is denumerable. Besides this trivial fact, the amount of properties specifiable by formulas clearly depends on the actual choice of the language $\mathcal{L}_{\mathrm{TL}\Gamma}$, i.e., the linguistic equipment of extensions added to the basic temporal logic language and thus achieving different expressiveness of $\mathcal{L}_{\mathrm{TL}\Gamma}$.

The different "description languages" $\mathcal{L}_{\mathrm{TL}\Gamma}$ also provide a first very rough classification of properties given by their syntactic membership to these languages. For a systematic treatment of properties it is useful to classify them with respect to the syntactic form of the formulas in a more detailed manner. We briefly describe (a part of) such a frequently used classification within the language $\mathcal{L}_{\mathrm{TL}\Gamma} = \mathcal{L}^{\mathrm{bp}}_{\mathrm{FOLTL}}(TSIG_\Gamma)$ (or $\mathcal{L}_{\mathrm{TL}\Gamma} = \mathcal{L}^{\mathrm{bp}}_{\mathrm{LTL}}(V_\Gamma)$ if Γ is propositional), i.e., the basic language extended by binary and past operators (including binary past operators as discussed in Sect. 3.6). For illustration we supplement the cases with a very simple lSTS example $\Gamma_{\alpha\beta}$ containing two actions α and β such that $exec\,\alpha$ and $exec\,\beta$ cannot become true in the same state.

The classification differentiates properties expressible by formulas of the form

$$\mathbf{pref}\ A$$

where **pref** is one of the four "significant" $\Box$-$\Diamond$-prefixes $\Box$, $\Diamond$, $\Diamond\Box$, and $\Box\Diamond$ according to Theorem 2.2.3 and A is a *past formula*, i.e., a formula containing no future operators.

- A property specifiable by a formula

  $$\Box A$$

  (or just by A since $\Box A \simeq A$) with a past formula A is called *safety property*. An example in $\Gamma_{\alpha\beta}$ is

  $$\Box(exec\,\beta \rightarrow \diamondminus exec\,\alpha)$$

  reading

  "whenever β is executed, α was executed before that".

- A property specifiable by a formula

  $$\Diamond A$$

  with a past formula A is called *response property*. An example in $\Gamma_{\alpha\beta}$ is

  $$\Diamond(\diamondminus exec\,\alpha \rightarrow exec\,\beta)$$

  reading

  "eventually a former execution of α will be responded to by executing β".

- A property specifiable by a formula

  $$\Diamond\Box A$$

  with a past formula A is called *persistence property*. An example in $\Gamma_{\alpha\beta}$ is

  $$\Diamond\Box\neg exec\,\alpha$$

  reading

  "eventually α will never more be executed".

The fourth $\Box$-$\Diamond$-prefix $\Box\Diamond$ does not provide a new class since $\Box\Diamond A \simeq \Diamond A$. So the properties $\Box\Diamond A$ (with past formulas A) are just the response properties.

These three classes of properties are not disjoint. Every safety property is in fact a response property and a persistence property as well since we have

$$\Box A \simeq \Diamond\boxminus A$$

and

$$\Box A \simeq \Diamond\Box\boxminus A.$$

These model equivalences are easily proved, e.g., the first one:

$$\begin{aligned}
\models_{\mathsf{K}} \Diamond \boxminus A &\Leftrightarrow \mathsf{K}_i^{(\xi)}(\Diamond \boxminus A) = \mathrm{tt} \ \text{ for every } \xi \text{ and } i \\
&\Leftrightarrow \mathsf{K}_j^{(\xi)}(\boxminus A) = \mathrm{tt} \ \text{ for some } j \geq i \text{ and every } \xi \text{ and } i \\
&\Leftrightarrow \mathsf{K}_k^{(\xi)}(A) = \mathrm{tt} \ \text{ for every } k \leq i \text{ and every } \xi \text{ and } i \\
&\Leftrightarrow \mathsf{K}_k^{(\xi)}(A) = \mathrm{tt} \ \text{ for every } \xi \text{ and } k \\
&\Leftrightarrow \models_{\mathsf{K}} \Box A.
\end{aligned}$$

The classification given here can be refined and extended. We do not follow this line but rather pick out now some simple cases of the classes for further treatment in the subsequent sections. A first kind are properties given by formulas

$$A \to \Box B$$

where A and B are state formulas of the system Γ. They are called *invariance properties* and form a subclass of the safety properties. This follows from

$$\begin{aligned}
&\mathsf{K}_i^{(\xi)}(A \to \Box B) = \mathrm{ff} \ \text{ for some } i \\
&\quad \Leftrightarrow \mathsf{K}_i^{(\xi)}(A) = \mathrm{tt} \text{ and } \mathsf{K}_i^{(\xi)}(\Box B) = \mathrm{ff} \ \text{ for some } i \\
&\quad \Leftrightarrow \mathsf{K}_i^{(\xi)}(A) = \mathrm{tt} \text{ and } \mathsf{K}_j^{(\xi)}(B) = \mathrm{ff} \ \text{ for some } i \text{ and some } j \geq i \\
&\quad \Leftrightarrow \mathsf{K}_j^{(\xi)}(\ominus A) = \mathrm{tt} \text{ and } \mathsf{K}_j^{(\xi)}(B) = \mathrm{ff} \ \text{ for some } j \\
&\quad \Leftrightarrow \mathsf{K}_j^{(\xi)}(\ominus A \to B) = \mathrm{ff} \ \text{ for some } j
\end{aligned}$$

which shows that $A \to \Box B \simeq \ominus A \to B$ and therefore

$$A \to \Box B \simeq \Box(\ominus A \to B)$$

because of $\ominus A \to B \simeq \Box(\ominus A \to B)$.

Note that invariance properties are expressible in the basic temporal logic without any extensions. A special case is given by formulas **true** $\to \Box B$ which can simply be written in the form of the logically equivalent

$$\Box B$$

and then are directly in the original form of safety properties. The specification with the model equivalent formula B would be even simpler but, unlike when writing axioms, here we mostly will prefer the notation with the temporal closure since it makes the temporal character a bit more apparent. If a system Γ has such a property $\Box B$ then B is also called a *global invariant* of Γ. As an example, the Towers of Hanoi property

$$\Box(DECR(pl_1) \wedge DECR(pl_2) \wedge DECR(pl_3))$$

describes a global invariant of Γ_{ToH}.

Using the extension "b" by binary operators, formulas

$$A \to B \ \mathbf{op} \ C$$

where **op** is a weak binary operator (**unless**, **unl**, **atnext**, etc.) and A, B, and C are state formulas of Γ specify another kind of property called *precedence properties*. All of them are again safety properties: for example,

$$A \rightarrow B \textbf{ before } C \simeq \Box(C \rightarrow B \textbf{ after } A)$$

because of

$$\begin{aligned}
&\mathsf{K}_i^{(\xi)}(A \rightarrow B \textbf{ before } C) = \mathsf{ff} \ \text{ for some } i \\
&\quad \Leftrightarrow \mathsf{K}_i^{(\xi)}(A) = \mathsf{tt} \text{ and } \mathsf{K}_i^{(\xi)}(B \textbf{ before } C) = \mathsf{ff} \ \text{ for some } i \\
&\quad \Leftrightarrow \mathsf{K}_i^{(\xi)}(A) = \mathsf{tt} \text{ and } \mathsf{K}_j^{(\xi)}(C) = \mathsf{tt} \ \text{ for some } i \text{ and some } j > i \\
&\quad\quad\ \text{and } \mathsf{K}_k^{(\xi)}(B) = \mathsf{ff} \ \text{ for } i < k < j \\
&\quad \Leftrightarrow \mathsf{K}_j^{(\xi)}(C) = \mathsf{tt} \text{ and } \mathsf{K}_j^{(\xi)}(B \textbf{ after } A) = \mathsf{ff} \ \text{ for some } j \\
&\quad \Leftrightarrow \mathsf{K}_j^{(\xi)}(C \rightarrow B \textbf{ after } A) = \mathsf{ff} \ \text{ for some } j
\end{aligned}$$

which shows that $A \rightarrow B$ **before** $C \simeq C \rightarrow B$ **after** A and proves the assertion.

According to the results of Sect. 3.1 this model equivalence can immediately be extended to the other strict binary operators. For the reflexive operators the argument runs analogously.

A simple example is

$$start_{\Gamma^l_{ToH}} \rightarrow \neg nil_{\Gamma^l_{ToH}} \textbf{ unl } A_{fin}$$

(with A_{fin} as before) specifying for the labeled Towers of Hanoi system Γ^l_{ToH} that

> "when starting to play the puzzle, in each step a move has to be made until the tower is on its destination place"

which is in fact a valid property of the system.

Note that the formula

$$\textbf{init} \rightarrow \neg nil_{\Gamma^l_{ToH}} \textbf{ unl } A_{fin}$$

would be another formalization of the informal phrase. It does, however, not fit into our syntactical framework since **init** is no state formula. So we choose here and in all analogous cases in the following (also with the other kinds of properties) the formulation with the initial condition *start* instead of **init**. Observe that in the case of invariance properties of this form it is easy to see (with the axiom (root) and the logical rules (init) and (alw)) that

$$\textbf{init} \rightarrow \Box B \vdash \Box B \vdash start \rightarrow \Box B \vdash \textbf{init} \rightarrow \Box B$$

which means that $start \rightarrow \Box B$ and **init** $\rightarrow \Box B$ are model equivalent and, moreover, both are model equivalent with $\Box B$.

Properties of the third kind we will consider are of the form

$$A \to \Diamond B$$

with state formulas A and B of Γ. They are called *eventuality properties* and are expressible again without any extensions of the basic temporal language. The property

$$start_{\Gamma_{ToH}} \to \Diamond A_{fin}$$

describing the goal of the Towers of Hanoi system is an example. Properties

$$\Diamond B$$

which are logically equivalent to **true** $\to \Diamond B$ are special cases and are of the form of a response property. In fact, all eventuality properties belong to this class because of

$$A \to \Diamond B \simeq \Diamond(\neg A \ \mathbf{backto}\ B)$$

which is proved by

$$\begin{aligned}
\mathsf{K}_i^{(\xi)}(A \to \Diamond B) = \mathsf{ff} &\Rightarrow \mathsf{K}_i^{(\xi)}(A) = \mathsf{tt} \text{ and } \mathsf{K}_j^{(\xi)}(B) = \mathsf{ff} \text{ for every } j \geq i \\
&\Rightarrow \mathsf{K}_j^{(\xi)}(\neg A \ \mathbf{backto}\ B) = \mathsf{ff} \text{ for every } j \geq i+1 \\
&\Rightarrow \mathsf{K}_{j+1}^{(\xi)}(\Diamond(\neg A \ \mathbf{backto}\ B)) = \mathsf{ff}
\end{aligned}$$

and

$$\begin{aligned}
&\mathsf{K}_i^{(\xi)}(\Diamond(\neg A \ \mathbf{backto}\ B)) = \mathsf{ff} \\
&\quad \Rightarrow \mathsf{K}_j^{(\xi)}(\neg A \ \mathbf{backto}\ B) = \mathsf{ff} \text{ for every } j \geq i \\
&\quad \Rightarrow \text{for every } j \geq i \text{ there is some } k < j \text{ such that} \\
&\qquad\ \mathsf{K}_k^{(\xi)}(A) = \mathsf{tt} \text{ and } \mathsf{K}_l^{(\xi)}(B) = \mathsf{ff} \text{ for } k \leq l \leq j \\
&\quad \Rightarrow \mathsf{K}_k^{(\xi)}(A) = \mathsf{tt} \text{ and } \mathsf{K}_l^{(\xi)}(B) = \mathsf{ff} \text{ for some } k \text{ and every } l \geq k \\
&\quad \Rightarrow \mathsf{K}_k^{(\xi)}(A \to \Diamond B) = \mathsf{ff} \text{ for some } k.
\end{aligned}$$

Summarizing, invariance, precedence, and eventuality properties are particular cases of safety and response properties. Although rather simple, these three kinds of properties have many interesting applications some of which will be investigated subsequently.

We recall at this point our decision to perform all these investigations in the framework of normal semantics. Of course, they could be transformed appropriately if initial validity semantics is used. For example, invariance properties would then have the general form

$$\Box(A \to \Box B)$$

(with state formulas A and B) and a similar adaption has to be performed for the other properties and all the other preceding and still following discussions.

Second Reading

We have classified system properties with respect to the syntactical form of their specifying formulas. There is another widely used semantical distinction of just two classes of properties. We consider this classification again only for the case of properties specified by formulas F of the language $\mathcal{L}_{\mathrm{FOLTL}}^{\mathrm{bp}}$. Such a property for a given transition system Γ is called *safety property* if, for every $\mathsf{K} = (\mathsf{S}_\Gamma, \mathsf{W})$, $\mathsf{W} = (\eta_0, \eta_1, \eta_2, \ldots)$, ξ, and $i \in \mathbb{N}$,

$$\begin{array}{lll} \mathsf{K}_i^{(\xi)}(F) = \mathsf{tt} & \Leftrightarrow & \text{for every } k > i \text{ there are infinitely many system states} \\ & & \overline{\eta}_k, \overline{\eta}_{k+1}, \overline{\eta}_{k+2}, \ldots \text{ such that } \overline{\mathsf{K}}_i^{(\xi)}(F) = \mathsf{tt} \text{ for } \overline{\mathsf{K}} = (\mathsf{S}_\Gamma, \overline{\mathsf{W}}) \\ & & \text{with } \overline{\mathsf{W}} = (\eta_0, \ldots, \eta_{k-1}, \overline{\eta}_k, \overline{\eta}_{k+1}, \overline{\eta}_{k+2}, \ldots). \end{array}$$

Informally this means that every run $(\eta_0, \eta_1, \eta_2, \ldots)$ of the system for which F does not hold in some η_i has a finite prefix $(\eta_0, \ldots, \eta_i, \ldots, \eta_{k-1})$ which cannot be "extended" to a run which has the property, even more intuitively: after some finite number of steps something "bad" must have happened in such a run which cannot be remedied by any further behaviour. Turning it around, a safety property means that "nothing bad ever happens".

The property is called *liveness property* if, for every $\mathsf{K} = (\mathsf{S}_\Gamma, \mathsf{W})$, $\mathsf{W} = (\eta_0, \eta_1, \eta_2, \ldots)$, ξ, and $i \in \mathbb{N}$, it is the case that

$$\begin{array}{l} \text{there are infinitely many system states } \overline{\eta}_k, \overline{\eta}_{k+1}, \overline{\eta}_{k+2}, \ldots \text{ such that} \\ \overline{\mathsf{K}}_i^{(\xi)}(F) = \mathsf{tt} \text{ for } \overline{\mathsf{K}} = (\mathsf{S}_\Gamma, \overline{\mathsf{W}}) \text{ with } \overline{\mathsf{W}} = (\eta_0, \ldots, \eta_{k-1}, \overline{\eta}_k, \overline{\eta}_{k+1}, \overline{\eta}_{k+2}, \ldots). \end{array}$$

This means informally that every finite prefix of a run can be extended such that it has the property, intuitively: "something good will happen".

Some interesting facts about these classes of properties can be proved. Some examples are:

- F is valid if and only if F is both a safety and a liveness property.
- There are properties which are neither safety nor liveness properties.
- If F_1 and F_2 are safety properties then so are $F_1 \wedge F_2$ and $F_1 \vee F_2$.

Referring to the system $\Gamma_{\alpha\beta}$ in the main text of this section for some simple examples, the formula

$$\mathit{exec}\,\alpha \ \mathbf{unless}\ \mathit{exec}\,\beta$$

is a safety property, while

$$\Diamond \mathit{exec}\,\beta$$

is a liveness property. The formula

$$\mathit{exec}\,\alpha \ \mathbf{until}\ \mathit{exec}\,\beta$$

is neither a safety nor a liveness property.

In general, the safety properties of this classification are exactly the safety properties of the syntactical classification. Liveness properties, however, are "not comparable" with the classes of that classification. Actually, every response or persistence property is logically equivalent to the conjunction of a safety and liveness property. For example, the above formula $\mathit{exec}\,\alpha$ **until** $\mathit{exec}\,\beta$ specifies a response property and is logically equivalent to $\mathit{exec}\,\alpha$ **unless** $\mathit{exec}\,\beta \wedge \Diamond \mathit{exec}\,\beta$.

7.2 Invariance Properties

Let $(\mathcal{L}_{\mathrm{TL}}, \mathcal{A})$ be a $\mathcal{C}$-FOLTL- (or $\mathcal{C}$-LTL-)theory for a class $\mathcal{C}$ of temporal structures. If Σ_{TL} is the formal system for the temporal logic with language $\mathcal{L}_{\mathrm{TL}}$ and F is a formula of $\mathcal{L}_{\mathrm{TL}}$ then $\mathcal{A} \vdash_{\Sigma_{\mathrm{TL}}} F$ implies $\mathcal{A} \vDash F$ because of the soundness of Σ_{TL}, and the latter implies $\vDash_{\mathsf{K}} F$ for every $\mathsf{K} \in \mathcal{C}$ by definition. So we have

$$\mathcal{A} \vdash_{\Sigma_{\mathrm{TL}}} F \;\Rightarrow\; \vDash_{\mathsf{K}} F \quad \text{for every } \mathsf{K} \in \mathcal{C}$$

which means that a sound way to prove a formula F to be valid in every temporal structure of $\mathcal{C}$ is to derive F within Σ_{TL} from $\mathcal{A}$.

This general observation can be directly applied to the verification of state systems. To show that such a system Γ has a property F means to prove that F is valid in every $\mathsf{K} \in \mathcal{C}_\Gamma$. Thus, a possible method for doing this is to show that

$$\mathcal{A}_\Gamma \vdash F$$

within the formal system for the chosen temporal logic of Γ.

In the following we want to introduce and discuss some basic *verification methods* for such derivations for the three kinds of properties picked out at the end of the previous section. We begin with invariance properties.

Verification methods for state systems depend (for all kinds of properties) on how the system is to be understood in the sense of the distinctions made in Chap. 6, formally: on the kind of the formal transition system representing it. To derive an invariance property

$$A \rightarrow \Box B$$

for a (non-labeled) STS Γ the main proof method is to apply one of the induction rules

(ind)	$A \rightarrow B, A \rightarrow \bigcirc A \vdash A \rightarrow \Box B$,
(ind1)	$A \rightarrow \bigcirc A \vdash A \rightarrow \Box A$,
(ind2)	$A \rightarrow B, B \rightarrow \bigcirc B \vdash A \rightarrow \Box B$

introduced in Sect. 2.3. The particular rule (ind1) can be applied to the frequently occurring case of safety properties of the form

$$A \rightarrow \Box A$$

expressing that whenever A holds in some state it will then hold permanently.

Example. The terminating counter Γ_{tcount} specified in Sect. 6.2 by ($\mathrm{data}_{\Gamma_{tcount}}$) and by the temporal axioms

(TC1)	$c \leq 100$,
(TC2)	$on \wedge c < 100 \rightarrow (on' \wedge c' = c + 1) \vee (\neg on' \wedge c' = c)$,

(TC3) $\neg on \wedge c < 100 \rightarrow (\neg on' \wedge c' = c) \vee (on' \wedge c' = 0)$,
(TC4) $c = 100 \rightarrow (on' \leftrightarrow on) \wedge c' = c$

has the property

$$c = 100 \rightarrow \Box(c = 100)$$

which is almost trivially derived with (ind1):

(1)	$c = 100 \rightarrow c' = 100$	(pred),(TC4)
(2)	$c = 100 \rightarrow \bigcirc(c = 100)$	(pred),(1)
(3)	$c = 100 \rightarrow \Box(c = 100)$	(ind1),(2)

Note that line (2) only describes the obvious transformation from the priming notation of line (1) into a formula with the operator $\bigcirc$ as required in (ind1). $\triangle$

In the general case of properties

$$A \rightarrow \Box B$$

one of the rules (ind) or (ind2) is adequate, but in most applications these rules cannot be directly applied with A or B taken from the given property: usually, the premises $A \rightarrow \bigcirc A$ or $B \rightarrow \bigcirc B$ will not be derivable. In fact, the crucial point of a derivation mostly will be to find an appropriate formula C for which $A \rightarrow C$ and $C \rightarrow B$ and (as the main task)

$$C \rightarrow \bigcirc C$$

can be derived. Applying (ind) we then get $C \rightarrow \Box B$ from which the desired formula $A \rightarrow \Box B$ is trivially obtained with (prop).

Example. The terminating counter above also has the property

$$c < 100 \rightarrow \Box(c = 100 \rightarrow on)$$

expressing that if $c < 100$ in some state then whenever c will (subsequently) have the value 100 the counter will be on. To derive this let

$$C \equiv c < 100 \vee (on \wedge c = 100).$$

We clearly have

(1)	$c < 100 \rightarrow C$	(taut)
(2)	$C \rightarrow (c = 100 \rightarrow on)$	(taut)

The main part of the proof is to derive $C \rightarrow \bigcirc C$:

(3)	$on \wedge c < 100 \rightarrow (on' \wedge c' = c + 1) \vee c' < 100$	(pred),(TC2)
(4)	$on \wedge c < 100 \rightarrow (on' \wedge (c' < 100 \vee c' = 100)) \vee c' < 100$	(pred),(data),(3)

(5)	$on \land c < 100 \rightarrow c' < 100 \lor (on' \land c' = 100)$	(prop),(4)
(6)	$\neg on \land c < 100 \rightarrow c' = c \lor c' = 0$	(prop),(TC3)
(7)	$\neg on \land c < 100 \rightarrow c' < 100$	(pred),(data),(6)
(8)	$\neg on \land c < 100 \rightarrow c' < 100 \lor (on' \land c' = 100)$	(prop),(7)
(9)	$c < 100 \rightarrow c' < 100 \lor (on' \land c' = 100)$	(prop),(5),(8)
(10)	$on \land c = 100 \rightarrow (on' \land c' = 100)$	(pred),(TC4)
(11)	$C \rightarrow c' < 100 \lor (on' \land c' = 100)$	(prop),(9),(10)

(Note that for brevity we write only (data) to indicate the usage of (data$_{\Gamma_{tcount}}$).) Again the derivation is performed in a notation with primed constants. The formula $c' < 100 \lor (on' \land c' = 100)$, however, is logically equivalent to $\bigcirc C$, so we finally obtain

(12)	$C \rightarrow \bigcirc C$	(pred),(11)
(13)	$C \rightarrow \Box(c = 100 \rightarrow on)$	(ind),(2),(12)
(14)	$c < 100 \rightarrow \Box(c = 100 \rightarrow on)$	(prop),(1),(13)

(In subsequent derivations we will not explicitly note a "translation" step as in line (12) but apply a rule like (ind) directly to the primed constant notation.) △

Turning now to the question how to derive global invariants, i.e., properties of the form

$$\Box A$$

we remark once more that such a property is specified by A as well, and this fact immediately indicates that the above induction rules are of no use in this case. For example, trying to apply (ind) for proving **true** $\rightarrow \Box A$ we had to prove the premises **true** $\rightarrow A$, which is equivalent to A, and the trivial **true** $\rightarrow \bigcirc$ **true**. For (ind2) the premises would be **true** $\rightarrow A$ and $A \rightarrow \bigcirc A$. So in both cases we had to prove A from which (if wanted) $\Box A$ is derived directly with the rule (alw).

In fact there is no general temporal logic device for deriving such a property $\Box A$ (or A) in an STS Γ if this is not rooted. Being a state formula, A will usually express some valid assertion about the involved data in this case and be an instance of (data$_\Gamma$).

The situation changes, however, if Γ is rooted with an initial condition $start_\Gamma$. In this case we obtain another useful induction rule

(indstart$_\Gamma$) $\quad start_\Gamma \rightarrow A, A \rightarrow \bigcirc A \vdash \Box A$

which can easily be derived with the axiom (root$_\Gamma$) and the rule (indinit) shown in Sect. 3.5.

Derivation of (indstart$_\Gamma$).

(1)	$start_\Gamma \rightarrow A$	assumption
(2)	$A \rightarrow \bigcirc A$	assumption
(3)	**init** $\rightarrow start_\Gamma$	(root$_\Gamma$)

(4) $\mathbf{init} \rightarrow A$ (prop),(1),(3)
(5) A (indinit),(2),(4)
(6) $\Box A$ (alw),(5) △

Example. We now prove the property $\Box A$ where

$$A \equiv DECR(pl_1) \wedge DECR(pl_2) \wedge DECR(pl_3)$$

for the rooted Towers of Hanoi system Γ_{ToH} of Sect. 6.3 with

$$start_{\Gamma_{ToH}} \equiv pl_1 = TOWER \wedge pl_2 = EMPTY \wedge pl_3 = EMPTY$$

and the axioms

$$\neg A_{fin} \rightarrow A_{123} \vee A_{132} \vee A_{213} \vee A_{231} \vee A_{312} \vee A_{321},$$
$$A_{fin} \rightarrow \circ A_{fin}$$

where

$$\begin{aligned} A_{ijk} \equiv\ & pl_i \neq EMPTY \wedge (pl_j \neq EMPTY \rightarrow TOP(pl_i) < TOP(pl_j)) \wedge \\ & pl'_i = POP(pl_i) \wedge pl'_j = PUSH(pl_j, TOP(pl_i)) \wedge pl'_k = pl_k, \\ A_{fin} \equiv\ & pl_1 = EMPTY \wedge pl_2 = TOWER \wedge pl_3 = EMPTY. \end{aligned}$$

The derivation runs as follows:

(1) $start_{\Gamma_{ToH}} \rightarrow A$ (data)
(2) $A_{fin} \rightarrow A$ (data)
(3) $\circ A_{fin} \rightarrow \circ A$ (T30),(2)
(4) $A_{fin} \rightarrow \circ A_{fin}$ (Γ)
(5) $A_{fin} \wedge A \rightarrow \circ A$ (prop),(3),(4)
(6) $\neg A_{fin} \wedge A \rightarrow \circ A$ (data),(Γ)
(7) $A \rightarrow \circ A$ (prop),(5),(6)
(8) $\Box A$ (indstart),(1),(7)

Note again that the references to (data$_{\Gamma_{ToH}}$) and (indstart$_{\Gamma_{ToH}}$) are not written out in their full detail. Moreover, in the justifications of lines (4) and (6) we do not note the respective axioms of Γ_{ToH} but indicate their use only by (Γ). We will continue in this way, particularly using the comment (Γ) "as can be seen from the specification axioms of the system" without justifying it in more detail. △

The induction rules discussed so far are generally applicable in (r)STSs. For labeled systems they can be still modified in a significant way. The main part in all the rules is to show a formula of the form

$$A \rightarrow \circ A$$

and in the case of a labeled system Γ this can be established in a particular way using the rule

$$\begin{array}{lll}(\text{trans}_\Gamma) & exec\lambda \land A \to \circ B & \text{for every } \lambda \in Act_\Gamma, \\ & nil_\Gamma \land A \to B & \\ & \vdash A \to \circ B & \text{if } B \text{ is a state formula of } \Gamma\end{array}$$

which can easily be derived with the axiom (nil_Γ) from Sect. 6.4 and can therefore be used in every (r)lSTS.

Derivation of (trans_Γ). Let $Act_\Gamma = \{\lambda_1, \ldots, \lambda_n\}$.

(1)	$exec\lambda \land A \to \circ B$ for every $\lambda \in Act_\Gamma$	assumption
(2)	$nil_\Gamma \land A \to B$	assumption
(3)	$nil_\Gamma \lor exec\lambda_1 \lor \ldots \lor exec\lambda_n$	(taut)
(4)	$nil_\Gamma \land A \to nil_\Gamma \land B$	(prop),(2)
(5)	$nil_\Gamma \land B \to \circ B$	(nil_Γ)
(6)	$nil_\Gamma \land A \to \circ B$	(prop),(4),(5)
(7)	$A \to \circ B$	(prop),(1),(3),(6) △

The informal meaning of this rule is that in order to prove that "A implies that B in the next state" it is sufficient to show that A is "transformed" to B by each action and A implies B in case no action is executed.

For notational convenience we now introduce the abbreviations

$$A \textbf{ invof } \lambda \equiv exec\lambda \land A \to \circ A$$

reading "A is an *invariant of* λ" and

$$A \textbf{ invof } Act_\Gamma \equiv \bigwedge_{\lambda \in Act_\Gamma} (A \textbf{ invof } \lambda)$$

meaning "A is an invariant of every $\lambda \in Act_\Gamma$". So if $A \equiv B$ in (trans_Γ) then the first premise of this rule can be written as A **invof** Act_Γ and the second premise becomes the tautology $nil_\Gamma \land A \to A$. Together this leads to the rule

$$A \textbf{ invof } Act_\Gamma \vdash A \to \circ A \quad \text{if } A \text{ is a state formula of } \Gamma$$

as a special case of (trans_Γ). Combining this rule with the induction rules we immediately obtain new ones which we call *invariant rules*. We note

$$\begin{array}{ll}(\text{inv}_\Gamma) & A \to B, A \textbf{ invof } Act_\Gamma \vdash A \to \Box B \quad \text{if } A \text{ is a state formula of } \Gamma, \\ (\text{inv1}_\Gamma) & A \textbf{ invof } Act_\Gamma \vdash A \to \Box A \quad \text{if } A \text{ is a state formula of } \Gamma, \\ (\text{invstart}_\Gamma) & start_\Gamma \to A, A \textbf{ invof } Act_\Gamma \vdash \Box A \quad \text{if } A \text{ is a state formula of } \Gamma\end{array}$$

which are transferred from the induction rules (ind), (ind1), and (indstart_Γ).

Examples. We consider two of the examples above in the setting of labeled systems. The terminating counter was not specified in its labeled version Γ^l_{tcount} in Chap. 6 but it should be evident that $Act_{\Gamma^l_{tcount}} = \{\lambda_{on}, \lambda_{off}, \lambda_c, \lambda_p\}$ and such a specification would contain axioms like

$$(1) \quad exec\lambda \rightarrow c < 100 \quad \text{for every } \lambda \in Act_{\Gamma^l_{tcount}}$$

("the counter is only executing an action if $c < 100$") or at least axioms from which this could be derived. The further derivation of the property

$$c = 100 \rightarrow \Box(c = 100)$$

is similarly trivial as before:

(2)	$exec\lambda \wedge c = 100 \rightarrow \circ(c = 100)$ for every $\lambda \in Act_{\Gamma^l_{tcount}}$		(pred),(data),(1)
(3)	$c = 100$ **invof** $Act_{\Gamma^l_{tcount}}$		(prop),(2)
(4)	$c = 100 \rightarrow \Box(c = 100)$		(inv1),(3)

The labeled Towers of Hanoi system Γ^l_{ToH} was specified in Sect. 6.4. We only note that again

$$start_{\Gamma^l_{ToH}} \equiv pl_1 = TOWER \wedge pl_2 = EMPTY \wedge pl_3 = EMPTY$$

and repeat the axioms

$$exec\lambda_{ij} \rightarrow pl_i \neq EMPTY \wedge (pl_j \neq EMPTY \rightarrow TOP(pl_i) < TOP(pl_j)),$$
$$exec\lambda_{ij} \rightarrow pl'_i = POP(pl_i) \wedge pl'_j = PUSH(pl_j, TOP(pl_i)) \wedge pl'_k = pl_k,$$

each for $\lambda_{ij} \in Act_{\Gamma^l_{ToH}}$ and with $k \neq i$, $k \neq j$. Using these axioms (indicated again simply by (Γ)) we can derive the property $\Box A$ where

$$A \equiv DECR(pl_1) \wedge DECR(pl_2) \wedge DECR(pl_3)$$

for Γ^l_{ToH} as follows:

(1)	$start_{\Gamma^l_{ToH}} \rightarrow A$	(data)
(2)	$exec\lambda_{ij} \wedge A \rightarrow \circ A$ for every $\lambda_{ij} \in Act_{\Gamma^l_{ToH}}$	(data),(Γ)
(3)	A **invof** $Act_{\Gamma^l_{ToH}}$	(prop),(2)
(4)	$\Box A$	(invstart),(1),(3)

Comparing this derivation with the proof for Γ_{ToH} above we observe that now we have no corresponding part to the line $A_{fin} \wedge A \rightarrow \circ A$ there. Informally this line showed the "invariance" of A under the assumption that the goal A_{fin} is reached. In the labeled system $nil_{\Gamma^l_{ToH}} \leftrightarrow A_{fin}$ is an axiom, so this case is implicitly dispatched by the axiom (nil$_{\Gamma^l_{ToH}}$) which is the basis of rule (trans$_{\Gamma^l_{ToH}}$). △

Note finally that in the invariant rules formulas are partially restricted to state formulas of the respective Γ induced by the corresponding restriction in the axiom (nil$_\Gamma$) and, hence, in the rule (trans$_\Gamma$). (There are no restrictions at all in the basic induction rules.) So, as remarked in Sect. 6.4, they could be strengthened but, as also announced there, the present form of the rules is obviously sufficient for the application to invariance properties $A \rightarrow \Box B$ in which A and B are state formulas of the system.

7.3 Precedence Properties

As in the case of safety properties, the basic proof methods for the derivation of a precedence property

$$A \to B \ \mathbf{op}\ C$$

for an STS are again immediately provided by the induction rules for the weak binary operators **op** developed in the corresponding logic FOLTL+b or LTL+b. We recall those introduced in Sect. 3.1:

(indunless)	$A \to \circ C \vee \circ(A \wedge B) \ \vdash\ A \to B \ \mathbf{unless}\ C,$
(indunl)	$A \to C \vee (B \wedge \circ A) \ \vdash\ A \to B \ \mathbf{unl}\ C,$
(indatnext)	$A \to \circ(C \to B) \wedge \circ(\neg C \to A) \ \vdash\ A \to B \ \mathbf{atnext}\ C,$
(indbefore)	$A \to \circ\neg C \wedge \circ(A \vee B) \ \vdash\ A \to B \ \mathbf{before}\ C.$

In each case the formula A plays a similar role as in the rule (ind). It "carries the induction": if holding in some state it has to hold – now under some particular circumstances – in the next state. Again it will often not be possible to apply the rules directly since for the formula A from the given property $A \to B\ \mathbf{op}\ C$ this will not be derivable. A better-suited formula D has then to be found for which $A \to D$ is derivable and which, taken instead of A, allows us to derive the premise of the corresponding rule. With the latter, $D \to B\ \mathbf{op}\ C$ is concluded which is then sufficient to obtain $A \to B\ \mathbf{op}\ C$.

Example. The (non-terminating) counter Γ_{count} specified in Sect. 6.2 with the temporal axioms

$$on \to (on' \wedge c' = c + 1) \vee (\neg on' \wedge c' = c),$$
$$\neg on \to (\neg on' \wedge c' = c) \vee (on' \wedge c' = 0)$$

has the property

$$\neg on \to c = 0 \ \mathbf{atnext}\ on$$

expressing that a switched off counter will get the value 0 when switched on next time. The derivation is very easy in this case by direct application of rule (indatnext):

(1)	$\neg on \to (\neg on' \wedge c' = c) \vee (on' \wedge c' = 0)$	(Γ)
(2)	$\neg on \to (on' \to c' = 0)$	(1)
(3)	$\neg on \to \circ(on \to c = 0) \wedge \circ(\neg on \to \neg on)$	(2)
(4)	$\neg on \to c = 0 \ \mathbf{atnext}\ on$	(indatnext),(3)

Observe that we continue shortening our comments in such derivations not only using again the shorthand (Γ) but now also leaving out the additional purely logical rules like (prop) or (pred) involved in steps (2) and (3). We will follow this line more and more, even omitting to note temporal logical laws like (T1),(T2),..., or data reasoning included in the axioms (data$_\Gamma$). This is to increase the understanding of a formal verification in content. Getting used to simple logical and data arguments we rely on them more implicitly and can thus better emphasize the substantial underlying proof ideas.

Another property of Γ_{count} is that whatever the value of the counter is it will not be decreased subsequently unless it is reset to 0. This is expressed by the formula

$$c = x \rightarrow c \geq x \ \mathbf{unl} \ c = 0$$

where x is a variable of sort NAT. Here the formula $c = x$ is not suitable for the induction but with

$$D \equiv c \geq x \vee c = 0$$

we can derive:

(1)	$c = x \rightarrow D$	(data)
(2)	$on \wedge c \geq x \rightarrow c' = c + 1 \vee c' = c$	(Γ)
(3)	$on \wedge c \geq x \rightarrow \bigcirc(c \geq x)$	(2)
(4)	$on \wedge D \rightarrow c = 0 \vee (c \geq x \wedge \bigcirc D)$	(3)
(5)	$\neg on \wedge c \geq x \rightarrow c' = c \vee c' = 0$	(Γ)
(6)	$\neg on \wedge c \geq x \rightarrow \bigcirc D$	(5)
(7)	$\neg on \wedge D \rightarrow c = 0 \vee (c \geq x \wedge \bigcirc D)$	(3)
(8)	$D \rightarrow c = 0 \vee (c \geq x \wedge \bigcirc D)$	(4),(7)
(9)	$D \rightarrow c \geq x \ \mathbf{unl} \ c = 0$	(indunl),(8)
(10)	$c = x \rightarrow c \geq x \ \mathbf{unl} \ c = 0$	(1),(9) △

Turning to labeled systems Γ we can again modify the above induction rules relating the state transitions to the actions of Γ. We get the new rules

(invunless$_\Gamma$) $exec\lambda \wedge A \rightarrow \bigcirc C \vee \bigcirc(A \wedge B)$ for every $\lambda \in Act_\Gamma$,
$nil_\Gamma \wedge A \rightarrow B \vee C$
$\vdash A \rightarrow B \ \mathbf{unless} \ C$ if A, B, and C are state formulas of Γ,

(invunl$_\Gamma$) $exec\lambda \wedge A \rightarrow C \vee (B \wedge \bigcirc A)$ for every $\lambda \in Act_\Gamma$,
$nil_\Gamma \wedge A \rightarrow B \vee C$
$\vdash A \rightarrow B \ \mathbf{unl} \ C$ if A, B, and C are state formulas of Γ,

(invatnext$_\Gamma$) $exec\lambda \wedge A \rightarrow \bigcirc(C \rightarrow B) \wedge \bigcirc(\neg C \rightarrow A)$ for every $\lambda \in Act_\Gamma$,
$nil_\Gamma \wedge A \rightarrow (C \rightarrow B)$
$\vdash A \rightarrow B \ \mathbf{atnext} \ C$ if A, B, and C are state formulas of Γ,

(invbefore$_\Gamma$) $exec\lambda \wedge A \rightarrow \bigcirc\neg C \wedge \bigcirc(A \vee B)$ for every $\lambda \in Act_\Gamma$,
$nil_\Gamma \wedge A \rightarrow \neg C$
$\vdash A \rightarrow B \ \mathbf{before} \ C$ if A, B, and C are state formulas of Γ.

We call these rules again *invariant rules*. In each case the formula A is similar to an invariant in the sense of the previous section. The derivations of the rules run along the same pattern using the derived rule (trans$_\Gamma$). We show only one of them:

Derivation of (invatnext$_\Gamma$).

(1)	$exec\lambda \land A \rightarrow \circ(C \rightarrow B) \land \circ(\neg C \rightarrow A)$ for every $\lambda \in Act_\Gamma$	assumption
(2)	$nil_\Gamma \land A \rightarrow (C \rightarrow B)$	assumption
(3)	$nil_\Gamma \land A \rightarrow (C \rightarrow B) \land (\neg C \rightarrow A)$	(prop),(2)
(4)	$A \rightarrow \circ(C \rightarrow B) \land \circ(\neg C \rightarrow A)$	(trans$_\Gamma$),(T15),(1),(3)
(5)	$A \rightarrow B$ **atnext** C	(indatnext),(4) △

It should be clear that the remark about the restrictions to state formulas of Γ carry over from the invariant rules in the previous section.

Example. We want to derive the properties of the previous example for the counter given by the l$_e$STS Γ^l_{count} specified in Sect. 6.4. The actions are λ_{on}, λ_{off}, λ_c,λ_p, and the axioms include

$$\begin{array}{l} exec\lambda \rightarrow on \quad \text{for } \lambda \in \{\lambda_{off}, \lambda_c\},\\ exec\lambda \rightarrow \neg on \quad \text{for } \lambda \in \{\lambda_{on}, \lambda_p\},\\ exec\lambda_{on} \rightarrow on' \land c' = 0,\\ exec\lambda_{off} \rightarrow \neg on' \land c' = c,\\ exec\lambda_c \rightarrow on' \land c' = c+1,\\ exec\lambda_p \rightarrow \neg on' \land c' = c. \end{array}$$

The property

$$\neg on \rightarrow c = 0 \textbf{ atnext } on$$

is then derived again very easily by direct application of (invatnext$_{\Gamma^l_{count}}$). We abbreviate $E \equiv \circ(on \rightarrow c = 0) \land \circ(\neg on \rightarrow \neg on)$ and have:

(1)	$exec\lambda_{on} \land \neg on \rightarrow E$	(Γ)
(2)	$exec\lambda_{off} \land \neg on \rightarrow E$	(Γ)
(3)	$exec\lambda_c \land \neg on \rightarrow E$	(Γ)
(4)	$exec\lambda_p \land \neg on \rightarrow E$	(Γ)
(5)	$nil_{\Gamma^l_{count}} \land \neg on \rightarrow (on \rightarrow c = 0)$	(taut)
(6)	$\neg on \rightarrow c = 0$ **atnext** on	(invatnext),(1)–(5)

For the property

$$c = x \rightarrow c \geq x \textbf{ unl } c = 0$$

we need again the formula $D \equiv c \geq x \lor c = 0$ and have:

(1)	$c = x \rightarrow D$	(data)
(2)	$exec\lambda_{on} \land D \rightarrow c = 0 \lor (c \geq x \land c' = 0)$	(Γ)
(3)	$exec\lambda_{off} \land D \rightarrow c = 0 \lor (c \geq x \land c' = c)$	(Γ)
(4)	$exec\lambda_c \land D \rightarrow c = 0 \lor (c \geq x \land c' = c+1)$	(Γ)

(5) $exec\lambda_p \land D \to c = 0 \lor (c \geq x \land c' = c)$ (Γ)
(6) $exec\lambda \land D \to c = 0 \lor (c \geq x \land \bigcirc(c \geq x \lor c = 0))$
for every $\lambda \in Act_{\Gamma^l_{count}}$ (2)–(5)
(7) $nil_{\Gamma^l_{count}} \land D \to (c \geq x \lor c = 0)$ (taut)
(8) $D \to c \geq x$ **unl** $c = 0$ (invunl),(6),(7)
(9) $c = x \to c \geq x$ **unl** $c = 0$ (1),(8) △

7.4 Eventuality Properties

As mentioned earlier, the only proof rules for eventuality properties

$$A \to \Diamond B$$

in the framework of propositional temporal logic developed so far are rules like

(som) $A \to \bigcirc B \vdash A \to \Diamond B$,
(chain) $A \to \Diamond B, B \to \Diamond C \vdash A \to \Diamond C$

providing a very simple *finite chain reasoning* method: in order to prove $A \to \Diamond B$ according to (chain) we have to prove two – or in general finitely many – "smaller steps" of the same kind. (som) is one simple way for establishing these steps.

Although often applicable, these rules are rather weak. A universal method is given by the rule

(wfr) $A \to \Diamond(B \lor \exists \bar{y}(\bar{y} \prec y \land A_y(\bar{y}))) \vdash \exists y A \to \Diamond B$
if B does not contain y,
for $y, \bar{y} \in \mathcal{X}_{WF}$.

introduced in Sect. 5.5. It is again an induction rule but induction is running over "objects" here instead of "computations" in the case of the propositional rules for invariance and precedence properties. Its formulation needs a linguistic first-order framework equipped with the special extension "w" providing some well-founded relation on distinguished objects.

Example. Consider a "bounded" counter system Γ_{bcount} by modifying the terminating counter Γ_{tcount} discussed in Sect. 6.2 in the following way: reaching the value 100 the counter does not terminate but is switched off. Furthermore, at most N pausing steps may be performed consecutively where N is some natural number constant. We do not write up an exact formalization as an STS but give immediately the temporal axioms specifying Γ_{bcount}:

$$c \leq 100 \land b \leq N,$$
$$on \land c < 100 \to (on' \land c' = c + 1) \lor (\neg on' \land c' = c \land b' = 0),$$
$$on \land c = 100 \to \neg on' \land c' = c \land b' = 0,$$
$$\neg on \land b < N \to (\neg on' \land c' = c \land b' = b + 1) \lor (on' \land c' = 0),$$
$$\neg on \land b = N \to on' \land c' = 0.$$

The additional system variable b (of sort NAT) counts the numbers of pausing steps. Note that for simplicity we do not exclude that at the very beginning the system might be forced to be switched on after less than N pausing steps if initially $b > 0$.

Γ_{bcount} has the property

$$\Diamond(c = 0)$$

expressing that a state where the counter has the value 0 will eventually be reached from any other state. To derive this property we first note that the underlying language $\mathcal{L}_{\mathrm{TL}}$ is based on the signature SIG_{Nat} containing the sort NAT and the predicate symbol $<$, which we take as the sort WF and the symbol $\prec$, thus viewing the language as being a language $\mathcal{L}^{\mathrm{w}}_{\mathrm{TL}}$. We then begin to show that $c > 0 \land \neg on$ implies that sometime $c = 0$ will hold. We want to apply the rule (wfr) and have to find an appropriate formula A which carries the induction. Taking

$$A \equiv y + b = N \land c > 0 \land \neg on$$

we obtain

$$\begin{array}{lll}
(1) & A \land b < N \to c' = 0 \lor (\neg on' \land c' = c \land b' = b + 1) & (\Gamma) \\
(2) & A \land b < N \to c' = 0 \lor (y + b' - 1 = N \land c' > 0 \land \neg on') & (1) \\
(3) & A \land b < N \to \bigcirc(c = 0 \lor A_y(y - 1)) & (2) \\
(4) & A \land b = N \to c' = 0 & (\Gamma) \\
(5) & b \leq N & (\Gamma) \\
(6) & A \to \bigcirc(c = 0 \lor A_y(y - 1)) & (3),(4),(5) \\
(7) & A \to \Diamond(c = 0 \lor \exists \bar{y}(\bar{y} < y \land A_y(\bar{y}))) & (\mathrm{som}),(6) \\
(8) & \exists y A \to \Diamond(c = 0) & (\mathrm{wfr}),(7) \\
(9) & \exists y(y + b = N) & (\mathrm{data}),(5) \\
(10) & c > 0 \land \neg on \to \exists y A & (9) \\
(11) & c > 0 \land \neg on \to \Diamond(c = 0) & (8),(10)
\end{array}$$

Next we show in a very similar way that if $c > 0 \land on$ then $c > 0 \land \neg on$ will eventually hold. With

$$B \equiv y + c = 100 \land c > 0 \land on$$

we get

$$\begin{array}{lll}
(12) & B \land c < 100 \to (c' = c \land \neg on) \lor (on' \land c' = c + 1) & (\Gamma) \\
(13) & B \land c < 100 \to & \\
 & \qquad (c' > 0 \land \neg on) \lor (y + c' - 1 = 100 \land c' > 0 \land on') & (12) \\
(14) & B \land c < 100 \to \bigcirc((c > 0 \land \neg on) \lor B_y(y - 1)) & (13) \\
(15) & B \land c = 100 \to c' > 0 \land \neg on' & (\Gamma) \\
(16) & c \leq 100 & (\Gamma) \\
(17) & B \to \bigcirc((c > 0 \land \neg on) \lor B_y(y - 1)) & (14),(15),(16) \\
(18) & B \to \Diamond((c > 0 \land \neg on) \lor \exists \bar{y}(\bar{y} < y \land B_y(y - 1))) & (\mathrm{som}),(17) \\
(19) & \exists y B \to \Diamond(c > 0 \land \neg on) & (\mathrm{wfr}),(18)
\end{array}$$

(20) $\exists y(y + c = 100)$ (data),(16)
(21) $c > 0 \land on \rightarrow \exists yB$ (20)
(22) $c > 0 \land on \rightarrow \Diamond(c > 0 \land \neg on)$ (19),(21)

Putting these results together we obtain

(23) $c > 0 \land on \rightarrow \Diamond(c = 0)$ (chain),(11),(22)
(24) $c > 0 \rightarrow \Diamond(c = 0)$ (11),(23)

This shows that $c = 0$ is eventually reached in the case of $c > 0$. If $c = 0$ this is trivial, so we can conclude the derivation by

(25) $c = 0 \rightarrow \Diamond(c = 0)$ (T5)
(26) $\Diamond(c = 0)$ (24),(25) △

As purely logical rules, (wfr) as well as (som) and (chain) can be applied in all kinds of transition systems. Turning to labeled systems Γ, the only direct starting point to gain new rules is to utilize the rule (trans$_\Gamma$) derived in Sect 7.2 and translate the rule (som) to

(som1$_\Gamma$) $exec\lambda \land A \rightarrow \bigcirc B$ for every $\lambda \in Act_\Gamma$,
$nil_\Gamma \land A \rightarrow B$
$\vdash A \rightarrow \Diamond B$ if B is a state formula of Γ.

This rule may be combined with (wfr) and then provides the (trivially derivable) version

(labwfr$_\Gamma$) $exec\lambda \land A \rightarrow \bigcirc(B \lor \exists \bar{y}(\bar{y} \prec y \land A_y(\bar{y})))$ for every $\lambda \in Act_\Gamma$,
$nil_\Gamma \land A \rightarrow B$
$\vdash \exists yA \rightarrow \Diamond B$ if A and B are state formulas of Γ and B does not contain y, for $y, \bar{y} \in \mathcal{X}_{WF}$.

of (wfr).

Another consideration deals with the first premise of (som1$_\Gamma$) requiring that the execution of every $\lambda \in Act$ leads from A to B. This is rather strong and it becomes weaker if the requirement has to be established only for some particular actions which cannot be delayed forever and if all the other actions, if not leading to B as well, leave A invariant. This idea is captured by the rule

(som2$_\Gamma$) $exec\lambda \land A \rightarrow \bigcirc B$ for every $\lambda \in Act_h \subseteq Act_\Gamma$,
$exec\lambda \land A \rightarrow \bigcirc(B \lor A)$ for every $\lambda \in Act_\Gamma \setminus Act_h$,
$\Box A \rightarrow \Diamond \bigvee_{\lambda \in Act_h} exec\lambda$
$\vdash A \rightarrow \Diamond B$ if A is a state formula of Γ

which is formulated again in the purely propositional framework. The elements of the subset Act_h of Act_Γ are called *helpful* actions. The third premise of the rule guarantees that, if A holds, then one of them is executed sometime (which also implies that the premise $nil_\Gamma \land A \rightarrow B$ of the rule above is no longer needed): otherwise, $\Box A$

would hold because of the invariance of A under $\lambda \in Act_\Gamma \setminus Act_h$ and this implies that some $\lambda \in Act_h$ is executed sometime which then would be a contradiction. The following derivation formalizes this idea.

Derivation of (som2$_\Gamma$). Let $C \equiv \bigvee_{\lambda \in Act_h} exec\lambda$.

(1)	$exec\lambda \land A \to \bigcirc B$ for every $\lambda \in Act_h$	assumption
(2)	$exec\lambda \land A \to \bigcirc(B \lor A)$ for every $\lambda \in Act_\Gamma \setminus Act_h$	assumption
(3)	$\Box A \to \Diamond C$	assumption
(4)	$exec\lambda \land \neg C \land A \land \Box\neg B \to \bigcirc A$ for every $\lambda \in Act_\Gamma \setminus Act_h$	(2)
(5)	$exec\lambda \land \neg C \land A \land \Box\neg B \to \bigcirc A$ for every $\lambda \in Act_h$	(taut)
(6)	$nil_\Gamma \land \neg C \land A \land \Box\neg B \to A$	(taut)
(7)	$\neg C \land A \land \Box\neg B \to \bigcirc A$	(trans$_\Gamma$),(4),(5),(6)
(8)	$\Box\neg(C \land A) \to \neg(C \land A) \land \bigcirc\Box\neg(C \land A)$	(ltl3)
(9)	$A \land \Box\neg(C \land A) \to A \land \neg C \land \bigcirc\Box\neg(C \land A)$	(8)
(10)	$A \land \Box\neg(C \land A) \land \Box\neg B \to \bigcirc(A \land \Box\neg(C \land A) \land \Box\neg B)$	(7),(9)
(11)	$A \land \Box\neg(C \land A) \land \Box\neg B \to \Box(A \land \Box\neg(C \land A) \land \Box\neg B)$	(ind1),(10)
(12)	$A \land \Box\neg(C \land A) \land \Box\neg B \to \Box A \land \Box\neg C$	(11)
(13)	$A \land \Box\neg B \to \neg\Box\neg(C \land A)$	(3),(12)
(14)	$A \land \Box\neg B \to \Diamond\bigcirc B$	(1),(13)
(15)	$A \to \Diamond B$	(14) △

Still the rule (som2$_\Gamma$) is not very useful in practice. It puts almost all of the proof problem on showing the third premise

$$\Box A \to \Diamond \bigvee_{\lambda \in Act_h} exec\lambda$$

which contains again the sometime operator. In many cases like those discussed in Sect. 6.5 this is in fact not possible without the additional requirement that the system is fair. Typically, $\Box A$ implies the eventual enabledness of some of the helpful actions and only the fairness assumption then guarantees that one of them will in fact be executed. Modifying (som2$_\Gamma$) along this line we obtain the rule

(fairsom$_\Gamma$) $exec\lambda \land A \to \bigcirc B$ for every $\lambda \in Act_h \subseteq Act_\Gamma$,
$exec\lambda \land A \to \bigcirc(B \lor A)$ for every $\lambda \in Act_\Gamma \setminus Act_h$,
$\Box A \to \Diamond \bigvee_{\lambda \in Act_h} enabled_\lambda$
$\vdash A \to \Diamond B$ if A is a state formula of Γ

which holds for any f(r)l$_e$STS Γ and is in this form applicable in many cases. The formal derivation of (fairsom$_\Gamma$) uses the fairness axiom

(fair$_\Gamma$) $\Box\Diamond enabled_\lambda \to \Diamond exec\lambda$ for every $\lambda \in Act_\Gamma$

given in Sect. 6.5.

Derivation of (fairsom$_\Gamma$).

(1)	$exec\lambda \wedge A \rightarrow \bigcirc B$ for every $\lambda \in Act_h$	assumption
(2)	$exec\lambda \wedge A \rightarrow \bigcirc(B \vee A)$ for every $\lambda \in Act_\Gamma \setminus Act_h$	assumption
(3)	$\Box A \rightarrow \Diamond \bigvee_{\lambda \in Act_h} enabled_\lambda$	assumption
(4)	$\Box A \rightarrow \Box\Diamond \bigvee_{\lambda \in Act_h} enabled_\lambda$	(T35),(3)
(5)	$\Box A \rightarrow \bigvee_{\lambda \in Act_h} \Box\Diamond enabled_\lambda$	(T20),(4)
(6)	$\Box A \rightarrow \bigvee_{\lambda \in Act_h} \Diamond exec\lambda$	(fair$_\Gamma$),(5)
(7)	$\Box A \rightarrow \Diamond \bigvee_{\lambda \in Act_h} exec\lambda$	(T19),(6)
(8)	$A \rightarrow \Diamond B$	(som2$_\Gamma$),(1), (2),(7) △

Example. The (original) counter system discussed in Chap. 6 does not have the property

$$\Diamond(c = 0)$$

since "unfair" execution sequences might never execute a switch on action. However, if we add (to the l$_e$STS Γ^l_{count}) the fairness requirement then the property becomes derivable. We need not note the corresponding fairness axiom explicitly; its use is hidden in the rule (fairsom$_\Gamma$). Besides that we apply temporal axioms of Γ^l_{count}, comprehended to

$$exec\lambda_{on} \rightarrow \neg on \wedge on' \wedge c' = 0,$$
$$exec\lambda_{off} \rightarrow on \wedge \neg on' \wedge c' = c,$$
$$exec\lambda_c \rightarrow on \wedge on' \wedge c' = c + 1,$$
$$exec\lambda_p \rightarrow \neg on \wedge \neg on' \wedge c' = c$$

and we recall that $enabled_{\lambda_{on}} \equiv \neg on$ and $enabled_{\lambda_{off}} \equiv on$.

We first show that $c > 0$ implies that eventually the counter will be switched off. With $Act_h = \{\lambda_{off}\}$ we get

(1)	$exec\lambda_{off} \wedge on \rightarrow \bigcirc\neg on$	(Γ)
(2)	$exec\lambda \wedge on \rightarrow \bigcirc(\neg on \vee on)$ for $\lambda \in \{\lambda_{on}, \lambda_c, \lambda_p\}$	(taut),(nex)
(3)	$\Box on \rightarrow \Diamond on$	(T8)
(4)	$\Box on \rightarrow \Diamond enabled_{\lambda_{off}}$	(Γ),(3)
(5)	$on \rightarrow \Diamond\neg on$	(fairsom),(1),(2),(4)
(6)	$c > 0 \wedge on \rightarrow \Diamond\neg on$	(5)
(7)	$c > 0 \wedge \neg on \rightarrow \Diamond\neg on$	(T5)
(8)	$c > 0 \rightarrow \Diamond\neg on$	(6),(7)

Next we show $\neg on \rightarrow \Diamond(c = 0)$ with $Act_h = \{\lambda_{on}\}$:

(9)	$exec\lambda_{on} \wedge \neg on \rightarrow \bigcirc(c = 0)$	(Γ)
(10)	$exec\lambda \wedge \neg on \rightarrow \bigcirc\neg on$ for $\lambda \in \{\lambda_{off}, \lambda_c, \lambda_p\}$	(Γ)
(11)	$exec\lambda \wedge \neg on \rightarrow \bigcirc(c = 0 \vee \neg on)$ for $\lambda \in \{\lambda_{off}, \lambda_c, \lambda_p\}$	(10)
(12)	$\Box\neg on \rightarrow \Diamond\neg on$	(T8)

(13) $\Box\neg on \to \Diamond enabled_{\lambda_{on}}$ (Γ),(12)
(14) $\neg on \to \Diamond(c = 0)$ (fairsom),(9),(11),(13)

Together we get

(15) $c > 0 \to \Diamond(c = 0)$ (chain),(8),(14)
(16) $c = 0 \to \Diamond(c = 0)$ (T5)
(17) $\Diamond(c = 0)$ (data),(15),16) △

The rule (fairsom$_\Gamma$) was developed from (som) in the context of fair labeled state systems. Similar modifications may be performed for the universal rule (wfr). The premise

$$A \to \Diamond(B \vee \exists\bar{y}(\bar{y} \prec y \wedge A_y(\bar{y})))$$

of (wfr) could be established with (som) by showing

$$A \to \bigcirc(B \vee \exists\bar{y}(\bar{y} \prec y \wedge A_y(\bar{y})))$$

and in the presence of (trans$_\Gamma$) this essentially amounts to showing

$$exec\lambda \wedge A \to \bigcirc(B \vee \exists\bar{y}(\bar{y} \prec y \wedge A_y(\bar{y}))) \quad \text{for every } \lambda \in Act_\Gamma$$

(if A and B are state formulas of the system). Again a weaker requirement is that this holds at least for "helpful" actions while for the others, if not leading to B, it is also sufficient to leave A invariant, i.e., to guarantee that their execution leads to a state in which A holds with the same value of y as before this execution. The choice of the helpful actions is again arbitrary and may even depend on y. We formalize this by introducing, for any f(r)l$_e$STS Γ and $\lambda \in Act_\Gamma$, the notation

$$H_\lambda$$

for an arbitrary rigid formula of $\mathcal{L}_{\mathrm{TL}\Gamma}$ and the abbreviations

$$E_\Gamma \equiv \bigvee_{\lambda \in Act_\Gamma} (H_\lambda \wedge enabled_\lambda),$$

$$\bar{y} \preceq y \equiv \bar{y} \prec y \vee \bar{y} = y.$$

Informally, the formula H_λ describes those "circumstances" (particularly values of y) under which λ is helpful. E_λ expresses that some helpful λ is enabled. The rule

(fairwfr$_\Gamma$)

$exec\lambda \wedge H_\lambda \wedge A \to \bigcirc(B \vee \exists\bar{y}(\bar{y} \prec y \wedge A_y(\bar{y})))$
for every $\lambda \in Act_\Gamma$,
$exec\lambda \wedge \neg H_\lambda \wedge A \to \bigcirc(B \vee \exists\bar{y}(\bar{y} \preceq y \wedge A_y(\bar{y})))$
for every $\lambda \in Act_\Gamma$,
$\Box A \to \Diamond(B \vee E_\Gamma)$
$\vdash \exists y A \to \Diamond B$ if A and B are state formulas of Γ
and B does not contain y,
for $y, \bar{y} \in \mathcal{X}_{WF}$.

then holds for Γ.

Derivation of (fairwfr$_\Gamma$). Let C_1, C_2, and D be the following abbreviations:
$C_1 \equiv \exists \bar{y}(\bar{y} \prec y \land A_y(\bar{y}))$, $C_2 \equiv \exists \bar{y}(\bar{y} \preceq y \land A_y(\bar{y}))$, $D \equiv \bigvee_{\lambda \in Act_\Gamma}(H_\lambda \land exec\lambda)$.

(1)	$exec\lambda \land H_\lambda \land A \rightarrow \circ(B \lor C_1)$ for every $\lambda \in Act_\Gamma$	assumption
(2)	$exec\lambda \land \neg H_\lambda \land A \rightarrow \circ(B \lor C_2)$ for every $\lambda \in Act_\Gamma$	assumption
(3)	$\Box A \rightarrow \Diamond(B \lor E_\Gamma)$	assumption
(4)	$A \rightarrow C_2$	(pred)
(5)	$exec\lambda \land C_2 \land \Box\neg B \rightarrow \circ C_2$ for every $\lambda \in Act_\Gamma$	(1),(2)
(6)	$(C_2 \land \Box\neg B)$ **invof** Act_Γ	(ltl3),(T15),(5)
(7)	$C_2 \land \Box\neg B \rightarrow \Box(C_2 \land \Box\neg B)$	(inv1$_\Gamma$),(6)
(8)	$A \land \Box\neg B \rightarrow \Box C_2$	(T18),(4),(7)
(9)	$A \land \Box\neg B \land \Box\neg C_1 \rightarrow \Box A \land \Box\neg B$	(8)
(10)	$\Box A \rightarrow \Box\Diamond(B \lor E_\Gamma)$	(T35),(3)
(11)	$\Box A \rightarrow \Box\Diamond B \lor \Box\Diamond E_\Gamma$	(T20),(10)
(12)	$A \land \Box\neg B \land \Box\neg C_1 \rightarrow \Box A \land \Box\Diamond E_\Gamma$	(ltl3),(9),(11)
(13)	$\Box\Diamond(H_\lambda \land enabled_\lambda) \rightarrow \Box\Diamond H_\lambda \land \Box\Diamond enabled_\lambda$ for every $\lambda \in Act_\Gamma$	(T26)
(14)	$\neg H_\lambda \rightarrow \circ\neg H_\lambda$ for every $\lambda \in Act_\Gamma$	(ltl6)
(15)	$\neg H_\lambda \rightarrow \Box\neg H_\lambda$ for every $\lambda \in Act_\Gamma$	(ind1),(14)
(16)	$\Diamond H_\lambda \rightarrow H_\lambda$ for every $\lambda \in Act_\Gamma$	(15)
(17)	$\Box\Diamond H_\lambda \rightarrow H_\lambda$ for every $\lambda \in Act_\Gamma$	(ltl3),(16)
(18)	$H_\lambda \rightarrow \circ H_\lambda$ for every $\lambda \in Act_\Gamma$	(ltl6)
(19)	$\Box\Diamond H_\lambda \rightarrow \Box H_\lambda$ for every $\lambda \in Act_\Gamma$	(ind2),(17),(18)
(20)	$\Box\Diamond(H_\lambda \land enabled_\lambda) \rightarrow \Box H_\lambda \land \Diamond exec\lambda$ for every $\lambda \in Act_\Gamma$	(fair$_\Gamma$),(13),(19)
(21)	$\Box\Diamond(H_\lambda \land enabled_\lambda) \rightarrow \Diamond(H_\lambda \land exec\lambda)$ for every $\lambda \in Act_\Gamma$	(T34),(20)
(22)	$\Box\Diamond E_\Gamma \rightarrow \Diamond D$	(T19),(T20),(21)
(23)	$A \land \Box\neg B \land \Box\neg C_1 \rightarrow \Box A \land \Diamond D \land \Box\neg B$	(12),(22)
(24)	$\Box A \land \Box\neg B \rightarrow (\Diamond D \rightarrow \Diamond(D \land A \land \Box\neg B))$	(T10),(T18),(T34)
(25)	$A \land \Box\neg B \land \Box\neg C_1 \rightarrow \Diamond(D \land A \land \Box\neg B)$	(23),(24)
(26)	$exec\lambda \land H_\lambda \land A \land \Box\neg B \rightarrow \Diamond C_1$ for every $\lambda \in Act_\Gamma$	(som),(T32),(1)
(27)	$A \land \Box\neg B \land \Box\neg C_1 \rightarrow \Diamond C_1$	(chain),(25),(26)
(28)	$A \rightarrow \Diamond(B \lor C_1)$	(27)
(29)	$\exists y A \rightarrow \Diamond B$	(wfr),(28) △

Example. Consider another modification $\Gamma_{wrcount}$ of the original counter system, a "counter without reset", which is to mean that the effect of the action λ_{on} is not resetting c to 0 but leaving c unchanged. In the specifying formulas in the above example we then have to change the first one to

$$exec\lambda_{on} \rightarrow \neg on \land on' \land c' = c.$$

If we assume this system to be fair then it has the property

$$c = 0 \rightarrow \Diamond(c = x)$$

stating that any value (of the variable x of sort NAT) will eventually be reached from $c = 0$. For the proof we fix – as in the first example of this section – WF and $\prec$ to be NAT and $<$, respectively (which means that $\preceq$ becomes $\leq$). We first show $\Diamond on$ by applying (fairsom$_{\Gamma_{wrcount}}$) with $Act_h = \{\lambda_{on}\}$:

(1)	$exec\lambda_{on} \land on \rightarrow \bigcirc on$	(Γ)
(2)	$exec\lambda \land \neg on \rightarrow \bigcirc(\neg on \lor on)$ for $\lambda \in \{\lambda_{off}, \lambda_c, \lambda_p\}$	(nex),(taut)
(3)	$\Box\neg on \rightarrow \Diamond enabled_{\lambda_{on}}$	(T8)
(4)	$\neg on \rightarrow \Diamond on$	(fairsom),(1),(2),(3)
(5)	$on \rightarrow \Diamond on$	(T5)
(6)	$\Diamond on$	(4),(5)

Let now

$$A \equiv y + c = x \land c < x$$

and

$$H_{\lambda_c} \equiv \mathbf{true},$$
$$H_\lambda \equiv \mathbf{false} \quad \text{for } \lambda \in \{\lambda_{on}, \lambda_{off}, \lambda_p\},$$

the latter expressing that λ_c is helpful and the other actions are not helpful (in any case). We then get

(7)	$exec\lambda_c \rightarrow c' = c + 1$	(Γ)
(8)	$exec\lambda_c \land A \land c < x - 1 \rightarrow \bigcirc A_y(y - 1)$	(7)
(9)	$exec\lambda_c \land A \land c = x - 1 \rightarrow \bigcirc(c = x)$	(7)
(10)	$exec\lambda_c \land H_{\lambda_c} \land A \rightarrow \bigcirc(c = x \lor \exists\bar{y}(\bar{y} < y \land A_y(\bar{y})))$	(8),(9)
(11)	$exec\lambda_c \land \neg H_{\lambda_c} \land A \rightarrow \bigcirc(c = x \lor \exists\bar{y}(\bar{y} \leq y \land A_y(\bar{y})))$	(taut)
(12)	$exec\lambda \land H_\lambda \land A \rightarrow \bigcirc(c = x \lor \exists\bar{y}(\bar{y} < y \land A_y(\bar{y})))$ for $\lambda \in \{\lambda_{on}, \lambda_{off}, \lambda_p\}$	(taut)
(13)	$exec\lambda \land A \rightarrow \bigcirc A$ for $\lambda \in \{\lambda_{on}, \lambda_{off}, \lambda_p\}$	(Γ)
(14)	$exec\lambda \land \neg H_\lambda \land A \rightarrow \bigcirc(c = x \lor \exists\bar{y}(\bar{y} \leq y \land A_y(\bar{y})))$ for $\lambda \in \{\lambda_{on}, \lambda_{off}, \lambda_p\}$	(13)
(15)	$\Box A \rightarrow \Diamond on$	(6)
(16)	$E_\Gamma \leftrightarrow enabled_{\lambda_c}$	(taut)
(17)	$\Box A \rightarrow \Diamond(c = x \lor E_\Gamma)$	(15),(16)
(18)	$\exists y A \rightarrow \Diamond(c = x)$	(fairwfr),(10),(11),(12),(14),(17)
(19)	$c = 0 \land x \neq 0 \rightarrow \exists y A$	(data)
(20)	$c = 0 \land x = 0 \rightarrow \Diamond(c = x)$	(T5)
(20)	$c = 0 \rightarrow \Diamond(c = x)$	(18),(19),(20) △

As mentioned already, the rule (wfr) and hence (fairwfr$_\Gamma$) as well formalize inductions over well-founded data sets, in our example the set of natural numbers. Proofs with the other purely propositional rules do not involve data at all but they can always be "encoded" into proofs with the universal rules. We conclude this section with a trivial example which makes the crucial idea of this fact evident.

Example. Consider a propositional frl$_e$STS Γ_{sw} modeling a system of two switches S_1 and S_2 represented by the set $V = \{on_1, on_2\}$ of system variables which show whether S_1 and S_2 are on or not. Three actions α_1, α_2, β may be continuously executed: α_1 switches S_1 on if it is off and leaves it on otherwise, α_2 does the same for S_2, and β does not change the switches at all. Fixing that both S_1 and S_2 are off at the beginning, Γ_{sw} is specified by

$$\begin{aligned} start_{\Gamma_{sw}} &\equiv \neg on_1 \wedge \neg on_2, \\ enabled_\lambda &\equiv \mathbf{true} \quad \text{for } \lambda \in \{\alpha_1, \alpha_2, \beta\} \end{aligned}$$

and the temporal axioms

$$\begin{aligned} &exec\,\alpha_1 \rightarrow on_1' \wedge (on_2' \leftrightarrow on_2), \\ &exec\,\alpha_2 \rightarrow (on_1' \leftrightarrow on_1) \wedge on_2', \\ &exec\,\beta \rightarrow (on_1' \leftrightarrow on_1) \wedge (on_2' \leftrightarrow on_2). \end{aligned}$$

Assuming fairness both α_1 and α_2 will be executed and, hence, will switch on S_1 and S_2 sometime. So Γ_{sw} has the property

$$start_{\Gamma_{sw}} \rightarrow \Diamond(on_1 \wedge on_2)$$

which is easily derived with (fairsom$_{\Gamma_{sw}}$) and (chain): with $Act_h = \{\alpha_1, \alpha_2\}$ we get

(1)	$exec\,\alpha_i \wedge start_{\Gamma_{sw}} \rightarrow \bigcirc(on_1 \vee on_2)$ for $i \in \{1, 2\}$	(Γ)
(2)	$exec\,\beta \wedge start_{\Gamma_{sw}} \rightarrow \bigcirc(on_1 \vee on_2 \vee start_{\Gamma_{sw}})$	(Γ)
(3)	$\Box start_{\Gamma_{sw}} \rightarrow \Diamond(enabled_{\alpha_1} \vee enabled_{\alpha_2})$	(taut),(T5)
(4)	$start_{\Gamma_{sw}} \rightarrow \Diamond(on_1 \vee on_2)$	(fairsom),(1),(2),(3)

In the same way we immediately get (with $Act_h = \{\alpha_2\}$)

(5)	$on_1 \wedge \neg on_2 \rightarrow \Diamond(on_1 \wedge on_2)$	(fairsom),(Γ)

and (with $Act_h = \{\alpha_1\}$)

(6)	$\neg on_1 \wedge on_2 \rightarrow \Diamond(on_1 \wedge on_2)$	(fairsom),(Γ)

which then yields

(7)	$start_{\Gamma_{sw}} \rightarrow \Diamond(on_1 \wedge on_2)$	(chain),(4),(5),(6)

There are no "inductive objects" in this system; the proof argues along the flow of any execution sequence through states in which $start_{\Gamma_{sw}}$, $on_1 \wedge \neg on_2$, $\neg on_1 \wedge on_2$, and finally $on_1 \wedge on_2$ hold. This can easily be described, however, by a decreasing sequence of natural numbers. Extending the underlying language $\mathcal{L}_{\mathrm{TL}\Gamma}$ to a first-order one based on SIG_{Nat}, and taking again NAT as WF and $<$ as $\prec$ we let

$$
\begin{aligned}
A &\equiv (\neg on_1 \wedge \neg on_2 \wedge y = 2) \vee (on_1 \wedge \neg on_2 \wedge y = 1) \vee (\neg on_1 \wedge on_2 \wedge y = 0),\\
H_{\alpha_1} &\equiv \neg on_1,\\
H_{\alpha_2} &\equiv \neg on_2,\\
H_\beta &\equiv \mathbf{false}.
\end{aligned}
$$

Then we may apply (fairwfr$_{\Gamma_{sw}}$) in the following alternative derivation. First we get

(1)	$H_{\alpha_1} \wedge A \rightarrow y = 2 \vee y = 0$	(prop)
(2)	$exec\,\alpha_1 \wedge A \wedge y = 2 \rightarrow \bigcirc A_y(1)$	(Γ)
(3)	$exec\,\alpha_1 \wedge A \wedge y = 0 \rightarrow \bigcirc(on_1 \wedge on_2)$	(Γ)
(4)	$exec\,\alpha_1 \wedge H_{\alpha_1} \wedge A \rightarrow$ $\bigcirc((on_1 \wedge on_2) \vee \exists \bar{y}(\bar{y} < y \wedge A_y(\bar{y})))$	(1),(2),(3)
(5)	$exec\,\alpha_1 \wedge \neg H_{\alpha_1} \wedge A \rightarrow \bigcirc A$	(Γ)

In the same way we obtain

(6)	$exec\,\alpha_2 \wedge H_{\alpha_2} \wedge A \rightarrow$ $\bigcirc((on_1 \wedge on_2) \vee \exists \bar{y}(\bar{y} < y \wedge A_y(\bar{y})))$	(Γ)
(7)	$exec\,\alpha_2 \wedge \neg H_{\alpha_2} \wedge A \rightarrow \bigcirc A$	(Γ)

For β the corresponding formulas are trivial:

(8)	$exec\,\beta \wedge H_\beta \wedge A \rightarrow$ $\bigcirc((on_1 \wedge on_2) \vee \exists \bar{y}(\bar{y} < y \wedge A_y(\bar{y})))$	(taut)
(9)	$exec\,\beta \wedge \neg H_\beta \wedge A \rightarrow \bigcirc A$	(Γ)

Finally we have

(10)	$\Box A \rightarrow \Diamond E_{\Gamma_{sw}}$	(T8)

since $E_{\Gamma_{sw}} \leftrightarrow \neg on_1 \vee \neg on_2$ is tautologically valid, and so we get

(11)	$\exists y A \rightarrow \Diamond(on_1 \wedge on_2)$	(fairwfr),(4)–(10)
(12)	$start_{\Gamma_{sw}} \rightarrow \exists y A$	(data)
(13)	$start_{\Gamma_{sw}} \rightarrow \Diamond(on_1 \wedge on_2)$	(11),(12) △

Although this second proof looks somewhat cumbersome it is actually more concise than the first one with the rule (fairsom). Its main part is to show the two first premises of rule (wfr) in lines (1)–(9), and the key idea for this is given by the definition of H_λ: the action α_1 is helpful when $\neg on$ holds, i.e., for the values 2 and 0 for y in A, α_2 is helpful for $y = 2$ and $y = 1$, and β is not helpful at all.

The derivation in lines (1)–(9) may more transparently be represented in a diagram as shown in Fig. 7.1. The nodes in this diagram – except the one labeled with $on_1 \wedge on_2$ – represent all possible values of y if A holds, together with the respective information encoded in A. Arrows $\Longrightarrow$ are labeled with helpful actions and point to those nodes representing what may hold after executing these actions in the corresponding states. Simple arrows $\longrightarrow$ show the same for non-helpful actions.

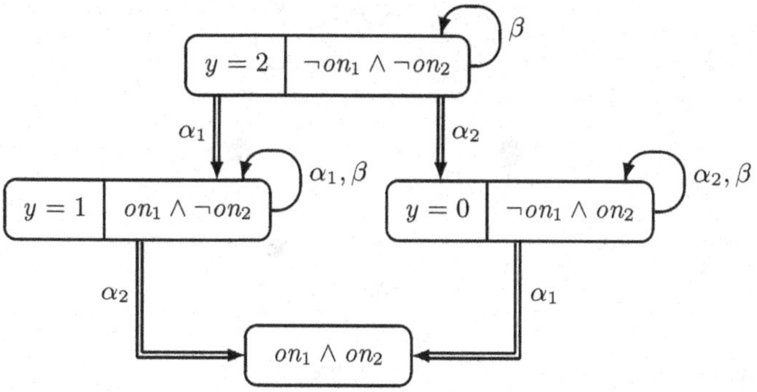

Fig. 7.1. A diagram representing a derivation

As mentioned already, the assumption of fairness is often needed for proving eventuality properties of systems. In fact, the rules (fairsom$_\Gamma$) and (fairwfr$_\Gamma$) are essentially based on the fairness axiom

(fair$_\Gamma$) $\quad \Box\Diamond enabled_\lambda \rightarrow \Diamond exec\,\lambda \quad$ for every $\lambda \in Act_\Gamma$.

We still note that in some applications this axiom may even be used directly (instead of its indirect usage in the rules).

Example. The fair printer system $\Gamma_{printer}$ specified in Sect. 6.5 has the property

$$req_1 \rightarrow \Diamond exec\,\beta_1$$

describing that, if the printer is requested by user U_1, then sometime it will execute the job for U_1. Recalling that $enabled_{\alpha_1} \equiv \neg req_1$, $enabled_{\beta_1} \equiv req_1$, and

$$exec\,\lambda \rightarrow (req_1' \leftrightarrow req_1) \quad \text{for } \lambda \in Act_{\Gamma_{printer}} \setminus \{\alpha_1, \beta_1\}$$

can be extracted from the specification axioms of $\Gamma_{printer}$, we obtain

(1)	$(req_1 \wedge \Box\neg exec\,\beta_1)$ **invof** $Act_{\Gamma_{printer}}$	(Γ),(ltl3)
(2)	$req_1 \wedge \Box\neg exec\,\beta_1 \rightarrow \Box(req_1 \wedge \Box\neg exec\,\beta_1)$	(inv1),(1)
(3)	$req_1 \wedge \Box\neg exec\,\beta_1 \rightarrow \Box req_1$	(2)
(4)	$\Box req_1 \rightarrow \Box\Diamond req_1$	(T5)
(5)	$\Box\Diamond req_1 \rightarrow \Diamond exec\,\beta_1$	(fair)
(6)	$req_1 \rightarrow \Diamond exec\,\beta_1$	(3),(4),(5) $\quad \triangle$

7.5 A Self-stabilizing Network

Summarizing the considerations of Chap. 6 and the preceding sections of this chapter we realize a bunch of linguistic features and formal methods which is at our disposal when facing the task of formally specifying and verifying a state system.

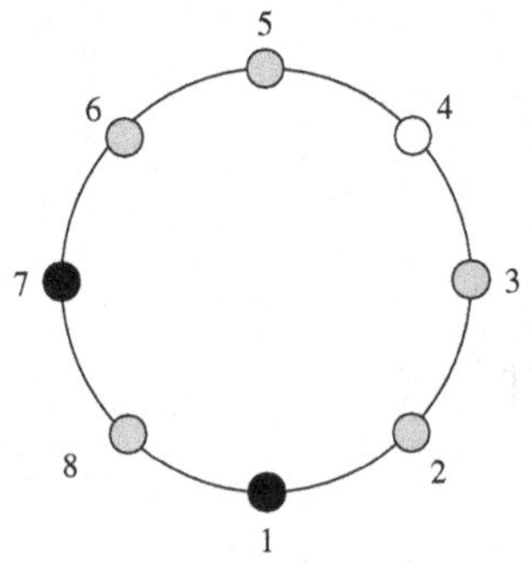

(a) A state of the system

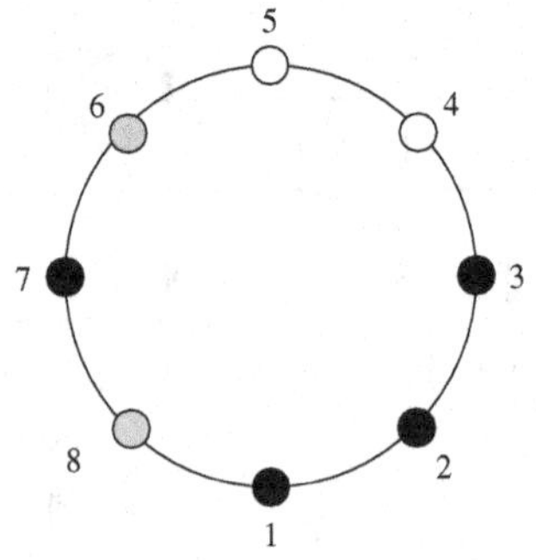

(b) State after three steps

Fig. 7.2. A network with 8 nodes

First of all, the system, in its formal representation as an STS, may be with or without initial condition, labeled or not, with or without fairness assumption. The appropriate temporal logic languages for specifying the system depend only slightly on this choice. Whenever the STS is rooted, the language should contain the feature of syntactic (or semantical) anchoring, i.e, the extension "p" by past operators or at least "i" by the particular formula **init** (or, alternatively, it should use the initial validity semantics). For non-rooted STSs any temporal logic language version is well suited.

The verification task has more influence on which language should be chosen. For describing invariance and eventuality properties there are no particular requirements while precedence properties need some extension, e.g., binary operators. For proving such properties there is a repertory of methods, and in the case of eventuality properties a further linguistic extension by well-founded relations could be necessary. (For dealing with other properties as indicated in Sect. 7.1, further extensions might be needed.)

In this and the next section we want to conclude the discussion with elaborating two more complicated examples of systems and their verification. Consider, firstly, a network system consisting of $n \geq 2$ nodes, enumerated by $1, \ldots, n$. Every node owns a register which is able to store values from the set $\mathbb{M} = \{0, 1, \ldots, N\}$ of natural numbers where $N \geq n - 1$ and which can be accessed (reading and writing) by the node. The nodes are arranged in a ring and every node is also allowed to read the register of its left neighbour. A state of the system is given by the valuation of the registers with values from $\mathbb{M}$. Fig. 7.2(a) depicts such a system with eight nodes using different hatchings to indicate three different register values.

The system starts running from some initial state. In every step one of the nodes may change the actual values $l_1, \ldots, l_n$ of the registers according to the following protocol:

- Node 1 may only execute a step if $l_1 = l_n$; by this step, l_1 is increased by 1 modulo $N + 1$; all other registers remain unchanged.

- Node i, $2 \leq i \leq n$, may only execute a step if $l_i \neq l_{i-1}$; by this step, the value l_{i-1} is copied into the own register of i replacing the present value l_i; all other registers remain unchanged.

Fig. 7.2(b) shows the system state resulting from (a) after executing three consecutive steps by nodes 2,3, and 5.

In general, several nodes are ready to execute a step in a state. For example, in state (a) of Fig. 7.2 node 2, 4, 5, 7, or 8 may execute. A state is called *stable* if there is one and only one node which may execute a step according to the protocol. Remarkably, such a system is *self-stabilizing*, which means that, starting from an arbitrary initial state and proceeding arbitrarily according to the protocol, it will eventually reach a stable state after finitely many steps and the states will remain stable from then on.

We want to prove this property formally and begin with specifying the system (for fixed n) understanding it as an $\mathrm{l_e}$STS $\Gamma_{ring} = (X, V, W, T, Act, \mathcal{E})$. For the moment we base Γ_{ring} on a signature SIG_{Nat} particularly containing N as an individual constant and a function symbol $\oplus^{(NAT\ NAT, NAT)}$ and supplied with its standard model N where $\oplus^{\mathsf{N}}$ is addition modulo $N + 1$. We do not write out all constituents of Γ_{ring} and note only

$$
\begin{aligned}
&Act = \{\beta_1, \ldots, \beta_n\},\\
&X = X_{NAT} = \{rg_1, \ldots, rg_n\},\\
&V = \{exec\lambda \mid \lambda \in Act\},\\
&enabled_{\beta_1} \equiv rg_1 = rg_n,\\
&enabled_{\beta_i} \equiv rg_i \neq rg_{i-1} \quad \text{for } 2 \leq i \leq n.
\end{aligned}
$$

For $1 \leq i \leq n$, β_i and rg_i represent the action of node i and the value of its register, respectively.

Choosing $\mathcal{L}_{\mathrm{FOLTL}}$ as the underlying language $\mathcal{L}_{\mathrm{TL}}$, a specification of Γ_{ring} is given by the temporal axioms ($\mathrm{nil}_{\Gamma_{ring}}$), ($\mathrm{action}_{\Gamma_{ring}}$), and

$$
\begin{aligned}
&\textstyle\bigwedge_{i=1}^{n} rg_i \leq N,\\
&enabled_{\beta_i} \rightarrow \neg nil_{\Gamma_{ring}} \quad \text{for } 1 \leq i \leq n,\\
&exec\,\beta_1 \rightarrow rg_1' = rg_1 \oplus 1,\\
&exec\,\beta_i \rightarrow rg_i' = rg_{i-1} \quad \text{for } 2 \leq i \leq n,\\
&exec\,\beta_i \rightarrow rg_j' = rg_j \quad \text{for } 1 \leq i, j \leq n, i \neq j
\end{aligned}
$$

which are evident from the informal description of the system. Note that the axioms in the second line mean that the system has to execute a node as long as this is possible.

Let now *stable* be the formula defined by

$$
stable \equiv \bigvee_{i=1}^{n} enabled_{\beta_i} \wedge \bigwedge_{\substack{i,j=1\\ i\neq j}}^{n} (enabled_{\beta_i} \rightarrow \neg enabled_{\beta_j})
$$

expressing that one and only one $\beta \in Act$ is enabled which just formalizes the "stability of a state". Then the self-stabilizing property of Γ_{ring} can be formalized by the two assertions

(a) $stable \rightarrow \Box stable.$
(b) $\Diamond\, stable.$

(b) expresses that a stable state will eventually be reached and (a) describes that whenever this is the case, the states will remain stable from then on.

We begin to prove the invariance property (a). To this end we derive the following "lemmas":

(a1) $\bigvee_{i=1}^{n} enabled_{\beta_i}.$
("In every state at least one node may execute".)

(a2) $\bigwedge_{i=1}^{n}(exec\,\beta_i \rightarrow \neg\bigcirc enabled_{\beta_i}).$
("Immediately after the execution of some node this is not able to execute again".)

(a3) $exec\,\beta_1 \rightarrow (enabled_{\beta_j} \leftrightarrow \bigcirc enabled_{\beta_j})$ for $3 \leq j \leq n$,
$exec\,\beta_i \rightarrow (enabled_{\beta_1} \leftrightarrow \bigcirc enabled_{\beta_1})$ for $2 \leq i \leq n-1$,
$exec\,\beta_i \rightarrow (enabled_{\beta_j} \leftrightarrow \bigcirc enabled_{\beta_j})$ for $2 \leq i,j \leq n, j \neq i, j \neq i+1$.
("After execution of a node i, for every node j except i and its right neighbour: j may execute if and only if it could do so before the execution of i as well".)

The informal proof idea for (a1) is simple: either $rg_i \neq rg_{i-1}$ holds for at least one $i > 1$ or all rg_i are equal which particularly means that $rg_1 = rg_n$. Formally this runs as follows.

Derivation of (a1).

(1)	$\bigwedge_{i=2}^{n} \neg enabled_{\beta_i} \rightarrow \bigwedge_{i=2}^{n} rg_i = rg_{i-1}$	(taut)
(2)	$\bigwedge_{i=2}^{n} rg_i = rg_{i-1} \rightarrow rg_1 = rg_n$	(pred)
(3)	$rg_1 = rg_n \rightarrow enabled_{\beta_1}$	(taut)
(4)	$\bigwedge_{i=2}^{n} \neg enabled_{\beta_i} \rightarrow enabled_{\beta_1}$	(1),(2),(3)
(5)	$\bigvee_{i=1}^{n} enabled_{\beta_i}$	(4) △

(a2) is evident for $i > 0$. Furthermore, $(k+1) \bmod (N+1) \neq k$ for arbitrary k because of $N+1 \geq n \geq 2$, and this implies (a2) also for $i = 0$.

Derivation of (a2).

(1)	$exec\,\beta_i \rightarrow rg'_i = rg_{i-1} \wedge rg'_{i-1} = rg_{i-1}$ for $2 \leq i \leq n$	(Γ)
(2)	$exec\,\beta_i \rightarrow \neg\bigcirc enabled_{\beta_i}$ for $2 \leq i \leq n$	(1)
(3)	$exec\,\beta_1 \rightarrow rg_1 = rg_n \wedge rg'_1 = rg_1 \oplus 1 \wedge rg'_n = rg_n$	(Γ)
(4)	$rg_1 \oplus 1 \neq rg_1$	(data)
(5)	$exec\,\beta_1 \rightarrow \neg\bigcirc enabled_{\beta_1}$	(3),(4)
(6)	$\bigwedge_{i=1}^{n}(exec\,\beta_i \rightarrow \neg\bigcirc enabled_{\beta_i})$	(2),(5) △

The main idea for proving (a3) is that the formula $enabled_{\beta_j}$ depends only on the register values of node j and its left neighbour, while the action β_i changes only the register value of node i.

Derivation of (a3).

(1) $exec\,\beta_1 \rightarrow rg'_{j-1} = rg_{j-1} \wedge rg'_j = rg_j$ for $3 \leq j \leq n$ (Γ)
(2) $exec\,\beta_1 \rightarrow (rg_j \neq rg_{j-1} \leftrightarrow rg'_j \neq rg'_{j-1})$ for $3 \leq j \leq n$ (1)
(3) $exec\,\beta_i \rightarrow rg'_1 = rg_1 \wedge rg'_n = rg_n$ for $2 \leq i \leq n-1$ (Γ)
(4) $exec\,\beta_i \rightarrow (rg_1 = rg_n \leftrightarrow rg'_1 = rg'_n)$ for $2 \leq i \leq n-1$ (3)
(5) $exec\,\beta_i \rightarrow rg'_{j-1} = rg_{j-1} \wedge rg'_j = rg_j$
for $2 \leq i,j \leq n, j \neq i, j \neq i+1$ (Γ)
(6) $exec\,\beta_i \rightarrow (rg_j \neq rg_{j-1} \leftrightarrow rg'_j \neq rg'_{j-1})$
for $2 \leq i,j \leq n, j \neq i, j \neq i+1$ (5)
(7) $exec\,\beta_1 \rightarrow (enabled_{\beta_j} \leftrightarrow \bigcirc enabled_{\beta_j})$ for $3 \leq j \leq n$ (2)
(8) $exec\,\beta_i \rightarrow (enabled_{\beta_1} \leftrightarrow \bigcirc enabled_{\beta_1})$ for $2 \leq i \leq n-1$ (4)
(9) $exec\,\beta_i \rightarrow (enabled_{\beta_j} \leftrightarrow \bigcirc enabled_{\beta_j})$
for $2 \leq i,j \leq n, j \neq i, j \neq i+1$ (6) △

After these preparations we are able to derive assertion (a). In a stable state there is exactly one enabled action β_i and after executing β_i, according to (a2) and (a3) no node except the right neighbour of i may execute. With (a1) it follows that the resulting state is again stable. So the formula *stable* is an invariant under every action of the system which then shows (a).

Derivation of (a).

(1) $\bigwedge_{i=1}^{n}(exec\,\beta_i \rightarrow enabled_{\beta_i})$ (Γ)
(2) $enabled_{\beta_i} \wedge stable \rightarrow \neg enabled_{\beta_j}$ for $1 \leq i,j \leq n, i \neq j$ (taut)
(3) $\bigvee_{i=1}^{n} \bigcirc enabled_{\beta_i}$ (a1),(nex)
(4) $exec\,\beta_1 \wedge stable \rightarrow \bigwedge_{j=3}^{n} \neg\bigcirc enabled_{\beta_j}$ (a3),(1),(2)
(5) $exec\,\beta_1 \wedge stable \rightarrow \bigcirc stable$ (a2),(3),(4)
(6) $exec\,\beta_i \wedge stable \rightarrow \neg\bigcirc enabled_{\beta_1}$ for $2 \leq i \leq n-1$ (a3),(1),(2)
(7) $exec\,\beta_i \wedge stable \rightarrow \neg\bigcirc enabled_{\beta_j}$
for $2 \leq i \leq n-1, 2 \leq j \leq n, j \neq i, j \neq i+1$ (a3),(1),(2)
(8) $exec\,\beta_i \wedge stable \rightarrow \bigcirc stable$ for $2 \leq i \leq n-1$ (a2),(3),(6),(7)
(9) $exec\,\beta_n \wedge stable \rightarrow \neg\bigcirc enabled_{\beta_j}$ for $2 \leq j \leq n-1$ (a3),(1),(2)
(10) $exec\,\beta_n \wedge stable \rightarrow \bigcirc stable$ (a2),(3),(9)
(11) *stable* **invof** *Act* (5),(8),(10)
(12) $stable \rightarrow \Box stable$ (inv1),(11) △

For the proof of the eventuality property (b) we now introduce some abbreviations for particular formulas:

$$C_i \equiv \bigwedge_{j=1}^{i} rg_j = rg_1 \quad \text{for } 1 \leq i \leq n,$$
$$D_{frv} \equiv \bigvee_{i=2}^{n}(x = rg_i \wedge \neg C_i),$$
$$D_{min} \equiv \neg D_{frv}(rg_1 \oplus x) \wedge \forall y(y < x \rightarrow D_{frv}(rg_1 \oplus y)).$$

In these formulas x is a variable of sort NAT and $D_{frv}(t)$ is used as a shorthand for $(D_{frv})_x(t)$ (t being a term). An analogous notation will be used for D_{min}.

Let us illustrate these notions by an example. Suppose $n = 6$, $N = 8$, and

$$\begin{aligned} rg_1 &= rg_2 = rg_3 = 4, \\ rg_4 &= 0, \\ rg_5 &= 4, \\ rg_6 &= 5 \end{aligned}$$

in some state. For $1 \leq i \leq n$, C_i expresses that the values of the first i registers $rg_1, \ldots, rg_i$ are equal. So, in the sample state, C_i holds for $i = 1, 2, 3$ and no other i. Note that C_1 holds in any case. D_{frv} expresses that $x = rg_j$ for some j for which C_j does not hold. So, D_{frv} holds exactly for those values x of registers (briefly called *free values*) which do not belong to the "first registers with equal values". In the example, these are 0, 4, and 5. Note that a register value may be free even if it is the value of some first equally valued registers. Finally, D_{min} expresses that the value of x is the smallest l (briefly called *minimal addition*) such that l added to rg_1 (modulo $N + 1$) is not a free value. Because of $4 \oplus 0 = 4$, $4 \oplus 1 = 5$, $4 \oplus 2 = 6$ we obtain that $D_{min}(2)$ holds in the example (and $D_{min}(t)$ does not hold if $t \neq 2$).

In the subsequent derivations we will use instances of $(data_{\Gamma_{ring}})$ axioms involving these formulas, in particular:

(b1) $\exists x(x \leq N \land D_{min})$

stating that the minimal addition really exists (under the numbers of $\mathbb{M}$). In order to see the validity of this axiom it suffices to note that (in any state) $\neg D_{frv}(rg_1 \oplus k)$ holds for some $k \in \mathbb{M}$, because then there is also a smallest such k. By definition, D_{frv} may hold only for $n - 1$ different values for x, but the values of $rg_1 \oplus k$ for $k \in \mathbb{M}$ are all $N + 1$ values of $\mathbb{M}$. Because of $N + 1 > n - 1$, $D_{frv}(rg_1 \oplus k)$ must therefore evaluate to false for at least one $k \in \mathbb{M}$.

Let us now prove the following list of further assertions:

(b2) $exec\,\beta_i \land C_j \to \circ C_j$ for $2 \leq i \leq n, 1 \leq j \leq n$.
("Every C_j is invariant under every $\beta \neq \beta_1$".)

(b3) $exec\,\beta_i \land \circ D_{frv} \to D_{frv}$ for $2 \leq i \leq n$.
("Any free value after execution of $\beta \neq \beta_1$ was a free value already before that".)

(b4) $exec\,\beta_1 \land \circ D_{frv} \to D_{frv} \lor x = rg_1$.
("After execution of β_1 at most the value of rg_1 might be added to the free values".)

(b5) $D_{min}(0) \land enabled_{\beta_j} \to \neg enabled_{\beta_1}$ for $2 \leq j \leq n$.
("If 0 is the minimal addition and node $j > 1$ may execute then node 1 is not able to execute".)

As in the proof of (a), these lemmas are quite straightforward consequences of the specification of Γ_{ring} and the above definitions. Again we give some short informal arguments explaining the respective formal derivations.

(b2) follows from the fact that if β_i is executed and C_j holds then j must be less than i because otherwise $rg_{i-1} = rg_i = rg_1$ and node i could not execute. Then $rg'_k = rg_k$ for $k < i$ and therefore $rg'_k = rg'_1$ for $k \leq j$ which implies $\bigcirc C_j$.

Derivation of (b2). Let $2 \leq i \leq n$ and $1 \leq j \leq n$.

(1)	$exec\,\beta_i \rightarrow rg_{i-1} \neq rg_i$	(Γ)
(2)	$exec\,\beta_i \rightarrow \neg C_i$	(1)
(3)	$exec\,\beta_i \wedge \neg C_i \wedge C_j \rightarrow \bigwedge_{k=1}^{j} rg'_k = rg_k$	(Γ)
(4)	$\bigwedge_{k=1}^{j} rg'_k = rg_k \rightarrow (\bigwedge_{k=1}^{j} rg_k = rg_1 \leftrightarrow \bigwedge_{k=1}^{j} rg'_k = rg'_1)$	(pred)
(5)	$exec\,\beta_i \wedge C_j \rightarrow \bigcirc C_j$	(2),(3),(4) △

For the proof of (b3) we observe that if β_i is executed and $\bigcirc D_{frv}$ holds then there is a $j, 2 \leq j \leq n$ such that $x = rg'_j$ and $\neg\bigcirc C_j$. With (b2) we get $\neg C_j$; hence $D_{frv}(rg_j)$. The assertion then follows from $rg_j = rg'_j = x$ in the case of $j \neq i$. If $j = i$ then $rg'_j = rg_{i-1}$ and $\neg C_{i-1}$ and this also implies D_{frv}.

Derivation of (b3). Let $2 \leq i \leq n$.

(1)	$\bigcirc D_{frv} \rightarrow \bigvee_{j=2}^{n}(x = rg'_j \wedge \bigcirc\neg C_j)$	(pred)
(2)	$exec\,\beta_i \wedge \bigcirc\neg C_j \rightarrow \neg C_j$ for $2 \leq j \leq n$	(b2)
(3)	$exec\,\beta_i \rightarrow rg'_j = rg_j$ for $2 \leq j \leq n, j \neq i$	(Γ)
(4)	$rg'_j = rg_j \wedge x = rg'_j \wedge \neg C_j \rightarrow D_{frv}$ for $2 \leq j \leq n$	(pred)
(5)	$exec\,\beta_i \wedge \bigcirc\neg C_j \wedge x = rg'_j \rightarrow D_{frv}$ for $2 \leq j \leq n, j \neq i$	(2),(3),(4)
(6)	$exec\,\beta_i \rightarrow rg'_i = rg_{i-1} \wedge rg'_{i-1} = rg_{i-1}$	(Γ)
(7)	$exec\,\beta_i \wedge C_{i-1} \rightarrow \bigcirc C_{i-1}$	(b2)
(8)	$\bigcirc C_{i-1} \wedge rg'_i = rg'_{i-1} \rightarrow \bigcirc C_i$	(pred)
(9)	$exec\,\beta_i \wedge \neg\bigcirc C_i \rightarrow \neg C_{i-1}$	(6),(7),(8)
(10)	$x = rg'_i \wedge rg'_i = rg_{i-1} \wedge \neg C_{i-1} \rightarrow D_{frv}$	(pred)
(11)	$exec\,\beta_i \wedge x = rg'_i \wedge \neg\bigcirc C_i \rightarrow D_{frv}$	(6),(9),(10)
(12)	$exec\,\beta_i \wedge \bigcirc D_{frv} \rightarrow D_{frv}$	(1),(5),(11) △

(b4) is a modification of (b3) for β_1 and follows from the fact that $\bigcirc D_{frv}$ implies $x = rg'_j$ for some $j > 1$ for which $\bigcirc\neg C_j$ holds and β_1 does not change rg_j. So if $x = rg_j = rg_1$ then we obtain (b4) immediately and otherwise $\neg C_j$ and hence D_{frv} are implied.

Derivation of (b4).

(1)	$\bigcirc D_{frv} \rightarrow \bigvee_{j=2}^{n} x = rg'_j$	(pred)
(2)	$exec\,\beta_1 \rightarrow rg'_j = rg_j$ for $2 \leq j \leq n$	(Γ)
(3)	$rg_j \neq rg_1 \rightarrow \neg C_j$ for $2 \leq j \leq n$	(pred)
(4)	$rg_j = x \wedge \neg C_j \rightarrow D_{frv}$ for $2 \leq j \leq n$	(pred)
(5)	$exec\,\beta_1 \wedge x = rg'_j \rightarrow D_{frv} \vee x = rg_1$ for $2 \leq j \leq n$	(2),(3),(4)
(6)	$exec\,\beta_1 \wedge \bigcirc D_{frv} \rightarrow D_{frv} \vee x = rg_1$	(1),(5) △

(b5) follows directly from the definitions: $enabled_{\beta_j}$ for $2 \le j \le n$ implies $D_{frv}(rg_n)$ and $D_{min}(0)$ implies $\neg D_{frv}(rg_1)$. So rg_1 and rg_n have different values.

Derivation of (b5). Let $2 \le j \le n$.

(1)	$rg_j \neq rg_{j-1} \rightarrow \neg C_n$	(pred)
(2)	$\neg C_n \rightarrow D_{frv}(rg_n)$	(pred)
(3)	$D_{min}(0) \rightarrow \neg D_{frv}(rg_1)$	(pred)
(4)	$D_{min}(0) \wedge enabled_{\beta_j} \rightarrow rg_1 \neq rg_n$	(1),(2),(3)
(5)	$D_{min}(0) \wedge enabled_{\beta_j} \rightarrow \neg enabled_{\beta_1}$	(4) △

Let us now approach the main proof of assertion (b). We want to apply the rule (labwfr$_\Gamma$) and have to find some appropriate well-founded set of data which decrease during execution of the system until a stable state is reached. A first starting point is the fact that the execution of β_1 decreases the minimal addition value (as long as this is not 0):

(b6) $exec\,\beta_1 \wedge D_{min} \wedge x > 0 \rightarrow \circ\exists y(y < x \wedge D_{min}(y))$.

For the proof of (b6) it suffices to show that for $x > 0$ the value of rg_1 in a state is different from the value of $rg_1 \oplus (x-1)$ in the state after execution of β_1. Then the latter value is not a free value after this execution by (b4) and the assertion follows from the fact that $\circ D_{min}(y)$ means that y is the least number with this property.

Derivation of (b6).

(1)	$exec\,\beta_1 \rightarrow rg_1' = rg_1 \oplus 1$	(Γ)
(2)	$D_{min} \rightarrow \neg D_{frv}(rg_1 \oplus x)$	(pred)
(3)	$x > 0 \rightarrow rg_1 \oplus x = (rg_1 \oplus 1) \oplus (x-1)$	(data)
(4)	$x > 0 \wedge x \le N \rightarrow rg_1 \oplus x \neq rg_1$	(data)
(5)	$exec\,\beta_1 \wedge x > 0 \wedge \neg D_{frv}(rg_1' \oplus (x-1)) \wedge rg_1' \oplus (x-1) \neq rg_1 \rightarrow$ $\neg\circ D_{frv}(rg_1 \oplus (x-1))$	(b4)
(6)	$x > 0 \wedge \neg D_{frv}(rg_1 \oplus (x-1)) \rightarrow \exists y(y < x \wedge D_{min}(y))$	(data)
(7)	$x > 0 \wedge \neg\circ D_{frv}(rg_1 \oplus (x-1)) \rightarrow \circ\exists y(y < x \wedge D_{min}(y))$	(6)
(8)	$D_{min} \rightarrow x \le N$	(b1),(data)
(9)	$exec\,\beta_1 \wedge D_{min} \wedge x > 0 \rightarrow \circ\exists y(y < x \wedge D_{min}(y))$	(1)–(5), (7),(8) △

Unfortunately the same assertion does not hold for actions $\beta \neq \beta_1$. We can only prove that these actions at least do not increase the minimal addition value:

(b7) $exec\,\beta_i \wedge D_{min} \rightarrow \circ\exists y(y \le x \wedge D_{min}(y))$ for $2 \le i \le n$.

Executions of nodes $i \neq 1$ do not change the value of rg_1 and do not increase the set of new register values according to (b3). From this (b7) follows because of the minimality property of y in $D_{min}(y)$.

Derivation of (b7). Let $2 \leq i \leq n$.

(1)	$D_{min} \rightarrow \neg D_{frv}(rg_1 \oplus x)$	(pred)
(2)	$D_{min} \land rg_1' = rg_1 \land \forall x(\circ D_{frv} \rightarrow D_{frv}) \rightarrow \neg \circ D_{frv}(rg_1 \oplus x)$	(1),(data)
(3)	$\neg D_{frv}(rg_1 \oplus x) \rightarrow \exists y(y \leq x \land D_{min}(y))$	(data)
(4)	$\neg \circ D_{frv}(rg_1 \oplus x) \rightarrow \circ \exists y(y \leq x \land D_{min}(y))$	(3)
(5)	$exec\,\beta_i \rightarrow rg_1' = rg_1$	(Γ)
(6)	$exec\,\beta_i \rightarrow (\circ D_{frv} \rightarrow D_{frv})$	(b3)
(7)	$exec\,\beta_i \land D_{min} \rightarrow \circ \exists y(y \leq x \land D_{min}(y))$	(2),(4), (5),(6) △

(b7) will help us at once but at the moment we still need values which are properly decreased by $\beta_2, \ldots, \beta_n$. From (a2) and (a3) we know that if one of these actions β_i is executed then its enabling condition $enabled_{\beta_i}$ is changing from true to false and all $enabled_{\beta_j}$ remain unchanged for $2 \leq j < i$. We may encode this considering the tuples

$$d = (d_2, \ldots, d_n) \in \mathbb{N}^{n-1}$$

with

$$d_i = \begin{cases} 1 & \text{if node } i \text{ is enabled,} \\ 0 & \text{otherwise} \end{cases}$$

for $2 \leq i \leq n$. Execution of any β_i, $i \neq 1$, then decreases the value of these tuples with respect to the lexicographical order on $\mathbb{N}^{n-1}$.

Together this discussion shows that the tuple

$$(d_1, d_2, \ldots, d_n) \in \mathbb{N}^n$$

where d_1 is the minimal addition and $d_2, \ldots, d_n$ are as described is decreased with respect to the lexicographical order on $\mathbb{N}^n$ by every execution step of the system as long as this is possible. This is the case at least as long as no stable state is reached since in non-stable states not all entries $d_1, \ldots, d_n$ can be 0 because of (a1).

To formalize this idea we now assume that the signature of Γ_{ring} extends SIG_{Nat} by a new sort $TUPLE$, n additional function symbols $SEL_1^{(TUPLE,NAT)}, \ldots, SEL_n^{(TUPLE,NAT)}$, and a predicate symbol $\prec^{(TUPLE\ TUPLE)}$. The corresponding structure N is extended by

$$TUPLE^{\mathsf{N}} = \mathbb{N}^n,$$
$$SEL_i^{\mathsf{N}}(m_1, \ldots, m_n) = m_i \quad \text{for } 1 \leq i \leq n$$

and $\prec^{\mathsf{N}}$, the (strict) lexicographical order on $\mathbb{N}^n$. Of course, this is a well-founded relation. The underlying language $\mathcal{L}_{\mathrm{TL}}$ can then be viewed as an $\mathcal{L}^{\mathrm{w}}_{\mathrm{FOLTL}}$ if we take the sort $TUPLE$ as WF.

To derive now assertion (b), let y be a variable of sort $TUPLE$,

$$A \equiv D_{min}(SEL_1(y)) \wedge \bigwedge_{i=2}^{n} ((enabled_{\beta_i} \rightarrow SEL_i(y) = 1) \wedge (\neg enabled_{\beta_i} \rightarrow SEL_i(y) = 0))$$

which formalizes the above coding, and

$$B \equiv \Box\neg stable \wedge A.$$

Derivation of (b).

(1) $exec\beta_i \rightarrow enabled_{\beta_i} \wedge \bigcirc\neg enabled_{\beta_i}$ for $2 \leq i \leq n$ — (Γ),(a2)

(2) $exec\beta_i \rightarrow \bigwedge_{j=2}^{i-1}(enabled_{\beta_j} \leftrightarrow \bigcirc enabled_{\beta_j})$ for $2 \leq i \leq n$ — (a3)

(3) $exec\beta_i \wedge A \rightarrow \bigcirc\exists\bar{y}(\bar{y} \prec y \wedge A_y(\bar{y}))$ for $2 \leq i \leq n$ — (1),(2),(b7)

(4) $\neg stable \rightarrow \bigvee_{i=2}^{n} enabled_{\beta_i}$ — (a1)

(5) $exec\beta_1 \rightarrow enabled_{\beta_1}$ — (Γ)

(6) $exec\beta_1 \wedge \neg stable \rightarrow (D_{min} \rightarrow x > 0)$ — (4),(5),(b5)

(7) $exec\beta_1 \wedge \neg stable \wedge A \rightarrow \bigcirc\exists\bar{y}(\bar{y} \prec y \wedge A_y(\bar{y}))$ — (b6),(6)

(8) $exec\lambda \wedge B \rightarrow \bigcirc(stable \vee \exists\bar{y}(\bar{y} \prec y \wedge B_y(\bar{y})))$ for every $\beta \in Act$ — (3),(7)

(9) $\mathrm{nil}_{\Gamma_{ring}} \wedge B \rightarrow stable$ — (Γ),(a1)

(10) $\exists yB \rightarrow \Diamond stable$ — (labwfr),(8),(9)

(11) $\exists yA \rightarrow \Diamond stable$ — (10)

(12) $\exists yA$ — (b1),(ltl4)

(13) $\Diamond stable$ — (11),(12) △

7.6 The Alternating Bit Protocol

Our second verification example deals with a protocol coordinating the data transmission between a *sender* and a *receiver*. The sender continuously gets messages as input and transmits them to the receiver which outputs them and sends back acknowledgements to the sender. Transmissions in both directions may be corrupted by the unreliable transmission medium. Nevertheless, the receiver should output the correct messages in the same order as they were input to the sender. A key for the solution of this problem is to send messages together with a control bit the value of which serves as the acknowledgement and has to alternate in an appropriate way.

We represent this *alternating bit protocol* by an frl$_e$STS Γ_{ABP} with

$$\begin{aligned}
&Act = \{\alpha_0, \alpha_1, \beta_0, \beta_1\},\\
&X = X_{NAT} \cup X_{MSG},\\
&X_{NAT} = \{sb, rb, wb, ack\},\\
&X_{MSG} = \{sm, rm\},\\
&V = \{exec\lambda \mid \lambda \in Act\},\\
&enabled_\lambda \equiv \mathbf{true} \quad \text{for } \lambda \in Act,\\
&start_{\Gamma_{ABP}} \equiv sb = 0 \wedge rb = 1 \wedge wb = 0 \wedge ack = 1 \wedge sm = FIRSTMSG.
\end{aligned}$$

The actions α_0 and α_1 constitute the sender (which we will refer to as system part Γ_{send} in the following); β_0 and β_1 are the actions of the receiver (Γ_{rec}). α_0 sends a package consisting of a message sm (of some sort MSG) and a bit sb to Γ_{rec} where it arrives on the "receive" variables rm and rb. α_1 checks acknowledgement ack and composes a new package consisting of the next message sm and sb with an alternated value if ack equals sb. (This also means that a package correctly arrived at Γ_{rec} may be corrupted again before being "realized" there.) β_0 and β_1 work analogously. β_0 checks the received bit rb and if this equals wb containing the value waited for then rm is output (and wb is alternated). β_1 sends the respective bit value back to Γ_{send} where it arrives on the variable ack. Note that we impose no "internal" order of the actions in Γ_{send} and Γ_{rec}, respectively, and that different ("non-contradictory") actions may even execute simultaneously. Fairness ensures that all actions happen continuously.

The initial condition describes the appropriate start of the system. The individual constant $FIRSTMSG$ (of sort MSG) represents the first message to be transmitted.

Again, we do not write out the definition of the states and the transition relation of Γ_{ABP} but proceed immediately to the specification of the system which is given by the temporal axioms (root$_{\Gamma_{ABP}}$) and

$$
\begin{aligned}
&exec\,\alpha_0 \rightarrow ((rm' = sm \land rb' = sb) \lor (rm' = ERR \land rb' = ERR)) \land \\
&\qquad\qquad unchanged(sb, wb, ack, sm),\\
&exec\,\alpha_1 \land sb = ack \rightarrow sm' = NEXTMSG(sm) \land sb' = sb \oplus 1 \land \\
&\qquad\qquad\qquad\qquad unchanged(rb, wb, ack, rm),\\
&exec\,\alpha_1 \land sb \neq ack \rightarrow unchanged(sb, rb, wb, ack, sm, rm),\\
&exec\,\beta_0 \land rb = wb \rightarrow wb' = wb \oplus 1 \land unchanged(sb, rb, ack, sm, rm),\\
&exec\,\beta_0 \land rb \neq wb \rightarrow unchanged(sb, rb, wb, ack, sm, rm),\\
&exec\,\beta_1 \rightarrow (ack' = wb \oplus 1 \lor ack' = ERR) \land unchanged(sb, rb, wb, sm, rm).
\end{aligned}
$$

(The axioms (nil$_{\Gamma_{ABP}}$) and (action$_{\Gamma_{ABP}}$) are derivable.) In these formulas we use the abbreviation

$$unchanged(a_1, \ldots, a_n) \equiv \bigwedge_{i=1}^{n} a_i' = a_i$$

for system variables $a_1, \ldots, a_n$. The function symbol $\oplus$ is interpreted as addition modulo 2. The axioms for α_0 and β_1 describe the two possibilities of a correct or a corrupted transmission, the latter resulting in some (recognizable) value represented by the individual constant ERR for both NAT and MSG. The acknowledgement value sent back by β_1 is $wb \oplus 1$ since wb is alternated by β_1 if this is executed with $rb = wb$. The axioms for α_1 and β_0 are evident, noting that $NEXTMSG^{(MSG\ MSG)}$ is a function symbol for fixing the order in which the messages are to be transmitted: for any message msg, $NEXTMSG(msg)$ is to follow msg.

The proper output performed by β_0 in case $rb = wb$ is not modeled in the axioms since it does not involve the system variables of Γ_{ABP}. Nevertheless, the formula

$$output \equiv exec\,\beta_0 \land rb = wb$$

represents the fact that the message contained in rm is output by Γ_{rec}.

The assertion that the messages are output in the right order cannot directly be expressed by a temporal formula. It is easy to see, however, that the two formulas

(a) $start_{\Gamma_{ABP}} \rightarrow rm = FIRSTMSG \ \mathbf{atnext}\ output,$
(b) $output \wedge rm = x \rightarrow rm = NEXTMSG(x) \ \mathbf{atnext}\ output$

provide an adequate formal representation of this claim. (a) says that the very first output message will be $FIRSTMSG$. (b) uses a variable x of sort MSG and states that after the output of any message x the next output message will be $NEXTMSG(x)$. Note that this does not include that the outputs will be performed at all. This aspect will be treated subsequently.

The derivations of (a) and (b) use the same main ideas. We first note three global invariants of Γ_{ABP}.

(c1) $\Box \neg nil_{\Gamma_{ABP}}$.
(c2) $\Box((sb = 0 \vee sb = 1) \wedge (wb = 0 \vee wb = 1))$.
(c3) $\Box((rb = wb \rightarrow wb = sb \wedge rm = sm) \wedge (sb = ack \rightarrow wb \neq sb))$.

(c1) follows from the formula (progress$_{\Gamma_{ABP}}$) generally derived in Sect. 6.5, and (c2) is trivially derived with (invstart$_{\Gamma_{ABP}}$). The proof of (c3) runs as follows.

Derivation of (c3). Let

$$A \equiv (rb = wb \rightarrow wb = sb \wedge rm = sm) \wedge (sb = ack \rightarrow wb \neq sb).$$

(1) $start_{\Gamma_{ABP}} \rightarrow A$ (pred)
(2) $exec\,\alpha_0 \wedge A \rightarrow \bigcirc((rm = sm \wedge rb = sb) \vee (rm = ERR \wedge rb = ERR)) \wedge \bigcirc(sb = ack \rightarrow wb \neq sb)$ (Γ)
(3) $rm = sm \wedge rb = sb \rightarrow (rb = wb \rightarrow wb = sb \wedge rm = sm)$ (pred)
(4) $rb = ERR \rightarrow rb \neq wb$ (c2)
(5) A **invof** α_0 (2),(3),(4)
(6) $exec\,\alpha_1 \wedge sb = ack \rightarrow sb' = sb \oplus 1 \wedge rb' = rb \wedge wb' = wb \wedge ack' = ack$ (Γ)
(7) $sb = ack \wedge A \rightarrow wb \neq sb \wedge rb \neq wb$ (pred)
(8) $exec\,\alpha_1 \wedge sb = ack \wedge A \rightarrow \bigcirc(rb \neq wb \wedge sb \neq ack)$ (6),(7)
(9) $exec\,\alpha_1 \wedge sb = ack \wedge A \rightarrow \bigcirc A$ (8)
(10) $exec\,\alpha_1 \wedge sb \neq ack \wedge A \rightarrow \bigcirc A$ (Γ)
(11) $exec\,\beta_0 \wedge rb = wb \rightarrow wb' = wb \oplus 1 \wedge sb' = sb \wedge rb' = rb \wedge ack' = ack$ (Γ)
(12) $rb = wb \wedge A \rightarrow wb = sb \wedge sb \neq ack$ (pred)
(13) $exec\,\beta_0 \wedge rb = wb \wedge A \rightarrow \bigcirc(rb \neq wb \wedge sb \neq ack)$ (11),(12)
(14) $exec\,\beta_0 \wedge rb = wb \wedge A \rightarrow \bigcirc A$ (13)
(15) $exec\,\beta_0 \wedge rb \neq wb \wedge A \rightarrow \bigcirc A$ (Γ)

(16) $exec\beta_1 \land A \to \bigcirc(ack = wb \oplus 1 \lor ack = ERR) \land$
$\qquad \bigcirc(rb = wb \to wb = sb \land rm = sm)$ (Γ)
(17) $ack = wb \oplus 1 \to (sb = ack \to wb \neq sb)$ (pred)
(18) $ack = ERR \to sb \neq ack$ (c2)
(19) A **invof** β_1 (16),(17),(18)
(20) A **invof** $Act_{\Gamma_{ABP}}$ (5),(9),(10)
(14),(15),(19)
(21) $\Box A$ (invstart),(1),(20) △

Let now

$$B_{first} \equiv wb = sb \land sm = FIRSTMSG,$$
$$B_{next} \equiv (wb = sb \to sm = NEXTMSG(x)) \land (wb \neq sb \to sm = x).$$

For these formulas we prove the following facts.

(c4) $\Box(rb = wb \land B_{first} \to rm = FIRSTMSG)$.
(c5) $\Box(rb = wb \land B_{next} \to rm = NEXTMSG(x))$.
(c6) B **invof** λ for $B \in \{B_{first}, B_{next}\}$ and $\lambda \in \{\alpha_0, \alpha_1, \beta_1\}$.

(c4) and (c5) are immediate consequences of (c3), and (c6) is derived as follows.

Derivation of (c6). Let $B \in \{B_{first}, B_{next}\}$.

(1) B **invof** λ for $\lambda \in \{\alpha_0, \beta_1\}$ (Γ)
(2) $exec\alpha_1 \land sb \neq ack \land B \to \bigcirc B$ (Γ)
(3) $B_{first} \to sb \neq ack$ (c3)
(4) $exec\alpha_1 \land sb = ack \land B_{first} \to \bigcirc B_{first}$ (3)
(5) $sb = ack \land B_{next} \to wb \neq sb \land sm = x$ (c3)
(6) $exec\alpha_1 \land sb = ack \land B_{next} \to$
$\qquad \bigcirc(sm = NEXTMSG(x) \land sb = wb)$ (5),(Γ),(c2)
(7) $exec\alpha_1 \land sb = ack \land B_{next} \to \bigcirc B_{next}$ (6)
(8) B **invof** λ for $\lambda \in \{\alpha_0, \alpha_1, \beta_1\}$ (1),(2),(4),(7) △

Let finally

$$C_{first} \equiv B_{first} \land \neg output,$$
$$C_{next} \equiv (output \to rm = x) \land (\neg output \to B_{next}).$$

The crucial step for the proof of (a) and (b) is to show

(c7) $C \to C^{rm}$ **atnext** $output$

for $C \in \{C_{first}, C_{next}\}$ where

$$C^{rm} \equiv \begin{cases} rm = FIRSTMSG & \text{if } C \equiv C_{first}, \\ rm = NEXTMSG(x) & \text{if } C \equiv C_{next}. \end{cases}$$

The derivation of (c7) applies the rule (invatnext$_{\Gamma_{ABP}}$).

Derivation of (c7). Let $C \in \{C_{first}, C_{next}\}$.

(1)	$exec\lambda \land C \rightarrow \bigcirc(output \rightarrow C^{rm}) \land \bigcirc(\neg output \rightarrow C)$ for $\lambda \in \{\alpha_0, \alpha_1, \beta_1\}$	(c4),(c5),(c6)
(2)	$exec\beta_0 \land rb \neq wb \land C \rightarrow \bigcirc(rb \neq wb \land C)$	(Γ)
(3)	$exec\beta_0 \land rb \neq wb \land C \rightarrow \bigcirc(output \rightarrow C^{rm}) \land \bigcirc(\neg output \rightarrow C)$	(2)
(4)	$exec\beta_0 \land rb = wb \rightarrow \neg C_{first}$	(taut)
(5)	$exec\beta_0 \land rb = wb \land C_{first} \rightarrow \bigcirc(output \rightarrow C^{rm}) \land \bigcirc(\neg output \rightarrow C_{first})$	(4)
(6)	$exec\beta_0 \land rb = wb \land C_{next} \rightarrow wb = sb \land sm = x$	(c3)
(7)	$exec\beta_0 \land rb = wb \land C_{next} \rightarrow \bigcirc(rb \neq wb \land wb \neq sb \land sm = x)$	(Γ),(6)
(8)	$exec\beta_0 \land rb = wb \land C_{next} \rightarrow \bigcirc(output \rightarrow C^{rm}) \land \bigcirc(\neg output \rightarrow C_{next})$	(7)
(9)	$exec\lambda \land C \rightarrow \bigcirc(output \rightarrow C^{rm}) \land \bigcirc(\neg output \rightarrow C)$ for every $\lambda \in Act_{\Gamma_{ABP}}$	(1),(3),(5),(8)
(10)	$nil_{\Gamma_{ABP}} \land C \rightarrow (output \rightarrow C^{rm})$	(c1)
(11)	$C \rightarrow C^{rm}$ **atnext** $output$	(invatnext), (9),(10) △

The assertions (a) and (b) follow now immediately from (c7).

Derivation of (a).

(1)	$start_{\Gamma_{ABP}} \rightarrow C_{first}$	(pred)
(2)	$C_{first} \rightarrow rm = FIRSTMSG$ **atnext** $output$	(c7)
(3)	$start_{\Gamma_{ABP}} \rightarrow rm = FIRSTMSG$ **atnext** $output$	(1),(2) △

Derivation of (b).

(1)	$output \land rm = x \rightarrow C_{next}$	(taut)
(2)	$C_{next} \rightarrow rm = NEXTMSG(x)$ **atnext** $output$	(c7)
(3)	$output \land rm = x \rightarrow rm = NEXTMSG(x)$ **atnext** $output$	(1),(2) △

The assertions (a) and (b) guarantee that, if messages are output by Γ_{rec} at all, the output will be in the correct order. We now want to show that in fact infinitely many messages are output. Together this states then that all input messages are transmitted and output correctly.

A first approach to what has to be proved is the formula

$$\Diamond output$$

stating that at every time there will be some subsequent output by Γ_{rec} and hence inducing infinitely many outputs. It is quite obvious, however, that this formula is not Γ_{ABP}-valid without additional assumptions. If the sending operation α_0 always fails then the variable rb will always receive the value ERR and no output will be performed. If sending the acknowledgement in β_1 always fails then Γ_{send} will not send new messages and Γ_{rec} will again perform no more outputs. So, continuous output is only guaranteed if, at every time, some eventual sending operation α_0 and β_1 will provide uncorrupted values. Moreover, these values must be read in α_1 and β_0, respectively, before a next corrupted transmission arrives.

These conditions can be described by the formulas

$$\begin{aligned} C_s &\equiv \Diamond(exec\,\alpha_1 \land ack \neq ERR), \\ C_r &\equiv \Diamond(exec\,\beta_0 \land rb \neq ERR) \end{aligned}$$

and our goal is to show the assertion under the additional assumptions C_s and C_r, i.e.,

(d) $\quad C_s, C_r \vdash \Diamond output.$

A proof of (d) may be viewed as an *assumption-commitment verification*: the desired behaviour expressed by $\Diamond output$ is a commitment of Γ_{ABP} under the assumption that the "environment" (the transmission medium in this case) behaves such that C_s and C_r hold.

For the proof we proceed again with a series of lemmas. Firstly we note

(d1) $\vdash \Diamond exec\,\alpha_0$,
(d2) $\vdash \Diamond exec\,\beta_1$

which result directly from the fairness axiom ($\mathrm{fair}_{\Gamma_{ABP}}$). Let now

$$\begin{aligned} D_1 &\equiv ack = wb \oplus 1 \lor ack = ERR, \\ D_2 &\equiv wb = sb \land (rb = sb \lor rb = ERR), \\ D_3 &\equiv rb = wb \lor rb = ERR. \end{aligned}$$

We show the following assertions.

(d3) $\Box\neg output \land D_1 \rightarrow \Box D_1$.
(d4) $\Box\neg output \land wb = sb \rightarrow \Box(wb = sb)$.
(d5) $\Box\neg output \land D_2 \rightarrow \Box D_3$.

These three formulas are not of the restricted syntactical form of invariance properties, but it is easy to overcome this technical problem here by recalling that, according to the Deduction Theorem, in order to prove (d3), (d4), (d5) it suffices to show

(d3') $\neg output \vdash D_1 \rightarrow \Box D_1$,
(d4') $\neg output \vdash wb = sb \rightarrow \Box(wb = sb)$,
(d5') $\neg output \vdash D_2 \rightarrow \Box D_3$

for which we can use the invariance rules of Sect. 7.2. (The applicability of the Deduction Theorem is ensured by results in earlier chapters.)

Derivation of (d3').

(1)	$\neg output$	assumption
(2)	D_1 **invof** λ for $\lambda \in \{\alpha_0, \alpha_1, \beta_1\}$	(Γ)
(3)	$exec\,\beta_0 \rightarrow rb \neq wb$	(1)
(4)	$exec\,\beta_0 \wedge rb \neq wb \wedge D_1 \rightarrow \bigcirc D_1$	(Γ)
(5)	D_1 **invof** β_0	(3),(4)
(6)	$D_1 \rightarrow \Box D_1$	(inv1),(2),(5) △

Derivation of (d4').

(1)	$\neg output$	assumption
(2)	$wb = sb$ **invof** λ for $\lambda \in \{\alpha_0, \beta_1\}$	(Γ)
(3)	$exec\,\alpha_1 \wedge wb = sb \rightarrow sb = ack$	(c3)
(4)	$exec\,\alpha_1 \wedge sb = ack \wedge wb = sb \rightarrow \bigcirc(wb = sb)$	(Γ)
(5)	$wb = sb$ **invof** α_1	(3),(4)
(6)	$wb = sb$ **invof** β_0	(1),(Γ)
(7)	$wb = sb \rightarrow \Box(wb = sb)$	(inv1),(2),(5),(6) △

Note that step (6) in this derivation comprehends the steps (3), (4), and (5) in the derivation of (d3') which are identical here and occur also in the following derivation.

Derivation of (d5').

(1)	$\neg output$	assumption
(2)	$D_2 \rightarrow D_3$	(pred)
(3)	D_2 **invof** λ for $\lambda \in \{\alpha_0, \beta_1\}$	(Γ)
(4)	$exec\,\alpha_1 \wedge wb = sb \rightarrow sb = ack$	(c3)
(5)	$exec\,\alpha_1 \wedge sb = ack \wedge D_2 \rightarrow \bigcirc D_2$	(Γ)
(6)	D_2 **invof** α_1	(4),(5)
(7)	D_2 **invof** β_0	(1),(Γ)
(8)	$D_2 \rightarrow \Box D_3$	(inv),(2),(3),(6),(7) △

To approach now the proof of the eventual output stated in assertion (d) we split this into the following two steps.

(d6) $C_s \vdash \Box\neg output \rightarrow \Diamond(wb = sb)$.
(d7) $C_r \vdash wb = sb \rightarrow \Diamond output$.

(d6) expresses that if Γ_{rec} never outputs a message then the bit sb sent by Γ_{send} will sometime be the expected one. Again, (d6) is not fitting into our simple property classes. It can be derived, however, directly by some purely logical arguments (and axioms of Γ_{ABP}) from the preceding lemmas. Roughly speaking, (d2) guarantees that sometime β_1 will be executed resulting in a state in which D_1 holds. From this it follows with the assumption C_s and (d3) that subsequently Γ_{send} will execute α_1 with $sb = ack$ and $wb \neq sb$ which will provide $wb = sb$. The formal derivation runs as follows.

Derivation of (d6).

(1)	C_s	assumption
(2)	$exec\,\beta_1 \to \bigcirc D_1$	(Γ)
(3)	$\Diamond D_1$	(d2),(2)
(4)	$D_1 \land wb \neq sb \to sb = ack \lor ack = ERR$	(c2)
(5)	$\Box(sb = ack \lor ack = ERR) \to \Diamond(exec\,\alpha_1 \land sb = ack)$	(1)
(6)	$\Box\neg output \land D_1 \land \Box(wb \neq sb) \to \Diamond(exec\,\alpha_1 \land sb = ack \land wb \neq sb)$	(d3),(4),(5)
(7)	$exec\,\alpha_1 \land sb = ack \land wb \neq sb \to \bigcirc(wb = sb)$	(Γ),(c2)
(8)	$\Box\neg output \land D_1 \to \Diamond(wb = sb)$	(6),(7)
(9)	$\Box\neg output \to \Diamond(wb = sb)$	(3),(8) △

The second step (d7) states that if $wb = sb$ in some state then there will be some eventual output. The proof runs similarly as for (d6), mainly using (d1) which sometime provides $rb = sb \lor rb = ERR$ and C_r which implies then with (d4) and (d5) that β_0 is executed eventually in a state where $rb = wb$ which is just the desired output action of Γ_{rec}.

Derivation of (d7).

(1)	C_r	assumption
(2)	$exec\,\alpha_0 \to \bigcirc(rb = sb \lor rb = ERR)$	(Γ)
(3)	$\Diamond(rb = sb \lor rb = ERR)$	(d1),(2)
(4)	$\Box\neg output \land wb = sb \to \Diamond(\Box\neg output \land D_2)$	(3),(d4)
(5)	$\Box\neg output \land D_2 \to \Diamond output$	(d5),(1)
(6)	$\Box\neg output \land wb = sb \to \Diamond output$	(4),(5)
(7)	$wb = sb \to \Diamond output$	(6) △

Finally it is easy to combine (d6) and (d7) for the proof of (d).

Derivation of (d).

(1)	C_s	assumption
(2)	C_r	assumption
(3)	$\Box\neg output \to \Diamond output$	(d6),(d7)
(4)	$\Diamond output$	(3) △

Bibliographical Notes

The application to the description and verification of system (more precisely: program) properties was already advocated in the very first papers on temporal logic, cf. Chap. 2.

The distinction between safety and liveness properties is originally due to Lamport [86]. Formal definitions of these classes appeared in [4, 5]. The classification of properties as described in Sect. 7.1 follows a (more detailed) hierarchy given by Manna and Pnueli [101], see also [102].

The idea of elaborating general (program) verification principles, i.e., proof rules for different property classes was addressed in a series of papers [95, 96, 97, 98] of Manna and Pnueli, see also [104]. Our presentation of the material mainly follows [83]. The use of diagrams to represent the derivations of properties was suggested in [103].

The self-stabilizing network example is due to [41]. The alternating bit protocol was introduced in [13] and is widely used as a non-trivial example for system verification. Our proof originates from [83].

8

Verification of Concurrent Programs

Programs are formal descriptions of algorithms the operational meaning of which can be viewed as state systems. In other words, a program is a formal (*algorithmic*) representation of such a state system, and a corresponding transition system – as another (*operational*) representation – may be understood as a formal definition of a *semantics* of the program. A temporal logic specification of the state system is then just a third (*axiomatic*) representation, often called *temporal logic semantics* of the program.

Verification of a program Π means verification of properties – now called *program properties* – of the state system (given by) Π. Temporal logic can be used for it along the general lines shown in Chap. 7: the verification is performed by formal derivations of the properties from the axiomatic specification within the logical framework. Actually, it was just this particular application which – historically – was the first aim of the development of temporal logic.

In general, program verification is a well-established important field in computer science and temporal logic is not the sole formal approach to it. In fact, for *sequential* (imperative) programs (which typically are transformational in the sense described in Sect. 6.2) there exist well-known proof methods like the *Hoare calculus* which are specially tailored and therefore most suited to these kinds of programs. The temporal logic treatment is universal in the sense that it is possible for all kinds of programs, but it shows its real power mainly in *concurrent*, particularly reactive programs on which we will therefore concentrate our subsequent considerations.

Concurrent programs with "interfering processes" usually involve *communication* between and *synchronization* of their components. For these tasks there exist algorithmic concepts following two different basic paradigms of *shared (program) variables* and *message passing*, respectively. We will treat both programming styles.

8.1 Programs as State Transition Systems

In order to work out the essentials of temporal logic program verification we fix the following simple framework. A concurrent program Π consists of a number np of (*sequential*) *processes* $\Pi_1, \dots, \Pi_{np}$ which are thought to be executed "in parallel" (*concurrently*) and each of which is a "sequential loop". The basic syntactical structure for this concept will be denoted by

$$\textbf{cobegin } \Pi_1 \parallel \dots \parallel \Pi_{np} \textbf{ coend}$$

and called *parallel statement.* As a formalization of concurrent execution we choose the *interleaving model* which means that

- every process in the parallel statement is to execute a sequence of distinguished *atomic steps*,
- a run of the parallel statement is created by sequentially (i.e., one after the other) executing single atomic steps of the processes such that steps belonging to different processes occur in arbitrary order but steps of the same process Π_i are executed in the order given by Π_i.

Consider, as an example, the parallel statement

$$PS \equiv \textbf{cobegin } \Pi_1 \parallel \Pi_2 \textbf{ coend}$$

with the two loops

$$\begin{aligned}\Pi_1 \equiv\ & \textbf{loop}\ \alpha_0 : a := 2 * a;\\ & \qquad\ \ \alpha_1 : b := b + 1\\ & \textbf{endloop},\\ \Pi_2 \equiv\ & \textbf{loop}\ \beta_0 : a := a + 1;\\ & \qquad\ \ \beta_1 : b := a\\ & \textbf{endloop}\end{aligned}$$

where $\alpha_0, \alpha_1, \beta_0, \beta_1$ are "names" for the four assignment statements in Π_1 and Π_2. Syntax and semantics of the **loop** construct will be defined precisely in the next section, but it should be clear already that Π_1 and Π_2 describe processes which continuously execute α_0 and α_1 (β_0 and β_1, respectively) in the order $\alpha_0, \alpha_1, \alpha_0, \alpha_1, \alpha_0, \dots$ ($\beta_0, \beta_1, \beta_0, \beta_1, \beta_0, \dots$).

Assuming that the four assignment statements are the atomic steps (and have the usual meaning which will be formalized shortly), a possible run of the parallel statement PS according to the interleaving model (starting with, say, $a = 0$ and $b = 0$) is depicted by

$$[0,0] \xrightarrow{\beta_0} [1,0] \xrightarrow{\alpha_0} [2,0] \xrightarrow{\alpha_1} [2,1] \xrightarrow{\alpha_0} [4,1] \xrightarrow{\beta_1} [4,4] \xrightarrow{\beta_0} [5,4] \xrightarrow{\dots} \dots$$

where the pairs $[\dots,\dots]$ denote the values of a and b.

Viewing the parallel statement together with the initialization $a = 0$ and $b = 0$ as (another representation of) an $\mathrm{rl_e}$STS Π it should be clear that

$$\begin{aligned}&Act_\Pi = \{\alpha_0, \alpha_1, \beta_0, \beta_1\},\\ &X_\Pi = \{a, b\},\end{aligned}$$

and that V_Π contains $exec\,\lambda$ for $\lambda \in Act_\Pi$. Any $\lambda \in Act_\Pi$ may only be executed if

"control in Π_1 or Π_2, respectively, is at λ".

For these enabling conditions which ensure the correct order of executions of the atomic steps within Π_1 and Π_2, respectively, we introduce additional propositional system variables

$$at\,\lambda$$

for $\lambda \in Act_\Pi$ with just this informal meaning. So the further definitions

$$\begin{aligned}
&V_\Pi = \{exec\,\lambda, at\,\lambda \mid \lambda \in Act_\Pi\},\\
&enabled_\lambda \equiv at\,\lambda \quad \text{for } \lambda \in Act_\Pi,\\
&start_\Pi \equiv at\,\alpha_0 \land at\,\beta_0 \land a = 0 \land b = 0,\\
&W_\Pi = \{\eta : X_\Pi \cup V_\Pi \to \mathbb{N} \cup \{\mathsf{ff},\mathsf{tt}\} \mid\\
&\qquad \eta(a), \eta(b) \in \mathbb{N},\ \eta(v) \in \{\mathsf{ff},\mathsf{tt}\} \text{ for } v \in V_\Pi,\\
&\qquad \eta \text{ admissible},\\
&\qquad \eta(exec\,\lambda) = \mathsf{tt} \text{ for exactly one } \lambda \in Act_\Pi,\\
&\qquad \eta(at\,\lambda) = \mathsf{tt} \text{ for exactly one } \lambda \in \{\alpha_0, \alpha_1\}\\
&\qquad\qquad\qquad \text{and exactly one } \lambda \in \{\beta_0, \beta_1\}\}
\end{aligned}$$

for Π are evident. The transition relation can be read directly from Π_1 and Π_2:

$$\begin{aligned}
T_\Pi = \{(\eta, \eta') \in W \times W \mid\ &\\
&\text{if } \eta(exec\,\alpha_0) = \mathsf{tt} \text{ then } \eta'(a) = 2 * \eta(a),\ \eta'(b) = \eta(b),\\
&\qquad\qquad\qquad\qquad\quad \eta'(at\,\alpha_1) = \mathsf{tt},\\
&\qquad\qquad\qquad\qquad\quad \eta'(at\,\lambda) = \eta(at\,\lambda) \text{ for } \lambda \in \{\beta_0, \beta_1\}\\
&\text{if } \eta(exec\,\alpha_1) = \mathsf{tt} \text{ then } \eta'(a) = \eta(a),\ \eta'(b) = \eta(b) + 1,\\
&\qquad\qquad\qquad\qquad\quad \eta'(at\,\alpha_0) = \mathsf{tt},\\
&\qquad\qquad\qquad\qquad\quad \eta'(at\,\lambda) = \eta(at\,\lambda) \text{ for } \lambda \in \{\beta_0, \beta_1\}\\
&\text{if } \eta(exec\,\beta_0) = \mathsf{tt} \text{ then } \eta'(a) = \eta(a) + 1,\ \eta'(b) = \eta(b),\\
&\qquad\qquad\qquad\qquad\quad \eta'(at\,\lambda) = \eta(at\,\lambda) \text{ for } \lambda \in \{\alpha_0, \alpha_1\}\\
&\qquad\qquad\qquad\qquad\quad \eta'(at\,\beta_1) = \mathsf{tt},\\
&\text{if } \eta(exec\,\beta_1) = \mathsf{tt} \text{ then } \eta'(a) = \eta(a),\ \eta'(b) = \eta(a),\\
&\qquad\qquad\qquad\qquad\quad \eta'(at\,\lambda) = \eta(at\,\lambda) \text{ for } \lambda \in \{\alpha_0, \alpha_1\}\\
&\qquad\qquad\qquad\qquad\quad \eta'(at\,\beta_0) = \mathsf{tt}\}.
\end{aligned}$$

Of course, the pairs (η, η') of T_Π do not only describe the change of the values of the "program variables" a and b but also the "flow of control" through the values of the additional system variables $at\,\lambda$. Note that in the clauses

$$\text{if } \eta(exec\,\lambda) = \mathsf{tt} \text{ then} \ldots$$

(for $\lambda = \alpha_0, \alpha_1, \beta_0, \beta_1$) it is not necessary to include that $\eta'(at\,\lambda) = \mathsf{ff}$ since this is implied in each case by the definition of W_Π.

The above sample run is formally represented by the execution sequence

$$[0,0,at\,\alpha_0,at\,\beta_0,\beta_0] \longrightarrow [1,0,at\,\alpha_0,at\,\beta_1,\alpha_0] \longrightarrow$$
$$[2,0,at\,\alpha_1,at\,\beta_1,\alpha_1] \longrightarrow [2,1,at\,\alpha_0,at\,\beta_1,\alpha_0] \longrightarrow$$
$$[4,1,at\,\alpha_1,at\,\beta_1,\beta_1] \longrightarrow [4,4,at\,\alpha_1,at\,\beta_0,\beta_0] \longrightarrow$$
$$[5,4,at\,\alpha_1,at\,\beta_1,\ldots] \longrightarrow \ldots$$

where the first two entries in a state $\eta = [\ldots]$ denote the values of a and b, the next two show those $at\,\lambda$ with $\eta(at\,\lambda) = \mathsf{tt}$, and the last entry displays the λ with $\eta(exec\,\lambda) = \mathsf{tt}$.

So far we consider Π as an $\mathrm{rl_e}$STS. Note, however, that because of the interleaving model of computation of Π, we face the typical situation which motivated the introduction of fairness into state transition systems in Sect. 6.5. For example, an execution sequence of Π like

$$[0,0,at\,\alpha_0,at\,\beta_0,\alpha_0] \longrightarrow [0,0,at\,\alpha_1,at\,\beta_0,\alpha_1] \longrightarrow$$
$$[0,1,at\,\alpha_0,at\,\beta_0,\alpha_0] \longrightarrow [0,1,at\,\alpha_1,at\,\beta_0,\alpha_1] \longrightarrow \ldots$$

never executing the statements of Π_2 distorts the intuitive meaning of "executing Π_1 and Π_2 in parallel". The additional fairness requirement obviously avoids such sequences and we make our approach more precise now by fixing that, in general, we will view concurrent programs as fair rooted (extended labeled) state transition systems.

Note also that after addition of fairness the clause

$$\eta(exec\,\lambda) = \mathsf{tt} \text{ for exactly one } \lambda \in Act_\Pi$$

in the above definition of W_Π for the example may be weakened to

$$\eta(exec\,\lambda) = \mathsf{tt} \text{ for at most one } \lambda \in Act_\Pi$$

since the stronger one follows from this and the fairness requirement (cf. Sect. 6.5). In fact, the latter clause will be more appropriate in subsequent cases since it includes situations in which the system "terminates" by executing no action any more.

There seems to be still another source for some adulteration of concurrent execution by the interleaving model. Consider the two actions

$$\alpha : a := a + 1$$

and

$$\beta : a := a - 1.$$

In reality, "parallel" execution of α and β on a computer with two processors sharing a common memory could produce different results on a depending on the different "speeds" of the single machine instructions involved by α and β. In the interleaving model α and β (viewed as atomic steps) are executed one after the other so that after their execution a will always have the same value as it had before.

In general, the problem arises if we view actions as indivisible in the interleaving computation which consist of more atomic steps in reality. But then interleaving with respect to these "smaller" actions, i.e., on a "finer" level of granularity of atomic steps, would adequately model the concurrent execution. Thus, at an appropriate "level of abstraction", interleaving can still be viewed as faithfully representing also this aspect of concurrency.

Although in many cases statements like $a := a + 1$ might not be an appropriate level of abstraction we will use such assignments or even more complex statements as atomic steps in subsequent programs. This is justified by the fact that any coherent block of statements (which might "implement" a complex one) can be made indivisible by means which will be shown in Sect. 8.3.

8.2 Shared-Variables Programs

We now want to make the cursory indications of the previous section more precise. As mentioned already, there are two main paradigms in concurrent programming and we begin here with programs in the shared variables style. To obtain a well-defined vehicle for our discussions we introduce a very simple programming language SVP for such programs. For any program Π of SVP (briefly: SVP *program*) we assume being given a signature SIG_Π and a structure S_Π for SIG_Π. Π has the syntactical form

var Δ
start J
cobegin $\Pi_1 \parallel \ldots \parallel \Pi_{np}$ **coend**

where $np \geq 1$. The case $np = 1$ which makes Π a *sequential program* is included for sake of generality. In fact, our treatment covers such programs without any particularities. As mentioned earlier, however, our real interest is focussed on concurrent programs with $np > 1$.

Δ is a list $\Delta_1; \ldots; \Delta_{nd}$ of *variable declarations* of the form

$$PV_1, \ldots, PV_{nv} : s$$

where s is a sort of SIG_Π and $PV_1, \ldots, PV_{nv}$ are called the *program variables* of sort s of Π. The *initialization* J is a formula of the language $\mathcal{L}_{\mathrm{FOL}}(SIG^0_\Pi)$, shortly denoted by $\mathcal{L}^0_\Pi$, where SIG^0_Π results from SIG_Π by adding the program variables (of each sort s) of Π to the individual constants (of the same sort) of SIG_Π.

Every Π_i, $i = 1, \ldots, np$, is a *process* formed according to the following syntactical rules.

process ::= **loop** *statement list* **endloop**

statement list ::= *labeled statement* | *labeled statement*; *statement list*

labeled statement ::= *label* : *statement*

statement ::= *simple statement* | *conditional statement simple statement* ::= *elementary statement* | *synchronization statement*

conditional statement ::=

if *condition* **then** *statement list* **else** *statement list* **endif**

synchronization statement ::=

await *condition* **then** *elementary statement*

with additionally fixing that

- a *label* is an element of some given set of labels, serving for identifying the statements,
- all labels occurring in Π are pairwise distinct,
- a *condition* is a closed formula of $\mathcal{L}^0_\Pi$.

The form of *elementary statements* is left open. A standard case will be that they are *assignments* written in the general form

$$a_1, \ldots, a_m := t_1, \ldots, t_m$$

$(m \geq 1)$ where $a_1, \ldots, a_m$ are program variables of Π and $t_1, \ldots, t_m$ are terms (of corresponding sorts) of $\mathcal{L}^0_\Pi$ not containing (logical) variables. For forthcoming application examples, however, we want to leave our options open to use also other forms.

The informal meaning of an SVP program Π is that its execution runs by interleaving the processes $\Pi_1, \ldots, \Pi_{np}$. The "flow of control" in each Π_i is defined as usual: statements of a statement list are executed sequentially in the order of the list. (This also fixes that we require elementary statements not to "leave" this normal flow of control by jumping somewhere else.) The execution of a conditional statement

if B **then** SL_1 **else** SL_2 **endif**

evaluates in a first step the condition B and then continues with the statement list SL_1 if B is true and with SL_2 otherwise. The statement list in **loop** ... **endloop** is to be repeated continuously.

The atomic steps of Π with respect to interleaving are

- executions of simple statements; these steps can be identified by the labels of the statements,
- the evaluation of the condition of a conditional statement together with the selection of the respective continuation; such a step can be referred to by the label of the conditional statement.

The effect of assignments is as usual: the (simultaneously determined) values of the right-hand terms are assigned to the corresponding left-hand program variables. The execution of a synchronization statement

await B **then** ES

consists of executing the elementary statement ES if B is true. If B is false then the

```
Π_exmp ≡ var a, b : NAT
         start a = 0 ∧ b = 1
         cobegin loop α0 : a := 2 * b;
                      α1 : if a < b then α2 : a := a + b
                                    else α3 : b := a + 1
                           endif;
                      α4 : a, b := a + 4, b + 1
                 endloop
                 ||
                 loop β0 : await a > 0 then a := a − 1;
                      β1 : b := b + 1
                 endloop
         coend
```

Fig. 8.1. A simple program example

	step	after the step: value of a	b	control at
	initially:	0	1	α_0 β_0
1	$\alpha_0 : a := 2 * b$	2	1	α_1 β_0
2	α_1 : determination of continuation	2	1	α_3 β_0
3	β_0 : **await** $a > 0$ **then** $a := a - 1$	1	1	α_3 β_1
4	$\alpha_3 : b := a + 1$	1	2	α_4 β_1
5	$\beta_1 : b := b + 1$	1	3	α_4 β_0
6	β_0 : **await** $a > 0$ **then** $a := a - 1$	0	3	α_4 β_1
7	$\alpha_4 : a, b := a + 4, b + 1$	4	4	α_0 β_1
8	$\alpha_0 : a := 2 * b$	8	4	α_1 β_1

Fig. 8.2. First steps of a possible run of Π_{exmp}

whole statement is not enabled to execute which means that it cannot be the next step in the interleaving computation of Π.

Fig. 8.1 shows an SVP program Π_{exmp} over SIG_{Nat} and N which illustrates the concepts of SVP. A possible prefix of a sequence of atomic steps executed according to the interleaving model is described by the table in Fig. 8.2. The run starts with $a = 0$, $b = 1$ and control being at α_0 and β_0. The first step can only be α_0 since the condition $a > 0$ in the synchronization statement β_0 is false. In the second step α_1 and β_0 are enabled and α_1, i.e., the evaluation of the condition $a < b$ together with the selection of continuation at α_3 is executed. β_0 is taken as the third step and so on.

Every statement list SL built according to the SVP syntax has the form

$$\lambda_1 : ST_1; \ldots ; \lambda_l : ST_l$$

($l \geq 1$) with labels $\lambda_1, \ldots, \lambda_l$ and statements $ST_1, \ldots, ST_l$. The label λ_1 will be denoted by $entry(SL)$. Moreover, any label λ in an SVP program occurs as some

λ_j, $1 \le j \le l$, in such an SL and we may associate with λ the label λ^{seq} in the following way. If $\lambda = \lambda_j$, $1 \le j \le l-1$, then $\lambda^{seq} = \lambda_{j+1}$. For $\lambda = \lambda_l$ we let $\lambda^{seq} = \bar{\lambda}^{seq}$ if SL is one of the statement lists in a conditional statement labeled by $\bar{\lambda}$, and $\lambda^{seq} = \lambda_1$ if SL is the statement list in a process $\Pi_i \equiv$ **loop** SL **endloop**. In the latter case, λ_1 is also denoted by $\lambda^{(i)}_{start}$.

For the first process of the program Π_{exmp} in Fig. 8.1, we have

$$\begin{aligned}
&\lambda^{(i)}_{start} = \alpha_0,\\
&\alpha_0^{seq} = \alpha_1,\\
&\alpha_1^{seq} = \alpha_2^{seq} = \alpha_3^{seq} = \alpha_4,\\
&\alpha_4^{seq} = \alpha_0.
\end{aligned}$$

The labels λ^{seq} keep track of the sequential "concatenation" structure of the statements in a process disregarding possible branching by conditional statements. The latter is additionally captured by associating two labels λ^{then} and λ^{else} with every label λ of a conditional statement **if** B **then** SL_1 **else** SL_2 **endif**: $\lambda^{then} = entry(SL_1)$ and $\lambda^{else} = entry(SL_2)$. Obviously, λ^{then} and λ^{else} are the labels where to continue if B is true or false, respectively. In Π_{exmp}, we have $\alpha_1^{then} = \alpha_2$ and $\alpha_1^{else} = \alpha_3$.

Let now Π be an SVP program over some SIG_Π and S_Π with processes $\Pi_1, \ldots, \Pi_{np}$ and initialization J. Let Lab_Π be the set of all labels occurring in Π and for every sort s of SIG_Π, let X_s^{prog} be the set of program variables of sort s of Π. According to the discussion in the previous section we view Π as an $\mathrm{frl_eSTS}$

$$\Pi = (X, V, W, T, Act, start, \mathcal{E})$$

over SIG_Π and S_Π defined as follows.

Every label of Lab_Π uniquely denotes an atomic step in the interleaving computation of Π and these steps are the actions which cause the transitions of the system. So Lab_Π may be taken as the set of actions:

$$Act = Lab_\Pi.$$

By Act_{Π_i} we will denote the set of labels occurring in Π_i. Moreover, we will from now on freely use the wording "statement λ" instead of "statement labeled by λ". In X and V we collect the program variables and the additional constructs for $\lambda \in Act$:

$$\begin{aligned}
&X_s = X_s^{prog} \quad \text{for every sort } s \text{ of } SIG_\Pi,\\
&V = \{exec\lambda, at\lambda \mid \lambda \in Act\}.
\end{aligned}$$

(Note that this also means that $\mathcal{L}^0_\Pi$ is a sublanguage of $\mathcal{L}_\Pi$ which is defined as in Sect. 6.2. Formulas of $\mathcal{L}^0_\Pi$ are formulas of $\mathcal{L}_\Pi$ without propositional constants from V.) The initial condition is

$$start \equiv \bigwedge_{i=1}^{np} at\lambda^{(i)}_{start} \wedge J$$

expressing that at the beginning the control is at the "start labels" of $\Pi_1, \ldots, \Pi_{np}$ and the initialization J holds. The enabling conditions are

$$enabled_\lambda \equiv \begin{cases} at\lambda \wedge B & \text{if } \lambda \text{ is a synchronization statement with condition } B,\\ at\lambda & \text{otherwise} \end{cases}$$

for every $\lambda \in Act$. The set of states is defined by

$$\begin{aligned} W = \{\eta : X \cup V \to |\mathsf{S}| \cup \{\mathsf{ff}, \mathsf{tt}\} \mid \\ & \eta(a) \in |\mathsf{S}|_s \text{ for } a \in X_s \text{ and every sort } s \text{ of } SIG_\Pi,\\ & \eta(v) \in \{\mathsf{ff}, \mathsf{tt}\} \text{ for } v \in V,\\ & \eta \text{ admissible},\\ & \eta(exec\lambda) = \mathsf{tt} \text{ for at most one } \lambda \in Act,\\ & \eta(at\lambda) = \mathsf{tt} \text{ for exactly one } \lambda \in Act_{\Pi_i} \ (i = 1, \ldots, np)\}. \end{aligned}$$

Finally,

$$\begin{aligned} &T = tot(T'),\\ &T' = \{(\eta, \eta') \in W \times W \mid \text{"description of transitions"}\} \end{aligned}$$

and "description of transitions" is a list of clauses

$$\text{if } \eta(exec\lambda) = \mathsf{tt} \text{ then} \ldots$$

for every $\lambda \in Act$ (as exemplified in the previous section). If λ is an elementary statement ES or a synchronization statement **await** B **then** ES in Π_i then this clause is of the form

$$\begin{aligned} \text{if } \eta(exec\lambda) = \mathsf{tt} \text{ then } & \text{"description of changes of program variables"},\\ & \eta'(at\lambda^{seq}) = \mathsf{tt},\\ & \eta'(at\bar{\lambda}) = \eta(at\bar{\lambda}) \text{ for every } \bar{\lambda} \in Act \setminus Act_{\Pi_i}. \end{aligned}$$

The "description of changes of program variables" depends on the form of the elementary statement ES. For ES being an assignment

$$a_1, \ldots, a_m := t_1, \ldots, t_m$$

we take

$$\begin{aligned} &\eta'(a_i) = \mathsf{S}_\Pi^{(\eta)}(t_i) && \text{for } i = 1, \ldots, m,\\ &\eta'(b) = \eta(b) && \text{for } b \in X \setminus \{a_1, \ldots, a_m\}. \end{aligned}$$

(Note that we write $\mathsf{S}_\Pi^{(\eta)}(t_i)$ omitting a variable valuation since t_i contains no variables.) If λ is a conditional statement with condition B in Π_i then the above clause is

$$\begin{aligned} \text{if } \eta(exec\lambda) = \mathsf{tt} \text{ then } & \eta'(a) = \eta(a) \text{ for every } a \in X,\\ & \eta'(at\bar{\lambda}) = \eta(at\bar{\lambda}) \text{ for every } \bar{\lambda} \in Act \setminus Act_{\Pi_i},\\ & \text{if } \mathsf{S}_\Pi^{(\eta)}(B) = \mathsf{tt} \text{ then } \eta'(at\lambda^{then}) = \mathsf{tt}\\ & \qquad \text{otherwise } \eta'(at\lambda^{else}) = \mathsf{tt}. \end{aligned}$$

$$
\begin{array}{lll}
\Pi_{exp} \equiv & \textbf{var}\ a, b, result : NAT \\
& \textbf{start}\ a = 2 \land b = N \land result = 1 \\
& \textbf{cobegin loop}\ \alpha_1 : \textbf{await}\ b \neq 0\ \textbf{then skip}\,; \\
& \qquad\qquad\quad \alpha_2 : \textbf{if}\ EVEN(b)\ \textbf{then}\ \alpha_3 : a, b := a * a, b/2 \\
& \qquad\qquad\qquad\qquad\qquad\qquad \textbf{else}\ \alpha_4 : b, result := b - 1, result * a \\
& \qquad\qquad\qquad \textbf{endif} \\
& \qquad\quad \textbf{endloop} \\
& \textbf{coend}
\end{array}
$$

Fig. 8.3. A transformational program

This schematic definition draws the state transition system directly from the syntactical form of the program. For the example Π_{exmp} in Fig. 8.1 we would get

$$
\begin{aligned}
& Act = \{\alpha_0, \alpha_1, \alpha_2, \alpha_3, \alpha_4, \beta_0, \beta_1\}, \\
& X = X_{Nat} = \{a, b\}, \\
& V = \{exec\lambda, at\lambda \mid \lambda \in Act\}, \\
& start \equiv at\alpha_0 \land at\beta_0 \land a = 0 \land b = 1, \\
& enabled_{\beta_0} \equiv at\beta_0 \land a > 0, \\
& enabled_\lambda \equiv at\lambda \quad \text{for } \lambda \in Act \setminus \{\beta_0\}.
\end{aligned}
$$

The state set W for Π_{exmp} is trivially taken from the general definition and the entries in the transition relation T amount to clauses like

$$
\begin{aligned}
\text{if } \eta(exec\alpha_0) = \mathsf{tt} \text{ then } & \eta'(a) = 2 * \eta(b), \\
& \eta'(b) = \eta(b), \\
& \eta'(at\alpha_1) = \mathsf{tt}, \\
& \eta'(at\lambda) = \eta(at\lambda) \text{ for } \lambda \in Act \setminus \{\beta_0, \beta_1\}
\end{aligned}
$$

and so on for the other actions.

Programs sometimes contain *boolean* program variables, i.e., program variables of a sort $BOOLEAN$ associated with operations like not, and, or, and the like and a two-element set of truth values as its domain. We include such program variables into the set X of the state system. Alternatively we could join them to the set V and then use $\neg$, $\land$, $\lor$ instead of not, and, or, etc. This approach would avoid the "duplication" of propositional logic and would be closer to system examples in Chap. 6: for example, the system variable on in the counter $\Gamma_{counter}$ was introduced as an element of $V_{\Gamma_{counter}}$ (and not of $X_{\Gamma_{counter}}$). The only reason for our decision for the present approach is the simplicity and uniformity of its general presentation.

We still note that (sequential or concurrent) SVP programs can also be transformational in the way that termination – represented as before – can be obtained by synchronization statements. A simple example is given by the (sequential) program Π_{exp} in Fig. 8.3 (containing a special elementary statement **skip** which does not change any program variable). It is easy to see that Π_{exp} computes the power 2^N for the natural number constant N in the sense that after some transition steps a state is reached in which control is at α_1, the program variable $result$ has the value 2^N, and which is then repeated forever since b has the value 0.

In concurrent reactive programs the "blocking" effect of the **await** concept is used for synchronization. Termination is just not the goal then but may happen unintentionally by "unfortunately" reaching a state in which the control in each process of the program is at some synchronization statement the enabling condition of which is false, so no action can be executed any more. Such an undesirable termination is called *deadlock*.

In the same way as the representation of an SVP program Π as a state system the temporal logic semantics $Th(\Pi)$ of Π can directly be drawn from the syntactical structure of Π without referring to the rather cumbersome $\mathrm{rfl_eSTS}$ view.

Let again Π be an SVP program over some SIG_Π and S_Π with processes $\Pi_1, \ldots, \Pi_{np}$ and the same denotations as above, and let $start_\Pi$, Act_Π, and $enabled_\lambda$ for $\lambda \in Act_\Pi$ be defined as before. The temporal signature $TSIG$ for the underlying language $\mathcal{L}_{\mathrm{TL}\Pi}(TSIG)$ of $Th(\Pi)$ is

$$TSIG = (SIG_\Pi, \mathbf{X}, \mathbf{V})$$

with

$$\mathbf{X}_s = X_s^{prog} \quad \text{for every sort } s \text{ of } SIG_\Pi,$$
$$\mathbf{V} = \{exec\lambda, at\lambda \mid \lambda \in Act_\Pi\}.$$

The set $\mathcal{A}$ of axioms of $Th(\Pi)$ consists of (data_Π), (root_Π), (nil_Π), (action_Π), (fair_Π) originating from our general investigations of Chap. 6 and the following additional axioms which describe the general requirements of the state set of Π and the possible transitions. Firstly, the axioms

$$(\mathrm{I}_\Pi) \qquad exec\lambda_1 \to \neg exec\lambda_2 \quad \text{for } \lambda_1, \lambda_2 \in Act_\Pi, \lambda_1 \neq \lambda_2,$$
$$(\mathrm{PC}_\Pi) \qquad at\lambda_1 \to \neg at\lambda_2 \quad \text{for } \lambda_1, \lambda_2 \in Act_{\Pi_i}, i = 1, \ldots, np, \lambda_1 \neq \lambda_2$$

express the interleaving principle and the "uniqueness of the program counters" in each Π_i. Note that (PC_Π) only describes "$\eta(at\lambda) = \mathsf{tt}$ for at most one $\lambda \in Act_{\Pi_i}$". The "exactly one" in this clause is derivable from the subsequent axioms. These "transition axioms" may be divided as follows: the axioms

$$(\mathrm{C1}_\Pi) \qquad exec\lambda \to \bigcirc at\lambda^{seq} \quad \text{for every simple statement } \lambda,$$
$$(\mathrm{C2}_\Pi) \qquad exec\lambda \to (B \wedge \bigcirc at\lambda^{then}) \vee (\neg B \wedge \bigcirc at\lambda^{else})$$
$$\text{for every conditional statement } \lambda : \textbf{if } B \textbf{ then } \ldots,$$
$$(\mathrm{C3}_\Pi) \qquad exec\lambda \wedge at\bar{\lambda} \to \bigcirc at\bar{\lambda} \quad \text{for every } \lambda \in Act_{\Pi_i}, \bar{\lambda} \in Act_\Pi \setminus Act_{\Pi_i},$$
$$i = 1, \ldots, np$$

describe the flow of control. (For better readability, we use the nexttime operator instead of the priming notation for propositional constants $at\lambda$.) The change of program variable values is expressed by

$$(\mathrm{PV1}_\Pi) \qquad exec\lambda \to \bigwedge_{a \in X} a' = a \quad \text{for every conditional statement } \lambda$$

and by an axiom of the general form

(PV2$_\Pi$) $\quad exec\lambda \rightarrow F$

with an appropriate formula F for every simple statement. For the standard case of an assignment

$$\lambda : a_1, \ldots, a_m := t_1, \ldots, t_m$$

or a synchronization statement

$$\lambda : \textbf{await } B \textbf{ then } a_1, \ldots, a_m := t_1, \ldots, t_m$$

(PV2$_\Pi$) becomes

(ASSIGN$_\Pi$) $\quad exec\lambda \rightarrow \bigwedge_{i=1}^{m} a_i' = t_i \wedge \bigwedge_{b \in X \setminus \{a_1, \ldots, a_m\}} b' = b.$

For illustration we give the complete list of temporal axioms for the sample program Π_{exmp} of Fig. 8.1.

(root$_{\Pi_{exmp}}$): $\quad \textbf{init} \rightarrow at\,\alpha_0 \wedge at\,\beta_0 \wedge a = 0 \wedge b = 1,$

(nil$_{\Pi_{exmp}}$): $\quad \bigwedge_{\lambda \in Act_{\Pi_{exmp}}} \neg exec\lambda \wedge A \rightarrow \bigcirc A$ if A is a state formula of Π_{exmp},

(action$_{\Pi_{exmp}}$): $\quad exec\lambda \rightarrow at\lambda$ for $\lambda \in Act_{\Pi_{exmp}} \setminus \{\beta_0\}$,
$exec\,\beta_0 \rightarrow at\,\beta_0 \wedge a > 0,$

(fair$_{\Pi_{exmp}}$): $\quad \Box\Diamond at\lambda \rightarrow \Diamond exec\lambda$ for $\lambda \in Act_{\Pi_{exmp}} \setminus \{\beta_0\}$,
$\Box\Diamond(at\,\beta_0 \wedge a > 0) \rightarrow \Diamond exec\,\beta_0,$

$(I_{\Pi_{exmp}})$: $\quad exec\lambda_1 \rightarrow \neg exec\lambda_2$ for $\lambda_1, \lambda_2 \in Act_{\Pi_{exmp}}, \lambda_1 \neq \lambda_2$,

$(PC_{\Pi_{exmp}})$: $\quad at\,\alpha_i \rightarrow \neg at\,\alpha_j$ for $i, j \in \{0, 1, 2, 3, 4\}, i \neq j$,
$at\,\beta_i \rightarrow \neg at\,\beta_j$ for $i, j \in \{0, 1\}, i \neq j$,

$(C1_{\Pi_{exmp}})$: $\quad exec\,\alpha_0 \rightarrow \bigcirc at\,\alpha_1,$
$exec\,\alpha_2 \rightarrow \bigcirc at\,\alpha_4,$
$exec\,\alpha_3 \rightarrow \bigcirc at\,\alpha_4,$
$exec\,\alpha_4 \rightarrow \bigcirc at\,\alpha_0,$
$exec\,\beta_0 \rightarrow \bigcirc at\,\beta_1,$
$exec\,\beta_1 \rightarrow \bigcirc at\,\beta_0,$

$(C2_{\Pi_{exmp}})$: $\quad exec\,\alpha_1 \rightarrow (a < b \wedge \bigcirc at\,\alpha_2) \vee (a \geq b \wedge \bigcirc at\,\alpha_3),$

$(C3_{\Pi_{exmp}})$: $\quad exec\,\alpha_i \wedge at\,\beta_j \rightarrow \bigcirc at\,\beta_j$ for $i \in \{0, 1, 2, 3, 4\}, j \in \{0, 1\}$,
$exec\,\beta_j \wedge at\,\alpha_i \rightarrow \bigcirc at\,\alpha_i$ for $i \in \{0, 1, 2, 3, 4\}, j \in \{0, 1\}$,

$(PV1_{\Pi_{exmp}})$: $\quad exec\,\alpha_1 \rightarrow a' = a \wedge b' = b,$

$(PV2_{\Pi_{exmp}})$: $\quad exec\,\alpha_0 \rightarrow a' = 2 * b \wedge b' = b,$
$exec\,\alpha_2 \rightarrow a' = a + b \wedge b' = b,$
$exec\,\alpha_3 \rightarrow a' = a \wedge b' = a + 1,$
$exec\,\alpha_4 \rightarrow a' = a + 4 \wedge b' = b + 1,$
$exec\,\beta_0 \rightarrow a' = a - 1 \wedge b' = b,$
$exec\,\beta_1 \rightarrow a' = a \wedge b' = b + 1.$

The list is rather long but it should be evident that it is almost trivial to "read it from the program text". The axioms ($I_{\Pi_{examp}}$) are included according to the general "translation". As in earlier examples in the previous chapters they are derivable here from the other axioms and could be omitted.

8.3 Program Properties

Synchronization and communication in concurrent programs induce a lot of program properties which arise naturally from typical requirements posed on the desired interaction of the involved processes. We give now a cursory overview of some of them in the framework of shared variables programs of SVP adding sporadically some examples of formal derivations. We follow again our simple classification given in Sect. 7.1 and begin with invariance properties.

A basic synchronization pattern of concurrent programming is induced by *exclusion* requirements. Assume, as the simplest case, a program Π with two processes Π_1 and Π_2 each of which contains a statement list SL_1 and SL_2, respectively, which are *critical sections* with the requirement that control of Π_1 and Π_2 should never be in these sections at the same time. If $\alpha_1, \ldots, \alpha_k$ and $\beta_1, \ldots, \beta_l$ are the statements of SL_1 and SL_2, respectively, then this *mutual exclusion* property can be specified by the formula

$$start_\Pi \land A \to \Box\neg\left(\bigvee_{i=1}^{k} at\,\alpha_i \land \bigvee_{j=1}^{l} at\,\beta_j\right)$$

where A might be some *precondition* holding (additionally to $start_\Pi$) at the beginning of every execution sequence of Π. If $A \equiv$ **true** then this description may be shortened to the global invariant

$$\Box\neg\left(\bigvee_{i=1}^{k} at\,\alpha_i \land \bigvee_{j=1}^{l} at\,\beta_j\right)$$

(according to the remarks in Sect. 7.1 where we also explained the use of $start_\Pi$ instead of **init** in such formulas).

A second basic synchronization pattern arises from the possible situation that the execution of some statement λ will generate a *fault* if some associated condition C_λ is violated. Synchronization should guarantee *fault freedom* by assuring that C_λ is true whenever control is at λ. The general form (with a possible precondition) of this property is

$$start_\Pi \land A \to \Box(at\,\lambda \to C_\lambda).$$

Example. Consider the well-known *producer-consumer* scheme given by the program Π_{pc} in Fig. 8.4. The first process Π_p of Π_{pc} – the producer – continuously produces in α_0 an object represented by the program variable obj of a sort $OBJECT$

$$
\begin{array}{l}
\Pi_{pc} \equiv \textbf{var } ex, bf, be : NAT; \\
\qquad\qquad obj, out : OBJECT; \\
\qquad\qquad b : BUFFER \\
\quad\;\; \textbf{start } ex = 1 \land bf = 0 \land be = CAP \\
\quad\;\; \textbf{cobegin loop } \alpha_0 : \textbf{produce } obj; \\
\qquad\qquad\qquad\qquad \alpha_1 : \textbf{await } be > 0 \textbf{ then } be := be - 1; \\
\qquad\qquad\qquad\qquad \alpha_2 : \textbf{await } ex = 1 \textbf{ then } ex := 0; \\
\qquad\qquad\qquad\qquad \alpha_3 : \textbf{store } obj \textbf{ in } b; \\
\qquad\qquad\qquad\qquad \alpha_4 : ex, bf := 1, bf + 1 \\
\qquad\qquad\quad \textbf{endloop} \\
\qquad\qquad\quad \| \\
\qquad\qquad\quad \textbf{loop } \beta_0 : \textbf{await } bf > 0 \textbf{ then } bf := bf - 1; \\
\qquad\qquad\qquad\qquad \beta_1 : \textbf{await } ex = 1 \textbf{ then } ex := 0; \\
\qquad\qquad\qquad\qquad \beta_2 : \textbf{remove } out \textbf{ from } b; \\
\qquad\qquad\qquad\qquad \beta_3 : ex, be := 1, be + 1; \\
\qquad\qquad\qquad\qquad \beta_4 : \textbf{consume } out \\
\qquad\qquad\quad \textbf{endloop} \\
\quad\;\; \textbf{coend}
\end{array}
$$

Fig. 8.4. The producer-consumer scheme

and stores it into a *buffer* b in α_3. b is of a sort $BUFFER$ which is endowed with two unary predicates $ISEMPTY$ and $ISFULL$ (with obvious interpretations) and a natural number CAP for the buffer capacity, i.e., the number of objects which can be stored in a buffer. b is shared with the second component Π_c of Π_{pc}, called consumer. This process continuously takes an object, represented by the program variable out, from b in β_2 and uses ("consumes") it in some internal computation in β_4. For simplicity these activities of the two processes are represented by elementary statements, thus fixing a level of abstraction which might be not realistic. As discussed in Sect. 8.1, the effects of the two concurrent accesses α_3 and β_2 to the buffer depend on how indivisible they are. In fact, they are critical sections in the present wording and it is just one particular purpose of the synchronization – organized by the remaining statements – to exclude them (at least) mutually, i.e., to guarantee the mutual exclusion property

$$\Box\neg(at\,\alpha_3 \land at\,\beta_2).$$

This does not make α_3 and β_2 "completely indivisible" but the interference of other actions of the processes with α_3 and β_2 is not critical. α_0 and β_4 are not critical at all in this sense, so the given abstraction does not really distort the analysis of the program.

Another requirement is that storing into the buffer is only possible if it is not full and for getting something from b it must not be empty. So the formulas

$$\Box(at\,\alpha_3 \rightarrow \neg ISFULL(b)),$$
$$\Box(at\,\beta_2 \rightarrow \neg ISEMPTY(b))$$

describe two properties of fault freedom. △

Synchronization of processes according to exclusion or fault freedom requirements may cause, if not performed carefully, new undesirable effects like deadlocks mentioned already in the previous section. Consider again a program with two processes Π_1 and Π_2. A deadlock is given by a state in which control is at some synchronization statement α in Π_1 and at another synchronization statement β in Π_2 and the enabling conditions of both α and β are false. So, the property of *deadlock freedom* that this cannot happen is generally specified by formulas

$$start_{\Pi} \land A \rightarrow \Box(at\,\alpha \land at\,\beta \rightarrow enabled_{\alpha} \lor enabled_{\beta})$$

for every pair α and β as described.

Example. In the producer-consumer program Π_{pc} of Fig. 8.4 deadlock freedom is guaranteed if CAP is not 0. This is described by the four formulas

$$\begin{aligned}
&start_{\Pi_{pc}} \land CAP > 0 \rightarrow \Box(at\,\alpha_1 \land at\,\beta_0 \rightarrow be > 0 \lor bf > 0),\\
&start_{\Pi_{pc}} \land CAP > 0 \rightarrow \Box(at\,\alpha_1 \land at\,\beta_1 \rightarrow be > 0 \lor ex = 1),\\
&start_{\Pi_{pc}} \land CAP > 0 \rightarrow \Box(at\,\alpha_2 \land at\,\beta_0 \rightarrow ex = 1 \lor bf > 0),\\
&start_{\Pi_{pc}} \land CAP > 0 \rightarrow \Box(at\,\alpha_2 \land at\,\beta_1 \rightarrow ex = 1)
\end{aligned}$$

which are easily drawn from the general form. △

The properties so far may be relevant in both reactive and transformational programs. For the latter case the property of *partial correctness* is additionally important. Assume that the goal of the computation of a transformational program Π is expressed by a formula B of $\mathcal{L}^0_{\Pi}$, often called a *postcondition* of Π. Partial correctness then means that

"whenever Π terminates, B will hold in the terminal state".

According to our former remarks a terminal state of an execution sequence of Π is characterized by the fact that no action is executed any more. So, partial correctness of Π may be expressed by a formula

$$start_{\Pi} \land A \rightarrow \Box(nil_{\Pi} \rightarrow B).$$

Example. Consider the program Π_{exp} shown in Fig. 8.3 in the previous section. Its postcondition describing the result of its execution is

$$result = 2^N$$

and since there is no precondition for this result, the partial correctness may be stated by the formula

$$start_{\Pi_{exp}} \rightarrow \Box(nil_{\Pi_{exp}} \rightarrow result = 2^N)$$

or in an even shorter way by formulating the postcondition as a global invariant. △

The verification of such properties, i.e., their derivation from the axioms of the corresponding temporal semantics, may use the complete repertory developed in Sect. 7.2. More particularly, since programs are labeled state systems, the invariant rules are applicable. Note that the fairness assumption introduced for compensating the interleaving model is not needed for proofs with these rules. The program specification axioms directly reflect the program text as we have seen in the previous section. We will not write them down explicitly in subsequent derivation examples but have them implicitly "in mind", and when using them in single derivation steps we will indicate this by (Π).

Example. We consider the producer-consumer program Π_{pc} in Fig. 8.4 and first verify the mutual exclusion property

$$\Box\neg(at\,\alpha_3 \wedge at\,\beta_2).$$

To this end we now have to specify the statements **produce** obj, **store** obj **in** b, **remove** out **from** b, and **consume** out a bit more precisely. We do not need to know too much about them but at least we fix that they have no particular enabling conditions and do not change the program variables ex, bf, and be the only purpose of which is to realize the synchronization. So we may assume that

$$enabled_\lambda \equiv at\,\lambda \quad \text{for } \lambda \in \{\alpha_0, \alpha_3, \beta_2, \beta_4\}$$

and that

(1) $exec\,\lambda \rightarrow ex' = ex \wedge bf' = bf \wedge be' = be \quad \text{for } \lambda \in \{\alpha_0, \alpha_3, \beta_2, \beta_4\}$

is a part of (or derivable from) the specification of these statements. Let now

$$\begin{aligned} A &\equiv at\,\alpha_3 \vee at\,\alpha_4, \\ B &\equiv at\,\beta_2 \vee at\,\beta_3, \\ C &\equiv (A \wedge \neg B \wedge ex = 0) \vee (\neg A \wedge B \wedge ex = 0) \vee (\neg A \wedge \neg B \wedge ex = 1). \end{aligned}$$

With $start_{\Pi_{pc}} \equiv at\,\alpha_0 \wedge at\,\beta_0 \wedge ex = 1 \wedge bf = 0 \wedge be = CAP$ it is clear that C holds at the beginning of Π_{pc}:

(2) $start_{\Pi_{pc}} \rightarrow C$ (pred)

Moreover, C is an invariant of every action of Π_{pc}. First we have trivially

(3) C **invof** λ for every $\lambda \in Act_{\Pi_{pc}} \setminus \{\alpha_2, \alpha_4, \beta_1, \beta_3\}$ (Π),(1)

For α_2 we get

(4) $exec\,\alpha_2 \rightarrow ex = 1 \wedge ex' = 0$ (Π)
(5) $exec\,\alpha_2 \wedge C \rightarrow \neg B \wedge \bigcirc A \wedge \bigcirc\neg B$ (4),(Π)
(6) C **invof** α_2 (4),(5)

and for α_4 the invariance is derived by

(7)	$exec\,\alpha_4 \rightarrow A \wedge \bigcirc\neg A$	(Π)
(8)	$exec\,\alpha_4 \wedge C \rightarrow \neg B \wedge ex = 0 \wedge \bigcirc\neg B \wedge ex' = 1$	(7),(Π)
(9)	C **invof** α_4	(7),(8)

In the same obvious way we obtain

(10) C **invof** β_1
(11) C **invof** β_3

and finally

(12)	C **invof** $Act_{\Pi_{pc}}$	(3),(6),(9),(10),(11)

Now we apply the rule (invstart$_{\Pi_{pc}}$) and get the desired property:

(13)	$\Box C$	(invstart),(2),(12)
(14)	$C \rightarrow \neg(at\,\alpha_3 \wedge at\,\beta_2)$	(taut)
(15)	$\Box\neg(at\,\alpha_3 \wedge at\,\beta_2)$	(13),(14)

Turning to the four formulas given above for expressing the deadlock freedom of Π_{pc}, the second, third, and fourth of them follow immediately from line (13) of this derivation:

(16)	$start_{\Pi_{pc}} \wedge CAP > 0 \rightarrow$ $\Box(at\,\alpha_1 \wedge at\,\beta_1 \rightarrow be > 0 \vee ex = 1)$	(prop),(13)
(17)	$start_{\Pi_{pc}} \wedge CAP > 0 \rightarrow$ $\Box(at\,\alpha_2 \wedge at\,\beta_0 \rightarrow ex = 1 \vee bf > 0)$	(prop),(13)
(18)	$start_{\Pi_{pc}} \wedge CAP > 0 \rightarrow \Box(at\,\alpha_2 \wedge at\,\beta_1 \rightarrow ex = 1)$	(prop),(13)

For deriving the first one of the four formulas we let

$$D \equiv (at\,\alpha_0 \vee at\,\alpha_1) \wedge (at\,\beta_0 \vee at\,\beta_4) \rightarrow be > 0 \vee bf > 0$$

and obtain

(19)	$start_{\Pi_{pc}} \wedge CAP > 0 \rightarrow D$	(pred)
(20)	$D \rightarrow (at\,\alpha_1 \wedge at\,\beta_0 \rightarrow be > 0 \vee bf > 0)$	(taut)
(21)	$exec\,\alpha_1 \rightarrow \bigcirc\neg(at\,\alpha_0 \vee at\,\alpha_1)$	(Π)
(22)	D **invof** α_1	(21)
(23)	$exec\,\alpha_4 \rightarrow bf' > 0$	(data),(Π)
(24)	D **invof** α_4	(23)
(25)	$exec\,\beta_0 \rightarrow \bigcirc\neg(at\,\beta_0 \vee at\,\beta_4)$	(Π)
(26)	D **invof** β_0	(25)
(27)	$exec\,\beta_3 \rightarrow be' > 0$	(data),(Π)
(28)	D **invof** β_3	(27)
(29)	D **invof** λ for every $\lambda \in Act_{\Pi_{pc}} \setminus \{\alpha_1, \alpha_4, \beta_0, \beta_3\}$	(Π),(1)
(30)	D **invof** $Act_{\Pi_{pc}}$	(22),(24),(26), (28),(29)
(31)	$D \rightarrow \Box(at\,\alpha_1 \wedge at\,\beta_0 \rightarrow be > 0 \vee bf > 0)$	(inv),(20),(30)

(32) $start_{\Pi_{pc}} \land CAP > 0 \rightarrow$
$$\Box(at\,\alpha_1 \land at\,\beta_0 \rightarrow be > 0 \lor bf > 0) \qquad (19),(31)$$

Note that only for this deadlock freedom formula concerning the statements α_1 and β_0 do we really need the precondition $CAP > 0$. △

Precedence properties of concurrent programs usually state temporal relationships of the occurrence of events. Simplest forms could be specified by formulas like

$$A \rightarrow exec\,\lambda_1 \textbf{ before } exec\,\lambda_2$$

or

$$A \rightarrow at\,\lambda_1 \textbf{ before } at\,\lambda_2$$

expressing that, if A holds in some state, then subsequently λ_1 will be executed before λ_2 or control will be at λ_1 before it will reach λ_2, respectively. More complicated forms, however, naturally arise as well. Examples are given by "output" actions which should occur in a special order, or when necessary or desired orderings of events in different processes according to some scheduling are to be described.

Examples. 1) Consider again the producer-consumer program Π_{pc} of Fig. 8.4 and assume that all objects produced and stored into the buffer b are pairwise distinct. If some object x is stored and another object y is not (yet) in b then a desirable property could be that x will be removed from b by the consumer before this (possibly) happens with y. Presupposing a predicate symbol $\in$ for membership of objects in the buffer (and $\notin$ for its negation) we can specify this by the formula

$$exec\,\alpha_3 \land obj = x \land y \notin b \land x \neq y \rightarrow$$
$$(exec\,\beta_2 \land out = x) \textbf{ before } (exec\,\beta_2 \land out = y)$$

where x and y are variables of sort $OBJECT$.

2) Consider a modification Π_{pcs} of the program Π_{pc} of Fig. 8.4 containing not only one but $nc > 1$ consumers, denoted by $\Pi_c^{(1)}, \ldots, \Pi_c^{(nc)}$. Whenever more than one of them is trying to take an object from the buffer, these processes are in a mutual competition for this and without additional assumptions it is not guaranteed that every one of the competitors will eventually be served. So there should be an additional *scheduler* process in Π_{pcs} organizing the access to the buffer for the consumers. This process could look like

loop γ_0 : **determine** $j \in \{1, \ldots, nc\}$;
γ_1 : **await** $next = 0$ **then** $next := j$
endloop

γ_0 determines in a not further specified appropriate way the index j of the consumer $\Pi_c^{(j)}$ who will be allowed to compete for the next buffer access with the producer. As soon as no other consumer is in this position, expressed by $next = 0$, this j

is assigned to the program variable $next$. Every $\Pi_c^{(i)}$ has a modified form: besides additionally resetting $next$ to 0 after its buffer access, it has a new entry statement

$$\beta_0^{(i)} : \mathbf{await}\ next = i$$

awaiting to be "the next admitted" consumer. (The statement **await** B abbreviates **await** B **then skip** where **skip** is as explained in the previous section.)

A reasonable requirement for the scheduler could be not to determine a next admitted consumer who is not requesting the access to the buffer. At first glance one might try to describe this property by

$$at\,\gamma_1 \wedge j = i \rightarrow at\,\beta_0^{(i)} \quad \text{for } i = 1, \ldots, nc$$

("if i is the result of the determination of j in γ_0 then $\Pi_c^{(i)}$ is waiting for being admitted"), but these formulas do not meet the intention precisely: $\Pi_i^{(i)}$ could already be the admitted consumer from the "previous round" of the scheduler, will use this grant now, and is then already scheduled to be the next admitted one again.

A more careful description is

$$\neg at\,\beta_0^{(i)} \rightarrow \neg(at\,\gamma_1 \wedge j = i)\ \mathbf{unl}\ at\,\beta_0^{(i)}$$

(for $i = 1, \ldots, nc$). This formula states that if $\Pi_c^{(i)}$ is not waiting for being next admitted then i will not be the result of the determination of j in γ_0 until $\Pi_c^{(i)}$ requests to be admitted. Observe that we have used here the non-strict operator **unl**. This excludes that γ_0 is executed with the result $j = i$ in the present state. Describing the property with the strict **unless** would need an additional (invariant) formula for this purpose:

$$\neg at\,\beta_0^{(i)} \rightarrow \neg(at\,\gamma_1 \wedge j = i)\ \mathbf{unless}\ at\,\beta_0^{(i)},$$
$$\Box(\neg at\,\beta_0^{(i)} \rightarrow \neg(exec\,\gamma_1 \wedge j = i)).$$

Of particular interest is the order in which the consumers are admitted for the buffer access. One possible strategy is that of first-come-first-served given by

$$at\,\beta_0^{(i)} \wedge \neg at\,\beta_0^{(k)} \rightarrow \neg(exec\,\gamma_1 \wedge j = k)\ \mathbf{unl}\ (exec\,\gamma_1 \wedge j = i)$$

or

$$at\,\beta_0^{(i)} \wedge \neg at\,\beta_0^{(k)} \rightarrow \neg(exec\,\gamma_1 \wedge j = k)\ \mathbf{unless}\ (exec\,\gamma_1 \wedge j = i),$$
$$\Box(at\,\beta_0^{(i)} \wedge \neg at\,\beta_0^{(k)} \rightarrow \neg(exec\,\gamma_1 \wedge j = k))$$

(for $i, k = 1, \ldots, nc, i \neq k$) stating that if $\Pi_c^{(i)}$ is waiting for admittance and $\Pi_c^{(k)}$ is not then this is not granted to $\Pi_c^{(k)}$ until $\Pi_c^{(i)}$ will be served.

Of course, all such properties may also be specified using other binary operators; we only give two transcriptions for the latter **unless** formula:

$$at\,\beta_0^{(i)} \wedge \neg at\,\beta_0^{(k)} \rightarrow (exec\,\gamma_1 \wedge j = i) \textbf{ before } (exec\,\gamma_1 \wedge j = k),$$
$$at\,\beta_0^{(i)} \wedge \neg at\,\beta_0^{(k)} \rightarrow (j = i) \textbf{ atnext } (exec\,\gamma_1 \wedge (j = i \vee j = k)).$$

The informal interpretation of the first formula is obvious and the second reads "if $\Pi_c^{(i)}$ is waiting for admittance and $\Pi_c^{(k)}$ is not then the next grant to $\Pi_c^{(i)}$ or $\Pi_c^{(k)}$ goes to $\Pi_c^{(i)}$". △

For the derivation of precedence properties the rules collected in Sect. 7.3 are the appropriate means. As in the case of invariance properties, the invariance rules developed there for labeled systems may usually be applied most profitably, and fairness is not needed for performing verifications with these rules.

Example. Let us prove the property of Π_{pc} given in the first example above. To be able to do this we have to specify the effect of the storing and removing actions α_3 and β_2 in more detail. We first fix that the formulas

$$exec\,\alpha_3 \rightarrow b' = INSERT(b, obj),$$
$$exec\,\beta_2 \rightarrow b' = DELETE(b, out)$$

are contained in $Th(\Pi_{pc})$ where $INSERT$ and $DELETE$ are appropriate function symbols with obvious interpretations (and the "usual" properties).

We also assume that the buffer is not changed by α_0 and β_4, and that the program variable out is not changed by α_0, α_3, and β_4. Hence the formulas

$$exec\,\lambda \rightarrow b' = b \quad \text{for } \lambda \in \{\alpha_0, \beta_4\},$$
$$exec\,\lambda \rightarrow out' = out \quad \text{for } \lambda \in \{\alpha_0, \alpha_3, \beta_4\}$$

should be contained in (or derivable from) $Th(\Pi_{pc})$.

Most important, however, the desired assertion only holds if the buffer b is in fact organized as a first-in-first-out queue. In order to specify this we assume being given a predicate symbol $AHEAD^{(BUFFER\ OBJECT\ OBJECT)}$ with the interpretation that

$$AHEAD(xb, x, y)$$

means that the (different) objects x and y are contained in the buffer xb and x "is ahead of" y. The queuing mechanism of b can then be specified by formulas at least containing

$$exec\,\alpha_3 \wedge obj = y \wedge x \in b \rightarrow AHEAD(b', x, y),$$
$$exec\,\alpha_3 \wedge AHEAD(b, x, y) \rightarrow AHEAD(b', x, y),$$
$$exec\,\beta_2 \wedge AHEAD(b, x, y) \rightarrow out \neq y$$

the informal meaning of which is evident. Let now

$$D \equiv exec\,\beta_2 \wedge out = x.$$

For better readability we will write $D(x)$ for D and $D(y)$ for $D_x(y)$. $D(x)$ and $D(y)$ express that an object x (y, respectively) is removed from the buffer by the consumer process. With the given assumptions we want to prove the assertion

$$execα_3 \land obj = x \land y \notin b \land x \neq y \rightarrow D(x) \text{ before } D(y).$$

To this end we let

$$\begin{aligned} A_1 &\equiv exec\alpha_3 \land obj = x \land y \notin b \land x \neq y, \\ A_2 &\equiv x \in b \land y \notin b, \\ A_3 &\equiv AHEAD(b, x, y), \\ A &\equiv (A_1 \lor A_2 \lor A_3) \land \neg D(x) \end{aligned}$$

and begin with showing that $A_1 \lor A_2 \lor A_3$ is an invariant of every action of Π_{pc} other than β_2.

(1)	$(A_1 \lor A_2 \lor A_3)$ **invof** λ for $\lambda \in Act_{\Pi_{pc}} \setminus \{\alpha_3, \beta_2\}$	(Π)
(2)	$exec\alpha_3 \land A_1 \rightarrow \circ A_2$	(Π)
(3)	$exec\alpha_3 \land A_2 \rightarrow \circ(A_2 \lor A_3)$	(Π)
(4)	A_3 **invof** α_3	(Π)
(5)	$(A_1 \lor A_2 \lor A_3)$ **invof** α_3	(2),(3),(4)

For β_2 we have

(6)	A_1 **invof** β_2	(Π)
(7)	$exec\beta_2 \land A_2 \land out \neq x \rightarrow \circ A_2$	(Π)
(8)	$exec\beta_2 \land A_3 \land out \neq x \rightarrow \circ A_3$	(Π)
(9)	$exec\beta_2 \land A \rightarrow \circ(A_1 \lor A_2 \lor A_3)$	(6),(7),(8)

We aim at using the rule (invbefore$_{\Pi_{pc}}$) for showing

$$A \rightarrow D(x) \text{ before } D(y)$$

and derive now the essential premise for this.

(10)	$A_1 \lor A_2 \lor A_3 \rightarrow x \neq y$	(pred)
(11)	$A \rightarrow \circ(x \neq y)$	(10),(ltl6)
(12)	$exec\lambda \land A \rightarrow \circ((A_1 \lor A_2 \lor A_3) \land x \neq y)$ for every $\lambda \in Act_{\Pi_{pc}}$	(1),(5),(9),(11)
(13)	$exec\lambda \land A \rightarrow \circ(A \lor (D(x) \land x \neq y))$ for every $\lambda \in Act_{\Pi_{pc}}$	(12)
(14)	$A \lor (D(x) \land x \neq y) \rightarrow \neg D(y)$	(Π)
(15)	$exec\lambda \land A \rightarrow \circ\neg D(y) \land \circ(A \lor D(x))$ for every $\lambda \in Act_{\Pi_{pc}}$	(13),(14)

With (15) we easily obtain

(16)	$nil_{\Pi_{pc}} \land A \rightarrow \neg D(y)$	(taut)
(17)	$A \rightarrow D(x)$ **before** $D(y)$	(invbefore), (15),(16)

and finally

(18) $execa_3 \land obj = x \land y \notin b \land x \neq y \rightarrow A$ (Π)
(19) $execa_3 \land obj = x \land y \notin b \land x \neq y \rightarrow D(x)$ **before** $D(y)$ (17),(18) △

Turning finally to eventuality properties, consider again a program with processes which are synchronized for some purposes. The synchronization might be "too strong" causing deadlocks, i.e., situations in which no action can be executed any more. But even if this is excluded, "local blocking" could occur in a single process. Assume a statement λ in some of the processes. If control is at λ it should be guaranteed that λ is eventually executed. This property is specified by

$$at\,\lambda \rightarrow \Diamond exec\,\lambda$$

and called *freedom of starvation* at λ. Related to this are *accessibility* properties of the form

$$at\,\lambda_1 \rightarrow \Diamond at\,\lambda_2$$

expressing that the process in question is not stuck at λ_1 but will sometime reach λ_2 from there. A more general form is

$$at\,\lambda_1 \land A \rightarrow \Diamond(at\,\lambda_2 \land B)$$

in which the formulas A and B are called *intermittent assertions.*

Example. In the producer-consumer program Π_{pc} of Fig. 8.4 relevant starvation formulas are

$$at\,\alpha_1 \rightarrow \Diamond exec\,\alpha_1$$

and the same for the other synchronization statements α_2, β_0, and β_1. (For the remaining actions starvation freedom is trivial because of the fairness assumption.) These properties can also be expressed by accessibility formulas, e.g.,

$$at\,\alpha_1 \rightarrow \Diamond at\,\alpha_2.$$

More general accessibilities in Π_{pc} concern the storing and removing actions α_3 and β_2. They are preceded by synchronization statements. If, say, the producer process "tries" to store, i.e., reaches α_1, it might be forced to wait, but after some time it should really reach the storing action:

$$at\,\alpha_1 \rightarrow \Diamond at\,\alpha_3.$$

For the consumer the analogous requirement is

$$at\,\beta_0 \rightarrow \Diamond at\,\beta_2.$$ △

For transformational programs Π essential eventuality properties are *termination* and *total correctness*. The general form of the former is

$$start_\Pi \land A \rightarrow \Diamond nil_\Pi$$

where A is again some precondition. Total correctness combines termination and partial correctness (with postcondition B) and is described by

$$start_{\Pi} \wedge A \rightarrow \Diamond(nil_{\Pi} \wedge B)$$

expressing that, provided A holds initially, Π will terminate and B will hold in the terminal state.

Example. Termination of program Π_{exp} in Fig. 8.3 of Sect. 7.1 is stated by

$$start_{\Pi_{exp}} \rightarrow \Diamond nil_{\Pi_{exp}}$$

and total correctness by

$$start_{\Pi_{exp}} \rightarrow \Diamond(nil_{\Pi_{exp}} \wedge result = 2^N). \qquad \triangle$$

For the formal verification of eventuality properties all the material of Sect. 7.4 may be used. Particularly this includes the rules (fairsom$_\Gamma$) and (fairwfr$_\Gamma$) for fair systems. In fact, the Π-validity of many eventuality properties of reactive programs Π is only assured by the fairness assumption for Π, so these rules are often inherently needed.

Example. We show the accessibility property

$$at\,\alpha_1 \rightarrow \Diamond at\,\alpha_3$$

for the producer-consumer program Π_{pc} of Fig. 8.4. First of all, however, we have to note that the validity of this property depends on the fact that the capacity CAP of the buffer is not 0. Hence, more precisely we could show

$$at\,\alpha_1 \wedge CAP > 0 \rightarrow \Diamond at\,\alpha_3.$$

Another possibility is to take $CAP > 0$ as a "global" assumption and derive the accessibility formula from it:

$$CAP > 0 \vdash at\,\alpha_1 \rightarrow \Diamond at\,\alpha_3.$$

(Noting that $CAP > 0 \leftrightarrow \Box(CAP > 0)$ is derivable for Π_{pc} and applying the Deduction Theorem and its converse, the two approaches can easily be seen to be equivalent.)

We follow the second idea and begin our derivation with

(1) $CAP > 0$ — assumption

From (1) and the four deadlock freedom formulas proved already in a preceding example we get by simple propositional reasoning:

(2) $\Box(at\,\alpha_1 \wedge at\,\beta_0 \rightarrow be > 0 \vee bf > 0)$
(3) $\Box(at\,\alpha_1 \wedge at\,\beta_1 \rightarrow be > 0 \vee ex = 1)$
(4) $\Box(at\,\alpha_2 \wedge at\,\beta_0 \rightarrow ex = 1 \vee bf > 0)$
(5) $\Box(at\,\alpha_2 \wedge at\,\beta_1 \rightarrow ex = 1)$

Furthermore we note the invariance property

(6) $\Box(at\,\beta_0 \lor at\,\beta_1 \lor at\,\beta_2 \lor at\,\beta_3 \lor at\,\beta_4)$

which is trivially proved with (invstart$_{\Pi_{pc}}$). For the main proof we first want to show

$$at\,\alpha_1 \to \Diamond at\,\alpha_2$$

with the rule (fairsom$_{\Pi_{pc}}$). Taking $Act_h = \{\alpha_1\}$ we immediately have

(7) $exec\,\alpha_1 \land at\,\alpha_1 \to \circ at\,\alpha_2$ (Π)
(8) $exec\,\lambda \land at\,\alpha_1 \to \circ(at\,\alpha_2 \land at\,\alpha_1)$
for every $\lambda \in Act_{\Pi_{pc}} \setminus \{\alpha_1\}$ (Π)

The essential part is to show the third premise of (fairsom$_{\Pi_{pc}}$) which reads

$$\Box at\,\alpha_1 \to \Diamond(at\,\alpha_1 \land be > 0)$$

here. We have

(9) $\Box at\,\alpha_1 \land be = 0 \land at\,\lambda \to enabled_\lambda$
for $\lambda \in \{\beta_0, \beta_1, \beta_2, \beta_3, \beta_4\}$ (2),(3)
(10) $\Box at\,\alpha_1 \land be = 0 \land at\,\lambda \to exec\,\lambda$
for $\lambda \in \{\beta_0, \beta_1, \beta_2, \beta_3, \beta_4\}$ (9),(Π)
(11) $\Box at\,\alpha_1 \land be = 0 \land at\,\beta_0 \to \circ(\Box at\,\alpha_1 \land be = 0 \land at\,\beta_1)$ (10),(Π)
(12) $\Box at\,\alpha_1 \land be = 0 \land at\,\beta_1 \to \circ(\Box at\,\alpha_1 \land be = 0 \land at\,\beta_2)$ (10),(Π)
(13) $\Box at\,\alpha_1 \land be = 0 \land at\,\beta_2 \to \circ(\Box at\,\alpha_1 \land be = 0 \land at\,\beta_3)$ (10),(Π)
(14) $\Box at\,\alpha_1 \land be = 0 \land at\,\beta_3 \to \circ(be > 0)$ (10),(Π)
(15) $\Box at\,\alpha_1 \land be = 0 \land at\,\beta_4 \to \circ(\Box at\,\alpha_1 \land be = 0 \land at\,\beta_0)$ (10),(Π)
(16) $\Box at\,\alpha_1 \land be = 0 \land at\,\lambda \to \Diamond(be > 0)$
for $\lambda \in \{\beta_0, \beta_1, \beta_2, \beta_3, \beta_4\}$ (11)–(15)
(17) $\Box at\,\alpha_1 \land be = 0 \to \Diamond(be > 0)$ (6),(16)
(18) $\Box at\,\alpha_1 \land be > 0 \to \Diamond(be > 0)$ (T5)
(19) $\Box at\,\alpha_1 \to \Diamond(be > 0)$ (17),(18)

With (19) we now get our first goal:

(20) $\Box at\,\alpha_1 \to \Diamond(at\,\alpha_1 \land be > 0)$ (19)
(21) $at\,\alpha_1 \to \Diamond at\,\alpha_2$ (fairsom), (7),(8),(20)

Taking now $Act_h = \{\alpha_2\}$ we have

(22) $exec\,\alpha_2 \land at\,\alpha_2 \to \circ at\,\alpha_3$ (Π)
(23) $exec\,\lambda \land at\,\alpha_2 \to \circ at\,\alpha_2$ for every $\lambda \in Act_{\Pi_{pc}} \setminus \{\alpha_2\}$ (Π)

It is evident that

$$\Box at\,\alpha_2 \to \Diamond(ex = 1)$$

can be shown in steps completely analogous to (9)–(19); so we get

(24) $at\alpha_1 \rightarrow \Diamond(at\alpha_2 \wedge ex = 1)$

as above and hence

(25) $at\alpha_2 \rightarrow \Diamond at\alpha_3$ (fairsom), (22),(23),(24)

which then yields the desired result:

(26) $at\alpha_1 \rightarrow \Diamond at\alpha_3$ (21),(25) △

8.4 A Mutual Exclusion Program

In this section we want to elaborate the verification of a program example in full detail. Fig. 8.5 shows the program Π_{Pet}, called *Peterson's algorithm*, which is another realization of mutual exclusion (for two processes). The critical sections of the processes Π_1 and Π_2 of Π_{Pet} are represented by the statements α_3 and β_3. The statements $\alpha_1, \alpha_2, \alpha_4$ and $\beta_1, \beta_2, \beta_4$ organize the synchronization and α_0 and β_0 represent the remaining parts of the processes which are not critical with respect to interference. (Observe again the notation **await** B for **await** B **then skip**.) A process Π_i, $i \in \{1,2\}$, intending to enter its critical section, signals this by setting a_i to 1. After leaving the critical section a_i is reset to 0. The program variable c is used to resolve conflicts when both processes try to enter their critical sections.

For $\alpha_0, \alpha_3, \beta_0, \beta_3$ we only fix that they have no particular enabling conditions and that they do not change the program variables a_1, a_2, and c:

```
ΠPet ≡ var a1, a2, c : NAT
       start a1 = 0 ∧ a2 = 0 ∧ c = 1
       cobegin loop α0 : noncritical;
                    α1 : a1, c := 1, 1;
                    α2 : await a2 = 0 ∨ c = 2;
                    α3 : critical;
                    α4 : a1 := 0
               endloop
               ||
               loop β0 : noncritical;
                    β1 : a2, c := 1, 2;
                    β2 : await a1 = 0 ∨ c = 1;
                    β3 : critical;
                    β4 : a2 := 0
               endloop
       coend
```

Fig. 8.5. Peterson's algorithm for mutual exclusion

$$enabled_\lambda \equiv at\,\lambda \quad \text{for } \lambda \in \{\alpha_0, \alpha_3, \beta_0, \beta_3\},$$
$$exec\,\lambda \to a_1' = a_1 \wedge a_2' = a_2 \wedge c' = c \quad \text{for } \lambda \in \{\alpha_0, \alpha_3, \beta_0, \beta_3\}.$$

Note, moreover, that

$$start_{\Pi_{Pet}} \equiv at\,\alpha_0 \wedge at\,\beta_0 \wedge a_1 = 0 \wedge a_2 = 0 \wedge c = 1.$$

Our first assertion is

(a) $\Box\neg(at\,\alpha_3 \wedge at\,\beta_3)$

stating the mutual exclusion property of Π_{Pet}. To derive this we introduce the abbreviation

$$at\,L \equiv \bigvee_{\lambda \in L} at\,\lambda$$

for any $L \subseteq Act_{\Pi_{Pet}}$ and let

$$A_1 \equiv (at\{\alpha_0, \alpha_1\} \leftrightarrow a_1 = 0) \wedge (at\{\alpha_2, \alpha_3, \alpha_4\} \leftrightarrow a_1 = 1),$$
$$A_2 \equiv (at\{\beta_0, \beta_1\} \leftrightarrow a_2 = 0) \wedge (at\{\beta_2, \beta_3, \beta_4\} \leftrightarrow a_2 = 1),$$
$$A_3 \equiv at\,\alpha_3 \to a_2 = 0 \vee c = 2,$$
$$A_4 \equiv at\,\beta_3 \to a_1 = 0 \vee c = 1,$$
$$A \equiv A_1 \wedge A_2 \wedge A_3 \wedge A_4\,.$$

We show the following properties for A:

(a1) A **invof** λ for every $\lambda \in Act_{\Pi_1}$.
(a2) A **invof** λ for every $\lambda \in Act_{\Pi_2}$.
(a3) $\Box A$.

Derivation of (a1).

(1)	A_2 **invof** λ for $\lambda \in \{\alpha_0, \alpha_1, \alpha_4\}$	(Π)
(2)	A_4 **invof** λ for $\lambda \in \{\alpha_2, \alpha_3\}$	(Π)
(3)	$exec\,\alpha_0 \wedge A \to at\,\alpha_0 \wedge a_1 = 0 \wedge \bigcirc(at\,\alpha_1 \wedge a_1 = 0)$	(Π)
(4)	A **invof** α_0	(1),(3)
(5)	$exec\,\alpha_1 \wedge A \to \bigcirc(at\,\alpha_2 \wedge a_1 = 1 \wedge c = 1)$	(Π)
(6)	A **invof** α_1	(1),(5)
(7)	$exec\,\alpha_2 \wedge A \to at\,\alpha_2 \wedge a_1 = 1 \wedge (a_2 = 0 \vee c = 2)$	(Π)
(8)	$exec\,\alpha_2 \wedge A \to \bigcirc(at\,\alpha_3 \wedge a_1 = 1 \wedge (a_2 = 0 \vee c = 2))$	(7),(Π)
(9)	A **invof** α_2	(2),(8)
(10)	$exec\,\alpha_3 \wedge A \to at\,\alpha_3 \wedge a_1 = 1 \wedge \bigcirc(at\,\alpha_4 \wedge a_1 = 1)$	(Π)
(11)	A **invof** α_3	(2),(10)
(12)	$exec\,\alpha_4 \wedge A \to \bigcirc(at\,\alpha_0 \wedge a_1 = 0)$	(Π)
(13)	A **invof** α_4	(1),(12)
(14)	A **invof** λ for every $\lambda \in Act_{\Pi_1}$	(4),(6),(9) (11),(13)

△

The derivation of (a2) is "symmetrical" and evident.

Derivation of (a3).

(1)	$start_{\Pi_{Pet}} \rightarrow A$	(Π)
(2)	A **invof** $Act_{\Pi_{Pet}}$	(a1),(a2)
(3)	$\Box A$	(invstart),(1),(2) △

With (a3) we are able now to prove (a) by showing that A implies that $at\alpha_3$ and $at\beta_3$ cannot both be true at the same time.

Derivation of (a).

(1)	$A \land at\alpha_3 \rightarrow a_2 = 0 \lor c = 2$	(taut)
(2)	$A \land a_2 = 0 \rightarrow \neg at\beta_3$	(taut)
(3)	$A \land at\alpha_3 \land at\beta_3 \rightarrow c = 2$	(1),(2),(Π)
(4)	$A \land at\beta_3 \rightarrow a_1 = 0 \lor c = 1$	(taut)
(5)	$A \land a_1 = 0 \rightarrow \neg at\alpha_3$	(taut)
(6)	$A \land at\alpha_3 \land at\beta_3 \rightarrow c = 1$	(4),(5),(Π)
(7)	$A \rightarrow \neg(at\alpha_3 \land at\beta_3)$	(3),(6)
(8)	$\Box\neg(at\alpha_3 \land at\beta_3)$	(a3),(7) △

Next we consider the relevant accessibility properties of Π_{Pet}. They are given by the assertions

(b) $at\alpha_1 \rightarrow \Diamond at\alpha_3$,
(c) $at\beta_1 \rightarrow \Diamond at\beta_3$

expressing for each of the two processes of Π_{Pet} that if it leaves its non-critical section and indicates its intention to enter the critical one then it will eventually proceed there.

We first derive (b) with the rule (fairsom$_{\Pi_{Pet}}$) in a similar way to how we showed the accessibility property for the producer-consumer program Π_{pc} in the previous section. To this end we need the following two invariance properties as lemmas.

(b1) $\Box(\bigvee_{i=0}^{4} at\beta_i)$.
(b2) $\Box(c = 1 \lor c = 2)$.

Both assertions can trivially be proved with the rule (invstart$_{\Pi_{Pet}}$). Note, by the way, that deadlock freedom, expressed by

$$\Box(at\alpha_2 \land at\beta_2 \rightarrow a_2 = 0 \lor c = 2 \lor a_1 = 0 \lor c = 1)$$

is an immediate consequence of (b2).

The first step for now deriving (b) is to show

(b3) $at\alpha_1 \rightarrow \Diamond at\alpha_2$

which is easy since α_1 is no synchronization statement. We use the rule (fairsom$_{\Pi_{Pet}}$) with $Act_h = \{\alpha_1\}$ (and $enabled_{\alpha_1} \equiv at\alpha_1$).

Derivation of (b3).

(1)	$\mathit{exec}\,\alpha_1 \wedge \mathit{at}\,\alpha_1 \rightarrow \bigcirc \mathit{at}\,\alpha_2$	(Π)
(2)	$\mathit{exec}\,\lambda \wedge \mathit{at}\,\alpha_1 \rightarrow \bigcirc(\mathit{at}\,\alpha_2 \vee \mathit{at}\,\alpha_1)$ for every $\lambda \in \mathit{Act}_{\Pi_{Pet}} \setminus \{\alpha_1\}$	(Π)
(3)	$\Box \mathit{at}\,\alpha_1 \rightarrow \Diamond \mathit{at}\,\alpha_1$	(T8)
(4)	$\mathit{at}\,\alpha_1 \rightarrow \Diamond \mathit{at}\,\alpha_2$	(fairsom),(1),(2),(3) △

The main part of the remaining task is to show

(b4) $\Box \mathit{at}\,\alpha_2 \rightarrow \Diamond(\mathit{at}\,\alpha_2 \wedge (a_2 = 0 \vee c = 2))$.

Derivation of (b4). Let $B \equiv \mathit{at}\,\alpha_2 \wedge (a_2 = 0 \vee c = 2)$.

(1)	$\Box \mathit{at}\,\alpha_2 \wedge \mathit{at}\,\beta_0 \rightarrow \mathit{exec}\,\beta_0 \wedge \bigcirc(\Box \mathit{at}\,\alpha_2 \wedge \mathit{at}\,\beta_1)$	(Π)
(2)	$\Box \mathit{at}\,\alpha_2 \wedge \mathit{at}\,\beta_1 \rightarrow \mathit{exec}\,\beta_1 \wedge \bigcirc(\Box \mathit{at}\,\alpha_2 \wedge \mathit{at}\,\beta_2)$	(Π)
(3)	$\Box \mathit{at}\,\alpha_2 \wedge \mathit{at}\,\beta_2 \wedge c = 1 \rightarrow \mathit{exec}\,\beta_2 \wedge \bigcirc(\Box \mathit{at}\,\alpha_2 \wedge \mathit{at}\,\beta_3)$	(Π)
(4)	$\Box \mathit{at}\,\alpha_2 \wedge \mathit{at}\,\beta_2 \wedge c = 2 \rightarrow B$	(ltl3),(T5)
(5)	$\Box \mathit{at}\,\alpha_2 \wedge \mathit{at}\,\beta_2 \rightarrow \bigcirc(\Box \mathit{at}\,\alpha_2 \wedge \mathit{at}\,\beta_3) \vee B$	(3),(4),(b2)
(6)	$\Box \mathit{at}\,\alpha_2 \wedge \mathit{at}\,\beta_3 \rightarrow \mathit{exec}\,\beta_3 \wedge \bigcirc(\Box \mathit{at}\,\alpha_2 \wedge \mathit{at}\,\beta_4)$	(Π)
(7)	$\Box \mathit{at}\,\alpha_2 \wedge \mathit{at}\,\beta_4 \rightarrow \mathit{exec}\,\beta_4 \wedge \bigcirc(a_2 = 0)$	(Π)
(8)	$\Box \mathit{at}\,\alpha_2 \wedge \mathit{at}\,\beta_4 \rightarrow \bigcirc B$	(7)
(9)	$\Box \mathit{at}\,\alpha_2 \wedge \mathit{at}\,\lambda \rightarrow \Diamond B$ for $\lambda \in \{\beta_0, \beta_1, \beta_2, \beta_3, \beta_4\}$	(1),(2),(5),(6),(8)
(10)	$\Box \mathit{at}\,\alpha_2 \rightarrow \Diamond B$	(9),(b1) △

With (b3) and (b4) we now obtain (b) applying (fairsom$_{\Pi_{Pet}}$) with $\mathit{Act}_h = \{\alpha_2\}$ (and $\mathit{enabled}_{\alpha_2} \equiv \mathit{at}\,\alpha_2 \wedge (a_2 = 0 \vee c = 2)$).

Derivation of (b).

(1)	$\mathit{exec}\,\alpha_2 \wedge \mathit{at}\,\alpha_2 \rightarrow \bigcirc \mathit{at}\,\alpha_3$	(Π)
(2)	$\mathit{exec}\,\lambda \wedge \mathit{at}\,\alpha_2 \rightarrow \bigcirc(\mathit{at}\,\alpha_3 \vee \mathit{at}\,\alpha_2)$ for every $\lambda \in \mathit{Act}_{\Pi_{Pet}} \setminus \{\alpha_2\}$	(Π)
(3)	$\mathit{at}\,\alpha_2 \rightarrow \Diamond \mathit{at}\,\alpha_3$	(fairsom),(1),(2),(b4)
(4)	$\mathit{at}\,\alpha_1 \rightarrow \Diamond \mathit{at}\,\alpha_3$	(b3),(3) △

It should be clear that the derivation of (c) runs quite symmetrically and need not be repeated. We rather want to show once more how such a proof can be carried out with the well-founded relation method as illustrated in a previous (trivial) example in Sect. 7.4: the flow of control leading from α_1 to α_3 (for assertion (b)) can be encoded by a decreasing sequence of natural numbers.

More concretely, the sort NAT is already present in Π_{Pet} and we assume that it is endowed with the relation $\leq$. Let

$$
\begin{aligned}
C \equiv\ & (\mathit{at}\,\alpha_1 \wedge y = 3) \vee \\
& (\mathit{at}\,\alpha_2 \wedge \mathit{at}\,\beta_2 \wedge c = 1 \wedge y = 2) \vee \\
& (\mathit{at}\,\alpha_2 \wedge (\mathit{at}\,\beta_3 \vee \mathit{at}\,\beta_4 \vee \mathit{at}\,\beta_0 \vee \mathit{at}\,\beta_1) \wedge y = 1) \vee \\
& (\mathit{at}\,\alpha_2 \wedge \mathit{at}\,\beta_2 \wedge c = 2 \wedge y = 0),
\end{aligned}
$$

$$\begin{aligned}
H_{\alpha_i} &\equiv \textbf{true} \quad \text{for } i = 0,1,2,3,4,\\
H_{\beta_1} &\equiv y = 1,\\
H_{\beta_2} &\equiv y = 2,\\
H_{\beta_j} &\equiv \textbf{false} \quad \text{for } j = 0,3,4.
\end{aligned}$$

For these formulas we show the following assertions.

(b5) $exec\lambda \land H_\lambda \land C \rightarrow \bigcirc(at\alpha_3 \lor \exists \bar{y}(\bar{y} < y \land C_y(\bar{y})))$
for every $\lambda \in Act_{\Pi_{Pet}}$.

(b6) $exec\lambda \land \neg H_\lambda \land C \rightarrow \bigcirc(at\alpha_3 \lor \exists \bar{y}(\bar{y} \leq y \land C_y(\bar{y})))$
for every $\lambda \in Act_{\Pi_{Pet}}$.

(b7) $\Box C \rightarrow \Diamond(at\alpha_3 \lor \bigvee_{\lambda \in Act_{\Pi_{Pet}}}(H_\lambda \land enabled_\lambda))$.

Recalling the discussion in Sect. 7.4, (b5) and (b6) informally mean that

> "helpful actions lead from a state where C holds with some value of y to α_3 or to a state where C holds with a smaller value of y"

and

> "non-helpful actions lead from a state where C holds with some value of y to α_3 or to a state where C holds with a value of y not greater than before".

According to the definition of H_λ, the actions $\alpha_0, \alpha_1, \alpha_2, \alpha_3, \alpha_4$ are helpful in any case, β_1 and β_2 are helpful for $y = 1$ and $y = 2$, respectively, and $\beta_0, \beta_3, \beta_4$ are not helpful at all.

We do not write out the full derivations of (b5) and (b6) but depict these proofs in Fig. 8.6 by a diagram as introduced in Sect. 7.4. In this diagram those (helpful or non-helpful) actions which may not be executed according to their enabling conditions do not occur as arrow labels. For them the respective formulas (b5) and (b6) are trivial in the formal derivations. Note that in the state encoded by $y = 0$, the action β_2 cannot be executed because of $at\alpha_2 \rightarrow a_1 = 1$ which follows from (a3).

For the proof of (b7) we show

(b7') $C \vdash \Diamond(at\alpha_3 \lor \bigvee_{\lambda \in Act_{\Pi_{Pet}}}(H_\lambda \land enabled_\lambda))$

from which (b7) follows with the Deduction Theorem 5.2.2. The derivation of (b7′) runs by checking all the cases given by the alternatives in C and uses the derived formula (progress$_{\Pi_{Pet}}$).

Derivation of (b7').

(1)	C	assumption
(2)	$y = 3 \lor y = 2 \lor y = 0 \rightarrow \bigvee_{\lambda \in Act_{\Pi_{Pet}}}(H_\lambda \land enabled_\lambda)$	(1)
(3)	$at\alpha_2 \land at\beta_3 \rightarrow \bigcirc(at\alpha_3 \lor (at\alpha_2 \land at\beta_4))$	(progress),(Π)
(4)	$at\alpha_2 \land at\beta_4 \rightarrow \bigcirc(at\alpha_3 \lor (at\alpha_2 \land at\beta_0))$	(progress),(Π)
(5)	$at\alpha_2 \land at\beta_0 \rightarrow \bigcirc(at\alpha_3 \lor (at\alpha_2 \land at\beta_1))$	(progress),(Π)
(6)	$at\alpha_2 \land at\beta_1 \land C \rightarrow H_{\beta_1} \land enabled_{\beta_1}$	(Π)
(7)	$y = 1 \rightarrow \Diamond(at\alpha_3 \lor \bigvee_{\lambda \in Act_{\Pi_{Pet}}}(H_\lambda \land enabled_\lambda))$	(1),(3)–(6)
(8)	$\Diamond(at\alpha_3 \lor \bigvee_{\lambda \in Act_{\Pi_{Pet}}}(H_\lambda \land enabled_\lambda))$	(1),(2),(7) △

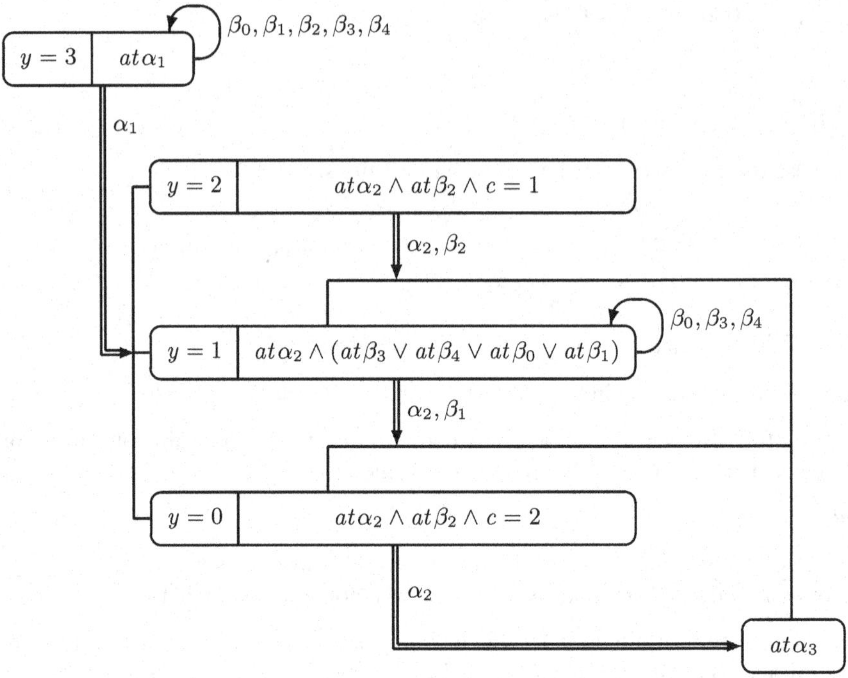

Fig. 8.6. Diagram for the proof of (b5) and (b6)

With (b5), (b6), and (b7) we now easily obtain (b).

Derivation of (b).

(1)	$\exists y C \to \Diamond at\,\alpha_3$	(fairwfr),(b5),(b6),(b7)
(2)	$at\,\alpha_1 \to C_y(3)$	(pred)
(3)	$at\,\alpha_1 \to \exists y C$	(2)
(4)	$at\,\alpha_1 \to \Diamond at\,\alpha_3$	(1),(3) △

Finally we analyse the "scheduling strategy" of Π_{Pet} which is controlled by the program variable c. Consider a situation where Π_1 is at α_2 trying to enter its critical section. If, at this time, Π_2 is not at β_2 or c's value is 2 then Π_1 will enter its critical section before Π_2 will do this next. If, on the other hand, Π_2 is at β_2 and $c = 1$ then Π_2 will enter its critical section ahead of Π_1 (and Π_1 will still be at α_2 at that time). These properties are specified by

(d) $at\,\alpha_2 \wedge (\neg at\,\beta_2 \vee c = 2) \to at\,\alpha_3$ **before** $at\,\beta_3$.

(e) $at\,\alpha_2 \wedge at\,\beta_2 \wedge c = 1 \to (at\,\alpha_2 \wedge at\,\beta_3)$ **before** $at\,\alpha_3$.

For the proof of (d) we use the lemma (a3) and the mutual exclusion property (a) and apply the derived formula (progress$_{\Pi_{Pet}}$) and the rule (invbefore$_{\Pi_{Pet}}$).

Derivation of (d). Let $D \equiv at\,\alpha_2 \wedge (\neg at\,\beta_2 \vee c = 2)$.

(1)	$exec\,\lambda \to \neg D$ for $\lambda \in \{\alpha_0, \alpha_1, \alpha_3, \alpha_4\}$	(Π)
(2)	$exec\,\alpha_2 \to \bigcirc(at\,\alpha_3 \wedge \neg at\,\beta_3)$	(Π),(a)
(3)	$exec\,\lambda \wedge D \to c = 2 \wedge \bigcirc(at\,\alpha_2 \wedge \neg at\,\beta_3 \wedge c = 2)$ for $\lambda \in \{\beta_0, \beta_1, \beta_3, \beta_4\}$	(Π)
(4)	$exec\,\beta_2 \to at\,\beta_2 \wedge (a_1 = 0 \vee c = 1)$	(Π)
(5)	$a_1 = 0 \to \neg at\,\alpha_2$	(a3)
(6)	$exec\,\beta_2 \to \neg D$	(4),(5)
(7)	$exec\,\lambda \wedge D \to \bigcirc \neg at\,\beta_3 \wedge \bigcirc(D \vee at\,\alpha_3)$ for $\lambda \in Act_{\Pi_{Pet}}$	(1),(2),(3),(6)
(8)	$at\,\beta_3 \to \neg \mathrm{nil}_{\Pi_{Pet}}$	(progress)
(9)	$\mathrm{nil}_{\Pi_{Pet}} \wedge D \to \neg at\,\beta_3$	(8)
(10)	$D \to at\,\alpha_3$ **before** $at\,\beta_3$	(invbefore),(7),(9) △

The proof of (e) runs quite similarly.

Derivation of (e). Let $D_1 \equiv at\,\alpha_2 \wedge at\,\beta_2 \wedge c = 1$, $D_2 \equiv at\,\alpha_2 \wedge at\,\beta_3$.

(1)	$exec\,\lambda \to \neg D_1$ for $\lambda \in Act_{\Pi_{Pet}} \setminus \{\alpha_2, \beta_2\}$	(Π)
(2)	$exec\,\alpha_2 \to a_2 = 0 \vee c = 2$	(Π)
(3)	$a_2 = 0 \to \neg at\,\beta_2$	(a3)
(4)	$exec\,\alpha_2 \to \neg D_1$	(2),(3)
(5)	$exec\,\beta_2 \wedge D_1 \to \bigcirc(D_2 \wedge \neg at\,\alpha_3)$	(Π)
(6)	$exec\,\lambda \wedge D_1 \to \bigcirc \neg at\,\alpha_3 \wedge \bigcirc(D_1 \vee D_2)$ for $\lambda \in Act_{\Pi_{Pet}}$	(1),(4),(5)
(7)	$at\,\alpha_3 \to \neg \mathrm{nil}_{\Pi_{Pet}}$	(progress)
(8)	$\mathrm{nil}_{\Pi_{Pet}} \wedge D_1 \to \neg at\,\alpha_3$	(7)
(9)	$D_1 \to D_2$ **before** $at\,\alpha_3$	(invbefore),(6),(8) △

This analysis may be summarized as follows: if Π_1 is trying to enter its critical section at α_2 then, in the case of (d), Π_1 will proceed to its critical section before Π_2 or, in the case of (e), Π_2 will do this before Π_1, but in the state this happens the situation of case (d) is given and Π_1 will enter its critical section before Π_2 may do this next time. I.e., if Π_1 is trying to enter its critical section then the entry of Π_2 into its critical section may be ahead of that of Π_1 at most once. This property, called *1-bounded overtaking*, can be specified in $\mathcal{L}_{\mathrm{TL}\Pi_{Pet}}$ in several ways. One possible formula is

(f) $at\,\alpha_2 \to \neg at\,\beta_3$ **unl** $(at\,\beta_3$ **unl** $(\neg at\,\beta_3$ **unl** $at\,\alpha_3))$

expressing that if Π_1 is at α_2 then before Π_1 will be in its critical section there will be three subsequent intervals in which Π_2 is not at β_3, is at β_3, and is not at β_3, respectively. (Each of these intervals may be empty.) Another formulation is

(f') $at\,\alpha_2 \to at\,\alpha_3$ **before** $at\,\beta_3 \vee (at\,\alpha_3$ **before** $at\,\beta_3)$ **atnext** $at\,\beta_3$

which reads that if Π_1 is at α_2 then Π_1 will be at α_3 before Π_2 will be at β_3 or this will be the case at least when Π_2 will be at β_3 next time.

Note that (f) and (f') (and possible further formulations of this property) are no longer of the syntactical form of our simple precedence properties defined in Sect. 7.3. Nevertheless they can rather simply be derived from (d) and (e). We show this for (f') applying the general rule (indatnext) which is not restricted to particular formulas.

Derivation of (f'). Let $D \equiv (at\alpha_2 \land at\beta_3)$ **before** $at\alpha_3$.

(1) $at\alpha_2 \land at\beta_3 \rightarrow at\alpha_3$ **before** $at\beta_3$ — (d),(Π)
(2) $D \rightarrow \bigcirc\neg at\alpha_3 \land \bigcirc((at\alpha_2 \land at\beta_3) \lor D)$ — (Tb16)
(3) $at\alpha_2 \rightarrow \bigcirc(at\alpha_2 \lor at\alpha_3)$ — (Π)
(4) $D \land at\alpha_2 \rightarrow \bigcirc at\alpha_2$ — (2),(3)
(5) $D \land at\alpha_2 \rightarrow \bigcirc(at\beta_3 \rightarrow at\alpha_3$ **before** $at\beta_3) \land$
$\bigcirc(\neg at\beta_3 \rightarrow D \land at\alpha_2)$ — (1),(2),(4)
(6) $D \land at\alpha_2 \rightarrow (at\alpha_3$ **before** $at\beta_3)$ **atnext** $at\beta_3$ — (indatnext),(5)
(7) $at\alpha_2 \land at\beta_2 \land c = 1 \rightarrow D \land at\alpha_2$ — (e)
(8) $at\alpha_2 \land \neg(at\beta_2 \land c = 1) \rightarrow at\alpha_3$ **before** $at\beta_3$ — (d)
(9) $at\alpha_2 \rightarrow at\alpha_3$ **before** $at\beta_3 \lor$
$(at\alpha_3$ **before** $at\beta_3)$ **atnext** $at\beta_3$ — (6),(7),(8),(b2) △

It should be clear that the symmetrical relationship described by

(g) $at\beta_2 \rightarrow \neg at\alpha_3$ **unl** $(at\alpha_3$ **unl** $(\neg at\alpha_3$ **unl** $at\beta_3))$

or

(g') $at\beta_2 \rightarrow at\beta_3$ **before** $at\alpha_3 \lor (at\beta_3$ **before** $at\alpha_3)$ **atnext** $at\alpha_3$

and expressing "if Π_2 is trying to enter its critical section then it may be overtaken by Π_1 at most once" holds as well and could be derived analogously.

8.5 Message Passing Programs

The second basic paradigm for realizing communication and synchronization of processes besides shared program variables is *message passing*. Concurrent programs following this concept are also called *distributed programs*. Message passing takes place between sending and receiving processes and can be organized in two different ways: *Asynchronous* message passing means that the sending process may send a message independently of whether the receiving process is ready to receive it. Sent messages are kept in some buffer until they are collected by the receiver. Using *synchronous* message passing the sender of a message can deliver it only when the receiving process is ready to accept it at the same moment. Symmetrically, a receiver can perform such an accepting action only when the sender is ready to send a message at the same moment. If a process is ready to send or to receive a message and the corresponding other process is not ready for the complementary operation then it has to wait until this will be the case.

On the abstract level of our investigations, asynchronous message passing does not show essentially new phenomena compared with the shared variables concept. In fact, an SVP example like the producer-consumer scheme in Sect. 8.3 could be viewed as organizing asynchronous communication between its processes. Synchronous communication is, however, a primitive concept with some new aspects not yet encountered in the previous sections. So we will concentrate only on the latter and as in the shared variables case we do this by defining a language for programs of this kind.

The language, briefly called MPP, is a very simple and somewhat modified version of the well-known prototype language CSP ("Communicating Sequential Processes"). For presentation, we adopt most of the syntactical definitions and notions from SVP. So, a program Π of MPP (briefly: MPP-*program*) is again based on a signature SIG_Π and a structure S_Π for SIG_Π and has the same form

var Δ
start J
cobegin $\Pi_1 \parallel \ldots \parallel \Pi_{np}$ **coend**

as an SVP program. The program variables listed in Δ, however, are no longer "global", i.e., (possibly) shared by all processes $\Pi_1, \ldots, \Pi_{np}$. Each of them is "local" for one of the processes and may not be accessed in the other processes.

The syntax for *statement list*, (*labeled*) *statement*, *simple statement*, and *conditional statement* is taken from SVP. Synchronization statements are now defined by

synchronization statement ::=
  await *condition* **then** *communication statement*
communication statement ::=
  channel ! *term* | *channel* ? *program variable*

where *channel* is an element of some given set of channels, the common use of which identifies those processes which are passing messages one to another. *term* is a term of the underlying language $\mathcal{L}^0_\Pi$. So, synchronization statements have the form

await B_1 **then** $ch_1!\,t$

or

await B_2 **then** $ch_2?\,a$

with conditions (i.e., closed formulas of $\mathcal{L}^0_\Pi$) B_1 and B_2. We will use the abbreviations

$ch_1!\,t$ and $ch_2?\,a$

for **await true then** $ch_1!\,t$ and **await true then** $ch_2?\,a$.

We say that two synchronization statements of a program Π *match* if they occur in different processes of Π, are of the two different forms above such that the channels ch_1 and ch_2 are identical, and the term t and the program variable a are of the same sort. Such statements represent sending (the value of) t from one process to another along a communication channel, represented by ch_1 ($\equiv ch_2$), and the assignment of the received value to the local program variable a. Their enabledness is influenced twofold: each of them is only ready to execute if the respective conditions B_1 and B_2 are true. Furthermore, characterizing synchronous message passing, both operations are possibly delayed until they can be performed together. The synchronous execution of two matching synchronization statements is an atomic step with respect to the interleaving computation of Π.

We restrict MPP to a *one-to-one* communication concept by requiring that for any communication statement with channel ch occurring in a process Π_i there is at most one other process Π_j containing communication statements which refer to the same channel ch.

Finally we generalize the syntactical definition of processes as follows.

$$\begin{aligned} &\mathit{process} ::= \textbf{loop}\ \mathit{statement\ list\ selection}\ \textbf{endloop} \\ &\mathit{statement\ list\ selection} ::= \mathit{statement\ list}\ | \\ &\qquad\qquad\qquad\qquad\qquad \mathit{statement\ list}\ \textbf{or}\ \mathit{statement\ list\ selection} \end{aligned}$$

A process has now the general form

$$\textbf{loop}\ SL_1\ \textbf{or}\ \dots\ \textbf{or}\ SL_n\ \textbf{endloop}$$

with $n \geq 1$ and statement lists $SL_1, \dots, SL_n$. For $n = 1$ we get back the previous form in SVP. The first (atomic) execution step of such a loop consists of selecting one of those statement lists, say SL_i, whose first statement is currently enabled, and executing the first step of SL_i. In subsequent steps the process proceeds with executing the rest of SL_i and then returns to the beginning. The selection of SL_i in case more than one of the first statements are enabled is nondeterministic. If none of them is enabled then the whole loop is not enabled as well.

Figure 8.7 shows an MPP-program Π_{mex} realizing mutual exclusion for (the first) two processes Π_1 and Π_2. It is based on a sort $SIGNAL$ with an individual constant $HELLO$ the interpretation of which is some "signal" $hello$. Whenever Π_1 or Π_2 wants to enter its critical section, it sends this signal on the channel ch_1 or ch_2, respectively, to the third process which coordinates the requests. It accepts the signal from one of the competitors and then waits for the next signal of the selected process indicating that its critical section is finished. After this both Π_1 and Π_2 may compete again in the same way. The program variable a is of no relevance and only needed for syntactical reasons.

Fig. 8.8 shows the first steps of a possible run of Π_{mex}. After step 2 both Π_1 and Π_2 intend to enter their critical section. In step 3 Π_2's signal is accepted by Π_3 which is represented by the simultaneous execution of the statements β_1 and γ_2. In step 5 the exit signal β_3 of Π_2 and the corresponding acceptance γ_3 are executed together.

```
Π_mex ≡ var a : SIGNAL
        start true
        cobegin loop α0 : noncritical;
                     α1 : ch1! HELLO;
                     α2 : critical;
                     α3 : ch1! HELLO
                endloop
                ||
                loop β0 : noncritical;
                     β1 : ch2! HELLO;
                     β2 : critical;
                     β3 : ch2! HELLO
                endloop
                ||
                loop γ0 : ch1? a;
                     γ1 : ch1? a
                     or
                     γ2 : ch2? a;
                     γ3 : ch2? a
                endloop
        coend
```

Fig. 8.7. An MPP-program for mutual exclusion

step	after the step:	control at		
	initially:	α_0	β_0	γ_0, γ_2
1 α_0		α_1	β_0	γ_0, γ_2
2 β_0		α_1	β_1	γ_0, γ_2
3 β_1, γ_2		α_1	β_2	γ_3
4 β_2		α_1	β_3	γ_3
5 β_3, γ_3		α_1	β_0	γ_0, γ_2
6 α_1, γ_0		α_2	β_0	γ_1
7 α_2		α_3	β_0	γ_1
8 α_3, γ_1		α_0	β_0	γ_0, γ_2

Fig. 8.8. First steps of a possible run of Π_{mex}

After that the analogous steps for Π_1 are performed. Note that for Π_3, being at the beginning of the loop is represented by being both at γ_0 and at γ_2.

We now adopt the definitions of $entry(SL)$ for a statement list SL and of λ^{then} and λ^{else} from Sect. 8.2 and modify the definitions of $\lambda^{(i)}_{start}$ and λ^{seq} as follows. $\lambda^{(i)}_{start}$ denotes the set

$$\{entry(SL_i) \mid i = 1, \ldots, n\}$$

for a process $\Pi_i \equiv$ **loop** SL_1 **or** ... **or** SL_n **endloop**, and λ^{seq} is now a set of labels as well. If λ occurs in the context

$$\ldots\lambda : ST_1 \; ; \; \bar{\lambda} : ST_2 \ldots$$

then $\lambda^{seq} = \{\bar{\lambda}\}$ and if it labels the last statement of one of the statement lists in a conditional statement $\bar{\lambda}$ then $\lambda^{seq} = \bar{\lambda}^{seq}$. If, finally, it labels the last statement of a statement list of process Π_i then $\lambda^{seq} = \lambda^{(i)}_{start}$.

Additionally, for every synchronization statement λ we let the set λ^{match} consist of all labels $\bar{\lambda}$ such that λ and $\bar{\lambda}$ label matching synchronization statements. For other statements λ we let $\lambda^{match} = \emptyset$.

Example. In Π_{mex} we have

$$\begin{aligned}
&\lambda^{(3)}_{start} = \{\gamma_0, \gamma_2\},\\
&\gamma_0^{seq} = \{\gamma_1\},\\
&\gamma_2^{seq} = \{\gamma_3\},\\
&\gamma_1^{seq} = \gamma_3^{seq} = \{\gamma_0, \gamma_3\},\\
&\gamma_0^{match} = \gamma_1^{match} = \{\alpha_1, \alpha_3\},\\
&\gamma_2^{match} = \gamma_3^{match} = \{\beta_1, \beta_3\},\\
&\alpha_0^{match} = \emptyset.
\end{aligned}$$

△

Let now Π be an MPP-program over some SIG_Π and S_Π with processes $\Pi_1, \ldots, \Pi_{np}$ and initialization J. Again we may view Π as an frl$_e$STS

$$\Pi = (X, V, W, T, Act, start, \mathcal{E})$$

over SIG_Π and S_Π. X, V, and Act are defined as for SVP programs in Sect. 8.2. The initial condition is

$$start \equiv \bigwedge_{i=1}^{np} \bigwedge_{\lambda \in \lambda^{(i)}_{start}} at\lambda \wedge J.$$

The enabling condition for a statement λ which is not a synchronization statement is

$$enabled_\lambda \equiv at\lambda$$

as before. If λ is a synchronization statement containing the condition B with $\lambda^{match} = \{\lambda_1, \ldots, \lambda_m\}$, and B_i are the conditions contained in λ_i, $i = 1, \ldots, m$, then we let

$$enabled_\lambda \equiv at\lambda \wedge B \wedge \bigvee_{i=1}^{m} (at_{\lambda_i} \wedge B_i)$$

which formalizes the informal explanations given for these statements. Note that $m = 0$ is not excluded in which case $enabled_\lambda$ is logically equivalent to **false**.

For defining the state set W and the transition relation T we observe from our example Π_{mex} that now the actions of Act (which are still represented by the labels occurring in Π) are not identical with the atomic steps in the interleaving computation of Π and some of them have to be executed together with another one in the same state. As remarked already in Sect. 6.4, however, the formalization of this is covered by the concept of the system variables $exec\lambda$ more than one of which may be true in a state.

We define the set W of states as for SVP programs in Sect. 8.2, only replacing the clauses

$$\eta(exec\lambda) = \mathsf{tt} \quad \text{for at most one } \lambda \in Act$$

and

$$\eta(at\lambda) = \mathsf{tt} \quad \text{for exactly one } \lambda \in Act_{\Pi_i} \quad (i = 1, \ldots, np)$$

by the three clauses

$$\begin{array}{l} \text{if } \eta(exec\lambda_1) = \mathsf{tt} \text{ then } \eta(exec\lambda_2) = \mathsf{ff} \\ \qquad\qquad \text{for every } \lambda_1, \lambda_2 \in Act, \lambda_1 \neq \lambda_2, \lambda_2 \notin \lambda_1^{match}, \\ \text{if } \eta(exec\lambda_1) = \mathsf{tt} \text{ for a synchronization statement } \lambda_1 \\ \qquad\qquad \text{then } \eta(exec\lambda_2) = \mathsf{tt} \text{ for some } \lambda_2 \in \lambda_1^{match}, \\ \text{for } i = 1, \ldots, np, \text{ either} \\ \qquad\qquad \eta(at\lambda) = \mathsf{tt} \text{ for every } \lambda \in \lambda_{start}^{(i)} \text{ and} \\ \qquad\qquad \eta(at\lambda) = \mathsf{ff} \text{ for every } \lambda \in Act_{\Pi_i} \setminus \lambda_{start}^{(i)} \\ \text{or} \\ \qquad\qquad \eta(at\lambda) = \mathsf{ff} \text{ for every } \lambda \in \lambda_{start}^{(i)} \text{ and} \\ \qquad\qquad \eta(at\lambda) = \mathsf{tt} \text{ for exactly one } \lambda \in Act_{\Pi_i} \setminus \lambda_{start}^{(i)}. \end{array}$$

These new clauses fix which $exec\lambda$ are true exclusively or together with another one and how the $at\lambda$ can be true if control is either at the beginning of a process or not.

T is also defined as for SVP programs; we only delete the clauses given there for synchronization statements. Instead, we include for every matching statement pair λ_1 : **await** B_1 **then** $ch!t$ in process Π_i and λ_2 : **await** B_2 **then** $ch?a$ in process Π_j, $i \neq j$, a clause

$$\begin{array}{l} \text{if } \eta(exec\lambda_1) = \eta(exec\lambda_2) = \mathsf{tt} \text{ then} \\ \qquad\qquad \eta'(a) = \eta(t), \\ \qquad\qquad \eta'(b) = \eta(b) \text{ for every } b \in X \setminus \{a\}, \\ \qquad\qquad \eta'(at\lambda) = \mathsf{tt} \text{ for every } \lambda \in \lambda_1^{seq} \cup \lambda_2^{seq}, \\ \qquad\qquad \eta'(at\lambda) = \eta(at\lambda) \text{ for every } \lambda \in Act \setminus (Act_{\Pi_i} \cup Act_{\Pi_j}). \end{array}$$

Example. For the program Π_{mex} of Fig. 8.7 we have

$$\begin{array}{l} Act = \{\alpha_0, \alpha_1, \alpha_2, \alpha_3, \beta_0, \beta_1, \beta_2, \beta_3, \gamma_0, \gamma_1, \gamma_2, \gamma_3\}, \\ X = X_{SIGNAL} = \{a\}, \end{array}$$

$$
\begin{aligned}
&V = \{exec\lambda, at\lambda \mid \lambda \in Act\},\\
&start \equiv at\alpha_0 \wedge at\beta_0 \wedge at\gamma_0 \wedge at\gamma_2 \wedge \mathbf{true},\\
&enabled_\lambda \equiv at\lambda \quad \text{for } \lambda \in \{\alpha_0, \alpha_2, \beta_0, \beta_2\},\\
&enabled_\lambda \equiv at\lambda \wedge (at\gamma_0 \vee at\gamma_1) \quad \text{for } \lambda \in \{\alpha_1, \alpha_3\},\\
&enabled_\lambda \equiv at\lambda \wedge (at\gamma_2 \vee at\gamma_3) \quad \text{for } \lambda \in \{\beta_1, \beta_3\},\\
&enabled_\lambda \equiv at\lambda \wedge (at\alpha_1 \vee at\alpha_3) \quad \text{for } \lambda \in \{\gamma_0, \gamma_1\},\\
&enabled_\lambda \equiv at\lambda \wedge (at\beta_1 \vee at\beta_3) \quad \text{for } \lambda \in \{\gamma_2, \gamma_3\}.
\end{aligned}
$$

The transition relation T for Π_{mex} contains pairs (η, η') with, e.g.,

$$
\begin{aligned}
&\eta(exec\alpha_3) = \eta(exec\gamma_1) = \mathsf{tt},\\
&\eta'(a) = hello,\\
&\eta'(at\alpha_0) = \eta'(at\gamma_0) = \eta'(at\gamma_2) = \mathsf{tt},\\
&\eta'(at\lambda) = \eta(at\lambda) \quad \text{for } \lambda \in \{\beta_0, \beta_1, \beta_2, \beta_3\}.
\end{aligned}
$$

△

The definition of an MPP-program Π as a state system also indicates how the temporal logic semantics $Th(\Pi)$ of Π has to be defined. Again we reuse the patterns from the SVP case. More precisely, the language $\mathcal{L}_{\mathrm{TL}\Pi}(TSIG)$ of $Th(\Pi)$ and the axioms (data$_\Pi$), (root$_\Pi$), (nil$_\Pi$), (action$_\Pi$), (fair$_\Pi$) are taken as before. (I$_\Pi$) and (PC$_\Pi$) are replaced by

(I1$^{mp}_\Pi$) $\quad exec\lambda_1 \rightarrow \neg exec\lambda_2 \quad$ for $\lambda_1, \lambda_2 \in Act_\Pi, \lambda_1 \neq \lambda_2, \lambda_2 \notin \lambda_1^{match}$,

(I2$^{mp}_\Pi$) $\quad exec\lambda_1 \rightarrow \bigvee_{\lambda_2 \in \lambda^{match}} exec\lambda_2 \quad$ for every synchronization statement λ_1,

(PC1$^{mp}_\Pi$) $\quad \left(\bigwedge_{\lambda \in L_i} at\lambda \wedge \bigwedge_{\lambda \in L'_i} \neg at\lambda\right) \vee \left(\bigwedge_{\lambda \in L_i} \neg at\lambda \wedge \bigvee_{\lambda \in L'_i} at\lambda\right)$

for $i = 1, \dots, np$,

(PC2$^{mp}_\Pi$) $\quad at\lambda_1 \rightarrow \neg at\lambda_2 \quad$ for $\lambda_1, \lambda_2 \in L'_i, i = 1, \dots, np, \lambda_1 \neq \lambda_2$

(with $L_i = \lambda^{(i)}_{start}$ and $L'_i = Act_\Pi \setminus \lambda^{(i)}_{start}$) reflecting the new clauses for the state set definition. (C1$_\Pi$) and (C3$_\Pi$) are modified, (C2$_\Pi$) is taken as before, and one more "control axiom" is added:

(C1$^{mp}_\Pi$) $\quad exec\lambda_1 \rightarrow \bigcirc \bigwedge_{\lambda_2 \in \lambda_1^{seq}} at\lambda_2 \quad$ for every simple statement λ_1,

(C2$^{mp}_\Pi$) $\quad exec\lambda \rightarrow (B \wedge \bigcirc at\lambda^{then}) \vee (\neg B \wedge \bigcirc at\lambda^{else})$

for every conditional statement λ : **if** B **then** ...,

(C3$^{mp}_\Pi$) $\quad exec\lambda \wedge at\bar{\lambda} \rightarrow \bigcirc at\bar{\lambda} \quad$ for every $\lambda \in Act_{\Pi_i}$,
λ not a synchronization statement,
$\bar{\lambda} \in Act_\Pi \setminus Act_{\Pi_i}, i = 1, \dots, np$,

(C4$^{mp}_\Pi$) $\quad exec\lambda_1 \wedge exec\lambda_2 \wedge at\bar{\lambda} \rightarrow \bigcirc at\bar{\lambda}$
for every $\lambda_1 \in Act_{\Pi_i}, \lambda_2 \in Act_{\Pi_j}$,
λ_1, λ_2 matching synchronization statements,
$\bar{\lambda} \in Act_\Pi \setminus (Act_{\Pi_i} \cup Act_{\Pi_j}), i, j = 1, \dots, np$.

Finally, the axiom ($\mathrm{PV1}_\Pi$) is now stated as

$$(\mathrm{PV1}_\Pi^{mp}) \qquad exec\,\lambda \rightarrow \bigwedge_{a \in X} a' = a \quad \text{for every conditional statement } \lambda$$

and

$$(\mathrm{COMM}_\Pi) \quad exec\,\lambda_1 \wedge exec\,\lambda_2 \;\rightarrow\; a' = t \wedge \bigwedge_{b \in X \setminus \{a\}} b' = b$$

for every matching pair λ_1 : **await** B_1 **then** $ch!t$ and λ_2 : **await** B_2 **then** $ch?a$

is added. The general form ($\mathrm{PV2}_\Pi$) is still taken for other statements and this becomes again (ASSIGN_Π) in the standard case of assignments.

Example. We list a few typical instances of the axioms for program Π_{mex} of Fig. 8.7.

$(\mathrm{I1}^{mp}_{\Pi_{mex}})$: $exec\,\alpha_1 \rightarrow \neg exec\,\lambda \quad \text{for } \lambda \in Act_{\Pi_{mex}} \setminus \{\gamma_0, \gamma_1\}, \alpha_1 \neq \lambda,$

$(\mathrm{I2}^{mp}_{\Pi_{mex}})$: $exec\,\beta_1 \rightarrow exec\,\gamma_2 \vee exec\,\gamma_3,$
$exec\,\gamma_0 \rightarrow exec\,\alpha_1 \vee exec\,\alpha_3,$

$(\mathrm{PC1}^{mp}_{\Pi_{mex}})$: $(at\,\gamma_0 \wedge at\,\gamma_2 \wedge \neg at\,\gamma_1 \wedge \neg at\,\gamma_3) \vee$
$(\neg at\,\gamma_0 \wedge \neg at\,\gamma_2 \wedge (at\,\gamma_1 \vee at\,\gamma_3)),$

$(\mathrm{PC2}^{mp}_{\Pi_{mex}})$: $at\,\gamma_i \rightarrow \neg at\,\gamma_j \quad \text{for } i, j \in \{1, 3\}, i \neq j,$

$(\mathrm{C1}^{mp}_{\Pi_{mex}})$: $exec\,\gamma_0 \rightarrow \bigcirc at\,\gamma_1,$
$exec\,\gamma_1 \rightarrow \bigcirc(at\,\gamma_0 \wedge at\,\gamma_2),$

$(\mathrm{C3}^{mp}_{\Pi_{mex}})$: $exec\,\alpha_0 \wedge at\,\gamma_2 \rightarrow \bigcirc at\,\gamma_2,$

$(\mathrm{C4}^{mp}_{\Pi_{mex}})$: $exec\,\alpha_1 \wedge exec\,\gamma_0 \wedge at\,\beta_0 \rightarrow \bigcirc at\,\beta_0,$

$(\mathrm{COMM}_{\Pi_{exp}})$: $exec\,\alpha_1 \wedge exec\,\gamma_0 \rightarrow a' = \mathit{HELLO}.$ △

Program properties like exclusions, fault freedom, deadlock and starvation freedom, partial or total correctness, termination, and the various accessibility and precedence properties discussed in Sect. 8.3 are also relevant for MPP-programs. Their specification is similar to as before if not identical. For their verification the same proof methods as for SVP programs can be used; the only difference is that they are applied to the modified temporal program axioms.

Example. The mutual exclusion property for the program Π_{mex} in Fig. 8.7 is specified by the formula

$$\Box\neg(at\,\alpha_2 \wedge at\,\beta_2)$$

which may be derived as follows. We let

$$A \equiv (at\,\alpha_2 \vee at\,\alpha_3 \leftrightarrow at\,\gamma_1) \wedge (at\,\beta_2 \vee at\,\beta_3 \leftrightarrow at\,\gamma_3)$$

and obtain

(1)	$exec\,\alpha_1 \rightarrow (exec\,\gamma_0 \lor exec\,\gamma_1)$	(Π)
(2)	$exec\,\gamma_0 \rightarrow (exec\,\alpha_1 \lor exec\,\alpha_3)$	(Π)
(3)	$exec\,\gamma_1 \land A \rightarrow \neg at\,\alpha_1$	(Π)
(4)	$exec\,\alpha_3 \land A \rightarrow \neg at\,\gamma_0$	(Π)
(5)	$A \rightarrow (exec\,\alpha_1 \leftrightarrow exec\,\gamma_0)$	(1)–(4)
(6)	$exec\,\alpha_1 \land exec\,\gamma_0 \rightarrow \neg at\,\gamma_3 \land \bigcirc(at\,\alpha_2 \land at\,\gamma_1 \land \neg at\,\gamma_3)$	(Π)
(7)	A **invof** λ for $\lambda \in \{\alpha_1, \gamma_0\}$	(5),(6),(Π)

In an analogous way we obtain

(8) A **invof** λ for $\lambda \in \{\alpha_3, \gamma_1\}$
(9) A **invof** λ for $\lambda \in \{\beta_1, \gamma_2\}$
(10) A **invof** λ for $\lambda \in \{\beta_3, \gamma_3\}$

and

(11) A **invof** λ for $\lambda \in \{\alpha_0, \alpha_2, \beta_0, \beta_2\}$

is trivial. Together we then have

(12)	A **invof** $Act_{\Pi_{mex}}$	(7)–(11)
(13)	$start_{\Pi_{mex}} \rightarrow A$	(Π)
(14)	$\Box A$	(invstart),(12),(13)
(15)	$\neg(at\,\gamma_1 \land at\,\gamma_3)$	(Π)
(16)	$A \rightarrow \neg(at\,\alpha_2 \land at\,\beta_2)$	(15)
(17)	$\Box\neg(at\,\alpha_2 \land at\,\beta_2)$	(14),(16) $\triangle$

8.6 A Producer-Consumer Program

We conclude this chapter with one more example. The program Π_{mpc} shown in Fig. 8.9 is an MPP version of the producer-consumer scheme discussed in Sect. 8.3. The first process Π_p of Π_{mpc} continuously produces an object obj and sends it to a third process Π_b which "manages" the buffer b. The second process Π_c, as the consumer continuously receives an object from Π_b, stores it locally on a, and then consumes it. Π_b uses a program variable bo counting the number of objects currently stored in b. It may receive an object from the producer on the program variable in – provided $bo < CAP$ where CAP is again the capacity of b – store it into b, and increase bo by 1. Alternatively – provided $bo > 0$ – it may send an object from b, represented by the program variable out, to the consumer, remove it from b, and decrease bo by 1.

Mutual exclusion of the buffer accesses is trivially guaranteed in Π_{mpc} since they are no longer performed by Π_p and Π_c but only by Π_b. The same holds for deadlock freedom. A deadlock could only occur when both Π_p and Π_c want to communicate with Π_b, control of the latter is at γ_0 and γ_3, and $bo < CAP$ and $bo > 0$ are both false. The formula

$$
\begin{array}{l}
\Pi_{mpc} \equiv \textbf{var } bo : NAT; \\
\qquad\qquad obj, a, in, out : OBJECT; \\
\qquad\qquad b : BUFFER \\
\qquad \textbf{start } bo = 0 \\
\qquad \textbf{cobegin loop } \alpha_0 : \textbf{produce } obj; \\
\qquad\qquad\qquad\qquad \alpha_1 : ch_1!\, obj \\
\qquad\qquad\quad \textbf{endloop} \\
\qquad\qquad\quad \| \\
\qquad\qquad\quad \textbf{loop } \beta_0 : ch_2?\, a; \\
\qquad\qquad\qquad\qquad \beta_1 : \textbf{consume } a \\
\qquad\qquad\quad \textbf{endloop} \\
\qquad\qquad\quad \| \\
\qquad\qquad\quad \textbf{loop } \gamma_0 : \textbf{await } bo < CAP \textbf{ then } ch_1?\, in; \\
\qquad\qquad\qquad\qquad \gamma_1 : \textbf{store } in \textbf{ in } b; \\
\qquad\qquad\qquad\qquad \gamma_2 : bo := bo + 1 \\
\qquad\qquad\qquad\qquad \textbf{or} \\
\qquad\qquad\qquad\qquad \gamma_3 : \textbf{await } bo > 0 \textbf{ then } ch_2!\, out; \\
\qquad\qquad\qquad\qquad \gamma_4 : \textbf{remove } out \textbf{ from } b; \\
\qquad\qquad\qquad\qquad \gamma_5 : bo := bo - 1 \\
\qquad\qquad\quad \textbf{endloop} \\
\qquad \textbf{coend}
\end{array}
$$

Fig. 8.9. An MPP-program for the producer-consumer scheme

$$
start_{\Pi_{mpc}} \land CAP > 0 \rightarrow \\
\qquad \Box(at\,\alpha_1 \land at\,\beta_0 \land at\,\gamma_0 \land at\,\gamma_3 \rightarrow bo < CAP \lor bo > 0)
$$

states that this will never happen (provided $CAP > 0$) and is trivial since, in any state, $bo < CAP$ or $bo \geq CAP > 0$.

The relevant eventuality properties of Π_{mpc} are not that trivial. If the producer wants to send obj to Π_b at α_1 then this will eventually be performed. This property can be specified by

$$at\,\alpha_1 \rightarrow \Diamond exec\,\alpha_1.$$

Of course, its Π_{mpc}-validity depends again on the fact that $CAP > 0$ which we take as an assumption, i.e., we assert

(a) $\quad CAP > 0 \vdash at\,\alpha_1 \rightarrow \Diamond exec\,\alpha_1.$

The analogous property for the consumer is

(b) $\quad CAP > 0 \vdash at\,\beta_0 \rightarrow \Diamond exec\,\beta_0.$

The proofs of both assertions are very similar; we show only (a). Note firstly that

$$
\begin{aligned}
enabled_{\alpha_1} &\equiv at\,\alpha_1 \land \textbf{true} \land at\,\gamma_0 \land bo < CAP, \\
enabled_{\beta_0} &\equiv at\,\beta_0 \land \textbf{true} \land at\,\gamma_3 \land bo > 0,
\end{aligned}
$$

$$
\begin{aligned}
enabled_{\gamma_0} &\equiv at\gamma_0 \wedge bo < CAP \wedge at\alpha_1 \wedge \mathbf{true},\\
enabled_{\gamma_3} &\equiv at\gamma_3 \wedge bo > 0 \wedge at\beta_0 \wedge \mathbf{true},\\
enabled_{\lambda} &\equiv at\lambda \quad \text{for } \lambda \in \{\alpha_0, \beta_1, \gamma_1, \gamma_2, \gamma_4, \gamma_5\}
\end{aligned}
$$

and that the invariance properties

(a1) $\Box(at\beta_0 \vee at\beta_1)$,
(a2) $\Box((at\gamma_0 \wedge at\gamma_3) \vee at\gamma_1 \vee at\gamma_2 \vee at\gamma_4 \vee at\gamma_5)$,
(a3) $at\alpha_1 \wedge \Box\neg exec\,\alpha_1 \rightarrow \Box at\alpha_1$

can easily be proved by direct application of (invstart$_{\Pi_{mpc}}$) in the case of (a1) and (a2) and of (inv$_{\Pi_{mpc}}$) in the case of (a3). Furthermore,

$$\Box(at\gamma_1 \vee at\gamma_2 \rightarrow bo < CAP) \wedge (\neg at\gamma_1 \wedge \neg at\gamma_2 \rightarrow bo \leq CAP)$$

is easily proved as well with (invstart$_{\Pi_{mpc}}$) and this obviously implies

(a4) $\Box(bo \leq CAP)$.

The essential part of proving (a) is to show

(a5) $CAP > 0 \vdash \Diamond(at\gamma_0 \wedge bo < CAP)$.

This can be derived with several applications of (fairsom$_{\Pi_{mpc}}$), but we choose the more compact proof with rule (fairwfr$_{\Pi_{mpc}}$) encoding the (helpful) flow of control into a decreasing sequence of natural numbers. So, taking NAT with $\leq$ as the well-founded relation framework, we let

$$
\begin{aligned}
A \equiv\ & (at\gamma_1 \wedge y = 5) \vee (at\gamma_2 \wedge y = 4) \vee\\
& (at\gamma_0 \wedge at\gamma_3 \wedge at\beta_1 \wedge bo = CAP \wedge y = 3) \vee\\
& (at\gamma_0 \wedge at\gamma_3 \wedge at\beta_0 \wedge bo = CAP \wedge y = 2) \vee\\
& (at\gamma_4 \wedge y = 1) \vee (at\gamma_5 \wedge y = 0),\\
H_{\alpha_0} \equiv\ & H_{\alpha_1} \equiv \mathbf{false},\\
H_{\beta_0} \equiv\ & H_{\beta_1} \equiv y = 2 \vee y = 3,\\
H_{\gamma_i} \equiv\ & y = 0 \vee y = 1 \vee y = 2 \vee y = 4 \vee y = 5 \quad \text{for every } i = 0,\ldots,5
\end{aligned}
$$

and show

(a6) $exec\lambda \wedge H_\lambda \wedge A \rightarrow \bigcirc((at\gamma_0 \wedge bo < CAP) \vee \exists \bar{y}(\bar{y} < y \wedge A_y(\bar{y})))$
for every $\lambda \in Act_{\Pi_{mpc}}$.
(a7) $exec\lambda \wedge \neg H_\lambda \wedge A \rightarrow \bigcirc((at\gamma_0 \wedge bo < CAP) \vee \exists \bar{y}(\bar{y} \leq y \wedge A_y(\bar{y})))$
for every $\lambda \in Act_{\Pi_{mpc}}$.
(a8) $CAP > 0 \vdash \Box A \rightarrow \Diamond((at\gamma_0 \wedge bo < CAP) \vee \bigvee_{\lambda \in Act_{\Pi_{mpc}}}(H_\lambda \wedge enabled_\lambda))$.

Again we do not write out the derivations for (a6) and (a7) but represent these proofs by the diagram shown in Fig. 8.10. The arguments depicted there should be clear according to the explanations in Sect. 8.4. Note that (a4) is used in the step in which γ_5 leads to $at\gamma_0 \wedge bo < CAP$. For the proof of (a8) we check all cases displayed in the formula A.

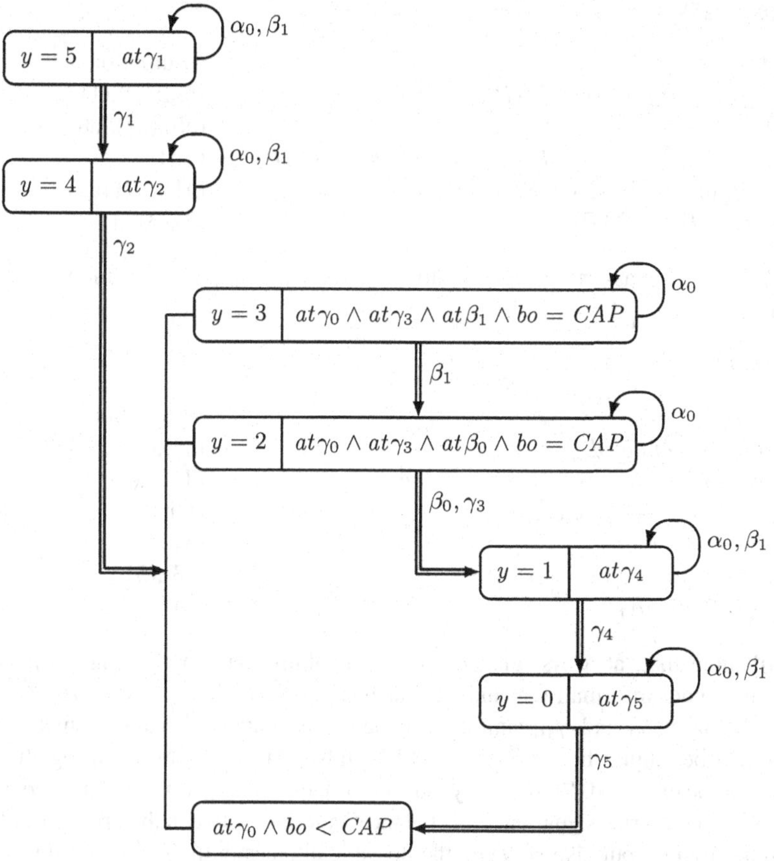

Fig. 8.10. Diagram for the proof of (a6) and (a7)

Derivation of (a8).

(1)	$CAP > 0$	assumption
(2)	$at\,\gamma_1 \wedge y = 5 \rightarrow H_{\gamma_1} \wedge enabled_{\gamma_1}$	(taut)
(3)	$at\,\gamma_2 \wedge y = 4 \rightarrow H_{\gamma_2} \wedge enabled_{\gamma_2}$	(taut)
(4)	$at\,\beta_1 \wedge y = 3 \rightarrow H_{\beta_1} \wedge enabled_{\beta_1}$	(taut)
(5)	$at\,\gamma_3 \wedge at\,\beta_0 \wedge bo = CAP \wedge y = 2 \rightarrow H_{\beta_0} \wedge enabled_{\beta_0}$	(1)
(6)	$at\,\gamma_4 \wedge y = 1 \rightarrow H_{\gamma_4} \wedge enabled_{\gamma_4}$	(taut)
(7)	$at\,\gamma_5 \wedge y = 0 \rightarrow H_{\gamma_5} \wedge enabled_{\gamma_5}$	(taut)
(8)	$A \rightarrow \bigvee_{\lambda \in Act_{\Pi_{mpc}}} (H_\lambda \wedge enabled_\lambda)$	(2)–(7)
(9)	$\Box A \rightarrow \Diamond((at\,\gamma_0 \wedge bo < CAP) \vee \bigvee_{\lambda \in Act_{\Pi_{mpc}}} (H_\lambda \wedge enabled_\lambda))$	(8) △

(a5) is now provided by applying ($\mathrm{fairwfr}_{\Pi_{mpc}}$) to (a6), (a7), and (a8).

Derivation of (a5).

(1)	$CAP > 0$	assumption
(2)	$\exists yA \rightarrow \Diamond(at\gamma_0 \wedge bo < CAP)$	(fairwfr),(1), (a6),(a7),(a8)
(3)	$at\gamma_0 \wedge at\gamma_3 \wedge bo < CAP \rightarrow \Diamond(at\gamma_0 \wedge bo < CAP)$	(T5)
(4)	$(at\gamma_0 \wedge at\gamma_3 \wedge bo < CAP) \vee \exists yA$	(a1),(a2),(a4)
(5)	$\Diamond(at\gamma_0 \wedge bo < CAP)$	(2),(3),(4) △

From (a5) the desired assertion (a) is finally obtained by a simple application of the fairness axiom (fair$_{\Pi_{mpc}}$).

Derivation of (a).

(1)	$CAP > 0$	assumption
(2)	$\Box at\alpha_1 \rightarrow \Diamond enabled_{\alpha_1}$	(a5),(1)
(3)	$\Box at\alpha_1 \rightarrow \Box\Diamond enabled_{\alpha_1}$	(T35),(2)
(4)	$\Box\Diamond enabled_{\alpha_1} \rightarrow \Diamond exec\alpha_1$	(fair)
(5)	$\Box at\alpha_1 \rightarrow \Diamond exec\alpha_1$	(3),(4)
(6)	$at\alpha_1 \wedge \Box\neg exec\alpha_1 \rightarrow \Diamond exec\alpha_1$	(a3),(5)
(7)	$at\alpha_1 \rightarrow \Diamond exec\alpha_1$	(6) △

We still note that, at a first glance, one might think that for proving (a) it is necessary to argue, informally speaking, that whenever Π_p waits at α_1 then Π_b, repeatedly being at γ_0 and γ_3, cannot permanently execute γ_3 because sometime the buffer will be empty; hence $bo > 0$ will be false. At that moment γ_0 together with α_1 would be executed. Remarkably, our proof does not need this but runs with a fairness argument. Fairness guarantees a "balance" not only between the processes of a concurrent program but also between the possible choices in the nondeterministic selection of Π_b proceeding with γ_0 or with γ_3 when reaching these points of control. This fact provides the eventual execution of α_1 without referring to the finite capacity of the buffer.

Second Reading

The investigations in Chaps. 6–8 were devoted to the temporal logical analysis of state systems in the following sense: a system is "explicitly" given by the definition of the single steps of all of its possible runs – in representation formalisms like transition systems or programs by a transition relation or a concrete program text, respectively. The analysis consists of

- the description (specification) of (mainly) these steps by temporal logic formulas of a typical shape like

  $$on \wedge c < 100 \rightarrow (on' \wedge c' = c + 1) \vee (\neg on' \wedge c' = c),$$
  $$exec\alpha_0 \rightarrow \bigcirc at\alpha_1,$$
  $$exec\alpha_0 \rightarrow a' = 2 * b \wedge b' = b$$

  (taken from examples in the previous text; cf. Sects. 6.2 and 8.2) in which the nexttime operator is (explicitly or implicitly) used to express the execution steps,

- the derivation of properties like

  $$c = 100 \rightarrow \Box(c = 100),$$
  $$\neg on \rightarrow c = 0 \ \mathbf{atnext}\ on,$$
  $$at\,\beta_0 \rightarrow \Diamond at\,\beta_1$$

  from the specification which hold for all system runs and typically use those temporal operators which express "behaviours" over "periods" of system states.

Another view is opened if we consider a state system not as explicitly given but take such "long-term" behaviour properties to specify the system "implicitly" (*descriptively*) by describing the *requirements* which have to be satisfied through ongoing runs when the system "evolves".

There are interesting applications connected with this view. One special example is given in the area of database systems. The entries in a database are permanently updated by *transactions* which are transition steps in our sense of state systems and which usually have to observe certain *integrity constraints* in order to reach consistency of the stored information with respect to the "real world" which is modeled by the system. Such constraints may be *dynamic* (*temporal*) restricting the long-term evolution of the database contents in some way. A typical example of such a constraint could be

- If an employee is dismissed then any re-employment of this person in the same year will be with the former salary.

This informal phrase can be described by a formula of temporal logic like

$$\begin{aligned} &\mathit{DISMISS}(\mathit{empl}) \land \mathit{YEAR} = x \land \mathit{SALARY} = y \rightarrow \\ &\qquad\qquad \Box(\mathit{EMPLOY}(\mathit{empl}) \land \mathit{YEAR} = x \rightarrow \mathit{SALARY} = y) \end{aligned}$$

(with an obvious signature) which is then a specifying requirement in the above sense. The challenge in this application is to find reasonable algorithmic means for *monitoring* such constraints during the runtime of the system, i.e., to ensure the correct database behaviour expressed by the constraints.

Another, more general application is *temporal logic programming*. Along the lines of "usual" logic programming, a temporal logic specification of the system requirements (typically written with some syntactical restrictions) is considered as a "program" itself, and the system evolves by "executing" this program.

As a simple example, recall the printer system considered in Sect. 6.5, but view it now in the following way: the system consists of two "parts", the environment given by the users U_1 and U_2 and, on the other hand, the printer "manager" who has to organize the allocations of the printer to the incoming requests from the users. The printer manager reacts on these arbitrary requests which are not under its own control. In fact, it is this part of the system which is to be "programmed" such that it satisfies some long-term requirements, e.g.:

- If the printer is requested by some user then eventually it has to print the job of that user.
- The printer is not printing for a user without being requested.
- The printer should always be printing for at most one of the users.

Using the system variables req_1 and req_2 ("there is a request from $U_{1/2}$") and the actions β_1 and β_2 ("the printer prints for $U_{1/2}$") as in Sect. 6.5, these requirements can be written as temporal logic formulas:

$$req_i \rightarrow \Diamond exec\,\beta_i \quad \text{for } i = 1, 2,$$
$$\neg req_i \rightarrow \neg exec\,\beta_i \ \mathbf{unl}\ req_i \quad \text{for } i = 1, 2,$$
$$\Box(exec\,\beta_1 \lor exec\,\beta_2).$$

The execution of this "program" is then to be performed by a procedure which causes a sequence of executions of β_1 and β_2 reacting on incoming requests and satisfying the three constraints.

We still remark that in the field of temporal logic programming another class of temporal logics, called *interval temporal logics*, is also successfully used. We will give a short outline of such logics in Sect. 10.2.

Bibliographical Notes

Deductive program verification has a long tradition in the computer science literature. One main stream originated from the pioneering work of Floyd [48] and Hoare [62]; a detailed description is given in [8].

The application of temporal logic to the verification of concurrent programs was just the main goal emphasized in the early papers which developed temporal logic. So the bibliographical remarks from the previous chapter are relevant here as well. Schneider's book [133] gives a detailed exposition of concurrent programming, properties, and verification.

The special phenomena and problems of concurrent programs are described in many textbooks, e.g., [7, 14, 28]. Peterson's algorithm was published in [118].

For applications of temporal logic in the area of data base systems see, e.g., [29, 93]. Approaches to temporal logic programming include [2, 12, 108, 110, 114].

9

Structured Specification

Formal system specification and verification are fundamental methods for the development of reliable software. In the preceding chapters we have shown at great length basic principles of how these can be performed in the framework of (linear) temporal logic.

For "real" applications, however, the approaches and means described so far are not yet polished enough. The development of a "large" system is a complicated task and in order to make it manageable it has to be structured in an appropriate manner.

In this chapter we address three important structuring concepts: *refinement*, *hiding*, and *composition*, and we study how these specification methods can be covered within temporal logic. A main key to the problem is the notion of *stuttering invariance* of temporal logic formulas. We present some special versions of temporal logic, subsumed under the name TLA (*Temporal Logic of Actions*), which are particularly tailored to respect this basic concept and thus may appropriately be used for structured specifications.

9.1 Refinement and Stuttering Invariance

One of the most important structuring concepts, known as*stepwise refinement*, is to consider system development as a process running through several levels of detail. Starting with the level of the user's view the development of the system specification proceeds in several steps, adding more and more details on how the user's requirements are realized. Considering the specifications of the system on the various levels, we so obtain the picture of a chain

$$\ldots \leadsto Spec_j \leadsto Spec_{j+1} \leadsto Spec_{j+2} \leadsto \ldots$$

of specifications where, with growing index k, $Spec_k$ contains more and more details but, of course, still fulfills – as a "correctness" property – the requirements specified in former levels. Any $Spec_k$ is called an *implementation* (or *refinement*) of a $Spec_l$ with $l < k$.

One typical ("behavioural") item with refinement is that "computations" which are regarded as one-step state transitions on a more abstract level are realized by a longer sequence of steps in an implementation. Also, these computations operate on additional system variables that represent the finer-grained detail of the refined system. As an example, let us consider again the counter system in its very first version as the STS Γ_{count} introduced in Sect. 6.2 and specified by the two axioms

$$\begin{aligned} C_1 &\equiv on \rightarrow (on' \wedge c' = c+1) \vee (\neg on' \wedge c' = c), \\ C_2 &\equiv \neg on \rightarrow (\neg on' \wedge c' = c) \vee (on' \wedge c' = 0). \end{aligned}$$

Imagine now the following implementation of Γ_{count}: the counting step from any value n of c to $n+1$ is realized by a more refined counting on the "first decimal", e.g., the step

$$17 \longrightarrow 18$$

on c is realized by counting

$$17.0 \longrightarrow 17.1 \longrightarrow 17.2 \longrightarrow 17.3 \longrightarrow \ldots \longrightarrow 17.9 \longrightarrow 18.0\,.$$

A specification of this implementation $\Gamma_{implcount}$ of Γ_{count} can be given by introducing an additional individual system variable *dec* for the value of the decimal and then taking the axioms

$$\begin{aligned} C_{impl1} \equiv\ & on \rightarrow (on' \wedge dec' = (dec+1) \bmod 10 \wedge \\ & \qquad\qquad (dec = 9 \rightarrow c' = c+1) \wedge (dec \neq 9 \rightarrow c' = c)) \vee \\ & \qquad (\neg on' \wedge c' = c \wedge dec' = dec), \\ C_{impl2} \equiv\ & \neg on \rightarrow (\neg on' \wedge c' = c \wedge dec' = dec) \vee \\ & \qquad (on' \wedge c' = 0 \wedge dec' = 0). \end{aligned}$$

The main difference compared to C_1 and C_2 is that the counting step

$$c' = c+1$$

of Γ_{count} is refined to

$$dec' = (dec+1) \bmod 10 \wedge (dec = 9 \rightarrow c' = c+1) \wedge (dec \neq 9 \rightarrow c' = c)$$

expressing that now in every step *dec* is increased by 1 and c remains unchanged except if *dec* changes from 9 to 0 in which case c is increased by 1. The other modifications in C_{impl1} and C_{impl2} are evident.

$\Gamma_{implcount}$ is more detailed than Γ_{count} and it is correct with respect to Γ_{count} in the sense that, related to the system variables on and c, the "behaviour" of $\Gamma_{implcount}$ agrees with that of Γ_{count}. In another wording used in Sect. 6.1, and disregarding the restriction to on and c in C_{impl1} and C_{impl2} for a moment, we would expect that

> "every model of the specification of $\Gamma_{implcount}$ is a model of the specification of Γ_{count}".

This expectation can formally be expressed by

$$\models_{\mathsf{K}} C_{impl1} \text{ and } \models_{\mathsf{K}} C_{impl2} \;\Rightarrow\; \models_{\mathsf{K}} C_1 \text{ and } \models_{\mathsf{K}} C_2 \qquad \text{for every "matching" temporal structure } \mathsf{K}$$

which means

$$C_{impl1}, C_{impl2} \models C_1 \quad \text{and} \quad C_{impl1}, C_{impl2} \models C_2.$$

(We view the formulas occurring here and in subsequent similar cases as belonging to a common temporal logic language. Note, moreover, that in general one would have to add relevant data axioms to the premises in these consequence relationships, but this is not necessary here.)

Let us now examine this formalization of the intended correctness relationship of the refinement. A typical temporal structure satisfying C_{impl1} and C_{impl2} is of the form (N, W) where W (representing a run of $\Gamma_{implcount}$) looks like

	...	η_i	η_{i+1}	η_{i+2}	...	η_{i+9}	η_{i+10}	η_{i+11}	η_{i+12}	...
on	...	tt	tt	tt	...	tt	tt	tt	tt	...
c	...	17	17	17	...	17	18	18	18	...
dec	...	0	1	2	...	9	0	1	2	...

and obviously does not satisfy C_1: for example, in the state η_i, on and on' are true but $c' = c + 1$ is not. This means that

$$C_{impl1}, C_{impl2} \models C_1$$

does not hold.

The crucial point of this problem comes out if we now really restrict this execution sequence W to what happens with on and c, i.e., to

$$\ldots \longrightarrow [\mathsf{tt}, 17] \longrightarrow [\mathsf{tt}, 17] \longrightarrow [\mathsf{tt}, 17] \longrightarrow \ldots \longrightarrow$$
$$[\mathsf{tt}, 17] \longrightarrow [\mathsf{tt}, 18] \longrightarrow [\mathsf{tt}, 18] \longrightarrow [\mathsf{tt}, 18] \longrightarrow \ldots$$

(written again in more compact form) and compare it with the corresponding execution sequence (of counting from 17 to 18)

$$\ldots \longrightarrow [\mathsf{tt}, 17] \longrightarrow [\mathsf{tt}, 18] \longrightarrow \ldots$$

of Γ_{count}. The first one contains steps of the form

$$[\mathsf{tt}, 17] \longrightarrow [\mathsf{tt}, 17]$$

which do not change the system variables on and c and are called *stuttering steps* (with respect to on and c). The specification formula C_1 of Γ_{count} satisfies the second execution sequence (not containing such steps) but it does not satisfy an execution sequence with stuttering steps.

In another wording we say that C_1 is not *stuttering invariant*. We will define this notion formally in Sect. 9.3; informally, a stuttering invariant formula A holds in some temporal structure (S, W) only if it holds in any $(\mathsf{S}, \mathsf{W}')$ such that the "restrictions" of W and W' to the flexible individual and propositional constants occurring in A only differ in containing more or less (finitely many) stuttering steps.

The observation pointed out here is the essential key to a possible solution to the problem. We should specify Γ_{count} in a manner that anticipates future refinements by allowing stuttering steps in its execution sequences; informally:

> "In any state transition of an execution step of Γ_{count}, the system variables on and c are changing according to C_1 or C_2, or they remain unchanged".

Formally this can be done by modifying C_1 to

$$C_1^r \equiv on \rightarrow (on' \wedge (c' = c + 1 \vee c' = c)) \vee (\neg on' \wedge c' = c)$$

and in fact C_1^r is stuttering invariant and

$$C_{impl1}, C_{impl2} \vDash C_1^r$$

holds as desired. Of course, the same modification can be applied to C_2 and it is easy to see that this does not really alter C_2, so with $C_2^r \equiv C_2$ we obtain

$$C_{impl1}, C_{impl2} \vDash C_2^r.$$

Following up on this idea, it should actually be applied to $\Gamma_{implcount}$ as well (which in turn could be refined in a next step). A specification suitable for refinement of this system according to the same pattern allows execution sequences in whose state transitions the system variables on, c, and dec are changed as described in C_{impl1} and C_{impl2} or remain unchanged. This is expressed by the stuttering invariant formulas

$$\begin{aligned}
C_{impl1}^r \equiv\ & on \rightarrow (on' \wedge (dec' = (dec + 1) \bmod 10 \wedge \\
& \qquad\qquad\qquad (dec = 9 \rightarrow c' = c + 1) \wedge \\
& \qquad\qquad\qquad (dec \neq 9 \rightarrow c' = c)) \vee \\
& \qquad\qquad (c' = c \wedge dec' = dec)) \vee \\
& \qquad (\neg on' \wedge c' = c \wedge dec' = dec), \\
C_{impl2}^r \equiv\ & C_{impl2}.
\end{aligned}$$

It is obvious that after this modification of C_{impl1} and C_{impl2}, the STS $\Gamma_{implcount}$ is still a correct refinement of Γ_{count}; formally:

$$C_{impl1}^r, C_{impl2}^r \vDash C_1^r \quad \text{and} \quad C_{impl1}^r, C_{impl2}^r \vDash C_2^r.$$

Indeed, if $\mathsf{K} = (\mathsf{N}, \mathsf{W})$ is a temporal structure satisfying C_{impl1}^r and C_{impl2}^r, and η_i is a state of W with $\eta_i(on) = \mathsf{tt}$ then for η_{i+1},

$\eta_{i+1}(on) = \mathsf{tt}$ and $\eta_{i+1}(c) = \eta_i(c) + 1$
or
$\eta_{i+1}(on) = \mathsf{tt}$ and $\eta_{i+1}(c) = \eta_i(c)$
or
$\eta_{i+1}(on) = \mathsf{ff}$ and $\eta_{i+1}(c) = \eta_i(c)$

holds. If $\eta_i(on) = \mathsf{ff}$ then

$$\eta_{i+1}(on) = \mathsf{ff} \text{ and } \eta_{i+1}(c) = \eta_i(c)$$
or
$$\eta_{i+1}(on) = \mathsf{tt} \text{ and } \eta_{i+1}(c) = 0.$$

This implies that C_1^r and C_2^r are valid in K.

Specifying state systems in a way as exemplified here enables an adequate temporal logic treatment of stepwise refinement of specifications. It should be observed, however, that the mere modification of "original" specification formulas to stuttering invariant ones induces a new undesired effect. For example, the specification by C_1^r above allows that the counter stays on and does not change the value of c forever, a behaviour which contradicts the intuition of the system and its implementation. But such adulterations can easily be remedied by adding formulas just excluding this, e.g.,

$$\Box on \rightarrow \Diamond(c' = c + 1)$$

in the case of Γ_{count}. This formula clearly does not change the validity of the refinement relationship.

We still remark that a consequence relationship like

$$C_{impl1}^r, C_{impl2}^r \vDash C_1^r$$

which holds after the modification of the specification formulas can be seen in the sense of Sect. 7.1: the formula C_1^r describes just a particular property which is $\Gamma_{implcount}$-valid. Hence it is evident that the above discussion immediately carries over to arbitrary system properties of an STS Γ which is specified in a stuttering invariant way. The properties should be expressed by stuttering invariant formulas F as well so that their intuitive Γ-validity is formally still implied by a relationship

$$\mathcal{A}_\Gamma \vDash F$$

as before. A simple example is the property of Γ_{count} informally saying that

"if the counter is on forever then the value of c is increasing in every step".

The former description

$$\Box on \rightarrow \Box(c' > c)$$

is not stuttering invariant; it should be modified to

$$\Box on \rightarrow \Box(c' > c \vee c' = c)$$

which then in fact is a consequence of C_1^r and C_2^r (and appropriate data axioms).

9.2 Basic TLA

The considerations in the previous section were carried out in the framework of the temporal logic FOLTL as used in the preceding chapters, and we have pointed out how formulas of this logic can be modified to stuttering invariant ones. A more rigorous way to enforce that specifications and properties are stuttering invariant is to tailor the temporal logic accordingly and to restrict it syntactically such that it does not contain formulas any more which are not stuttering invariant. A logic which realizes this idea is TLA (*Temporal Logic of Actions*).

We introduce TLA in this section in a "basic" form (starting, however, immediately with a first-order version); the extension to "full" TLA will be motivated and defined in Sect. 9.5. Following the intention, TLA restricts the syntax of FOLTL (taken in its FOLTL$'$ version defined in Sect. 5.4). Traditionally it is equipped with initial validity semantics. We present it in this form, i.e., as a sublogic of FOLTL$_0$ ("FOLTL with initial validity semantics").

The discussion in Sect. 9.1 indicates that the nexttime operator is the essential source for formulas not being stuttering invariant. Therefore the basic idea for TLA is to restrict the free use of this operator, permitting it only in a way in which it occurs in formulas specifying transition steps. Let us consider again the counter system Γ_{count} as studied in Sect. 9.1. An easy calculation shows that the stuttering invariant specification formula C_1^{τ} used there is logically equivalent to $C_1 \vee c' = c$, and therefore

$$\Box(C_1 \vee c' = c)$$

which is stuttering invariant as well could be taken as an appropriate specification formula if initial validity semantics is assumed. TLA restricts FOLTL$_0$ just by allowing the nexttime operator (or the priming notation) only in a form like this (analogously also for propositional system variables); more precisely: TLA is FOLTL$_0$ with the restrictions that

- the nexttime operator $\bigcirc$ is not used explicitly but only in the form of the priming notation (including primed flexible propositional constants),
- primed flexible constants may only occur in formulas of the form $\Box(A \vee a' = a)$ or $\Box(A \vee (v' \leftrightarrow v))$ where a and v are flexible individual or propositional constants, respectively, and A may not contain other temporal operators than the "priming operator".

The special formulas in this definition are distinguished by writing them as

$$\Box[A]_e$$

(read: "always square A sub e") for $e \equiv a$ or $e \equiv v$, respectively. Note that, in general, the "expression" A itself is not a formula then. It is used to describe "the proper" transition steps. (In TLA terminology, A is called *action* which explains the name of the logic; we will see shortly that this has to do something with an action in the sense of Sect. 6.4 but it should not be confused with that notion.)

Let us give also an explicit definition of TLA on its own, taking $\Box[\_]_\_$ as a separate operator. Given a temporal signature $TSIG = (SIG, \mathbf{X}, \mathbf{V})$, $SIG = (\mathbf{S}, \mathbf{F}, \mathbf{P})$, the language $\mathcal{L}_{\mathrm{FOL}}(SIG^+)$ with the set $\mathcal{X} = \bigcup_{s \in \mathbf{S}} \mathcal{X}_s$ of variables is defined as in Sect. 5.1. The alphabet of a *(basic first-order) language* $\mathcal{L}_{\mathrm{TLA}}(TSIG)$ (also shortly: $\mathcal{L}_{\mathrm{TLA}}$) *of* TLA is given by

- all symbols of $\mathcal{L}_{\mathrm{FOL}}(SIG^+)$,
- the symbols $\Box \mid ' \mid [\mid]$.

Terms (with *their sorts*) are those of $\mathcal{L}_{\mathrm{FOL}}(SIG^+)$ with the additional rule

- If $a \in \mathbf{X}$ then a' is a term of the same sort as a.

The formulas of $\mathcal{L}_{\mathrm{TLA}}$ are defined together with a second syntactical type of *pre-formulas* by simultaneous induction. *Atomic pre-formulas* are the atomic formulas of $\mathcal{L}_{\mathrm{FOL}}(SIG^+)$; those which contain no primed individual constants are called *atomic formulas*.

Inductive Definition of *formulas* (of $\mathcal{L}_{\mathrm{TLA}}(TSIG)$).

1. Every atomic pre-formula is a pre-formula.
2. Every atomic formula is a formula.
3. **false** is a pre-formula and a formula.
4. If A and B are pre-formulas then $(A \to B)$ is a pre-formula; if they are formulas then $(A \to B)$ is a formula.
5. If $v \in \mathbf{V}$ then v' is a pre-formula.
6. If A is a pre-formula and $e \in \mathbf{X} \cup \mathbf{V}$ then $\Box[A]_e$ is a formula.
7. If A is a formula then $\Box A$ is a formula.
8. If A is a pre-formula and x is a variable then $\exists x A$ is a pre-formula; if A is a formula then $\exists x A$ is a formula.

We adopt all relevant abbreviations, notions and notational conventions from FOLTL. Furthermore we let, for $\mathbf{U} = \{e_1, \ldots, e_n\} \subseteq \mathbf{X} \cup \mathbf{V}$,

$$\Box[A]_{\mathbf{U}} \equiv \Box[A]_{e_1} \wedge \ldots \wedge \Box[A]_{e_n}$$

and

$$\Diamond\langle A\rangle_{\mathbf{U}} \equiv \neg\Box[\neg A]_{e_1} \vee \ldots \vee \neg\Box[\neg A]_{e_n}.$$

(We will also write $\Box[A]_{e_1,\ldots,e_n}$ for $\Box[A]_{\mathbf{U}}$ and analogously for $\Diamond\langle A\rangle_{\mathbf{U}}$.)

The semantics of $\mathcal{L}_{\mathrm{TLA}}$ is given by defining, for a temporal structure K for $TSIG$, a variable valuation ξ, and $i \in \mathbb{N}$, the truth value $\mathsf{K}_i^{(\xi)}(F)$ for pre-formulas and formulas F just as in Sects. 5.1 and 5.4, viewing v' as $\bigcirc v$ for $v \in \mathbf{V}$ and understanding a formula $\Box[A]_e$ as explained above. This means that

$$\mathsf{K}_i^{(\xi)}(v') = \mathsf{K}_{i+1}^{(\xi)}(v),$$
$$\mathsf{K}_i^{(\xi)}(\Box[A]_e) = \mathsf{tt} \Leftrightarrow \mathsf{K}_j^{(\xi)}(A) = \mathsf{tt} \text{ or } \mathsf{K}_{j+1}^{(\xi)}(e) = \mathsf{K}_j^{(\xi)}(e) \text{ for every } j \geq i.$$

For the new abbreviations we then obtain

$$\begin{aligned}
\mathsf{K}_i^{(\xi)}(\Box[A]_{\mathbf{U}}) = \mathsf{tt} \;&\Leftrightarrow\; \mathsf{K}_j^{(\xi)}(A) = \mathsf{tt} \text{ or } \mathsf{K}_{j+1}^{(\xi)}(e) = \mathsf{K}_j^{(\xi)}(e) \text{ for every } e \in \mathbf{U} \\
&\qquad \text{for every } j \geq i, \\
\mathsf{K}_i^{(\xi)}(\Diamond\langle A\rangle_{\mathbf{U}}) = \mathsf{tt} \;&\Leftrightarrow\; \text{there is } j \geq i \text{ such that} \\
&\qquad \mathsf{K}_j^{(\xi)}(A) = \mathsf{tt} \text{ and } \mathsf{K}_{j+1}^{(\xi)}(e) \neq \mathsf{K}_j^{(\xi)}(e) \text{ for some } e \in \mathbf{U}.
\end{aligned}$$

For formulas A and formula sets $\mathcal{F}$, the notions of initial validity in K ($\overset{0}{\vDash}_{\mathsf{K}} A$), initial consequence ($\mathcal{F} \overset{0}{\vDash} A$), and (universal) initial validity ($\overset{0}{\vDash} A$) are defined as in Sect. 2.6.

Example. Let $TSIG = (SIG_{Nat}, \{a\}, \{v\})$ be a temporal signature with SIG_{Nat} as usual, x a variable of sort NAT. Then

$$A \equiv a = x \wedge v \wedge \Box[(v \rightarrow v') \wedge a' = a + 1]_{a,v} \rightarrow \Box(a \geq x \wedge v)$$

is a formula of $\mathcal{L}_{\mathrm{TLA}}(TSIG)$. For any temporal structure K for $TSIG$ with data component N and variable valuation ξ we have (using notation from Sect. 5.4)

$$\begin{aligned}
&\mathsf{K}_0^{(\xi)}(a = x \wedge v \wedge \Box[(v \rightarrow v') \wedge a' = a + 1]_{a,v}) = \mathsf{tt} \\
&\quad \Rightarrow \mathsf{K}_0^{(\xi)}(a) = \xi(a) \text{ and} \\
&\qquad \mathsf{K}_0^{(\xi)}(v) = \mathsf{tt} \text{ and} \\
&\qquad \mathsf{K}_j^{(\xi)}((v \rightarrow v') \wedge a' = a + 1) = \mathsf{tt} \text{ or} \\
&\qquad\quad \mathsf{K}_{j+1}^{(\xi)}(a) = \mathsf{K}_j^{(\xi)}(a) \text{ and } \mathsf{K}_{j+1}^{(\xi)}(v) = \mathsf{K}_j^{(\xi)}(v) \\
&\qquad\qquad\qquad\qquad\qquad\qquad\qquad\qquad \text{for every } j \geq 0 \\
&\quad \Rightarrow \mathsf{K}_1^{(\xi)}(a) = \xi(a) \text{ or } \mathsf{K}_1^{(\xi)}(a) = \xi(a) + 1 \\
&\qquad \text{and} \\
&\qquad \mathsf{K}_1^{(\xi)}(v) = \mathsf{tt} \\
&\qquad \text{and} \\
&\qquad \mathsf{K}_j^{(\xi)}((v \rightarrow v') \wedge a' = a + 1) = \mathsf{tt} \text{ or} \\
&\qquad\quad \mathsf{K}_{j+1}^{(\xi)}(a) = \mathsf{K}_j^{(\xi)}(a) \text{ and } \mathsf{K}_{j+1}^{(\xi)}(v) = \mathsf{K}_j^{(\xi)}(v) \\
&\qquad\qquad\qquad\qquad\qquad\qquad\qquad\qquad \text{for every } j \geq 1 \\
&\quad \vdots \\
&\quad \Rightarrow \mathsf{K}_j^{(\xi)}(a) \geq \xi(a) \text{ and } \mathsf{K}_j^{(\xi)}(v) \text{ for every } j \in \mathbb{N} \\
&\quad \Rightarrow \mathsf{K}_0^{(\xi)}(\Box(a \geq x \wedge v)) = \mathsf{tt}
\end{aligned}$$

which means that $\overset{0}{\vDash}_{\mathsf{K}} A$. △

We will prove in Sect. 9.3 that every formula of TLA is in fact stuttering invariant. We will also discuss there how to axiomatize TLA.

A specification of an STS Γ can be written in TLA as indicated by our examples. In general, the description of the possible "state changes" of Γ within the pre-formula A of specification formulas $\Box[A]_{\mathbf{U}}$ can be carried out in different ways (as it is the case in FOLTL specifications). It is customary to write TLA system specifications in a standard form where the transition relation of Γ together with the possible stuttering steps is described by one single formula

$$\Box[A_\Gamma]_{\mathbf{U}}$$

(instead of several formulas we were used to so far) where A_Γ is a disjunction of all possible transitions of Γ. In our example of the counter system Γ_{count} we obtain this form with

$$A_{\Gamma_{count}} \equiv A_{on} \vee A_{off} \vee A_c \vee A_p$$

where

$$\begin{aligned}
A_{on} &\equiv \neg on \wedge on' \wedge c' = 0,\\
A_{off} &\equiv on \wedge \neg on' \wedge c' = c,\\
A_c &\equiv on \wedge on' \wedge c' = c + 1,\\
A_p &\equiv \neg on \wedge \neg on' \wedge c' = c.
\end{aligned}$$

A_p describes a stuttering transition (with respect to on and c), and can equivalently be omitted from the definition of $A_{\Gamma_{count}}$. This description is very close to the specification of Γ^l_{count} in Sect. 6.4 and easy to understand. So the (main part of the) stuttering invariant specification of Γ_{count} is then given by the formula

$$\Box[A_{\Gamma_{count}}]_{on,c}\,.$$

As mentioned already we should, however, still add a formula excluding infinitely many stuttering steps with respect to c if the counter is on. An appropriate TLA formula for such a *progress condition* is

$$\Box(\Box on \to \Diamond\langle c' = c + 1\rangle_c).$$

It is trivial that rooted STSs can be specified by just adding the initial condition of the STS to the specification formulas. Moreover, TLA can easily be applied to labeled STSs. One has essentially to change the transition descriptions a bit. For example, taking the counter in its version Γ^l_{count} of Sect. 6.4, A_{on} should then read

$$exec\,\lambda_{on} \wedge on' \wedge c' = 0$$

and similarly for the other constituents. Fairness can be included in the same way as in Sect. 6.5. We should mention, however, that typical TLA specifications avoid the explicit use of action "names" and assume a state system to be represented by an "unlabeled" STS. The actions in the sense of Sect. 6.4 are implicitly represented by the disjunction constituents of the pre-formula A_Γ in the specification formula $[A_\Gamma]_{\mathbf{U}}$ and these can also be used for expressing fairness. In Γ_{count}, fairness with respect to the switching on action expressed by A_{on} can be expressed by

$$\Box\Diamond\neg on \to \Box\Diamond\langle A_{on}\rangle_{on,c}\,.$$

$$
\begin{array}{lll}
\Pi_{Pet} \equiv & \textbf{var } a_1, a_2, c : NAT & \\
& \textbf{start } a_1 = 0 \wedge a_2 = 0 \wedge c = 1 & \\
& \textbf{cobegin loop } \alpha_0 : \textbf{noncritical}; & \\
& \qquad\qquad \alpha_1 : a_1, c := 1, 1; & \\
& \qquad\qquad \alpha_2 : \textbf{await } a_2 = 0 \vee c = 2; & \\
& \qquad\qquad \alpha_3 : \textbf{critical}; & \\
& \qquad\qquad \alpha_4 : a_1 := 0 & \\
& \qquad \textbf{endloop} & \\
& \qquad \| & \\
& \qquad \textbf{loop } \beta_0 : \textbf{noncritical}; & \\
& \qquad\qquad \beta_1 : a_2, c := 1, 2; & \\
& \qquad\qquad \beta_2 : \textbf{await } a_1 = 0 \vee c = 1; & \\
& \qquad\qquad \beta_3 : \textbf{critical}; & \\
& \qquad\qquad \beta_4 : a_2 := 0 & \\
& \qquad \textbf{endloop} & \\
& \textbf{coend} &
\end{array}
$$

Fig. 9.1. Peterson's algorithm again

Note that in this context, progress conditions may be viewed as weak fairness conditions as well (cf. Sect. 6.5).

Summarizing, a TLA specification of a system Γ consists of a formula $\Box[A_\Gamma]_{\mathbf{U}}$, possibly further formulas like $start_\Gamma$ and formulas expressing (strong or weak) fairness conditions, and, if Γ is not propositional, data axioms (data$_\Gamma$). Actually, the temporal axioms of a TLA specification are usually given by one single formula

$$F_\Gamma \equiv start_\Gamma \wedge \Box[A_\Gamma]_{\mathbf{U}} \wedge fair_\Gamma$$

where $fair_\Gamma$ is the conjunction of the fairness formulas.

Let us illustrate this discussion by one more example. Figure 9.1 shows again Peterson's algorithm studied in Sect. 8.4. A ("standard") TLA specification of this program is given by (data$_{\Pi_{Pet}}$) and the formula

$$F_{\Pi_{Pet}} \equiv start_{\Pi_{Pet}} \wedge \Box[A_{\Pi_{Pet}}]_{\mathbf{U}_{Pet}} \wedge fair_{\Pi_{Pet}}$$

where, with $Lab_{Pet} = \{\alpha_i, \beta_i \mid 0 \le i \le 4\}$,

$$\mathbf{U}_{Pet} = \{at\lambda \mid \lambda \in Lab_{Pet}\} \cup \{a_1, a_2, c\}$$

and

$$
\begin{aligned}
start_{\Pi_{Pet}} &\equiv at\alpha_0 \wedge at\beta_0 \wedge a_1 = 0 \wedge a_2 = 0 \wedge c = 1, \\
A_{\Pi_{Pet}} &\equiv \bigvee_{\lambda \in Lab_{Pet}} A_\lambda, \\
A_{\alpha_0} &\equiv step(\alpha_0, \alpha_1) \wedge a_1' = a_1 \wedge a_2' = a_2 \wedge c' = c, \\
A_{\alpha_1} &\equiv step(\alpha_1, \alpha_2) \wedge a_1' = 1 \wedge a_2' = a_2 \wedge c' = 1,
\end{aligned}
$$

$$
\begin{aligned}
A_{\alpha_2} &\equiv \mathit{step}(\alpha_2,\alpha_3) \land (a_2 = 0 \lor c = 2) \land a_1' = a_1 \land a_2' = a_2 \land c' = c,\\
A_{\alpha_3} &\equiv \mathit{step}(\alpha_3,\alpha_4) \land a_1' = a_1 \land a_2' = a_2 \land c' = c,\\
A_{\alpha_4} &\equiv \mathit{step}(\alpha_4,\alpha_0) \land a_1' = 0 \land a_2' = a_2 \land c' = c,\\
A_{\beta_0} &\equiv \mathit{step}(\beta_0,\beta_1) \land a_1' = a_1 \land a_2' = a_2 \land c' = c,\\
A_{\beta_1} &\equiv \mathit{step}(\beta_1,\beta_2) \land a_1' = a_1 \land a_2' = 1 \land c' = 2,\\
A_{\beta_2} &\equiv \mathit{step}(\beta_2,\beta_3) \land (a_1 = 0 \lor c = 1) \land a_1' = a_1 \land a_2' = a_2 \land c' = c,\\
A_{\beta_3} &\equiv \mathit{step}(\beta_3,\beta_4) \land a_1' = a_1 \land a_2' = a_2 \land c' = c,\\
A_{\beta_4} &\equiv \mathit{step}(\beta_4,\beta_0) \land a_1' = a_1 \land a_2' = 0 \land c' = c,\\
\mathit{fair}_{\Pi_{Pet}} &\equiv \bigwedge_{\lambda \in \mathit{Lab}_{Pet} \setminus \{\alpha_0,\beta_0\}} (\Diamond\Box \mathit{enabled}_\lambda \rightarrow \Box\Diamond\langle A_\lambda\rangle_{\mathbf{U}_{Pet}}).
\end{aligned}
$$

We use here formulas $\mathit{enabled}_\lambda$ for $\lambda \in \mathit{Lab}_{Pet}$ as generally defined in Sect. 8.2, e.g.,

$$
\begin{aligned}
\mathit{enabled}_{\alpha_0} &\equiv at\,\alpha_0,\\
\mathit{enabled}_{\alpha_2} &\equiv at\,\alpha_2 \land (a_2 = 0 \lor c = 2),
\end{aligned}
$$

and so on, and the abbreviations

$$
\mathit{step}(\lambda_1,\lambda_2) \;\equiv\; at\,\lambda_1 \land \neg at\,\lambda_1' \land at\,\lambda_2' \land \bigwedge_{\lambda \in \mathit{Lab}_{Pet} \setminus \{\lambda_1,\lambda_2\}} (at\,\lambda' \leftrightarrow at\,\lambda)
$$

for $\lambda_1, \lambda_2 \in \mathit{Lab}_{Pet}$. (Observe that the elements of Lab_{Pet} are not handled as actions; the formulas $at\,\lambda$ act as "program counters".)

In TLA, fairness assumptions are by convention written explicitly as part of the specification instead of expressing them by a generic axiom. It is therefore natural to specify fairness "per action", as briefly indicated at the end of Sect. 6.5. For the present example, we have assumed weak fairness for all actions except (those represented by) A_{α_0} and A_{β_0}. This corresponds to the idea that a process may remain forever in the non-critical section but should not block either in its critical section or during the entry and exit protocols of Peterson's algorithm. A close inspection of the proof of the accessibility properties in Sect. 8.4 (including the derivation of the rule (fairsom$_\Gamma$) in Sect. 7.4) shows that they can still be derived from these weaker fairness assumptions.

Many relevant system properties, in particular invariance and eventuality properties, can be described as before since the corresponding formulas

$$\Box(A \rightarrow \Box B)$$

and

$$\Box(A \rightarrow \Diamond B)$$

are TLA formulas as well. How to (deductively) verify properties from the specification will be discussed in Sect. 9.4.

9.3 Generalized TLA

The temporal logic TLA restricts the free use of the nexttime operator, thereby ensuring that formulas become stuttering invariant. Actually, this restriction is quite strong and could be weakened to allow for more stuttering invariant formulas. Concerning application, such a weakening would enable the formulation of more properties of systems. Consider, e.g., a property of the kind

> "Whenever an action α has occurred, only an action β is allowed to change the value of a".

A reasonable formalization in the TLA sense would be of a form

$$\Box\big[A_\alpha \to \Box[A_\beta]_a\big]_e$$

which seems to cause no problems with respect to stuttering but is not a TLA formula.

Besides this application aspect, another annoying effect of the strong syntactical restriction in TLA concerns the logic itself: it is a severe obstacle to a reasonable axiomatization of TLA. Consider, e.g., the induction rule (ind) from Sect. 2.3, written as

(ind$_0$) $\quad \Box(A \to B), \Box(A \to \bigcirc A) \vdash \Box(A \to \Box B)$

in Sect. 2.6 for initial validity semantics. This rule is quite fundamental for all kinds of deductions of formulas of the shape

$$\Box(A \to \Box B)$$

but we cannot take it as a rule in TLA because it uses a formula $\bigcirc A$ which is no TLA formula (and there is also no admissible "equivalent" for it if the formula A contains temporal operators). Attempts to solve this problem within TLA are not very satisfactory.

In view of such observations we extend TLA now by introducing a more liberal syntax, still observing, of course, that formulas remain stuttering invariant. The extended logic is called GTLA (*Generalized* TLA) and, in fact, it will particularly permit a reasonable proof-theoretical treatment.

The main idea of GTLA is to reintroduce the nexttime operator $\bigcirc$ and to generalize the definition of pre-formulas. In particular, $\bigcirc A$ is a pre-formula for an arbitrary formula A, whereas TLA allows only the restricted forms a' and v' to appear in pre-formulas.

Formally, given a temporal signature $TSIG$, a language $\mathcal{L}_{\mathrm{GTLA}}(TSIG)$ (again shortly: $\mathcal{L}_{\mathrm{GTLA}}$) is obtained from $\mathcal{L}_{\mathrm{TLA}}(TSIG)$ by adding the symbol $\bigcirc$ to the alphabet and replacing the formation rule

5. If $v \in \mathbf{V}$ then v' is a pre-formula

of TLA by

5_G. If A is a formula then A and $\bigcirc A$ are pre-formulas.

Note that, for avoiding redundancy, one can then simplify rule 3 to

3_G. **false** is a formula.

As in TLA, $\Box[\_]_\_$ is considered to be a separate operator and $[A]_e$ itself is not a formula. Indeed, it would not be stuttering invariant. However, we introduce the latter now as an abbreviation for a special pre-formula:

$$[A]_e \;\equiv\; A \lor e' = e.$$

(For uniformity, here and subsequently $e' = e$ denotes $e' \leftrightarrow e$ for $e \in \mathbf{V}$.) Of course, other abbreviations, notations, etc. are used as before, and it is evident that every TLA formula, understanding v' as $\bigcirc v$ for flexible propositional constants, is a GTLA formula as well. The example

$$\Box\big[A_\alpha \to \Box[A_\beta]_a\big]_e$$

from the beginning of this section is also a GTLA formula.

Given a temporal structure K for the underlying $TSIG$, the evaluation $\mathsf{K}_i^{(\xi)}$ is defined as before; in particular we have again

$$\mathsf{K}_i^{(\xi)}(\bigcirc A) = \mathsf{K}_{i+1}^{(\xi)}(A).$$

For the abbreviation above we obtain

$$\mathsf{K}_i^{(\xi)}([A]_e) = \mathsf{tt} \;\Leftrightarrow\; \mathsf{K}_i^{(\xi)}(A) = \mathsf{tt} \text{ or } \mathsf{K}_{i+1}^{(\xi)}(e) = \mathsf{K}_i^{(\xi)}(e).$$

As *validity in* K we define

$$\models_{\mathsf{K}} A \;\Leftrightarrow\; \mathsf{K}_i^{(\xi)}(A) = \mathsf{tt} \text{ for every } i \text{ and every } \xi$$

which means that, extending this to the notions of consequence ($\mathcal{F} \models A$) and (universal) validity ($\models A$), we obtain a normal semantics of $\mathcal{L}_{\mathrm{GTLA}}$ as usual. This choice (which makes GTLA a sublogic of FOLTL if we identify formulas $\Box[A]_e$ with $\Box(A \lor e' = e)$) may appear somewhat strange since TLA was equipped with initial validity semantics. It will, however, simplify the axiomatization aimed at for GTLA and the intended application in the TLA sense remains still feasible.

Example. Let $TSIG = (SIG_{Nat}, \{a, b\}, \emptyset)$ be a temporal signature with SIG_{Nat} as usual. Then

$$A \;\equiv\; \Box\big[\Box[a' > b]_a \lor \bigcirc\Box(a > 0)\big]_b$$

is a formula of $\mathcal{L}_{\mathrm{GTLA}}(TSIG)$ (but not a TLA formula). Let $\mathsf{K} = (\mathsf{N}, \mathsf{W})$, W given by

	η_0	η_1	η_2	η_3	η_4	...
a	3	2	0	5	5	...(5 forever)...
b	4	7	7	3	8	...(arbitrary)...

We calculate (for arbitrary ξ):

$$\mathsf{K}_0^{(\xi)}(a' > b \lor a' = a) = \mathsf{ff},\ \mathsf{K}_0^{(\xi)}(\bigcirc\Box(a > 0)) = \mathsf{ff},\ \mathsf{K}_1^{(\xi)}(b) \neq \mathsf{K}_0^{(\xi)}(b)$$
$$\Rightarrow \mathsf{K}_0^{(\xi)}(A) = \mathsf{ff}.$$
$$\mathsf{K}_2^{(\xi)}(b) = \mathsf{K}_1^{(\xi)}(b),\ \mathsf{K}_j^{(\xi)}(\bigcirc\Box(a > 0)) = \mathsf{tt} \text{ for } j \geq 2$$
$$\Rightarrow \mathsf{K}_i^{(\xi)}(A) = \mathsf{tt} \text{ for } i \geq 1.$$

△

The formulas of GTLA are to be stuttering invariant. We set out now to define this notion formally. Let $TSIG = (SIG, \mathbf{X}, \mathbf{V})$ be a temporal signature and $\mathbf{U} \subseteq \mathbf{X} \cup \mathbf{V}$. For two states η and η' (of some temporal structure(s) for $TSIG$) let

$$\eta =_{\mathbf{U}} \eta' \quad \Leftrightarrow \quad \eta(e) = \eta'(e) \text{ for every } e \in \mathbf{U}.$$

Furthermore we define, for $\mathsf{W} = (\eta_0, \eta_1, \eta_2, \ldots)$, the mapping $\vartheta_{\mathbf{U}}^{\mathsf{W}} : \mathbb{N} \to \mathbb{N}$ inductively by

$$\vartheta_{\mathbf{U}}^{\mathsf{W}}(0) = 0,$$
$$\vartheta_{\mathbf{U}}^{\mathsf{W}}(i+1) = \begin{cases} \vartheta_{\mathbf{U}}^{\mathsf{W}}(i) & \text{if } \eta_{i+1} =_{\mathbf{U}} \eta_i \text{ and } \eta_j \neq_{\mathbf{U}} \eta_i \text{ for some } j > i, \\ \vartheta_{\mathbf{U}}^{\mathsf{W}}(i) + 1 & \text{otherwise.} \end{cases}$$

Observe that $\vartheta_{\mathbf{U}}^{\mathsf{W}}$ is monotonic and surjective. In particular, given any $k \in \mathbb{N}$ there is at least one, but only finitely many $j \in \mathbb{N}$ such that $\vartheta_{\mathbf{U}}^{\mathsf{W}}(j) = k$.

The infinite sequence

$$\Theta_{\mathbf{U}}(\mathsf{W}) = (\eta_{i_0}, \eta_{i_1}, \eta_{i_2}, \ldots)$$

of states of W where

$$i_k = \min\{j \in \mathbb{N} \mid \vartheta_{\mathbf{U}}^{\mathsf{W}}(j) = k\} \qquad (\text{for } k \in \mathbb{N})$$

is called $\mathbf{U}$-*stuttering free variant* of W. It is obtained from W by "cutting out" all finite subsequences of states which have the same values on all $e \in \mathbf{U}$.

Example. Let W be given by

	η_0	η_1	η_2	η_3	η_4	η_5	η_6	η_7	...
v	tt	ff	ff	ff	tt	tt	ff	tt	...
a	4	4	4	7	6	6	6	6	...(6 forever)...
b	6	2	3	3	8	1	2	4	...

Then we have:

$$\Theta_{\{v\}}(\mathsf{W}) = (\eta_0, \eta_1, \eta_4, \eta_6, \eta_7, \ldots),$$
$$\Theta_{\{a\}}(\mathsf{W}) = (\eta_0, \eta_3, \eta_4, \eta_5, \eta_6, \eta_7, \ldots),$$
$$\Theta_{\{v,a\}}(\mathsf{W}) = (\eta_0, \eta_1, \eta_3, \eta_4, \eta_6, \eta_7, \ldots).$$

△

It is easy to see that the transformation $\Theta_{\mathbf{U}}$ is idempotent. The following lemma slightly generalizes this observation.

Lemma 9.3.1. *If* $\mathbf{U}' \subseteq \mathbf{U}$ *then* $\Theta_{\mathbf{U}'}(\Theta_{\mathbf{U}}(\mathsf{W})) =_{\mathbf{U}'} \Theta_{\mathbf{U}'}(\mathsf{W})$.

Proof. Let $\mathsf{W} = (\eta_0, \eta_1, \eta_2, \ldots)$, $\Theta_{\mathbf{U}}(\mathsf{W}) = (\eta_{i_0}, \eta_{i_1}, \eta_{i_2}, \ldots)$, and $\Theta_{\mathbf{U}'}(\mathsf{W}) = (\eta_{j_0}, \eta_{j_1}, \eta_{j_2}, \ldots)$. By definition, we know that $\eta_l =_{\mathbf{U}} \eta_{l+1}$ for all l where $i_k \leq l < i_{k+1}$, and by the assumption $\mathbf{U}' \subseteq \mathbf{U}$ it follows that $\eta_l =_{\mathbf{U}'} \eta_{l+1}$ for all such l. Hence, $(j_0, j_1, j_2, \ldots)$ must be a subsequence of $(i_0, i_1, i_2, \ldots)$ except if there is some $j \in \mathbb{N}$ such that $\eta_l =_{\mathbf{U}'} \eta_{l+1}$ holds for all $l \geq j$. In the latter case, the smallest such j must be one of the i_k, and then we have, again by definition, $\eta_{i_l} =_{\mathbf{U}} \eta_j$ for all $l \geq k$. In either case, the assertion of the lemma follows. △

For two state sequences $\mathsf{W}_1 = (\eta_0^{(1)}, \eta_1^{(1)}, \eta_2^{(1)}, \ldots)$, $\mathsf{W}_2 = (\eta_0^{(2)}, \eta_1^{(2)}, \eta_2^{(2)}, \ldots)$ we let now

$$\mathsf{W}_1 =_{\mathbf{U}} \mathsf{W}_2 \;\Leftrightarrow\; \eta_i^{(1)} =_{\mathbf{U}} \eta_i^{(2)} \text{ for every } i \in \mathbb{N}$$

and define the relation $\simeq_{\mathbf{U}}$, called **U**-*stuttering equivalence* by

$$\mathsf{W}_1 \simeq_{\mathbf{U}} \mathsf{W}_2 \;\Leftrightarrow\; \Theta_{\mathbf{U}}(\mathsf{W}_1) =_{\mathbf{U}} \Theta_{\mathbf{U}}(\mathsf{W}_2).$$

Clearly, $\simeq_{\mathbf{U}}$ is an equivalence relation. The following lemma lists some additional facts about this relation. Adapting some notation from Sect. 2.1, for $\mathsf{W} = (\eta_0, \eta_1, \eta_2, \ldots)$ and $i \in \mathbb{N}$, the sequence $(\eta_i, \eta_{i+1}, \eta_{i+2}, \ldots)$ is denoted by W^i. It is evident from the definitions that if $\vartheta_{\mathbf{U}}^{\mathsf{W}}(i) = k$ and $\overline{\mathsf{W}} = \Theta_{\mathbf{U}}(\mathsf{W}) = (\eta_{i_0}, \eta_{i_1}, \eta_{i_2}, \ldots)$ then

$$\Theta_{\mathbf{U}}(\mathsf{W}^i) = (\eta_{i_k}, \eta_{i_{k+1}}, \eta_{i_{k+2}}, \ldots) = \overline{\mathsf{W}}^k.$$

Lemma 9.3.2. *Let* $\mathsf{W}_1 = (\eta_0^{(1)}, \eta_1^{(1)}, \eta_2^{(1)}, \ldots)$, $\mathsf{W}_2 = (\eta_0^{(2)}, \eta_1^{(2)}, \eta_2^{(2)}, \ldots)$, *and* $\mathsf{W}_1 \simeq_{\mathbf{U}} \mathsf{W}_2$.

a) $\eta_0^{(1)} =_{\mathbf{U}} \eta_0^{(2)}$.
b) If $\mathbf{U}' \subseteq \mathbf{U}$ *then* $\mathsf{W}_1 \simeq_{\mathbf{U}'} \mathsf{W}_2$.
c) For every $i \in \mathbb{N}$ *there is some* $j \in \mathbb{N}$ *such that* $\mathsf{W}_1^i \simeq_{\mathbf{U}} \mathsf{W}_2^j$ *and* $\mathsf{W}_1^{i+1} \simeq_{\mathbf{U}} \mathsf{W}_2^k$ *where* $k = j$ *or* $k = j+1$.

Proof. a) With $\min\{j \in \mathbb{N} \mid \vartheta_{\mathbf{U}}^{\mathsf{W}_1}(j) = 0\} = 0$ we have $\Theta_{\mathbf{U}}(\mathsf{W}_1) = (\eta_0^{(1)}, \ldots)$; in the same way we obtain $\Theta_{\mathbf{U}}(\mathsf{W}_2) = (\eta_0^{(2)}, \ldots)$, and the assumption then implies $\eta_0^{(1)} =_{\mathbf{U}} \eta_0^{(2)}$.

b) Observe first that for any W, W', and $\mathbf{U}$, if $\mathsf{W} =_{\mathbf{U}} \mathsf{W}'$ then $\vartheta_{\mathbf{U}}^{\mathsf{W}} = \vartheta_{\mathbf{U}}^{\mathsf{W}'}$. Now, because $\mathsf{W}_1 \simeq_{\mathbf{U}} \mathsf{W}_2$ we have $\Theta_{\mathbf{U}}(\mathsf{W}_1) =_{\mathbf{U}} \Theta_{\mathbf{U}}(\mathsf{W}_2)$ by definition, and the assumption $\mathbf{U}' \subseteq \mathbf{U}$ implies that $\Theta_{\mathbf{U}}(\mathsf{W}_1) =_{\mathbf{U}'} \Theta_{\mathbf{U}}(\mathsf{W}_2)$. Writing $\overline{\mathsf{W}}_i$ for $\Theta_{\mathbf{U}}(\mathsf{W}_i)$, the observation above shows that $\vartheta_{\mathbf{U}'}^{\overline{\mathsf{W}}_1} = \vartheta_{\mathbf{U}'}^{\overline{\mathsf{W}}_2}$. Together with $\overline{\mathsf{W}}_1 =_{\mathbf{U}'} \overline{\mathsf{W}}_2$ we obtain $\Theta_{\mathbf{U}'}(\overline{\mathsf{W}}_1) =_{\mathbf{U}'} \Theta_{\mathbf{U}'}(\overline{\mathsf{W}}_2)$, and the assertion follows with the help of Lemma 9.3.1.

c) Let $i \in \mathbb{N}$, $k = \vartheta_{\mathbf{U}}^{W_1}(i)$, and $j = \max\{l \in \mathbb{N} \mid \vartheta_{\mathbf{U}}^{W_2}(l) = k\}$. (Note that j is well-defined because the set is non-empty and finite.) Then we have $\vartheta_{\mathbf{U}}^{W_2}(j) = k$ and for $\overline{W}_1 = \Theta_{\mathbf{U}}(W_1)$ and $\overline{W}_2 = \Theta_{\mathbf{U}}(W_2)$ we obtain by the above remark and the assumption that $\Theta_{\mathbf{U}}(W_1^i) = \overline{W}_1^k =_{\mathbf{U}} \overline{W}_2^k = \Theta_{\mathbf{U}}(W_2^j)$, i.e., $W_1^i \simeq_{\mathbf{U}} W_2^j$. If $\vartheta_{\mathbf{U}}^{W_1}(i+1) = \vartheta_{\mathbf{U}}^{W_1}(i) = k$ then we get $W_1^{i+1} \simeq_{\mathbf{U}} W_2^j$ in the same way. Moreover, we have $\vartheta_{\mathbf{U}}^{W_2}(j+1) \neq \vartheta_{\mathbf{U}}^{W_2}(j)$ by the definition of j and therefore $\vartheta_{\mathbf{U}}^{W_2}(j+1) = \vartheta_{\mathbf{U}}^{W_2}(j) + 1 = k+1$. So, if $\vartheta_{\mathbf{U}}^{W_1}(i+1) = \vartheta_{\mathbf{U}}^{W_1}(i) + 1 = k+1$ then $\Theta_{\mathbf{U}}(W_1^{i+1}) = \overline{W}_1^{k+1} =_{\mathbf{U}} \overline{W}_2^{k+1} = \Theta_{\mathbf{U}}(W_2^{j+1})$ again with the same arguments and this means $W_1^{i+1} \simeq_{\mathbf{U}} W_2^{j+1}$. △

Now, following the earlier informal explanations and observing the TLA format of specifications and properties, stuttering invariance of a formula A (of any first-order linear temporal logic) is to mean that, if we evaluate A (with some underlying variable valuation) in the initial states of temporal structures with the same data component and stuttering equivalent state sequences, then these evaluations provide equal truth values. This is formally defined as follows.

Definition. Let $TSIG = (SIG, \mathbf{X}, \mathbf{V})$ be a temporal signature, $\mathcal{L}_{\mathrm{TL}}(TSIG)$ be a (first-order) linear temporal logic language. A formula A of $\mathcal{L}_{\mathrm{TL}}(TSIG)$ is called *stuttering invariant* if

$$\mathsf{K}_0^{(\xi)}(A) = \mathsf{K}_0'^{(\xi)}(A)$$

holds for all variable valuations ξ, and for all temporal structures $\mathsf{K} = (\mathsf{S}, \mathsf{W})$ and $\mathsf{K}' = (\mathsf{S}, \mathsf{W}')$ for $TSIG$ with $\mathsf{W} \simeq_{\mathbf{U}(A)} \mathsf{W}'$ where $\mathbf{U}(A) \subseteq \mathbf{X} \cup \mathbf{V}$ is the set of flexible individual and propositional constants occurring in A.

We formulate now the desired result. It says that all formulas of GTLA, hence all formulas of TLA, are stuttering invariant in the sense already used informally in Sect. 9.2. Proving the theorem we will use an adaption of Lemma 2.1.5 to GTLA; its proof carries over from Sect. 2.1 and is not repeated here.

Theorem 9.3.3. *Every formula of a language $\mathcal{L}_{\mathrm{GTLA}}$ is stuttering invariant.*

Proof. We simultaneously prove for arbitrary temporal structures $\mathsf{K} = (\mathsf{S}, \mathsf{W})$, $\mathsf{W} = (\eta_0, \eta_1, \eta_2, \ldots)$, and $\hat{\mathsf{K}} = (\mathsf{S}, \hat{\mathsf{W}})$, $\hat{\mathsf{W}} = (\hat{\eta}_0, \hat{\eta}_1, \hat{\eta}_2, \ldots)$, and arbitrary variable valuation ξ the assertions

a) if A is a formula and $\mathsf{W} \simeq_{\mathbf{U}(A)} \hat{\mathsf{W}}$ then $\mathsf{K}_0^{(\xi)}(A) = \hat{\mathsf{K}}_0^{(\xi)}(A)$,
b) if A is a pre-formula, $\mathsf{W} \simeq_{\mathbf{U}(A)} \hat{\mathsf{W}}$, and $\mathsf{W}^1 \simeq_{\mathbf{U}(A)} \hat{\mathsf{W}}^1$ then $\mathsf{K}_0^{(\xi)}(A) = \hat{\mathsf{K}}_0^{(\xi)}(A)$

by structural induction on A. Part a) is just the claim of the theorem.

For assertion a) we consider the different cases in the definition of formulas A.

1. A is an atomic formula: By Lemma 9.3.2 a) we have $\eta_0(e) = \hat{\eta}_0(e)$ for every $e \in \mathbf{U}(A)$ from the assumption and this implies $\mathsf{K}_0^{(\xi)}(A) = \hat{\mathsf{K}}_0^{(\xi)}(A)$.
2. $A \equiv$ **false**: Then $\mathsf{K}_0^{(\xi)}(A) = \mathsf{ff} = \hat{\mathsf{K}}_0^{(\xi)}(A)$.

3. $A \equiv B \to C$ with formulas A and B: Then $\mathbf{U}(B) \subseteq \mathbf{U}(A)$ and $\mathbf{U}(C) \subseteq \mathbf{U}(A)$. The assumption implies $\mathsf{W} \simeq_{\mathbf{U}(B)} \hat{\mathsf{W}}$ and $\mathsf{W} \simeq_{\mathbf{U}(C)} \hat{\mathsf{W}}$ by Lemma 9.3.2 b). The induction hypothesis for assertion a) provides $\mathsf{K}_0^{(\xi)}(B) = \hat{\mathsf{K}}_0^{(\xi)}(B)$ and $\mathsf{K}_0^{(\xi)}(C) = \hat{\mathsf{K}}_0^{(\xi)}(C)$, which imply the assertion.
4. $A \equiv \Box[B]_e$ with a pre-formula B: Assume first that $\hat{\mathsf{K}}_0^{(\xi)}(A) = \mathsf{tt}$; we will show that $\mathsf{K}_0^{(\xi)}(A) = \mathsf{tt}$. For an arbitrary $i \in \mathbb{N}$, let j be chosen according to Lemma 9.3.2 c). We get $\mathsf{W}^i \simeq_{\mathbf{U}(A)} \hat{\mathsf{W}}^j$; hence $\eta_i(e) = \hat{\eta}_j(e)$ by Lemma 9.3.2 a). If $\hat{\eta}_{j+1}(e) = \hat{\eta}_j(e)$ or $\mathsf{W}^{i+1} \simeq_{\mathbf{U}(A)} \hat{\mathsf{W}}^j$ then $\eta_{i+1}(e) = \eta_i(e)$, and therefore $\mathsf{K}_i^{(\xi)}([B]_e) = \mathsf{tt}$. Otherwise, again using Lemma 9.3.2 a), it must be the case that $\mathsf{W}^{i+1} \simeq_{\mathbf{U}(A)} \hat{\mathsf{W}}^{j+1}$ and also $\hat{\mathsf{K}}_j^{(\xi)}(B) = \mathsf{tt}$. Since $\mathbf{U}(B) \subseteq \mathbf{U}(A)$ we get $\mathsf{K}_i^{(\xi)}(B) = \hat{\mathsf{K}}_j^{(\xi)}(B) = \mathsf{tt}$ by Lemma 9.3.2 b), the induction hypothesis for assertion b) applied to B, and adapting Lemma 2.1.5. Again, this implies $\mathsf{K}_i^{(\xi)}([B]_e) = \mathsf{tt}$, and since i was chosen arbitrarily, it follows that $\mathsf{K}_0^{(\xi)}(A) = \mathsf{tt}$. Symmetrically we show that $\mathsf{K}_0^{(\xi)}(A) = \mathsf{tt}$ implies $\hat{\mathsf{K}}_0^{(\xi)}(A) = \mathsf{tt}$, which then shows the assertion.
5. $A \equiv \Box B$ with a formula B: Assume first that $\hat{\mathsf{K}}_0^{(\xi)}(A) = \mathsf{tt}$; we will show that $\mathsf{K}_0^{(\xi)}(A) = \mathsf{tt}$. For an arbitrary $i \in \mathbb{N}$, let j again be chosen according to Lemma 9.3.2 c). We have $\mathsf{W}^i \simeq_{\mathbf{U}(A)} \hat{\mathsf{W}}^j$, and with $\mathbf{U}(B) = \mathbf{U}(A)$ we obtain $\mathsf{K}_i^{(\xi)}(B) = \hat{\mathsf{K}}_j^{(\xi)}(B) = \mathsf{tt}$ by the induction hypothesis for assertion a), again adapting Lemma 2.1.5. Since i was chosen arbitrarily, this proves $\mathsf{K}_0^{(\xi)}(A) = \mathsf{tt}$, and the assertion is proved with an analogous argument as in the previous case.
6. $A \equiv \exists x B$ with a formula B: Then $\mathbf{U}(B) = \mathbf{U}(A)$, and the induction hypothesis for assertion a) provides $\mathsf{K}_0^{(\xi')}(B) = \hat{\mathsf{K}}_0^{(\xi')}(B)$ for any valuation ξ', which implies the assertion.

Turning to assertion b) we have to consider the formation rules for pre-formulas.

1. A is an atomic pre-formula: By Lemma 9.3.2 a) we have $\eta_0(e) = \hat{\eta}_0(e)$ and $\eta_1(e) = \hat{\eta}_1(e)$ for every $e \in \mathbf{U}(A)$ from the assumptions and this implies $\mathsf{K}_0^{(\xi)}(A) = \hat{\mathsf{K}}_0^{(\xi)}(A)$.
2. A is a formula: Then the assertion follows immediately from the induction hypothesis for assertion a).
3. $A \equiv \circ B$ with a formula B: Then the assumption $\mathsf{W}^1 \simeq_{\mathbf{U}(A)} \hat{\mathsf{W}}^1$ and the induction hypothesis for assumption a) applied to B imply $\mathsf{K}_1^{(\xi)}(B) = \hat{\mathsf{K}}_1^{(\xi)}(B)$; hence $\mathsf{K}_0^{(\xi)}(A) = \hat{\mathsf{K}}_0^{(\xi)}(A)$.
4. $A \equiv B \to C$ or $A \equiv \exists x B$ with pre-formulas A and B: In these cases the proof runs as for assertion a). △

Let us now illustrate the "logical contents" of GTLA by noting that the relationship

$$\mathcal{F} \cup \{A\} \models B \Leftrightarrow \mathcal{F} \models \Box A \to B \qquad \text{if } A \text{ is closed}$$

holds as in FOLTL, and by giving some valid formulas including a few proofs. First of all, it is clear that any valid formula of FOLTL which is a GTLA formula is now valid as well. Particularly the laws (T1)–(T42) from Sects. 2.2 and 5.1 are also laws of GTLA whenever they are formulas at all. Some examples are:

(T9) $\Diamond\Box A \rightarrow \Box\Diamond A$,
(T18) $\Box(A \wedge B) \leftrightarrow \Box A \wedge \Box B$,
(T41) $\exists x \Diamond A \leftrightarrow \Diamond \exists x A$.

Other laws of FOLTL can be "translated" to valid GTLA formulas in an obvious way, e.g.:

($\mathrm{T1}_{GTLA}$) $\Box[\neg\bigcirc A \leftrightarrow \bigcirc\neg A]_e$,
($\mathrm{T14}_{GTLA}$) $\Box[\bigcirc(A \rightarrow B) \leftrightarrow \bigcirc A \rightarrow \bigcirc B]_e$,
($\mathrm{T28}_{GTLA}$) $\Box[\Box A \leftrightarrow A \wedge \bigcirc\Box A]_e$,
($\mathrm{T39}_{GTLA}$) $\Box[\exists x \bigcirc A \leftrightarrow \bigcirc\exists x A]_e$

as modifications of (T1), (T14), (T28), and (T39).

Proof of ($\mathrm{T14}_{GTLA}$). For arbitrary K, i, ξ, and $j \geq i$ we have

$$\mathsf{K}_j^{(\xi)}(\bigcirc(A \rightarrow B)) = \mathrm{tt} \Leftrightarrow \mathsf{K}_j^{(\xi)}(\bigcirc A \rightarrow \bigcirc B) = \mathrm{tt}$$

as in the proof of (T14) in Sect. 2.2. This implies

$$\mathsf{K}_j^{(\xi)}(\bigcirc(A \rightarrow B)) \leftrightarrow \bigcirc A \rightarrow \bigcirc B) = \mathrm{tt};$$

hence

$$\mathsf{K}_i^{(\xi)}(\Box[\bigcirc(A \rightarrow B) \leftrightarrow \bigcirc A \rightarrow \bigcirc B]_e) = \mathrm{tt}. \qquad \triangle$$

The latter laws use the characteristic GTLA operator $\Box[\_]_e$. The following list shows some more valid formulas concerning this construction.

(GT1) $\Box\big[[A]_e \rightarrow A\big]_e$,
(GT2) $\Box A \rightarrow \Box[\bigcirc A]_e$,
(GT3) $\Box\big[[A]_e\big]_e \leftrightarrow \Box[A]_e$,
(GT4) $\Box\big[\Box[A]_{e_1} \rightarrow [A]_{e_1}\big]_{e_2}$,
(GT5) $\Box[A]_{e_1} \rightarrow \Box\big[[A]_{e_1}\big]_{e_2}$,
(GT6) $\Box\big[[A]_{e_1}\big]_{e_2} \leftrightarrow \Box\big[[A]_{e_2}\big]_{e_1}$.

Proof of (GT4). For arbitrary K, i, ξ, and $j \geq i$ we have

$$\begin{aligned}\mathsf{K}_j^{(\xi)}(\Box[A]_{e_1}) = \mathrm{tt} &\Rightarrow \mathsf{K}_k^{(\xi)}(A) = \mathrm{tt} \text{ or } \mathsf{K}_{k+1}^{(\xi)}(e_1) = \mathsf{K}_k^{(\xi)}(e_1) \text{ for every } k \geq j\\ &\Rightarrow \mathsf{K}_j^{(\xi)}(A) = \mathrm{tt} \text{ or } \mathsf{K}_{j+1}^{(\xi)}(e_1) = \mathsf{K}_j^{(\xi)}(e_1)\\ &\Rightarrow \mathsf{K}_j^{(\xi)}([A]_{e_1}) = \mathrm{tt};\end{aligned}$$

thus

$$\mathsf{K}_j^{(\xi)}(\Box[A]_{e_1} \to [A]_{e_1}) = \mathsf{tt}$$

and therefore

$$\mathsf{K}_i^{(\xi)}(\Box\big[\Box[A]_{e_1} \to [A]_{e_1}\big]_{e_2}) = \mathsf{tt}. \qquad \triangle$$

Finally we turn now to an axiomatization of GTLA. We begin with a formal system Σ_{pGTLA} as follows. (Tautologically valid GTLA formulas are defined as earlier and for pre-formulas this notion can be adopted just as well.)

Axioms

(taut) All tautologically valid formulas,
(taut_{pf}) $\Box[A]_e$ if A is a tautologically valid pre-formula,
(gtla1) $\Box A \to A$,
(gtla2) $\Box A \to \Box[A]_e$,
(gtla3) $\Box A \to \Box[\circ\Box A]_e$,
(gtla4) $\Box[A \to B]_e \to (\Box[A]_e \to \Box[B]_e)$,
(gtla5) $\Box[e' \neq e]_e$,
(gtla6) $\Box[\neg\circ A \leftrightarrow \circ\neg A]_e$,
(gtla7) $\Box[\circ(A \to B) \to (\circ A \to \circ B)]_e$,
(gtla8) $\Box\big[\Box[A]_{e_1} \to [A]_{e_1}\big]_{e_2}$,
(gtla9) $\Box[A]_{e_1} \to \Box\big[\circ\Box[A]_{e_1}\big]_{e_2}$,
(gtla10) $\Box\big[[A]_{e_1} \land \circ\Box[A]_{e_1} \;\to\; \Box[A]_{e_1}\big]_{e_2}$,
(gtla11) $\Box\big[\circ\Box A \to \Box[\circ A]_{e_1}\big]_{e_2}$.

Rules

(mp) $A, A \to B \vdash B$,
(alw) $A \vdash \Box A$,
(ind_{pf}) $A \to B, \Box[A \to \circ A]_{\mathsf{U}(A)} \vdash A \to \Box B$.

Σ_{pGTLA} is a sound and weakly complete axiomatization of the "propositional fragment" of GTLA. Referring to our introductory discussion of this section we observe that (ind_{pf}) is now an appropriate adaption of the (normal semantics) induction rule (ind) of LTL. Some useful derived rules are:

(mp_{pf}) $\Box[A]_e, \Box[A \to B]_e \vdash \Box[B]_e$,
(ch_{pf}) $\Box[A \to B]_e, \Box[B \to C]_e \vdash \Box[A \to C]_e$,
(alw_{pf}) $A \vdash \Box[A]_e$.

We give, as an example, a derivation of (mp_{pf}).

Derivation of (mp_{pf}).

(1)	$\Box[A]_e$	assumption
(2)	$\Box[A \to B]_e$	assumption
(3)	$\Box[A \to B]_e \to (\Box[A]_e \to \Box[B]_e)$	(gtla4)
(4)	$\Box[A]_e \to \Box[B]_e$	(mp),(2),(3)
(5)	$\Box[B]_e$	(mp),(1),(4) $\triangle$

As an example for the usage of these additional rules we show a simple derivation of the law (GT1) given above.

Derivation of (GT1).

(1)	$\Box[e' \neq e]_e$	(gtla5)
(2)	$\Box\big[e' \neq e \to ([A]_e \to A)\big]_e$	(taut$_{pf}$)
(3)	$\Box\big[[A]_e \to A\big]_e$	(mp$_{pf}$),(1),(2) △

Most of the axioms and rules of Σ_{pGTLA} are appropriate transcriptions from Σ_{LTL}. An extension of Σ_{pGTLA} to a formal system Σ_{GTLA} for the full first-order GTLA is obtained by adding analogous adaptions of FOLTL axioms and rules. We give only the following obvious examples concerning the existential quantifier.

Additional axioms

(gtla12) $A_x(t) \;\to\; \exists x A$ if t is substitutable for x in A,
(gtla13) $\Box[A_x(t) \;\to\; \exists x A]_e$ if t is substitutable for x in A,
(gtla14) $\Box[\bigcirc\exists x A \;\to\; \exists x \bigcirc A]_e$.

Additional rules

(par) $A \to B \vdash \exists x A \to B$ if there is no free occurrence of x in B,
(par$_{pf}$) $\Box[A \to B]_e \vdash \Box[\exists x A \to B]_e$ if there is no free occurrence of x in B.

This formal system shows that the axiomatization of GTLA can be solved in a satisfactory way (from the "purely logical" point of view; practical aspects will be discussed in the next section). According to the introductory comments we should still remark how it can be applied to TLA. Of course, because of the different semantics, an arbitrary TLA consequence relationship

$$\mathcal{F} \overset{0}{\models} A$$

cannot be proved in general by deriving A from $\mathcal{F}$ in Σ_{GTLA}. However, universal validity of formulas is independent of the chosen semantics as in LTL (cf. Theorem 2.6.4), so we have at least

$$\vdash_{\Sigma_{\mathrm{GTLA}}} A \;\Rightarrow\; \overset{0}{\models} A$$

for every TLA formula A. Furthermore, if $\mathcal{F} = \{A_1, \ldots, A_n\}$ is finite then we have

$$\mathcal{F} \overset{0}{\models} A \;\Leftrightarrow\; \overset{0}{\models} A_1 \wedge \ldots \wedge A_n \to A$$

in TLA (again as in Sect. 2.6, cf. Theorem 2.6.3); so we obtain

$$\vdash_{\Sigma_{\mathrm{GTLA}}} A_1 \wedge \ldots \wedge A_n \to A \;\;\Rightarrow\;\; A_1, \ldots, A_n \overset{0}{\models} A$$

for TLA formulas $A_1, \ldots, A_n, A$.

A similar use of Σ_{GTLA} with even infinite $\mathcal{F}$ will be shown in the following section. Summarizing, we find that in many applications Σ_{GTLA} is an appropriate tool for deriving also TLA consequence relationships.

9.4 System Verification with GTLA

The idea of deductive verification of a property F_{prop} of an STS Γ, as studied in Chaps. 7 and 8, is to derive F_{prop} from the set of specification axioms $\mathcal{A}_\Gamma$ of Γ within some formal system. Expressed semantically this means to show the consequence relationship

$$(*) \qquad \mathcal{A}_\Gamma \vDash F_{prop}$$

(of normal semantics). If we now use the standard form of TLA (or GTLA) specifications as introduced in Sect. 9.2 then $\mathcal{A}_\Gamma$ consists of the set $\mathcal{A}_{data}$ of the relevant data axioms (data_Γ) and the formula

$$F_\Gamma \equiv start_\Gamma \wedge \Box[A_\Gamma]_{\mathrm{U}} \wedge fair_\Gamma$$

(in its general form with initial condition and fairness) which is to be understood with initial validity semantics. This means that F_Γ may be assumed to be initially valid in every $\mathsf{K} \in \mathcal{C}_\Gamma$ where

$$\mathcal{C}_\Gamma = \{\mathsf{K} = (\mathsf{S}_\Gamma, \mathsf{W}_\Gamma) \mid \mathsf{W}_\Gamma \text{ is an execution sequence of } \Gamma\}$$

as in Sect. 6.2.

Modifying the terminology of Sect.7.1, let us now call a property (specified by a formula) F_{iprop} a valid *initial property* of Γ if F_{iprop} is initially valid in every $\mathsf{K} \in \mathcal{C}_\Gamma$. Clearly, any property F_{prop} of Γ considered with respect to normal semantics can be reformulated as the initial property $\Box F_{prop}$.

Formulating system properties as initial properties the verification task $(*)$ becomes to show

$$\vDash_{\mathsf{K}} \mathcal{A}_{data}, \overset{0}{\vDash}_{\mathsf{K}} F_\Gamma \Rightarrow \overset{0}{\vDash}_{\mathsf{K}} F_{iprop}$$

(for arbitrary K). Writing $\Box\mathcal{A}_{data}$ for the formula set $\{\Box A \mid A \in \mathcal{A}_{data}\}$ we have $\vDash_{\mathsf{K}} \mathcal{A}_{data} \Leftrightarrow \overset{0}{\vDash}_{\mathsf{K}} \Box\mathcal{A}_{data}$ by Lemma 2.6.1 b); so this amounts to

$$\Box\mathcal{A}_{data} \cup \{F_\Gamma\} \overset{0}{\vDash} F_{iprop}$$

and immediately leads to another verification format which, in fact, is typically used for (G)TLA verifications: by the Theorems 2.6.3 and 2.6.2 b), the latter initial consequence relationship is equivalent to

$$\mathcal{A}_{data} \vDash F_\Gamma \to F_{iprop}$$

which means that $F_\Gamma \to F_{iprop}$ is S_Γ-valid in the sense of Sect. 5.1. (Note that the results from Sect. 2.6 used here can easily be transferred.)

As mentioned already in Sect. 9.1 the verification of implementation correctness should be just a particular instance of the general verification problem. In fact, if F_Γ is the specification of a refinement of a system Γ' specified by $F_{\Gamma'}$ then

$$F_\Gamma \to F_{\Gamma'}$$

is just the adequate correctness formula.

To summarize, apart from the description of system properties as initial properties we need not care any more about the different semantics. The verification can be carried out by deriving

$$\mathcal{A}_{data} \vdash F_\Gamma \to F_{iprop}$$

within, e.g., the formal system Σ_{GTLA}.

We illustrate the described method by two examples. Firstly we now formally verify the implementation correctness of the counter system discussed in Sects. 9.1 and 9.2. Taking the system without an initial condition and ignoring any kind of fairness, the "high level" specification is given by the formula

$$F_{count} \equiv \Box[A_{\Gamma_{count}}]_{on,c}$$

(cf. Sect. 9.2) where

$$A_{\Gamma_{count}} \equiv A_{on} \lor A_{off} \lor A_c \lor A_p$$

and

$$\begin{aligned}
A_{on} &\equiv \neg on \land on' \land c' = 0,\\
A_{off} &\equiv on \land \neg on' \land c' = c,\\
A_c &\equiv on \land on' \land c' = c + 1,\\
A_p &\equiv \neg on \land \neg on' \land c' = c.
\end{aligned}$$

The implementation of Γ_{count} is analogously given by

$$F_{implcount} \equiv \Box[A_{\Gamma_{implcount}}]_{on,c,dec}$$

where

$$\begin{aligned}
A_{\Gamma_{implcount}} &\equiv A_{on} \lor A_{off} \lor B_c \lor A_p,\\
B_c &\equiv on \land on' \land dec' = (dec + 1) \bmod 10 \land\\
&\qquad (dec = 9 \to c' = c + 1) \land\\
&\qquad (dec \neq 9 \to c' = c).
\end{aligned}$$

The implementation correctness is expressed by

$$F_{implcount} \to F_{count}$$

and is easily derived as follows:

(1)	$\Box[A_{\Gamma_{implcount}} \to [A_{\Gamma_{count}}]_{on}]_{on}$	(taut_{pf})
(2)	$\Box[A_{\Gamma_{implcount}}]_{on} \to \Box[[A_{\Gamma_{count}}]_{on}]_{on}$	(mp),(gtla4),(1)
(3)	$\Box[A_{\Gamma_{implcount}}]_{on} \to \Box[A_{\Gamma_{count}}]_{on}$	(prop), (GT3),(2)
(4)	$\Box[A_{\Gamma_{implcount}} \to [A_{\Gamma_{count}}]_c]_c$	(taut_{pf})
(5)	$\Box[A_{\Gamma_{implcount}}]_c \to \Box[[A_{\Gamma_{count}}]_c]_c$	(mp),(gtla4),(4)
(6)	$\Box[A_{\Gamma_{implcount}}]_c \to \Box[A_{\Gamma_{count}}]_c$	(prop), (GT3),(5)
(7)	$\Box[A_{\Gamma_{implcount}}]_{on,c} \to F_{count}$	(prop),(3),(6)
(8)	$F_{implcount} \to F_{count}$	(prop),(7)

(The rule (prop) is defined and used as in earlier chapters. Its justification by Theorem 2.3.2 carries over as well.)

The substantial point of this proof is the fact that the two pre-formulas

$$A_{\Gamma_{implcount}} \rightarrow [A_{\Gamma_{count}}]_{on},$$
$$A_{\Gamma_{implcount}} \rightarrow [A_{\Gamma_{count}}]_{c}$$

are tautologically valid. They provide the lines (1) and (4) in the derivation and are then manipulated within formulas of the form $\Box[\_]_{\_}$. This observation holds quite generally: facts (and arguments) concerned with pre-formulas have to be "encoded" within formulas since only formulas are handled by the formal system Σ_{GTLA}. Coming back to a remark made already in the previous section we thus find that Σ_{GTLA} is a satisfactory solution of the axiomatization problem of (G)TLA, but it might be rather cumbersome to use it in practice. This could particularly be the case if the arguments are really data dependent and not only the axiom (taut$_{pf}$) – as in the present example – but more sophisticated first-order reasoning is needed.

If we are prepared to trade the "logical purism" for a pragmatic approach to deductive system verification, we can instead carry out the formal proof within full first-order logic, i.e., within the formal system Σ_{FOLTL} where we can handle both pre-formulas and formulas of GTLA simply as FOLTL formulas. Of course, we continue considering $[A]_e$ as an abbreviation for $A \vee e' = e$ and, hence, $\Box[A]_e$ simply as $\Box(A \vee e' = e)$. The following trivial lemma justifies this method.

Lemma 9.4.1. *Let $\mathcal{F}$ be a set of GTLA formulas and let A be a GTLA formula. If $\mathcal{F} \vdash_{\Sigma_{\mathrm{FOLTL}}} A$ then $\mathcal{F} \models A$ with respect to the GTLA semantics.*

Proof. By Theorem 5.2.1, $\mathcal{F} \vdash_{\Sigma_{\mathrm{FOLTL}}} A$ implies $\mathcal{F} \models A$ within FOLTL. According to the definition of GTLA as a sublogic of FOLTL we can immediately conclude that $\mathcal{F} \models A$ holds with respect to the GTLA semantics as well. △

Applying this approach in our example above we could verify the implementation correctness by deriving $F_{implcount} \rightarrow F_{count}$ within Σ_{FOLTL} as follows.

(1)	$A_{\Gamma_{implcount}} \rightarrow [A_{\Gamma_{count}}]_{on}$	(taut)
(2)	$\Box[A_{\Gamma_{implcount}}]_{on} \rightarrow \Box[A_{\Gamma_{count}}]_{on}$	(T22),(1)
(3)	$A_{\Gamma_{implcount}} \rightarrow [A_{\Gamma_{count}}]_{c}$	(taut)
(4)	$\Box[A_{\Gamma_{implcount}}]_{c} \rightarrow \Box[A_{\Gamma_{count}}]_{c}$	(T22),(3)
(5)	$\Box[A_{\Gamma_{implcount}}]_{on,c} \rightarrow F_{count}$	(prop),(2),(4)
(6)	$F_{implcount} \rightarrow F_{count}$	(prop),(5)

It is easy to see that the "encoded" steps (1)–(3) and (4)–(6) in the former Σ_{GTLA} derivation are now "directly" performed in steps (1)–(2) and (3)–(4).

Our second verification example deals with Peterson's algorithm as specified in Sect. 9.3 by the formula $F_{\Pi_{Pet}}$. We prove the mutual exclusion property which was already formulated as $\Box\neg(at\,\alpha_3 \wedge at\,\beta_3)$ in Sect. 8.4. This is also a suitable initial property formula, so we have to derive

$$F_{\Pi_{Pet}} \rightarrow \Box\neg(at\,\alpha_3 \wedge at\,\beta_3).$$

We perform this proof now only with the second method and derive the formula within Σ_{FOLTL}. Actually, we may follow the main proof idea from the corresponding derivation in Sect. 8.4 and adjust it to the present context. So let

$$\begin{aligned} B_1 &\equiv (at\{\alpha_0,\alpha_1\} \leftrightarrow a_1 = 0) \wedge (at\{\alpha_2,\alpha_3,\alpha_4\} \leftrightarrow a_1 = 1), \\ B_2 &\equiv (at\{\beta_0,\beta_1\} \leftrightarrow a_2 = 0) \wedge (at\{\beta_2,\beta_3,\beta_4\} \leftrightarrow a_2 = 1), \\ B_3 &\equiv at\,\alpha_3 \rightarrow a_2 = 0 \vee c = 2, \\ B_4 &\equiv at\,\beta_3 \rightarrow a_1 = 0 \vee c = 1, \\ B &\equiv B_1 \wedge B_2 \wedge B_3 \wedge B_4 \end{aligned}$$

where the notation $at\,L$ for $L \subseteq Lab_{Pet}$ is used as before. Structuring the proof similarly as in Sect. 8.4 (observe only some renaming) we show:

(a1) $A_\lambda \wedge B \rightarrow \bigcirc B$ for every $\lambda \in Lab_{Pet}$.
(a2) $F_{\Pi_{Pet}} \rightarrow \Box B$.

Derivation of (a1) for $\lambda = \alpha_0$.

(1)	$A_{\alpha_0} \wedge B_2 \rightarrow \bigcirc B_2$	(Π)
(2)	$A_{\alpha_0} \wedge B \rightarrow at\,\alpha_0 \wedge a_1 = 0 \wedge \bigcirc(at\,\alpha_1 \wedge a_1 = 0)$	(Π)
(3)	$A_{\alpha_0} \wedge B \rightarrow \bigcirc B$	(1),(2) △

(We write again (Π) to indicate the application of the specification formulas.) The derivation of (a1) for the other cases for λ runs along the same line by transferring the corresponding steps in the derivation in Sect. 8.4.

Derivation of (a2).

(1)	$start_{\Pi_{Pet}} \rightarrow B$	(Π)
(2)	$F_{\Pi_{Pet}} \rightarrow \Box[A_{\Pi_{Pet}}]_{\mathbf{U}_{Pet}} \wedge B$	(1)
(3)	$A_{\Pi_{Pet}} \wedge B \rightarrow \bigcirc B$	(a1)
(4)	$[A_{\Pi_{Pet}}]_{\mathbf{U}_{Pet}} \wedge B \rightarrow \bigcirc B$	(3)
(5)	$\Box[A_{\Pi_{Pet}}]_{\mathbf{U}_{Pet}} \wedge B \rightarrow \bigcirc(\Box[A_{\Pi_{Pet}}]_{\mathbf{U}_{Pet}} \wedge B)$	(4)
(6)	$F_{\Pi_{Pet}} \rightarrow \Box(\Box[A_{\Pi_{Pet}}]_{\mathbf{U}_{Pet}} \wedge B)$	(ind2),(2),(5)
(7)	$F_{\Pi_{Pet}} \rightarrow \Box B$	(6) △

Now the formula

$$B \rightarrow \neg(at\,\alpha_3 \wedge at\,\beta_3)$$

can be derived exactly as in Sect. 8.4 and from this and (a2) the mutual exclusion property

$$F_{\Pi_{Pet}} \rightarrow \Box\neg(at\,\alpha_3 \wedge at\,\beta_3)$$

follows immediately.

This derivation is based on the induction rule (ind2) of FOLTL. We still remark that we could also introduce specially tailored *invariant rules* like those given in Sect. 7.2, e.g, a rule (invstart$'_\Gamma$) $\quad start_\Gamma \to B,\, A_\lambda \land B \to \circ B$ for every $\lambda \in \Lambda \vdash F_\Gamma \to \Box B$

where $F_\Gamma \equiv start_\Gamma \land \Box[A_\Gamma]_{\mathbf{U}} \land fair_\Gamma$ with $A_\Gamma \equiv \bigvee_{\lambda\in\Lambda} A_\lambda$, and B contains no temporal operators and no flexible constants not contained in $\mathbf{U}$. With this rule (the derivation of which is easy to extract from the above proof), the derivation of (a2) could be given in the form

(1)	$start_{\Pi_{Pet}} \to B$	(Π)
(2)	$A_\lambda \land B \to \circ B$ for every $\lambda \in Lab_{Pet}$	(a1)
(3)	$F_{\Pi_{Pet}} \to \Box B$	(invstart'),(1),(2)

which then directly reflects the corresponding proof part in Sect. 8.4.

9.5 Hiding of Internal System Variables

We have stated in Sect. 9.2 that TLA system specifications are usually written in the form

$$F_\Gamma \equiv start_\Gamma \land \Box[A_\Gamma]_{\mathbf{U}} \land fair_\Gamma .$$

The formula F_Γ describes all possible executions of a system; the "level of detail" of this specification is determined by the underlying temporal signature $TSIG$. From a computer science perspective, F_Γ is likely to "reveal too much information" in the sense that it does not distinguish between the internal details of a system and its external interface. Continuing the running example of the counter, imagine that internally some elementary "tick" events are counted but that only every tenth tick is to be displayed externally. A specification of such a device (still with the ability to switch it on or off, and ignoring fairness conditions for a moment) is given by the formula

$$F_{implcount}$$

defined in Sect. 9.4 as $\Box[A_{\Gamma_{implcount}}]_{on,c,dec}$, except that this formula does not make any difference between the "internal" counter dec and the "external" display c. Taking into account this distinction, the specification should really express that

> "there exists an internal system variable dec behaving as given by $F_{implcount}$".

Technically this suggests we *hide* the internal system variable dec by existentially quantifying "over it". The specification would therefore be written in the form

$$F_{extimplcount} \equiv \exists dec\, F_{implcount} ,$$

thus restricting the "visible" system variables (that occur "free"in the specification) to just on and c.

Turning to refinement, we have shown in Sect. 9.4 that the counter with decimals is a correct refinement of the counter specification F_{count}, formally expressed as

$F_{implcount} \to F_{count}.$

Because the variable *dec* does not occur in F_{count}, it is easy to see (and confirmed by proof rules for existential quantification) that the implication

$F_{extimplcount} \to F_{count}$

therefore holds as well. In other words, the specification $F_{extimplcount}$ with an "invisible" decimal is a correct implementation of the high-level counter specification.

For this example, we may indeed expect the two specifications F_{count} and $F_{extimplcount}$ of the counter to be indistinguishable, and therefore expect that the implication

$F_{count} \to F_{extimplcount}$

holds as well: the free variables of the formula $F_{extimplcount}$ are just those of the formula F_{count}, and they can change in the same ways. An external observer should not be able to tell if the counter display is derived from an invisible tick counter.

But consider now an execution sequence of the form

$[\mathsf{tt}, 16] \longrightarrow [\mathsf{tt}, 17] \longrightarrow \ldots \longrightarrow [\mathsf{tt}, 17] \longrightarrow [\mathsf{tt}, 18] \longrightarrow \ldots$

with a number k of stuttering steps $[\mathsf{tt}, 17] \longrightarrow [\mathsf{tt}, 17]$. For every k, F_{count} is true in the state denoted by $[\mathsf{tt}, 16]$. The formula $\exists dec\, F_{implcount}$ is also true in this state if $k \geq 9$; however, for $k < 9$ this is not the case. Take, e.g., the sequence

$[\mathsf{tt}, 16] \longrightarrow [\mathsf{tt}, 17] \longrightarrow [\mathsf{tt}, 17] \longrightarrow [\mathsf{tt}, 18] \longrightarrow \ldots$

with $k = 1$. It is not possible to find a sequence of values of *dec* which make $F_{implcount}$ true: such a sequence must associate $dec = 9$ with the state $[\mathsf{tt}, 16]$, $dec = 0$ and $dec = 1$ with the next two states, and then there is no possible value of *dec* in the state $[\mathsf{tt}, 18]$.

The essential reason for this fact is again that the formula $\exists dec\, F_{implcount}$ is not stuttering invariant. In Sect. 9.1, we were able to enforce stuttering invariance by restricting the temporal logic FOLTL to a syntactically identified subset TLA. In the present situation, the problem is due to the semantics of quantification, which can result in $\exists x F$ being stuttering sensitive even if F is stuttering invariant. The solution is to introduce a new operator of existential quantification whose semantics is defined in a way that guarantees stuttering invariance.

For this purpose, we assume an additional set $\mathcal{X}^{fl} = \bigcup_{s \in \mathbf{S}} \mathcal{X}^{fl}_s$ of flexible individual variables, just as in Sect. 5.6 for FOLTL. We also assume a set $\mathcal{V}^{fl}$ of flexible propositional variables, in analogy to the language $\mathcal{L}^{\mathrm{q}}_{\mathrm{LTL}}$ in Sect. 3.3 (where the corresponding set was denoted by $\mathcal{V}$). A language $\mathcal{L}^{\mathrm{q}}_{\mathrm{GTLA}}(TSIG)$ of the logic GTLA+q is obtained as the extension of some language $\mathcal{L}_{\mathrm{GTLA}}(TSIG)$ of GTLA by the sets $\mathcal{X}^{fl}$ and $\mathcal{V}^{fl}$, a new existential quantifier denoted by $\boldsymbol{\exists}$, and by adding the formation rule

- If A is a formula and $w \in \mathcal{X}^{fl} \cup \mathcal{V}^{fl}$ is a flexible propositional or individual variable then $\boldsymbol{\exists} w A$ is a formula to the syntactical definition of GTLA. For defining the semantics of $\boldsymbol{\exists}$ we recall the relation $\sim_w$ defined in Sects. 3.3 and 5.6 such that, for two flexible variable valuations Ξ and Ξ', $\Xi \sim_w \Xi'$ informally means that Ξ and Ξ' have "pointwise equal" values for all flexible variables except possibly w. This relation was used to define the semantics of the (flexible) quantifier $\exists$ by

$$\mathsf{K}_i^{(\xi,\Xi)}(\exists w A) = \mathsf{tt} \Leftrightarrow \text{ there is a } \Xi' \text{ such that } \Xi \sim_w \Xi' \text{ and } \mathsf{K}_i^{(\xi,\Xi')}(A) = \mathsf{tt}.$$

For the operator $\boldsymbol{\exists}$ we modify this definition in the following way. We first extend the stuttering notions from Sect. 9.3 to the new kind of language. For any temporal structure $\mathsf{K} = (\mathsf{S}, \mathsf{W})$ for $TSIG$, $\mathsf{W} = (\eta_0, \eta_1, \eta_2, \ldots)$, and any flexible variable valuation $\Xi = (\xi_0, \xi_1, \xi_2, \ldots)$ for $\mathcal{X}^{fl} \cup \mathcal{V}^{fl}$, the "union" $\mathsf{W} \cup \Xi$ is the sequence $(\eta_0 \cup \xi_0, \eta_1 \cup \xi_1, \eta_2 \cup \xi_2, \ldots)$ of mappings

$$\eta_i \cup \xi_i : \mathbf{X} \cup \mathbf{V} \cup \mathcal{X}^{fl} \cup \mathcal{V}^{fl} \to |\mathsf{S}| \cup \{\mathsf{ff}, \mathsf{tt}\}$$

where

$$\begin{aligned} \eta_i \cup \xi_i(e) &= \eta_i(e) && \text{for } e \in \mathbf{X} \cup \mathbf{V}, \\ \eta_i \cup \xi_i(w) &= \xi_i(w) && \text{for } w \in \mathcal{X}^{fl} \cup \mathcal{V}^{fl}. \end{aligned}$$

We adopt, just by replacing state sequences W by sequences $\mathsf{W} \cup \Xi$, the definitions from Sect. 9.3, particularly

$$\Theta_{\mathbf{U}}(\mathsf{W} \cup \Xi) = (\eta_{i_0} \cup \xi_{i_0}, \eta_{i_1} \cup \xi_{i_1}, \eta_{i_2} \cup \xi_{i_2}, \ldots)$$

for any $\mathbf{U} \subseteq \mathbf{X} \cup \mathbf{V} \cup \mathcal{X}^{fl} \cup \mathcal{V}^{fl}$ and

$$\mathsf{W}_1 \cup \Xi_1 \simeq_{\mathbf{U}} \mathsf{W}_2 \cup \Xi_2 \Leftrightarrow \Theta_{\mathbf{U}}(\mathsf{W}_1 \cup \Xi_1) =_{\mathbf{U}} \Theta_{\mathbf{U}}(\mathsf{W}_2 \cup \Xi_2).$$

Now the semantics of $\boldsymbol{\exists}$ is given by

$$\begin{aligned} \mathsf{K}_i^{(\xi,\Xi)}(\boldsymbol{\exists} w A) = \mathsf{tt} \Leftrightarrow \; & \text{there are } \mathsf{K}' = (\mathsf{S}, \mathsf{W}'), \Xi', \text{ and } \Xi'' \text{ such that} \\ & \mathsf{W} \cup \Xi \simeq_{\mathbf{U}(A)} \mathsf{W}' \cup \Xi', \; \Xi' \sim_w \Xi'', \text{ and} \\ & \mathsf{K}_i'^{(\xi,\Xi'')}(A) = \mathsf{tt} \end{aligned}$$

for $\mathsf{K} = (\mathsf{S}, \mathsf{W})$. Comparing this clause with the one for $\exists$, it roughly means that no longer Ξ itself, but a "stuttering equivalent version" of Ξ has to be "equal up to w" to an appropriate valuation (now Ξ'').

Every formula of the new shape is indeed stuttering invariant again where this notion is now redefined as follows:

Definition. Let $TSIG = (SIG, \mathbf{X}, \mathbf{V})$ be a temporal signature. A formula A of $\mathcal{L}^{\mathrm{q}}_{\mathrm{GTLA}}(TSIG)$ is called *stuttering invariant* if

$$\mathsf{K}_0^{(\xi,\Xi)}(A) = \mathsf{K}_0'^{(\xi,\Xi')}(A)$$

holds for all variable valuations ξ, temporal structures $\mathsf{K} = (\mathsf{S}, \mathsf{W})$ and $\mathsf{K}' = (\mathsf{S}, \mathsf{W}')$ for $TSIG$, and flexible variable valuations Ξ and Ξ' with $\mathsf{W} \cup \Xi \simeq_{\mathbf{U}(A)} \mathsf{W}' \cup \Xi'$ where $\mathbf{U}(A) \subseteq \mathbf{X} \cup \mathbf{V} \cup \mathcal{X}^{fl} \cup \mathcal{V}^{fl}$ is the set of flexible individual and propositional constants and variables occurring free in A.

Theorem 9.5.1. *Every formula of a language $\mathcal{L}^{q}_{\mathrm{GTLA}}$ is stuttering invariant.*

Proof. The proof of Theorem 9.3.3 can be adapted to the present situation (with the assumption $\mathsf{W} \cup \Xi \simeq_{\mathbf{U}(A)} \hat{\mathsf{W}} \cup \hat{\Xi}$). We only have to extend it for the additional case of a formula $A \equiv \exists w B$. So, let $\mathsf{K}_0^{(\xi,\Xi)}(A) = \mathsf{tt}$. Then there are $\mathsf{K}' = (\mathsf{S}, \mathsf{W}')$, Ξ', and Ξ'' such that $\mathsf{W} \cup \Xi \simeq_{\mathbf{U}(A)} \mathsf{W}' \cup \Xi'$, $\Xi' \sim_w \Xi''$, and $\mathsf{K}'^{(\xi,\Xi'')}(B) = \mathsf{tt}$. Then we also have $\hat{\mathsf{W}} \cup \hat{\Xi} \simeq_{\mathbf{U}(A)} \mathsf{W}' \cup \Xi'$ by the assumption and this immediately implies $\hat{\mathsf{K}}_0^{(\xi,\hat{\Xi})}(A) = \mathsf{tt}$. The opposite direction follows by symmetry, so we obtain $\mathsf{K}_0^{(\xi,\Xi)}(A) = \hat{\mathsf{K}}_0^{(\xi,\hat{\Xi})}(A)$. △

GTLA+q can be axiomatized, even in a weakly complete way with respect to its propositional fragment. We do not go into the details, we only list

- $A_w(B) \rightarrow \exists w A$,
- $A_w(t) \rightarrow \exists w A$,
- $\Diamond \exists w A \rightarrow \exists w \Diamond A$,
- $\Diamond \langle \exists w A \rangle_e \rightarrow \exists w \Diamond \langle A \rangle_e$,
- $\Diamond \langle A \wedge \bigcirc \exists w B \rangle_e \rightarrow \exists w \Diamond \langle A \wedge \bigcirc B \rangle_e$ if there is no free occurrence of w in A

as some examples of helpful axioms and note that the particularization rule

- $A \rightarrow B \vdash \exists w A \rightarrow B$ if there is no free occurrence of w in B

can be taken in its usual form for $\exists$ as well.

Coming back to our example, the application of the new operator in the announced way works as desired: we obtain that

$$F_{count} \rightarrow \exists dec\ F_{implcount}$$

is N-valid. In this formula, *dec* is now in fact a flexible individual variable and we assume the priming notation of Sect. 5.4 to be extended to flexible variables in an obvious way. To see the N-validity of this implication formally, let $\mathsf{K} = (\mathsf{N}, \mathsf{W})$ be a temporal structure and η_i be a state of W. Assume $\mathsf{K}_i^{(\xi,\Xi)}(F_{count}) = \mathsf{tt}$ for some ξ and Ξ. To find appropriate W', Ξ', and Ξ'' such that $\mathsf{K}_i'^{(\xi,\Xi'')}(F_{implcount}) = \mathsf{tt}$ for $\mathsf{K}' = (\mathsf{N}, \mathsf{W}')$ we adopt "steps" $(\ldots, \eta_j \cup \xi_j, \eta_{j+1} \cup \xi_{j+1}, \ldots)$ from $\mathsf{W} \cup \Xi$ to $\mathsf{W}' \cup \Xi'$ (and choose Ξ'' accordingly) in all cases except those where

$$\eta_j(on) = \eta_{j+1}(on) = \ldots = \eta_{j+k+2}(on) = \mathsf{tt},$$
$$\eta_j(c) = \eta_{j+1}(c) = \ldots = \eta_{j+k+1}(c),$$
$$\eta_{j+k+2}(c) = \eta_{j+k+1}(c) + 1$$

hold for some $k < 9$. In this case we "stretch" $\mathsf{W} \cup \Xi$ to $\mathsf{W}' \cup \Xi'$ by introducing a sufficient number of stuttering steps such that we obtain Ξ'' then by evaluating *dec* with $0, 1, 2, \ldots, 9$ from the state with the index $j+1$ on. For example, let $\mathsf{W} \cup \Xi$ be given by

		j							
on	...	tt	tt	tt	tt	ff	ff	tt	...
c	...	16	17	17	18	18	18	0	...
dec	...		7	4	5	3	2	6	...

(We write simply j for $\eta_j \cup \xi_j$ and omit the other entries in the "header line".) Then the first three lines of the matrix

		j														
on	...	tt	tt	tt	tt	tt	tt	tt	tt	tt	tt	tt	tt	ff	ff	tt ...
c	...	16	17	17	17	17	17	17	17	17	17	17	18	18	18	0 ...
dec	...		7	4	4	4	4	4	4	4	4	4	5	3	2	6 ...
dec	...		0	1	2	3	4	5	6	7	8	9	0	0	0	0 ...

show $\mathsf{W}' \cup \Xi'$, and Ξ'' is obtained by taking the fourth instead of the third line.

The semantic definition of $\exists$ in terms of additional "stretching" must be reflected in the axiomatization of the quantifier. We again omit the details, but only show an example of an axiom (for the first-order case) useful for introducing a "stuttering variable" w that enforces certain numbers of stuttering steps between changes of the externally visible system variable e:

$$\begin{aligned}&\exists w(w = t_1 \land\\ &\quad \Box[(w > 0 \land w' = w - 1 \land e' = e) \lor (w = 0 \land e' \neq e \land w' = t_2)]_{w,e} \land\\ &\quad \Box\Diamond(w = 0)).\end{aligned}$$

In this formula, t_1 and t_2 are terms of sort NAT that do not contain the "stuttering variable" w. When the value of w is n for some $n \in \mathbb{N}$, it enforces at least n stuttering steps with respect to e. Initially, w is set to (the value of) t_1. There are two types of transitions: the first decrements w and leaves e unchanged, the second changes the visible variables and sets w to t_2. The latter type of transition is possible only if $w = 0$ holds, that is, if no more stuttering transitions are necessary. The final conjunct $\Box\Diamond(w = 0)$ asserts that "counting-down transitions" eventually occur whenever w is non-zero. In the counter example, t_1 and t_2 would both be chosen as 9.

In the light of the above discussion we arrive at a somewhat generalized form of system specifications in (G)TLA: they are typically of the form

$$F_\Gamma \equiv \exists w_1 \ldots \exists w_m(start_\Gamma \land \Box[A_\Gamma]_{\mathbf{U}} \land fair_\Gamma)$$

where the variables $w_1, \ldots, w_m \in \mathbf{U}$ represent the internal system variables of the specification. ($\mathbf{U}$ is now a subset of $\mathbf{X} \cup \mathbf{V} \cup \mathcal{X}^{fl} \cup \mathcal{V}^{fl}$). When proving a refinement relationship

$$F_{implΓ} \to F_\Gamma$$

an important step in the proof consists in finding "witnesses" for the hidden variables w_i in F_Γ, for example by an application of the axiom

$$A_w(t) \rightarrow \exists wA.$$

The "witness term" t is usually called a "refinement mapping".

We have studied the "hiding operator" $\exists$ in the framework of GTLA. Of course, it could also have been introduced in (basic) TLA. The resulting logic (equipped with initial validity semantics) is what we announced as "full" TLA in Sect. 9.2.

The syntax of GTLA allows more formulas than can be built in TLA, and there are GTLA formulas which cannot equivalently be expressed in basic TLA. Interestingly, however, this different expressivity of the two logics disappears when they are extended by the operator $\exists$ (and endowed with the same semantics). More precisely:

- for every GTLA+q formula A there is a formula A^* of (full) TLA such that $\models A \leftrightarrow A^*$.

(This formulation refers to normal semantics; transferring Theorem 2.6.4 shows that it holds for initial validity semantics as well.) Actually, A^* can systematically be constructed from A. We only illustrate this construction by means of an example. Let

$$A \equiv \Box\big[\Box v_1 \rightarrow \bigcirc\exists w_1 \Box[v_2 \rightarrow \bigcirc\Box w_1]_{v_2}\big]_{v_1}$$

where v_1 and v_2 are flexible propositional constants and w_1 is a flexible propositional variable. (Observe that A is not a TLA formula.) In a first step the subformula $\exists w_1 \Box[v_2 \rightarrow \bigcirc\Box w_1]_{v_2}$ of A is "represented" by a (fresh) flexible propositional variable:

$$A^+ \equiv \exists w_2(\Box(w_2 \leftrightarrow \exists w_1 \Box[v_2 \rightarrow \bigcirc\Box w_1]_{v_2}) \land (\Box[\Box v_1 \rightarrow w_2']_{v_1}).$$

The second step transforms those subformulas of A^+ inside some $\Box[\_]_\_$ which are not allowed in TLA, i.e., the formulas $v_2 \rightarrow \bigcirc\Box w_1$ and $\Box v_1 \rightarrow w_2'$. Their "inadmissible" parts $\Box w_1$ and $\Box v_1$ are again represented by additional flexible variables:

$$\begin{aligned} A^* \equiv \exists w_2(\Box(w_2 \leftrightarrow \exists w_1 \exists w_3(\Box(w_3 \leftrightarrow \Box w_1) \land \Box[v_2 \rightarrow w_3']_{v_2})) \land \\ \exists w_4(\Box(w_4 \leftrightarrow \Box v_1) \land \Box[w_4 \rightarrow w_2']_{v_1}))\,. \end{aligned}$$

A^* is a TLA formula and from the construction it is quite evident that it has the desired property. Moreover, it is not hard to see how to define a procedure that carries out the construction for an arbitrary formula of GTLA+q.

9.6 Composition of System Components

Systems are often *composed* of smaller components. Actually, system composition occurs in different versions, depending on how the interaction between the components is organized. We illustrate how this structuring method can be described within (G)TLA by the particular case of *open* systems: any system (component) interacts with an environment which may be other components. The interaction takes place by receiving inputs from the environment and delivering outputs to it. In order to simplify the discussion we consider only the composition of two components and we represent the input and output interfaces of each component by system variables in and out, respectively. Inputs are "arriving" on in and out receives the outputs. Assuming $a_1, \dots, a_n$ to be the internal system variables, a component Γ of this kind is in general specified in (G)TLA by a formula

$$F_\Gamma \equiv start_\Gamma \wedge \Box[A_\Gamma]_{\mathbf{U}_\Gamma} \wedge fair_\Gamma$$

where

$$\mathbf{U}_\Gamma = \{a_1, \dots, a_n, in, out\}.$$

(As described in Sect. 9.5, hiding of the internal variables could be expressed by quantifying "over them" with $\exists$.) The set $\mathbf{U}_\Gamma$ contains all relevant variables. The specification A_Γ describes the transitions of Γ, which may occur in reaction to changes of the input variable.

This concept, however, still needs to be made a bit more precise. In the sense of Chap. 8, the component and its environment are running concurrently and this concurrency can be represented by different "computation models" which fix whether changes of the input variable may or may not occur simultaneously with actions concerning the other system variables. (G)TLA does not commit to any particular model of computation: it is encoded in the specification, which has to "synchronize" actions of different components in an appropriate way. We apply here again a version of the *interleaving model* in which changes of the input variable in and the output variable out do not take place simultaneously. (This notion of interleaving is slightly different from the one described in Sect. 8.1.) Therefore, A_Γ should be given such that

$$A_\Gamma \rightarrow in' = in \vee out' = out$$

is S_Γ-valid (as a pre-formula).

Let us give an example. Assume SIG_{queue} to be a signature for *queues* (of, say, natural numbers) containing (at least) the function symbols

$$EMPTY, APPEND, HEAD, TAIL$$

which are interpreted by a structure Q with the empty queue ε and the usual queue operations of appending a number to a queue, returning the head, and returning the tail of a queue, respectively. Based on SIG_{queue} we consider the specification

$$F_{queue} \equiv start_{\Gamma_{queue}} \wedge \Box[A_{\Gamma_{queue}}]_{a,out}$$

(we omit fairness aspects) of a system Γ_{queue} where

$$\begin{aligned}
start_{\Gamma_{queue}} &\equiv a = EMPTY,\\
A_{enq} &\equiv in' \neq in \wedge a' = APPEND(in', a) \wedge out' = out,\\
A_{deq} &\equiv a \neq EMPTY \wedge out' = HEAD(a) \wedge a' = TAIL(a) \wedge in' = in,\\
A_{\Gamma_{queue}} &\equiv A_{enq} \vee A_{deq}.
\end{aligned}$$

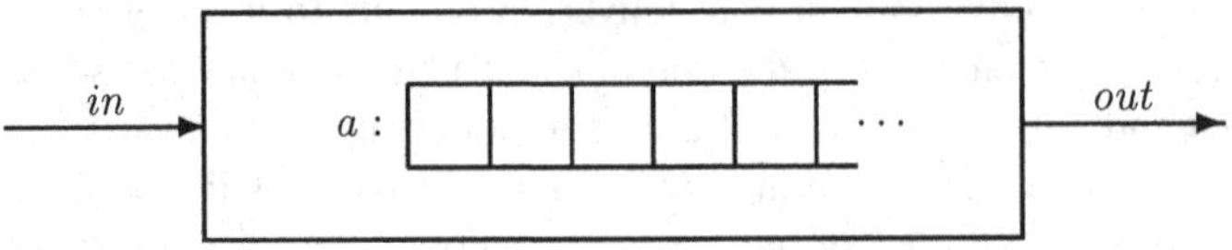

Fig. 9.2. A queue

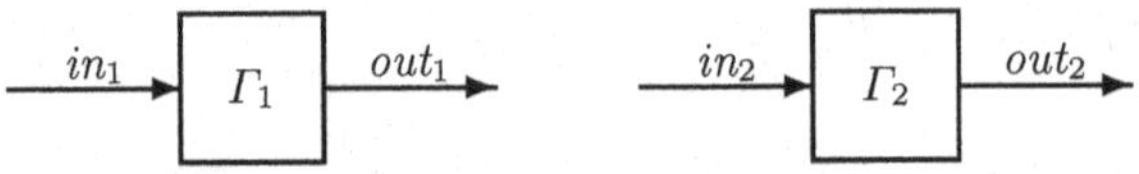

(a) Two components Γ_1 and Γ_2

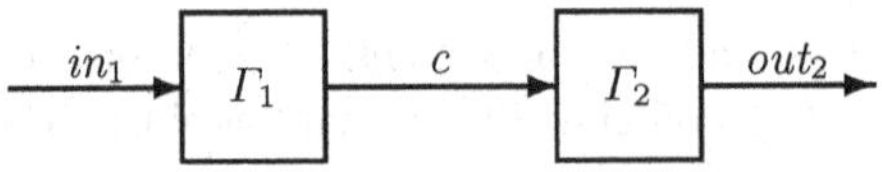

(b) The composition of Γ_1 and Γ_2

Fig. 9.3. Composition of system components

Γ_{queue} may be depicted as in Fig. 9.2. It has one internal system variable a which stores the incoming numbers such that input and output works in a first-in-first-out manner. A_{enq} and A_{deq} describe the "enqueuing" and "dequeuing" actions, respectively: the queue adds the new input value to its queue whenever in changes, and it may dequeue an element whenever the queue is non-empty. The conjuncts $in' = in$ and $out' = out$ in the definitions of these actions ensure the above "interleaving condition". An example of an execution sequence is:

$$[\varepsilon, 0, 0] \longrightarrow [(5), 5, 0] \longrightarrow [(3, 5), 3, 0] \longrightarrow [(3), 3, 5] \longrightarrow [(8, 3), 8, 5] \longrightarrow \ldots$$

where a state η is represented by $[\eta(a), \eta(in), \eta(out)]$. As intended, simultaneous changes of the input and output "channels" are impossible, and the change of the input channel is synchronized with the update of the queue.

The kind of composition of (two) components we want to describe now is to link up the output of one component with the input of the other, as depicted in Fig. 9.3. The system variable c represents the "connection" of out_1 with in_2. As an example, we consider the composition $\Gamma_{cqueues}$ of two queues Γ_{queue}. We hide now the two internal system variables; so, after some renaming, a straightforward specification of $\Gamma_{cqueues}$ is given by

$$F_{cqueues} \equiv \exists w_1 \exists w_2 (start_{\Gamma_{cqueues}} \wedge \Box[A_{\Gamma_{cqueues}}]_{w_1, w_2, c, out})$$

where

$$\begin{aligned}
start_{\Gamma_{cqueues}} &\equiv w_1 = EMPTY \wedge w_2 = EMPTY \wedge c = EMPTY, \\
A^{(1)}_{enq} &\equiv in' \neq in \wedge w_1' = APPEND(in, w_1) \wedge c' = c \wedge \\
&\qquad w_2' = w_2 \wedge out' = out,
\end{aligned}$$

$$\begin{aligned}
A^{(1)}_{deq} &\equiv w_1 \neq EMPTY \wedge c' = HEAD(w_1) \wedge w_1' = TAIL(w_1) \wedge \\
&\qquad in' = in \wedge w_2' = w_2 \wedge out' = out, \\
A^{(2)}_{enq} &\equiv c' \neq c \wedge w_2' = APPEND(c, w_2) \wedge out' = out \wedge \\
&\qquad in' = in \wedge w_1' = w_1, \\
A^{(2)}_{deq} &\equiv w_2 \neq EMPTY \wedge out' = HEAD(w_2) \wedge w_2' = TAIL(w_2) \wedge \\
&\qquad c' = c \wedge w_1' = w_1 \wedge in' = in, \\
A_{\Gamma_{cqueues}} &\equiv A^{(1)}_{enq} \vee A^{(1)}_{deq} \vee A^{(2)}_{enq} \vee A^{(2)}_{deq}.
\end{aligned}$$

The "logical composition" of the separate specifications of the two single queues is expressed in a somehow "interweaved" disjunction in $A_{\Gamma_{cqueues}}$ which describes all (interleaving) actions of the components. Actually, there is an equivalent description which combines the separate specifications in a more "direct" way by (essentially) building their logical conjunction.

To find this, consider first the two internal system variables represented by the flexible variables w_1 and w_2. Their interleaved changes are described by disjunctions of the form

$$B \equiv (w_1' = t_1 \wedge w_2' = w_2) \vee (w_2' = t_2 \wedge w_1' = w_1)$$

with terms t_1 and t_2 not containing w_2 and w_1, respectively. It is easy to see from the definition of the operator $\exists$ that the formula

$$\exists w_1 \exists w_2 B \leftrightarrow \exists w_1 (w_1' = t_1) \wedge \exists w_2 (w_2' = t_2)$$

is valid. Of course, the same does not hold for the system variables in and out since they are "free". However, if we explicitly include the pre-formulas $out' = out$ and $in' = in$ in the specifications of the (actions of the) first and second queue, respectively, then the stuttering invariance (with respect to in and out) of these specifications provide again the possibility to describe the interleaving actions by a conjunction. Finally, the two queues synchronize on the channel c: a dequeue action of the first queue occurs simultaneously with an enqueue of the second one. Indeed, using these arguments it turns out that the specification $F_{cqueues}$ is logically equivalent to the formula

$$\exists w_1 F^{(1)}_{queue} \wedge \exists w_2 F^{(2)}_{queue}$$

where $F^{(1)}_{queue}$ and $F^{(2)}_{queue}$ are the specifications of the two single queues, modified as follows:

$$\begin{aligned}
F^{(1)}_{queue} &\equiv start^{(1)}_{\Gamma_{queue}} \wedge \Box[A^{(1)}_{\Gamma_{queue}} \wedge out' = out]_{in, w_1, c, out}\,, \\
F^{(2)}_{queue} &\equiv start^{(2)}_{\Gamma_{queue}} \wedge \Box[A^{(2)}_{\Gamma_{queue}} \wedge in' = in]_{in, c, w_2, out}\,,
\end{aligned}$$

and $start^{(1)}_{\Gamma_{queue}}$ and $A^{(1)}_{\Gamma_{queue}}$ are $start_{\Gamma_{queue}}$ and $A_{\Gamma_{queue}}$ where a and out are replaced by w_1 and c, respectively, and $start^{(2)}_{\Gamma_{queue}}$ and $A^{(2)}_{\Gamma_{queue}}$ result analogously by replacing a and in by w_2 and c.

The observation made in this example carries over to the general case. If

$$F_{\Gamma_1} \equiv \exists w_1^{(1)} \ldots \exists w_n^{(1)}(start_{\Gamma_1} \wedge \Box[A_{\Gamma_1}]_{\mathbf{U}_{\Gamma_1}})$$

and

$$F_{\Gamma_2} \equiv \exists w_1^{(2)} \ldots \exists w_m^{(2)}(start_{\Gamma_2} \wedge \Box[A_{\Gamma_2}]_{\mathbf{U}_{\Gamma_2}})$$

are specifications of two components Γ_1 and Γ_2 (now with hidden internal system variables) then the behaviour of the composition Γ of Γ_1 and Γ_2 is given by

$$F_\Gamma \equiv F^*_{\Gamma_1} \wedge F^*_{\Gamma_2}$$

where $F^*_{\Gamma_1}$ results from F_{Γ_1} by replacing *out* by c and then $\Box[A^*_{\Gamma_1}]_{\mathbf{U}^*_{\Gamma_1}}$ (which is the result of this replacement) by

$$\Box[A^*_{\Gamma_1} \wedge out' = out]_{\mathbf{U}^*_{\Gamma_1} \cup \{out\}},$$

and $F^*_{\Gamma_2}$ results from F_{Γ_2} by analogously replacing in by c and then $\Box[A^*_{\Gamma_2}]_{\mathbf{U}^*_{\Gamma_2}}$ by

$$\Box[A^*_{\Gamma_2} \wedge in' = in]_{\mathbf{U}^*_{\Gamma_1} \cup \{in\}}.$$

So the composition of two components is logically described by the conjunction of the single specifications. (This holds also if fairness formulas are added.) Besides the trivial replacements of *out* and *in* by c, these specifications have only to be modified by the additions $out' = out$ and $c' = c$, respectively. This modification is induced by the underlying interleaving model.

We finally remark that a composition Γ of Γ_1 and Γ_2 could also be understood as an *implementation* of some other system $\overline{\Gamma}$ (extending the usage of this notion in the previous sections). For example, the composition of the two queues above implements just a single queue again. Similiarly as in earlier cases this can be expressed by the "correctness" formula

$$\exists w_1 F^{(1)}_{queue} \wedge \exists w_2 F^{(2)}_{queue} \rightarrow \exists w F_{queue}$$

where F_{queue} is the original queue specification (with w instead of a). This formula is in fact Q-valid. The opposite "completeness" relationship is obtained by hiding the internal "connection" variable c. So, taking c now directly as a flexible individual variable, the formula

$$\exists w F_{queue} \rightarrow \exists c(\exists w_1 F^{(1)}_{queue} \wedge \exists w_2 F^{(2)}_{queue})$$

describes this relationship, which intuitively asserts that it is impossible to tell from looking at the "external interface" provided by *in* and *out* whether a queue is internally implemented as the composition of two queues.

Bibliographical Notes

Concepts of refinement have long been studied for formal methods for the development of computer systems [3, 9, 19, 42].

Lamport suggested that specifications of reactive systems should be stuttering invariant and introduced TLA [88], where he also proposed to represent composition by conjunction and hiding by existential quantification. The logic GTLA and its axiomatization were introduced in [109]. Pnueli [123] proposed a temporal logic for refinement that is similar to TLA. Peled and Wilke proved that all properties expressible in propositional LTL+b that are stuttering invariant can be written without using the nexttime operator [116]. Similarly, all stuttering invariant properties expressible in LTL (without binary operators) can be written in GTLA without quantification over propositional variables [69].

Compositional methods aim at managing the complexity of developing big systems by decomposing the problems of specification and verification along the module boundaries. Different components of a system may mutually make assumptions about each other, and verifying that these assumptions are all satisfied in the overall system poses interesting problems. Within the context of temporal logic, Pnueli [122] made an early suggestion that triggered much work on the problem. We only refer to the excellent overviews [39, 40] of compositional approaches to specification and verification.

10

Other Temporal Logics

A common feature of all versions of temporal logics investigated so far is that they are based on the paradigm of linearly ordered time. More precisely, formulas are evaluated over sequences of "time points", with $\mathbb{N}$ as index set and the linear order $<$ on $\mathbb{N}$ as the basis for the semantics of the temporal operators.

Additionally to the numerous syntactical and semantical variations in previous chapters we briefly sketch here some more modifications of such logics including possible generalizations to other linearly ordered time models and *spatial-temporal logics*.

The main focus of this chapter, however, is to discuss some important temporal logics based on "non-linear time models". The most popular of them, *branching time* temporal logic CTL ("computation tree logic"), is widely used in connection with verification techniques which we will encounter in Chap. 11. We restrict ourselves to a propositional logic treatment in these cases. Particularly for CTL, this is sufficient for the intended applications. First-order versions could easily be defined in all cases along the lines shown for LTL in Chap. 5.

10.1 Further Modifications of Linear Temporal Logic

In the preceding chapters we have extensively studied many variants of propositional and first-order linear temporal logics. The variations were given by different choices of the linguistic means (particularly the numerous logical operators), i.e., the syntax of the respective logical language, or by different semantics. The borderline between these principal sources of modifications is not unique: an operator like $\exists$ introduced in Sect. 9.5 as a new syntactical element could also be viewed as just the existential quantifier with a modified semantics.

We want to sketch in this section some more examples of syntactical and semantical modifications. To begin with another syntactical aspect, we recall our "design decision" in Sect. 5.1 where we chose propositional and individual constants as the flexible symbols in FOLTL. In some presentations of first-order temporal logic one can find another choice: flexible predicate symbols. A language $\mathcal{L}_{\mathrm{FOLTL}^{\mathrm{fp}}}(TSIG)$ of such a logic FOLTL^{fp} can be defined as follows. A temporal signature $TSIG = (SIG, \mathbf{R})$ is given in this case by a signature $SIG = (\mathbf{S}, \mathbf{F}, \mathbf{P})$ and $\mathbf{R} = \bigcup_{\vec{s} \in \mathbf{S}^*} \mathbf{R}^{(\vec{s})}$ where $\mathbf{R}^{(\vec{s})}$, for every $\vec{s} \in \mathbf{S}^*$, is a set of *flexible predicate symbols*. Terms and formulas are built as usual, by handling the new flexible predicate symbols like rigid ones. A temporal structure $\mathsf{K} = (\mathsf{S}, \mathsf{W})$ for a temporal signature $TSIG = (SIG, \mathbf{R})$ is defined as in FOLTL, with the difference that a state η_i of W now associates a mapping

$$p^{\eta_i} : |\mathsf{S}|_{s_1} \times \ldots \times |\mathsf{S}|_{s_n} \to \{\mathsf{ff}, \mathsf{tt}\}$$

with every $p \in \mathbf{R}^{(s_1 \ldots s_n)}$. Given a variable valuation ξ, the evaluation of terms is as in FOL and for atomic formulas the clause

$$\mathsf{S}^{(\xi,\eta_i)}(p(t_1, \ldots, t_n)) = p^{\eta_i}(\mathsf{S}^{(\xi,\eta_i)}(t_1), \ldots, \mathsf{S}^{(\xi,\eta_i)}(t_n)) \quad \text{for } p \in \mathbf{R}$$

has to be added. All further semantical definitions are verbally adopted from FOLTL.

We do not want to investigate this logic in detail; we only point out its relationship to the "original" FOLTL. The two logics are not "directly" comparable with respect to the expressibility notions of Sect. 4.1, but we may state, as a first observation, that FOLTL can be "embedded" into FOLTL^{fp} which means in a somewhat modified sense that whatever is "describable" in FOLTL can also be described in FOLTL^{fp}. More formally: given a language $\mathcal{L}_{\text{FOLTL}}(TSIG)$, there is a language $\mathcal{L}_{\text{FOLTL}^{\text{fp}}}(TSIG^*)$ (with the same variables) such that for every formula A of $\mathcal{L}_{\text{FOLTL}}(TSIG)$ we can construct a formula A^* of $\mathcal{L}_{\text{FOLTL}^{\text{fp}}}(TSIG^*)$, and for every temporal structure K for $TSIG$ we can construct a temporal structure K^* for $TSIG^*$ such that

$$\mathsf{K}_i^{*(\xi)}(A^*) = \mathsf{K}_i^{(\xi)}(A)$$

holds for every K, ξ, and i. This assertion is quite trivial. The flexible propositional constants of $TSIG$ are directly included as elements of $\mathbf{R}^{(\varepsilon)}$ in $TSIG^*$, and any flexible individual constant a of sort s in $TSIG$ can be encoded in a way which is known already from classical FOL (for rigid symbols) and can immediately be applied in the present situation. $TSIG^*$ contains a flexible predicate symbol $p_a \in \mathbf{R}^{(s)}$ for every such a with the informal meaning that, in any state, p_a is true for exactly that element of the domain which is the value of a. A formula like, e.g., $a < b$ of $\mathcal{L}_{\text{FOLTL}}(TSIG)$ is encoded by the formula

$$p_a(x) \wedge p_b(y) \to x < y$$

of $\mathcal{L}_{\text{FOLTL}^{\text{fp}}}(TSIG^*)$ and, in fact, this definition meets the requirement if we formalize the idea by defining, for $\mathsf{K} = (\mathsf{S}, \mathsf{W})$, $\mathsf{W} = (\eta_0, \eta_1, \eta_2, \ldots)$, the temporal structure K^* by $\mathsf{K}^* = (\mathsf{S}, \mathsf{W}^*)$, $\mathsf{W} = (\eta_0^*, \eta_1^*, \eta_2^*, \ldots)$, with

$$p_a^{\eta_i^*}(d) = \mathsf{tt} \Leftrightarrow \eta_i(a) = d$$

for every $i \in \mathbb{N}$. It is evident that every occurrence of flexible individual constants can be eliminated in this way. Furthermore, generalizing this argument a bit, we also see that *flexible function symbols* (with definitions analogous to those above) would not bring in additional descriptive power. Such a symbol f could be encoded by a flexible predicate symbol p_f with

$$p_f^{\eta_i^*}(d_1, \ldots, d_n, d_{n+1}) = \mathsf{tt} \Leftrightarrow f^{\eta_i^*}(d_1, \ldots, d_n) = d_{n+1}.$$

Conversely, FOLTL^{fp} can also be embedded into FOLTL, but this is not entirely obvious. Consider, as an example, the (atomic) formula

$$p(t_1, t_2)$$

with a flexible predicate symbol p (and t_1, t_2 rigid). An approach for an encoding is to describe the truth value of this formula in a state η_i by a formula

$$isin(t_1, t_2, a_p)$$

where a_p is a flexible individual constant which has the set

$$\{(d_1, d_2) \mid \text{“}p(d_1, d_2) \text{ is true in } \eta_i\text{”}\}$$

as value in η_i, and $isin$ is a (rigid) predicate symbol which, applied as shown, just asserts that the pair of the values of t_1 and t_2 is contained in the set (that is the value of) a_p.

To make this idea formally precise, let $\mathcal{L}_{\mathrm{FOLTL^{fp}}}$ be a language over a temporal signature $TSIG = (SIG, \mathbf{R})$. The encoding language $\mathcal{L}_{\mathrm{FOLTL}}$ is based on the temporal signature $TSIG^* = (SIG^*, \mathbf{X}, \emptyset)$ where

- SIG^* extends $SIG = (\mathbf{S}, \mathbf{F}, \mathbf{P})$ by adding, for every $\vec{s} = s_1 \ldots s_n \in \mathbf{S}^*$ with $\mathbf{R}^{(\vec{s})} \neq \emptyset$, a sort $[s_1, \ldots, s_n]$ to $\mathbf{S}$ and defines $\mathbf{P}^{(s_1 \ldots s_n [s_1, \ldots, s_n])} = \{isin_{\vec{s}}\}$ with a new predicate symbol $isin_{\vec{s}}$.
- $\mathbf{X} = \{a_p \mid p \in \mathbf{R}\}$ where a_p is of sort $[s_1, \ldots, s_n]$ if $p \in \mathbf{R}^{(s_1 \ldots s_n)}$.

Continuing immediately with the construction of the temporal structure K^* for $TSIG^*$ from a temporal structure $\mathsf{K} = (\mathsf{S}, \mathsf{W})$ for $TSIG$, we define $\mathsf{K}^* = (\mathsf{S}^*, \mathsf{W}^*)$ where

- S^* is S extended by the domains

  $$|\mathbf{S}_{[s_1, \ldots, s_n]}| = 2^{|\mathsf{S}_{s_1}| \times \ldots \times |\mathsf{S}_{s_n}|}$$

  for the new sorts $[s_1, \ldots, s_n]$ in SIG^* and by associating the mappings $isin^{\mathsf{S}^*}_{s_1 \ldots s_n}$ with the new predicate symbols $isin_{s_1 \ldots s_n}$ in $\mathbf{P}$ which are given by

  $$isin^{\mathsf{S}^*}_{s_1 \ldots s_n}(d_1, \ldots, d_n, d_{n+1}) = \mathsf{tt} \Leftrightarrow (d_1, \ldots, d_n) \in d_{n+1},$$

- the states $\eta_i^* : \mathbf{X} \to |\mathbf{S}_{[s_1, \ldots, s_n]}|$ of W^* are given by

  $$\eta_i^*(a_p) = \{(d_1, \ldots, d_n) \in |\mathbf{S}_{[s_1, \ldots, s_n]}| \mid p^{\eta_i}(d_1, \ldots, d_n) = \mathsf{tt}\}$$

  for every $a_p \in \mathbf{X}$, $i \in \mathbb{N}$.

Observe that these definitions imply that all terms t of $\mathcal{L}_{\mathrm{FOLTL}^{\mathrm{fp}}}(TSIG)$ are terms of $\mathcal{L}_{\mathrm{FOLTL}}(TSIG^*)$ as well and $\mathsf{S}^{*(\xi,\eta_i^*)}(t) = \mathsf{S}^{(\xi,\eta_i)}(t)$ holds for every i and ξ.

Following the idea shown above, finally the formula A^* of $\mathcal{L}_{\mathrm{FOLTL}}(TSIG^*)$ is inductively defined according to the syntactic structure of the formula A of $\mathcal{L}_{\mathrm{FOLTL}^{\mathrm{fp}}}(TSIG)$.

1. $A \equiv p(t_1,\dots,t_n)$ with $p \in \mathbf{R}^{(s_1\dots s_n)}$: Then
$$A^* \equiv isin_{s_1\dots s_n}(t_1,\dots,t_n,a_p).$$
2. $A \equiv p(t_1,\dots,t_n)$ with $p \in \mathbf{P}$ or $A \equiv t_1 = t_2$ or $A \equiv$ **false**: Then $A^* \equiv A$.
3. $A \equiv B \rightarrow C$ or $A \equiv \bigcirc B$ or $A \equiv \Box B$ or $A \equiv \exists x B$: Then $A^* \equiv B^* \rightarrow C^*$, $A^* \equiv \bigcirc B^*$, $A^* \equiv \Box B^*$, $A^* \equiv \exists x B^*$, respectively, where B^* and C^* are the results of this construction for B and C.

These definitions provide the desired encoding result.

Theorem 10.1.1. *With the constructions defined above,*
$$\mathsf{K}_i^{*(\xi)}(A^*) = \mathsf{K}_i^{(\xi)}(A)$$
holds for every formula A of $\mathcal{L}_{\mathrm{FOLTL}^{\mathrm{fp}}}(TSIG)$, temporal structure K for TSIG, variable valuation ξ, and $i \in \mathbb{N}$.

Proof. The proof runs by structural induction on A.

1. $A \equiv p(t_1,\dots,t_n)$ with $p \in \mathbf{R}^{(s_1\dots s_n)}$: Then we have (using the above remark)
$$\begin{aligned}\mathsf{K}_i^{*(\xi)}(A^*) = \mathsf{tt} &\Leftrightarrow \mathsf{K}_i^{*(\xi)}(isin_{s_1\dots s_n}(t_1,\dots,t_n,a_p)) = \mathsf{tt}\\ &\Leftrightarrow isin^{\mathsf{S}^*}_{s_1\dots s_n}(\mathsf{S}^{*(\xi,\eta_i^*)}(t_1),\dots \mathsf{S}^{*(\xi,\eta_i^*)}(t_n),\mathsf{S}^{*(\xi,\eta_i^*)}(a_p))\\ &\qquad\qquad = \mathsf{tt}\\ &\Leftrightarrow isin^{\mathsf{S}^*}_{s_1\dots s_n}(\mathsf{S}^{(\xi,\eta_i)}(t_1),\dots \mathsf{S}^{(\xi,\eta_i)}(t_n),\eta_i^*(a_p)) = \mathsf{tt}\\ &\Leftrightarrow (\mathsf{S}^{(\xi,\eta_i)}(t_1),\dots \mathsf{S}^{(\xi,\eta_i)}(t_n)) \in \eta_i^*(a_p)\\ &\Leftrightarrow p^{\eta_i}(\mathsf{S}^{(\xi,\eta_i)}(t_1),\dots \mathsf{S}^{(\xi,\eta_i)}(t_n)) = \mathsf{tt}\\ &\Leftrightarrow \mathsf{K}_i^{(\xi)}(A) = \mathsf{tt}.\end{aligned}$$
2. $A \equiv p(t_1,\dots,t_n)$ with $p \in \mathbf{P}$ or $A \equiv t_1 = t_2$ or $A \equiv$ **false**: Then A does not contain flexible predicate symbols and by definition of K^* we have
$$\mathsf{K}_i^{*(\xi)}(A^*) = \mathsf{K}_i^{*(\xi)}(A) = \mathsf{K}_i^{(\xi)}(A).$$
3. $A \equiv B \rightarrow C$ or $A \equiv \bigcirc B$ or $A \equiv \Box B$ or $A \equiv \exists x B$: Using the respective induction hypothesis, we have in the first case
$$\begin{aligned}\mathsf{K}_i^{*(\xi)}(A^*) = \mathsf{tt} &\Leftrightarrow \mathsf{K}_i^{*(\xi)}(B^* \rightarrow C^*) = \mathsf{tt}\\ &\Leftrightarrow \mathsf{K}_i^{*(\xi)}(B^*) = \mathsf{ff} \text{ or } \mathsf{K}_i^{*(\xi)}(C^*) = \mathsf{tt}\\ &\Leftrightarrow \mathsf{K}_i^{(\xi)}(B) = \mathsf{ff} \text{ or } \mathsf{K}_i^{(\xi)}(C) = \mathsf{tt}\\ &\Leftrightarrow \mathsf{K}_i^{(\xi)}(A) = \mathsf{tt},\end{aligned}$$

and the other cases run analogously. △

FOLTL^{fp} appears not very appropriate for the applications (mainly) considered in this book (with the exception of applications to database systems as briefly sketched in a Second Reading paragraph in Sect. 8.6). This version of FOLTL may be profitably used, however, in theoretical investigations, even of FOLTL, since results can be transferred from FOLTL^{fp} to FOLTL by relationships like the one we have just proved.

For the modification of the semantics of LTL or FOLTL there are manifold possibilities on different "levels". For example, one can define, following patterns in classical logic which we briefly mentioned in Sect. 2.1, semantics which characterize *three-valued, probabilistic, intuitionistic* and other temporal logics departing from the usual two-truth-values paradigm. We briefly illustrate the case of a (basic) intuitionistic propositional temporal logic ILTL. In particular, intuitionistic logics treat negation in a special way, so we define a language $\mathcal{L}_{\mathrm{ILTL}}(\mathbf{V})$ as in the case of LTL with the difference that we take the operators $\neg$, $\vee$, $\wedge$, and $\Diamond$ instead of **false** as symbols of the underlying alphabet (in addition to $\rightarrow$, $\bigcirc$, and $\Box$), together with the corresponding syntactical rule

- If A and B are formulas then $\neg A$, $(A \vee B)$, $(A \wedge B)$, and $\Diamond A$ are formulas

instead of the rule for **false**.

For the definition of semantics, a temporal structure $\mathsf{K}^{int} = (\mathcal{J}, \Subset)$ for the set $\mathbf{V}$ of propositional constants is now given by a non-empty set $\mathcal{J}$ of state sequences $(\eta_0, \eta_1, \eta_2, \ldots)$ with states η_i as in LTL and a partial order $\Subset$ on $\mathcal{J}$. We require that whenever $(\eta_0, \eta_1, \eta_2, \ldots) \Subset (\eta'_0, \eta'_1, \eta'_2, \ldots)$ and $\eta_i(v) = \mathsf{tt}$ then also $\eta'_i(v) = \mathsf{tt}$, for all $i \in \mathbb{N}$ and $v \in \mathbf{V}$. Given such a temporal structure K^{int}, a value $\mathsf{K}_i(A) \in \{\mathsf{ff}, \mathsf{tt}\}$ is inductively defined for every formula A, every $\mathsf{K} \in \mathcal{J}$, and $i \in \mathbb{N}$.

1. $\mathsf{K}_i(v) = \mathsf{tt} \Leftrightarrow \eta'_i(v)$ for some $\mathsf{K}' = (\eta'_0, \eta'_1, \eta'_2, \ldots) \in \mathcal{J}$ with $\mathsf{K}' \Subset \mathsf{K}$ for $v \in \mathbf{V}$.
2. $\mathsf{K}_i(\neg A) = \mathsf{tt} \Leftrightarrow \mathsf{K}'_i(A) = \mathsf{ff}$ for every $\mathsf{K}' \in \mathcal{J}$ with $\mathsf{K} \Subset \mathsf{K}'$.
3. $\mathsf{K}_i(A \vee B) = \mathsf{tt} \Leftrightarrow \mathsf{K}_i(A) = \mathsf{tt}$ or $\mathsf{K}_i(B) = \mathsf{tt}$.
4. $\mathsf{K}_i(A \wedge B) = \mathsf{tt} \Leftrightarrow \mathsf{K}_i(A) = \mathsf{tt}$ and $\mathsf{K}_i(B) = \mathsf{tt}$.
5. $\mathsf{K}_i(A \rightarrow B) = \mathsf{tt} \Leftrightarrow \mathsf{K}'_i(A) = \mathsf{ff}$ or $\mathsf{K}'_i(B) = \mathsf{tt}$ for every $\mathsf{K}' \in \mathcal{J}$ with $\mathsf{K} \Subset \mathsf{K}'$.
6. $\mathsf{K}_i(\bigcirc A) = \mathsf{K}_{i+1}(A)$.
7. $\mathsf{K}_i(\Box A) = \mathsf{tt} \Leftrightarrow \mathsf{K}_j(A) = \mathsf{tt}$ for every $j \geq i$.
8. $\mathsf{K}_i(\Diamond A) = \mathsf{tt} \Leftrightarrow \mathsf{K}_j(A) = \mathsf{tt}$ for some $j \geq i$.

A formula A of $\mathcal{L}_{\mathrm{ILTL}}(\mathbf{V})$ is called *valid in the temporal structure* K^{int} for $\mathbf{V}$ if $\mathsf{K}_i(A) = \mathsf{tt}$ for every $\mathsf{K} \in \mathcal{J}$ and every $i \in \mathbb{N}$. *Consequence* and *universal validity* are defined as usual.

These definitions transfer the semantical features of "usual" intuitionistic logic to temporal logic. A temporal structure is now a collection of "LTL state sequences", and the order $\Subset$ is informally understood as a possible "growth of knowledge" about the truth of formulas in these state sequences (formalized by the compatibility condition for the relation $\trianglelefteq$). The new definitions concern the classical operators and have only "indirect" influence on the temporal operators. These have the semantics as before, but some typical laws of LTL no longer hold in ILTL, e.g., the operators $\Box$ and $\Diamond$ are no longer dual to each other: the implication $\Diamond A \rightarrow \neg\Box\neg A$ is valid, but the opposite direction

$$\neg\Box\neg A \rightarrow \Diamond A$$

is not.

Intuitionistic logic may be applied in systems with "incomplete information" where the handling of negation is of crucial importance.

All variants of linear temporal logic which we have shown so far exhibit still one common feature: formulas are evaluated by state sequences $(\eta_i)_{i \in \mathbb{N}}$. Recalling the statement in Sect. 2.1 that the characteristic paradigm of linear temporal logic is to be based on a linearly ordered, discrete time model, we observe that within this frame the standard index set ("time model") $\mathbb{N}$ of such state sequences may also be replaced by some other set with a discrete linear order relation.

A simple example of this kind is a semantics where, in the basic propositional case, a temporal structure $\mathsf{K} = (\eta_0, \eta_1, \eta_2, \ldots)$ is a finite or infinite sequence of states. In applications to state systems, the inclusion of finite sequences would enable us to model finite (e.g.: terminating) system runs in a more direct way than with the standard semantics. On the other hand, one has to take some care then of the nexttime operator. Analogously to the previous operators of the logic LTL+p one should introduce a *weak* and a *strong nexttime operator*. Denoting the first again by $\bigcirc$ and the second by $\odot$, an appropriate definition would be as follows.

- $\mathsf{K}_i(\bigcirc A) = \mathsf{tt} \;\Leftrightarrow\;$ if η_{i+1} exists in K then $\mathsf{K}_{i+1}(A) = \mathsf{tt}$.
- $\mathsf{K}_i(\odot A) = \mathsf{tt} \;\Leftrightarrow\;$ η_{i+1} exists in K and $\mathsf{K}_{i+1}(A) = \mathsf{tt}$.

Of course, the semantics of the always operator could be defined as before.

Going a step further one can restrict temporal structures to be only finite sequences. Certain logics of this kind are called *interval temporal logics* and are of their own specific importance. Their basic ideas will be given separately in the next section.

Another modification which is "opposite" to "cutting off" temporal structures is to take the set $\mathbb{Z}$ of integers as a time model, i.e., to define a temporal structure to be a state sequence

$$(\eta_i)_{i \in \mathbb{Z}} .$$

With such a semantics (again based on the natural order $<$) no initial state would be distinguished. Furthermore, it is evident that for any logic containing only future operators, there would be no difference to the former semantics since, informally speaking, then no formula evaluated in some η_i refers to states η_j with $j < i$, so the shape of the state sequence "behind" η_i is irrelevant. The introduction of past operators, however, becomes simpler. Like the one nexttime operator $\bigcirc$ (in the standard case), one single previous operator $\ominus$ would be enough:

- $\mathsf{K}_i(\ominus A) = \mathsf{K}_{i-1}(A)$.

Relating this semantics to state systems, it reflects the general case of systems represented by not necessarily rooted STSs. Rooted systems could still be handled (with some technical changes) referring exclusively to the initial condition of a system for describing the beginnings of its runs.

We still remark that, characterizing linear temporal logic, one can also omit the requirement of discreteness of time: the set $\mathbb{R}$ of real numbers would be an obvious example. With such a semantics the nexttime operator makes no sense any more. So, in the basic version, there would be only the operator $\Box$ (and its dual $\Diamond$) with the usual semantical definition. Such a logic then rather appears as a particular *modal logic*, with past and maybe binary operators as a *tense logic* (cf. the Second Reading paragraphs in Sects. 2.3 and 3.6 for some remarks about these kinds of logics). So we do not pursue this idea here. Arguing from the point of view of applications, we remark that such a logic would no longer reflect the "discreteness" of state systems in the sense shown in Chap. 6. Applying temporal logic to *real-time systems* (which, at a first glance, could be thought of as an application area) one typically treats times as special data which may be, e.g., values of "clock variables".

We conclude this survey by mentioning *spatial-temporal logics* which open a new *spatial* dimension – besides the temporal one – for changeable truth and falsity of formulas by viewing a state as a somehow structured and changeable collection of "local" states distributed over different "locations". (Of course, the locations referred to in this context are unrelated to locations of automata as in Chap. 4 or in Sect. 6.4.) Such logics may be applied, e.g., in systems with *mobile agents* which, in fact, can be seen to be determined by their local state variables, to be "associated" to some location, and to be able to change this association during a run.

We illustrate the idea by a simple propositional logic STL which extends LTL by a spatial aspect. For the definition of a language $\mathcal{L}_{\mathrm{STL}}(\mathbf{V},\mathbf{L})$ of STL the alphabet of $\mathcal{L}_{\mathrm{LTL}}(\mathbf{V})$ (for some $\mathbf{V}$) is enriched by a non-empty set $\mathbf{L}$ of *locations* which contains a distinguished *reference location* r, and the symbols $[$ and $]$. Formulas are built as in LTL and additionally with the formation rule

- If A is a formula and n is a location then $\mathsf{n}[A]$ is a formula.

The special element r of $\mathbf{L}$ represents a location which exists in every state and to which all other existing locations (in a state) are "connected" in the spatial structure. A formula $\mathsf{n}[A]$ informally means

"A holds at location n, provided this location exists".

By the dualization

$$\mathsf{n}\langle A\rangle \equiv \neg\mathsf{n}[\neg A]$$

one obtains formulas expressing

"Location n exists and A holds there".

For defining the semantics, a *spatial-temporal structure* $\mathsf{K} = (\eta_0, \eta_1, \eta_2, \ldots)$ for $\mathbf{V}$ and $\mathbf{L}$ is now an infinite sequence of states $\eta_i = (\mathbf{L}_i, \leftrightharpoons_i, \zeta_i)$ where, for every $i \in \mathbb{N}$,

- $\mathbf{L}_i \subseteq \mathbf{L}$ is a subset of $\mathbf{L}$ with $\mathsf{r} \in \mathbf{L}_i$,
- $\leftrightharpoons_i$ is a binary *connection* relation on $\mathbf{L}_i$ such that $\mathsf{n} \leftrightharpoons_i \mathsf{r}$ for every $\mathsf{n} \in \mathbf{L}_i$,
- $\zeta_i : \mathbf{L}_i \times \mathbf{V} \to \{\mathsf{ff}, \mathsf{tt}\}$ associates a truth value with every $v \in \mathbf{V}$ "at a location from $\mathbf{L}_i$".

The relations $\leftrightharpoons_i$ formalize the idea that the set of locations existing in a state is "structured" somehow. In this simple STL this structure is not specified more concretely; it is only required that every existing location is always connected with the reference location r. A refinement to trees (with root r) could be a natural, more particular choice.

Given such a K, $\mathsf{K}_{i,\mathsf{m}}(A) \in \{\mathsf{ff}, \mathsf{tt}\}$ (the "truth value of A in the ith state at location m") is defined for every formula A, every $i \in \mathbb{N}$, and every $\mathsf{m} \in \mathbf{L}$.

1. $\mathsf{K}_{i,\mathsf{m}}(v) = \mathsf{tt} \Leftrightarrow \mathsf{m} \in \mathbf{L}_i$ and $\zeta_i(\mathsf{m}, v) = \mathsf{tt}$ for $v \in \mathbf{V}$.
2. $\mathsf{K}_{i,\mathsf{m}}(\mathbf{false}) = \mathsf{ff}$.
3. $\mathsf{K}_{i,\mathsf{m}}(A \to B) = \mathsf{tt} \Leftrightarrow \mathsf{K}_{i,\mathsf{m}}(A) = \mathsf{ff}$ or $\mathsf{K}_{i,\mathsf{m}}(B) = \mathsf{tt}$.
4. $\mathsf{K}_{i,\mathsf{m}}(\bigcirc A) = \mathsf{tt} \Leftrightarrow \mathsf{m} \in \mathbf{L}_{i+1}$ and $\mathsf{K}_{i+1,\mathsf{m}}(A) = \mathsf{tt}$.
5. $\mathsf{K}_{i,\mathsf{m}}(\Box A) = \mathsf{tt} \Leftrightarrow$ for every $j \geq i$:
   if $\mathsf{m} \in \mathbf{L}_{i+k}$ for every $k \leq j$ then $\mathsf{K}_{j,\mathsf{m}}(A) = \mathsf{tt}$.
6. $\mathsf{K}_{i,\mathsf{m}}(\mathsf{n}[A]) = \mathsf{tt} \Leftrightarrow$ if $\mathsf{n} \in \mathbf{L}_i$ and $\mathsf{n} \leftrightharpoons_i \mathsf{m}$ then $\mathsf{K}_{i,\mathsf{n}}(A) = \mathsf{tt}$.

The last clause formalizes the above informal intention (additionally requesting that n be connected with m). The semantics of $\bigcirc$ and $\Box$ is modified according to the fact that locations may "disappear": the truth of $\bigcirc A$ at m requests that m exists in the next state and $\mathsf{K}_{i,\mathsf{m}}(\Box A)$ is now defined to mean that $\Box A$ holds in a state at location m if

"A holds in all subsequent states at m as long as m exists".

Finally, a formula A of $\mathcal{L}_{\mathrm{STL}}(\mathbf{V}, \mathbf{L})$ is called *valid* in a spatial-temporal structure K for $\mathbf{V}$ and $\mathbf{L}$ if $\mathsf{K}_{i,\mathsf{r}}(A) = \mathsf{tt}$ for every $i \in \mathbb{N}$, i.e., if

"A holds in every state at r".

Consequence and universal validity are defined as usual. For example,

$$\begin{array}{l} \mathsf{n}[A \to B] \to (\mathsf{n}[A] \to \mathsf{n}[B]), \\ \neg\mathsf{n}[A] \to \mathsf{n}[\neg A], \\ \bigcirc\neg A \to \neg\bigcirc A, \\ \bigcirc\neg\mathsf{n}[A] \to \mathsf{n}[\neg\bigcirc A], \\ \Box\mathsf{n}[A] \to \mathsf{n}[\Box A] \end{array}$$

are some valid formulas of STL.

10.2 Interval Temporal Logics

As indicated in the previous section, restricting temporal structures to finite sequences of states leads to a special class of logics called *(finite) interval temporal logics*. The temporal structures define finite *state intervals* and formulas are interpreted in these intervals.

One main application area of such logics is the field of *temporal logic programming* (cf. our short remarks about this field in the Second Reading paragraph in Sect. 8.6). We do not enter this topic, as it is beyond the scope of this book, but we want to give in this section at least a short outline of the basic ideas of interval temporal logics.

We illustrate the concepts in the style of LTL by means of a basic propositional interval temporal logic ITL. Given a set $\mathbf{V}$ of propositional constants the alphabet of a language $\mathcal{L}_{\mathrm{ITL}}(\mathbf{V})$ (shortly: $\mathcal{L}_{\mathrm{ITL}}$) of ITL is given by

- all propositional constants of $\mathbf{V}$,
- the symbols **false** | $\rightarrow$ | $\bigcirc$ | **chop** | (|).

The new (binary) *chop operator* **chop**, just enabled by the semantical concept of finite intervals, is characteristic for ITL and allows us to describe "sequential composition". The operator $\Box$ is not included in this list since it can be defined by **chop**.

Inductive Definition of *formulas* (of $\mathcal{L}_{\mathrm{ITL}}(\mathbf{V})$).

1. Every propositional constant of $\mathbf{V}$ is a formula.
2. **false** is a formula.
3. If A and B are formulas then $(A \rightarrow B)$ is a formula.
4. If A and B are formulas then $\bigcirc A$ and $(A$ **chop** $B)$ are formulas.

Further useful operators are the usual classical ones and (among others):

$$\begin{aligned}
&\odot A \equiv \neg\bigcirc\neg A,\\
&\Diamond A \equiv \textbf{true chop } A,\\
&\Box A \equiv \neg\Diamond\neg A,\\
&\textbf{empty} \equiv \bigcirc\textbf{false}.
\end{aligned}$$

Operator priorities are applied as before, including the convention that the binary operator **chop** has higher priority than the classical binary operators.

For the semantical machinery we define, as announced, an *(interval) temporal structure* for some set $\mathbf{V}$ of propositional constants to be a finite non-empty sequence $\mathsf{K} = (\eta_0, \ldots, \eta_{|\mathsf{K}|})$ of mappings (*states*)

$$\eta_i : \mathbf{V} \rightarrow \{\mathsf{ff}, \mathsf{tt}\}.$$

$|\mathsf{K}|$ is called the length of K. Furthermore, we let, for $0 \leq i \leq |\mathsf{K}|$,

$$\begin{aligned}
{}^{i}\mathsf{K} &= (\eta_0, \ldots, \eta_i),\\
\mathsf{K}^{i} &= (\eta_i, \ldots, \eta_{|\mathsf{K}|})
\end{aligned}$$

denote the prefix "up to η_i" and the suffix "from η_i on" of K, respectively, both being again interval temporal structures (in Sect. 2.1 we introduced the notation K^i already for infinite K). Observe that

$$(\mathsf{K}^i)^k = \mathsf{K}^{i+k}$$

and

$$^k(\mathsf{K}^i) = (^{i+k}\mathsf{K})^i$$

hold for arbitrary i, k with $0 \le i \le |\mathsf{K}|$ and $0 \le k \le |\mathsf{K}^i|$.

ITL is typically endowed with initial validity semantics as discussed in Sect. 2.6. Quite generally, our standard way of defining validity of formulas was to define the truth values $\mathsf{K}_i(F)$ of formulas F for "every state η_i in K", and initial validity of F in a temporal structure K was determined by the value $\mathsf{K}_0(F)$. We briefly mentioned already in Sect. 2.6 that this latter notion can also be obtained in a technically somewhat different way. In fact, this modified definition is often taken for ITL and it reflects the "interval idea" more obviously. The difference is to define – instead of the truth value $\mathsf{K}_i(F)$ in a single state – the truth value $\mathsf{K}(F)$ of F "in the state interval K". We apply this technique for ITL by the following inductive clauses:

1. $\mathsf{K}(v) = \eta_0(v)$ for $v \in \mathbf{V}$.
2. $\mathsf{K}(\mathbf{false}) = \mathsf{ff}$.
3. $\mathsf{K}(A \to B) = \mathsf{tt} \Leftrightarrow \mathsf{K}(A) = \mathsf{ff}$ or $\mathsf{K}(B) = \mathsf{tt}$.
4. $\mathsf{K}(\bigcirc A) = \mathsf{tt} \Leftrightarrow$ if $|\mathsf{K}| > 0$ then $\mathsf{K}^1(A) = \mathsf{tt}$.
5. $\mathsf{K}(A \ \mathbf{chop}\ B) = \mathsf{tt} \Leftrightarrow {}^j\mathsf{K}(A) = \mathsf{tt}$ and $\mathsf{K}^j(B) = \mathsf{tt}$ for some $j, 0 \le j \le |\mathsf{K}|$.

In the informal wording of above, a formula $\bigcirc A$ holds in an interval if, provided this interval has length at least 1 (i.e., at least two states), A holds in the interval obtained by "moving the start" one state into the future. Note that $\bigcirc$ is again a weak version in the sense that this next state may not exist; $\odot$ is the corresponding strong version. For the evaluation of the formula A **chop** B, the interval is divided into two sub-intervals in which A and B, respectively, are evaluated. Note that these sub-intervals have one common state: the "end state" of the first and the "start state" of the second one. For the other operators we get the following additional clauses:

6. $\mathsf{K}(\odot A) = \mathsf{tt} \Leftrightarrow |\mathsf{K}| > 0$ and $\mathsf{K}^1(A) = \mathsf{tt}$
7. $\mathsf{K}(\Diamond A) = \mathsf{tt} \Leftrightarrow \mathsf{K}^j(A) = \mathsf{tt}$ for some $j, 0 \le j \le |\mathsf{K}|$.
8. $\mathsf{K}(\Box A) = \mathsf{tt} \Leftrightarrow \mathsf{K}^j(A) = \mathsf{tt}$ for every $j, 0 \le j \le |\mathsf{K}|$.
9. $\mathsf{K}(\mathbf{empty}) = \mathsf{tt} \Leftrightarrow |\mathsf{K}| = 0$.

So, $\Diamond$ and $\Box$ have the expected meaning and **empty** expresses that the state sequence consists of just one state. We prove, as an example, the clause for $\Box A$.

$$\begin{aligned}
\mathsf{K}(\Box A) = \mathsf{tt} &\Leftrightarrow \mathsf{K}(\neg(\mathbf{true\ chop}\ \neg A)) = \mathsf{tt}\\
&\Leftrightarrow \mathsf{K}(\mathbf{true\ chop}\ \neg A) = \mathsf{ff}\\
&\Leftrightarrow \text{there is no } j, 0 \le j \le |\mathsf{K}| \text{ such that}\\
&\qquad {}^j\mathsf{K}(\mathbf{true}) = \mathsf{tt} \text{ and } \mathsf{K}^j(\neg A) = \mathsf{tt}\\
&\Leftrightarrow \mathsf{K}^j(A) = \mathsf{tt} \text{ for every } j, 0 \le j \le |\mathsf{K}|.
\end{aligned}$$

To conclude the semantical definitions, the validity of a formula A in some K can now "directly" be determined by $\mathsf{K}(A)$.

Definition. A formula A of $\mathcal{L}_{\mathrm{ITL}}(\mathbf{V})$ is called *valid in the temporal structure* K for $\mathbf{V}$ (or K *satisfies* A), denoted by $\models_{\mathsf{K}} A$, if $\mathsf{K}(A) = \mathsf{tt}$. A is called a *consequence of* a set $\mathcal{F}$ of formulas ($\mathcal{F} \models A$) if $\models_{\mathsf{K}} A$ holds for every K such that $\models_{\mathsf{K}} B$ for all $B \in \mathcal{F}$. A is called *(universally) valid* ($\models A$) if $\emptyset \models A$.

Example. Let $A \equiv \bigcirc(v_1 \to v_2)$, $B \equiv \Box(v_1 \vee v_2)$, $C \equiv v_1$ **chop** $(\neg v_1 \wedge v_2)$ with $v_1, v_2 \in \mathbf{V}$, and K with $|\mathsf{K}| = 6$ be given by

	η_0	η_1	η_2	η_3	η_4	η_5	η_6
v_1	tt	tt	ff	tt	ff	tt	tt
v_2	ff	tt	ff	tt	tt	tt	ff

We have:

$$\mathsf{K}^1(v_2) = \eta_1(v_2) = \mathsf{tt} \;\Rightarrow\; \mathsf{K}(A) = \mathsf{tt}.$$

$$\mathsf{K}^2(v_1) = \eta_2(v_1) = \mathsf{ff} \text{ and } \mathsf{K}^2(v_2) = \eta_2(v_2) = \mathsf{ff} \;\Rightarrow\; \mathsf{K}^2(v_1 \vee v_2) = \mathsf{ff}$$
$$\Rightarrow\; \mathsf{K}(B) = \mathsf{ff}.$$

$${}^4\mathsf{K}(v_1) = \eta_0(v_1) = \mathsf{tt},\ \mathsf{K}^4(\neg v_1) = \eta_4(\neg v_1) = \mathsf{tt},\ \mathsf{K}^4(v_2) = \eta_4(v_2) = \mathsf{tt}$$
$$\Rightarrow\; \mathsf{K}(C) = \mathsf{tt}.$$

Thus, A and C are valid in K, B is not. △

The above semantical definitions reflect the "interval idea" but, as indicated already, they do have the same results as we would obtain with the standard style given in Sect. 2.6 for LTL_0. In that context, $\mathsf{K}_i(F)$ would be defined for formulas F of the form $v \in \mathbf{V}$, **false**, and $A \to B$ as usual, for $\bigcirc A$ by

- $\mathsf{K}_i(\bigcirc A) = \mathsf{tt} \;\Leftrightarrow\;$ if $|\mathsf{K}| > 0$ then $\mathsf{K}_{i+1}(A) = \mathsf{tt}$

as explained in Sect. 10.1, and for A **chop** B by

- $\mathsf{K}_i(A \textbf{ chop } B) = \mathsf{tt} \;\Leftrightarrow\; {}^j\mathsf{K}_i(A) = \mathsf{tt}$ and $\mathsf{K}_j(B) = \mathsf{tt}$ for some $j, i \le j \le |\mathsf{K}|$.

Denoting (initial) validity in K with $\overset{0}{\models}$ as in LTL_0 we then would define

$$\overset{0}{\models}_{\mathsf{K}} A \;\Leftrightarrow\; \mathsf{K}_0(A) = \mathsf{tt}.$$

Let us prove the equivalence of this validity definition with the above one. For this we first transfer the assertion of Lemma 2.1.5 to the present situation.

Lemma 10.2.1. *Let* K *be a temporal structure,* $i, k \in \mathbb{N}$ *such that* $i + k \le |\mathsf{K}|$. *Then* $\mathsf{K}^k_i(F) = \mathsf{K}_{k+i}(F)$ *for every formula* F *of* $\mathcal{L}_{\mathrm{ITL}}$.

Proof. The proof runs by structural induction on F and the cases $v \in \mathbf{V}$, **false**, and $A \to B$ for F can be taken from the proof of Lemma 2.1.5 (with some renaming). Observe now that $|\mathsf{K}^k| = |\mathsf{K}| - k$. Applying the induction hypothesis, for $F \equiv \bigcirc A$ we then have

$$\begin{aligned} \mathsf{K}_i^k(\bigcirc A) = \mathsf{tt} &\Leftrightarrow \text{ if } |\mathsf{K}^k| > i \text{ then } \mathsf{K}_{i+1}^k(A) = \mathsf{tt} \\ &\Leftrightarrow \text{ if } |\mathsf{K}| > k+i \text{ then } \mathsf{K}_{k+i+1}(A) = \mathsf{tt} \\ &\Leftrightarrow \mathsf{K}_{k+i}(\bigcirc A) = \mathsf{tt}, \end{aligned}$$

and for $F \equiv A$ **chop** B we have

$$\begin{aligned} \mathsf{K}_i^k(A \textbf{ chop } B) = \mathsf{tt} &\Leftrightarrow {}^j(\mathsf{K}^k)_i(A) = \mathsf{tt} \text{ and } \mathsf{K}_j^k(B) = \mathsf{tt} \\ &\qquad \text{for some } j,\ i \le j \le |\mathsf{K}^k| \\ &\Leftrightarrow ({}^{k+j}\mathsf{K})_i^k(A) = \mathsf{tt} \text{ and } \mathsf{K}_j^k(B) = \mathsf{tt} \\ &\qquad \text{for some } j,\ i \le j \le |\mathsf{K}^k| \\ &\Leftrightarrow {}^{k+j}\mathsf{K}_{k+i}(A) = \mathsf{tt} \text{ and } \mathsf{K}_{k+j}(B) = \mathsf{tt} \\ &\qquad \text{for some } k+j,\ k+i \le k+j \le |\mathsf{K}| \\ &\Leftrightarrow \mathsf{K}_{k+i}(A \textbf{ chop } B) = \mathsf{tt}. \end{aligned}$$

△

With this lemma the equivalence of the notions of validity in some K and, hence, of consequence and universal validity given by the two different approaches are easily proved.

Theorem 10.2.2. *Let* K *be a temporal structure. Then*

$$\models_{\mathsf{K}} F \Leftrightarrow \overset{0}{\models}_{\mathsf{K}} F$$

holds for every formula F of $\mathcal{L}_{\text{ITL}}$.

Proof. According to the definitions we have to show $\mathsf{K}(F) = \mathsf{K}_0(F)$ and this is proved by structural induction on F. Applying the induction hypothesis in the cases 3–5 and Lemma 10.2.1 in 4 and 5 we have:

1. $\mathsf{K}(v) = \eta_0(v) = \mathsf{K}_0(v)$ for $v \in \mathbf{N}$.
2. $\mathsf{K}(\textbf{false}) = \mathsf{ff} = \mathsf{K}_0(\textbf{false})$.
3. $$\begin{aligned} \mathsf{K}(A \to B) = \mathsf{tt} &\Leftrightarrow \mathsf{K}(A) = \mathsf{ff} \text{ or } \mathsf{K}(B) = \mathsf{tt} \\ &\Leftrightarrow \mathsf{K}_0(A) = \mathsf{ff} \text{ or } \mathsf{K}_0(B) = \mathsf{tt} \\ &\Leftrightarrow \mathsf{K}_0(A \to B) = \mathsf{tt}. \end{aligned}$$
4. $$\begin{aligned} \mathsf{K}(\bigcirc A) = \mathsf{tt} &\Leftrightarrow \text{ if } |\mathsf{K}| > 0 \text{ then } \mathsf{K}^1(A) = \mathsf{tt} \\ &\Leftrightarrow \text{ if } |\mathsf{K}| > 0 \text{ then } \mathsf{K}_0^1(A) = \mathsf{tt} \\ &\Leftrightarrow \text{ if } |\mathsf{K}| > 0 \text{ then } \mathsf{K}_1(A) = \mathsf{tt} \\ &\Leftrightarrow \mathsf{K}_0(\bigcirc A) = \mathsf{tt}. \end{aligned}$$
5. $$\begin{aligned} \mathsf{K}(A \textbf{ chop } B) = \mathsf{tt} &\Leftrightarrow {}^j\mathsf{K}(A) = \mathsf{tt} \text{ and } \mathsf{K}^j(B) = \mathsf{tt} \text{ for some } j, 0 \le j \le |\mathsf{K}| \\ &\Leftrightarrow {}^j\mathsf{K}_0(A) = \mathsf{tt} \text{ and } \mathsf{K}_0^j(B) = \mathsf{tt} \text{ for some } j, 0 \le j \le |\mathsf{K}| \\ &\Leftrightarrow {}^j\mathsf{K}_0(A) = \mathsf{tt} \text{ and } \mathsf{K}_j(B) = \mathsf{tt} \text{ for some } j, 0 \le j \le |\mathsf{K}| \\ &\Leftrightarrow \mathsf{K}_0(A \textbf{ chop } B) = \mathsf{tt}. \end{aligned}$$ △

Summarizing this discussion, we may say that ITL is LTL_0 "on finite temporal structures" and extended by the chop operator which inherently relies on the finiteness of temporal structures. Observe also that the semantics of the original LTL_0

could indeed be defined in the way chosen here for ITL since it is easy to show analogously to Theorem 10.2.2 that a formula F of some $\mathcal{L}_{\text{LTL}}(\mathbf{V})$ is initially valid in some (infinite) temporal structure K for $\mathbf{V}$ if and only if $\mathsf{K}(F) = \mathsf{tt}$ where $\mathsf{K}(F)$ is defined inductively by the clauses 1–3 as for ITL and

- $\mathsf{K}(\bigcirc A) = \mathsf{tt} \;\Leftrightarrow\; \mathsf{K}^1(A) = \mathsf{tt}$,
- $\mathsf{K}(\Box A) = \mathsf{tt} \;\Leftrightarrow\; \mathsf{K}^j(A) = \mathsf{tt}$ for every $j \in \mathbb{N}$

(where the notation K^i is now used as in Sect. 2.1).

We note that ITL is decidable and can be axiomatized, and list some characteristic laws of ITL involving the chop operator.

(IT1) $\;\textbf{empty chop}\; A \leftrightarrow A$,
(IT2) $\;\odot A \;\textbf{chop}\; B \leftrightarrow \odot(A \;\textbf{chop}\; B)$,
(IT3) $\;(A \vee B) \;\textbf{chop}\; C \leftrightarrow A \;\textbf{chop}\; C \vee B \;\textbf{chop}\; C$,
(IT4) $\;A \;\textbf{chop}\; (B \vee C) \leftrightarrow A \;\textbf{chop}\; B \vee A \;\textbf{chop}\; C$,
(IT5) $\;A \;\textbf{chop}\; (B \;\textbf{chop}\; C) \leftrightarrow (A \;\textbf{chop}\; B) \;\textbf{chop}\; C$.

For example, the simple calculation

$$\begin{aligned}
\mathsf{K}(\odot A \;\textbf{chop}\; B) = \mathsf{tt} &\Leftrightarrow {}^j\mathsf{K}(\odot A) = \mathsf{tt} \text{ and } \mathsf{K}^j(B) = \mathsf{tt} \\
&\qquad \text{for some } j,\, 0 \le j \le |\mathsf{K}| \\
&\Leftrightarrow |\mathsf{K}| > 0 \text{ and } ({}^j\mathsf{K})^1(A) = \mathsf{tt} \text{ and } \mathsf{K}^j(B) = \mathsf{tt} \\
&\qquad \text{for some } j,\, 1 \le j \le |\mathsf{K}| \\
&\Leftrightarrow |\mathsf{K}| > 0 \text{ and } {}^{j-1}(\mathsf{K}^1)(A) = \mathsf{tt} \text{ and } (\mathsf{K}^1)^{j-1}(B) = \mathsf{tt} \\
&\qquad \text{for some } j-1,\, 0 \le j-1 \le |\mathsf{K}^1| \\
&\Leftrightarrow |\mathsf{K}| > 0 \text{ and } \mathsf{K}^1(A \;\textbf{chop}\; B) = \mathsf{tt} \\
&\Leftrightarrow \mathsf{K}(\odot(A \;\textbf{chop}\; B)) = \mathsf{tt}
\end{aligned}$$

proves (IT2).

Like LTL, ITL can be extended or modified in various ways. We only mention one special extension by a (binary) *projection operator* **proj** which is used as another characteristic feature of interval temporal logics. Its semantics is given by

- $\mathsf{K}(A \;\textbf{proj}\; B) = \mathsf{tt} \;\Leftrightarrow\;$ there are $m, j_0, \ldots, j_m \in \mathbb{N}$ such that $0 = j_0 < j_1 < \ldots < j_m = |\mathsf{K}|$ and $({}^{j_{k+1}}\mathsf{K})^{j_k}(A) = \mathsf{tt}$ for every $k, 0 \le k < m$ and $\overline{\mathsf{K}}(B) = \mathsf{tt}$ for $\overline{\mathsf{K}} = (\eta_{j_0}, \eta_{j_1}, \ldots, \eta_{j_m})$

(where $\mathsf{K} = (\eta_0, \ldots, \eta_{|\mathsf{K}|})$). So, A **proj** B informally means that the interval under consideration can be divided into a series of sub-intervals such that A holds in each of them and B holds in the interval formed from the end points of these sub-intervals. An important use of **proj** is in describing "iteration". For example, a *star operator* could be introduced by

$$A^* \equiv A \;\textbf{proj true}.$$

A^* expresses that A "holds repeatedly (some number of times)".

10.3 Branching Time Temporal Logics

Formulas of linear temporal logics (or more precisely, *linear time temporal logics*) are semantically interpreted over state sequences which may model execution sequences of state systems. The formulas are therefore able to express behavioural properties of such sequences. Consider once more the Towers of Hanoi system repeatedly treated in Chap. 6 as one of our first examples of a state system and formalized as Γ_{ToH} in Sect. 6.3. Taking it with three stones, its possible execution sequences going through a particular state, e.g., $[3, 21, \varepsilon]$ look like

$$\ldots \longrightarrow [3,21,\varepsilon] \longrightarrow [3,2,1] \longrightarrow [32,\varepsilon,1] \longrightarrow [321,\varepsilon,\varepsilon] \longrightarrow \ldots,$$
$$\ldots \longrightarrow [3,21,\varepsilon] \longrightarrow [\varepsilon,21,3] \longrightarrow [1,2,3] \longrightarrow [1,\varepsilon,32] \longrightarrow \ldots,$$
$$\ldots \longrightarrow [3,21,\varepsilon] \longrightarrow [\varepsilon,21,3] \longrightarrow [\varepsilon,2,31] \longrightarrow [2,\varepsilon,31] \longrightarrow \ldots,$$

etc.

The set of all these execution sequences may be systematically comprehended in a *computation tree* as shown in Fig. 10.1. Every "branch" (i.e., infinite sequence of states connected by arrows) in this tree represents one execution sequence.

As mentioned in Sect. 7.1, the property

$$\Box(DECR(pl_1) \land DECR(pl_2) \land DECR(pl_3))$$

is a valid property of Γ_{ToH} which informally means that it holds in every execution sequence of Γ_{ToH}. So, relating this fact to the computation tree of Γ_{ToH} we may say that this property holds on every branch of the tree (with arbitrary "starting point"). The property

$$start_{\Gamma_{ToH}} \rightarrow \Diamond A_{fin}$$

with $A_{fin} \equiv pl_1 = EMPTY \land pl_2 = TOWER \land pl_3 = EMPTY$ does not hold on every branch of the tree: most of the possible execution sequences do not lead to the goal of the puzzle. We only may assert that there exists some "successful" sequence of moves or, again related to the computation tree,

> "if $start_{\Gamma_{ToH}}$ holds in a state then there is a branch starting from that state on which $\Diamond A_{fin}$ holds".

It might be desirable to formulate and verify assertions of this kind but linear time temporal logics evidently provide no means to do this. From the linguistic point of view we would need some language construct to express the phrase

> "there is an execution sequence such that ..."

and approaching a temporal logic with such a linguistic feature we have to change the semantical basis used up to now. Following the computation tree idea, formulas are then to be interpreted over sets of sequences which are given by a tree-like ("branching") structure. In other words, the basic concept of a temporal structure should no longer be defined to be one single sequence

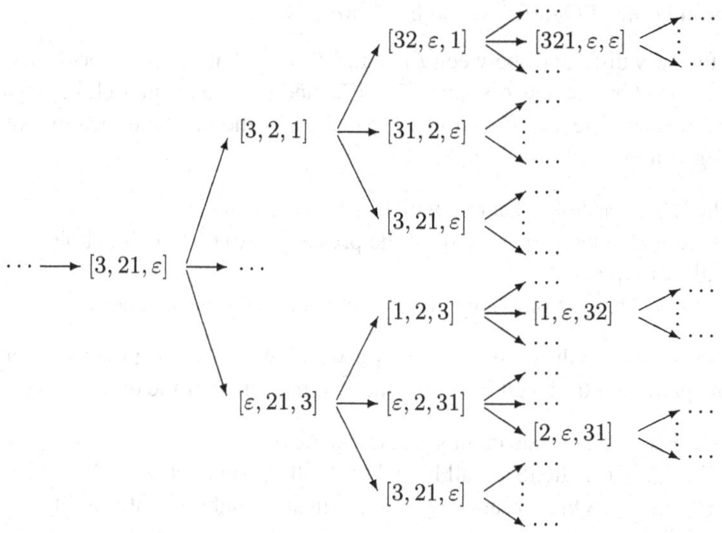

Fig. 10.1. A computation tree

$$\dots \longrightarrow \eta_i \longrightarrow \eta_{i+1} \longrightarrow \eta_{i+2} \longrightarrow \dots$$

of states but rather a collection of states connected by a "successor relation" which does not necessarily induce a linear order and therefore in general contains state sequences as various different branches of the structure.

As we could view the states of a state sequence as "time points" on a (linear) time scale, we may then regard the states as reflecting a time structure in which the "flow of time" is branching at each time point to (possibly) more than one successor point. This view explains why a temporal logic with this semantical basis is called a *branching time* temporal logic.

We develop now – analogously to LTL – a basic propositional logic BTL of this kind. The operators of this logic combine the expressibility of the existence of branches in the state structure with the possibility of speaking (as in LTL) about the "next" state, "all subsequent" states, and "some subsequent" state on the branches. Formally this is captured by the following definitions.

Given a set **V** of *propositional constants* the alphabet of a (*basic*) *language* $\mathcal{L}_{\mathrm{BTL}}(\mathbf{V})$ (also shortly: $\mathcal{L}_{\mathrm{BTL}}$) *of propositional branching time temporal logic* is given by

- all propositional constants of **V**,
- the symbols **false** | $\rightarrow$ | E◯ | E□ | E◇ | (|) .

Inductive Definition of *formulas* (of $\mathcal{L}_{\mathrm{BTL}}(\mathbf{V})$).

1. Every propositional constant of **V** is a formula.
2. **false** is a formula.
3. If A and B are formulas then $(A \rightarrow B)$ is a formula.

4. If A is a formula then $\mathsf{E}\bigcirc A$, $\mathsf{E}\Box A$, and $\mathsf{E}\Diamond A$ are formulas.

Linguistically, the only difference between $\mathcal{L}_{\mathrm{LTL}}$ and $\mathcal{L}_{\mathrm{BTL}}$ is that the operators $\bigcirc$ and $\Box$ (and $\Diamond$) are replaced by the new operators $\mathsf{E}\bigcirc$, $\mathsf{E}\Box$, and $\mathsf{E}\Diamond$. The symbol E in these notations indicates the existential assertion on branches, so the informal meaning of the operators is given by the following phrases:

$\mathsf{E}\bigcirc A$: "There is a successor state in which A holds",
$\mathsf{E}\Box A$: "There is a branch (starting from the present state) on which A holds in all subsequent states",
$\mathsf{E}\Diamond A$: "There is a branch on which A holds in some subsequent state".

Further operators, including the classical ones (for which we adopt the priority order from LTL), can again be introduced by abbreviations, in particular the dualizations

$\mathsf{A}\bigcirc A \equiv \neg\mathsf{E}\bigcirc\neg A$ ("A holds in all successor states"),
$\mathsf{A}\Box A \equiv \neg\mathsf{E}\Diamond\neg A$ ("A holds on all branches in all subsequent states"),
$\mathsf{A}\Diamond A \equiv \neg\mathsf{E}\Box\neg A$ ("On all branches, A holds in some subsequent state").

It will come out immediately by the semantical definitions that the duality relationships are not as simple as they are in the case of $\bigcirc$, $\Box$, and $\Diamond$: the operator $\mathsf{E}\bigcirc$ is not self-dual and $\mathsf{E}\Box$ and $\mathsf{E}\Diamond$ are not dual to each other.

As pointed out, the semantics of $\mathcal{L}_{\mathrm{BTL}}$ is based on a time model in which each time point may have more than one successor. In order to develop this idea formally, a pair $(I, \twoheadrightarrow)$ where I is a non-empty set (of "time points") and $\twoheadrightarrow$ is a total binary relation on I is called a *branching time structure*. $\twoheadrightarrow$ represents the successor relation on time points. A *fullpath* in I is an infinite sequence $(\iota_0, \iota_1, \iota_2, \ldots)$ of elements of I with $\iota_k \twoheadrightarrow \iota_{k+1}$ for $k \in \mathbb{N}$.

Let now $\mathbf{V}$ be a set of propositional constants. A (*branching time*) *temporal structure* $\mathsf{K} = (\{\eta_\iota\}_{\iota\in I}, \twoheadrightarrow)$ for $\mathbf{V}$ is given by a branching time structure $(I, \twoheadrightarrow)$ and a multiset $\{\eta_\iota\}_{\iota\in I}$ of *states*

$$\eta_\iota : \mathbf{V} \to \{\mathsf{ff}, \mathsf{tt}\}.$$

Observe that in general there is no distinguished initial state in K and that I (and therefore $\{\eta_\iota\}_{\iota\in I}$ as well) may be finite. Infinite state sequences are provided by the fact that $\twoheadrightarrow$ is total. Furthermore, it is evident that a "linear time" temporal structure $(\eta_0, \eta_1, \eta_2, \ldots)$ as defined in Sect. 2.1 is just a special case of such a structure with $I = \mathbb{N}$ and $i \twoheadrightarrow j \Leftrightarrow j = i + 1$.

For a temporal structure $\mathsf{K} = (\{\eta_\iota\}_{\iota\in I}, \twoheadrightarrow)$ we inductively define the truth value $\mathsf{K}_\iota(F)$ of a formula F of $\mathcal{L}_{\mathrm{BTL}}$ "in state η_ι" as follows ($\iota \in I$):

1. $\mathsf{K}_\iota(v) = \eta_\iota(v)$ for $v \in \mathbf{V}$.
2. $\mathsf{K}_\iota(\mathbf{false}) = \mathsf{ff}$.
3. $\mathsf{K}_\iota(A \to B) = \mathsf{tt} \Leftrightarrow \mathsf{K}_\iota(A) = \mathsf{ff}$ or $\mathsf{K}_\iota(B) = \mathsf{tt}$.
4. $\mathsf{K}_\iota(\mathsf{E}\bigcirc A) = \mathsf{tt} \Leftrightarrow \mathsf{K}_\kappa(A) = \mathsf{tt}$ for some κ with $\iota \twoheadrightarrow \kappa$.
5. $\mathsf{K}_\iota(\mathsf{E}\Box A) = \mathsf{tt} \Leftrightarrow$ there is a fullpath $(\iota_0, \iota_1, \iota_2, \ldots)$ in I with $\iota_0 = \iota$ and $\mathsf{K}_{\iota_k}(A) = \mathsf{tt}$ for every $k \in \mathbb{N}$.

6. $\mathsf{K}_\iota(\mathsf{E}\Diamond A) = \mathsf{tt} \Leftrightarrow$ there is a fullpath $(\iota_0, \iota_1, \iota_2, \ldots)$ in I with $\iota_0 = \iota$ and $\mathsf{K}_{\iota_k}(A) = \mathsf{tt}$ for some $k \in \mathbb{N}$.

A fullpath $(\iota_0, \iota_1, \iota_2, \ldots)$ in I represents a state sequence $(\eta_{\iota_0}, \eta_{\iota_1}, \eta_{\iota_2}, \ldots)$ as a branch "in K", so these formal definitions realize the intentions discussed above. Furthermore, they induce the following additional clauses for the dual operators:

7. $\mathsf{K}_\iota(\mathsf{A}\bigcirc A) = \mathsf{tt} \Leftrightarrow \mathsf{K}_\kappa(A) = \mathsf{tt}$ for every κ with $\iota \twoheadrightarrow \kappa$.
8. $\mathsf{K}_\iota(\mathsf{A}\Box A) = \mathsf{tt} \Leftrightarrow$ for every fullpath $(\iota_0, \iota_1, \iota_2, \ldots)$ in I with $\iota_0 = \iota$, $\mathsf{K}_{\iota_k}(A) = \mathsf{tt}$ for every $k \in \mathbb{N}$.
9. $\mathsf{K}_\iota(\mathsf{A}\Diamond A) = \mathsf{tt} \Leftrightarrow$ for every fullpath $(\iota_0, \iota_1, \iota_2, \ldots)$ in I with $\iota_0 = \iota$, $\mathsf{K}_{\iota_k}(A) = \mathsf{tt}$ for some $k \in \mathbb{N}$.

Example. Let $A \equiv \mathsf{E}\Box(v_1 \vee v_2) \wedge \mathsf{A}\bigcirc v_2$ with $v_1, v_2 \in \mathbf{V}$, and let K be given by $I = \{1,2,3\}$, $\twoheadrightarrow = \{(1,2),(1,3),(2,1),(2,3),(3,3)\}$ and

	η_1	η_2	η_3
v_1	tt	tt	ff
v_2	ff	tt	tt

$(1,2,1,3,3,3,\ldots)$ is a fullpath in I representing the state sequence

$$(\eta_1, \eta_2, \eta_1, \eta_3, \eta_3, \eta_3, \ldots).$$

Other fullpaths are $(1,3,3,3,\ldots)$, $(2,1,2,1,2,\ldots)$, $(3,3,3,\ldots)$, and so on. We compute:

$$\begin{aligned}
&\mathsf{K}_1(v_1 \vee v_2) = \mathsf{K}_3(v_1 \vee v_2) = \mathsf{tt} \Rightarrow \\
&\qquad \mathsf{K}_1(\mathsf{E}\Box(v_1 \vee v_2)) = \mathsf{tt} \quad \text{with the fullpath } (1,3,3,3,\ldots) \text{ and} \\
&\qquad \mathsf{K}_3(\mathsf{E}\Box(v_1 \vee v_2)) = \mathsf{tt} \quad \text{with the fullpath } (3,3,3,\ldots), \\
&\mathsf{K}_2(v_2) = \mathsf{K}_3(v_2) = \mathsf{tt} \Rightarrow \mathsf{K}_1(\mathsf{A}\bigcirc v_2) = \mathsf{K}_3(\mathsf{A}\bigcirc v_2) = \mathsf{tt};
\end{aligned}$$

hence together: $\mathsf{K}_1(A) = \mathsf{K}_3(A) = \mathsf{tt}$. On the other hand:

$$\mathsf{K}_1(v_2) = \mathsf{ff} \Rightarrow \mathsf{K}_2(\mathsf{A}\bigcirc v_2) = \mathsf{ff} \Rightarrow \mathsf{K}_2(A) = \mathsf{ff}. \qquad \triangle$$

The definitions of validity and consequence follow the usual pattern.

Definition. A formula A of $\mathcal{L}_{\mathrm{BTL}}(\mathbf{V})$ is called *valid in the temporal structure* $\mathsf{K} = (\{\eta_\iota\}_{\iota \in I}, \twoheadrightarrow)$ for $\mathbf{V}$ (or K *satisfies* A), denoted by $\models_{\mathsf{K}} A$, if $\mathsf{K}_\iota(A) = \mathsf{tt}$ for every $\iota \in I$. A is called a *consequence of* a set $\mathcal{F}$ of formulas ($\mathcal{F} \models A$) if $\models_{\mathsf{K}} A$ holds for every K such that $\models_{\mathsf{K}} B$ for all $B \in \mathcal{F}$. A is called *(universally) valid* ($\models A$) if $\emptyset \models A$.

Example. The formula

$$\mathsf{E}\Box A \leftrightarrow A \wedge \mathsf{E}\bigcirc\mathsf{E}\Box A$$

describing a fixpoint characterization of the operator $\mathsf{E}\Box$ is valid:

$$
\begin{aligned}
\mathsf{K}_\iota(\mathsf{E}\Box A) = \mathrm{tt} &\Leftrightarrow \text{there is a fullpath } (\iota_0, \iota_1, \iota_2, \ldots) \text{ with } \iota_0 = \iota \text{ and} \\
&\qquad \mathsf{K}_{\iota_k}(A) = \mathrm{tt} \text{ for every } k \in \mathbb{N} \\
&\Leftrightarrow \mathsf{K}_\iota(A) = \mathrm{tt} \text{ and} \\
&\qquad\qquad \text{there is } \kappa \text{ with } \iota \twoheadrightarrow \kappa \text{ and a fullpath} \\
&\qquad\qquad (\kappa_0, \kappa_1, \kappa_2, \ldots) = (\iota_1, \iota_2, \iota_3, \ldots) \\
&\qquad\qquad \text{with } \kappa_0 = \kappa \text{ and } \mathsf{K}_{\kappa_j}(A) = \mathrm{tt} \text{ for every } j \in \mathbb{N} \\
&\Leftrightarrow \mathsf{K}_\iota(A) = \mathrm{tt} \text{ and } \mathsf{K}_\kappa(\mathsf{E}\Box A) = \mathrm{tt} \text{ for some } \kappa \text{ with } \iota \twoheadrightarrow \kappa \\
&\Leftrightarrow \mathsf{K}_\iota(A) = \mathrm{tt} \text{ and } \mathsf{K}_\iota(\mathsf{E}\bigcirc\mathsf{E}\Box A) = \mathrm{tt} \\
&\Leftrightarrow \mathsf{K}_\iota(A \wedge \mathsf{E}\bigcirc\mathsf{E}\Box A) = \mathrm{tt}. \qquad \triangle
\end{aligned}
$$

There are fixpoint characterizations for the operators $\mathsf{E}\Diamond$, $\mathsf{A}\Box$, and $\mathsf{A}\Diamond$ as well. We note the complete list:

(BT1) $\mathsf{E}\Box A \leftrightarrow A \wedge \mathsf{E}\bigcirc\mathsf{E}\Box A$,
(BT2) $\mathsf{E}\Diamond A \leftrightarrow A \vee \mathsf{E}\bigcirc\mathsf{E}\Diamond A$,
(BT3) $\mathsf{A}\Box A \leftrightarrow A \wedge \mathsf{A}\bigcirc\mathsf{A}\Box A$,
(BT4) $\mathsf{A}\Diamond A \leftrightarrow A \vee \mathsf{A}\bigcirc\mathsf{A}\Diamond A$.

Of course, many other logical laws, some of them similar to those in LTL, are also available. We show only a few examples.

(BT5) $\mathsf{A}\bigcirc A \rightarrow \mathsf{E}\bigcirc A$,
(BT6) $\mathsf{E}\Box A \rightarrow \mathsf{E}\bigcirc A$,
(BT7) $\mathsf{E}\Box\mathsf{E}\Box A \leftrightarrow \mathsf{E}\Box A$,
(BT8) $\mathsf{E}\bigcirc\mathsf{E}\Box A \rightarrow \mathsf{E}\Box\mathsf{E}\bigcirc A$,
(BT9) $\mathsf{E}\bigcirc(A \wedge B) \rightarrow \mathsf{E}\bigcirc A \wedge \mathsf{E}\bigcirc B$,
(BT10) $\mathsf{E}\bigcirc(A \rightarrow B) \leftrightarrow \mathsf{A}\bigcirc A \rightarrow \mathsf{E}\bigcirc B$,
(BT11) $\mathsf{E}\Diamond(A \vee B) \leftrightarrow \mathsf{E}\Diamond A \vee \mathsf{E}\Diamond B$,
(BT12) $\mathsf{E}\Box(A \wedge B) \rightarrow \mathsf{E}\Box A \wedge \mathsf{E}\Box B$.

BTL is decidable with an exponential time complexity, and the following formal system Σ_{BTL} provides a sound and weakly complete axiomatization.

Axioms

(taut) All tautologically valid formulas,
(btl1) $\mathsf{E}\bigcirc$**true**,
(btl2) $\mathsf{E}\bigcirc(A \vee B) \leftrightarrow \mathsf{E}\bigcirc A \vee \mathsf{E}\bigcirc B$,
(btl3) $\mathsf{E}\Box A \leftrightarrow A \wedge \mathsf{E}\bigcirc\mathsf{E}\Box A$,
(btl4) $\mathsf{E}\Diamond A \leftrightarrow A \vee \mathsf{E}\bigcirc\mathsf{E}\Diamond A$.

Rules

(mp) $A, A \rightarrow B \vdash B$,
(nexb) $A \rightarrow B \vdash \mathsf{E}\bigcirc A \rightarrow \mathsf{E}\bigcirc B$,
(indb1) $A \rightarrow B, A \rightarrow \mathsf{E}\bigcirc A \vdash A \rightarrow \mathsf{E}\Box B$,
(indb2) $A \rightarrow \neg B, A \rightarrow \mathsf{A}\bigcirc(A \vee \neg\mathsf{E}\Diamond B) \vdash A \rightarrow \neg\mathsf{E}\Diamond B$.

These axioms and rules are easy to interpret. (The notion of tautological validity is adapted in an obvious way.) Particularly, the axioms include the fixpoint characterizations (BT1) and (BT2). Note that the axiom (btl1) means that each state does have a successor. To illustrate the use of Σ_{BTL} we give a simple example of a derivation. (The application of the rule (prop) can be justified as in Sect. 2.3 for LTL.)

Derivation of (BT8).

(1)	$\mathsf{E}\Box A \to A$	(prop),(btl3)
(2)	$\mathsf{E}\bigcirc\mathsf{E}\Box A \to \mathsf{E}\bigcirc A$	(nexb),(1)
(3)	$\mathsf{E}\Box A \to \mathsf{E}\bigcirc\mathsf{E}\Box A$	(prop),(btl3)
(4)	$\mathsf{E}\bigcirc\mathsf{E}\Box A \to \mathsf{E}\bigcirc\mathsf{E}\bigcirc\mathsf{E}\Box A$	(nexb),(3)
(5)	$\mathsf{E}\bigcirc\mathsf{E}\Box A \to \mathsf{E}\Box\mathsf{E}\bigcirc A$	(indb1),(2),(4) △

Let us see now how BTL can be applied to state systems. We formally refer again to transition systems as defined in Sect. 6.2 and since BTL is a propositional logic we restrict the considerations to propositional STSs. Let

$$\Gamma = (\emptyset, V, W, T)$$

be such an STS with the set V of system variables, the set W of (system) states $\eta : V \to \{\mathsf{ff}, \mathsf{tt}\}$, and the (total) transition relation $T \subseteq W \times W$. The relationship to BTL is now immediate: Γ induces a language $\mathcal{L}_{\text{BTL}\Gamma} = \mathcal{L}_{\text{BTL}}(V)$ and a temporal structure $\mathsf{K}^\Gamma = (W, \twoheadrightarrow)$ in which, informally speaking, we take W as the state multiset $\{\eta_\iota\}_{\iota\in I}$ and let "T induce $\twoheadrightarrow$". Technically, W is a set; so (W, T) is a branching time structure and we can define

$$\mathsf{K}^\Gamma = (\{\eta_\iota\}_{\iota\in W}, T)$$

where $\eta_\iota = \iota$ for every $\iota \in W$ ("every state of W is its own index in $\{\eta_\iota\}_{\iota\in W}$"). Clearly we have then $\{\eta_\iota\}_{\iota\in W} = W$, so we also may simply write

$$\mathsf{K}^\Gamma = (W, T)$$

for this temporal structure (and $\mathsf{K}_\eta(F)$ for the truth value of some F "in a state $\eta \in W$"). A fullpath $(\eta_0, \eta_1, \eta_2, \ldots)$ in W represents itself as a state sequence "in K^Γ".

Example. Consider the oscillator circuit shown in Sect. 6.1 and formalized in Sect. 6.2 as STS Γ_{osc} with $V = \{b_0, b_1, b_2\}$, $W = \{\eta : V \to \{\mathsf{ff}, \mathsf{tt}\}\}$, and

$$\begin{aligned} T = \{(\eta, \eta') \in W \times W \mid \\ & \eta'(b_0) = \eta(b_0), \\ & \eta'(b_1) = \mathsf{tt} \Leftrightarrow \eta(b_0) \neq \eta(b_1), \\ & \eta'(b_2) = \mathsf{tt} \Leftrightarrow \eta(b_2) = \mathsf{tt} \text{ if and only if } \eta(b_0) = \eta(b_1) = \mathsf{ff}\}. \end{aligned}$$

For the states η, η' with

$$\eta(b_0) = \mathsf{tt},\ \eta(b_1) = \mathsf{tt},\ \eta(b_2) = \mathsf{ff},$$
$$\eta'(b_0) = \mathsf{tt},\ \eta'(b_1) = \mathsf{ff},\ \eta'(b_2) = \mathsf{tt}$$

we find $(\eta, \eta') \in T$ and $(\eta', \eta) \in T$, so $(\eta, \eta', \eta, \eta', \eta, \ldots)$ is a fullpath in W and "in $\mathsf{K}^{\Gamma_{osc}}$". It describes the execution sequence

$$011 \longrightarrow 101 \longrightarrow 011 \longrightarrow 101 \longrightarrow 011 \longrightarrow \ldots$$

of Γ_{osc} shown in Sect. 6.2. △

In general, the fullpaths of the temporal structure K^{Γ} represent the execution sequences of the STS Γ and properties of Γ may be expressed by formulas in the language $\mathcal{L}_{\mathrm{BTL}\Gamma}$. Again we say that Γ *has the property* (expressed by the formula) F if F is Γ-valid, and this latter notion is now defined directly through K^{Γ}.

Definition. Let Γ be a propositional STS. A formula A of $\mathcal{L}_{\mathrm{BTL}\Gamma}$ is called *Γ-valid* if A is valid in K^{Γ}.

According to our previous discussions in Chaps. 6 and 7 (cf. also the Second Reading paragraph in Sect. 8.6) system properties occur as specification axioms describing (mainly) the possible single steps of the system or as "long-term" behaviour properties which one might want to prove for the system runs. Typical formulas in LTL or FOLTL expressing specification axioms are of the form

$$A \rightarrow \bigcirc(B_1 \vee \ldots \vee B_n)$$

(if not using a priming notation) where $B_1, \ldots, B_n$ describe possible successor states of states in which A holds. In the present situation, the temporal structure K^{Γ} comprehending the computation tree structure of the system Γ should be specified. This can be done by axioms of the form

$$A \rightarrow (\mathsf{E}\bigcirc B_1 \vee \ldots \vee \mathsf{E}\bigcirc B_n) \wedge \mathsf{A}\bigcirc(B_1 \vee \ldots \vee B_n)$$

which says (more precisely than above) that the states described by $B_1, \ldots, B_n$ are exactly those which will follow states described by A.

Actually, we do not pursue such a use of BTL as specification language. Branching time logics are typically used for describing system properties in the sense of Chap. 7 together with another verification method (cf. Chap. 11) which does not need specification axioms of a system. So turning to this kind of property, it is easy to see in the first place that invariance and eventuality properties are now expressible by formulas of the form

$$A \rightarrow \mathsf{A}\Box B$$

and

$$A \rightarrow \mathsf{A}\Diamond B,$$

respectively (with "state formulas" A and B as before). The operators $\Box$ and $\Diamond$ in the linear temporal logic formulations are now replaced by $\mathsf{A}\Box$ and $\mathsf{A}\Diamond$ which express that $\Box B$ and $\Diamond B$ hold "on all runs". However, one reason which we gave for the introduction of BTL was that it could also be desirable to describe properties which hold only for some runs and it is clear that this can be done now with the operators $\mathsf{E}\Box$ and $\mathsf{E}\Diamond$. In particular, formulas of the form

$$A \rightarrow \mathsf{E}\Diamond B$$

constitute now an interesting new class of system properties called *reachability properties*. Referring to the introductory motivation in this section, the formula

$$start_{\Gamma_{ToH}} \rightarrow \mathsf{E}\Diamond A_{fin}$$

(where we imagine for a moment that we have extended BTL to a first-order version) describes an example of such a property, it just expresses the desired informal phrase and, in fact, such properties can not be expressed in linear temporal logic. On the other hand, however, there are properties (e.g.: fairness constraints) expressible in LTL, but not in BTL.

Generally, LTL and BTL are incomparable with respect to expressibility in a formal sense. We will make this statement precise in the following section and indicate here one part of it only informally. Consider a formula of LTL of the form

$$\Diamond\Box A.$$

The "natural" translation $\mathsf{A}\Diamond\Box A$ into BTL is not possible since this is no BTL formula. The only remaining candidate to express $\Diamond\Box A$ in BTL then seems to be

$$\mathsf{A}\Diamond\mathsf{A}\Box A$$

but this formula does not mean the same thing as $\Diamond\Box A$. It says that any run will reach a state η such that A will hold in all states of all continuations from η on. The common prefix up to η together with the different continuations are different runs, and stating $\Diamond\Box A$ means that in each of these runs there is a state from which A holds permanently, but η need not necessarily be the same for all runs.

10.4 The Logics CTL and CTL*

Like LTL, the basic branching time logic BTL can be extended in various ways. An important extension widely used in applications is the *computation tree logic* CTL. This logic is the branching time counterpart of LTL+b, i.e., it results from BTL by adding some binary operator (under E and A). A usual choice of this operator for CTL is **until** or its non-strict version **unt**. We fix it here by taking the non-strict **unt**, so we add the binary operator **Eunt** to BTL which then allows for building formulas of the form

$$A \ \mathbf{Eunt} \ B.$$

The operator $\mathsf{E}\Diamond$ can be expressed by **Eunt** (as we will see below), so the syntax of CTL may be defined as follows.

Given a set $\mathbf{V}$ of *propositional constants* the alphabet of a *language* $\mathcal{L}_{\mathrm{CTL}}(\mathbf{V})$ (also shortly: $\mathcal{L}_{\mathrm{CTL}}$) *of (propositional)* CTL consists of all propositional constants of $\mathbf{V}$ and the symbols

$$\mathbf{false} \mid \rightarrow \mid \mathsf{E}\bigcirc \mid \mathsf{E}\Box \mid \mathbf{Eunt} \mid (\mid) .$$

false and all propositional constants of $\mathbf{V}$ are formulas and if A and B are formulas then so are $(A \rightarrow B)$, $\mathsf{E}\bigcirc A$, $\mathsf{E}\Box A$, and $(A\ \mathbf{Eunt}\ B)$. The informal meaning of the latter formula is

> "There is a branch on which B will hold in some subsequent state and A holds on this branch until that state".

(For some reasons which will become clear shortly this new kind of formula is also written in the form $\mathsf{E}(A\ \mathbf{unt}\ B)$.)

The operator $\mathsf{E}\Diamond$ can now be introduced as

$$\mathsf{E}\Diamond A \ \equiv\ \mathbf{true}\ \mathbf{Eunt}\ A,$$

the operators $\mathsf{A}\bigcirc$, $\mathsf{A}\Box$, $\mathsf{A}\Diamond$ can be defined as in BTL, and furthermore we may abbreviate:

$$A\ \mathbf{Aunt}\ B \ \equiv\ \neg(\neg B\ \mathbf{Eunt}\ (\neg A \wedge \neg B)) \wedge \neg \mathsf{E}\Box \neg B$$

(**Eunt** has a higher binding priority than the classical binary operators) with the informal meaning

> "On every branch B will hold in some subsequent state and A holds on these branches until that state".

The semantics of CTL takes over the semantical framework and definitions of BTL only extending the definition of $\mathsf{K}_\iota(A)$ by the clause

- $\mathsf{K}_\iota(A\ \mathbf{Eunt}\ B) = \mathsf{tt} \Leftrightarrow$ there is a fullpath $(\iota_0, \iota_1, \iota_2, \ldots)$ in I with $\iota_0 = \iota$ and $\mathsf{K}_{\iota_j}(B) = \mathsf{tt}$ for some $j \in \mathbb{N}$ and $\mathsf{K}_{\iota_k}(A) = \mathsf{tt}$ for every $k, 0 \le k < j$.

For A **Aunt** B we then get

- $\mathsf{K}_\iota(A\ \mathbf{Aunt}\ B) = \mathsf{tt} \Leftrightarrow$ for every fullpath $(\iota_0, \iota_1, \iota_2, \ldots)$ in I with $\iota_0 = \iota$ there is $j \in \mathbb{N}$ with $\mathsf{K}_{\iota_j}(B) = \mathsf{tt}$ and $\mathsf{K}_{\iota_k}(A) = \mathsf{tt}$ for every $k, 0 \le k < j$

and for $\mathsf{E}\Diamond A$ we get back in fact the clause we had already in BTL:

$$\begin{aligned}
\mathsf{K}_\iota(\mathsf{E}\Diamond A) = \mathsf{tt} &\Leftrightarrow \mathsf{K}_\iota(\mathbf{true}\ \mathbf{Eunt}\ A) = \mathsf{tt} \\
&\Leftrightarrow \text{there is a fullpath } (\iota_0, \iota_1, \iota_2, \ldots) \text{ in } I \text{ with } \iota_0 = \iota \text{ and} \\
&\quad\ \mathsf{K}_{\iota_j}(B) = \mathsf{tt} \text{ for some } j \in \mathbb{N} \text{ and} \\
&\quad\ \mathsf{K}_{\iota_k}(\mathbf{true}) = \mathsf{tt} \text{ for every } k, 0 \le k < j \\
&\Leftrightarrow \text{there is a fullpath } (\iota_0, \iota_1, \iota_2, \ldots) \text{ in } I \text{ with } \iota_0 = \iota \text{ and} \\
&\quad\ \mathsf{K}_{\iota_j}(B) = \mathsf{tt} \text{ for some } j \in \mathbb{N}.
\end{aligned}$$

Example. Let $A \equiv v_1$ **Eunt** $(v_1 \wedge v_2)$ with $v_1, v_2 \in \mathbf{V}$, and let K be the temporal structure with $I = \{1,2,3\}$, $\twoheadrightarrow\ = \{(1,2),(1,3),(2,1),(2,3),(3,3)\}$ and

	η_1	η_2	η_3
v_1	tt	tt	ff
v_2	ff	tt	tt

as considered already in Sect. 10.3. We have $\mathsf{K}_2(v_1 \wedge v_2) = \mathsf{tt}$ and $\mathsf{K}_1(v_1) = \mathsf{tt}$, so we get

$$\mathsf{K}_1(A) = \mathsf{tt}$$

with a fullpath $(1,2,\ldots)$ and

$$\mathsf{K}_2(A) = \mathsf{tt}$$

with $(2,\ldots)$. However, $\mathsf{K}_3(v_1 \wedge v_2) = \mathsf{ff}$ and there is only the fullpath $(3,3,3,\ldots)$ starting with 3, so

$$\mathsf{K}_3(A) = \mathsf{ff}. \qquad \triangle$$

Valid formulas containing the new operator include particularly the fixpoint characterization

(CT1) $\quad A\ \mathbf{Eunt}\ B \leftrightarrow B \vee (A \wedge \mathsf{E}\bigcirc(A\ \mathbf{Eunt}\ B))$

which is an adaption of the law (Tb13) of LTL+b and can be proved as follows.

$\mathsf{K}_\iota(A\ \mathbf{Eunt}\ B) = \mathsf{tt} \Leftrightarrow$ there is a fullpath $(\iota_0, \iota_1, \iota_2, \ldots)$ in I with $\iota_0 = \iota$ and
$\mathsf{K}_{\iota_j}(B) = \mathsf{tt}$ for some $j \in \mathbb{N}$ and
$\mathsf{K}_{\iota_k}(A) = \mathsf{tt}$ for every $k, 0 \le k < j$

$\Leftrightarrow \mathsf{K}_\iota(B) = \mathsf{tt}$
or
there is a fullpath $(\iota_0, \iota_1, \iota_2, \ldots)$ in I with $\iota_0 = \iota$ and
$\mathsf{K}_{\iota_j}(B) = \mathsf{tt}$ for some $j > 0$ and
$\mathsf{K}_{\iota_k}(A) = \mathsf{tt}$ for every $k, 0 \le k < j$

$\Leftrightarrow \mathsf{K}_\iota(B) = \mathsf{tt}$
or
$\mathsf{K}_\iota(B) = \mathsf{tt}$ and
there is a $\kappa \in I$ with $\iota \twoheadrightarrow \kappa$ and
a fullpath $(\kappa_0, \kappa_1, \kappa_2, \ldots)$ in I with $\kappa_0 = \kappa$ and
$\mathsf{K}_{\kappa_j}(B) = \mathsf{tt}$ for some $j \in \mathbb{N}$ and
$\mathsf{K}_{\kappa_k}(A) = \mathsf{tt}$ for every $k, 0 \le k < j$

$\Leftrightarrow \mathsf{K}_\iota(B \vee (A \wedge \mathsf{E}\bigcirc(A\ \mathbf{Eunt}\ B))) = \mathsf{tt}.$

Some examples of further valid formulas of CTL are:

(CT2) $\quad A\ \mathbf{Eunt}\ B \rightarrow \mathsf{E}\Diamond B,$

(CT3) $\mathsf{E}\bigcirc(A\ \mathbf{Eunt}\ B) \leftrightarrow \mathsf{E}\bigcirc A\ \mathbf{Eunt}\ \mathsf{E}\bigcirc B$,
(CT4) $A\ \mathbf{Eunt}\ C \vee B\ \mathbf{Eunt}\ C \rightarrow (A \vee B)\ \mathbf{Eunt}\ C$,
(CT5) $(A \wedge B)\ \mathbf{Eunt}\ C \rightarrow A\ \mathbf{Eunt}\ C \wedge B\ \mathbf{Eunt}\ C$,
(CT6) $A\ \mathbf{Eunt}\ (B \vee C) \leftrightarrow A\ \mathbf{Eunt}\ B \vee A\ \mathbf{Eunt}\ C$,
(CT7) $A\ \mathbf{Eunt}\ (B \wedge C) \rightarrow A\ \mathbf{Eunt}\ B \wedge A\ \mathbf{Eunt}\ C$.

Like BTL, CTL is decidable (again with exponential time complexity) and for an axiomatization of CTL we may modify the formal system Σ_{BTL} in the following way.

Axioms

(taut) All tautologically valid formulas,
(btl1) $\mathsf{E}\bigcirc\mathbf{true}$,
(btl2) $\mathsf{E}\bigcirc(A \vee B) \leftrightarrow \mathsf{E}\bigcirc A \vee \mathsf{E}\bigcirc B$,
(btl3) $\mathsf{E}\Box A \leftrightarrow A \wedge \mathsf{E}\bigcirc\mathsf{E}\Box A$,
(ctl) $A\ \mathbf{Eunt}\ B \leftrightarrow B \vee (A \wedge \mathsf{E}\bigcirc(A\ \mathbf{Eunt}\ B))$.

Rules

(mp) $A, A \rightarrow B \vdash B$,
(nexb) $A \rightarrow B \vdash \mathsf{E}\bigcirc A \rightarrow \mathsf{E}\bigcirc B$,
(indb1) $A \rightarrow B, A \rightarrow \mathsf{E}\bigcirc A \vdash A \rightarrow \mathsf{E}\Box B$,
(indc) $A \rightarrow \neg C, A \rightarrow \mathsf{A}\bigcirc(A \vee \neg(B\ \mathbf{Eunt}\ C)) \vdash A \rightarrow \neg(B\ \mathbf{Eunt}\ C)$.

This formal system Σ_{CTL} results from Σ_{BTL} by replacing the axiom (btl4) and the rule (indb2) for $\mathsf{E}\Diamond$ by an axiom (ctl) and a rule (indc) for **Eunt**. Σ_{CTL} is sound and weakly complete. As an example for its use we derive the law (CT2).

Derivation of (CT2). We use $\mathsf{E}\Diamond A \equiv \mathbf{true}\ \mathbf{Eunt}\ A$ and $\mathsf{A}\bigcirc A \equiv \neg\mathsf{E}\bigcirc\neg A$ as abbreviations and the rule (prop) as before.

(1)	$\neg\mathsf{E}\Diamond B \rightarrow \neg B$	(prop),(ctl)
(2)	$\neg\mathsf{E}\Diamond B \rightarrow \neg(\mathbf{true} \wedge \mathsf{E}\bigcirc\mathsf{E}\Diamond B)$	(prop),(ctl)
(3)	$\neg\mathsf{E}\Diamond B \rightarrow \neg\mathsf{E}\bigcirc\mathsf{E}\Diamond B$	(prop),(2)
(4)	$\neg\neg\mathsf{E}\Diamond B \rightarrow \mathsf{E}\Diamond B$	(taut)
(5)	$\neg\mathsf{E}\bigcirc\mathsf{E}\Diamond B \rightarrow \mathsf{A}\bigcirc\neg\mathsf{E}\Diamond B$	(nexb),(prop),(4)
(6)	$\neg(\neg\mathsf{E}\Diamond B \vee \neg(A\ \mathbf{Eunt}\ B)) \rightarrow \neg\neg\mathsf{E}\Diamond B$	(taut)
(7)	$\mathsf{A}\bigcirc\neg\mathsf{E}\Diamond B \rightarrow \mathsf{A}\bigcirc(\neg\mathsf{E}\Diamond B \vee \neg(A\ \mathbf{Eunt}\ B))$	(nexb),(prop),(6)
(8)	$\neg\mathsf{E}\Diamond B \rightarrow \mathsf{A}\bigcirc(\neg\mathsf{E}\Diamond B \vee \neg(A\ \mathbf{Eunt}\ B))$	(prop),(3),(5),(7)
(9)	$\neg\mathsf{E}\Diamond B \rightarrow \neg(A\ \mathbf{Eunt}\ B)$	(indc),(1),(8)
(10)	$A\ \mathbf{Eunt}\ B \rightarrow \mathsf{E}\Diamond B$	(prop),(9) △

The application of CTL to state systems runs as with BTL. The definitions of K^{Γ} and of Γ-validity for a (propositional) STS Γ are taken over; the new linguistic means allow now for the description of further system properties, especially by formulas of the form

$$A \rightarrow B\ \mathbf{Aunt}\ C$$

which express properties similar to precedence properties as defined in Sect. 7.1. The difference is that **Aunt** is a strong operator in the sense of Sect. 3.1 (B **Aunt** C says that C has to become true on the branches considered) whereas precedence properties are built with weak binary operators. Recalling the law (Tb3) from Sect. 3.1, one could think of defining a "weak version" **Aunl** of **Aunt** by

$$A \mathbf{\ Aunl\ } B \equiv A \mathbf{\ Aunt\ } B \lor \mathsf{A}\Box A$$

but this means

> "On every branch, B will hold sometime and A will hold until then, or A holds permanently on every branch".

What we want to express, however, is

> "On every branch, B will hold sometime and A will hold until then or A holds permanently".

This is different from the first phrase and, in fact, it cannot be expressed in CTL.

In general, the systematic relationship between various views of binary operators gets lost in CTL. Another observation is that CTL is still incomparable with LTL (or LTL+b) regarding expressibility: the LTL formulas mentioned as not expressible in BTL in the previous section are not expressible in CTL either.

Such deficiencies could be overcome by a still more powerful extension CTL* of BTL. The weakness of CTL in the cases discussed here comes from the fact that the "branch quantifiers" E and A are strictly bound to one temporal operator and formulas like $\mathsf{A}\Diamond\Box$ or $\mathsf{A}(A \mathbf{\ unt\ } B \lor \Box A)$ (this "translates" the above non-expressible phrase) are not allowed by the syntax of CTL. In CTL* just this limitation is dropped.

To define CTL*, let $\mathbf{V}$ be a set of propositional constants. The alphabet of a *language* $\mathcal{L}_{\mathrm{CTL}^*}(\mathbf{V})$ (also shortly: $\mathcal{L}_{\mathrm{CTL}^*}$) *of propositional branching time temporal logic* consists of all propositional constants of $\mathbf{V}$ and the symbols

$$\mathbf{false} \mid \rightarrow \mid \bigcirc \mid \mathbf{unt} \mid \mathsf{E} \mid (\mid) .$$

So we now use the quantifier symbol E for its own. The operators $\bigcirc$ and **unt** are taken as basis for the "linear time aspect on single branches".

The formulas of $\mathcal{L}_{\mathrm{CTL}^*}(\mathbf{V})$ are defined together with a second (auxiliary) syntactical type of *path formulas* by a simultaneous induction.

Inductive Definition of *formulas* (of $\mathcal{L}_{\mathrm{CTL}^*}(\mathbf{V})$).

1. Every propositional constant of $\mathbf{V}$ is a formula.
2. **false** is a formula.
3. If A and B are formulas then $(A \rightarrow B)$ is a formula.
4. If A is a path formula then $\mathsf{E}A$ is a formula.
5. Every formula is a path formula.
6. If A and B are path formulas then $(A \rightarrow B)$ is a path formula.
7. If A and B are path formulas then $\bigcirc A$ and $(A \mathbf{\ unt\ } B)$ are path formulas.

(Formulas are often called *state formulas* in order to distinguish them more explicitly from path formulas. Since we have introduced this notion already in another context in Sect. 6.2 we prefer to use simply "formula" here.)

Further operators can be introduced as expected, e.g.,

$$\begin{aligned} \mathsf{A}A &\equiv \neg\mathsf{E}\neg A, \\ \Diamond A &\equiv \textbf{true unt } A, \\ \Box A &\equiv \neg\Diamond\neg A \end{aligned}$$

and priority rules analogous to the previous ones are adopted.

The semantics of CTL* is again based on the same notion of temporal structures $\mathsf{K} = (\{\eta_\iota\}_{\iota \in I}, \twoheadrightarrow)$ as in BTL and CTL. For $\iota \in I$, fullpath $\pi = (\iota_0, \iota_1, \iota_2, \ldots)$ in I, and $j \in \mathbb{N}$ we let $\pi^j = (\iota_j, \iota_{j+1}, \iota_{j+2}, \ldots)$ and define the truth values $\mathsf{K}_\iota(A)$ for formulas and $\mathsf{K}_\pi(A)$ for path formulas inductively as follows:

1. $\mathsf{K}_\iota(v) = \eta_\iota(v)$ for $v \in \mathbf{V}$.
2. $\mathsf{K}_\iota(\textbf{false}) = \mathsf{ff}$.
3. $\mathsf{K}_\iota(A \to B) = \mathsf{tt} \Leftrightarrow \mathsf{K}_\iota(A) = \mathsf{ff}$ or $\mathsf{K}_\iota(B) = \mathsf{tt}$.
4. $\mathsf{K}_\iota(\mathsf{E}A) = \mathsf{tt} \Leftrightarrow$ there is a fullpath $\pi' = (\iota'_0, \iota'_1, \iota'_2, \ldots)$ in I with $\iota'_0 = \iota$ and $\mathsf{K}_{\pi'}(A) = \mathsf{tt}$.
5. $\mathsf{K}_\pi(A) = \mathsf{K}_{\iota_0}(A)$ for formulas A.
6. $\mathsf{K}_\pi(A \to B) = \mathsf{tt} \Leftrightarrow \mathsf{K}_\pi(A) = \mathsf{ff}$ or $\mathsf{K}_\pi(B) = \mathsf{tt}$.
7. $\mathsf{K}_\pi(\bigcirc A) = \mathsf{K}_{\pi^1}(A)$.
8. $\mathsf{K}_\pi(A \textbf{ unt } B) = \mathsf{tt} \Leftrightarrow \mathsf{K}_{\pi^j}(B) = \mathsf{tt}$ for some $j \geq 0$ and $\mathsf{K}_{\pi^k}(A) = \mathsf{tt}$ for every $k, 0 \leq k < j$.

The clauses implied for the further operators are evident, e.g.:

9. $\mathsf{K}_\iota(\mathsf{A}A) = \mathsf{tt} \Leftrightarrow \mathsf{K}_{\pi'}(A) = \mathsf{tt}$ for every fullpath $\pi' = (\iota'_0, \iota'_1, \iota'_2, \ldots)$ in I with $\iota'_0 = \iota$.
10. $\mathsf{K}_\pi(\Diamond A) = \mathsf{tt} \Leftrightarrow \mathsf{K}_{\pi^j}(A) = \mathsf{tt}$ for some $j \geq 0$.
11. $\mathsf{K}_\pi(\Box A) = \mathsf{tt} \Leftrightarrow \mathsf{K}_{\pi^j}(A) = \mathsf{tt}$ for every $j \geq 0$.

Validity of formulas and the consequence relation are defined as in BTL and CTL.

Example. For $v_1, v_2 \in \mathbf{V}$, $A \equiv \mathsf{E}(\bigcirc\neg v_1 \to \Box v_2)$ is a formula of $\mathcal{L}_{\mathrm{CTL}^*}(\mathbf{V})$. Let K be as above with $I = \{1, 2, 3\}$, $\twoheadrightarrow = \{(1,2), (1,3), (2,1), (2,3), (3,3)\}$ and

	η_1	η_2	η_3
v_1	tt	tt	ff
v_2	ff	tt	tt

For the fullpath $\pi = (1, 2, 1, 2, \ldots)$ we have $\mathsf{K}_\pi(\bigcirc\neg v_1) = \mathsf{K}_2(\neg v_1) = \mathsf{ff}$ because of $\eta_2(v_1) = \mathsf{tt}$; hence $\mathsf{K}_\pi(\bigcirc\neg v_1 \to \Box v_2) = \mathsf{tt}$, and therefore

$$\mathsf{K}_1(A) = \mathsf{tt}.$$

In the same way we calculate $\mathsf{K}_2(A) = \mathsf{tt}$ with the fullpath $(2, 1, 2, 1, \ldots)$ and, finally, $\mathsf{K}_3(A) = \mathsf{tt}$ is obtained with the fullpath $\pi' = (3, 3, 3, 3, \ldots)$ for which we have $\mathsf{K}_{\pi'}(\Box v_2) = \mathsf{tt}$ because of $\mathsf{K}_3(v_2) = \eta_3(v_2) = \mathsf{tt}$. This means that A is valid in K. △

Mainly because of the high (double exponential) complexity of its decision procedures, CTL* is not widely used in practice. So we do not treat it in more detail, but we still want to point out its relationships to LTL, BTL, and CTL.

Every CTL formula is a CTL* formula as well (with coinciding semantics) if we write formulas

$$A \ \mathsf{\textbf{Eunt}}\ B$$

with the operator **Eunt** in the form

$$\mathsf{E}(A \ \textbf{unt}\ B).$$

(We mentioned already that this notation is often used in CTL instead of ours.) So CTL and, hence, also BTL are sublogics of CTL*.

The case of LTL is not so clear at first glance since LTL formulas are not covered by the syntax of CTL* formulas and, moreover, the semantical frameworks are different in both logics. In order to enable a comparison we might base the semantics of LTL on the branching time concept of temporal structures. This runs in an analogous way as we could take transition systems as semantical basis for LTL as mentioned at the end of Sect. 6.2 and summarized in Theorem 6.2.1. We may define a formula A of a language $\mathcal{L}_{\mathrm{LTL}}(\mathbf{V})$ to be K-*valid* for a branching time temporal structure $\mathsf{K} = (\{\eta_\iota\}_{\iota \in I}, \twoheadrightarrow)$ for $\mathbf{V}$ if

"A is valid in the LTL sense in every state sequence in K",

formally: if

$$\overline{\mathsf{K}}_{\iota_j}(A) = \mathsf{tt} \qquad \text{(in the LTL sense)}$$

holds for every fullpath $(\iota_0, \iota_1, \iota_2, \ldots)$ in I, $\overline{\mathsf{K}} = (\eta_{\iota_0}, \eta_{\iota_1}, \eta_{\iota_2}, \ldots)$, and every $j \in \mathbb{N}$. An immediate transcription of the proof of Theorem 6.2.1 shows that A is valid if and only if it is K-valid for every such K.

More interestingly in the present context, if A is a formula of $\mathcal{L}_{\mathrm{LTL}}(\mathbf{V})$ then $\mathsf{A}A$ is a formula of $\mathcal{L}_{\mathrm{CTL^*}}(\mathbf{V})$ and, in fact, this formula characterizes the same structures as A.

Theorem 10.4.1. *For every formula A of $\mathcal{L}_{\mathrm{LTL}}(\mathbf{V})$ and every branching time temporal structure K for $\mathbf{V}$, the formula $\mathsf{A}A$ of $\mathcal{L}_{\mathrm{CTL^*}}(\mathbf{V})$ is valid in K if and only if A is K-valid.*

Proof. Let $\mathsf{K} = (\{\eta_\iota\}_{\iota \in I}, \twoheadrightarrow)$ be a temporal structure for $\mathbf{V}$, F be a formula of $\mathcal{L}_{\mathrm{LTL}}(\mathbf{V})$.

a) We first show by induction on F that

$$\mathsf{K}_\pi(F) = \overline{\mathsf{K}}_{\kappa_0}(F) \qquad (\overline{\mathsf{K}}_{\kappa_0}(F) \text{ in the LTL sense})$$

holds for every fullpath $\pi = (\kappa_0, \kappa_1, \kappa_2, \ldots)$ in I and $\overline{\mathsf{K}} = (\eta_{\kappa_0}, \eta_{\kappa_1}, \eta_{\kappa_2}, \ldots)$. For $v \in \mathbf{V}$ we have $\mathsf{K}_\pi(v) = \mathsf{K}_{\kappa_0}(v) = \eta_{\kappa_0}(v) = \overline{\mathsf{K}}_{\kappa_0}(v)$, and **false** and $A \rightarrow B$ are trivial as usual. Applying the induction hypothesis, we have

$$\mathsf{K}_\pi(\bigcirc A) = \mathsf{K}_{\pi^1}(A) = \overline{\mathsf{K}}_{\kappa_1}(A) = \overline{\mathsf{K}}_{\kappa_0}(\bigcirc A)$$

for $\bigcirc A$ and

$$\begin{aligned}\mathsf{K}_\pi(\Box A) = \mathsf{tt} &\Leftrightarrow \mathsf{K}_{\pi^j}(A) = \mathsf{tt} \text{ for every } j \geq 0\\ &\Leftrightarrow \mathsf{K}_{\kappa_j}(A) = \mathsf{tt} \text{ for every } j \geq 0\\ &\Leftrightarrow \mathsf{K}_{\kappa_0}(\Box A) = \mathsf{tt}\end{aligned}$$

for $\Box A$.

b) Let now $\mathsf{A}A$ be valid in K, $(\iota_0, \iota_1, \iota_2, \ldots)$ be a fullpath in I, and $j \in \mathbb{N}$. Then $\mathsf{K}_\iota(\mathsf{A}A) = \mathsf{tt}$ for all ι, so $\mathsf{K}_{\iota_j}(\mathsf{A}A) = \mathsf{tt}$ and therefore $\mathsf{K}_\pi(A) = \mathsf{tt}$ for every fullpath $\pi = (\iota_j, \ldots)$, particularly for $\pi = (\iota_j, \iota_{j+1}, \iota_{j+2}, \ldots)$. So we obtain $\overline{\mathsf{K}}_{\iota_j}(A) = \mathsf{tt}$ by a) which means that A is K-valid.

c) For the opposite direction, let A be K-valid, $\iota \in I$, and $\pi = (\iota, \ldots)$ be a fullpath in I. Then $\overline{\mathsf{K}}_\iota(A) = \mathsf{tt}$; hence $\mathsf{K}_\pi(A) = \mathsf{tt}$ by a) and this means that $\mathsf{A}A$ is valid in K. △

Slightly generalizing a notion used earlier, this theorem says that the LTL formula A and the CTL* formula $\mathsf{A}A$ are "model equivalent" (with respect to branching time temporal structures K). If K is some K^Γ for a transition system Γ then K-validity of A means just Γ-validity in the sense of Sect. 7.1, so we can conclude that a system Γ has a property described by A if and only if it has the property described by $\mathsf{A}A$.

Putting all together we find that CTL* allows us to express system properties which can be formulated in LTL, BTL, or CTL. Furthermore, the "interpretation" of LTL in the common CTL* framework enables now the formal treatment of mutual expressibility of formulas of these various logics in the sense of Sect. 4.1. Particularly, we say that an LTL formula A is expressible in BTL (or CTL) if there is a BTL (CTL) formula B such that (the CTL* formula) $\mathsf{A}A \leftrightarrow B$ is valid. The other way round, a BTL (CTL) formula A is expressible in LTL if there is an LTL formula B such that $A \leftrightarrow \mathsf{A}B$ is valid.

With these formal notions we may state, as announced at the end of the previous section, the incomparability of LTL with BTL (and CTL) in a formal way. For example, we argued already informally that the LTL formula $\Diamond\Box A$ and the BTL formula $\mathsf{A}\Diamond\mathsf{A}\Box A$ do not "mean the same". According to the present considerations this amounts to the formal statement that the CTL* formula $\mathsf{A}\Diamond\Box A \leftrightarrow \mathsf{A}\Diamond\mathsf{A}\Box A$ is not valid. This fact is easily seen by taking the temporal structure $\mathsf{K} = (\{\eta_\iota\}_{\iota \in I}, \twoheadrightarrow)$ with $I = \{1, 2, 3\}$, $\twoheadrightarrow = \{(1,1), (1,2), (2,3), (3,3)\}$ and such that $\eta_1(A) = \eta_3(A) = \mathsf{tt}$ and $\eta_2(A) = \mathsf{ff}$. Then all execution sequences starting with η_1 will either stay in η_1 forever or reach at some time η_3 where they will stay. Hence we have

$$\mathsf{K}_1(\mathsf{A}\Diamond\Box A) = \mathsf{tt}.$$

But in the sequence which stays in η_1 forever there is no state such that from there $\Box A$ will hold on all possible continuations since such continuations may also go through η_2. This means

$$\mathsf{K}_1(\mathsf{A}\Diamond\mathsf{A}\Box A) = \mathsf{ff}$$

and shows the desired assertion.

As a more general result it can be shown that, in fact, the LTL formula $\Diamond\Box A$ is not expressible (for arbitrary A) in CTL (and, hence, not in BTL). The proof of this fact is somewhat cumbersome and not carried out here. The "opposite incomparability" is provided by the following theorem which also justifies now our assertion in Sect. 10.3 about the non-expressibility of reachability properties in LTL.

Theorem 10.4.2. *The* BTL *(and* CTL*) formula* $\mathsf{E}\Diamond A$ *is (in general) not expressible in* LTL.

Proof. Let v be a propositional constant and assume that there is an LTL formula B such that $\mathsf{E}\Diamond v \leftrightarrow \mathsf{A}B$ is valid. Let $I = \{1,2\}$, $\twoheadrightarrow = \{(1,1),(1,2),(2,2)\}$, and $\mathsf{K} = (\{\eta_\iota\}_{\iota\in I}, \twoheadrightarrow)$ such that $\eta_1(v) = \mathrm{ff}$ and $\eta_2(v) = \mathrm{tt}$. Then $\mathsf{K}_1(\mathsf{E}\Diamond v) = \mathrm{tt}$ with the fullpath $(1,2,2,\ldots)$ in I and therefore $\mathsf{K}_1(\mathsf{A}B) = \mathrm{tt}$ which means $\mathsf{K}_\pi(B) = \mathrm{tt}$ for every fullpath π in I. Let now K' result from K by deleting the element 2 from I and the pairs $(1,2)$ and $(2,2)$ from $\twoheadrightarrow$. The only fullpath in $I \setminus \{2\}$ with the new $\twoheadrightarrow$ is $(1,1,1,\ldots)$ and this is also a fullpath in I, so we obtain $\mathsf{K}'_\pi(B) = \mathrm{tt}$; hence $\mathsf{K}'_1(\mathsf{A}B) = \mathrm{tt}$. But we also have $\mathsf{K}'_\pi(\Diamond v) = \mathrm{ff}$ and therefore $\mathsf{K}'_1(\mathsf{E}\Diamond v) = \mathrm{ff}$. This contradicts the assumed validity of $\mathsf{E}\Diamond v \leftrightarrow \mathsf{A}B$ and proves the assertion. △

Of course, the expressive power of CTL* can be compared "directly" with that of BTL or CTL and it is easy to see that, e.g., the CTL* formula

$$\mathsf{E}\Box\Diamond A$$

cannot be expressed in these logics (nor in LTL in the above sense). So, adapting a notion of Sect. 4.1, we may say that CTL* is more expressive than each of LTL, BTL, and CTL.

Second Reading

In earlier Second Reading paragraphs we already compared (linear time) temporal with modal logics. In the branching time framework this comparison provides some new insights. Recalling the modal logic notions from Sect. 2.3, it is evident that a branching time temporal structure $\mathsf{K} = (\{\eta_\iota\}_{\iota\in I}, \twoheadrightarrow)$ is just the same as a modal logic Kripke structure with a total accessibility relation. This observation, together with the remarks given in the above main text about LTL in the branching time framework, provides a direct comparison of temporal and modal logic expressibility.

Writing out the semantical definitions of the modal necessity and possibility operators $\Box$ and $\Diamond$ for $\mathsf{K} = (\{\eta_\iota\}_{\iota\in I}, \twoheadrightarrow)$ we obtain

$$\mathsf{K}_\iota(\Box A) = \mathrm{tt} \Leftrightarrow \mathsf{K}_\kappa(A) = \mathrm{tt} \text{ for every } \kappa \text{ with } \iota \lhd \kappa,$$
$$\mathsf{K}_\iota(\Diamond A) = \mathrm{tt} \Leftrightarrow \mathsf{K}_\kappa(A) = \mathrm{tt} \text{ for some } \kappa \text{ with } \iota \lhd \kappa$$

and find as a first trivial fact that this coincides with the semantics of the branching time operators $\mathsf{A}\bigcirc$ and $\mathsf{E}\bigcirc$. In other words: the sublogic of BTL with only these latter operators would be nothing but modal logic (with total accessibility relation), and richer branching time temporal logics can be viewed as extensions of this basic modal logic.

A particular extension is the modal μ-calculus MμC which extends modal logic by the fixpoint operators μ and ν and was briefly sketched in the Second Reading paragraph in Sect. 3.2. Observing the fixpoint characterizations

(BT1) $\mathsf{E}\Box A \leftrightarrow A \land \mathsf{E}\circ\mathsf{E}\Box A$,
(CT1) A **Eunt** $B \leftrightarrow B \lor (A \land \mathsf{E}\circ(A$ **Eunt** $B))$

of the operators $\mathsf{E}\Box$ and **Eunt** and recalling the discussions in Sect. 3.2 about LTL+μ, it is easy to see that these operators can be expressed with μ and ν. This means that for every formula A of some $\mathcal{L}_{\text{CTL}}(\mathbf{V})$ there is an MμC formula A^* such that, for every temporal (or Kripke) structure $\mathsf{K} = (\{\eta_\iota\}_{\iota \in I}, \twoheadrightarrow)$ for $\mathbf{V}$,

$$\mathsf{K}_\iota(A) = \mathsf{K}_\iota(A^*)$$

holds for every $\iota \in I$. A^* is defined inductively by $v^* \equiv v$ for $v \in \mathbf{V}$, $\mathbf{false}^* \equiv \mathbf{false}$, $(A \rightarrow B)^* \equiv A^* \rightarrow B^*$, and

$$(\mathsf{E}\circ A)^* \equiv \Diamond A^*,$$
$$(\mathsf{E}\Box A)^* \equiv \nu u(A^* \land \Diamond u),$$
$$(A \textbf{ Eunt } B)^* \equiv \mu u(B^* \lor (A^* \land \Diamond u)).$$

So, in the notation of Sect. 4.1, we may write CTL $\leq$ MμC. Actually, by a more complicated translation it can be shown that CTL* $\leq$ MμC (and, hence, LTL $\leq$ MμC) hold as well.

These observations also imply that the modal μ-calculus can be viewed (up to the totality of accessibility) as an extension BTL+μ of BTL (even without $\mathsf{E}\Box$) by fixpoint operators which is the branching time counterpart of LTL+μ and turns out in this way to be of considerable expressive power. System properties expressible in MμC (or BTL+μ) are called *regular*. An example of a *non-regular* property (not expressible in MμC) is

"In every subsequent state, A will have been true in more previous states than B".

It follows that such a property cannot be expressed in LTL (including its extensions), CTL, or even CTL*. One possibility to express them is to extend MμC in some appropriate way.

10.5 Temporal Logics for True Concurrency Modeling

The branching time logics BTL, CTL, and CTL* can be extended or modified in various ways. We show a simple example which – together with other approaches briefly exemplified at the end of this section – give rise to an interesting application to state systems different from the kind described so far.

The example, called *partial order temporal logic* POTL, is just BTL extended by *past operators*, corresponding to LTL+p in the linear time framework. The time model is branching also "in the past", i.e., a state in a temporal structure may have not only different successors but also different predecessors. So we enrich BTL with operators $\mathsf{E}\ominus$, $\mathsf{E}\boxminus$, and $\mathsf{E}\diamondminus$ with the following informal meaning.

$\mathsf{E}\ominus A$: "There is a predecessor state in which A holds",
$\mathsf{E}\boxminus A$: "There is a branch of past states (ending in the present state) on which A holds in all states",
$\mathsf{E}\diamondminus A$: "There is a branch of past states on which A holds in some state".

Formally a language $\mathcal{L}_{\text{POTL}}(\mathbf{V})$ (shortly: $\mathcal{L}_{\text{POTL}}$) of POTL for a given set $\mathbf{V}$ of propositional constants results from $\mathcal{L}_{\text{BTL}}(\mathbf{V})$ by adding the symbols $\mathsf{E}\ominus$, $\mathsf{E}\boxminus$, and $\mathsf{E}\diamondminus$ to the alphabet and the clause

- If A is a formula then $\mathsf{E}\ominus A$, $\mathsf{E}\boxminus A$, and $\mathsf{E}\diamondminus A$ are formulas

to the inductive definition of formulas.

For the semantics, a *partial order time structure* $(I, \twoheadrightarrow)$ is given by a non-empty set I and a total binary relation $\twoheadrightarrow$ on I with the additional requirement that the inverse relation $\twoheadleftarrow$ of $\twoheadrightarrow$ (i.e., the relation with $d_1 \twoheadleftarrow d_2 \Leftrightarrow d_2 \twoheadrightarrow d_1$) is total as well. Fullpaths in the previous sense (with respect to $\twoheadrightarrow$) are now called *forward fullpaths*, and a *backward fullpath* in I is an infinite sequence $(\iota_0, \iota_1, \iota_2, \ldots)$ of elements of I with $\iota_k \twoheadleftarrow \iota_{k+1}$ for $k \in \mathbb{N}$. A (*partial order*) *temporal structure* $\mathsf{K} = (\{\eta_\iota\}_{\iota \in I}, \twoheadrightarrow)$ for some set $\mathbf{V}$ of propositional constants is defined as in BTL with the difference that $(I, \twoheadrightarrow)$ is now a partial order time structure.

The definition of $\mathsf{K}_\iota(F)$ for formulas is adopted from BTL (with forward fullpaths) and extended by

- $\mathsf{K}_\iota(\mathsf{E}\ominus A) = \mathsf{tt} \Leftrightarrow \mathsf{K}_\kappa(A) = \mathsf{tt}$ for some κ with $\iota \twoheadleftarrow \kappa$.
- $\mathsf{K}_\iota(\mathsf{E}\boxminus A) = \mathsf{tt} \Leftrightarrow$ there is a backward fullpath $(\iota_0, \iota_1, \iota_2, \ldots)$ in I with $\iota_0 = \iota$ and $\mathsf{K}_{\iota_k}(A) = \mathsf{tt}$ for every $k \in \mathbb{N}$.
- $\mathsf{K}_\iota(\mathsf{E}\diamondminus A) = \mathsf{tt} \Leftrightarrow$ there is a backward fullpath $(\iota_0, \iota_1, \iota_2, \ldots)$ in I with $\iota_0 = \iota$ and $\mathsf{K}_{\iota_k}(A) = \mathsf{tt}$ for some $k \in \mathbb{N}$.

Observe that, analogously to the case of LTL with $\mathbb{Z}$ as time model (cf. Sect. 10.1), there is no need for distinguishing weak and strong versions of $\mathsf{E}\ominus$ since $\twoheadleftarrow$ is total. The definition of validity and consequence is as in BTL.

Clearly, dual operators can be introduced as usual by

$\mathsf{A}\ominus A \equiv \neg\mathsf{E}\ominus\neg A$ ("A holds in all predecessor states"),
$\mathsf{A}\boxminus A \equiv \neg\mathsf{E}\diamondminus\neg A$ ("A holds on all backward branches in all preceding states"),
$\mathsf{A}\diamondminus A \equiv \neg\mathsf{E}\boxminus\neg A$ ("On all backward branches, A holds in some preceding state")

and they have the expected semantics:

- $\mathsf{K}_\iota(\mathsf{A}\ominus A) = \mathsf{tt} \Leftrightarrow \mathsf{K}_\kappa(A) = \mathsf{tt}$ for every κ with $\iota \twoheadleftarrow \kappa$.
- $\mathsf{K}_\iota(\mathsf{A}\boxminus A) = \mathsf{tt} \Leftrightarrow$ for every backward fullpath $(\iota_0, \iota_1, \iota_2, \ldots)$ in I with $\iota_0 = \iota$, $\mathsf{K}_{\iota_k}(A) = \mathsf{tt}$ for every $k \in \mathbb{N}$.
- $\mathsf{K}_\iota(\mathsf{A}\diamondminus A) = \mathsf{tt} \Leftrightarrow$ for every backward fullpath $(\iota_0, \iota_1, \iota_2, \ldots)$ in I with $\iota_0 = \iota$, $\mathsf{K}_{\iota_k}(A) = \mathsf{tt}$ for some $k \in \mathbb{N}$.

Example. Let $A \equiv \mathsf{E}\ominus\mathsf{E}\Box v_2 \to \mathsf{A}\diamondminus(v_1 \wedge v_2)$ with $v_1, v_2 \in \mathbf{V}$. The branching time temporal structure K as considered in the example in Sects. 10.3 and 10.4, i.e., with $I = \{1, 2, 3\}$, $\twoheadrightarrow = \{(1, 2), (1, 3), (2, 1), (2, 3), (3, 3)\}$ and

	η_1	η_2	η_3
v_1	tt	tt	ff
v_2	ff	tt	tt

is also a partial order temporal structure for $\mathbf{V}$ since $\twoheadleftarrow$ is total. We have:

$\mathsf{K}_2(\mathsf{E}\Box v_2) = \mathsf{tt}$ with the forward fullpath $(2, 3, 3, 3, \ldots) \Rightarrow$
$\quad \mathsf{K}_1(\mathsf{E}\ominus\mathsf{E}\Box v_2) = \mathsf{K}_3(\mathsf{E}\ominus\mathsf{E}\Box v_2) = \mathsf{tt}$,
$\mathsf{K}_1(v_2) = \mathsf{ff} \Rightarrow \mathsf{K}_1(\mathsf{E}\Box v_2) = \mathsf{ff} \Rightarrow \mathsf{K}_2(\mathsf{E}\ominus\mathsf{E}\Box v_2) = \mathsf{ff}$,
$\mathsf{K}_2(v_1 \wedge v_2) = \mathsf{tt}, \mathsf{K}_3(v_1 \wedge v_2) = \mathsf{ff} \Rightarrow$
$\quad \mathsf{K}_1(\mathsf{A}\diamondminus(v_1 \wedge v_2)) = \mathsf{tt}$ and
$\quad \mathsf{K}_3(\mathsf{A}\diamondminus(v_1 \wedge v_2)) = \mathsf{ff}$ because of the backward fullpath $(3, 3, 3, \ldots)$.

Together we obtain $\mathsf{K}_1(A) = \mathsf{K}_2(A) = \mathsf{tt}$ and $\mathsf{K}_3(A) = \mathsf{ff}$. △

POTL is decidable and a sound and weakly complete formal system Σ_{POTL} can be obtained by extending Σ_{BTL} by the following axioms and rules.

Additional axioms

(potl1) $\mathsf{E}\ominus\mathbf{true}$,
(potl2) $\mathsf{E}\ominus(A \vee B) \leftrightarrow \mathsf{E}\ominus A \vee \mathsf{E}\ominus B$,
(potl3) $\mathsf{E}\boxminus A \leftrightarrow A \wedge \mathsf{E}\ominus\mathsf{E}\boxminus A$,
(potl4) $\mathsf{E}\diamondminus A \leftrightarrow A \vee \mathsf{E}\ominus\mathsf{E}\diamondminus A$,
(potl5) $A \rightarrow \mathsf{A}\ominus\mathsf{E}\bigcirc A$,
(potl6) $A \rightarrow \mathsf{A}\bigcirc\mathsf{E}\ominus A$.

Additional rules

(prevpo) $A \rightarrow B \vdash \mathsf{E}\ominus A \rightarrow \mathsf{E}\ominus B$,
(indpo1) $A \rightarrow B, A \rightarrow \mathsf{E}\ominus A \vdash A \rightarrow \mathsf{E}\boxminus B$,
(indpo2) $A \rightarrow \neg B, A \rightarrow \mathsf{A}\ominus(A \vee \neg\mathsf{E}\diamondminus B) \vdash A \rightarrow \neg\mathsf{E}\diamondminus B$.

These additions are easily understood from previous discussions. (potl5) and (potl6) are counterparts of the axioms (pltl5) and (pltl6) in LTL+p (cf. Sect. 3.4).

POTL can be applied to state systems along the lines pointed out in Sects. 10.3 and 10.4. In this logic system properties like

$$\mathsf{A}\Box(A \rightarrow \mathsf{A}\diamondminus B)$$

("all subsequent states in which A holds will be preceded by a state in which B holds") can be formulated which are safety properties in the terminology of Sect. 7.1 if A and B do not contain temporal operators. However, many other properties like, e.g.,

$$\mathsf{A}\Box(A \rightarrow \mathsf{E}\diamondminus B)$$

("all subsequent states in which A holds can be reached from a state in which B holds") cannot be expressed in linear temporal logic. On the other hand, the same arguments as in BTL and CTL imply that there are properties expressible in LTL but not in POTL.

Actually, POTL was designed for applications to state systems with another intention. To explain this, let us come back to our discussion about linear and branching time modeling at the beginning of Sect. 10.3. State systems (which we want to speak and reason about) are characterized by a set of possible runs and, as formalized in the transition system model, such runs are sequences (i.e., linearly ordered sets) of states. Linear time temporal logics are designed to make statements about single sequences, whereas branching time logics (and also POTL) can formulate and argue about statements which concern the whole set of state sequences by taking the branching structure of the set as semantical basis.

A special kind of state system are systems of concurrently running sequential processes. Such systems can be represented by transition systems using the concept of interleaving (together with fairness) as we discussed in detail in Chap. 8. However, there exist also other formal (*true concurrency*) models of such systems which may be more appropriate for handling certain problems. In these representations some "concurrent transitions" have to be executed in some relative order but others need not be forced into such an order by interleaving; they may be left unordered. This implies that a single run is then represented by a partially ordered set of states. A simple example is given by two processes running through "local" states $\eta_0, \eta_1, \eta_2, \ldots$ and $\eta'_0, \eta'_1, \eta'_2, \ldots$, respectively. Some states η_i and η'_j represent critical sections (cf. Sect. 8.3) which are to be mutually excluded. A run could look like

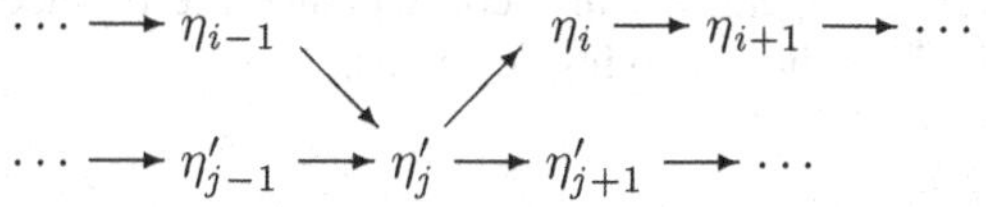

where η_i occurs after η'_j but other states are mutually unordered (assuming that they are "non-critical"). The logic POTL is designed to treat such models. This also means that it comes back to the linear temporal logic application style: one temporal structure of the logic represents one run of the system.

We do not pursue such models and their temporal logic treatment in detail, but we want to indicate the great variety of possibilities by sketching another temporal logic, called (*discrete*) *event structure logic* DESL, for which a more complicated partial order system model is used and directly taken as semantical basis (cf. again our remarks at the end of Sect. 6.2).

In this modeling the behaviour of a system is represented by a (*discrete*) *event structure* $(I, \rightarrowtriangle, \curlyvee)$ consisting of a non-empty set I of *events*, an irreflexive, antisymmetric, and intransitive binary relation $\rightarrowtriangle$ on I, and an irreflexive, symmetric binary relation $\curlyvee$ on I, called *conflict relation*, with the property that for any events $\iota_1, \iota_2, \iota_3 \in I$, if $\iota_1 \curlyvee \iota_2$ and $\iota_2 \rightarrowtriangle^* \iota_3$ then $\iota_1 \curlyvee \iota_3$. The relation $\rightarrowtriangle^*$ is the reflexive transitive closure of $\rightarrowtriangle$ and called *causality relation*. Informally, a system is thought of as a set of event occurrences, $\rightarrowtriangle^*$ represents its "inherent sequential flow", events "in conflict" may not both occur, and events which are neither comparable by $\rightarrowtriangle^*$ nor in conflict may occur concurrently. The condition on $\curlyvee$ means that in the "past" of any event no two events may be in conflict.

A language $\mathcal{L}_{\mathrm{DESL}}(\mathbf{V})$ (for a set $\mathbf{V}$ of propositional constants) of DESL is defined as usual with the temporal operators $\bigcirc$, $\Box$, $\ominus$, $\boxminus$, and $\boxed{\curlyvee}$. The first four refer to the partial order $\rightarrowtriangle^*$ of events but unlike in POTL, they do not include quantification on branches. The (unary) operator $\boxed{\curlyvee}$ refers to the conflict relation, a formula $\boxed{\curlyvee} A$

informally means

"A holds in all states which are in conflict with the present one."

Formally, the semantics of $\mathcal{L}_{\mathrm{DESL}}$ is based on the notion of an (*event*) *temporal structure* $\mathsf{K} = (\{\eta_\iota\}_{\iota \in I}, \mathrel{-\!\!\triangleright}, \curlyvee)$ for $\mathbf{V}$ which is given by an event structure $(I, \mathrel{-\!\!\triangleright}, \curlyvee)$ and a multiset $\{\eta_\iota\}_{\iota \in I}$ of states defined as before. According to the informal meaning, the definition of $\mathsf{K}_\iota(F)$ for formulas F built with the temporal operators of DESL is given as follows:

- $\mathsf{K}_\iota(\bigcirc A) = \mathrm{tt} \Leftrightarrow \mathsf{K}_\kappa(A) = \mathrm{tt}$ for every κ such that $\iota \mathrel{-\!\!\triangleright} \kappa$.
- $\mathsf{K}_\iota(\Box A) = \mathrm{tt} \Leftrightarrow \mathsf{K}_\kappa(A) = \mathrm{tt}$ for every κ such that $\iota \mathrel{-\!\!\triangleright}^* \kappa$.
- $\mathsf{K}_\iota(\ominus A) = \mathrm{tt} \Leftrightarrow \mathsf{K}_\kappa(A) = \mathrm{tt}$ for every κ such that $\kappa \mathrel{-\!\!\triangleright} \iota$.
- $\mathsf{K}_\iota(\boxminus A) = \mathrm{tt} \Leftrightarrow \mathsf{K}_\kappa(A) = \mathrm{tt}$ for every κ such that $\kappa \mathrel{-\!\!\triangleright}^* \iota$.
- $\mathsf{K}_\iota(\boxed{\curlyvee} A) = \mathrm{tt} \Leftrightarrow \mathsf{K}_\kappa(A) = \mathrm{tt}$ for every κ such that $\iota \curlyvee \kappa$.

Observe that the clauses for $\bigcirc$, $\Box$, $\ominus$, and $\boxminus$ resemble the corresponding definitions in LTL+p with the difference that $\mathbb{N}$ is replaced by I and the linear order on $\mathbb{N}$ is replaced by the partial order $\mathrel{-\!\!\triangleright}^*$. (Cf. also our remarks about modal logic in the Second Reading paragraph in Sect. 2.3.) Validity and consequence are defined as before. Typical laws of the logic include the following formulas.

(ET1) $\Box A \to \Box\Box A$,
(ET2) $\boxminus A \to \boxminus\boxminus A$,
(ET3) $\Box A \to A \wedge \bigcirc\Box A$,
(ET4) $\boxminus A \to A \wedge \ominus\boxminus A$,
(ET5) $A \to \ominus\bigcirc A$,
(ET6) $A \to \bigcirc\ominus A$,
(ET7) $\boxed{\curlyvee}(A \to B) \to (\boxed{\curlyvee} A \to \boxed{\curlyvee} B)$,
(ET8) $A \to \boxed{\curlyvee}\neg\boxed{\curlyvee}\neg A$,
(ET9) $\boxed{\curlyvee} A \to \boxed{\curlyvee}\Box A$.

(ET8) expresses the symmetry of the relation $\curlyvee$ and (ET9) is given by its "inheritance property". This can easily be seen when proving it:

$$\begin{aligned} \mathsf{K}_\iota(\boxed{\curlyvee} A) = \mathrm{tt} &\Rightarrow \mathsf{K}_\kappa(A) = \mathrm{tt} \text{ for every } \kappa \text{ such that } \iota \curlyvee \kappa \\ &\Rightarrow \mathsf{K}_{\kappa'}(A) = \mathrm{tt} \text{ for every } \kappa \text{ and } \kappa' \text{ such that } \iota \curlyvee \kappa \text{ and } \kappa \mathrel{-\!\!\triangleright}^* \kappa' \\ &\Rightarrow \mathsf{K}_\kappa(\Box A) = \mathrm{tt} \text{ for every } \kappa \text{ such that } \iota \curlyvee \kappa \\ &\Rightarrow \mathsf{K}_\iota(\boxed{\curlyvee}\Box A) = \mathrm{tt}. \end{aligned}$$

DESL is decidable and can be axiomatized. Describing system properties is similar to linear temporal logics (with another understanding of system runs) as far as the use of the operators $\bigcirc$, $\Box$, $\ominus$, $\boxminus$ is concerned. The operator $\boxed{\curlyvee}$ is used for expressing *conflict freeness*: the informal meaning of $\boxed{\curlyvee} A$ noted above can also be understood as saying

"All states in which $\neg A$ holds are not in conflict".

Bibliographical Notes

The embedding of FOLTL^{fp} into FOLTL is due to [107]. Correspondence theory is a prominent field of study of modal logic that is dedicated to the study of different semantical conditions on the accessibility relation of Kripke structures and their representation by the axioms of the logics. Within temporal logic, many semantic variations have been studied in [58, 151]. Temporal logics for real-time systems are studied, e.g., in [6, 135]. Spatial-temporal logics for mobile agents were first introduced in connection with process calculi [26]; our presentation mainly follows [74, 161].

The interval temporal logic ITL was first introduced by Moszkowski [110] in connection with temporal logic programming. Its decision problems and axiomatization are studied in [22, 111].

The investigation of branching time temporal logics originated with [15]. Their studies have generated a large body of research and we cannot pretend to do justice to this field in our exposition; see [45, 67] for elementary presentations. The formal system Σ_{BTL} and its extension to CTL presented here are inspired by [117]. There has been a long controversy about the relative merits of linear time and branching time temporal logics for system specification, started by [87]. Vardi [154] evokes key arguments of that discussion and puts them in perspective. A study of temporal logics for expressing non-regular properties appears in [89].

Partial-order temporal logics have also attracted considerable attention, and different languages have been suggested emphasizing different aspects of partial-order structures and their use for modeling distributed systems. Besides [117], we would like to mention [17, 113].

11

System Verification by Model Checking

In this last chapter we come back to the verification of (properties of) state systems. Verification means to show that the system in question has some property (expressed by a formula) F. In its basic deductive form treated at great length in Chap. 7, this is performed by deriving F from specification axioms using the proof-theoretical means of the underlying temporal logic.

We now study an alternative approach called *model checking*. This is a method for *semantical* system verification not using any deductive means of the logic. Moreover, it does not use a temporal logic system specification but refers to the respective system in a more "direct" way.

Model checking is used as an algorithmic method and it can be applied for different temporal logics. In any case, it presupposes some assumptions on the decidability of the verification task. We treat the method for *finite state systems* which ensure these assumptions, and we concentrate on LTL and CTL as underlying logics. In Sects. 11.2–11.5 the basics of the model checking approach are studied in detail. Some short comments on more advanced techniques in Sect. 11.6 conclude the considerations.

11.1 Finite State Systems

To verify some property F for a state (transition) system Γ means to show that F is Γ-valid. Γ-validity is a semantical notion, whereas the "deductive" approach to verification by deriving F within a formal system of temporal logic from a set $\mathcal{A}_\Gamma$ of specification axioms for Γ (or some modification of this as in Sect. 9.4) is a proof-theoretical one. It is justified because of the argument chain

$$\mathcal{A}_\Gamma \vdash F \;\Rightarrow\; \mathcal{A}_\Gamma \vDash F \;\Rightarrow\; F \text{ is } \Gamma\text{-valid}$$

(cf. Sect. 7.2).

Another approach could be to carry out the proof of the desired assertion on the semantical level itself either by showing $\mathcal{A}_\Gamma \vDash F$ or even "directly", i.e., without any reference to specification axioms, by just using the definition of Γ-validity. In general, the proof-theoretical approach appears more attractive than such semantical methods since derivations are formal, schematic activities and may be supported by at least semi-automatic means. General semantical reasoning is not that "mechanical" – unless the underlying logic is "poor" enough. (In fact, this is one methodological purpose of introducing formal systems in logics.)

These findings may, however, change in special situations. For example, if the underlying temporal logic is propositional (and $\mathcal{A}_\Gamma$ is finite) then the semantical relationship $\mathcal{A}_\Gamma \models F$ is decidable and might – in principle – be established even algorithmically. It could be shown without using a formal proof system, e.g., by applying the methods discussed in Sect. 2.5. Clearly, systems ("directly") formalized as propositional STSs are examples for this special case and, as indicated in Sects. 6.1 and 6.2 by the circuit system Γ_{osc}, there are in fact real applications of this kind.

The restriction to propositional STSs and their corresponding propositional temporal logic is not as strong as it may seem at a first glance. In general, first-order STSs are beyond the borderline of reasonable semantical approaches. In many applications, however, state systems formalized as such STSs do not really need the full power of first-order logic but can, in fact, also be represented by a propositional STS (in other words: the first-order STS can be encoded as propositional STS) and system properties can be formulated in propositional temporal logic.

An important class of such state systems is given by *finite state systems*, i.e., systems with only finitely many states. Consider, as an example, the terminating counter Γ_{tcount} of Sect. 6.2 with the system variables on and c. The possible values of c in arbitrary states are restricted to the set $\{0, 1, \dots, 100\}$, so the set of all states of Γ_{tcount} is clearly finite. Let now

$$cval_0, cval_1, \dots, cval_{100}$$

be new propositional system variables and $\widetilde{V} = \{on, cval_0, cval_1, \dots, cval_{100}\}$. For every state η of Γ_{tcount} let

$$\widetilde{\eta} : \widetilde{V} \to \{\mathsf{ff}, \mathsf{tt}\}$$

be defined by $\widetilde{\eta}(on) = \eta(on)$ and

$$\widetilde{\eta}(cval_k) = \mathsf{tt} \Leftrightarrow \eta(c) = k \quad \text{for } 0 \le k \le 100.$$

Every such $\widetilde{\eta}$ contains "the same information" as the original η: the value for the system variable on is the same and the value $\eta(c) = k$ of the individual system variable c is encoded by $\widetilde{\eta}(cval_k) = \mathsf{tt}$. So let $\widetilde{W}$ be the set of all such $\widetilde{\eta}$ and define

$$\widetilde{T} = tot(\widetilde{T}')$$

where

$$\begin{aligned}\widetilde{T}' = \{&([\mathsf{tt}, cval_k], [\mathsf{tt}, cval_{k+1}]), ([\mathsf{tt}, cval_k], [\mathsf{ff}, cval_k]),\\ &([\mathsf{ff}, cval_k], [\mathsf{ff}, cval_k]), ([\mathsf{ff}, cval_k], [\mathsf{tt}, cval_0]) \mid 0 \le k \le 99\}\end{aligned}$$

(the second component in $[\ldots,\ldots]$ denotes the $cval_k$ with $\widetilde{\eta}(cval_k) = \mathsf{tt}$). The propositional STS

$$\widetilde{\Gamma}_{tcount} = (\emptyset, \widetilde{V}, \widetilde{W}, \widetilde{T})$$

obviously represents the same state system as the first-order STS Γ_{tcount}. For example, a run of the system represented by the execution sequence

$$[\mathsf{ff}, 32] \longrightarrow [\mathsf{tt}, 0] \longrightarrow [\mathsf{tt}, 1] \longrightarrow \ldots$$

of Γ_{tcount} is described by

$$[\mathsf{ff}, cval_{32}] \longrightarrow [\mathsf{tt}, cval_0] \longrightarrow [\mathsf{tt}, cval_1] \longrightarrow \ldots$$

in $\widetilde{\Gamma}_{tcount}$.

System properties described within some first-order temporal logic with respect to Γ_{tcount} can be expressed in a propositional temporal logic corresponding to $\widetilde{\Gamma}_{tcount}$. For example, the property

$$c = x \rightarrow c \geq x \ \mathbf{unl}\ c = 0$$

is "translated" to

$$\bigwedge_{i=0}^{100} \Big(cval_i \rightarrow \Big(\bigvee_{j=i}^{100} cval_j \Big) \ \mathbf{unl}\ cval_0 \Big).$$

A property like "there is a number n and an execution sequence in which the counter value will eventually be different from n" which could be written as

$$\exists x \mathsf{E}\Diamond(c \neq x)$$

in some first-order extension of BTL is propositionally expressed by

$$\bigvee_{i=0}^{100} \mathsf{E}\Diamond\neg cval_i\,.$$

It is easy to see from the example how this construction works in general. If a first-order STS Γ represents a finite state system then the domains $|\mathsf{S}_\Gamma|_s$ (i.e., the sets of possible values of individual system variables) can be chosen to be finite for every sort $s \in \mathbf{S}_\Gamma$ and Γ is encoded by a propositional STS $\widetilde{\Gamma} = (\emptyset, \widetilde{V}, \widetilde{W}, \widetilde{T})$ where

- $\widetilde{V} = V_\Gamma \cup \bigcup_{a \in X_\Gamma} V_a$ with $V_a = \{aval_d \mid d \in |\mathsf{S}_\Gamma|_s\}$ for every a of sort s (V_Γ and all V_a being pairwise disjoint),
- any state $\eta \in W_\Gamma$ is encoded by $\widetilde{\eta} : \widetilde{V} \rightarrow \{\mathsf{ff}, \mathsf{tt}\}$ with $\widetilde{\eta}(v) = \eta(v)$ for $v \in V_\Gamma$ and

$$\widetilde{\eta}(aval_d) = \mathsf{tt} \Leftrightarrow \eta(a) = d \quad \text{for } aval_d \in V_a, a \in X_\Gamma$$

and $\widetilde{W_\Gamma}$ is the set of all such states $\widetilde{\eta}$; this set is finite,
- $\widetilde{T}$ is the set of all pairs $(\widetilde{\eta}, \widetilde{\eta}') \in \widetilde{W} \times \widetilde{W}$ such that $\widetilde{\eta}$ and $\widetilde{\eta}'$ encode η and η' with $(\eta, \eta') \in T_\Gamma$.

The translation of properties of Γ into the propositional temporal logic corresponding to $\widetilde{\Gamma}$ has no special temporal aspect and is well known from classical logic. Apart from some simple technical details concerning variables and function symbols the main principles are:

- atomic formulas $p(a, b, \ldots)$ with $a, b, \ldots \in X_\Gamma$ are translated to

$$\bigvee_{p^{\mathsf{S}_\Gamma}(d_a, d_b, \ldots) = \mathsf{tt}} (aval_{d_a} \wedge bval_{d_b} \wedge \ldots)$$

(with an analogous translation of formulas $a = b$),
- quantification of formulas with $\exists$ or $\forall$ runs only over finitely many values and is replaced by disjunction or conjunction, respectively.

(Observe that formulas with free variables as in the example can also be viewed as universally closed.)

Summarizing the whole discussion we may assume without loss of generality that an STS representing a finite state system is propositional and has only finitely many states. According to our general definitions in Sect. 6.2 the set V of (propositional) system variables may be infinite. However, because of the finiteness of the state set, it is quite easy to encode an infinite V by a finite one. Moreover, we mentioned in Sect. 6.2 that the general choice was made only for some "theoretical" reasons whereas in practical applications V is usually finite. (This fact is not invalidated by the above encoding of first-order finite state systems into propositional ones.) So we assume that the set V is finite itself. (Note that the state set and also the transition relation are then "automatically" finite.)

We give the following separate definition for this case.

Definition. A *finite* (*state*) *transition system* (briefly: FSTS) $\Psi = (V, W, T)$ is given by

- a finite set V of *system* (or *state*) *variables*,
- a set W of (*system*) *states* $\eta : V \to \{\mathsf{ff}, \mathsf{tt}\}$,
- a total *transition relation* $T \subseteq W \times W$.

In the following considerations any FSTS will (also) be handled as a propositional STS and notions of *successor state*, *execution sequence*, etc., and notations like $\Psi(V)$, W_Ψ, etc. will be adopted from Sect. 6.2.

Finite transition systems may be depicted in a graphical representation as *transition diagrams.* States η are given by nodes in the diagram "containing" those system variables v with $\eta(v) = \mathsf{tt}$, and arrows between the nodes represent the transition relation. For example, the FSTS $\widetilde{\Gamma}_{tcount}$ from above is represented by the transition diagram in Fig. 11.1 (where we write c_k instead of $cval_k$). The node containing

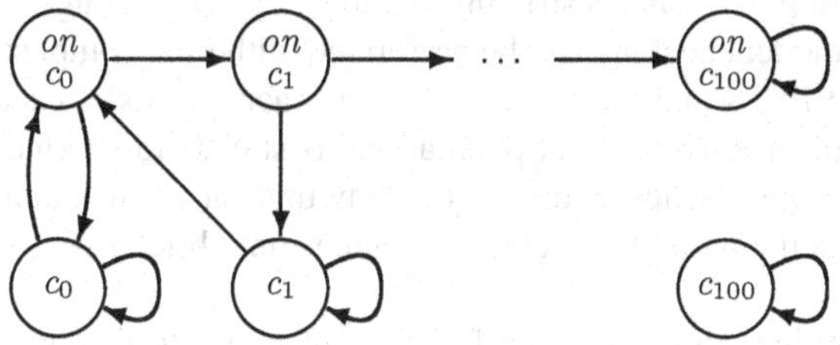

Fig. 11.1. Transition diagram for a counter

only c_1 represents the state $[\mathsf{ff}, c_1]$, the arrow from this node to that with on and c_0 represents the pair $([\mathsf{ff}, c_1], [\mathsf{tt}, c_0])$ of the transition relation.

The temporal logic language of an FSTS Ψ is some propositional one. A (temporal logic) specification of Ψ is given by a set $\mathcal{A}_\Psi$ of formulas of this language. For example, a specification of the terminating counter in its propositional form Γ_{tcount} above could be given by the axioms

$$\bigvee_{k=0}^{100} cval_k,$$
$$cval_k \rightarrow \neg cval_j \qquad \text{for } 0 \leq k, j \leq 100,\ k \neq j,$$
$$on \wedge cval_k \rightarrow (on' \wedge cval'_{k+1}) \vee (\neg on' \wedge cval'_k) \qquad \text{for } 0 \leq k < 100,$$
$$\neg on \wedge cval_k \rightarrow (\neg on' \wedge cval'_k) \vee (on' \wedge cval'_0) \qquad \text{for } 0 \leq k < 100,$$
$$cval_{100} \rightarrow (on' \leftrightarrow on) \wedge cval'_{100}.$$

The first two of these axioms describe that c has a (unique) value in the interval from 0 to 100 and the other three axioms are trivially taken from the first-order axioms given for Γ_{tcount} in Sect. 6.2.

Coming back finally to the discussion at the beginning of this section, we may now say that the semantical verification of some property F for a finite state system – formally represented as an FSTS Ψ – takes place within an (algorithmically treatable) propositional temporal logic framework, and it means to show $\mathcal{A}_\Psi \models F$ or to check whether F is Ψ-valid. The latter approach is called *(temporal logic) model checking*.

To show some consequence relationship $\mathcal{A}_\Psi \models F$ (for finite $\mathcal{A}_\Psi$), a decision procedure like the one presented in Sect. 2.5 might be used. For example, if the axioms of $\mathcal{A}_\Psi$ and F are LTL formulas then $\mathcal{A}_\Psi \models F$ can be shown by constructing a tableau for the PNP $(\mathcal{A}_\Psi, \{F\})$. Model checking algorithms are usually more efficient and, hence, more attractive in practice than such procedures since they use the FSTS Ψ "directly" whereas the axioms of $\mathcal{A}_\Psi$ "encode" Ψ and, in general, the decision procedures cannot take advantage of the special form of these formulas. For this reason we will focus on the model checking approach in the following sections.

Concerning complexity, model checking algorithms themselves depend on which temporal logic is used to describe the system property F. In the case of linear temporal logic model checking algorithms have time complexity linear in the size of the FSTS Ψ and exponential in the length of F. Model checking with the branching time logic CTL* has the same complexity, but restricting the logic to CTL changes the situation significantly. CTL model checking can be performed with time complexity linear both in the size of the FSTS and the formula. So, in practice, model checking with CTL has been established as the most popular and best elaborated kind of all the semantical verification approaches, and we will study this variant in detail in Sects. 11.3–11.5. Model checking with linear temporal logic is only briefly sketched in the next section.

Compared with the definitions in Chap. 6, an FSTS corresponds to the "basic" case of STSs introduced in Sect. 6.2. Of course, we can extend the considerations to the more refined kinds of transition systems. We restrict ourselves to the context of verification by model checking and consider, firstly, systems in which certain initial states are distinguished. In Sect. 6.3 such rooted STSs were defined to be endowed with a formula *start* which could immediately be used for specification purposes. Although specification is not relevant in the model checking approach, we can define *rooted* FSTSs in the same way, but we can also come back to what was already mentioned in Sect. 6.3 and represent such systems "more directly" by explicitly adding the set $W_0 \subseteq W$ of initial states to the FSTS definition. In any case, however, one must take care then to formulate properties in a way which takes into account that only execution sequences are considered which begin in an initial state.

Labeled systems in the sense of Sect. 6.4 need no particular treatment at all in the present context. System variables of the form $exec\,\lambda$ are propositional and therefore permitted in FSTSs (if they are needed for describing system properties). Enabling conditions were useful for specification but do not provide more information than what can directly be described in the transition relation of the system.

Example. The printer system shown in Sect. 6.5 can immediately be written as an FSTS $\Psi_{printer} = (V, W, T)$ where

$$
\begin{aligned}
V = \{&exec\lambda \mid \lambda \in \{\alpha_1, \alpha_2, \beta_1, \beta_2, \gamma\}\} \cup \{req_1, req_2\},\\
W = \{&\eta : V \to \{\mathsf{ff}, \mathsf{tt}\} \mid\\
&\quad \text{if } \eta(exec\alpha_1) = \mathsf{tt} \text{ then } \eta(req_1) = \mathsf{ff},\\
&\quad \text{if } \eta(exec\alpha_2) = \mathsf{tt} \text{ then } \eta(req_2) = \mathsf{ff},\\
&\quad \text{if } \eta(exec\beta_1) = \mathsf{tt} \text{ then } \eta(req_1) = \mathsf{tt},\\
&\quad \text{if } \eta(exec\beta_2) = \mathsf{tt} \text{ then } \eta(req_1) = \mathsf{tt},\\
&\quad \eta(exec\lambda) = \mathsf{tt} \text{ for exactly one } \lambda \in \{\alpha_1, \alpha_2, \beta_1, \beta_2, \gamma\}\},\\
T = \{&(\eta, \eta') \in W \times W \mid\\
&\quad \text{if } \eta(exec\alpha_1) = \mathsf{tt} \text{ then } \eta'(req_1) = \mathsf{tt}, \eta'(req_2) = \eta(req_2),\\
&\quad \text{if } \eta(exec\alpha_2) = \mathsf{tt} \text{ then } \eta'(req_1) = \eta(req_1), \eta'(req_2) = \mathsf{tt},\\
&\quad \text{if } \eta(exec\beta_1) = \mathsf{tt} \text{ then } \eta'(req_1) = \mathsf{ff}, \eta'(req_2) = \eta(req_2),\\
&\quad \text{if } \eta(exec\beta_2) = \mathsf{tt} \text{ then } \eta'(req_1) = \eta(req_1), \eta'(req_2) = \mathsf{ff},\\
&\quad \text{if } \eta(exec\gamma) = \mathsf{tt} \text{ then } \eta'(req_1) = \eta(req_1), \eta'(req_2) = \eta(req_2)\}.
\end{aligned}
$$

Additionally assuming that the system starts in a state where there is no user request we would obtain a rooted FSTS with the initial condition

$$\neg req_1 \land \neg req_2$$

or the set

$$W_0 = \{\eta \in W \mid \eta(req_1) = \eta(req_2) = \mathsf{ff}\}$$

of initial states. The property described by the formula $req_1 \rightarrow \Diamond exec\,\beta_1$ (cf. Sect. 7.4) for the non-rooted version should be formulated as

$$\neg req_1 \wedge \neg req_2 \rightarrow \Box(req_1 \rightarrow \Diamond exec\,\beta_1)$$

(in both cases) if the system is rooted. △

Actually we used the system $\Gamma_{printer}$ in Sect. 6.5 to motivate the concept of fairness. Of course, fairness assumptions may be relevant when concerning the verifiability of properties of an FSTS as well and we will study this issue separately and in more detail in Sect. 11.4.

11.2 LTL Model Checking

According to the definition of Ψ-validity in Sect. 6.2, to verify by model checking that an FSTS Ψ has a property F which is described in a (propositional) linear temporal logic means to show that all execution sequences W_Ψ of Ψ (which are now just temporal structures) satisfy F. Algorithms for this task typically use some tableau construction, and in fact, restricting the logic to the basic LTL, we may directly take the construction presented in Sect. 2.5 and modify it a little to provide an LTL model checking algorithm.

Consider, as an example, the FSTS $\Psi(\{v_1, v_2\})$ given by the transition diagram

(denoting the two states of Ψ by η_1 and η_2) and let

$$A \equiv v_1 \vee v_2 \rightarrow \Box v_1.$$

Clearly, A is Ψ-valid but not universally valid. The latter fact is reflected by the tableau $\mathcal{T}_\mathcal{P}$ for the PNP $\mathcal{P} = (\emptyset, \{A\})$ shown in Fig. 11.2. (We use an extended form with the rule $(\vee^+)$ for disjunction and omit the set parentheses in the graphical representation since all non-empty formula sets contain exactly one element.) $\mathcal{T}_\mathcal{P}$ is successful, so $\neg A$ is satisfiable. Let us examine this observation somewhat more precisely.

The tableau contains all possible "attempts" of how $\neg A$ could be satisfied. Nodes $\mathcal{Q}$ particularly indicate how the propositional constants of A should be evaluated by tt (if contained in $pos(\mathcal{Q})$) or ff (if contained in $neg(\mathcal{Q})$) in the states of a satisfying

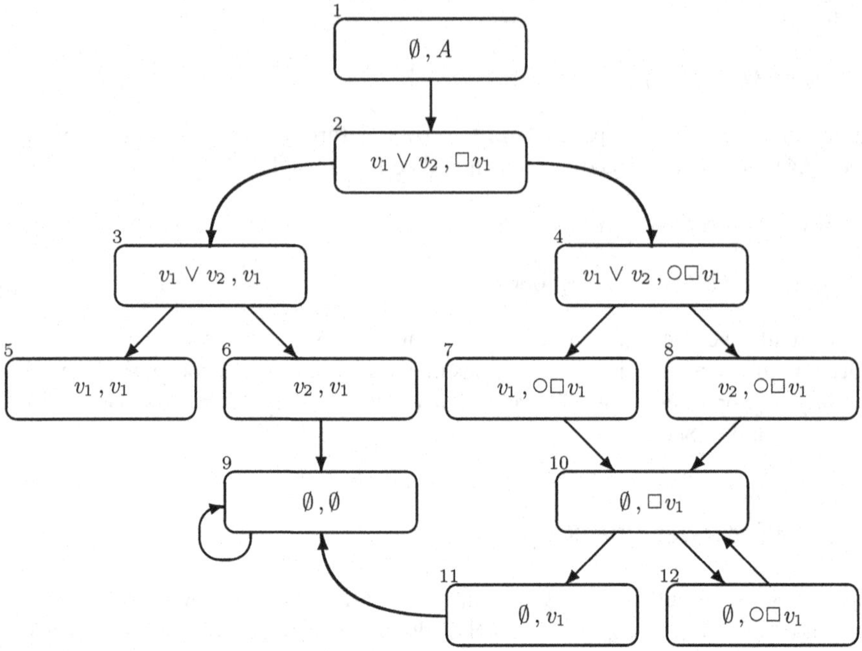

Fig. 11.2. Tableau for $(\emptyset, \{A\})$, $A \equiv v_1 \vee v_2 \rightarrow \Box v_1$

temporal structure K. A closed node like the one marked 5 is "contradictory" and not helpful for finding K since it contains v_1 both positively and negatively.

The definition of closed nodes reflects the fact that we look for an arbitrary K, so "contradictions" are only given by nodes according to the clause $(C1)$, i.e., satisfying condition $(\perp)$ and their propagation through the tableau by the inductive clauses $(C2)$ and $(C3)$.

Turning now to the Ψ-validity of the formula A, it is in fact quite easy to modify the tableau $\mathcal{T}_{\mathcal{P}}$ along these basic ideas such that this fact can be drawn from it in a similar usage. An arbitrary formula F is Ψ-valid if and only if there is no temporal structure W_Ψ containing a state η in which F has the truth value ff. Such an η can be any state of Ψ. So the modified tableau in our example should comprehend all attempts for all $\eta \in W_\Psi$ of how to satisfy $\neg A$ by some W_Ψ "at state η"; in other words, how to make $\neg A$ true in η under the assumption that the continuation of η in any temporal structure under consideration is given by the transition relation of Ψ.

Consider, e.g., the state η_1. Looking for a possibility to make $\neg A$ true in η_1 within some W_Ψ means that the nodes 1–8 in $\mathcal{T}_{\mathcal{P}}$ which do not involve any step according to the tableau condition $(\bigcirc)$ must be "consistent" with the definition of η_1. Node 5 is still "contradictory in itself", but nodes 6 and 8 which both suggest a state η with $\eta(v_2) = \mathsf{tt}$ can now also be viewed as closed (without any successor node) since this contradicts $\eta_1(v_2) = \mathsf{ff}$.

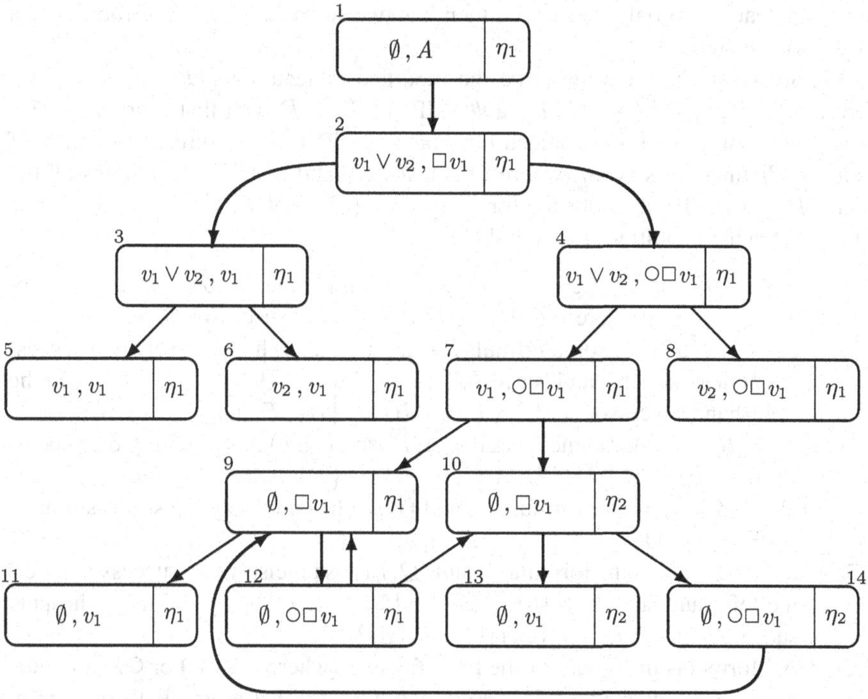

Fig. 11.3. Modified tableau

Node 10 is reached by a step according to ($\bigcirc$) and therefore deals with the possible successor nodes of η_1 in W_Ψ. These are η_1 and η_2, so we may split the node 10 into two instants which have to be consistent with η_1 and η_2, respectively, and proceed then in the same way. A tableau following this idea could look like the one in Fig. 11.3

Each node is augmented with the additional information about which state of Ψ it should be consistent with. Nodes 9 and 10 are the two nodes corresponding to the former node 10. The successors of node 12 are nodes 9 and 10 as for node 7, and the successor of node 14 is node 9 since η_1 is the only successor state of η_2 in Ψ. The nodes 5, 6, 8, 11, and 13 are to be seen as closed, the latter two because of $\eta_1(v_1) = \eta_2(v_1) = \mathsf{tt}$. So, applying the propagation rules $(C2)$ and $(C3)$, the root 1 of this tableau would turn out to be closed which shows that $\neg A$ cannot be made true in state η_1 in a temporal structure W_Ψ. Observe that if we change Ψ such that $\eta_2(v_1) = \mathsf{ff}$ then node 13 would not be closed (and would have some successor node), and thus the root would not be closed either. In fact, A would then not be valid in any execution sequence $\mathsf{W}_\Psi = (\ldots, \eta_1, \eta_2, \ldots)$.

So far, we have only considered how $\neg A$ could be true in state η_1, and the tableau in Fig. 11.3 reflects this. We could build now another such modified tableau for η_2 (in general: for all states of the FSTS) or, more concisely, we may identify equal nodes, i.e., nodes with equal PNP and equal state information and thus melt these single tableaux into only one which then has two roots (in general: n roots for an FSTS with n states).

Summarizing, we may describe the modified tableau construction as follows. Given an FSTS $\Psi = (V, W, T)$, a Ψ-PNP is a PNP $\mathcal{P}$ such that every $F \in \mathcal{F}_{\mathcal{P}}$ is a formula of $\mathcal{L}_{\mathrm{LTL}}(V)$. A tableau for Ψ and a Ψ-PNP $\mathcal{P}$ is a directed graph $\mathcal{T}$ of pairwise distinct pairs $(\mathcal{Q}, \eta)$ where $\mathcal{Q}$ is a Ψ-PNP and $\eta \in W$. $\mathcal{T}$ contains all the pairs $(\mathcal{P}, \eta)$, $\eta \in W$, as roots and for every node $(\mathcal{Q}, \eta)$ of $\mathcal{T}$, $\mathcal{Q} = (\mathcal{F}^+, \mathcal{F}^-)$, one of the following conditions has to hold:

($\bot$) **false** $\in \mathcal{F}^+$ or $\mathcal{F}^+ \cap \mathcal{F}^- \neq \emptyset$ or $\eta(v) = \mathsf{ff}$ for some $v \in \mathcal{F}^+$ or $\eta(v) = \mathsf{tt}$ for some $v \in \mathcal{F}^-$ (where $v \in V$), and $(\mathcal{Q}, \eta)$ has no successor node.

($\rightarrow^+$) $A \rightarrow B \in \mathcal{F}^+$ for some formulas A, B, and $(\mathcal{Q}, \eta)$ has precisely two successor nodes: the left-hand successor $((\mathcal{F}^+ \setminus \{A \rightarrow B\}, \mathcal{F}^- \cup \{A\}), \eta)$ and the right-hand successor $(((\mathcal{F}^+ \setminus \{A \rightarrow B\}) \cup \{B\}, \mathcal{F}^-), \eta)$.

($\rightarrow^-$) $A \rightarrow B \in \mathcal{F}^-$ for some formulas A, B, and $(\mathcal{Q}, \eta)$ has precisely the successor node $((\mathcal{F}^+ \cup \{A\}, (\mathcal{F}^- \setminus \{A \rightarrow B\}) \cup \{B\}), \eta)$.

($\Box^+$) $\Box A \in \mathcal{F}^+$ for some formula A, and $(\mathcal{Q}, \eta)$ has precisely the successor node $(((\mathcal{F}^+ \setminus \{\Box A\}) \cup \{A, \bigcirc\Box A\}, \mathcal{F}^-), \eta)$.

($\Box^-$) $\Box A \in \mathcal{F}^-$ for some formula A, and $(\mathcal{Q}, \eta)$ has precisely two successor nodes: the left-hand successor $((\mathcal{F}^+, (\mathcal{F}^- \setminus \{\Box A\}) \cup \{A\}), \eta)$ and the right-hand successor $((\mathcal{F}^+, (\mathcal{F}^- \setminus \{\Box A\}) \cup \{\bigcirc\Box A\}), \eta)$.

($\bigcirc$) All formulas in $\mathcal{F}_{\mathcal{Q}}$ are of the form **false**, v (where $v \in V$) or $\bigcirc A$ for some formula A, node $(\mathcal{Q}, \eta)$ does not satisfy ($\bot$), and has precisely the successor nodes $((\sigma_1(\mathcal{Q}), \sigma_3(\mathcal{Q})), \eta')$ with all η' such that $(\eta, \eta') \in T$.

(Again, σ_1 and σ_3 are the functions defined in Sect. 2.4.) Note that because of the finiteness of the state set W there are only finitely many possible nodes for making up the tableau.

The set of closed nodes of such a tableau $\mathcal{T}$ is defined as in the original construction:

($C1$) All nodes $(\mathcal{Q}, \eta)$ of $\mathcal{T}$ that satisfy condition ($\bot$) are closed.

($C2$) Every node $(\mathcal{Q}, \eta)$ of $\mathcal{T}$ all of whose successors are closed is closed.

($C3$) If $(\mathcal{Q}, \eta)$ is a node and A is a formula such that $\Box A \in neg(\mathcal{Q})$ and every path from $(\mathcal{Q}, \eta)$ to nodes $(\mathcal{Q}', \eta')$ with $A \in neg(\mathcal{Q}')$ contains some closed node then $(\mathcal{Q}, \eta)$ is itself closed.

(We have listed only conditions for expansion and pruning steps with respect to the basic LTL operators. Extensions for derived operators can be given in the same way as in the original definition.)

We do not go into proof details, but it should be quite evident from the elaborated proofs in Sect. 2.5 and the above considerations that the former (appropriately modified) lemmas can easily be transferred to the present situation providing the desired model checking algorithm: given an FSTS $\Psi(V)$ and a formula F of $\mathcal{L}_{\mathrm{LTL}}(V)$, in order to decide whether F is Ψ-valid one can construct a tableau for Ψ and the Ψ-PNP $(\emptyset, \{F\})$ and decide whether all of its roots are closed.

We finally note that this verification method can easily be adapted to the case of rooted FSTSs: if, e.g., a system is given with an initial condition $start$ then the roots of the tableau are the pairs $(\mathcal{P}', \eta)$ where $\mathcal{P}' = (pos(\mathcal{P}) \cup \{start\}, neg(\mathcal{P}))$.

We have observed a close connection between the tableau construction and Büchi automata in Sect. 4.4, and this connection has been very fruitful for deriving model checking algorithms for LTL. We sketch the practically important case where Γ is a rooted FSTS given with a designated set W_0 of – for simplicity – precisely one initial state η_0 (cf. Sect. 11.1), and where one is interested in the validity of an initial property F in the sense of Sect. 9.4. This means that $\mathsf{K}_0(F) = \mathsf{tt}$ holds for all temporal structures K that arise from execution sequences of Γ starting at state η_0. Equivalently, there does not exist any execution sequence from η_0 such that $\mathsf{K}_0(F) = \mathsf{ff}$ holds for the corresponding temporal structure. According to Theorem 4.4.1, this means that no such structure is accepted by the Büchi automaton $\Omega_{(\emptyset,\{F\})}$. Furthermore, a rooted FSTS Γ itself resembles an automaton (with trivial acceptance condition), and a product construction similar to the one described in Theorem 4.3.1 can be used to construct a Büchi automaton "synchronizing" Γ and $\Omega_{(\emptyset,\{F\})}$. This automaton defines the empty language if and only if F is (initially) Γ-valid, and language emptiness of Büchi automata can be decided by Theorem 4.3.8. In fact, the proof of this theorem provides the idea to compute an element of the language when it is non-empty, and graph search algorithms employed to determine emptiness yield such a witness in a direct way. In the context of model checking, a witness of the product automaton represents a counterexample: an execution of Γ from η_0 that does not satisfy F. The ability to produce counterexamples makes model checking an attractive approach in practice.

More precisely, the locations of the product automaton are pairs (η, q) where η is a state of Γ and q is a location of $\Omega_{(\emptyset,\{F\})}$. The initial locations are of the form (η_0, q_0) for initial locations q_0 of $\Omega_{(\emptyset,\{F\})}$. The transition formulas of the product automaton synchronize possible transitions of Γ and of $\Omega_{(\emptyset,\{F\})}$ as follows:

$$\delta((\eta, q), (\eta', q')) = \begin{cases} \textbf{true} & \text{if } (\eta, \eta') \in T_\Gamma \text{ and } \models_{\eta} \delta(q, q'), \\ \textbf{false} & \text{otherwise.} \end{cases}$$

The set of acceptance locations of the product automaton is the set of all pairs (η, q_f) such that q_f is an accepting location of $\Omega_{(\emptyset,\{F\})}$.

The size of the automaton is the product of the sizes of Γ and of $\Omega_{(\emptyset,\{F\})}$, and the latter can be exponential in the size of the formula F, as we have observed in Sect. 4.4. However, formulas are often quite short, and the linear factor contributed by Γ is often the limiting one; this is the infamous *state explosion problem* of model checking. So-called "on-the-fly" algorithms alleviate the problem by interleaving the emptiness check and the construction of the product automaton, thus avoiding the explicit construction (and storage in computer memory) of the latter.

11.3 CTL Model Checking

Model checking has been successfully applied particularly in the CTL framework. Recalling the remarks about the application of BTL to state systems in Sect. 10.3 (which can be carried over to CTL as well), an FSTS $\Psi = (V, W, T)$ induces in this case a language $\mathcal{L}_{\mathrm{CTL}\Psi} = \mathcal{L}_{\mathrm{CTL}}(V)$ and a temporal structure $\mathsf{K}^{\Psi} = (\{\eta_\iota\}_{\iota \in W}, T)$ for V with $\eta_\iota = \iota$ for every $\iota \in W$, briefly denoted by

$$\mathsf{K}^{\Psi} = (W, T).$$

A property of Ψ is given by a formula F of $\mathcal{L}_{\mathrm{CTL}\Psi}$ and to verify by model checking that Ψ has this property means, according to the definition of Ψ-validity, to show that F is valid in K^{Ψ}, i.e., that

$$\mathsf{K}^{\Psi}_{\eta}(F) = \mathsf{tt} \quad \text{for every } \eta \in W.$$

(If Ψ is rooted with a set W_0 of initial states, we may be more interested in determining if $\mathsf{K}^{\Psi}_{\eta}(F) = \mathsf{tt}$ holds for all $\eta \in W_0$. The techniques described in the following are easily adapted to this situation.)

There are several different approaches to perform this task algorithmically. We present here one method which particularly allows for quite efficient implementation. The idea is to determine all states $\eta \in W$ with $\mathsf{K}^{\Psi}_{\eta}(F) = \mathsf{tt}$ and then check whether these are all states of W. The latter part is trivial, so, introducing the notation

$$[\![F]\!]_{\Psi} = \{\eta \in W \mid \mathsf{K}^{\Psi}_{\eta}(F) = \mathsf{tt}\}$$

(for arbitrary formulas F of $\mathcal{L}_{\mathrm{CTL}\Psi}$), we may fix the essential part of this CTL model checking approach as follows:

- Given an FSTS Ψ and a formula F of $\mathcal{L}_{\mathrm{CTL}\Psi}$, determine the set $[\![F]\!]_{\Psi}$.

We call $[\![F]\!]_{\Psi}$ the *satisfaction set* of F (with respect to Ψ), and for simplicity we will often write $[\![F]\!]$ instead of $[\![F]\!]_{\Psi}$ and also K_{η} instead of K^{Ψ}_{η} if the context of the given Ψ is clear. The notation $[\![F]\!]_{\Psi}$ resembles the similar notation $[\![F]\!]^{\Xi}_{\mathsf{K}}$ introduced in Sect. 3.2. In fact, we will shortly come back also to some techniques discussed there.

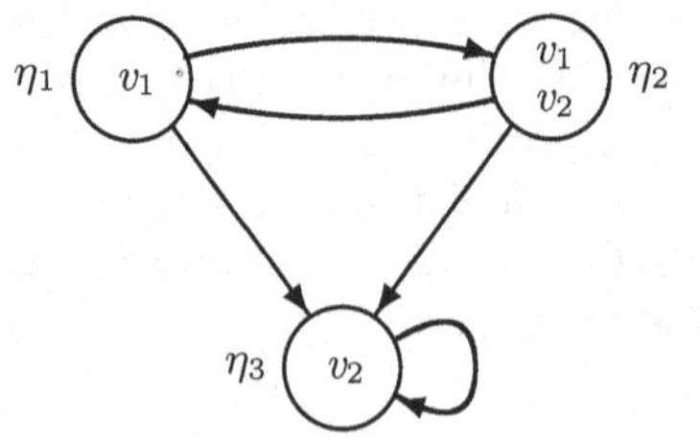

Fig. 11.4. An FSTS Ψ_{examp}

Example. Let $\Psi_{exmp}(\{v_1, v_2\})$ be the FSTS represented by the transition diagram in Fig. 11.4. Then

$$\mathsf{K}^{\Psi_{exmp}} = (\{\eta_1, \eta_2, \eta_3\}, \{(\eta_1, \eta_2), (\eta_1, \eta_3), (\eta_2, \eta_1), (\eta_2, \eta_3), (\eta_3, \eta_3)\}).$$

Up to some renamings, $\mathsf{K}^{\Psi_{exmp}}$ is just the temporal structure $\mathsf{K} = (\{\eta_\iota\}_{\iota \in \{1,2,3\}}, \twoheadrightarrow)$ from Sect. 10.4 which was defined by $\twoheadrightarrow = \{(1,2), (1,3), (2,1), (2,3), (3,3)\}$ and

	η_1	η_2	η_3
v_1	tt	tt	ff
v_2	ff	tt	tt

For the formula $A \equiv v_1$ **Eunt** $(v_1 \wedge v_2)$ we found there that $\mathsf{K}_1(A) = \mathsf{K}_2(A) = \mathsf{tt}$ and $\mathsf{K}_3(A) = \mathsf{ff}$. With respect to the notation used for $\mathsf{K}^{\Psi_{exmp}}$ we write this now as $\mathsf{K}_{\eta_1}(A) = \mathsf{K}_{\eta_2}(A) = \mathsf{tt}$ and $\mathsf{K}_{\eta_3}(A) = \mathsf{ff}$, so we have $[\![A]\!] = \{\eta_1, \eta_2\}$. △

In general, given $\Psi = (V, W, T)$, the set $[\![F]\!]$ can be determined recursively with respect to the formula F and, since W and T are finite, this provides in fact an algorithm for computing it. We begin with the obvious cases concerning the classical logical connectives of CTL:

- $[\![v]\!] = \{\eta \in W \mid \mathsf{K}_\eta(v) = \mathsf{tt}\}$
  $= \{\eta \in W \mid \eta(v) = \mathsf{tt}\}$ for $v \in V$.
- $[\![\mathbf{false}]\!] = \emptyset$.
- $[\![A \to B]\!] = \{\eta \in W \mid \mathsf{K}_\eta(A \to B) = \mathsf{tt}\}$
  $= \{\eta \in W \mid \mathsf{K}_\eta(A) = \mathsf{ff}$ or $\mathsf{K}_\eta(B) = \mathsf{tt}\}$
  $= (W \setminus [\![A]\!]) \cup [\![B]\!]$.

The third clause states the fact (which occurred implicitly already in the setting of Sect. 3.2) that the classical implication operator $\to$ is represented by some set operations on $[\![A]\!]$ and $[\![B]\!]$. It is clear that this extends also to the derived operators $\neg, \vee, \wedge$ in the following way:

$$[\![\neg A]\!] = W \setminus [\![A]\!].$$
$$[\![A \vee B]\!] = [\![A]\!] \cup [\![B]\!].$$
$$[\![A \wedge B]\!] = [\![A]\!] \cap [\![B]\!].$$

Turning to the proper CTL operators $\mathsf{E}\bigcirc$, $\mathsf{E}\Box$, and **Eunt**, the first of them is still easy. Denoting the *inverse image* operation of the relation T by T^{-1} (which means $T^{-1}(W') = \{\eta \in W \mid$ there exists $\eta' \in W'$ with $(\eta, \eta') \in T\}$ for $W' \subseteq W$) we have

$$\begin{aligned}[\![\mathsf{E}\bigcirc A]\!] &= \{\eta \in W \mid \mathsf{K}_{\eta'}(A) = \mathsf{tt} \text{ for some } \eta' \text{ with } (\eta, \eta') \in T\}\\ &= T^{-1}([\![A]\!]).\end{aligned}$$

Example. Let Ψ_{exmp} be the FSTS of the previous example. According to the clauses up to now we have

$$
\begin{aligned}
&[\![v_1]\!] = \{\eta_1, \eta_2\},\\
&[\![v_2]\!] = \{\eta_2, \eta_3\},\\
&[\![\neg v_1]\!] = W \setminus \{\eta_1, \eta_2\} = \{\eta_3\},\\
&[\![v_1 \wedge v_2]\!] = [\![v_1]\!] \cap [\![v_2]\!] = \{\eta_1, \eta_2\} \cap \{\eta_2, \eta_3\} = \{\eta_2\},\\
&[\![\neg v_1 \vee v_2]\!] = [\![\neg v_1]\!] \cup [\![v_2]\!] = \{\eta_3\} \cup \{\eta_2, \eta_3\} = \{\eta_2, \eta_3\},\\
&[\![\mathsf{E}\!\bigcirc v_1]\!] = T^{-1}([\![v_1]\!]) = T^{-1}(\{\eta_1, \eta_2\}) = \{\eta_1, \eta_2\}.
\end{aligned}
$$

These results are informally quite evident from the transition diagram. For example, $[\![\mathsf{E}\!\bigcirc v_1]\!]$ is the set of those nodes for which there is an arrow to another node which contains v_1. These are just η_1 and η_2. △

The remaining cases of the operators $\mathsf{E}\Box$ and **Eunt** are somewhat more difficult. For their treatment we recall, as basic idea, that these operators satisfy the fixpoint characterizations

(BT1) $\mathsf{E}\Box A \leftrightarrow A \wedge \mathsf{E}\!\bigcirc\!\mathsf{E}\Box A$,
(CT1) $A\ \mathbf{Eunt}\ B \leftrightarrow B \vee (A \wedge \mathsf{E}\!\bigcirc(A\ \mathbf{Eunt}\ B))$

(cf. Sects. 10.3 and 10.4). This fact indicates that we can characterize the corresponding satisfaction sets as fixpoints of certain functions, quite similarly to how this was elaborated in Sect. 3.2 for the case of linear temporal logic operators. In the present situation we consider, for a given FSTS $\Psi = (V, W, T)$, functions

$$\Upsilon : 2^W \to 2^W$$

and recall that some $Z \subseteq W$ is a fixpoint of such an Υ if $\Upsilon(Z) = Z$. Furthermore, fixpoints can be compared by set inclusion, so least and greatest fixpoints may be distinguished among them.

Consider now the function

$$\Upsilon_A(Z) = [\![A]\!] \cap T^{-1}(Z)$$

(for some given formula A of $\mathcal{L}_{\mathrm{CTL}\Psi}$). From similar definitions in Sect 3.2 and the equivalence (BT1) it should be quite evident that this function tackles the case $\mathsf{E}\Box A$.

Theorem 11.3.1. $[\![\mathsf{E}\Box A]\!]$ *is the greatest fixpoint of* Υ_A.

Proof. We have

$$
\begin{aligned}
\eta \in [\![\mathsf{E}\Box A]\!] &\Leftrightarrow \mathsf{K}_\eta(\mathsf{E}\Box A) = \mathrm{tt}\\
&\Leftrightarrow \text{there is a fullpath } (\eta_0, \eta_1, \eta_2, \ldots) \text{ in } W \text{ with } \eta_0 = \eta\\
&\ \text{and } \mathsf{K}_{\eta_k}(A) = \mathrm{tt} \text{ for every } k \in \mathbb{N}\\
&\Leftrightarrow \mathsf{K}_\eta(A) = \mathrm{tt} \text{ and there exists } \eta' \in [\![\mathsf{E}\Box A]\!] \text{ with } (\eta, \eta') \in T\\
&\Leftrightarrow \eta \in [\![A]\!] \text{ and } \eta \in T^{-1}([\![\mathsf{E}\Box A]\!])\\
&\Leftrightarrow \eta \in \Upsilon_A([\![\mathsf{E}\Box A]\!]),
\end{aligned}
$$

so $[\![\mathsf{E}\Box A]\!]$ is a fixpoint of Υ_A.

Let now Z be an arbitrary fixpoint of Υ_A and $\eta_0 \in Z$. So, $Z = \Upsilon_A(Z)$ and therefore $\eta_0 \in [\![A]\!]$ and $(\eta_0, \eta_1) \in T$ for some $\eta_1 \in Z$. Applying the same argument for η_1 and continuing inductively, we find a fullpath $(\eta_0, \eta_1, \eta_2, \ldots)$ in W such that $\eta_i \in [\![A]\!]$, i.e., $\mathsf{K}_{\eta_i}(A) = \mathsf{tt}$ for all $i \in \mathbb{N}$. This means that $\eta_0 \in [\![\mathsf{E}\Box A]\!]$ and therefore $Z \subseteq [\![\mathsf{E}\Box A]\!]$. So $[\![\mathsf{E}\Box A]\!]$ is in fact the greatest fixpoint of Υ_A. △

Turning to the case of A **Eunt** B and following the equivalence (CT1), we define the function

$$\Upsilon_{A,B}(Z) = [\![B]\!] \cup ([\![A]\!] \cap T^{-1}(Z))$$

(for formulas A and B of $\mathcal{L}_{\mathrm{CTL}\Psi}$) and obtain the following result.

Theorem 11.3.2. *$[\![A \textbf{ Eunt } B]\!]$ is the least fixpoint of $\Upsilon_{A,B}$.*

Proof. As in the previous proof we first find that $[\![A \textbf{ Eunt } B]\!]$ is a fixpoint of $\Upsilon_{A,B}$ because of

$$\begin{aligned}
\eta \in [\![A \textbf{ Eunt } B]\!] &\Leftrightarrow \mathsf{K}_\eta(A \textbf{ Eunt } B) = \mathsf{tt} \\
&\Leftrightarrow \text{there is a fullpath } (\eta_0, \eta_1, \eta_2, \ldots) \text{ in } W \text{ with } \eta_0 = \eta \\
&\qquad \text{and } \mathsf{K}_{\eta_j}(B) = \mathsf{tt} \text{ for some } j \in \mathbb{N} \\
&\qquad \text{and } \mathsf{K}_{\eta_k}(A) = \mathsf{tt} \text{ for every } k, 0 \le k < j \\
&\Leftrightarrow \mathsf{K}_\eta(B) = \mathsf{tt} \\
&\qquad\quad \text{or} \\
&\qquad \mathsf{K}_\eta(A) = \mathsf{tt} \\
&\qquad \text{and there exists } \eta' \in [\![A \textbf{ Eunt } B]\!] \text{ with } (\eta, \eta') \in T \\
&\Leftrightarrow \eta \in [\![B]\!] \text{ or } \eta \in [\![A]\!] \cap T^{-1}([\![A \textbf{ Eunt } B]\!]) \\
&\Leftrightarrow \eta \in \Upsilon_{A,B}([\![A \textbf{ Eunt } B]\!]).
\end{aligned}$$

Let now Z be an arbitrary fixpoint of $\Upsilon_{A,B}$, i.e.,

$$Z = \Upsilon_{A,B}(Z) = [\![B]\!] \cup ([\![A]\!] \cap T^{-1}(Z)).$$

It remains to show that $[\![A \textbf{ Eunt } B]\!] \subseteq Z$ so that $[\![A \textbf{ Eunt } B]\!]$ is the least fixpoint of $\Upsilon_{A,B}$. Let $\eta_0 \in [\![A \textbf{ Eunt } B]\!]$. This means that there is a fullpath $(\eta_0, \eta_1, \eta_2, \ldots)$ in W and some $j \in \mathbb{N}$ such that $\mathsf{K}_{\eta_j}(B) = \mathsf{tt}$ and $\mathsf{K}_{\eta_k}(A) = \mathsf{tt}$ for $0 \le k < j$. The number j depends on η_0 and to show the claim we prove now by induction on this j that $\eta_0 \in Z$.

If $j = 0$ then $\mathsf{K}_{\eta_0}(B) = \mathsf{tt}$, so $\eta_0 \in [\![B]\!]$ and $\eta_0 \in Z$ is clear. For $j > 0$ we obtain $\mathsf{K}_{\eta_0}(A) = \mathsf{tt}$; hence $\eta_0 \in [\![A]\!]$. Moreover, considering the fullpath

$$(\eta'_0, \eta'_1, \ldots, \eta'_l, \ldots) = (\eta_1, \eta_2, \ldots, \eta_j, \ldots)$$

we find that $\mathsf{K}_{\eta'_l}(B) = \mathsf{K}_{\eta_j}(B) = \mathsf{tt}$ and $\mathsf{K}_{\eta'_k}(A) = \mathsf{tt}$ for every $k, 0 \le k < l$. This implies $\eta_1 = \eta'_0 \in [\![A \textbf{ Eunt } B]\!]$ and because of $l < j$ we may apply the induction hypothesis to the case of η_1 and obtain $\eta_1 \in Z$. With $(\eta_0, \eta_1) \in T$ we get altogether

$$\eta_0 \in [\![A]\!] \cap T^{-1}(Z)$$

and therefore $\eta_0 \in Z$. △

In order to obtain an algorithm from the preceding theorems about $[\![\mathsf{E}\Box A]\!]$ and $[\![A \ \mathbf{Eunt} \ B]\!]$ we recall from Sect. 3.2 that in general, given a set $\mathbb{D}$, a function $\Upsilon : 2^{\mathbb{D}} \to 2^{\mathbb{D}}$ is called monotone if $\Upsilon(\mathbb{E}_1) \subseteq \Upsilon(\mathbb{E}_2)$ for $\mathbb{E}_1, \mathbb{E}_2 \subseteq \mathbb{D}$ with $\mathbb{E}_1 \subseteq \mathbb{E}_2$. Theorem 3.2.1 gives characterizations of the least and the greatest fixpoints, respectively, of a monotone Υ. If, additionally, the set $\mathbb{D}$ is finite, which is the case in our application here with $\mathbb{D} = W$, then we are able to modify this theorem in a way such that simple procedures for computing these fixpoints can be derived.

To show this we start with the following simple lemma. (We write $\Upsilon^i(\mathbb{E})$ to denote i applications of Υ to $\mathbb{E}$; more formally: $\Upsilon^0(\mathbb{E}) = \mathbb{E}$ and $\Upsilon^{i+1}(\mathbb{E}) = \Upsilon(\Upsilon^i(\mathbb{E}))$ for every $i \in \mathbb{N}$.)

Lemma 11.3.3. *Let $\mathbb{D}$ be a set and $\Upsilon : 2^{\mathbb{D}} \to 2^{\mathbb{D}}$ a monotone function. Then, for every $i \in \mathbb{N}$,*

a) $\Upsilon^i(\emptyset) \subseteq \Upsilon^{i+1}(\emptyset)$.
b) $\Upsilon^i(\mathbb{D}) \supseteq \Upsilon^{i+1}(\mathbb{D})$.

Proof. The proofs for both a) and b) run by induction in i. For $i = 0$ we have $\Upsilon^0(\emptyset) = \emptyset \subseteq \Upsilon^1(\emptyset)$ and $\Upsilon^0(\mathbb{D}) = \mathbb{D} \supseteq \Upsilon^1(\mathbb{D})$, and with the induction hypothesis (for i) we obtain

$$\Upsilon^{i+1}(\emptyset) = \Upsilon(\Upsilon^i(\emptyset)) \subseteq \Upsilon(\Upsilon^{i+1}(\emptyset)) = \Upsilon^{i+2}(\emptyset),$$
$$\Upsilon^{i+1}(\mathbb{D}) = \Upsilon(\Upsilon^i(\mathbb{D})) \supseteq \Upsilon(\Upsilon^{i+1}(\mathbb{D})) = \Upsilon^{i+2}(\mathbb{D})$$

since Υ is monotone. △

Theorem 11.3.4. *Let $\mathbb{D}$ be a finite set and $\Upsilon : 2^{\mathbb{D}} \to 2^{\mathbb{D}}$ a monotone function. Then the following assertions hold.*

a) There is some $m \in \mathbb{N}$ such that $\Upsilon^{m+1}(\emptyset) = \Upsilon^m(\emptyset)$ and $\Upsilon^m(\emptyset)$ is the least fixpoint of Υ.
b) There is some $m \in \mathbb{N}$ such that $\Upsilon^{m+1}(\mathbb{D}) = \Upsilon^m(\mathbb{D})$ and $\Upsilon^m(\mathbb{D})$ is the greatest fixpoint of Υ.

Proof. a) By Lemma 11.3.3 a) we have

$$\Upsilon^0(\emptyset) \subseteq \Upsilon^1(\emptyset) \subseteq \Upsilon^2(\emptyset) \subseteq \ldots.$$

The assumption that $\Upsilon^i(\emptyset) \neq \Upsilon^{i+1}(\emptyset)$ holds for all $i \in \mathbb{N}$ would imply that this is an infinite chain of subsets of $\mathbb{D}$ with permanently increasing numbers of elements. This cannot be since $\mathbb{D}$ is finite; hence $\Upsilon^{m+1}(\emptyset) = \Upsilon^m(\emptyset)$ for some $m \in \mathbb{N}$. This also means that $\Upsilon(\Upsilon^m(\emptyset)) = \Upsilon^{m+1}(\emptyset) = \Upsilon^m(\emptyset)$, so $\Upsilon^m(\emptyset)$ is a fixpoint of Υ.

Furthermore, if $\mathbb{E}$ is another fixpoint of Υ then we find by induction on i that $\Upsilon^i(\emptyset) \subseteq \mathbb{E}$ for every $i \in \mathbb{N}$: $\Upsilon^0(\emptyset) = \emptyset \subseteq \mathbb{E}$ is trivial and with the monotonicity of Υ and the induction hypothesis we obtain $\Upsilon^{i+1}(\emptyset) = \Upsilon(\Upsilon^i(\emptyset)) \subseteq \Upsilon(\mathbb{E}) = \mathbb{E}$.

So we have $\Upsilon^m(\emptyset) \subseteq \mathbb{E}$ and taking all together, $\Upsilon^m(\emptyset)$ is the least fixpoint of Υ.

b) The proof of this part is symmetrical, using Lemma 11.3.3 b). △

This theorem provides the announced procedures for computing the least or the greatest fixpoint in the case of a monotone function $\Upsilon : 2^{\mathbb{D}} \to 2^{\mathbb{D}}$ and finite $\mathbb{D}$. One has to compute successively the sets

$$\Upsilon^0(\emptyset), \Upsilon^1(\emptyset), \Upsilon^2(\emptyset), \ldots$$

or

$$\Upsilon^0(\mathbb{D}), \Upsilon^1(\mathbb{D}), \Upsilon^2(\mathbb{D}), \ldots,$$

respectively, until $\Upsilon^{m+1}(\ldots) = \Upsilon^m(\ldots)$ holds. The set $\Upsilon^m(\ldots)$ is then the least (greatest) fixpoint of Υ. Theorem 11.3.4 particularly ensures that these procedures terminate. (Actually, it is easy to see from the proof that in both cases the number of elements of $\mathbb{D}$ is an upper bound for the number of necessary iterations computing the $\Upsilon^i(\ldots)$ until the fixpoint is found.)

In order to apply this general result now to the computation of $[\![\mathsf{E}\Box A]\!]$ and $[\![A\ \mathbf{Eunt}\ B]\!]$, it is only left to show that the functions Υ_A and $\Upsilon_{A,B}$ defined above are monotone.

Lemma 11.3.5. *The functions Υ_A and $\Upsilon_{A,B}$ are monotone.*

Proof. Let $Z_1, Z_2 \subseteq W$, $Z_1 \subseteq Z_2$. If $\eta \in \Upsilon_A(Z_1)$ then $\eta \in [\![A]\!]$ and there exists some $\eta' \in Z_1$ with $(\eta, \eta') \in T$. For this η' we have also $\eta' \in Z_2$ which implies $\eta \in \Upsilon_A(Z_2)$ and shows that Υ_A is monotone.

If $\eta \in \Upsilon_{A,B}(Z_1)$ then $\eta \in [\![B]\!]$ in which case $\eta \in \Upsilon_{A,B}(Z_2)$ is trivial or, otherwise, $\eta \in [\![A]\!]$ and $(\eta, \eta') \in T$ for some $\eta' \in Z_1$, so $\eta \in \Upsilon_{A,B}(Z_2)$ as in the case of Υ_A. Thus, $\Upsilon_{A,B}$ is monotone as well. △

Putting now all together, the satisfaction sets $[\![\mathsf{E}\Box A]\!]$ and $[\![A\ \mathbf{Eunt}\ B]\!]$ can be computed as induced by Theorem 11.3.4. More precisely, we have the following two procedures.

- Computation of $[\![\mathsf{E}\Box A]\!]$:
  Compute successively the sets $Z_0, Z_1, Z_2, \ldots$, inductively defined by
  $Z_0 = W$,
  $Z_{i+1} = [\![A]\!] \cap T^{-1}(Z_i)$,
  until $Z_{m+1} = Z_m$ holds for some $m \in \mathbb{N}$.
  Then $[\![\mathsf{E}\Box A]\!] = Z_m$.

- Computation of $[\![A\ \mathbf{Eunt}\ B]\!]$:
  Compute successively the sets $Z_0, Z_1, Z_2, \ldots$, inductively defined by
  $Z_0 = \emptyset$,
  $Z_{i+1} = [\![B]\!] \cup ([\![A]\!] \cap T^{-1}(Z_i))$,
  until $Z_{m+1} = Z_m$ holds for some $m \in \mathbb{N}$.
  Then $[\![A\ \mathbf{Eunt}\ B]\!] = Z_m$.

Example. For the FSTS Ψ_{examp} in Fig. 11.4 we have already computed that

$$\begin{aligned}
&[\![v_1]\!] = \{\eta_1, \eta_2\},\\
&[\![v_1 \wedge v_2]\!] = \{\eta_2\},\\
&[\![\neg v_1 \vee v_2]\!] = \{\eta_2, \eta_3\}.
\end{aligned}$$

Let us now determine $[\![\mathsf{E}\Box(\neg v_1 \vee v_2)]\!]$ and $[\![v_1 \textbf{ Eunt } (v_1 \wedge v_2)]\!]$ with the above procedures. Applying the first one we have:

$$\begin{aligned}
Z_0 &= W,\\
Z_1 &= [\![\neg v_1 \vee v_2]\!] \cap T^{-1}(W)\\
&= \{\eta_2, \eta_3\} \cap W\\
&= \{\eta_2, \eta_3\},\\
Z_2 &= [\![\neg v_1 \vee v_2]\!] \cap T^{-1}(\{\eta_2, \eta_3\})\\
&= \{\eta_2, \eta_3\} \cap W\\
&= Z_1.
\end{aligned}$$

This means that

$$[\![\mathsf{E}\Box(\neg v_1 \vee v_2)]\!] = \{\eta_2, \eta_3\}.$$

To compute $[\![v_1 \textbf{ Eunt } (v_1 \wedge v_2)]\!]$ we take the second procedure:

$$\begin{aligned}
Z_0 &= \emptyset,\\
Z_1 &= [\![v_1 \wedge v_2]\!] \cup ([\![v_1]\!] \cap T^{-1}(\emptyset))\\
&= \{\eta_2\} \cup (\{\eta_1, \eta_2\} \cap \emptyset)\\
&= \{\eta_2\},\\
Z_2 &= [\![v_1 \wedge v_2]\!] \cup ([\![v_1]\!] \cap T^{-1}(\{\eta_2\}))\\
&= \{\eta_2\} \cup (\{\eta_1, \eta_2\} \cap \{\eta_1\})\\
&= \{\eta_1, \eta_2\},\\
Z_3 &= [\![v_1 \wedge v_2]\!] \cup ([\![v_1]\!] \cap T^{-1}(\{\eta_1, \eta_2\}))\\
&= \{\eta_2\} \cup (\{\eta_1, \eta_2\} \cap \{\eta_1, \eta_2\})\\
&= \{\eta_1, \eta_2\}\\
&= Z_2.
\end{aligned}$$

So we obtain

$$[\![v_1 \textbf{ Eunt } (v_1 \wedge v_2)]\!] = \{\eta_1, \eta_2\}$$

and this coincides with what we found already at the beginning of this section. △

Summarizing our considerations, we have reached the announced goal: we have a (recursive) algorithm which, given an FSTS Ψ and a formula F of $\mathcal{L}_{\mathrm{CTL}\Psi}$, computes the satisfaction set $[\![F]\!]_\Psi$ and thus solves the CTL model checking problem. The algorithm is given by the clauses

$$\begin{aligned}
&[\![v]\!]_\Psi = \{\eta \in W \mid \eta(v) = \mathsf{tt}\} \quad \text{for } v \in V,\\
&[\![\mathbf{false}]\!]_\Psi = \emptyset,\\
&[\![A \to B]\!]_\Psi = (W \setminus [\![A]\!]) \cup [\![B]\!],\\
&[\![\mathsf{E}\bigcirc A]\!]_\Psi = T^{-1}([\![A]\!]),
\end{aligned}$$

and the two iterative "subroutines" for the cases $\mathsf{E}\Box A$ and A **Eunt** B.

Similarly as in the case of LTL model checking (cf. Sect. 11.2), witnesses and counterexamples that explain why CTL formulas hold or fail to hold can be computed as a "by-product" of the computation of satisfaction sets. As we have already remarked for the LTL case, this ability of model checking algorithms, beyond being mere decision procedures, makes them attractive for use in industrial practice. Consider a formula of the form $\mathsf{E}\Box A$, a state $\eta_0 \in [\![\mathsf{E}\Box A]\!]$, and let $T(\eta) = \{\eta' \in W \mid (\eta, \eta') \in T\}$ denote the set of successor states of an $\eta \in W$ with respect to the transition relation T of Ψ. The set $[\![\mathsf{E}\Box A]\!] \cap T(\eta_0)$ cannot be empty since $\mathsf{K}_{\eta_0}(\mathsf{E}\Box A) = \mathsf{tt}$ implies $\mathsf{K}_{\eta'}(\mathsf{E}\Box A) = \mathsf{tt}$ for some $\eta' \in T(\eta_0)$. Choosing an arbitrary $\eta_1 \in [\![\mathsf{E}\Box A]\!] \cap T(\eta_0)$ and continuing in the same way we find states $\eta_2, \eta_3, \eta_4, \ldots$ from the intersections of $[\![\mathsf{E}\Box A]\!]$ with $T(\eta_1), T(\eta_2), T(\eta_3), \ldots$. So the fact that $\eta_0 \in [\![\mathsf{E}\Box A]\!]$ holds does not only tell us that there is a fullpath starting with η_0 on which A holds in every state; the fullpath

$$(\eta_0, \eta_1, \eta_2, \eta_3, \ldots)$$

constructed in this way is a *witness* for this: we have $\mathsf{K}_{\eta_i}(A) = \mathsf{tt}$ for all $i \in \mathbb{N}$.

Example. In the previous example we saw that $[\![\mathsf{E}\Box(\neg v_1 \vee v_2)]\!] = \{\eta_2, \eta_3\}$. With $T(\eta_2) = \{\eta_1, \eta_3\}$, $[\![\mathsf{E}\Box(\neg v_1 \vee v_2)]\!] \cap T(\eta_2) = \{\eta_3\}$, and $T(\eta_3) = \{\eta_3\}$ we obtain the fullpath

$$(\eta_2, \eta_3, \eta_3, \eta_3, \ldots)$$

as (the only) witness for $\mathsf{E}\Box(\neg v_1 \vee v_2)$ being true in η_2. △

With similar constructions witnesses for formulas F of the form $\mathsf{E}\bigcirc A$, $\mathsf{E}\Diamond A$, or A **Eunt** B (with respect to some state $\eta_0 \in [\![F]\!]$) can be found. Dually, if we consider a formula $\mathsf{A}\Box A$ and a state $\eta_0 \notin [\![\mathsf{A}\Box A]\!]$ then $\eta_0 \in [\![\mathsf{E}\Diamond\neg A]\!]$ and a witness for $\mathsf{E}\Diamond\neg A$ is a *counterexample* for $\mathsf{A}\Box A$: a fullpath on which A will not be true in all states. Counterexamples for $\mathsf{A}\bigcirc A$, $\mathsf{A}\Diamond A$, or A **Aunt** B can be computed in a similar manner.

Analyzing the complexity of the CTL model checking algorithm, observe that at least one state is added (when computing $[\![$**Eunt** $A]\!]$) or removed (when computing $[\![\mathsf{E}\Box A]\!]$) at each iteration of the fixpoint computation. Therefore, the computation takes at most $|W|$ iterations. The cost of computing the functions at each iteration can be linear in δ, and therefore (at worst) quadratic in $|W|$. In order to compute $[\![F]\!]$ for a CTL formula F, sets $[\![A]\!]$ have to be computed for each subformula of F, whose number is linear in the length of F. Overall, the complexity of the algorithm is therefore linear in the length of F and cubic in $|W|$.

An improved algorithm is still linear in the length of F, but only quadratic in $|W|$ (and therefore linear in the size of Γ, which is dominated by the transition relation). The idea for computing $[\![A \ \mathsf{Eunt}\ B]\!]$ is to perform a backward search starting from the states in $[\![B]\!]$ (which has already been computed). For $[\![\mathsf{E}\Box A]\!]$, the graph of Γ is first restricted to those states satisfying A, and the algorithm enumerates the strongly connected components of this subgraph. Now, $[\![\mathsf{E}\Box A]\!]$ consists of all states from which such a graph component is reachable, which can be found using a breadth-first backward search.

11.4 Fairness Constraints

As we have seen in earlier chapters, the validity (and, hence, the verifiability) of system properties may require assumptions about certain fairness conditions. In case of a linear temporal logic framework the inclusion of such conditions into the verification process is easy since they can be expressed adequately by formulas of the underlying logic. In deductive verifications the set $\mathcal{A}_{fair}$ of these formulas is added to the specification of the system, so the formulas may be used as assumptions in deductions. In a tableau model checking algorithm the verification process for a property F checks whether $\neg F$ is satisfiable. In the algorithm presented in Sect. 11.2 this is done (in the basic FSTS case) by constructing a tableau for the FSTS Ψ under consideration and the Ψ-PNP $(\emptyset, \{F\})$. To include the fairness assumptions of $\mathcal{A}_{fair}$ means that the satisfiability of $\neg F$ has to be checked under the additional condition that the formulas of $\mathcal{A}_{fair}$ have to be true in every state of a temporal structure W_Ψ. Obviously this can be achieved by constructing a tableau for Ψ and the Ψ-PNP

$$(\{\Box A \mid A \in \mathcal{A}_{fair}\}, \{F\}).$$

Turning to the CTL framework we face the fact (cf. the corresponding remarks in Sects. 10.3 and 10.4) that "usual" fairness conditions cannot be expressed as CTL formulas. However, fairness can be taken into consideration in CTL model checking in several other ways. We describe in the following one such method and we begin with illustrating it by an example.

Consider the printer system $\Psi_{printer}$ with the system variables $exec\,\alpha_1$, $exec\,\alpha_2$, $exec\,\beta_1$, $exec\,\beta_2$, $exec\,\gamma$, req_1, req_2 given in the example at the end of Sect. 11.1. Recalling the discussion of the corresponding STS $\Gamma_{printer}$ in Sect. 6.5 and transferring it to the present situation, $\Psi_{printer}$ should be considered as a *fair* FSTS which means to restrict the "relevant" execution sequences of $\Psi_{printer}$ to those which fulfil the fairness assumptions, e.g.,

- if req_1 is true in infinitely many states then so is $exec\,\beta_1$,
- if req_2 is true in infinitely many states then so is $exec\,\beta_2$.

If $exec\,\beta_1$ (or $exec\,\beta_2$) is true in a state then $\neg req_1$ (or $\neg req_2$) is true in the successor state, respectively. Moreover, if req_1 (or req_2) is true in a state and $\neg req_1$ ($\neg req_2$) is true in some subsequent state then $exec\,\beta_1$ ($exec\,\beta_2$) must be true "in between". So it is evident that these assumptions are equivalent to

- $\neg req_1$ is true in infinitely many states,

- $\neg req_2$ is true in infinitely many states.

(The fairness conditions for $exec\,\alpha_1$ and $exec\,\alpha_2$ can be treated analogously.)

Restrictions of this kind can in fact be introduced into CTL model checking algorithms. So we generally model the fairness of an FSTS $\Psi = (V, W, T)$ by endowing it with a finite set $\mathcal{H}$ of formulas of $\mathcal{L}_{\mathrm{CTL}\Psi}$, called *fairness constraints*, and define a fullpath $(\eta_0, \eta_1, \eta_2, \ldots)$ in W to be *fair* (with respect to $\mathcal{H}$) if, for every $C \in \mathcal{H}$, $\mathsf{K}^{\Psi}_{\eta_k}(C) = \mathsf{tt}$ holds for infinitely many $k \in \mathbb{N}$. The Ψ-validity of a formula with respect to $\mathcal{H}$ is given by restricting the range of the "path quantifiers" E and A in the truth evaluation of formulas to fair fullpaths. (This kind of fairness is often called *simple* and is in general weaker than strong fairness.)

Relating these definitions to the CTL model checking method of Sect. 11.3, the algorithm shown there has to be modified such that it computes, for given $\mathcal{H}$, the following new satisfaction sets for formulas $\mathsf{E}\bigcirc A$, $\mathsf{E}\Box A$, and A **Eunt** B:

$$\begin{aligned}
[\![\mathsf{E}\bigcirc A]\!]^{\mathcal{H}}_{\Psi} = \{\eta \in W \mid{} & \text{there is a fair fullpath } (\eta_0, \eta_1, \eta_2, \ldots) \text{ in } W \text{ with} \\
& \eta_0 = \eta \text{ and } \mathsf{K}^{\Psi}_{\eta_1}(A) = \mathsf{tt}\}, \\
[\![\mathsf{E}\Box A]\!]^{\mathcal{H}}_{\Psi} = \{\eta \in W \mid{} & \text{there is a fair fullpath } (\eta_0, \eta_1, \eta_2, \ldots) \text{ in } W \text{ with} \\
& \eta_0 = \eta \text{ and } \mathsf{K}^{\Psi}_{\eta_k}(A) = \mathsf{tt} \text{ for every } k \in \mathbb{N}\}, \\
[\![A \;\mathbf{Eunt}\; B]\!]^{\mathcal{H}}_{\Psi} = \{\eta \in W \mid{} & \text{there is a fair fullpath } (\eta_0, \eta_1, \eta_2, \ldots) \text{ in } W \text{ with} \\
& \eta_0 = \eta \text{ and } \mathsf{K}^{\Psi}_{\eta_j}(B) = \mathsf{tt} \text{ for some } j \in \mathbb{N} \text{ and} \\
& \mathsf{K}^{\Psi}_{\eta_k}(A) = \mathsf{tt} \text{ for every } k, 0 \le k < j\}.
\end{aligned}$$

We want to show that these sets can be constructed similarly as before and we begin with the case of $[\![\mathsf{E}\Box A]\!]^{\mathcal{H}}$. (We again omit the index Ψ in the given context.) We first recall from Sect. 11.3 that, for arbitrary formulas A and B of $\mathcal{L}_{\mathrm{CTL}\Psi}$, the "normal" satisfaction set $[\![A \;\mathbf{Eunt}\; B]\!]$ is the least fixpoint of the function $\Upsilon_{A,B} : 2^W \to 2^W$,

$$\Upsilon_{A,B}(Z) = [\![B]\!] \cup ([\![A]\!] \cap T^{-1}(Z)).$$

Let $\Upsilon_{A,Z'} : 2^W \to 2^W$ for any fixed $Z' \subseteq W$ be defined by

$$\Upsilon_{A,Z'}(Z) = Z' \cup ([\![A]\!] \cap T^{-1}(Z)).$$

Slightly abusing notation, we write $[\![A \;\mathbf{Eunt}\; Z']\!]$ for the least fixpoint of $\Upsilon_{A,Z'}$, and inspecting the proof of Theorem 11.3.2 it is evident that

$$\begin{aligned}
[\![A \;\mathbf{Eunt}\; Z']\!] = \{\eta \in W \mid{} & \text{there is a fullpath } (\eta_0, \eta_1, \eta_2, \ldots) \text{ in } W \text{ with} \\
& \eta_0 = \eta \text{ and } \eta_j \in Z' \text{ for some } j \in \mathbb{N} \text{ and} \\
& \mathsf{K}^{\Psi}_{\eta_k}(A) = \mathsf{tt} \text{ for every } k, 0 \le k < j\}.
\end{aligned}$$

Let now $\Upsilon'_A : 2^W \to 2^W$ be defined by

$$\Upsilon'_A(Z) = [\![A]\!] \cap \bigcap_{C \in \mathcal{H}} T^{-1}([\![A \;\mathbf{Eunt}\; (Z \cap [\![C]\!])]\!]).$$

Υ'_A is a modification of $\Upsilon_A(Z) = [\![A]\!] \cap T^{-1}(Z)$ which was used to characterize $[\![\mathsf{E}\Box A]\!]$ in Sect. 11.3 and, in fact, we obtain a corresponding result to Theorem 11.3.1:

Theorem 11.4.1. *$[\![\mathsf{E}\Box A]\!]^{\mathcal{H}}$ is the greatest fixpoint of Υ'_A.*

Proof. If $\eta_0 \in [\![\mathsf{E}\Box A]\!]^{\mathcal{H}}$ then there is a fair fullpath $(\eta_0, \eta_1, \eta_2, \ldots)$ in W with $\mathsf{K}_{\eta_k}(A) = \mathsf{tt}$ for every $k \in \mathbb{N}$. $(\eta_1, \eta_2, \eta_3, \ldots)$ is a fair fullpath as well, so we find that for every $C \in \mathcal{H}$ there is $j \geq 1$ such that $\eta_j \in [\![\mathsf{E}\Box A]\!]^{\mathcal{H}} \cap [\![C]\!]$. We obtain $\eta_0 \in T^{-1}([\![A \ \mathbf{Eunt}\ ([\![\mathsf{E}\Box A]\!]^{\mathcal{H}} \cap [\![C]\!])]\!])$ for every C; hence

$$\eta_0 \in [\![A]\!] \cap \bigcap_{C \in \mathcal{H}} T^{-1}([\![A \ \mathbf{Eunt}\ ([\![\mathsf{E}\Box A]\!]^{\mathcal{H}} \cap [\![C]\!])]\!])$$

which means $\eta_0 \in \Upsilon'_A([\![\mathsf{E}\Box A]\!]^{\mathcal{H}})$.

On the other hand, if $\eta_0 \in \Upsilon'_A([\![\mathsf{E}\Box A]\!]^{\mathcal{H}})$ then $\mathsf{K}_{\eta_0}(A) = \mathsf{tt}$ and there is a fullpath $(\eta_1, \eta_2, \eta_3, \ldots)$ with $(\eta_0, \eta_1) \in T$, $\eta_j \in [\![\mathsf{E}\Box A]\!]^{\mathcal{H}}$ for some $j \geq 1$, and $\mathsf{K}_{\eta_k}(A) = \mathsf{tt}$ for $1 \leq k < j$. So there is a fair fullpath $(\eta'_j, \eta'_{j+1}, \eta'_{j+2}, \ldots)$ with $\eta'_j = \eta_j$ and $\mathsf{K}_{\eta'_k}(A) = \mathsf{tt}$ for every $k \geq j$. With the fair fullpath $(\eta_0, \eta_1, \ldots, \eta_j, \eta'_{j+1}, \eta'_{j+2}, \ldots)$ we find that $\eta_0 \in [\![\mathsf{E}\Box A]\!]^{\mathcal{H}}$; thus together we obtain $\Upsilon'_A([\![\mathsf{E}\Box A]\!]^{\mathcal{H}}) = [\![\mathsf{E}\Box A]\!]^{\mathcal{H}}$, i.e., $[\![\mathsf{E}\Box A]\!]^{\mathcal{H}}$ is a fixpoint of Υ'_A.

Let now Z be an arbitrary fixpoint of Υ'_A, $\eta_0 \in Z$, and $\mathcal{H} = \{C_1, \ldots, C_n\}$. So $Z = \Upsilon'_A(Z)$ and therefore $\mathsf{K}_{\eta_0}(A) = \mathsf{tt}$ and there is a fullpath with a finite prefix $(\eta_1, \ldots, \eta_j)$ such that $(\eta_0, \eta_1) \in T$, $\mathsf{K}_{\eta_k}(A) = \mathsf{tt}$ for $1 \leq k < j$, and $\eta_j \in Z \cap [\![C_1]\!]$. Since $\eta_j \in Z$ we find in the same way that $\mathsf{K}_{\eta_j}(A) = \mathsf{tt}$ and there is $(\eta'_{j+1}, \ldots, \eta'_l)$ such that $(\eta_j, \eta'_{j+1}) \in T$, $\mathsf{K}_{\eta'_k}(A) = \mathsf{tt}$ for $j{+}1 \leq k < l$, $\eta'_l \in Z \cap [\![C_2]\!]$, and so on for the other $C_3, \ldots, C_n$. This yields a state sequence $(\eta_0, \ldots, \overline{\eta})$ and applying the same argument to $\overline{\eta}$ and continuing inductively, we obtain a fair fullpath $(\eta_0, \eta_1, \eta_2, \ldots)$ in W with $\mathsf{K}_{\eta_k}(A) = \mathsf{tt}$ for every $k \in \mathbb{N}$. This means $\eta_0 \in [\![\mathsf{E}\Box A]\!]^{\mathcal{H}}$ and shows $Z \subseteq [\![\mathsf{E}\Box A]\!]^{\mathcal{H}}$. So $[\![\mathsf{E}\Box A]\!]^{\mathcal{H}}$ is in fact the greatest fixpoint of Υ'_A. △

We still need the monotonicity of Υ'_A.

Lemma 11.4.2. *The function Υ'_A is monotone.*

Proof. Let $Z_1, Z_2 \subseteq W$, $Z_1 \subseteq Z_2$, and $\eta_0 \in \Upsilon'_A(Z_1)$. Then $\eta_0 \in [\![A]\!]$ and there is a fullpath $(\eta_1, \eta_2, \eta_3, \ldots)$ with $(\eta_0, \eta_1) \in T$ and such that, for every $C \in \mathcal{H}$, there is $j \geq 1$ with $\eta_j \in Z_1 \cap [\![C]\!]$ and $\mathsf{K}_{\eta_k}(A) = \mathsf{tt}$ for $1 \leq k < j$. Then also $\eta_j \in Z_2 \cap [\![C]\!]$; so we obtain $\eta_0 \in \Upsilon'_A(Z_2)$ which proves the assertion. △

Taking these results it follows that $[\![\mathsf{E}\Box A]\!]^{\mathcal{H}}$ can be computed according to Theorem 11.3.4 b) by starting with $Z_0 = W$ and then computing successively the sets

$$Z_{i+1} = \Upsilon'_A(Z_i)$$

until $Z_{m+1} = Z_m$ holds for some $m \in \mathbb{N}$. Then Z_m is just $[\![\mathsf{E}\Box A]\!]^{\mathcal{H}}$. Observe that in each iteration step the computation of the set $[\![A \ \mathbf{Eunt}\ (Z_i \cap [\![C]\!])]\!]$ can be performed as described in Sect. 11.3 for sets $[\![A \ \mathbf{Eunt}\ B]\!]$: starting with $Z'_0 = \emptyset$ one iterates by

$$Z'_{i+1} = (Z_i \cap [\![C]\!]) \cup ([\![A]\!] \cap T^{-1}(Z'_i)).$$

Having a procedure for computing $[\![\mathsf{E}\Box A]\!]^{\mathcal{H}}$, the remaining cases of $[\![\mathsf{E}\bigcirc A]\!]^{\mathcal{H}}$ and $[\![A \ \mathbf{Eunt}\ B]\!]^{\mathcal{H}}$ can be handled quite easily. The set

$$W_{fair} = [\![\mathsf{E}\Box\mathbf{true}]\!]^{\mathcal{H}}$$

comprises all those states η of W for which there is a fair fullpath in W beginning with η. Using this set we obtain

$$\begin{aligned}[\![\mathsf{E}\bigcirc A]\!]^{\mathcal{H}} &= \{\eta \in W \mid \text{there is a fair fullpath } (\eta_0, \eta_1, \eta_2, \ldots) \text{ in } W \text{ with} \\ &\qquad \eta_0 = \eta \text{ and } \mathsf{K}_{\eta_1}(A) = \mathsf{tt}\} \\ &= \{\eta \in W \mid \mathsf{K}_{\eta_1}(A) = \mathsf{tt} \text{ for some } \eta_1 \text{ with } (\eta, \eta_1) \in W \text{ and} \\ &\qquad \text{there is a fair fullpath } (\eta_1, \eta_2, \eta_3, \ldots) \text{ in } W\} \\ &= T^{-1}([\![A]\!] \cap W_{fair})\end{aligned}$$

and (using again the above notation for the least fixpoint of $\Upsilon_{A,Z'}$)

$$\begin{aligned}[\![A \text{ } \mathsf{Eunt} \text{ } B]\!]^{\mathcal{H}} &= \{\eta \in W \mid \text{there is a fair fullpath } (\eta_0, \eta_1, \eta_2, \ldots) \text{ in } W \text{ with} \\ &\qquad \eta_0 = \eta \text{ and } \mathsf{K}_{\eta_j}(B) = \mathsf{tt} \text{ for some } j \in \mathbb{N} \text{ and} \\ &\qquad \mathsf{K}_{\eta_k}(A) = \mathsf{tt} \text{ for every } k, 0 \le k < j\} \\ &= \{\eta \in W \mid \text{there is a fullpath } (\eta_0, \eta_1, \eta_2, \ldots) \text{ in } W \text{ with} \\ &\qquad \eta_0 = \eta \text{ and } \mathsf{K}_{\eta_j}(B) = \mathsf{tt} \text{ for some } j \in \mathbb{N} \text{ and} \\ &\qquad \mathsf{K}_{\eta_k}(A) = \mathsf{tt} \text{ for every } k, 0 \le k < j \text{ and} \\ &\qquad \text{there is a fair fullpath } (\eta_j, \eta'_{j+1}, \eta'_{j+2}, \ldots)\} \\ &= [\![A \text{ } \mathsf{Eunt} \text{ } ([\![B]\!] \cap W_{fair})]\!].\end{aligned}$$

Both sets can be computed with the algorithms given in Sect. 11.3 and the procedure for $[\![\mathsf{E}\Box A]\!]^{\mathcal{H}}$, applied to $A \equiv \mathbf{true}$.

Summarizing, we see that the algorithm for computing satisfaction sets $[\![F]\!]$ in the presence of simple fairness constraints is a straightforward variant of the ordinary one. For the temporal subformulas of F, the sets $[\![\mathsf{E}\bigcirc A]\!]^{\mathcal{H}}$, $[\![\mathsf{E}\Box A]\!]^{\mathcal{H}}$, and $[\![A \text{ } \mathsf{Eunt} \text{ } B]\!]^{\mathcal{H}}$ are computed as described above. For the remaining subformulas, the algorithm remains unchanged. The results of such computations, however, have to be interpreted with some care compared with the "normal" case. If no fairness is involved, the Ψ-validity of F is decided by finally checking whether $W = [\![F]\!]$ holds. But if fairness is taken into account then W may contain states which are not in W_{fair} and these, of course, need not be contained in $[\![F]\!]$. So, what has to be checked then is whether $W_{fair} \subseteq [\![F]\!]$ holds.

Finally we remark that witnesses and counterexamples can be found also if fairness constraints are involved. This works in a similar way as indicated at the end of the previous section for the case without fairness.

11.5 Symbolic CTL Model Checking

The CTL model checking algorithm elaborated in Sect. 11.3 manipulates sets of states using the operations union, intersection, and difference and the inverse image operation of a transition relation. We mentioned already that the algorithm can be implemented quite efficiently. This is achieved by an adequate data structure, called *binary decision diagrams*, which in fact allows for an efficient realization of such sets and operations.

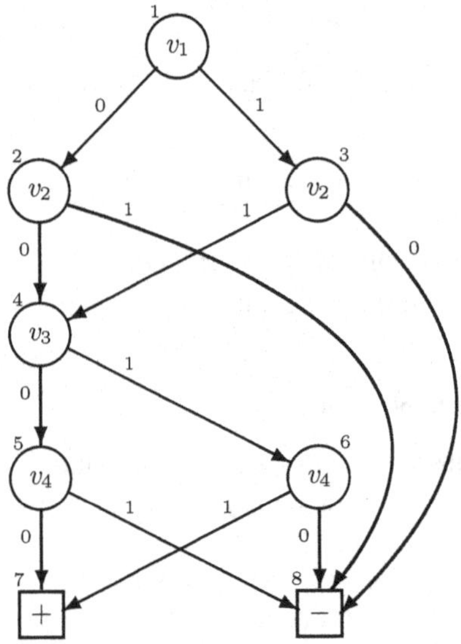

Fig. 11.5. A binary decision diagram $\mathcal{B}_{exmp}$

In general, binary decision diagrams are intended to represent *boolean functions*. We adapt their definition here directly to our present goal of representing sets of states of a finite state transition system.

Definition. A *binary decision diagram* (briefly: BDD) (with respect to a set V) is a rooted directed acyclic graph with the following properties:

- Every non-terminal node g is labeled by an element $var(g)$ of V and has precisely two successor nodes $zero(g)$ and $one(g)$.
- Every terminal node g is labeled by either $+$ or $-$.

Example. Figure 11.5 shows a BDD $\mathcal{B}_{exmp}$ with respect to $V_4 = \{v_1, v_2, v_3, v_4\}$. Terminal nodes are displayed by squares, edges leading to successors $zero(\ldots)$ or $one(\ldots)$ are labeled by 0 or 1, respectively. (As in earlier graphs, the nodes are marked by numbers 1–8 for identification.) △

Let now $V = \{v_1, \ldots, v_m\}$, $W(V)$ be the set of all mappings $\eta : V \to \{\mathsf{tt}, \mathsf{ff}\}$, and $\mathcal{B}$ be a BDD with respect to V. Every node g of $\mathcal{B}$ determines a set $Z_g \subseteq W(V)$ of such mappings (i.e., states) as follows.

- If g is terminal then $Z_g = W(V)$ if g is labeled by $+$ and $Z_g = \emptyset$ if g is labeled by $-$.
- If g is non-terminal and $var(g) = v_i$ $(1 \le i \le m)$ then

$$\begin{aligned} Z_g = (&\{\eta \in W(V) \mid \eta(v_i) = \mathsf{ff}\} \cap Z_{zero(g)}) \cup \\ (&\{\eta \in W(V) \mid \eta(v_i) = \mathsf{tt}\} \cap Z_{one(g)}). \end{aligned}$$

We denote Z_g for the root g of $\mathcal{B}$ by $Z_{\mathcal{D}}$ and say that $\mathcal{B}$ determines the state set $Z_{\mathcal{D}}$.

Example. For the BDD $\mathcal{B}_{examp}$ in Fig. 11.5 we find the following sets Z_1–Z_8 for the nodes (marked by) 1–8. (We briefly write $\{\ldots\}$ instead of $\{\eta \in W(V_4) \mid \ldots\}$ for sets of states under consideration.)

$Z_7 = W(V_4)$.
$Z_8 = \emptyset$.
$Z_5 = (\{\eta(v_4) = \mathsf{ff}\} \cap Z_7) \cup (\{\eta(v_4) = \mathsf{tt}\} \cap Z_8) = \{\eta(v_4) = \mathsf{ff}\}$.
$Z_6 = (\{\eta(v_4) = \mathsf{ff}\} \cap Z_8) \cup (\{\eta(v_4) = \mathsf{tt}\} \cap Z_7) = \{\eta(v_4) = \mathsf{tt}\}$.
$Z_4 = (\{\eta(v_3) = \mathsf{ff}\} \cap Z_5) \cup (\{\eta(v_3) = \mathsf{tt}\} \cap Z_6) = \{\eta(v_3) = \eta(v_4)\}$.
$Z_2 = (\{\eta(v_2) = \mathsf{ff}\} \cap Z_4) \cup (\{\eta(v_2) = \mathsf{tt}\} \cap Z_8) = \{\eta(v_2) = \mathsf{ff}, \eta(v_3) = \eta(v_4)\}$.
$Z_3 = (\{\eta(v_2) = \mathsf{ff}\} \cap Z_8) \cup (\{\eta(v_2) = \mathsf{tt}\} \cap Z_4) = \{\eta(v_2) = \mathsf{tt}, \eta(v_3) = \eta(v_4)\}$.
$Z_1 = (\{\eta(v_1) = \mathsf{ff}\} \cap Z_2) \cup (\{\eta(v_1) = \mathsf{tt}\} \cap Z_3)$
$\quad = \{\eta(v_1) = \eta(v_2), \eta(v_3) = \eta(v_4)\}$.

$Z_{\mathcal{D}}$ is Z_1; in full notation: $Z_{\mathcal{D}} = \{\eta \in W(V_4) \mid \eta(v_1) = \eta(v_2), \eta(v_3) = \eta(v_4)\}$. △

The definition of the set $Z_{\mathcal{D}}$ determined by some BDD $\mathcal{B}$ can be understood quite intuitively as follows. Assume that on every path (this notion is used as in earlier cases) from the root of $\mathcal{B}$ to a terminal node there is, for every $v \in V$, at most one occurrence of v as a node label. Then the path determines a state η given by $\eta(v) = \mathsf{tt}$ whenever the path proceeds from a node labeled with v to its *one*-successor and by $\eta(v) = \mathsf{ff}$ if it goes to the *zero*-successor. Then $\eta \in Z_{\mathcal{D}}$ if and only if the terminal node at the end of the path is labeled with $+$. For example, in $\mathcal{B}_{examp}$ the path through the nodes $1, 3, 4, 5, 7$ provides the state η with $\eta(v_1) = \mathsf{tt}$, $\eta(v_2) = \mathsf{tt}$, $\eta(v_3) = \mathsf{ff}$, $\eta(v_4) = \mathsf{ff}$ which belongs to $Z_{\mathcal{D}}$. Any state η' with $\eta'(v_1) = \mathsf{tt}$ and $\eta'(v_2) = \mathsf{ff}$ given by the path through $1, 3, 8$ does not belong to $Z_{\mathcal{D}}$.

It is evident that, in general, sets of states can be represented by binary decision diagrams with quite different structure. In applications like the one intended here it is desirable to have distinguished *canonical* representations which are unique. To obtain them we firstly restrict ourselves to *ordered* binary decision diagrams (briefly: OBDDs). An OBDD $\mathcal{B}$ is a BDD (with respect to V) with the property that there is a linear order $\lessdot$ on V such that for any node g in $\mathcal{B}$, if g has a non-terminal successor node g' then $var(g) \lessdot var(g')$. More intuitively: on all paths from the root to a terminal node, the elements of V labeling the nodes occur in the same order (possibly missing some of them). For example, taking the order $v_1 \lessdot v_2 \lessdot v_3 \lessdot v_4$, the BDD $\mathcal{B}_{examp}$ is ordered.

Given an OBDD $\mathcal{B}$, a canonical OBDD is obtained by repeatedly applying the following three transformations (which do not alter the state set determined by $\mathcal{B}$):

- Removal of duplicate terminals:
  Delete all terminal nodes with label $+$ except one and redirect all edges leading to the deleted nodes to the remaining one. Proceed in the same way with the terminal nodes with label $-$.
- Removal of duplicate non-terminals:
  If $var(g) = var(g')$, $zero(g) = zero(g')$, and $one(g) = one(g')$ for some non-

terminal nodes g and g' then delete one of them, say g, and redirect all edges leading to g to g'.

- Removal of redundant tests:
  If $zero(g) = one(g)$ ($= g'$) for some non-terminal node g then delete g and redirect all edges leading to g to g'.

An OBDD is called *reduced* if none of these *reduction* transformations can be applied. It can be shown that for any state set Z and fixed order $\lessdot$ on V there is a unique reduced OBDD $\mathcal{B}$ which determines Z. We denote this OBDD by $\mathcal{B}(Z)$. Of course, $\mathcal{B}(Z)$ depends on how V is ordered, and it should be noted that different orders may in fact lead to OBDD representations of significantly different size. Algorithms to find the "optimal" order are beyond practicable complexity but there exist good heuristic methods which usually provide reasonable results to this problem in practice.

Let us now come to the representation of the necessary set operations in the framework of reduced OBDDs. We first introduce an auxiliary operation defined as follows. For $\eta \in W(V)$, $v \in V$, $\mathsf{x} \in \{\mathsf{ff}, \mathsf{tt}\}$ let $\eta_{v \mapsto \mathsf{x}} \in W(V)$ be given by

$$\eta_{v\mapsto \mathsf{x}}(v) = \mathsf{x},$$
$$\eta_{v\mapsto \mathsf{x}}(v') = \eta(v') \qquad \text{for } v' \neq v.$$

The *restriction* $Z_{v\mapsto \mathsf{x}}$ of some $Z \in W(V)$ is the state set

$$Z_{v\mapsto \mathsf{x}} = \{\eta \in W(V) \mid \eta_{v\mapsto \mathsf{x}} \in Z\}.$$

This operation is represented by the following BDD restriction transformation.

- Construction of $\mathcal{B}(Z_{v\mapsto \mathsf{x}})$ from $\mathcal{B}(Z)$:
  - Delete all edges from a node g with $var(g) = v$ to $zero(g)$ if $\mathsf{x} = \mathsf{tt}$ or to $one(g)$ if $\mathsf{x} = \mathsf{ff}$, respectively, and delete all nodes which then are no longer reachable by a path from the root.
  - Delete all nodes g with $var(g) = v$ and redirect all edges leading to such nodes to $zero(g)$ if $\mathsf{x} = \mathsf{ff}$ or to $one(g)$ if $\mathsf{x} = \mathsf{tt}$, respectively.
  - Apply the reduction transformations to obtain a reduced OBDD.

Example. As seen in the previous example, the state set

$$Z = \{\eta \in W(V_4) \mid \eta(v_1) = \eta(v_2), \eta(v_3) = \eta(v_4)\}$$

is represented by the BDD $\mathcal{B}_{exmp}$ of Fig 11.5 which is in fact a reduced OBDD. We have

$$Z_{v_4\mapsto \mathsf{tt}} = \{\eta \in W(V_4) \mid \eta_{v_4\mapsto \mathsf{tt}} \in Z\}$$

where $\eta_{v_4\mapsto \mathsf{tt}}(v) = \eta(v)$ for $v \in \{v_1, v_2, v_3\}$ and $\eta_{v_4\mapsto \mathsf{tt}}(v_4) = \mathsf{tt}$; thus

$$Z_{v_4\mapsto \mathsf{tt}} = \{\eta \in W(V_4) \mid \eta(v_1) = \eta(v_2), \eta(v_3) = \mathsf{tt}\}.$$

Applying the above construction to $\mathcal{B}_{exmp}$ we obtain (without any reduction transformations) the reduced OBDD shown in Fig. 11.6 which represents $Z_{v_4\mapsto \mathsf{tt}}$. △

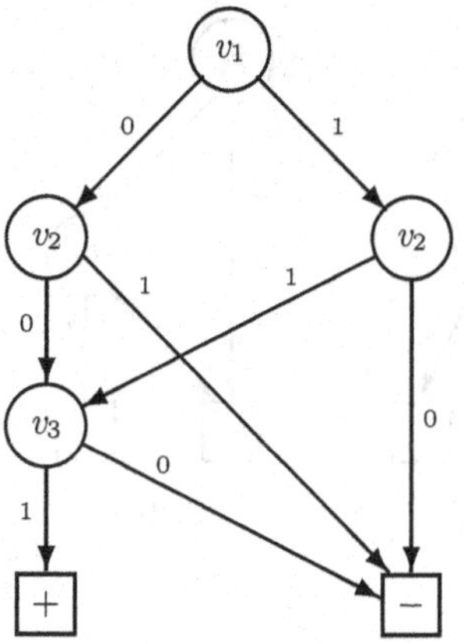

Fig. 11.6. A restriction of $\mathcal{B}_{exmp}$

With the restriction operation we are now able to give constructions for set union $\cup$, intersection $\cap$, and difference $\setminus$, and we can do this even in a uniform way for these operations. The key idea is to use the *Shannon expansion* (applied to state sets), i.e., the fact that if $\circledast$ denotes $\cup$, $\cap$, or $\setminus$ then

$$\begin{aligned} Z \circledast Z' &= (\{\eta \in W(V) \mid \eta(v) = \mathsf{ff}\} \cap (Z \circledast Z')) \cup \\ &\quad\ (\{\eta \in W(V) \mid \eta(v) = \mathsf{tt}\} \cap (Z \circledast Z')) \\ &= (\{\eta \in W(V) \mid \eta(v) = \mathsf{ff}\} \cap \{\eta \in W(V) \mid \eta_{v \mapsto \mathsf{ff}} \in Z \circledast Z'\}) \cup \\ &\quad\ (\{\eta \in W(V) \mid \eta(v) = \mathsf{tt}\} \cap \{\eta \in W(V) \mid \eta_{v \mapsto \mathsf{tt}} \in Z \circledast Z'\}) \\ &= (\{\eta \in W(V) \mid \eta(v) = \mathsf{ff}\} \cap (Z_{v \mapsto \mathsf{ff}} \circledast Z'_{v \mapsto \mathsf{ff}})) \cup \\ &\quad\ (\{\eta \in W(V) \mid \eta(v) = \mathsf{tt}\} \cap (Z_{v \mapsto \mathsf{tt}} \circledast Z'_{v \mapsto \mathsf{tt}})) \end{aligned}$$

holds for arbitrary $Z, Z' \subseteq W(V)$, and $v \in V$. Comparing this equation for $Z \circledast Z'$ with the general definition of $Z_{\mathcal{D}}$ for a BDD $\mathcal{B}$, it is easy to see that the construction of $\mathcal{B}(Z \circledast Z')$ can be organized recursively. As v in the expansion we take the "least occurring" element of V. This v labels the root of $\mathcal{B}(Z \circledast Z')$ and the *zero*- and *one*-edges lead to the diagrams for $Z_{v \mapsto \mathsf{ff}} \circledast Z'_{v \mapsto \mathsf{ff}}$ and $Z_{v \mapsto \mathsf{tt}} \circledast Z'_{v \mapsto \mathsf{tt}}$, respectively. The recursion terminates if both diagrams which are to be combined consist only of a single terminal node.

- Construction of $\mathcal{B}(Z \circledast Z')$ from $\mathcal{B}(Z)$ and $\mathcal{B}(Z')$
  ($\circledast$ denotes the union $\cup$, intersection $\cap$, or difference $\setminus$ of sets; g and g' denote the roots of Z and Z', respectively):
  - If g and g' are terminal then $\mathcal{B}(Z \circledast Z')$ has only one node which is terminal and labeled by $+$ if and only if
    - at least one of g or g' is labeled by $+$ in case $\circledast$ is $\cup$,
    - both g and g' are labeled by $+$ in case $\circledast$ is $\cap$,
    - g is labeled by $+$ and g' by $-$ in case $\circledast$ is $\setminus$.
  - If g is non-terminal, $var(g) = v$, and g' is terminal or non-terminal with $v \lessdot var(g')$ or $v = var(g')$ then construct $\mathcal{B}_0 = \mathcal{B}(Z_{v \mapsto \mathsf{ff}} \circledast Z'_{v \mapsto \mathsf{ff}})$ and

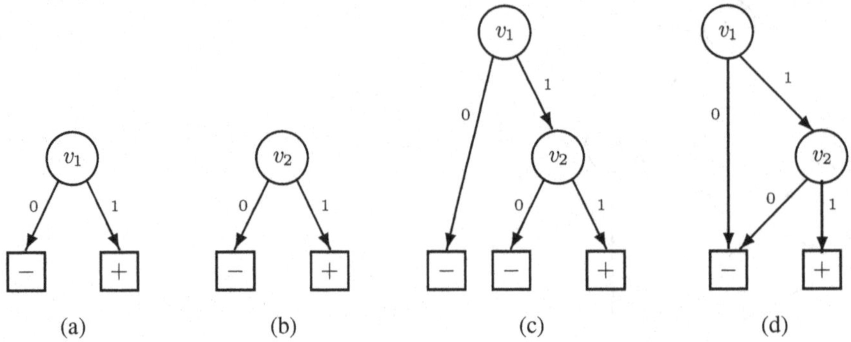

Fig. 11.7. Construction steps for a set intersection

$\mathcal{B}_1 = \mathcal{B}(Z_{v \mapsto \text{tt}} \circledast Z'_{v \mapsto \text{tt}})$. Then $\mathcal{B}(Z \circledast Z')$ is the OBDD with root g and the roots of $\mathcal{B}_0$ and $\mathcal{B}_1$ as $zero(g)$ and $one(g)$, respectively.
- The case that g' is non-terminal and g is terminal or non-terminal with a label not less than the label of g' with respect to the order $\lessdot$ is handled symmetrically.
- Apply the reduction transformations to obtain a reduced OBDD.

Example. Let $Z = \{\eta \in W(V_4) \mid \eta(v_1) = \text{tt}\}$, $Z' = \{\eta \in W(V_4) \mid \eta(v_2) = \text{tt}\}$, and assume again $v_1 \lessdot v_2$. Figure 11.7 shows the essential steps when constructing $\mathcal{B}(Z \cap Z')$. The OBDDs (a) and (b) represent Z and Z'. Let $\mathcal{B}_+$ and $\mathcal{B}_-$ denote the trivial OBDDs consisting of just a terminal node which is labeled by $+$ or $-$, respectively. Then we have by the restriction construction

$$\mathcal{B}(Z_{v_1 \mapsto \text{ff}}) = \mathcal{B}(Z'_{v_2 \mapsto \text{ff}}) = \mathcal{B}_- ,$$
$$\mathcal{B}(Z_{v_1 \mapsto \text{tt}}) = \mathcal{B}(Z'_{v_2 \mapsto \text{tt}}) = \mathcal{B}_+ ,$$

and both $\mathcal{B}(Z'_{v_1 \mapsto \text{ff}})$ and $\mathcal{B}(Z'_{v_1 \mapsto \text{tt}})$ are the OBDD (b). The root of $\mathcal{B}(Z \cap Z')$ has to be labeled by v_1 and the *zero*- and *one*-successors of the root are the roots of $\mathcal{B}(Z_{v_1 \mapsto \text{ff}} \cap Z'_{v_1 \mapsto \text{ff}})$ and $\mathcal{B}(Z_{v_1 \mapsto \text{tt}} \cap Z'_{v_1 \mapsto \text{tt}})$, respectively. The construction of these diagrams provides $\mathcal{B}_-$ for the first and the OBDD (b) for the second one. Putting them together yields the OBDD (c) which is finally reduced to the OBDD (d). △

Besides set operations we have to represent the transition relation T of a given FSTS Ψ and its inverse image operation. For this purpose, let $V^c = \{v^c \mid v \in V\}$ be a "copy" of V. For $\eta_1, \eta_2 \in W(V)$ we define $\eta_1 \times \eta_2 \in W(V \cup V^c)$ by

$$\eta_1 \times \eta_2(v) = \eta_1(v) \qquad \text{for } v \in V,$$
$$\eta_1 \times \eta_2(v^c) = \eta_2(v) \qquad \text{for } v^c \in V^c.$$

With T we associate now a subset $T^\times$ of $W(V \cup V^c)$:

$$T^\times = \{\eta_1 \times \eta_2 \in W(V \cup V^c) \mid (\eta_1, \eta_2) \in T\}.$$

$T^\times$ is a set of states (with respect to the set $V \cup V^c$ of system variables), and we represent T by the reduced OBDD $\mathcal{B}(T^\times)$.

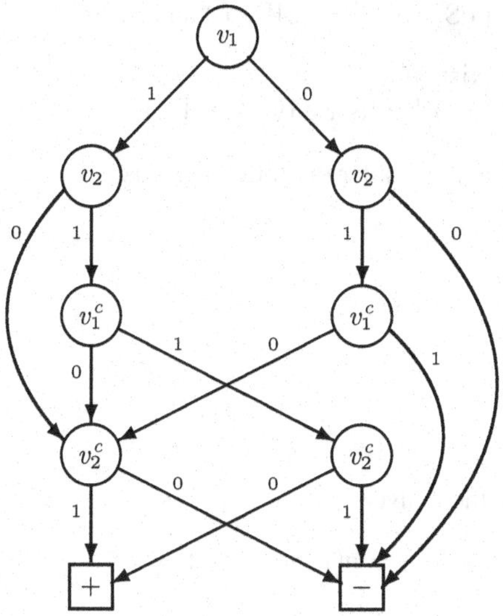

Fig. 11.8. A binary decision diagram for a transition relation

Example. Consider the FSTS $\Psi_{examp} = (\{v_1, v_2\}, \{\eta_1, \eta_2, \eta_3\}, T)$ of Sect. 11.3 with $\eta_1(v_1) = \eta_2(v_1) = \eta_2(v_2) = \eta_3(v_2) = \text{tt}$, $\eta_3(v_1) = \eta_1(v_2) = \text{ff}$, and

$$T = \{(\eta_1, \eta_2), (\eta_1, \eta_3), (\eta_2, \eta_1), (\eta_2, \eta_3), (\eta_3, \eta_3)\}.$$

Then we have

$$T^\times = \{\eta_1 \times \eta_2, \eta_1 \times \eta_3, \eta_2 \times \eta_1, \eta_2 \times \eta_3, \eta_3 \times \eta_3\}$$

where the elements of $T^\times$ are mappings $\{v_1, v_2, v_1^c, v_2^c\} \to \{\text{ff}, \text{tt}\}$ given by

	$\eta_1 \times \eta_2$	$\eta_1 \times \eta_3$	$\eta_2 \times \eta_1$	$\eta_2 \times \eta_3$	$\eta_3 \times \eta_3$
v_1	tt	tt	tt	tt	ff
v_2	ff	ff	tt	tt	tt
v_1^c	tt	ff	tt	ff	ff
v_2^c	tt	tt	ff	tt	tt

Figure 11.8 shows a OBDD representation of $T^\times$. For example, the path from the root of this BDD along the edges labeled by $1, 1, 1, 0$ represents $\eta_2 \times \eta_1$; hence the pair (η_2, η_1) of T. △

For representing the inverse image operation we first observe that, for an arbitrary state set Z and system variable v we have

$$(*) \qquad \eta \in Z_{v \mapsto \text{ff}} \cup Z_{v \mapsto \text{tt}} \Leftrightarrow \text{there exists } \overline{\eta} \in Z \text{ with } \eta(\overline{v}) = \overline{\eta}(\overline{v}) \text{ for } \overline{v} \neq v$$

since $\eta \in Z_{v \mapsto \text{ff}} \cup Z_{v \mapsto \text{tt}} \Leftrightarrow \eta_{v \mapsto \text{ff}} \in Z$ or $\eta_{v \mapsto \text{tt}} \in Z$.

Let now Z be a subset of $W(V)$ for an FSTS $\Psi = (V, W, T)$ and

$$Z^c = \{\eta_1 \times \eta_2 \in W(V \cup V^c) \mid \text{there exists } \eta \in Z \text{ with } \eta_2(v^c) = \eta(v) \text{ for every } v^c \in V^c\}.$$

Furthermore, let again $V = \{v_1, \dots, v_m\}$ and consider the following sets:

$$\begin{aligned}
Z^{(0)} &= Z^c \cap T^\times, \\
Z^{(1)} &= Z^{(0)}_{v_1^c \mapsto \mathsf{ff}} \cup Z^{(0)}_{v_1^c \mapsto \mathsf{tt}}, \\
Z^{(2)} &= Z^{(1)}_{v_2^c \mapsto \mathsf{ff}} \cup Z^{(1)}_{v_2^c \mapsto \mathsf{tt}}, \\
&\vdots \\
Z^{(m)} &= Z^{(m-1)}_{v_m^c \mapsto \mathsf{ff}} \cup Z^{(m-1)}_{v_m^c \mapsto \mathsf{tt}}.
\end{aligned}$$

Using the assertions $(*)$ above n times we then have

$$\begin{aligned}
\overline{\eta} \in Z^{(m)} &\Leftrightarrow \text{there exists } \overline{\eta} \in Z^{(0)} \text{ with } \overline{\eta}(v) = \eta(v) \text{ for } v \in V \\
&\Leftrightarrow \text{there exists } \eta \times \eta' \in Z^c \cap T^\times \\
&\Leftrightarrow \text{there exists } \eta' \in Z \text{ with } (\eta, \eta') \in T.
\end{aligned}$$

Due to the construction of $Z^{(m)}$ the OBDD $\mathcal{B}(Z^{(m)})$ does not contain any nodes with labels from V^c, so, according to this equivalence, this OBDD can also be viewed as determining the set of those $\eta \in W(V)$ for which there exists $\eta' \in Z$ with $(\eta, \eta') \in T$ which is just $T^{-1}(Z)$.

Following a similar argument, an OBDD for Z^c is given by an OBDD for the set $\{\eta^c \in W(V^c) \mid \eta^c(v^c) = \eta(v), \eta \in Z\}$. Thus the inverse image operation can be represented in the following way.

- Construction of $\mathcal{B}(T^{-1}(Z))$ from $\mathcal{B}(T^\times)$ and $\mathcal{B}(Z)$
  Construct $\mathcal{B}(Z^c)$ by replacing all labels v of non-terminal nodes in $\mathcal{B}(Z)$ by v^c, and then construct successively $\mathcal{B}(Z^{(0)}), \mathcal{B}(Z^{(1)}), \dots, \mathcal{B}(Z^{(m)})$ for the sets $Z^{(0)}, Z^{(1)}, \dots, Z^{(m)}$ defined above.
  Then $\mathcal{B}(Z^{(m)})$ is $\mathcal{B}(T^{-1}(Z))$.

Example. Consider again the FSTS Ψ_{examp} from the previous example. The OBDD representation of its transition relation T was given in Fig. 11.8. The stepwise construction of $\mathcal{B}(T^{-1}(Z))$ for $Z = \{\eta_2\}$ is shown in Fig. 11.9. The OBDDs (a), (b), (c), and (d) represent the sets Z^c, $Z^{(0)}$, $Z^{(1)}$, and $Z^{(2)}$, respectively. So (d) is $\mathcal{B}(T^{-1}(Z)) = \mathcal{B}(\{\eta_1\})$. △

The model checking algorithm of Sect. 11.3 computes the satisfaction set $[\![F]\!]_\Psi$ for given FSTS Ψ and formula F of $\mathcal{L}_{\mathrm{CTL}\Psi}$. Summarizing the preceding efforts, it is clear now that this algorithm can be implemented by manipulating reduced OBDDs as representations of state sets. The OBDD constructions for set union, intersection, or difference are applied wherever these operations are used in the clauses of the algorithm. The case $F \equiv \mathsf{E}\bigcirc A$ is handled by constructing $\mathcal{B}(T^{-1}(W(A)))$, and such inverse image constructions are also applied in the iteration steps of the procedures

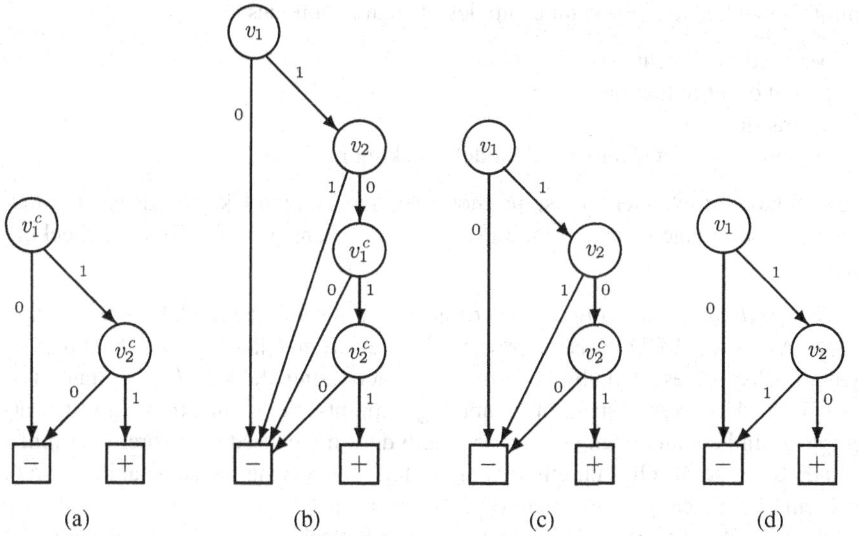

Fig. 11.9. Construction steps for an inverse image

for formulas E□A and A **Eunt** B. The termination check in these latter procedures needs to compare reduced OBDDs and determine whether they represent the same set. Because of their canonical form this is easily carried out by checking whether they are equal.

The representation of satisfaction sets of formulas by BDDs is often called *symbolic*, emphasizing that the size of a representing BDD depends on the structure of the underlying formula rather than on the size of the set: for example, the empty set and the set of all states as satisfaction sets of **false** and **true** are both represented by diagrams with just one node (the diagrams $\mathcal{B}_-$ and $\mathcal{B}_+$ introduced in an example above). Consequently, the algorithm of Sect. 11.3 in the OBDD implementation is called a *symbolic model checking* technique.

In practice a concrete model checking system realizing the algorithm typically offers an input language in which the user can formulate the FSTS, possible fairness constraints, and the formula(s) to be checked. Often the implementation does not really "strictly translate" the "abstract" algorithm but utilizes certain optimizations. After running the algorithm the model checker either confirms that the property holds or reports that it is violated. In cases where this feature is applicable, a witness or counterexample is delivered as well.

11.6 Further Model Checking Techniques

In the previous sections we have discussed some basics of the model checking approach to system verification. Based on these, there are many advanced techniques which were designed to improve and extend the practical applicability of the method.

Among others, some important examples of such techniques are

- bounded model checking,
- partial order reduction,
- abstraction,
- combination of deductive and model checking methods.

We conclude this chapter with some short comments on these keywords just to illustrate the wide range of useful modifications and extensions of the model checking idea.

Bounded model checking can be considered as a symbolic model checking technique. As in the BDD-based approach, the transition relation T of the FSTS is symbolically represented: by a formula characterizing the set $T^{\times}$ of states (cf. Sect. 11.5). However, instead of computing fixpoints, the verification algorithm attempts to find counterexamples whose length does not exceed some pre-determined bound. To do so, it relies on efficient algorithms for solving the satisfiability (SAT) problem of classical propositional logic PL, cf. Sect. 1.1.

We describe the principle of bounded model checking for LTL. Consider some state η_0 of an FSTS Ψ and a formula $\Box A$, where A is non-temporal. A counterexample to $\Box A$ starting from η_0 is provided by a finite prefix

$$\eta_0 \longrightarrow \eta_1 \longrightarrow \ldots \longrightarrow \eta_k$$

of an execution sequence that reaches a state η_k in which A does not hold. An algorithm for bounded model checking searches for such prefixes up to some fixed length $k \in \mathbb{N}$. If a state in which A does not hold is found in this way then the corresponding finite state sequence is a *finite counterexample* (for $\Box A$ and η_0 in Ψ), showing that $\Box A$ does not hold in η_0. Otherwise, the search is repeated with a larger k. The repetition stops when some previously known upper bound is reached or – without final decision – when the process runs out of available resources.

For formulas $\Diamond A$ (for non-temporal A) a finite counterexample cannot be of the simple form above, but it must have some "loop structure"

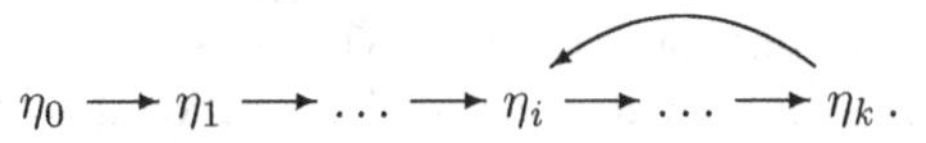

If A is false in all $\eta_0, \ldots, \eta_k$ then such a loop is a finite counterexample to the formula $\Diamond A$ in η_0. This idea can be extended to arbitrary LTL formulas.

For an LTL formula F, a state η of the FSTS Ψ, and $k \in \mathbb{N}$, a formula $F_k^{(\Psi,\eta)}$ of PL is associated such that $F_k^{(\Psi,\eta)}$ is satisfiable if and only if there is a finite counterexample of length k for F and η in Ψ.

We illustrate the definition of $F_k^{(\Psi,\eta)}$ by an example. Consider the FSTS Ψ_{examp} from earlier examples given by the transition diagram in Fig. 11.10 and the formula $F \equiv \Diamond(\neg v_1 \vee v_2)$. Let $k = 1$ and

$$A_T \equiv (v_1 \wedge \neg v_2 \wedge v_2^c) \vee (v_1 \wedge v_2 \wedge (v_1^c \leftrightarrow \neg v_2^c)) \vee (\neg v_1 \wedge v_2 \wedge \neg v_1^c \wedge v_2^c).$$

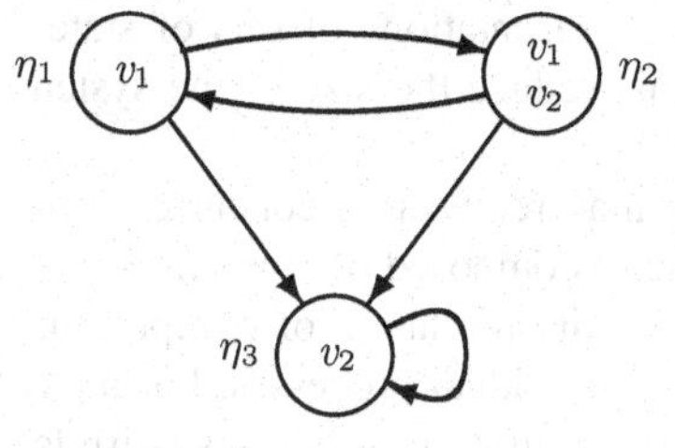

Fig. 11.10. The FSTS Ψ_{examp} again

This formula describes the transition relation of Ψ_{examp} using copies v_1^c and v_2^c of the system variables v_1 and v_2 as in Sect. 11.5 (cf. Fig. 11.8). Thus, the formula

$$A_1 \equiv v_1 \wedge v_2 \wedge A_T$$

describes all state sequences $\eta_2 \longrightarrow \eta'$ of length 1 in Ψ. Moreover, let A_T^c result from A_T by replacing v_1 and v_2 by v_1^c and v_2^c and the latter by further copies v_1^{cc} and v_2^{cc}, respectively. Then the formula

$$A_2 \equiv A_1 \wedge ((A_T^c \wedge v_1^{cc} \wedge v_2^{cc}) \vee (A_T^c \wedge (v_1^{cc} \leftrightarrow v_1^c) \wedge (v_2^{cc} \leftrightarrow v_2^c)))$$

describes all such sequences $\eta_2 \longrightarrow \eta'$ which contain a loop (from η' to η_2 or to η'). Then it is evident that the formula

$$F_1^{(\Psi_{examp},\eta_2)} \equiv A_2 \wedge (\neg v_1 \vee v_2) \wedge (\neg v_1^c \vee v_2^c)$$

encodes F in the desired way. In fact, this formula is satisfied by the valuation

$$\begin{array}{lll} v_1 \mapsto \mathsf{tt}, & v_1^c \mapsto \mathsf{ff}, & v_1^{cc} \mapsto \mathsf{ff}, \\ v_2 \mapsto \mathsf{tt}, & v_2^c \mapsto \mathsf{tt}, & v_1^{cc} \mapsto \mathsf{tt} \end{array}$$

which corresponds to the finite counterexample

$$\eta_2 \longrightarrow \eta_3 \circlearrowleft$$

for F. Observe that a state sequence is a counterexample for F if and only if it is a witness for the CTL formula $F' \equiv \mathsf{E}\Box(\neg v_1 \vee v_2)$. The result agrees with earlier examples in Sect. 11.3 where we found that F' is true in η_2, with the (infinite) witness

$$\eta_2 \longrightarrow \eta_3 \longrightarrow \eta_3 \longrightarrow \eta_3 \longrightarrow \ldots.$$

This sequence is just the "unfolded" finite counterexample for F.

Turning to the next item of our short list of further model checking techniques, we have observed in Sect. 11.2 that the state explosion problem is the main limitation to the application of model checking. Symbolic model checking algorithms attempt to alleviate this limitation by providing compact representations of sets of states. Alternatively, approaches have been considered that reduce the size of the system that needs to be analysed during model checking.

An FSTS Ψ to be verified by model checking may represent a concurrent program as studied in Chap. 8 (more generally: a system composed of concurrent processes with some "interaction"). In this case the transition relation of Ψ represents all possible interleavings of the atomic steps of the individual processes. For many properties, however, the relative order of such steps in different processes is irrelevant and it suffices to consider only some representative interleaving sequences. This particularly holds when only little synchronization takes place between the concurrent processes. *Partial order reduction* techniques are designed to reduce the number of such sequences, i.e., execution sequences of Ψ and, as a consequence, the number of states, which have to be considered in the model checking process.

The main problem for finding an appropriate reduction is to detect only from the "local" knowledge available at a given state when some interleaving may be omitted. A simple idea would be to connect this with the *commutativity* of two atomic steps α and β which means that the state reached after executing them does not depend on the order of their execution and may be depicted by

$$\eta_1 \xrightarrow{\alpha} \eta_2 \xrightarrow{\beta} \eta_3 \qquad \text{and} \qquad \eta_1 \xrightarrow{\beta} \eta_2' \xrightarrow{\alpha} \eta_3 .$$

To omit one of these sequences, however, is dangerous: the states η_2 and η_2' may have successors other than η_3 which may not be explored if the respective sequence is ignored. Moreover, the property to be checked might be quite sensitive to the choice of the intermediate states η_2 and η_2'.

Algorithms embodying partial order reduction techniques differ in how these problems are dealt with efficiently and in a way appropriate for the systems of interest. We show, as an example, one possible selection of conditions such that one of the above two sequences could be ignored in the model checking process.

We say that two atomic steps α and β commute in a state η where they are both enabled (i.e., there are $(\eta, \eta') \in T_\Psi$ "caused by α" and $(\eta, \eta'') \in T_\Psi$ "caused by β") if all of the following hold:

- β is enabled in all possible successors of η reached by executing α,
- α is enabled in all possible successors of η reached by executing β,
- the states reachable from η by executing α followed by β are the same as those reachable by executing first β, then α.

When model checking an LTL formula F over Ψ, the atomic step β can be delayed (i.e., the second sequence in the illustration above can be ignored) if the following conditions are satisfied.

- F is stuttering invariant (in the sense of Sect. 9.3).
- The atomic step β does not modify the values of the system variables occurring in F.
- The step β commutes with all atomic steps γ of Ψ, in all states where β and γ are simultaneously enabled.

In practice, deciding whether two atomic actions commute can be costly, and the third condition above is approximated by sufficient syntactic conditions. For example, the assignment to a local variable of a process commutes with all steps that do not modify the variables of the expression in the right-hand side of the assignment.

Abstraction is another technique for decreasing the number of states and transitions which have to be considered when model checking is applied to a system. Recall from Sect. 11.1 that an FSTS may be an encoding of a first-order STS. Such systems manipulate data and are a particular application area for this technique.

Abstraction is based on the observation that system properties in such cases often involve only simple relationships between the data values occurring during execution. The idea is to find an abstraction mapping between the data of the given systems and a small set of "abstract" data with the goal that when extending this mapping to states and transitions one obtains an abstract version of the system which is smaller and still sufficient for the verification of the property under consideration. More precisely: the property holds of the given system if it can be proved for the abstract one.

On the first-order STS level the abstraction mapping can typically be understood to be realized by functions φ_a for every individual system variable a of the given system. Assume that the domain $\mathbb{D}$ of possible values of a is partitioned into sets $\mathbb{D}_1, \ldots, \mathbb{D}_n$. The set $\{d_1, \ldots, d_n\}$ is a (finite) set of abstract values for a (called abstract data domain) and the abstraction mapping φ_a is given by

$$\varphi_a(d) = d_i \quad \text{if } d \in \mathbb{D}_i$$

for every element $d \in \mathbb{D}$. In an encoding FSTS we then have n propositional system variables $aval_1, \ldots, aval_n$ encoding the abstract values, i.e., with the meaning that

$$\widetilde{\eta}(aval_i) = \mathsf{tt} \Leftrightarrow \eta(a) \in \mathbb{D}_i \quad \text{for } 1 \le i \le n.$$

($\widetilde{\eta}$ denotes the encoding of the original state η as in Sect. 11.1.) The appropriate partition of $\mathbb{D}$ depends on the application. In the general case, it has to be defined by the user. Observe that the abstraction technique therefore is not an entirely automatic method in the same way that standard model checking is. Full automation can be recovered for pre-defined abstract domains, such as partitioning the integers into zero, strictly positive and strictly negative integers. Abstraction may be applicable if the original domain $\mathbb{D}$ is infinite, so the given system is not a finite state system.

Again we give a simple example for illustration. The counter system Γ_{count} introduced in Sect. 6.2 has (under some fairness assumptions) the property

$$\Diamond(c = 0).$$

Γ_{count} has infinitely many states since the values of c may be any natural number, but it is quite obvious from the possible transitions (and can also be seen by an inspection of the formal derivation of this formula in Sect. 7.4) that realizing the fact that any (fair) execution sequence will eventually reach a state with $c = 0$ does not really refer to the concrete values of c. The only relevant "information" about c is whether

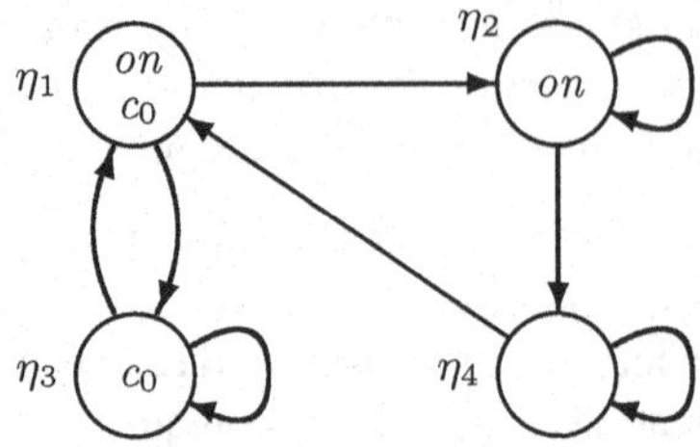

Fig. 11.11. Transition diagram of an abstract FSTS

it equals 0 or not. Thus, a partition of $\mathbb{N}$ into the sets $\mathbb{D}_1 = \{0\}$ and $\mathbb{D}_2 = \mathbb{N} \setminus \mathbb{D}_1$ provides a faithful abstract finite state system which can be represented as an FSTS with the system variables on and c_0 and the transition diagram depicted in Fig. 11.11. The system variable c_0 stands for "the value of c is 0" and, e.g., the arrow from η_4 to η_1 represents the transition of switching the counter on in a state where it is off and $c \neq 0$. All counting steps are represented by arrows leading to η_2, i.e., to the state in which the counter is on and $c \neq 0$. Under suitable fairness assumptions, the formula $\Diamond(c = 0)$ can easily be verified for this FSTS and the result can be transferred back to Γ_{count}.

Instead of defining an abstraction mapping, a reduced system can be obtained by a quotient construction with respect to an equivalence relation. This idea underlies a technique known as *symmetry reduction* that identifies system states that agree "up to permutation". For example, systems are often composed of processes that behave identically, and for many properties the precise identity of a process performing a certain step can be ignored.

The idea of abstraction also is a natural basis for combining deductive and model checking methods for system verification. Among several possible approaches, we mention just one that is directly related to abstraction as just sketched. The abstraction mapping maps concrete to abstract systems. Thus, it works "semantically" and in complex cases it might be difficult to see that the abstract system reflects the concrete one in a correct way. The idea of the method is to formalize this step by some deductive procedure between specifications of the systems on the two levels. Moreover, the specification of the abstract system may be represented in a form of a *predicate diagram* which can directly be viewed as (the transition diagram of) an FSTS verifiable by model checking.

We use again the counter system Γ_{count} as a simple example to indicate the basic idea. A specification of Γ_{count} was given in Sect. 6.2 by the two axioms

$$on \rightarrow (on' \land c' = c + 1) \lor (\neg on' \land c' = c),$$
$$\neg on \rightarrow (\neg on' \land c' = c) \lor (on' \land c' = 0).$$

An adequate predicate diagram for the system (and the property $\Diamond(c = 0)$ to be proved) could be as given in Fig. 11.12. Its one-to-one correspondence to the transition diagram depicted for the above abstraction example is evident: $c = 0$ can

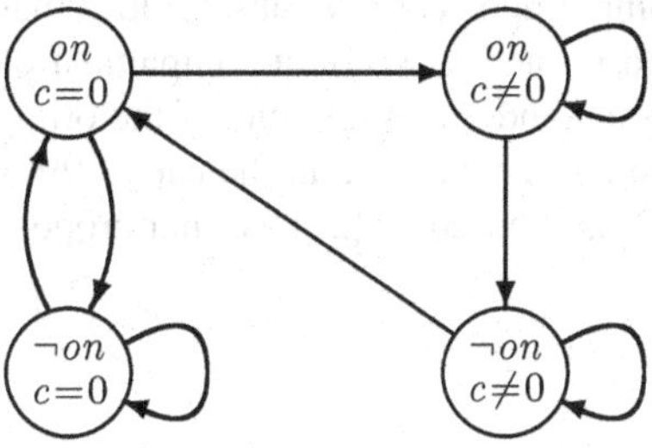

Fig. 11.12. Predicate diagram for a counter

be viewed as (another notation of) a propositional system variable, and negations mean that a system variable has the value ff. So, model checking can be performed as before.

On the other hand, the nodes of the predicate diagram can be read as formulas by combining their atomic formulas by conjunction. Interpreting the arrows still as possible "transitions" from a state to a successor state, the diagram represents the formulas

$$\begin{aligned}
&on \wedge c = 0 \rightarrow (\neg on' \wedge c' = 0) \vee (on' \wedge c' \neq 0),\\
&on \wedge c \neq 0 \rightarrow (on' \wedge c' \neq 0) \vee (\neg on' \wedge c' \neq 0),\\
&\neg on \wedge c = 0 \rightarrow (\neg on' \wedge c' = 0) \vee (on' \wedge c' = 0),\\
&\neg on \wedge c \neq 0 \rightarrow (\neg on' \wedge c' \neq 0) \vee (on' \wedge c' = 0)
\end{aligned}$$

which specify the abstract system. These formulas are derivable from the axioms of Γ_{count}. Therefore, any safety property verified for the predicate diagram holds for Γ_{count} as well. The technique can be extended to arbitrary temporal properties when fairness hypotheses are faithfully represented in the predicate diagram.

Bibliographical Notes

The idea of using model checking as a verification technique for reactive systems was first proposed in 1981 [30, 127] and has since matured into a domain of its own, with specialized conferences and industrial applications. In-depth presentations of model checking for finite state systems can be found in [16, 33, 35, 65, 67]. BDD-based methods for symbolic model checking were introduced by McMillan [106]; see [23] for original work on BDDs.

Bounded model checking was first proposed by Biere et al. [18]. Partial-order reduction methods exist in many variants; see [47, 56, 64, 115, 150] among other publications. Abstraction-based model checking techniques were initially considered in [32, 37, 94]. They are now often studied in connection with methods for combining model checking and deductive techniques, typically in the framework of predicate abstraction [59]. In particular, the paradigm of counterexample guided abstraction refinement [10, 31, 61] is based on computing successive abstractions that are submitted to finite state model checkers and refined based on a comparison of the counterexample reported for the abstract model and the executions of the original system. The technique of symmetry reduction was developed in the early 1990s [34, 46, 68]. Our presentation of predicate diagrams is based on [27]; similar proposals are [20, 38, 72].

List of Temporal Logic Laws

We give here a compact list of laws of the various temporal logics, particularly including those which are frequently used throughout the book. Furthermore, we note some of the corresponding formal systems.

Laws of Basic LTL

(T1)	$\neg\bigcirc A \leftrightarrow \bigcirc\neg A$
(T2)	$\neg\Box A \leftrightarrow \Diamond\neg A$
(T3)	$\neg\Diamond A \leftrightarrow \Box\neg A$
(T4)	$\Box A \rightarrow A$
(T5)	$A \rightarrow \Diamond A$
(T6)	$\Box A \rightarrow \bigcirc A$
(T7)	$\bigcirc A \rightarrow \Diamond A$
(T8)	$\Box A \rightarrow \Diamond A$
(T9)	$\Diamond\Box A \rightarrow \Box\Diamond A$
(T10)	$\Box\Box A \leftrightarrow \Box A$
(T11)	$\Diamond\Diamond A \leftrightarrow \Diamond A$
(T12)	$\Box\bigcirc A \leftrightarrow \bigcirc\Box A$
(T13)	$\Diamond\bigcirc A \leftrightarrow \bigcirc\Diamond A$
(T14)	$\bigcirc(A \rightarrow B) \leftrightarrow \bigcirc A \rightarrow \bigcirc B$
(T15)	$\bigcirc(A \wedge B) \leftrightarrow \bigcirc A \wedge \bigcirc B$
(T16)	$\bigcirc(A \vee B) \leftrightarrow \bigcirc A \vee \bigcirc B$
(T17)	$\bigcirc(A \leftrightarrow B) \leftrightarrow (\bigcirc A \leftrightarrow \bigcirc B)$
(T18)	$\Box(A \wedge B) \leftrightarrow \Box A \wedge \Box B$
(T19)	$\Diamond(A \vee B) \leftrightarrow \Diamond A \vee \Diamond B$
(T20)	$\Box\Diamond(A \vee B) \leftrightarrow \Box\Diamond A \vee \Box\Diamond B$
(T21)	$\Diamond\Box(A \wedge B) \leftrightarrow \Diamond\Box A \wedge \Diamond\Box B$
(T22)	$\Box(A \rightarrow B) \rightarrow (\Box A \rightarrow \Box B)$
(T23)	$\Box A \vee \Box B \rightarrow \Box(A \vee B)$
(T24)	$(\Diamond A \rightarrow \Diamond B) \rightarrow \Diamond(A \rightarrow B)$

(T25) $\Diamond(A \land B) \rightarrow \Diamond A \land \Diamond B$
(T26) $\Box\Diamond(A \land B) \rightarrow \Box\Diamond A \land \Box\Diamond B$
(T27) $\Diamond\Box A \lor \Diamond\Box B \rightarrow \Diamond\Box(A \lor B)$
(T28) $\Box A \leftrightarrow A \land \bigcirc\Box A$
(T29) $\Diamond A \leftrightarrow A \lor \bigcirc\Diamond A$
(T30) $\Box(A \rightarrow B) \rightarrow (\bigcirc A \rightarrow \bigcirc B)$
(T31) $\Box(A \rightarrow B) \rightarrow (\Diamond A \rightarrow \Diamond B)$
(T32) $\Box A \rightarrow (\bigcirc B \rightarrow \bigcirc(A \land B))$
(T33) $\Box A \rightarrow (\Box B \rightarrow \Box(A \land B))$
(T34) $\Box A \rightarrow (\Diamond B \rightarrow \Diamond(A \land B))$
(T35) $\Box(\Box A \rightarrow B) \rightarrow (\Box A \rightarrow \Box B)$
(T36) $\Box(A \rightarrow \Diamond B) \rightarrow (\Diamond A \rightarrow \Diamond B)$
(T37) $\Diamond\Box\Diamond A \leftrightarrow \Box\Diamond A$
(T38) $\Box\Diamond\Box A \leftrightarrow \Diamond\Box A$

Laws for Binary Operators in LTL

(Tb1) $A \;\mathbf{until}\; B \leftrightarrow \bigcirc\Diamond B \land A \;\mathbf{unless}\; B$
(Tb2) $A \;\mathbf{unless}\; B \leftrightarrow \bigcirc(A \;\mathbf{unl}\; B)$
(Tb3) $A \;\mathbf{unl}\; B \leftrightarrow A \;\mathbf{unt}\; B \lor \Box A$
(Tb4) $A \;\mathbf{unt}\; B \leftrightarrow B \lor (A \land A \;\mathbf{until}\; B)$
(Tb5) $A \;\mathbf{unless}\; B \leftrightarrow B \;\mathbf{atnext}\; (A \rightarrow B)$
(Tb6) $A \;\mathbf{atnext}\; B \leftrightarrow B \;\mathbf{before}\; (\neg A \land B)$
(Tb7) $A \;\mathbf{before}\; B \leftrightarrow \neg(A \lor B) \;\mathbf{unless}\; (A \land \neg B)$
(Tb8) $\bigcirc A \leftrightarrow A \;\mathbf{atnext}\; \mathbf{true}$
(Tb9) $\Box A \leftrightarrow A \land A \;\mathbf{unless}\; \mathbf{false}$
(Tb10) $\Box A \leftrightarrow A \;\mathbf{unl}\; \mathbf{false}$
(Tb11) $A \;\mathbf{until}\; B \leftrightarrow \bigcirc B \lor \bigcirc(A \land A \;\mathbf{until}\; B)$
(Tb12) $A \;\mathbf{unless}\; B \leftrightarrow \bigcirc B \lor \bigcirc(A \land A \;\mathbf{unless}\; B)$
(Tb13) $A \;\mathbf{unt}\; B \leftrightarrow B \lor (A \land \bigcirc(A \;\mathbf{unt}\; B))$
(Tb14) $A \;\mathbf{unl}\; B \leftrightarrow B \lor (A \land \bigcirc(A \;\mathbf{unl}\; B))$
(Tb15) $A \;\mathbf{atnext}\; B \leftrightarrow \bigcirc(B \rightarrow A) \land \bigcirc(\neg B \rightarrow A \;\mathbf{atnext}\; B)$
(Tb16) $A \;\mathbf{before}\; B \leftrightarrow \bigcirc\neg B \land \bigcirc(A \lor A \;\mathbf{before}\; B)$
(Tb17) $\neg(A \;\mathbf{unless}\; B) \leftrightarrow \bigcirc\neg B \land \bigcirc(\neg A \lor \neg(A \;\mathbf{unless}\; B))$
(Tb18) $\Box(\neg B \rightarrow A) \rightarrow A \;\mathbf{unl}\; B$
(Tb19) $\bigcirc(A \;\mathbf{unl}\; B) \leftrightarrow \bigcirc A \;\mathbf{unl}\; \bigcirc B$
(Tb20) $(A \land B) \;\mathbf{unl}\; C \leftrightarrow A \;\mathbf{unl}\; C \land B \;\mathbf{unl}\; C$
(Tb21) $A \;\mathbf{unl}\; (B \lor C) \leftrightarrow A \;\mathbf{unl}\; B \lor A \;\mathbf{unl}\; C$
(Tb22) $A \;\mathbf{unl}\; (B \land C) \rightarrow A \;\mathbf{unl}\; B \land A \;\mathbf{unl}\; C$
(Tb23) $A \;\mathbf{unl}\; (A \;\mathbf{unl}\; B) \leftrightarrow A \;\mathbf{unl}\; B$
(Tb24) $(A \;\mathbf{unl}\; B) \;\mathbf{unl}\; B \leftrightarrow A \;\mathbf{unl}\; B$
(Tb25) $\Box(B \rightarrow A) \rightarrow A \;\mathbf{atnext}\; B$
(Tb26) $\bigcirc(A \;\mathbf{atnext}\; B) \leftrightarrow \bigcirc A \;\mathbf{atnext}\; \bigcirc B$
(Tb27) $(A \land B) \;\mathbf{atnext}\; C \leftrightarrow A \;\mathbf{atnext}\; C \land B \;\mathbf{atnext}\; C$
(Tb28) $(A \lor B) \;\mathbf{atnext}\; C \leftrightarrow A \;\mathbf{atnext}\; C \lor B \;\mathbf{atnext}\; C$

(Tb29) A **atnext** $(B \vee C) \rightarrow A$ **atnext** $B \vee A$ **atnext** C

Laws for Fixpoint Operators in LTL

(Tμ1) $\Box A \leftrightarrow \nu u(A \wedge \bigcirc u)$
(Tμ2) $\Diamond A \leftrightarrow \mu u(A \vee \bigcirc u)$
(Tμ3) A **until** $B \leftrightarrow \mu u(\bigcirc B \vee \bigcirc(A \wedge u))$
(Tμ4) A **unless** $B \leftrightarrow \nu u(\bigcirc B \vee \bigcirc(A \wedge u))$
(Tμ5) A **unt** $B \leftrightarrow \mu u(B \vee (A \wedge \bigcirc u))$
(Tμ6) A **unl** $B \leftrightarrow \nu u(B \vee (A \wedge \bigcirc u))$
(Tμ7) A **atnext** $B \leftrightarrow \nu u(\bigcirc(B \rightarrow A) \wedge \bigcirc(\neg B \rightarrow u))$
(Tμ8) A **before** $B \leftrightarrow \nu u(\bigcirc\neg B \wedge \bigcirc(A \vee u))$

Laws for Propositional Quantification in LTL

(Tq1) $\forall u A \rightarrow A_u(B)$
(Tq2) $\forall u \bigcirc A \leftrightarrow \bigcirc \forall u A$
(Tq3) $\forall u \Box A \leftrightarrow \Box \forall u A$
(Tq4) $\exists u \Diamond A \leftrightarrow \Diamond \exists u A$
(Tq5) $\Box(A \vee B) \rightarrow \exists u \Box((A \wedge u) \vee (B \wedge \neg u))$

Laws for Past Operators in LTL

(Tp1) $\circleddash A \rightarrow \neg\ominus$ **false**
(Tp2) $\circleddash\neg A \rightarrow \neg\circleddash A$
(Tp3) $\neg\ominus A \leftrightarrow \circleddash\neg A$
(Tp4) $A \rightarrow \ominus\bigcirc A$
(Tp5) $A \rightarrow \bigcirc\circleddash A$
(Tp6) $\ominus(A \rightarrow B) \leftrightarrow \ominus A \rightarrow \ominus B$
(Tp7) $\ominus(A \wedge B) \leftrightarrow \ominus A \wedge \ominus B$
(Tp8) $\circleddash(A \wedge B) \leftrightarrow \circleddash A \wedge \circleddash B$

Laws of First-Order LTL

(T39) $\exists x \bigcirc A \leftrightarrow \bigcirc \exists x A$
(T40) $\forall x \bigcirc A \leftrightarrow \bigcirc \forall x A$
(T41) $\exists x \Diamond A \leftrightarrow \Diamond \exists x A$
(T42) $\forall x \Box A \leftrightarrow \Box \forall x A$
(Tb30) $\exists x(A$ **unl** $B) \leftrightarrow A$ **unl** $(\exists x B)$
if there is no free occurrence of x in A
(Tb31) $\forall x(A$ **unl** $B) \leftrightarrow (\forall x A)$ **unl** B
if there is no free occurrence of x in B
(Tb32) $\exists x(A$ **atnext** $B) \leftrightarrow (\exists x A)$ **atnext** B
if there is no free occurrence of x in B
(Tb33) $\forall x(A$ **atnext** $B) \leftrightarrow (\forall x A)$ **atnext** B
if there is no free occurrence of x in B

Derivation Rules of Linear Temporal Logic

(nex) $A \vdash \bigcirc A$
(alw) $A \vdash \Box A$
(ind) $A \to B, A \to \bigcirc A \vdash A \to \Box B$
(ind1) $A \to \bigcirc A \vdash A \to \Box A$
(ind2) $A \to B, B \to \bigcirc B \vdash A \to \Box B$
(som) $A \to \bigcirc B \vdash A \to \Diamond B$
(chain) $A \to \Diamond B, B \to \Diamond C \vdash A \to \Diamond C$
(indunless) $A \to \bigcirc C \lor \bigcirc(A \land B) \vdash A \to B$ **unless** C
(indunl) $A \to C \lor (B \land \bigcirc A) \vdash A \to B$ **unl** C
(indatnext) $A \to \bigcirc(C \to B) \land \bigcirc(\neg C \to A) \vdash A \to B$ **atnext** C
(indbefore) $A \to \bigcirc\neg C \land \bigcirc(A \lor B) \vdash A \to B$ **before** C
(μ-ind) $A_u(B) \to B \vdash \mu u A \to B$ if there is no free occurrence of u in B
(qltl-ind) $F \to \exists \mathbf{u}_2 \bigcirc((\mathbf{u}_2 \leftrightarrow \mathbf{u}_1) \land F_{\mathbf{u}_1}(\mathbf{u}_2))$
$\vdash F \to \exists \mathbf{u}_2((\mathbf{u}_2 \leftrightarrow \mathbf{u}_1) \land \Box F_{\mathbf{u}_1}(\mathbf{u}_2))$
if every occurrence of variables u_1^i in F is in the scope of at most one $\bigcirc$ operator and no other temporal operator
(indpast) $A \to B, A \to \ominus A \vdash A \to \boxminus B$
(indinit) **init** $\to A, A \to \bigcirc A \vdash A$
(wfr) $A \to \Diamond(B \lor \exists \bar{y}(\bar{y} \prec y \land A_y(\bar{y}))) \vdash \exists y A \to \Diamond B$
if B does not contain y, for $y, \bar{y} \in \mathcal{X}_{WF}$

Laws of Generalized TLA

(GT1) $\Box\big[[A]_e \to A\big]_e$
(GT2) $\Box A \to \Box[\bigcirc A]_e$
(GT3) $\Box\big[[A]_e\big]_e \leftrightarrow \Box[A]_e$
(GT4) $\Box\big[\Box[A]_{e_1} \to [A]_{e_1}\big]_{e_2}$
(GT5) $\Box[A]_{e_1} \to \Box\big[[A]_{e_1}\big]_{e_2}$
(GT6) $\Box\big[[A]_{e_1}\big]_{e_2} \leftrightarrow \Box\big[[A]_{e_2}\big]_{e_1}$

Laws of Interval Temporal Logic

(IT1) **empty chop** $A \leftrightarrow A$
(IT2) $\odot A$ **chop** $B \leftrightarrow \odot(A$ **chop** $B)$
(IT3) $(A \lor B)$ **chop** $C \leftrightarrow A$ **chop** $C \lor B$ **chop** C
(IT4) A **chop** $(B \lor C) \leftrightarrow A$ **chop** $B \lor A$ **chop** C
(IT5) A **chop** $(B$ **chop** $C) \leftrightarrow (A$ **chop** $B)$ **chop** C

Laws of BTL and CTL

(BT1)	$\mathsf{E}\Box A \leftrightarrow A \land \mathsf{E}\bigcirc\mathsf{E}\Box A$
(BT2)	$\mathsf{E}\Diamond A \leftrightarrow A \lor \mathsf{E}\bigcirc\mathsf{E}\Diamond A$
(BT3)	$\mathsf{A}\Box A \leftrightarrow A \land \mathsf{A}\bigcirc\mathsf{A}\Box A$
(BT4)	$\mathsf{A}\Diamond A \leftrightarrow A \lor \mathsf{A}\bigcirc\mathsf{A}\Diamond A$
(BT5)	$\mathsf{A}\bigcirc A \rightarrow \mathsf{E}\bigcirc A$
(BT6)	$\mathsf{E}\Box A \rightarrow \mathsf{E}\bigcirc A$
(BT7)	$\mathsf{E}\Box\mathsf{E}\Box A \leftrightarrow \mathsf{E}\Box A$
(BT8)	$\mathsf{E}\bigcirc\mathsf{E}\Box A \rightarrow \mathsf{E}\Box\mathsf{E}\bigcirc A$
(BT9)	$\mathsf{E}\bigcirc(A \land B) \rightarrow \mathsf{E}\bigcirc A \land \mathsf{E}\bigcirc B$
(BT10)	$\mathsf{E}\bigcirc(A \rightarrow B) \leftrightarrow \mathsf{A}\bigcirc A \rightarrow \mathsf{E}\bigcirc B$
(BT11)	$\mathsf{E}\Diamond(A \lor B) \leftrightarrow \mathsf{E}\Diamond A \lor \mathsf{E}\Diamond B$
(BT12)	$\mathsf{E}\Box(A \land B) \rightarrow \mathsf{E}\Box A \land \mathsf{E}\Box B$
(CT1)	$A\ \mathbf{Eunt}\ B \leftrightarrow B \lor (A \land \mathsf{E}\bigcirc(A\ \mathbf{Eunt}\ B))$
(CT2)	$A\ \mathbf{Eunt}\ B \rightarrow \mathsf{E}\Diamond B$
(CT3)	$\mathsf{E}\bigcirc(A\ \mathbf{Eunt}\ B) \leftrightarrow \mathsf{E}\bigcirc A\ \mathbf{Eunt}\ \mathsf{E}\bigcirc B$
(CT4)	$A\ \mathbf{Eunt}\ C \lor B\ \mathbf{Eunt}\ C \rightarrow (A \lor B)\ \mathbf{Eunt}\ C$
(CT5)	$(A \land B)\ \mathbf{Eunt}\ C \rightarrow A\ \mathbf{Eunt}\ C \land B\ \mathbf{Eunt}\ C$
(CT6)	$A\ \mathbf{Eunt}\ (B \lor C) \leftrightarrow A\ \mathbf{Eunt}\ B \lor A\ \mathbf{Eunt}\ C$
(CT7)	$A\ \mathbf{Eunt}\ (B \land C) \rightarrow A\ \mathbf{Eunt}\ B \land A\ \mathbf{Eunt}\ C$

Derivation Rules of Branching Time Temporal Logic

(nexb)	$A \rightarrow B \vdash \mathsf{E}\bigcirc A \rightarrow \mathsf{E}\bigcirc B$
(indb1)	$A \rightarrow B, A \rightarrow \mathsf{E}\bigcirc A \vdash A \rightarrow \mathsf{E}\Box B$
(indb2)	$A \rightarrow \neg B, A \rightarrow \mathsf{A}\bigcirc(A \lor \neg\mathsf{E}\Diamond B) \vdash A \rightarrow \neg\mathsf{E}\Diamond B$
(indc)	$A \rightarrow \neg C, A \rightarrow \mathsf{A}\bigcirc(A \lor \neg(B\ \mathbf{Eunt}\ C)) \vdash A \rightarrow \neg(B\ \mathbf{Eunt}\ C)$

The Formal System Σ_{LTL}

(taut)	All tautologically valid formulas
(ltl1)	$\neg\bigcirc A \leftrightarrow \bigcirc\neg A$
(ltl2)	$\bigcirc(A \rightarrow B) \rightarrow (\bigcirc A \rightarrow \bigcirc B)$
(ltl3)	$\Box A \rightarrow A \land \bigcirc\Box A$
(mp)	$A, A \rightarrow B \vdash B$
(nex)	$A \vdash \bigcirc A$
(ind)	$A \rightarrow B, A \rightarrow \bigcirc A \vdash A \rightarrow \Box B$

Additional Axioms and Rules for Extensions of LTL

(until1)	$A\ \mathbf{until}\ B \leftrightarrow \bigcirc B \lor \bigcirc(A \land A\ \mathbf{until}\ B)$
(until2)	$A\ \mathbf{until}\ B \rightarrow \bigcirc\Diamond B$
(unless1)	$A\ \mathbf{unless}\ B \leftrightarrow \bigcirc B \lor \bigcirc(A \land A\ \mathbf{unless}\ B)$

(unless2) $\circ\Box A \rightarrow A$ **unless** B

(atnext1) A **atnext** $B \leftrightarrow \circ(B \rightarrow A) \wedge \circ(\neg B \rightarrow A$ **atnext** $B)$

(atnext2) $\circ\Box\neg B \rightarrow A$ **atnext** B

(before1) A **before** $B \leftrightarrow \circ\neg B \wedge \circ(A \vee A$ **before** $B)$

(before2) $\circ\Box\neg B \rightarrow A$ **before** B

(μ-rec) $A_u(\mu u A) \rightarrow \mu u A$

(μ-ind) $A_u(B) \rightarrow B \vdash \mu u A \rightarrow B$ if there is no free occurrence of u in B

(qltl1) $A_u(B) \rightarrow \exists u A$

(qltl2) $\exists u \circ A \leftrightarrow \circ \exists u A$

(qltl3) $\exists u(u \wedge \circ\Box\neg u)$

(qltl-part) $A \rightarrow B \vdash \exists u A \rightarrow B$ if there is no free occurrence of u in B

(qltl-ind) $F \rightarrow \exists \mathbf{u}_2 \circ((\mathbf{u}_2 \leftrightarrow \mathbf{u}_1) \wedge F_{\mathbf{u}_1}(\mathbf{u}_2))$
$\vdash F \rightarrow \exists \mathbf{u}_2((\mathbf{u}_2 \leftrightarrow \mathbf{u}_1) \wedge \Box F_{\mathbf{u}_1}(\mathbf{u}_2))$
if every occurrence of variables u_1^i in F is in the scope of at most one $\circ$ operator and no other temporal operator

(pltl1) $⊜\neg A \rightarrow \neg ⊜ A$

(pltl2) $\ominus(A \rightarrow B) \rightarrow (\ominus A \rightarrow \ominus B)$

(pltl3) $\boxminus A \rightarrow A \wedge \ominus\boxminus A$

(pltl4) $\diamondminus\ominus$ **false**

(pltl5) $A \rightarrow \ominus\circ A$

(pltl6) $A \rightarrow \circ⊜ A$

(prev) $A \vdash \ominus A$

(indpast) $A \rightarrow B, A \rightarrow \ominus A \vdash A \rightarrow \boxminus B$

(iltl) $\circ\neg$**init**

(init) **init** $\rightarrow \Box A \vdash A$

(since) A **since** $B \leftrightarrow ⊜ B \vee ⊜(A \wedge A$ **since** $B)$

(backto) A **backto** $B \leftrightarrow \ominus B \vee \ominus(A \wedge A$ **backto** $B)$

(atlast) A **atlast** $B \leftrightarrow \ominus(B \rightarrow A) \wedge \ominus(\neg B \rightarrow A$ **atlast** $B)$

(after) A **after** $B \leftrightarrow \ominus\neg B \wedge \ominus(A \vee A$ **after** $B)$

The Formal System Σ_{FOLTL}

(taut) All tautologically valid formulas

(ltl1) $\neg\circ A \leftrightarrow \circ\neg A$

(ltl2) $\circ(A \rightarrow B) \rightarrow (\circ A \rightarrow \circ B)$

(ltl3) $\Box A \rightarrow A \wedge \circ\Box A$

(ltl4) $A_x(t) \rightarrow \exists x A$ if t is substitutable for x in A

(ltl5) $\circ\exists x A \rightarrow \exists x \circ A$

(ltl6) $A \rightarrow \circ A$ if A is rigid

(eq1) $x = x$

(eq2) $x = y \rightarrow (A \rightarrow A_x(y))$ if A is non-temporal

(mp) $A, A \rightarrow B \vdash B$

(nex) $A \vdash \circ A$
(ind) $A \to B, A \to \circ A \vdash A \to \Box B$
(par) $A \to B \vdash \exists x A \to B$ if there is no free occurrence of x in B

The Formal System Σ_{pGTLA}

(taut) All tautologically valid formulas
(taut$_{pf}$) $\Box[A]_e$ if A is a tautologically valid pre-formula
(gtla1) $\Box A \to A$
(gtla2) $\Box A \to \Box[A]_e$
(gtla3) $\Box A \to \Box[\circ\Box A]_e$
(gtla4) $\Box[A \to B]_e \to (\Box[A]_e \to \Box[B]_e)$
(gtla5) $\Box[e' \neq e]_e$
(gtla6) $\Box[\neg\circ A \leftrightarrow \circ\neg A]_e$
(gtla7) $\Box[\circ(A \to B) \to (\circ A \to \circ B)]_e$
(gtla8) $\Box\big[\Box[A]_{e_1} \to [A]_{e_1}\big]_{e_2}$
(gtla9) $\Box[A]_{e_1} \to \Box\big[\circ\Box[A]_{e_1}\big]_{e_2}$
(gtla10) $\Box\big[[A]_{e_1} \land \circ\Box[A]_{e_1} \to \Box[A]_{e_1}\big]_{e_2}$
(gtla11) $\Box\big[\circ\Box A \to \Box[\circ A]_{e_1}\big]_{e_2}$
(mp) $A, A \to B \vdash B$
(alw) $A \vdash \Box A$
(ind$_{pf}$) $A \to B, \Box[A \to \circ A]_{\mathbf{U}(A)} \vdash A \to \Box B$

The Formal System Σ_{BTL}

(taut) All tautologically valid formulas
(btl1) $\mathsf{E}\circ\mathbf{true}$
(btl2) $\mathsf{E}\circ(A \lor B) \leftrightarrow \mathsf{E}\circ A \lor \mathsf{E}\circ B$
(btl3) $\mathsf{E}\Box A \leftrightarrow A \land \mathsf{E}\circ\mathsf{E}\Box A$
(btl4) $\mathsf{E}\Diamond A \leftrightarrow A \lor \mathsf{E}\circ\mathsf{E}\Diamond A$
(mp) $A, A \to B \vdash B$
(nexb) $A \to B \vdash \mathsf{E}\circ A \to \mathsf{E}\circ B$
(indb1) $A \to B, A \to \mathsf{E}\circ A \vdash A \to \mathsf{E}\Box B$
(indb2) $A \to \neg B, A \to \mathsf{A}\circ(A \lor \neg\mathsf{E}\Diamond B) \vdash A \to \neg\mathsf{E}\Diamond B$

The Formal System Σ_{CTL}

(taut) All tautologically valid formulas
(btl1) $\mathsf{E}\circ\mathbf{true}$
(btl2) $\mathsf{E}\circ(A \lor B) \leftrightarrow \mathsf{E}\circ A \lor \mathsf{E}\circ B$
(btl3) $\mathsf{E}\Box A \leftrightarrow A \land \mathsf{E}\circ\mathsf{E}\Box A$
(ctl) $A\ \mathbf{Eunt}\ B \leftrightarrow B \lor (A \land \mathsf{E}\circ(A\ \mathbf{Eunt}\ B))$
(mp) $A, A \to B \vdash B$

(nexb) $A \to B \vdash \mathsf{E}\bigcirc A \to \mathsf{E}\bigcirc B$
(indb1) $A \to B, A \to \mathsf{E}\bigcirc A \vdash A \to \mathsf{E}\Box B$
(indc) $A \to \neg C, A \to \mathsf{A}\bigcirc(A \lor \neg(B \mathbf{~Eunt~} C)) \vdash A \to \neg(B \mathbf{~Eunt~} C)$

References

1. ABADI, M. The power of temporal proofs. *Theoretical Computer Science 65*, 1 (June 1989), pp. 35–84. See Corrigendum in TCS 70 (1990), p. 275.
2. ABADI, M. AND MANNA, Z. Temporal logic programming. In *Symp. Logic Programming* (San Francisco, California, 1987), IEEE Computer Society, pp. 4–16.
3. ABRIAL, J.-R. *The B-Book: Assigning Programs to Meanings.* Cambridge University Press, Cambridge, UK, 1996.
4. ALPERN, B. AND SCHNEIDER, F. B. Defining liveness. *Information Processing Letters 21*, 4 (1985), pp. 181–185.
5. ALPERN, B. AND SCHNEIDER, F. B. Recognizing safety and liveness. *Distributed Computing 2* (1987), pp. 117–126.
6. ALUR, R. AND HENZINGER, T. A. A really temporal logic. *Journal of the ACM 41* (1994), pp. 181–204.
7. ANDREWS, G. R. *Foundations of Multithreaded, Parallel, and Distributed Programming*. Addison-Wesley, 2000.
8. APT, K. R. AND OLDEROG, E.-R. *Verification of sequential and concurrent programs.* Springer, New York, 1991.
9. BACK, R. AND VON WRIGHT, J. *Refinement calculus – A systematic introduction.* Springer, New York, 1998.
10. BALL, T. AND RAJAMANI, S. K. The SLAM project: Debugging system software via static analysis. In *29th Ann. Symp. Principles of Programming Languages* (Portland, Oregon, 2002), pp. 1–3.
11. BANIEQBAL, B. AND BARRINGER, H. Temporal logic with fixpoints. In *Temporal Logic in Specification* (Altrincham, UK, 1987), B. Banieqbal, H. Barringer, and A. Pnueli, Eds., vol. 398 of *Lecture Notes in Computer Science*, Springer, pp. 62–74.
12. BARRINGER, H., FISHER, M., GABBAY, D. M., GOUGH, G., AND OWENS, R. METATEM: A framework for programming in temporal logic. In *Stepwise Refinement of Distributed Systems* (Mook, The Netherlands, 1989), J. W. de Bakker, W.-P. de Roever, and G. Rozenberg, Eds., vol. 430 of *Lecture Notes in Computer Science*, Springer, pp. 94–129.
13. BARTLETT, K. A., SCANTLEBURY, R. A., AND WILKINSON, P. T. A note on reliable full-duplex transmission over half-duplex links. *Communications of the ACM 12* (1969), pp. 260–261.
14. BEN-ARI, M. *Principles of Concurrent and Distributed Programming*, 2nd ed. Addison-Wesley, Harlow, UK, 2006.

15. BEN-ARI, M., PNUELI, A., AND MANNA, Z. The temporal logic of branching time. *Acta Informatica 20* (1983), pp. 207–226.
16. BÉRARD, B., BIDOIT, M., FINKEL, A., LAROUSSINIE, F., PETIT, A., PETRUCCI, L., AND SCHNOEBELEN, P. *Systems and Software Verification. Model-Checking Techniques and Tools.* Springer, 2001.
17. BHAT, G. AND PELED, D. Adding partial orders to linear temporal logic. *Fundamenta Informaticae 36*, 1 (1998), pp. 1–21.
18. BIERE, A., CIMATTI, A., CLARKE, E., STRICHMAN, O., AND ZHU, Y. Bounded model checking. In *Highly Dependable Software*, vol. 58 of *Advances in Computers*. Academic Press, 2003.
19. BJØRNER, D. AND JONES, C. B. *Formal Specification and Software Development.* Prentice Hall, 1982.
20. BJØRNER, N., BROWNE, A., COLON, M., FINKBEINER, B., MANNA, Z., SIPMA, H., AND URIBE, T. Verifying temporal properties of reactive systems: A STeP tutorial. *Formal Methods in System Design 16* (2000), pp. 227–270.
21. BLACKBURN, P., DE RIJKE, M., AND VENEMA, Y. *Modal Logic*, vol. 53 of *Cambridge Tracts in Theoretical Computer Science.* Cambridge University Press, Cambridge, UK, 2001.
22. BOWMAN, H. AND THOMPSON, S. A decision procedure and complete axiomatization of finite interval temporal logic with projection. *Journal of Logic and Computation 13* (2003), pp. 195–239.
23. BRYANT, R. E. Symbolic boolean manipulations with ordered binary decision diagrams. *ACM Computing Surveys 24*, 3 (1992), pp. 293–317.
24. BÜCHI, J. R. On a decision method in restricted second-order arithmetics. In *Intl. Cong. Logic, Method and Philosophy of Science* (1962), Stanford University Press, pp. 1–12.
25. BURSTALL, M. Program proving as hand simulation with a little induction. In *IFIP Congress 1974* (Stockholm, Sweden, 1974), North-Holland, pp. 308–312.
26. CAIRES, L. AND CARDELLI, L. A spatial logic for concurrency (part I). *Information and Computation 186*, 2 (2003), pp. 194–235.
27. CANSELL, D., MÉRY, D., AND MERZ, S. Diagram refinements for the design of reactive systems. *Journal of Universal Computer Science 7*, 2 (2001), pp. 159–174.
28. CHANDY, K. M. AND MISRA, J. *Parallel Program Design: A Foundation.* Addison-Wesley, 1988.
29. CHOMICKI, J. AND TOMAN, D. Temporal logic in information systems. BRICS Lecture Series LS-97-1, Department of Computer Science, University of Aarhus, 1997.
30. CLARKE, E. M. AND EMERSON, E. A. Synthesis of synchronization skeletons for branching time temporal logic. In *Workshop Logic of Programs* (Yorktown Heights, N.Y., 1981), D. Kozen, Ed., vol. 131 of *Lecture Notes in Computer Science*, Springer, pp. 52–71.
31. CLARKE, E. M., GRUMBERG, O., JHA, S., LU, Y., AND VEITH, H. Counterexample-guided abstraction refinement for symbolic model checking. *Journal of the ACM 50*, 5 (2003), pp. 752–794.
32. CLARKE, E. M., GRUMBERG, O., AND LONG, D. E. Model checking and abstraction. *ACM Trans. Program. Lang. Syst. 16*, 5 (1994), pp. 1512–1542.
33. CLARKE, E. M., GRUMBERG, O., AND PELED, D. *Model Checking.* MIT Press, Cambridge, Mass., 1999.
34. CLARKE, E. M., JHA, S., ENDERS, R., AND FILKORN, T. Exploiting symmetry in temporal logic model checking. *Formal Methods in System Design 9*, 1-2 (1996), pp. 77–104.

35. CLARKE, E. M. AND SCHLINGLOFF, H. Model checking. In *Handbook of Automated Deduction*, A. Robinson and A. Voronkov, Eds., vol. II. Elsevier Science, 2000, pp. 1635–1790.
36. CLIFFORD, J. Tense logic and the logic of change. *Logique et Analyse 34* (1966), pp. 219–230.
37. DAMS, D., GRUMBERG, O., AND GERTH, R. Abstract interpretation of reactive systems: Abstractions preserving $\forall$CTL*, $\exists$CTL* and CTL*. In *IFIP Work. Conf. Programming Concepts, Methods, and Calculi* (Amsterdam, The Netherlands, 1994), E.-R. Olderog, Ed., Elsevier Science, pp. 561–581.
38. DE ALFARO, L., MANNA, Z., SIPMA, H. B., AND URIBE, T. Visual verification of reactive systems. In *Third Intl. Workshop Tools and Algorithms for the Construction and Analysis of Systems* (Enschede, The Netherlands, 1997), E. Brinksma, Ed., vol. 1217 of *Lecture Notes in Computer Science*, Springer, pp. 334–350.
39. DE ROEVER, W.-P., DE BOER, F., HANNEMANN, U., HOOMAN, J., LAKHNECH, Y., POEL, M., AND ZWIERS, J. *Concurrency Verification: Introduction to Compositional and Noncompositional Methods*. Cambridge University Press, Cambridge, UK, 2001.
40. DE ROEVER, W.-P., LANGMAACK, H., AND PNUELI, A., Eds. *Compositionality: The Significant Difference* (1998), vol. 1536 of *Lecture Notes in Computer Science*, Springer.
41. DIJKSTRA, E. W. Self-stabilizing systems in spite of distributed control. *Communications of the ACM 17*, 11 (1974), pp. 643–644.
42. DIJKSTRA, E. W. *A Discipline of Programming*. Prentice Hall, 1976.
43. EBBINGHAUS, H., FLUM, J., AND THOMAS, W. *Einführung in die Mathematische Logik*. Wissenschaftliche Buchgesellschaft, Darmstadt, Germany, 1978.
44. EMERSON, E. A. Alternative semantics for temporal logics. *Theoretical Computer Science 26* (1983), pp. 121–130.
45. EMERSON, E. A. Temporal and modal logic. In *Handbook of theoretical computer science*, J. van Leeuwen, Ed., vol. B: Formal Models and Semantics. Elsevier, 1990, pp. 997–1071.
46. EMERSON, E. A. AND SISTLA, A. P. Symmetry and model checking. *Formal Methods in System Design 9*, 1-2 (1996), pp. 105–131.
47. ESPARZA, J. Model checking using net unfoldings. *Science of Computer Programming 23* (1994), pp. 151–195.
48. FLOYD, R. Assigning meaning to programs. In *Symposium on Applied Mathematics 19, Mathematical Aspects of Computer Science* (New York, 1967), J. T. Schwartz, Ed., American Mathematical Society, pp. 19–32.
49. FRANCEZ, N. *Fairness*. Springer, New York, 1986.
50. FREGE, G. *Begriffsschrift, eine der arithmetischen nachgebildete Formelsprache des reinen Denkens*. Louis Nebert, Halle, Germany, 1879.
51. FRENCH, T. AND REYNOLDS, M. A sound and complete proof system for QPTL. *Advances in Modal Logic 4* (2002), pp. 1–20.
52. GABBAY, D. M., HODKINSON, I., AND REYNOLDS, M. *Temporal Logic: Mathematical Foundations and Computational Aspects*, vol. 1. Clarendon Press, Oxford, UK, 1994.
53. GABBAY, D. M., PNUELI, A., SHELAH, S., AND STAVI, J. On the temporal analysis of fairness. In *7th Ann. Symp. Principles of Programming Languages* (Las Vegas, Nevada, 1980), pp. 163–173.
54. GASTIN, P. AND ODDOUX, D. Fast LTL to Büchi automata translation. In *13th Intl. Conf. Computer Aided Verification* (Paris, France, 2001), G. Berry, H. Comon, and A. Finkel, Eds., vol. 2102 of *Lecture Notes in Computer Science*, Springer, pp. 53–65.

55. GERTH, R., PELED, D., VARDI, M. Y., AND WOLPER, P. Simple on-the-fly automatic verification of linear temporal logic. In *Protocol Specification, Testing, and Verification* (Warsaw, Poland, 1995), Chapman & Hall, pp. 3–18.
56. GODEFROID, P. AND WOLPER, P. A partial approach to model checking. *Information and Computation 110*, 2 (1994), pp. 305–326.
57. GÖDEL, K. Über formal unentscheidbare Sätze der Principia Mathematica und verwandter Systeme. *Monatshefte für Mathematik und Physik 38* (1931), pp. 173–198.
58. GOLDBLATT, R. *Logics of Time and Computation*, vol. 7 of *CSLI Lecture Notes*. CSLI, Stanford, California, 1987.
59. GRAF, S. AND SAÏDI, H. Construction of abstract state graphs with PVS. In *9th Intl. Conf. Computer Aided Verification* (Haifa, Israel, 1997), O. Grumberg, Ed., vol. 1254 of *Lecture Notes in Computer Science*, Springer, pp. 72–83.
60. HAMILTON, A. G. *Logic for Mathematicians*, revised ed. Cambridge University Press, Cambridge, UK, 1988.
61. HENZINGER, T. A., JHALA, R., MAJUMDAR, R., AND MCMILLAN, K. L. Abstractions from proofs. In *31st Symp. Principles of Programming Languages* (Venice, Italy, 2004), ACM Press, pp. 232–244.
62. HOARE, C. A. R. An axiomatic basis for computer programming. *Communications of the ACM 12* (1969), pp. 576–580.
63. HODKINSON, I., WOLTER, F., AND ZAKHARYASCHEV, M. Decidable fragments of first-order temporal logics. *Annals of Pure and Applied Logic 106* (2000), pp. 85–134.
64. HOLZMANN, G. AND PELED, D. An improvement in formal verification. In *IFIP Conf. Formal Description Techniques* (Bern, Switzerland, 1994), Chapman & Hall, pp. 197–214.
65. HOLZMANN, G. J. *The SPIN Model Checker*. Addison-Wesley, 2003.
66. HUGHES, G. E. AND CRESSWELL, M. J. *An Introduction to Modal Logic*. Methuen, London, UK, 1968.
67. HUTH, M. AND RYAN, M. D. *Logic in Computer Science: Modelling and Reasoning about Systems*, 2nd ed. Cambridge University Press, Cambridge, UK, 2004.
68. IP, C. N. AND DILL, D. L. Better verification through symmetry. *Formal Methods in System Design 9*, 1-2 (1996), pp. 41–75.
69. KAMINSKI, M. Invariance under stuttering in a temporal logic of actions. *Theoretical Computer Science 368*, 1-2 (2006), pp. 50–63.
70. KAMP, H. W. *Tense logic and the theory of linear order*. PhD thesis, UCLA, Los Angeles, California, 1968.
71. KELLER, R. M. Formal verification of parallel programs. *Communications of the ACM 19* (1976), pp. 371–384.
72. KESTEN, Y. AND PNUELI, A. Verification by augmented finitary abstraction. *Information and Computation 163*, 1 (2000), pp. 203–243.
73. KESTEN, Y. AND PNUELI, A. Complete proof system for QPTL. *Journal of Logic and Computation 12*, 5 (2002), pp. 701–745.
74. KNAPP, A., MERZ, S., WIRSING, M., AND ZAPPE, J. Specification and refinement of mobile systems in MTLA and Mobile UML. *Theoretical Computer Science 351*, 2 (2006), pp. 184–202.
75. KOZEN, D. Results on the propositional mu-calculus. *Theoretical Computer Science 27* (1983), pp. 333–354.
76. KRIPKE, S. A. Semantical analysis of modal logic I. *Z. Math. Logik Grundlagen Math. 9* (1963), pp. 67–96.
77. KRÖGER, F. Logical rules of natural reasoning about programs. In *Intl. Coll. Automata, Logic and Programming* (Edinburgh, UK, 1976), Edinburgh University Press, pp. 87–98.

78. KRÖGER, F. LAR: A logic of algorithmic reasoning. *Acta Informatica 8* (1977), pp. 243–266.
79. KRÖGER, F. A uniform logical basis for the description, specification and verification of programs. In *IFIP Work. Conf. Formal Description of Programming Concepts* (St. Andrews, Canada, 1978), North-Holland, pp. 441–457.
80. KRÖGER, F. On temporal program verification rules. *RAIRO Informatique Théorique et Applications 19* (1985), pp. 261–280.
81. KRÖGER, F. On the interpretability of arithmetic in temporal logic. *Theoretical Computer Science 73* (1990), pp. 47–60.
82. KRÖGER, F. A generalized nexttime operator in temporal logic. *Journal of Computer and Systems Sciences 29* (1984), pp. 80–98.
83. KRÖGER, F. *Temporal Logic of Programs.* Springer, Berlin-Heidelberg, 1987.
84. KUPFERMAN, O. AND VARDI, M. Y. Weak alternating automata are not so weak. In *5th Israeli Symp. Theory of Computing and Systems* (1997), IEEE Computer Society, pp. 147–158.
85. KUPFERMAN, O. AND VARDI, M. Y. Complementation constructions for nondeterministic automata on infinite words. In *11th Intl. Conf. Tools and Algorithms for the Construction and Analysis of Systems* (Edinburgh, UK, 2005), N. Halbwachs and L. Zuck, Eds., vol. 3440 of *Lecture Notes in Computer Science*, Springer, pp. 206–221.
86. LAMPORT, L. Proving the correctness of multiprocess programs. *IEEE Transactions on Software Engineering SE-3(2)* (1977), pp. 125–143.
87. LAMPORT, L. 'Sometime' is sometimes 'not never'. In *7th Ann. Symp. Principles of Programming Languages* (Las Vegas, Nevada, January 1980), ACM Press, pp. 174–185.
88. LAMPORT, L. The Temporal Logic of Actions. *ACM Trans. Program. Lang. Syst. 16*, 3 (1994), pp. 872–923.
89. LANGE, M. *Temporal Logics Beyond Regularity.* Habilitationsschrift, Ludwig-Maximilians-Universität München, Munich, Germany, 2007.
90. LEMMON, E. J. AND SCOTT, D. *An Introduction to Modal Logic*, vol. 11 of *American Philosophical Quarterly Monograph Series.* Basil Blackwell, Oxford, UK, 1977. edited by K. Segerberg.
91. LESSKE, F. Constructive specifications of abstract data types using temporal logic. In *2nd Intl. Symp. Logical Foundations of Computer Science* (Tver, Russia, 1992), A. Nerode and M. A. Taitslin, Eds., vol. 620 of *Lecture Notes in Computer Science*, Springer, pp. 269–280.
92. LICHTENSTEIN, O., PNUELI, A., AND ZUCK, L. The glory of the past. In *Logics of Programs* (Brooklyn College, New York, 1985), R. Parikh, Ed., vol. 193 of *Lecture Notes in Computer Science*, Springer, pp. 196–218.
93. LIPECK, U. W. AND SAAKE, G. Monitoring dynamic integrity constraints based on temporal logic. *Information Systems 12* (1987), pp. 255–269.
94. LOISEAUX, C., GRAF, S., SIFAKIS, J., BOUAJJANI, A., AND BENSALEM, S. Property preserving abstractions for the verification of concurrent systems. *Formal Methods in System Design 6* (1995), pp. 11–44.
95. MANNA, Z. AND PNUELI, A. Verification of concurrent programs: Temporal proof principles. In *Workshop Logic of Programs* (Yorktown Heights, New York, 1981), D. Kozen, Ed., vol. 131 of *Lecture Notes in Computer Science*, Springer, pp. 200–252.
96. MANNA, Z. AND PNUELI, A. Verification of concurrent programs: The temporal framework. In *The correctness problem in computer science*, R. S. Boyer and J. S. Moore, Eds. Academic Press, 1982, pp. 215–273.

97. MANNA, Z. AND PNUELI, A. How to cook a temporal proof system for your pet language. In *10th Ann. Symp. Principles of Programming Languages* (Austin, Texas, 1983), pp. 141–154.
98. MANNA, Z. AND PNUELI, A. Proving precedence properties: The temporal way. In *10th Intl. Coll. Automata, Languages and Programming* (Barcelona, Spain, 1983), J. Diaz, Ed., vol. 154 of *Lecture Notes in Computer Science*, Springer, pp. 491–512.
99. MANNA, Z. AND PNUELI, A. Verification of concurrent programs: A temporal proof system. In *Foundations of computer science IV*, vol. 159 of *Mathematical Centre Tracts*. CWI, Amsterdam, 1983, pp. 163–255.
100. MANNA, Z. AND PNUELI, A. The anchored version of the temporal framework. In *Linear Time, Branching Time and Partial Order in Logics and Models for Concurrency*, J. W. de Bakker, W.-P. de Roever, and G. Rozenberg, Eds., vol. 354 of *Lecture Notes in Computer Science*. Springer, 1989, pp. 201–284.
101. MANNA, Z. AND PNUELI, A. A hierarchy of temporal properties. In *9th Symp. Principles of Distributed Programming* (Vancouver, Canada, 1990), pp. 377–408.
102. MANNA, Z. AND PNUELI, A. *The Temporal Logic of Reactive and Concurrent Systems – Specification.* Springer, New York, 1992.
103. MANNA, Z. AND PNUELI, A. Temporal verification diagrams. In *Intl. Conf. Theoretical Aspects of Computer Software* (Sendai, Japan, 1994), M. Hagiya and J. C. Mitchell, Eds., vol. 789 of *Lecture Notes in Computer Science*, Springer, pp. 726–765.
104. MANNA, Z. AND PNUELI, A. *The Temporal Logic of Reactive and Concurrent Systems – Safety.* Springer, New York, 1995.
105. MANZANO, M. *Extensions of First Order Logic*, vol. 19 of *Cambridge Tracts in Theoretical Computer Science.* Cambridge University Press, Cambridge, UK, 1996.
106. MCMILLAN, K. L. *Symbolic Model Checking.* Kluwer Academic Publishers, 1993.
107. MERZ, S. Decidability and incompleteness results for first-order temporal logics of linear time. *Journal of Applied Non-Classical Logic 2*, 2 (1992).
108. MERZ, S. Efficiently executable temporal logic programs. In *Executable Modal and Temporal Logics* (Chambéry, France, 1995), M. Fisher and R. Owens, Eds., vol. 897 of *Lecture Notes in Computer Science*, Springer, pp. 69–85.
109. MERZ, S. A more complete TLA. In *World Cong. Formal Methods* (Toulouse, France, 1999), J. M. Wing, J. Woodcock, and J. Davies, Eds., vol. 1709 of *Lecture Notes in Computer Science*, Springer, pp. 1226–1244.
110. MOSZKOWSKI, B. C. *Executing Temporal Logic.* Cambridge University Press, Cambridge, UK, 1986.
111. MOSZKOWSKI, B. C. A complete axiomatization of interval temporal logic with infinite time. In *15th Ann. Symp. Logics in Computer Science* (Santa Barbara, California, 2000), IEEE Computer Society, pp. 241–252.
112. MULLER, D. E., SAOUDI, A., AND SCHUPP, P. E. Weak alternating automata give a simple explanation of why most temporal and dynamic logics are decidable in exponential time. In *3rd IEEE Symp. on Logic in Computer Science* (Edinburgh, UK, 1988), IEEE Press, pp. 422–427.
113. NIEBERT, P. A ν-calculus with local views for systems of sequential agents. In *20th Intl. Symp. Mathematical Foundations of Computer Science* (Prague, Czech Republic, 1995), J. Wiedermann and P. Hájek, Eds., vol. 969 of *Lecture Notes in Computer Science*, Springer, pp. 563–573.
114. ORGUN, M. A. AND MA, W. An overview of temporal and modal logic programming. In *First Intl. Conf. Temporal Logic* (Bonn, Germany, 1994), D. M. Gabbay and H. J. Ohlbach, Eds., vol. 827 of *Lecture Notes in Computer Science*, Springer, pp. 445–479.

115. PELED, D. Combining partial order reductions with on-the-fly model-checking. *Formal Methods in System Design 8*, 1 (1996), pp. 39–64.
116. PELED, D. AND WILKE, T. Stutter-invariant temporal properties are expressible without the next-time operator. *Information Processing Letters 63*, 5 (1997), pp. 243–246.
117. PENCZEK, W. Branching time and partial order in temporal logics. In *Time and Logic – A Computational Approach*, L. Bolc and A. Szalas, Eds. UCL Press, London, 1994, pp. 179–228.
118. PETERSON, G. L. Myths about the mutual exclusion problem. *Information Processing Letters 12* (1981), pp. 115–116.
119. PETRI, C. A. *Kommunikation mit Automaten.* Schriften des Institutes für Instrumentelle Mathematik, Bonn, Germany, 1962.
120. PNUELI, A. The temporal logic of programs. In *18th Ann. Symp. Foundations of Computer Science* (Providence, Rhode Island, 1977), IEEE, pp. 46–57.
121. PNUELI, A. The temporal semantics of concurrent programs. *Theoretical Computer Science 13* (1981), pp. 45–60.
122. PNUELI, A. In transition from global to modular temporal reasoning about programs. In *Logics and Models of Concurrent Systems*, K. R. Apt, Ed., vol. 193 of *Lecture Notes in Computer Science.* Springer, 1985, pp. 123–144.
123. PNUELI, A. System specification and refinement in temporal logic. In *Foundations of Software Technology and Theoretical Computer Science* (New Delhi, India, 1992), R. K. Shyamasundar, Ed., vol. 652 of *Lecture Notes in Computer Science*, Springer, pp. 1–38.
124. PRATT, V. R. A decidable μ-calculus: Preliminary report. In *22nd Ann. Symp. Foundations of Computer Science* (Nashville, Tennessee, 1981), IEEE Computer Society, pp. 421–427.
125. PRIOR, A. N. *Time and modality.* Oxford University Press, Oxford, UK, 1957.
126. PRIOR, A. N. *Past, Present and Future.* Oxford University Press, Oxford, UK, 1967.
127. QUEILLE, J. P. AND SIFAKIS, J. Specification and verification of concurrent systems in Cesar. In *5th Intl. Symp. Programming* (Torino, Italy, 1981), vol. 137 of *Lecture Notes in Computer Science*, Springer, pp. 337–351.
128. QUEILLE, J. P. AND SIFAKIS, J. Fairness and related properties in transition systems – a temporal logic to deal with fairness. *Acta Informatica 19* (1983), pp. 195–220.
129. REISIG, W. *Petri Nets: An Introduction.* Springer, Berlin-Heidelberg, 1985.
130. RESCHER, N. AND URQUHART, A. *Temporal Logic.* Springer, New York, 1971.
131. SAFRA, S. On the complexity of ω-automata. In *29th IEEE Symp. Foundations of Computer Science* (White Plains, New York, 1988), IEEE Computer Society, pp. 319–327.
132. SCHLINGLOFF, H. *Beweistheoretische Untersuchungen zur temporalen Logik.* Diplomarbeit, Technische Universität München, Institut für Informatik, Munich, Germany, 1983.
133. SCHNEIDER, F. B. *On Concurrent Programming.* Springer, New York, 1997.
134. SCHNEIDER, K. *Verification of Reactive Systems.* Springer, New York, 2004.
135. SCHOBBENS, P.-Y., RASKIN, J.-F., AND HENZINGER, T. A. Axioms for real-time logics. *Theoretical Computer Science 274*, 1-2 (2002), pp. 151–182.
136. SEGERBERG, C. On the logic of tomorrow. *Theoria 33* (1967), pp. 45–52.
137. SHOENFIELD, J. R. *Mathematical Logic.* Addison-Wesley, Reading, Mass., 1967.
138. SISTLA, A. P. *Theoretical issues in the design of distributed and concurrent systems.* PhD thesis, Harvard Univ., Cambridge, MA, 1983.
139. SISTLA, A. P., VARDI, M. Y., AND WOLPER, P. The complementation problem for Büchi automata with applications to temporal logic. *Theoretical Computer Science 49* (1987), pp. 217–237.

140. STIRLING, C. *Modal and Temporal Properties of Processes*. Springer, New York, 2001.
141. SZALAS, A. Concerning the semantic consequence relation in first-order temporal logic. *Theoretical Computer Science 47* (1986), pp. 329–334.
142. SZALAS, A. Arithmetical axiomatization of first-order temporal logic. *Information Processing Letters 26* (1987), pp. 111–116.
143. SZALAS, A. A complete axiomatic characterization of first-order temporal logic of linear time. *Theoretical Computer Science* (1987), pp. 199–214.
144. SZALAS, A. Towards the temporal approach to abstract data types. *Fundamenta Informaticae 11* (1988), pp. 49–64.
145. SZALAS, A. Temporal logic of programs: a standard approach. In *Time and Logic – A Computational Approach*, L. Bolc and A. Szalas, Eds. UCL Press, London, UK, 1994, pp. 1–50.
146. SZALAS, A. AND HOLENDERSKI, L. Incompleteness of first-order temporal logic with until. *Theoretical Computer Science 57* (1988), pp. 317–325.
147. THOMAS, W. Automata on infinite objects. In *Handbook of Theoretical Computer Science*, J. van Leeuwen, Ed., vol. B: Formal Models and Semantics. Elsevier Science, Amsterdam, 1990, pp. 133–194.
148. THOMAS, W. Languages, automata, and logic. In *Handbook of Formal Language Theory*, G. Rozenberg and A. Salomaa, Eds., vol. III. Springer, New York, 1997, pp. 389–455.
149. THOMAS, W. Complementation of Büchi automata revisited. In *Jewels are Forever, Contributions on Theoretical Computer Science in Honor of Arto Salomaa*, J. Karhumäki, Ed. Springer, 2000, pp. 109–122.
150. VALMARI, A. The state explosion problem. In *Lectures on Petri Nets I: Basic Models*, vol. 1491 of *Lecture Notes in Computer Science*. Springer, 1998, pp. 429–528.
151. VAN BENTHEM, J. *The Logic of Time*, vol. 156 of *Synthese Library*. Reidel, Dordrecht, The Netherlands, 1983. Revised and expanded edition, 1991.
152. VARDI, M. Y. Verification of concurrent programs: The automata-theoretic framework. In *Second Symp. Logic in Computer Science* (Ithaca, New York, 1987), IEEE, pp. 167–176.
153. VARDI, M. Y. Alternating automata and program verification. In *Computer Science Today*, J. van Leeuwen, Ed., vol. 1000 of *Lecture Notes in Computer Science*. Springer, 1995, pp. 471–485.
154. VARDI, M. Y. Branching vs. linear time – final showdown. In *Intl. Conf. Tools and Algorithms for the Construction and Analysis of Systems* (Genova, Italy, 2001), T. Margaria and W. Yi, Eds., vol. 2031 of *Lecture Notes in Computer Science*, Springer, pp. 1–22.
155. VARDI, M. Y. AND WOLPER, P. Reasoning about infinite computations. *Information and Computation 115*, 1 (1994), pp. 1–37.
156. VON WRIGHT, G. H. Always. *Theoria 34* (1968), pp. 208–221.
157. WALUKIEWICZ, I. Completeness of Kozen's axiomatisation of the propositional μ-calculus. *Information and Computation 157*, 1-2 (2000), pp. 142–182.
158. WHITEHEAD, A. N. AND RUSSELL, B. *Principia Mathematica (3 vols)*. Cambridge University Press, Cambridge, UK, 1910–13. 2nd edition 1925–27.
159. WOLPER, P. Temporal logic can be more expressive. *Information and Control 56* (1983), pp. 72–93.
160. WOLPER, P. The tableau method for temporal logic: an overview. *Logique et Analyse 28* (1985), pp. 119–136.
161. ZAPPE, J. *Towards a Mobile Temporal Logic of Actions*. PhD thesis, Ludwig-Maximilians-Universität München, Munich, Germany, 2005.

Index

K. Jensen
Coloured Petri Nets
Basic Concepts, Analysis Methods and Practical Use, Vol. 1
2nd ed.

K. Jensen
Coloured Petri Nets
Basic Concepts, *Analysis Methods* and Practical Use, Vol. 2

K. Jensen
Coloured Petri Nets
Basic Concepts, Analysis Methods and *Practical Use*, Vol. 3

A. Nait Abdallah
The Logic of Partial Information

Z. Fülöp, H.Vogler
Syntax-Directed Semantics
Formal Models Based on Tree Transducers

A. de Luca, S. Varricchio
Finiteness and Regularity in Semigroups and Formal Languages

E. Best, R. Devillers, M. Koutny
Petri Net Algebra

S.P. Demri, E.S. Orlowska
Incomplete Information: Structure, Inference, Complexity

J.C.M. Baeten, C.A. Middelburg
Process Algebra with Timing

L.A. Hemaspaandra, L. Torenvliet
Theory of Semi-Feasible Algorithms

E. Fink, D. Wood
Restricted-Orientation Convexity

Zhou Chaochen, M.R. Hansen
Duration Calculus
A Formal Approach to Real-Time Systems

M. Große-Rhode
Semantic Integration of Heterogeneous Software Specifications

H. Ehrig, K. Ehrig, U. Prange, G. Taentzer
Fundamentals of Algebraic Graph Transformation

W. Michiels, E. Aarts, J. Korst
Theoretical Aspects of Local Search

D. Bjørner, M.C. Henson (Eds.)
Logics of Specification Languages

J. Esparza, K. Heljanko
Unfoldings
A Partial-Order Approach to Model Checking

Texts in Theoretical Computer Science · An EATCS Series

P. Clote, E. Kranakis
Boolean Functions and Computation Models

L.A. Hemaspaandra, M. Ogihara
The Complexity Theory Companion

C.S. Calude
Information and Randomness
An Algorithmic Perspective 2nd ed.

J. Hromkovič
Theoretical Computer Science
Introduction to Automata, Computability, Complexity, Algorithmics, Randomization, Communication and Cryptography

K. Schneider
Verification of Reactive Systems
Formal Methods and Algorithms

S. Ronchi Della Rocca, L. Paolini
The Parametric Lambda Calculus
A Metamodel for Computation

Y. Bertot, P. Castéran
Interactive Theorem Proving and Program Development
Coq'Art: The Calculus of Inductive Constructions

L. Libkin
Elements of Finite Model Theory

M. Hutter
Universal Artificial Intelligence
Sequential Decisions Based on Algorithmic Probability

G. Păun, G. Rozenberg, A. Salomaa
DNA Computing
New Computing Paradigms
2nd corr. printing

W. Kluge
Abstract Computing Machines
A Lambda Calculus Perspective

J. Hromkovič
Design and Analysis of Randomized Algorithms
Introduction to Design Paradigms

J. Hromkovič
Dissemination of Information in Communication Networks
Broadcasting, Gossiping, Leader Election, and Fault Tolerance

R. Kurki-Suonio
A Practical Theory of Reactive Systems
Incremental Modeling of Dynamic Behaviors

F. Drewes
Grammatical Picture Generation
A Tree-Based Approach

J. Flum, M. Grohe
Parameterized Complexity Theory

D. Bjørner
Software Engineering 1
Abstraction and Modelling

D. Bjørner
Software Engineering 2
Specification of Systems and Languages

D. Bjørner
Software Engineering 3
Domains, Requirements, and Software Design

E. Grädel et al.
Finite Model Theory and Its Applications

W. Fokkink
Modelling Distributed Systems

S. Bandyopadhyay
Dissemination of Information in Optical Networks
From Technology to Algorithms

F. Kröger, S. Merz
Temporal Logic and State Systems